DATE DUE

THE BANANA WARS

CENTRAL AMERICA
AND THE
CARIBBEAN SEA
Circa 1900

0   50   100   200   300 miles

One Inch equals 150 Miles

Key West 100 miles Nor

Havan

Trocha

CARIB

MEXICO

BRITISH
HONDURAS
(BELIZE)

GUATEMALA

HONDURAS

EL SALVADOR

Ocotal

Puerto
Cabezas

NICARAGUA

Corinto

L. Managua

León

Managua

L. Nicaragua

Granada

Bluefields

COSTA RICA

PANAM

ISTHMUS OF
PANAMA
1900

Colón

Panama
Railroad

Matachin

Panama
City

PACIFIC OCEAN

N

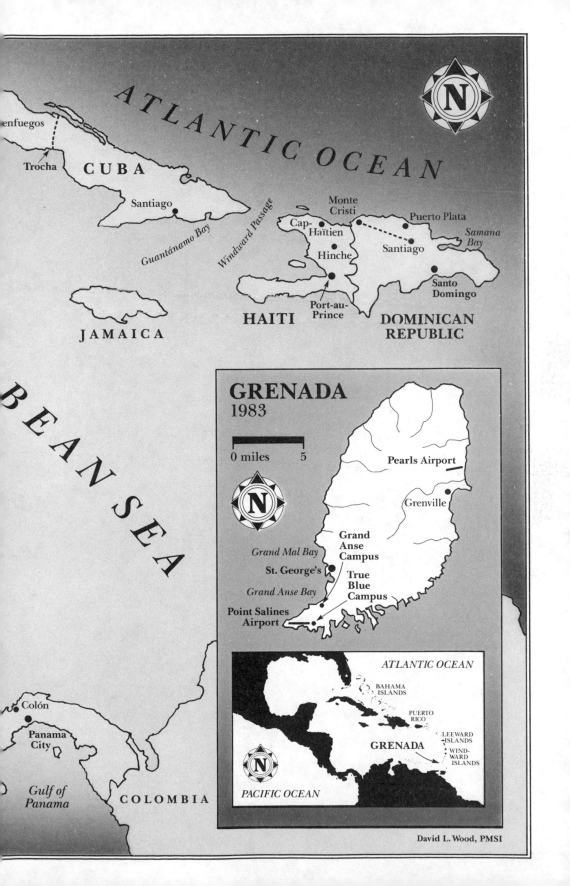

ATLANTIC OCEAN

enfuegos

Trocha

CUBA

Santiago

Guantánamo Bay

Windward Passage

Monte
Cristi

Cap-
Haïtien

Puerto Plata

Hinche

Santiago

*Samana
Bay*

Port-au-
Prince

Santo
Domingo

HAITI

DOMINICAN
REPUBLIC

JAMAICA

BEAN SEA

Colón

Panama
City

*Gulf of
Panama*

COLOMBIA

GRENADA
1983

0 miles   5

Pearls Airport

Grenville

**Grand
Anse
Campus**

Grand Mal Bay

St. George's

Grand Anse Bay

**True
Blue
Campus**

**Point Salines
Airport**

ATLANTIC OCEAN

BAHAMA
ISLANDS

PUERTO
RICO

GRENADA

LEEWARD
ISLANDS

WIND-
WARD
ISLANDS

PACIFIC OCEAN

David L. Wood, PMSI

ALSO BY IVAN MUSICANT

Battleship at War
U.S. Armored Cruisers

THE
BANANA
WARS

A History of United States
Military Intervention in Latin America
from the Spanish-American War
to the Invasion of Panama

IVAN MUSICANT

MACMILLAN PUBLISHING COMPANY
New York

Dedicated to the memory and service of
Vice Admiral Edwin B. Hooper, USN,
1909–1986, Director of Naval History

Macmillan Publishing Company
866 Third Avenue, New York, NY 10022
Collier Macmillan Canada, Inc.

Library of Congress Cataloging-in-Publication Data

Musicant, Ivan, 1943–
    The banana wars : a history of United States military intervention
in Latin America from the Spanish-American War to the invasion of
Panama / Ivan Musicant.
        p.   cm.
    Includes bibliographical references and index.
    ISBN 0-02-588210-4
    1. Latin America—Foreign relations—United States.   2. United
States—Foreign relations—Latin America.   3. Intervention
(International law)   4. United States—Military policy.   5. United
States—History, Military.   I. Title.
F1418.M96   1990   89-29657   CIP
327.7308—dc20

Macmillan books are available at special discounts for bulk purchases for sales promotions, premiums, fund-raising, or educational use.
For details, contact:
    Special Sales Director
    Macmillan Publishing Company
    866 Third Avenue
    New York, NY 10022

10 9 8 7 6 5 4 3 2 1

PRINTED IN THE UNITED STATES OF AMERICA

CONTENTS

ACKNOWLEDGMENTS

To the many people who have aided in the compilation of this book go my sincerest thanks.

For their cheerful and dedicated assistance, without which this work could not have reached fruition, from the History and Museums Division, United States Marine Corps, Robert Aguilina, Benis Frank, Michael Miller, Kenneth Smith-Christmas, Patricia Morgan, Evelyn Englander; from the United States Army Center for Military History, Robert Slonaker, Randy Hackenburg, Geffery Hoskins; from the Military History Branch, National Archives and Records Service, Richard von Doenhoff; from the Minnesota Historical Society, Wiley Pope, Faustino Avoloz, Marlin Heisse, Alissa Wiener; from the Wisconsin State Historical Society, James Hanson; for his knowledge of nineteeenth-century technology, Mr. John Bowditch of the Thomas Edison Institute; for the use of their enormous resources and the granting of special privileges, the University of Minnesota libraries.

I am thankful to the United States Naval Institute for their assistance with many of the photographs, and for their publication of the Dominican Republic chapter in *Naval History*, under the title of "Uncle Joe's Flying Column."

I would especially like to recognize Captain Edward L. Beach, USN (Ret.) and Lieutenant Colonel Littleton W. T. Waller III, USMC (Ret.) for their most kind reception and the use of the papers of their forebears; for cheerfully responding to my endless questions relating to command, Rear Admiral Raymond P. Hunter, USN (Ret.), Major General Jonas Platt, USMC (Ret.), Captain James G. Ross, USN (Ret.); for their knowledge regarding contemporary Latin American issues, Colonel John D. Waghelstein, USA (Ret.), Lieutenant Colonel Robert Kemp, USA, Lieutenant Colonel Ed Fitzsimmons, USA, Lieutenant Colonel Vince Santillo, USAF, Lieutenant Colonel Thomas Qualy, USA (Ret.); for a thousand intangibles, Colonel Donald Patton, USAR.

For the loan of materials from his library, Dr. Robert Scheina, Historian, United States Coast Guard; for his help in locating critical portions of the bibliography, Colonel John E. Greenwood, USMC (Ret.), Editor, *Marine Corps Gazette*; for his vast and first-hand knowledge of irregular warfare, Mr. William J. Hatton, ex-Sergeant, USMC; in appreciation of his continuous support and criticism, Mr. Rex Pickett, ex-Captain, USMC.

For their diligent and excellent work, thanks to my editor, Ms. Amy Fastenberg of the Macmillan Publishing Company, and copy editor, Mr. Fred Chase.

Lastly, thanks to the most fascinating person I have ever met, Major General Walter Greatsinger Farrell, USMC (Ret.).

INTRODUCTION

The accident of strategic geography dictates political events. Even a cursory glance at a map showing the northern half of the Western Hemisphere will indicate the geographic domination of the United States over its Central American and Caribbean neighbors. The formations of the land and sea masses, and their strategic relationship to the northern colossus, led inevitably to a quadraspheric American "empire." In their military and naval aspects, the founding and policing of this Central American and Caribbean realm, de facto and de jure, are colloquially termed the Banana Wars.

To be sure, there were many social, political, and economic factors that dictated United States military intervention into the region. But in the main, these came on the back of the overriding strategic consideration, specifically the need to create a Caribbean bulwark shielding the Atlantic approaches to America's hemispheric jugular vein, the isthmus and canal of Panama; from this premise, all else flowed.

Although there are prologues and epilogues, the classic period of the Banana Wars occurred roughly in the first third of the twentieth century. The Spanish-American War evicted Spain from the Americas and the Philippines and fully established the United States as a major imperial player on the world's stage. Cuba passed from a Spanish colony into an American protectorate. Though this situation proved temporary, the acquisition of permanent naval facilities at Guantánamo Bay, Cuba, coupled with Spain's cession of Puerto Rico, provided the necessary sentry boxes to guard the Central American isthmus and nailed shut the key Atlantic gates into the Caribbean.

Panama, even before the canal, was of vital strategic interest to the United States. Prior to 1903 it had been a department of Colombia, and in mid-nineteenth century bilateral treaties, the United States accepted the right and obligation to maintain the free flow of commerce across the isthmian line of transit, whatever its mode.

By late century, the isthmus had assumed paramount importance to the United States Navy, now recovering from its post–Civil War malaise. Indeed, the American naval renaissance and the rise of the United States as an empire and world arbiter were parallel and symbiotic. If anyone needed a lesson regarding the absolute strategic necessity for an isthmian canal, it came during the Spanish-American War, when fleet units were forced 15,000 miles and sixty-six days "round the Horn" to deploy from the Pacific to the Atlantic. Future conflicts with maritime powers would doubtless require a more rapid concentration of the fleet. When the United States acquired its eastern albatross—the Philippines—from Spain in 1898 (an event coincident with Japanese naval and imperial expansion), American hegemony over an isthmian canal route was ensured.

Once the purely strategic linchpins of empire—Guantánamo Bay, Cuba; Puerto Rico; and the Panama Canal Zone—were in place, it behooved successive American governments to maintain U.S. paramountcy in the region, as well as to promote political, 1nomic, and social stability within the empire's tactical boundaries. With the ascendancy of the United States Navy to second place, in a three-way tie with Germany and France, who, together with Great Britain, the world's naval leader, held substantial economic interests in the region, the Monroe Doctrine ceased to be an international joke. "The Monroe Doctrine," said Theodore Roosevelt, "is as strong as the United States Navy, and no stronger."

European colonization in the hemisphere was no longer an issue, but European military intervention, to safeguard investments and nationals, was. The Caribbean and Central American states, notably Haiti, the Dominican Republic, Honduras, and beginning in 1909, Nicaragua, were convulsed with endemic internal strife. By the time of Theodore Roosevelt's administration, the presence of expeditionary European naval forces to keep the peace and restore order in America's front yard could no longer be tolerated.

To cement America's newfound role as quadraspheric constable, Roosevelt devised his controversial Corollary to the Monroe Doctrine whereby the United States could militarily and unilaterally intervene in any regional state where the political, economic, or social conditions invited a European protective response in force. It was Woodrow Wilson's invocation of the Corollary that provided for the intervention and nineteen-year occupation of Haiti by the Marine Corps and for the establishment of an ill-conceived American military government under the navy and the Marine Corps in the Dominican Republic.

The most controversial and indefensible motivation for the Banana Wars was dollar diplomacy, the economic stepchild of the Roosevelt Corollary. Begun, at least officially, during the Taft administration, and carried through by Wilson, Harding, and Coolidge, it was used to foster economic stability through the infusion of American capital, often combined with high-handed diplomatic coercion, into the empire. It had the unfortunate (at least from the native standpoint) result of transforming the Latin and Caribbean nations into economic vassals of the United States. This was especially so for Cuba, the Dominican Republic, and Nicaragua. In the case of Nicaragua, a 1927 military intervention "to protect American interests" brought the United States into its first conflict against a charismatic foe steeped in the new ideology of national liberation, Augusto Sandino and his *Sandinistas*.

The tools of American intervention varied, from the all-arms national crusade of the Spanish-American War and the multi-regiment 1906 Army of Cuban Pacification, to the occasional cruiser or gunboat and her handful of bluejackets and marines in less sweeping involvements. Before the Spanish-American War and the 1903 occupation of the Panama Canal Zone, cruising vessels of the fleet were dispatched to the trouble spots. But after the acquisition of permanent Caribbean bases at the Zone and at Guantánamo Bay, their permanent marine garrisons ensured quick deployment to any point in the Caribbean or the Pacific coast of Nicaragua.

Technology advanced enormously during the Banana Wars.

The thirty-year span between the Spanish-American War and the second Nicaragua campaign witnessed the passing of the "coffee grinder" Gatling gun for the water-cooled machine gun; the tethered kite balloon for all-metal aircraft; the coal-eating, black-powder fleet to the steam turbine, the swift light cruiser, and the fleet aircraft carrier.

The attitude of the American people toward the acquisition and policing of the empire varied across the political spectrum and over time. The delirium of the national crusade for the Spanish-American War, which to be sure had its anti-imperialist detractors, soon gave way to general ennui on the subject of America's hemispheric military endeavors. The odd cruiser and gunboat, the few companies of marines, even the dozen regiments of the Army of Cuban Pacification evoked little dissent, save for the traditional, and mainly midwestern, anti-interventionist press.

A marked change occurred however in the years immediately following World War I. The anti-imperialism of the postwar years was bolstered by reports of American atrocity, both real and imagined, from occupied Haiti and the Dominican Republic and led to the creation of significant movements in the American left for a withdrawal from empire. These movements were strongest in the late 1920's during the vicious guerrilla war against the strangely idolized Sandino and his *Sandinista* following in Nicaragua. It was a revulsion against an American external policy not seen again until the Vietnam War.

This work takes no broad strokes in either sweeping approval or condemnation of the politico-military rationale for American military commitments in Central America and the Caribbean. In the case of Panama for example, once the United States assumed great-power status with all its trials and responsibilities, intervention and dominance of an isthmian canal zone was an important and necessary step for legitimate strategic reasons. It was accomplished without bloodshed, and with the full approval of the indigenous population, though not of its former Colombian master. Additionally, the United States Army's military government in Cuba, albeit with condescending paternalism, guided that country out of the ravages of its revolutionary struggle with Spain, and sincerely attempted to plant lasting democratic institutions. The intervention in Haiti, though decried by the American left, pulled that unhappy land from the abyss of complete social collapse, and the nineteen-year occupation, notwithstanding several serious errors in colonial policy, proved to be the most prosperous and stable period in Haitian history.

On the other hand, the 1912 Cuban and 1927 Nicaraguan interventions, which fell under the rubric of dollar diplomacy and were taken primarily to protect America's economic interests, were unnecessary from both the strategic and social standpoints, and drew the opprobrium of even the military personnel involved.

As of this writing in January 1990, the corrupt drama in Panama, with the canal still a vital hemispheric asset, has brought yet another chapter to the Banana Wars, as might the pathetic social conditions of a ruthlessly self-destructive Haiti.

1:

EMPIRE BY DEFAULT
1898

It has been a splendid little war; begun with the highest motives, carried on with magnificent intelligence and spirit, favored by that fortune which loves the brave.

–John Hay, American ambassador to Great Britain, to Colonel Theodore Roosevelt, 1st United States Volunteer Cavalry

The night lay heavy over Havana. On board the battleship *Maine,* the anchor watch mustered, and lights in the wardroom and berthing spaces were extinguished. Under the muzzles of the after 10-inch guns, a group of officers escaped the stifling heat of the 'tween decks and puffed away at some excellent local cigars. Aft, in his cabin, the battleship's bespectacled, walrus-mustached skipper, Captain Charles Sigsbee, finished a letter to his wife. Forward, a bugler began sounding taps. Sigsbee put down his pen and listened. As its last notes died away, so did America's innocence. They were a swan song to her often noisy, but always small-time role as a bit player on the world's stage. Sigsbee folded his letter and placed it in the envelope. Three bells in the evening watch, February 15, 1898, dawn of the American century.

An enormous, ear-shattering, volcanic blast of fire rent the night. From stem to quarterdeck, foretop to bilge keel, the *Maine* vomited forth a horrifying conflagration of flame, gas, and smoke. Ammunition cooked off, the whole forward half of the ship blew apart and she sank into the harbor mud. Out of 350 officers and men, 252 were dead.

The news took four hours to reach Washington. Navy Secretary John D. Long was roused from sleep and handed a message from Sigsbee: "*Maine* blown up in Havana Harbor at nine-forty tonight and destroyed. Many wounded and doubtless more killed and drowned. . . . Public opinion should be suspended until further report." President McKinley was informed a few minutes later. The night watchman remembered him pacing the floor in stupefied disbelief, murmuring over and over, "The *Maine* blown up! The *Maine* blown up!"[1]

With a high heart, the United States marched off to war; the parties and people united in a national crusade. The cause was just, the motive pure: to lift the rotting yoke of imperial Spain from a prostrate, bleeding Cuba. But there were also those who, harboring dreams of a new Manifest Destiny, envisioned a much closer association with Cuba, say as a state of the Union.

The plight of the Pearl of the Antilles, Spain's "ever faithful isle," tugged mightily at America's conscience; at least that was true. It didn't seem to matter that publishing giants William Randolph Hearst and Joseph Pulitzer were locked in mortal combat and that to build newspaper circulation they fed the nation outrageous tales of Spanish perfidy and atrocity. When Hearst's *New York Journal* artist Frederick Remington wired the boss, "Everything is quiet. There is no trouble here. There will be no war [between Spain and the United States]," Hearst shot back, "You furnish the pictures and I'll furnish the war." And so they did.[2]

It also did not seem to matter that the Cuban rebels, united under the Liberation Army, had played a role equal to the Spaniards in bringing the Cuban people to their present state of wretchedness. The guerrilla war for independence, described by an American participant as containing "a larger amount of lying than any before or since," was a war of internal destabilization.[3]

The economy of the island, mainly based on sugar and tobacco, lay as prostrate as the people. Mounted columns of the Liberation Army crossed the countryside, laying the torch to foreign-owned plantations and causing massive rural unemployment. Smallholders were not exempt. Frederick Funston, a future general in the United States Army, fought for a time as a rebel volunteer in Oriente (Santiago) Province. The rebel pack trains, he noted, "scoured the country, taking from the miserable people the last sweet potato, ear of corn or banana that could be found."[4]

Spain, however, was hardly a blameless innocent. Never known for a policy of tolerant colonialism, her methods of quashing the rebellion were brutal and ultimately ineffective. Against an insurgent force that never amounted to more than 25,000 ill-armed rural laborers and peasants, leavened by a number of exiled Cubans and American filibusters,* Spain fielded a reasonably first-class army that eventually mustered 200,000 men. But the Spanish tactics were faulty. Instead of pursuing the rebels with mobile detachments of cavalry and mounted infantry, they relied instead on heavy regiments of foot, entrenched in the towns, and left the countryside to the predations of the Liberation Army.

In February 1896 there arrived a new and remorseless Captain General, Valeriano Weyler. An able continental soldier, he was devoid of political understanding and instantly became the lightning rod of the American press. The *New York Journal* provided the world with his sobriquet which has lasted to the present day: the Butcher. Weyler did little to dispel the name. In one of his first proclamations he made plain to the Cuban people that punishment for aiding the rebels was death.

Militarily, Weyler's tactics were far more suited to the high plains of Andalusia or the rocky wastes of Morocco than to the jungles of Cuba. Advancing east and west from Havana Province with his slow-moving infantry, he built a series of *trochas*, fortified lines, reinforcing them with cordons of barbed wire and blockhouses. Cuba was girthed in armored belts, and the Spanish regiments, far from having their mobility increased, were tied to their defense. As the Liberation Army probed for weak points, confused, indecisive but destructive combats popped all along the lines.

The insurgent campaign of economic destabilization increased, bringing the island to the brink of starvation. Weyler thereupon issued his most damaging decree, the infamous *reconcentrado* or concentration camp order. To completely deny the Liberation Army any support in the countryside, all rural Cubans—men, women, children—were removed from their villages and plots and packed into the garrison towns. No civilian was permitted into the rural districts without a passport and any so caught were subject to confiscation of property or death. Provision was made for the cultivation of certain areas to provide food for the *reconcentrados*, but the fields were systematically raided and the seedbeds uprooted by the rebels.[5]

In high spate American reporters flocked to Cuba, crowding

---

*From the Spanish *filibustero*, meaning "freebooter."

the bars of Havana and filling their notebooks with stock tales of Spanish atrocities, rapes, sundry horrors, and the glorious exploits of the Liberation Army. This propaganda became the most potent weapon in the rebel arsenal. "Without a press," said General Máximo Gómez, the rebels' nominal commander in chief, "we shall get nowhere."[6]

In the United States, treble-shotted broadsides exploded from the front pages, resurrecting the old Anglo-Saxon caricature of the sleazy, corrupt, and cruel Spaniard. "Blood on the roadsides, blood in the fields, blood on the doorsteps, blood, blood, blood," shrieked Joseph Pulitzer's *New York World*. "Is there no nation wise enough, brave enough, and strong enough to restore peace in this blood-smitten land?"[7]

And so it went. The revolutionary havoc and starvation wrought by the Liberation Army was met by the counter-revolutionary firing squad, mass arrests, incarceration in Cuba's inhuman prisons, and continuing abject misery of the population.

In the United States, public opinion, for a time, was held in check by the neutralist, anti-expansion policies of Democratic President Grover Cleveland. During his second tenure in office (1892–1896), the Republican outs fumed against his administration, accusing it of "brutal stupidity and cowardice." In 1896, William McKinley and the Republicans recaptured the White House. "A kindly soul in a spineless body," McKinley shocked the jingoist elements of his party by showing no great stomach for war with Spain over the issue of starving Cuba.[8]

In Spain, a new, Liberal ministry began implementing a futile policy for Cuban autonomy. In one of its first acts of conciliation, Weyler was sacked and replaced by the more tolerant General Ramón Blanco.

At once he issued orders to alleviate the suffering. A fixed, daily ration was issued to all *reconcentrados*; medical care—however rudimentary—was provided; and rural industry was reorganized as quickly as circumstances permitted. It was all too little, though, and far too late. From the provincial capital of Matanzas, the American consul reported to the State Department, "The scenes of misery and distress daily observed are beyond belief. General Blanco's order is inoperative and to no avail."[9]

In December, William McKinley presented his first annual message to Congress. Cuba constituted a major theme, and on the Spanish thumb he gave the screw a good half turn. He branded the reconcentration policy "not civilized warfare" but "extermination" and claimed matters could no longer be allowed to proceed fruitlessly. Of the possible American options, official recognition of rebel belligerency and even Cuban independence were mentioned. But as for actual American military intervention, i.e., a war with Spain to free Cuba, the President, to the consternation of the yellow press and the jingo wing of the party, waffled. Instead he naively suggested a "neutral" American presence imposing a "rational compromise" between the warring parties. The absurdity of such a suggestion was evident. Spain, with her hotly defended sense of national honor, would hardly stand aside while United States troops landed in Cuba to restore order.[10]

Until 1898 there was much talk and agitation for war, but it was not yet inevitable. This greatly frustrated the dynamic and impetuous Assistant Secretary of the Navy, Theodore Roosevelt, who felt "very sorry not to see us make the experiment of trying to land ... and to feed and clothe, an expeditionary force [in Cuba], if only for the sake of learning from our blunders." But with the new year, events did begin an inexorable march toward open conflict.[11]

On January 12, 1898, a pro-Spanish mob rioted in Havana. Several uniformed officers participated, and with shouts of "Death to Blanco and Autonomy," they ransacked the autonomist newspaper offices. The United States consul general, an ardent supporter of the rebel cause, wired the State Department that American citizens might be in danger and that warships "should be ready to move promptly."[12]

There were cruisers and gunboats aplenty, running down filibustering expeditions off the Florida coast. But if a major disturbance should occur in Havana, then a vessel of considerable force, with a strong complement of marines, would be best on the scene. Fortunately, the battleship *Maine* had just emerged from drydock, her bottom newly cleaned, and she now swung to her hook at Key West, awaiting orders.

For ten days, while Havana reverted to its usual somnolence, McKinley pondered the dilemma. United States warships had not visited Cuban ports since the revolution erupted in 1895 and to send one now might be viewed as provocative. Yet if Americans were attacked by the mob and there was no protection on the spot his vacillation would be raw meat to the Democrats. McKinley then hit upon a brilliant idea; he would send the *Maine* as a token of American friendship! The Secretary of the Navy informed the press that normal courtesy visits to Cuba were resumed and the coming of the *Maine* to Havana must not be "looked upon in any other aspect."[13]

Not surprisingly the Spanish "aspect" was somewhat different. Their ambassador in Washington, Enrique Dupuy de Lôme, "unofficially" threatened a declaration of war according to Republican Senator Henry Cabot Lodge. He was told "quietly and decidedly" that sailing orders had already been cabled and "he quieted down." From Madrid came the uncomfortable reply that since courtesy visits were back on the agenda, the armored cruiser *Vizcaya* would shortly call at New York.[14]

In late morning, January 25, the white and buff *Maine* passed under the guns of Havana's El Morro, fired a national salute to the Spanish flag, and came to rest at buoy No. 4 opposite the great shears of the navy yard. "Secure the special sea and anchor detail," intoned the boatswain's mate of the watch. "Up ditty boxes; Sweepers, man your brooms."

"Ship quietly arrived 11 A.M. today," wired the consul. "No demonstration so far, salutes exchanged. All quiet."[15]

And there she sat, brightwork gleaming in the flyblown Havana sun. Watches changed in monotonous four-hour regularity. Formal calls were paid and received, and with the exception of extra marine sentries posted at night, the *Maine* might have been tied up at Norfolk. Peace reigned profoundly.

But in Spain, there was concern. The American fleet's movements—the *Maine* at Havana, the cruiser *Marblehead* to Matanzas, and the annual winter cruise of the North Atlantic Squadron to its southern drill grounds—all gave rise to apprehension. The Foreign Minister wired de Lôme of his "increasing anxiety." The maneuvers and courtesy calls might, through some mischance, bring about a conflict. "We are trying," read the ambassador, "to avoid it at any cost [and are] making heroic efforts to maintain ourselves in the severest rectitude."[16]

On the day de Lôme received the cable, a diplomatic storm of the most dangerous sort broke in Washington and New York. It crashed down on the Spanish ambassador's head and fanned anew the simmering embers of war fever. The previous December he had written an analysis of McKinley's annual Congressional address to a friend in Cuba. It was an accurate, if wholly unflattering description of the President. In blunt and devastating language, McKinley was depicted as "weak and a bidder for the admiration of the crowd, besides being a would-be politician who tries to leave a door open behind himself while keeping on good terms with the jingoes of his party."[17]

The letter was a private correspondence but somehow had been purloined by a rebel agent in the Havana post office. From there it made its way to the Washington bureau of Mr. Hearst's *New York Journal.* The State Department was stunned. De Lôme had committed the unspeakable crime of *lèse-majesté,* and was no longer welcome in the United States; a demand was made for his immediate recall.

The publication of the letter hardened positions on both sides of the Atlantic. Americans of all parties were convinced of Spanish insincerity. To Senator Lodge it "revealed the utter hollowness of all the Spanish professions." From Madrid, Ambassador Stewart Woodford wired the State Department, "Spanish feeling grows more bitter against the United States each day . . . the Spanish Government will make no further concession, and will insist upon their own time to crush the [Cuban] rebellion."[18]

One week later the broken *Maine* made war all but certain. The yellow press wallowed in the catastrophe. There was no doubt in the mind of William Randolph Hearst. On the front page of the *New York Journal* his artists drew the battleship riding peaceably to her moorings, a Spanish mine floating under her keel. "The War Ship *Maine* Was Split in Two by an Enemy's Infernal Machine," screamed the eight-column head. A reward of $50,000 was offered "For the Detection of the Perpetrator of the *Maine* Outrage."[19]

Whether an accident or a deliberate act no one will ever know with final certainty, and Captain Sigsbee's initial reaction was as confused as the most uninformed landsman. "Probably the *Maine* was destroyed by mine," he wired Secretary Long, "perhaps by accident." In Washington, the battle lines were drawn. Secretary Long noticed how opinions were colored by political bias; "a conservative . . . is sure that it was an accident . . . a jingo is equally sure it was by design." The Secretary himself was inclined toward the accident theory but he suspended judgment.[20]

Long immediately ordered a court of inquiry. Composed of four distinguished naval officers it met three weeks at Havana and Key West. The court, while no whitewash botch, relied over-much on inconsistent testimony and left no record of its deliberative analysis. Technical experts in ordnance were not called, as the members felt their own knowledge sufficient. Great emphasis was placed on the testimony of navy divers, whose reports on the configuration of the ruptured keel and armored deck seemed to indicate an external explosion, "probably a submarine mine." Such was the court's verdict, and in the context of the rapidly deteriorating relations between the United States and Spain it was the only one that could be expected. Had the *Maine* blown up in an American or friendly foreign port, it is doubtful whether the results would have been so construed. An analysis of the wreck conducted in 1911 and later postmortems of existing data have reasonably determined that a coal bunker fire over-heated an adjacent powder magazine thereby causing the explosion.[21]

The court of inquiry appended no blame. There was not the slightest conclusive evidence of Spanish complicity, an act tanta-mount to national suicide. But there was no dampening of the American hysteria and even the opposition press excoriated the President for not demanding an immediate declaration of war. "Mr. McKinley may not have sufficient backbone even to resent an offense so gross as this," opined the *New Orleans Times-Democrat*, "but war in this country is declared by Congress." So rife were the rumor mills that the Associated Press found it necessary to issue a blanket denial. The fleet had *not* been ordered to Havana; Consul Lee had *not* been assassinated; the Cabinet and Congress were *not* in special session; President McKinley was *not* at the Capitol. The situation, it concluded, "is decidedly quiet."[22]

Yet "the slightest spark," Secretary Long noted in his diary, "is liable to result in war." Since the catastrophe he had spent long hours at his desk, and was much in need of a day's rest. On Friday afternoon, February 25, he quit early for home, leaving the hum-drum work of the department in the hands of his capable, belli-cose, and impulsive assistant secretary, Theodore Roosevelt. When Long returned after a "splendid" night's sleep, he found not only the routine matters taken care of but the fleet in the process of mobilization and on a virtual war footing. "Roosevelt," he jotted, "has come very near causing more of an explosion than happened on the *Maine* . . . the very devil seemed to possess him yesterday afternoon."[23]

Whatever Roosevelt's motives, his actions were essentially correct. The nation *was* moving toward war and McKinley, whom he described as having "no more backbone than a chocolate éclair," could do nothing to stem the feverish agitation. When war came, the navy, unlike the army, was ready and in place to fight.[24]

On March 6, McKinley himself took a giant step down the war path. Summoning "Uncle Joe" Cannon, the steel hayseed from Illinois and chairman of the powerful House Appropriations Committee, the President stated bluntly, "I must have money to get ready for war." Cannon, who foresaw the crisis, had already gone over the treasury accounts. An outright withdrawal of $50 million could be done without taxation or bonding. Would the President draft a note for the request? This McKinley refused on the tissue-thin excuse that while the United States was still negotiating with Spain, a presidential request could be interpreted as a war message and that he, standing before the world, would be accused of "double-dealing."[25]

Could the committee, McKinley asked, introduce the bill on its own motion? Cannon agreed in principle. The President's water came in a heavy bucket and Uncle Joe, hardly the political naïf, was not about to carry it alone. If he wanted the committee to act on its "own" motion, McKinley would have to draft the language. The President, Cannon remembered, "walked over to the table and wrote on a telegraph blank a single sentence: 'For national defense, fifty million dollars,' and I put the slip of paper in my pocket."[26]

Three days later, the famous Fifty Million Bill came up for its Congressional vote and passed unanimously through both houses. Coming so quickly upon de Lôme's diplomatic debacle and the tragedy of the *Maine,* the hasty legislation signaled a death knell for any Spanish hopes of conciliation with the United States. From Madrid Ambassador Woodford cabled the President. The appropriation "has not excited the Spaniards—it has stunned them. The ministry and the press are simply stunned."[27]

The question of Cuban intervention now passed from "if" to "when." The fickle hand of domestic politics bore down heavily and Damoclean threads snapped one by one. On March 28, McKinley released to Congress the court of inquiry report on the destruction of the *Maine.* While fixing no responsibility "upon any person or persons," its conclusion of an external cause stood Spain guilty in the minds of the public and the cry of "Remember the *Maine!*" entered the American lexicon.[28]

In Madrid Ambassador Woodford received the last, desperate proposals from the Spanish government. Nearly every American demand was met. They would assume reparations for the loss of the *Maine*. The *reconcentrado* decrees in Cuba were revoked and relocation funds appropriated. They even went so far as to grant a military truce should the rebels request it. Lastly, an autonomist Cuban government, already in place in Havana, would decide the question of permanent peace when it met in a month's time. If peace, Woodford was told, is what President McKinley sincerely desired, he would accept these final positions. If not, Spain was prepared to go down fighting rather than surrender her empire.

Reining in the national mood required a leader made of sterner stuff than William McKinley. He dismissed Spain's concessions as inconsequential, but hesitated in taking bold, offensive action. As he attempted to shirk responsibilty for military appropriations, so McKinley now announced his intention to lay the entire matter of national policy toward Cuba in the lap of Congress.

On April 11 the President's message was read aloud from the well of the House of Representatives. "The war in Cuba," the clerk began, "is of such a nature that short of subjugation or extermination a final military victory for either side seems impracticable." Spain's intransigence toward a United States–dictated peace was "disappointing" and so, the address continued, "the Executive is brought to the end of his effort."[29]

For the future, McKinley excluded outright recognition of the insurrectionists as neither "wise nor prudent." Such a commitment might subject the United States to "embarrassing" obligations with a new Cuban regime. With this reservation, McKinley deemed that "the forcible intervention of the United States as a neutral to stop the war is justifiable on rational grounds."[30]

In summation he asked Congress for authorization to end the war, secure the establishment of a stable government, "and to use the military and naval forces of the United States as may be necessary for these purposes."[31]

Only after he had hurled the meat into the cage did McKinley, almost casually, mention Spain's acceptance of nearly all American demands. The Congress, he was certain, would give this matter "its just and careful attention."[32]

Congress debated for a week and on April 19 presented the famous Joint Resolution for the President's signature. It was a terse, four-point document and indistinguishable from a declaration of war. At Spain's feet were thrown unconditional and nonnegotiable demands for the immediate abrogation of its sovereignty and government in Cuba. If she refused, the President was given the power to mobilize and employ "the entire land and naval forces of the United States" and the warrant to federalize the state national guards for active service.[33]

The fourth paragraph, inserted almost as an afterthought, was the most interesting and managed to preserve at the last moment America's honor. If the cry over the decades had called for unshackling Cuba from a foreign yoke, the United States, in good conscience, could not flagrantly assume Spain's imperial legacy. The paragraph, introduced as an amendment by Senator Henry Teller of Colorado, passed into the Joint Resolution with neither debate nor dissenting vote. "The United States," it stated, "hereby disclaims any disposition or intention to exercise sovereignty, jurisdiction, or control over said island, except for the pacification thereof, and asserts its determination when that is accomplished to leave the government and control of the island to its people." Any lingering desire by annexationists and expansionists to incorporate Cuba into the United States was shattered forever.[34]

If the Joint Resolution was not a literal declaration of war Spain certainly considered it to be one. On April 20, within minutes of McKinley's signature on the document, the Spanish ambassador requested his passports and entrained for Canada. In Madrid Ambassador Woodford presented the resolution to the Spanish government. According to State Department instructions, if a "full and satisfactory" reply were not received in three days, the President would proceed "without further notice."[35]

The Spanish foreign ministry refused the note with icy silence. Diplomatic relations, Woodford was told, had ceased with McKinley's signature. The next morning, April 22, before the formal declarations of war, the North Atlantic Squadron heaved in its anchors at Key West, and steamed off to blockade the Cuban coast. On Sunday, April 24, came Spain's lawful declaration, and the next day the United States Congress followed suit, declaring war retroactive to April 21.

Martial spirit was at a fever pitch. Thousands flocked to recruiting offices. In every town Civil War veterans exhorted the nation's youth to embark on the great crusade. State militias drilled in courthouse squares, while avid recruits struck studio poses for the obligatory parlor photograph.

To defeat Spain's sizable army in Cuba—150,000 veteran troops, 40,000 insular volunteers—the Regular Army of the United States, tough, capable, and inured to hardship through decades of Indian wars on the frontier, mustered barely 28,000 of all ranks. They were spread across the continent in dusty little posts and antiquated coastal forts, and were totally unprepared to take the offensive in a modern war. Secretary of War Russell Alger, a well-meaning bungler, and his overworked and under-staffed department made a complete hash of mobilization. Since the *Maine* explosion, other than increasing the army's rolls by two artillery regiments (and that forced by act of Congress), they took virtually no action to prepare the army for active, overseas cam-paigning.

So narrowly did Alger and McKinley interpret the national defense clause of the Fifty Million Bill that it was not until actual hostilities were declared that the War Department was permitted to purchase its necessary matériel. In the end, Secretary Alger would be served up as the scapegoat for the army's woeful logistic shortcomings.[36]

But rallying eager recruits to the colors proved no problem. At a stroke, Congress doubled the strength of the Regulars. The federalization of the National Guard and the establishment of volunteer regiments added nearly 200,000 men. Gentlemen of high standing flocked to Washington, offering up their services "on the altar of patriotism." William Randolph Hearst, who had done more to precipitate the conflict than anyone else, save per-haps Butcher Weyler, begged to organize and equip a regiment. McKinley, to his credit, declined the gift. Others were more for-tunate. Theodore Roosevelt soon resigned his post in the Navy Department and, with Colonel Leonard Wood, raised the excel-lent 1st United States Volunteer Cavalry Regiment, the famed Rough Riders.

At first it rather seemed like playing at war. One western governor was dismayed that his fine state regiment was forced to live under canvas. "But what if it rains?" he implored. Many a dashing young National Guardsman who fancied himself a soldier because he could cross a stretch of level ground without stepping on his feet was brought up short to the reality of his insignificance by the hard-bitten, long-service sergeants of the Regulars.

"God always looks after the fools and the United States," Bismarck once said. If so, in the spring of 1898 He needed a hefty hand. Nearly a quarter of a million men lacked equipment and there was hardly a scrap in the nation's larder. There was not a yard of khaki uniform cloth in the United States, and the troops, save for the privately equipped Rough Riders, were outfitted for tropical campaigning in blue, winter service dress. Everything had to be made or bought: uniforms, tentage, wagons, ambulances, horses, harness, field guns, small arms, ammunition, everything.

By great exertion most of the troops and gear lurched to their appointed places in one of five great camps across the country.* Yet within weeks, the cursing, apoplectic Regular officers sorted out the initial chaos. Brigades formed, and then divisions, until seven army corps—thirty-five regiments of foot, thirteen of horse, seven artillery, and three engineer—were mustered, equipped, and drilled. On May 25, just over a month since the declaration of war, the first expeditionary force sailed from San Francisco to the Philippines, where on the far side of the globe the navy had struck the first blow.

The Spanish-American War was perforce a naval war, and it proved a perfect theater for the renascent United States Navy to test Alfred Thayer Mahan's theories of force concentration and sea control. This involved maintaining command of the seas by concentrating the major fleet units at the decisive strategic point to intercept and destroy the enemy. Thus, unlike the War Department, whose political bureaucracy dithered in the weeks following the *Maine* debacle, the Department of the Navy, under Secretaries Long and Roosevelt, moved ahead with strenuous activity. Seamen whose enlistments were about to expire found themselves retained for the duration. Coal stocks were topped off, ammunition distributed, and vessels recalled from distant stations. A pair of 6-inch-gunned Brazilian cruisers building in British yards, along with a number of foreign auxiliaries and seagoing civilian yachts, were purchased to augment the fleet. In late February, on the day of the navy secretary's much needed rest, Assistant Secretary Roosevelt cabled Commodore George Dewey, commanding the United States Asiatic Squadron. "Keep full of

---

*The camps were located in Chickamauga Park, Georgia; Falls Church, Virginia; Mobile, Alabama; San Francisco, California; and Tampa, Florida.

coal," he ordered, and in the event of war assume "offensive operations in Philippine Islands."[37]

But in the western Atlantic, where the outcome of the war would be decided (and in accordance with Mahan's theories), it was imperative that strength be concentrated at the decisive strategic point—the Caribbean basin. Loading ammunition and coal in San Francisco, the new battleship *Oregon* was ordered through the Straits of Magellan to join Rear Admiral William Sampson's North Atlantic Squadron at Key West. Without mishap, she completed the 15,000 mile passage in a remarkable sixty-six days.

Of far greater importance than a tactical reinforcement to the fleet, the voyage of the *Oregon* made manifest to the navy and the nation the absolute strategic necessity for a Central American isthmian canal. In the future, the United States Navy would doubtlessly confront forces far more aggressive than those of a doddering Spain, and the canal would provide the hemispheric key for a rapid concentration of the fleet on either coast. It was a lesson that left a deep impression on that studious disciple of Mahan's, the bespectacled Assistant Secretary of the Navy, soon to serve as a lieutenant colonel of volunteer cavalry.

Neither Spain nor the United States manned a fleet which, so far as numbers were concerned, could match a first-class European navy. But anyone who could interpret a table of organization should have had little doubt as to the probable outcome of the impending actions at sea. The United States Navy had available for service four modern first-class battleships and one second-class battleship; a pair of fast, powerful armored cruisers equal to any afloat; eleven protected and three unprotected cruisers of varying age and utility; seventeen gunboats; eight torpedo boats; six coast defense monitors of doubtful worth; and a dynamite cruiser. This fighting fleet was augmented by a sizable train of colliers, supply and repair vessels, armed tugs and yachts, revenue cutters, and auxiliary cruisers.* In total weight of broadside, it outgunned the Spanish Navy by three to one.

It also maintained other, less tangible advantages. Operating

---

*Cruisers of the day came with several identifications. An armored cruiser, the most powerful of the genre, was fitted with vertical side armor as well as an armored deck below the ship's waterline. Protected cruisers were fitted with the deck only, while unprotected and lesser types dispensed with virtually all armor. The dynamite cruiser *Vesuvius* was an odd duck, fitted with three 15-inch, pneumatic, dynamite-throwing tubes. Auxiliary cruisers were fast, armed merchant vessels, officered and manned by the navy.

on interior lines of communications, the fleet's advanced, shore-based logistic support at Key West was as little as 100 and never more than 900 miles from the scene of active operations. The navy's morale, top to bottom, as indeed the nation's, was very high. The fleet was entering the peak of its material and strategic renaissance and it was eager to test its mettle.

The Spanish Navy by contrast was a drowsy, moth-eaten organization, gone to seed with the remnant empire it was honor-bound to defend. About the only thing it possessed in abundance was the unquestioned bravery of its officers and seamen. Although her Navy List was impressive, the numbers were very deceptive. There was but one obsolete battleship and an even more ancient broadside ironclad. The strength of the Spanish Navy, such as it was, lay in a quartet of up-to-date, swift armored cruisers (with four more in various states of completion) and seven new, very fast torpedo-boat destroyers. For the rest, it was mostly a collection of superannuated junk. Several of the vessels in the Caribbean and Philippines were incapable of getting up steam. Of the warships in home waters, the two battleships had yet to complete their modernization, and the most powerful of Spain's armored cruisers, the *Cristóbal Colón*, would sail to her doom mounting a pair of 10-inch wooden dummies in place of her main armament.

Yet there was a school of professional opinion that gave Spain the edge. The *London Engineer* found it "difficult to see where the usefulness of these heavily-armed floating citadels [the American battleships] comes in except to capture and sink the *Pelayo* [the one true Spanish battleship]." Of American enlisted seamen, many of whom were immigrants, the *Engineer* was even more scathing. "Naval warfare," it noted, "is a grim and ghastly reality . . . and no hirelings of an alien state are likely to come well out of such a terrible ordeal."[38]

Even the noted navalist Frederick T. Jane, compiler of *Fighting Ships*,* had his doubts. "The *Cristóbal Colón*," he wrote in April 1898, "and the other armored Spanish ships should be more than sufficient to stop any blockade of Havana."[39]

"A fine set of fellows," remarked British officers at Hong Kong as they watched Dewey's Asiatic Squadron get up steam and depart for Manila Bay, "but unhappily we shall never see them again."[40]

No one, it seemed, paid any attention to Rear Admiral Pascual

---

*Since 1897 the generally accepted annual compendium of the world's navies.

Cervera, commander of the Spanish fleet that would soon sail to the war zone. A kindly, generous man, he was a fatal pessimist and knew the unpalatable truth. "The conflict is fast coming upon us," he wrote to the Minister of Marine, "and the *Colón* has not received her big guns; the *Carlos V* has not been delivered, and her artillery is not yet mounted; the *Pelayo* is not ready for want of finishing her redoubt . . . the *Vittoria* has no ordnance, and of the *Numancia* [the broadside ironclad] we had better not speak." The vessels enumerated by the admiral comprised nearly half of Spain's theoretical battle fleet.[41]

In early April, two weeks before the declarations of war, Cervera sailed to the Cape Verde islands to await political developments. The movement caused a tremendous panic along America's eastern seabord; absolute hysteria reigned. Everywhere, badly frightened, ill-informed citizens concocted nightmarish visions of the Spanish cruisers bombarding their cities, landing troops, and holding up towns for ransom. Nervous Boston bankers removed their specie and securities and deposited them in Worcester, fifty miles inland.

Incessant appeals were made to the War and Navy departments. "They wanted guns everywhere," Secretary of War Alger remembered, "mines in all rivers and harbors on the map." Before his resignation, Assistant Navy Secretary Roosevelt was besieged by a group of New England Congressmen demanding ships to defend "Portland, Maine, Jekyll Island, Narragansett Pier, and other points of like importance." To assuage their fear Roosevelt ordered north a Civil War monitor manned by twenty-one members of the New Jersey Naval Militia. This, he mirthfully noted, "satisfied Portland entirely!" albeit the craft was "useless against any war vessel more modern than one of Hamilkar's galleys."[42]

What was not a laughing matter, however, was the temporary weakening of the North Atlantic Squadron. The naval war would be won or lost in the Caribbean, not off Martha's Vinyard. Even if Cervera managed to lob a few shells at New York or Boston, it was of no great military import, and he could not sustain the operation without a ready supply of coal.

But the clamor of the coastal cities for protection forced the Navy Department into unsatisfactory compromises. The North Atlantic Squadron was split. The main group under Rear Admiral William Sampson was based at Key West, ready to assume the offensive against Cuba and Puerto Rico. The second force, the

Flying Squadron, commanded by Commodore W. S. Schley, operated from Norfolk for the roving protection of the Atlantic coast. For a time the fleet was further stripped of several cruisers by the creation of the Northern Patrol Squadron.

On April 29 Cervera upped anchor and steamed off from the Cape Verde islands into the North Atlantic void.

Two days later, across the world, across the ocean that is Pacific in name only, the Asiatic Squadron, blacked out and cleared for action, crept south by east off Bataan. "As darkness slowly descended the scene took on a character at once soothing and disturbing," Lieutenant Bradley Fiske of the gunboat *Petrel* remembered; "soothing, because everything was so beautiful and so calm; disturbing, because of the grim preparations evident . . . the men lay, or sat, or stood by their guns."[43]

While mess cooks served out black coffee and hardtack to the men at their stations, the big, 8-inch gunned *Olympia* led the cruisers *Baltimore, Raleigh, Boston,* and gunboats *Concord* and *Petrel* darkly, silently, and with only the monotonous throb of the engines and the swish of the water alongside, past the harbor forts, past the silent batteries of rocky Corregidor and into the fold of Manila Bay.

Straight ahead lay the city, its lights visible in the predawn ink. To starboard, Sangley Point came into view. Behind its batteries sheltered the relics of a dying empire: pathetic vessels, steaming aimlessly or anchored in the mud.

"There were seven of them in line," remembered the *Olympia*'s navigator, "they were cleared for action, and their crews animated by rounds of regulation cheers and the display of battle-flags."[44]

The first shell splash went up, the shell lofted a mile short by the batteries on Sangley Point. Then more fire, faster, but all of it wild. Through the geysers of foaming sea, the American line advanced, each ship keeping rigid and perfect station in line ahead. A round suddenly burst directly over the flagship *Olympia*. On her bridge, florid, walrus-faced, and deceptively jovial, Commodore George Dewey steadied his binoculars on the jumble of masts and smoke; it was time. He turned to his flag captain, "You may fire when ready, Gridley."

Back and forth, for two hours, the *Olympia* led the squadron through a series of flat ovals and figure eights. The Spanish vessels according to the ship's navigator, "now and then [made] isolated and ineffectual rushes in advance—rushes which had no rational significance except as demonstrations of the point of honor. They were mere flourishes of desperation inspired by defeat."[45]

With the morning sun still low in the eastern sky, Dewey signaled a temporary retirement to count his remaining ammunition and to give the hands some breakfast. On hearing the order one *Olympia* seaman shouted to the bridge, "For God's sake, Captain, don't let us stop now. To hell with breakfast!"[46]

At 11:00 A.M. the squadron resumed fire, and after another hour of battle, the Spanish were annihilated.

At San Francisco, 11,000 troops of the VIII Corps boarded their transports and steamed for the Philippines. On August 13, Manila surrendered after token resistance. The Filipinos, in sporadic revolt against Spain since 1896, were greatly surprised when they learned of the exchange from one imperial master to another and they rose in insurrection against the new American rule. It was a bloody, brutal, and protracted affair. It took three years for the United States Army and Marine Corps to "pacify" the archipelago; a hard victory for what would prove to be a costly strategic albatross. The bill came due a scant half century in the future, and was expensive indeed.

In the Caribbean the hunt for the elusive Cervera consumed the energy and coal of Admiral Sampson's North Atlantic Squadron. The destruction or neutralization of the Spanish fleet was the grand-tactical key to the whole Cuban campaign. While the fleet remained free and afloat, no expedition could sail for an invasion of the island.

Sampson guessed that the Spanish would coal first at San Juan, Puerto Rico. With his armored cruiser flagship the *New York,* battleships *Iowa* and *Indiana,* two monitors and a torpedo boat, he steamed to investigate. But the place, save for an ancient French cruiser, was empty of warships and Sampson had to satisfy himself with an ineffective bombardment of the harbor forts.

Cervera, his bottoms foul, crawled the sea at an agonizing seven knots. Instead of San Juan, he touched land far to the east, at Martinique. The French, however, refused coal, and the depleted vessels were forced to Dutch Curaçao. Cervera was able to partly fill his bunkers there but options were now limited, making offensive operations impossible. Aside from empty bunkers, the fleet's engines and boilers were in a horrible state. Worse, having slipped into the Caribbean at its eastern end, Havana and the whole of Cuba's Atlantic coast were inaccessible. The only haven in reach, Santiago de Cuba, lay 700 miles north in the notch of the island's great fish tail. On May 19, without having sighted a hostile ship, the Spanish fleet, amidst cheers and congratulations, rode up-channel and moored off the town.

Schley's Flying Squadron, meanwhile, had come down from Hampton Roads and went steaming around Cuba's south coast. It was possible the Spanish fleet had put into Cienfuegos. Schley took his time getting there, and after a leisurely reconnaissance, he came up empty.

Evidence, however, was fast accumulating that pointed to Santiago de Cuba as Cervera's bolt hole. Schley got word by fast dispatch vessel and at six knots, through mounting seas, he headed east. But his coal was running low and though the Flying Squadron had a wheezy collier in company, the rolling swells made coaling at sea impossible. When only twenty miles from Santiago, Schley signaled his ships to return to Key West.

He was delayed by engine trouble and was still near Santiago when an auxiliary cruiser steamed up, bringing word from Washington: "All Department's information indicates Spanish division is still at Santiago . . . and that the enemy, if therein, does not leave without decisive action." Schley was a dashing, courageous officer, but his response contained neither dash nor courage: "Much to be regretted . . . forced to proceed for coal to Key West."*[47]

But fortune smiled. The seas moderated, coaling commenced, and in the evening of May 28 Schley took station off Santiago. The next morning any remaining doubt was dispelled. From their perches his lookouts spotted the *Colón* poking about in the outer roads. On June 1 Rear Admiral Sampson hove up with the North Atlantic Squadron and assumed overall command. Concentration of force at the decisive point had been achieved.

The American vessels assumed station for close blockade. At the apex of a semicircle, about five miles to sea, rode the battleships *Iowa, Indiana, Massachusetts, Oregon,* and the little *Texas.* On the flanks were the armored cruiser flagships, Sampson's

---

*Departmental communications with the fleet off eastern Cuba were maintained by vessels shuttling back and forth to the cable station at Môle St. Nicholas, Haiti.

New York and Schley's *Brooklyn*. Smaller craft—cruisers, torpedo boats, armed yachts—patrolled inshore.

But the Spanish still constituted a "fleet in being." By just rotting at his moorings Cervera exerted a restraining effect on American operations. So long as his ships could get up steam, the possibilities of escape and interference were ever present.

Mines and shore batteries precluded Sampson from rushing the anchorage and imitating Nelson's annihilation of the French fleet at the Battle of the Nile in 1798. His alternative was an attempt to plug the channel with a blockship. The collier *Merrimac* was chosen and manned with a picked crew of volunteers to scuttle her in the narrows. But the daring plan went awry. The vessel was spotted and Spanish shore batteries quickly disabled her steering gear. Drifting, she sank, only partially blocking the channel. Several attempts to silence the batteries by bombardment showed no effect.

Holding bare steerage way, the blockading fleet ate prodigiously into its coal. Key West was a good 900 miles away, too far for continuous daily logistic support. A forward base was necessary. On June 10, east about forty miles, a detached force landed 850 marines to seize the excellent anchorage of Guantánamo Bay.

It was now the turn of the army. Admiral Sampson cabled Washington for sufficient troops to capture the enemy's harbor works. Once the army had done, he could send in his small craft to clear the minefields, then storm the inner anchorage with the heavy ships of the fleet.

At Tampa, Florida, Major General William Shafter, the corpulent commander of the V Corps, loaded his 25,000 men into their transports. It was a logistic nightmare of the first order. Vessels there were, chartered by the War Department and fitted with bunks for the men and stalls for the horses and mules. But port and loading facilities were virtually nonexistent. Worse yet, only a single-track railroad led from the base camps to the dock.

War Department paperwork compounded the chaos. "There are over 300 [railway] cars loaded with war material along the roads about Tampa," reported General Nelson Miles, the army's commander in chief. "Stores are sent to the quartermaster at Tampa, but the invoices and bills of lading have not been received . . . officers are obliged to break open seals and hunt from car to car to ascertain whether they contain clothing, grain, balloon material, horse equipments, ammunition, siege guns, commissary stores, etc."[48]

Regimental officers learned there were only enough berthing spaces in the transports for about 18,000 men. In a mad scramble, units broke camp. Those lucky enough managed to find trains; the others marched, but it mattered little. Lieutenant Colonel Roosevelt of the Rough Riders jotted in his diary, "Worst confusion yet. [Railroad] system is utterly mismanaged. No military at head. No allotment of transports. No plans."[49]

The 6th Infantry grabbed a stock train and were forced to stand for hours in soft manure while the cars were shunted about in a baking midday sun. On the other hand, the black troopers of the 10th Cavalry managed to get aboard a train whose luxury coaches came equipped with ice water, but they had nothing to eat. A white officer who attempted to make arrangements with a local restaurant was refused accommodation on the grounds that it would ruin business.*

At dockside it was no better. Lieutenant Colonel Roosevelt learned that his regiment's ship, the *Yucatan,* had also been allotted to two others. "I ran down to my men," he wrote, "and rushed them to the dock . . . holding the gangplank against the Second Infantry and Seventy-first New York."[50]

By June 14, it had all somehow been done, and the convoy, under the protection of the navy, sailed for Cuba. Six days later they hove into view off the mountainous coast of Oriente Province.

For the first and only time in the campaign, the army and navy chiefs held a combined council of war. Before any troops landed, Sampson and Shafter met ashore with General Calixto García, the bullet-scarred commander of the Liberation Army in eastern Cuba. The first order of business was to cover the landing. Several hundred Spanish troops were in the immediate vicinity of the beaches, and García promised to keep them busy with a diversionary attack.

But of the main point, the army's mission, there seems to have been no firm decision. Sampson returned to his flagship assuming the army would skirt the city and concentrate instead on destroying the harbor fortifications.

On June 22 the troops went ashore at Daiquirí, eighteen miles

---

*In the Regular Army's order of battle, four regiments, the 9th and 10th cavalry, and the 24th and 25 infantry, were black units; the officers were white. All were assigned to the V Corps and comprised ten percent of its strength.

east of Santiago. The landing sites were pounded by rough surf, and a high ridgeline covered the beaches for twenty miles. Had the local Spanish Army, 12,000 seasoned troops within easy call, displayed even moderate initiative, they could have turned the landing into a bloody shambles and thrown the invaders back with disastrous losses. Instead, they withdrew inland.

Specialized landing craft lay four decades in the future, and the regiments, towed willy-nilly by the fleet's steam launches, came ashore in ships' boats. Horses and mules were pushed from the transports to make their own way through the surf. All but a half-dozen made it. When one group of artillery mounts lost their direction and headed out to sea, an alert bugler sounded the recall. Obediently the horses wheeled about and swam ashore. Despite the disorganization, by day's end 6,000 troops were ashore.

The crusading nature of the war imbued the men with deep emotions of patriotism. The first general ashore, old "Fighting Joe" Wheeler, late of the Confederate cavalry and the United States Congress, ordered some Rough Riders to hoist the flag over a Spanish blockhouse. The troops, noted a correspondent, spent a quarter hour in "whistle shrieks, cheers, yells, drum flares, bugle calls and patriotic songs." When a regimental band played "The Star-Spangled Banner" they fell quiet. Then "three full-lunged hurrahs crashed against the hill, and the salute to the flag was complete."[51]

The first meeting of the United States and Cuban Liberation armies was also met by shouts and went well. *"Viva Cuba libre"* from the Americans was met by *"Vivan los Americanos"* from the insurgents. The rebels were heroes to the American mind right out of the ragged, Valley Forge tradition. "The day of the landing at Daiquirí," wrote a reporter for the *Washington Star,* "Castillo's regiment was coming through. The strings of cloth which answered for shirts and other garments could hardly be said to clothe the nakedness of the men."[52]

At first the Americans shared their rations generously with both insurgent and refugee alike. But fraternity quickly led to contempt and then disgust. Every soldier of the V Corps was considered a mark, a veritable cornucopia by the Liberation Army, to be ready on every occasion to disgorge his food, clothing, and tobacco. On both sides the spirit of solidarity soon melted away.

On June 23 a forward base was established along the coast at Siboney and the advance commenced. But Shafter and Sampson, as the navy was soon to learn, were not in accord regarding the objective. If the harbor forts were the principal target, as they were according to Sampson's naval logic, the point regiment would have stepped out along the coastal railroad to within four miles of El Morro and her attendant batteries, then executed a column-right, inland, to cut them off from Santiago city. The works could then be stormed from the rear.

But the next day Wheeler launched his dismounted cavalry troopers into the jungle against a strong Spanish position at Las Guásimas. At odds of about one to two, the Regulars and Rough Riders drove the Spanish out and opened the road to the main enemy lines around Kettle and San Juan hills.

Sampson, on learning of the action, considered it a feint, or at most a tactical necessity to eliminate any flanking threat to the coastal march. Days later, much to his astonishment, came a message from Shafter outlining the army's principal objective, the city of Santiago de Cuba.

The strain of a tropical campaign in the height of the rainy season took its toll on the V Corps. Heat exhaustion, typhoid, and the onset of the dread yellow fever thinned the ranks. Worse yet, 8,000 Spanish troops were reported coming in from the west to bolster the Santiago garrison. Shafter's command barely outnumbered the enemy, and should those reinforcements arrive, the odds would tip; he resolved to attack the city on July 1.

The plan was faulty and as a result the battle, as the Duke of Wellington said of Waterloo, was "a near run thing." On the extreme right, against the isolated and weakly held Spanish outpost of El Caney, Shafter deployed nearly half his attacking force, Lawton's reinforced 2nd Division.* On the left, three miles south, came the main thrust, the 1st and Cavalry divisions, assaulting the outer Spanish trench lines around Kettle and San Juan hills.

Naturally suited for defense, these hillocks faced an expanse of open ground, and the Spanish had fairly well fortified the positions. Barbed wire was strung in front of the rifle pits, stone forts and blockhouses anchored the trenches. Once past the line of departure the Americans, in their winter blue, would lay naked of cover, exposed on a scraggly glacis to a withering fire.

On the night before the attack, war correspondent Richard

---

*The divisions were small, only one-third the size of their American World War I counterparts. On parade, Wheeler's Cavalry Division mustered just over 2,500 troopers, and Lawton's infantry division approximately 6,200.

Harding Davis made his rounds. "Above us," he later penned in his notebook, "the tropical moon hung white and clear in the dark purple sky, pierced with millions of white stars. . . . Before the moon rose again, every sixth man who had slept in the mist that night was either killed or wounded."[53]

At dawn Lawton opened the attack on El Caney, and he found a determined little Spanish garrison, 520 men, who had no thought of surrender. Outranged, the antiquated, black-powder American artillery was ineffective against the position's stone fort. Black powder also proved the bane of the 2nd Massachusetts Infantry. Like most of the federalized National Guard regiments, they were equipped with obsolete, single-shot Springfields whose discharges provided ready targets for the modern, smokeless Spanish Mausers.

The attack on El Caney, supposed to last two hours at most, bogged down, and by mid-afternoon there was little progress. Only when the enemy had run short of ammunition enabling the American artillery to deploy within range, could the assault be pressed home.

"The line is now being formed for the final rush," wrote Lieutenant James A. Moss of the black 25th Infantry. "Men are still dropping by the wayside, but on, on, up, up, they go, those dusky boys in blue!"[54]

Just after 4:00 P.M. the stone fort, key to the position, was taken by storm. Two hundred and thirty-five men, fully half the Spanish defenders, were killed or wounded, and most of the remainder were taken prisoner. Lawton's units suffered likewise, eighty-one dead, 360 wounded.

The major land battle for Santiago, the assault up Kettle and San Juan hills, has rightly entered the hagiography of American military history as one of its most heroic minor performances. It is only the popular but erroneous version of the battle, falsely depicting mounted Rough Riders leading the charge, that has denigrated this bloody little action into a seeming comic opera.

The fight at first went badly. The deployment of the 1st and Cavalry divisions to the line of departure was a confused trek down enemy-observed roads and jungle trails. A Signal Corps observation balloon, towed along with the troops, provided an aiming point for the Spanish artillery—new Krupp smokeless quick-firers that completely outranged and silenced the American guns. "It was thoroughly evident," wrote Hearst's artist Frederick

Remington, "that the Spaniards had the range of everything in the country."[55]

Marching up the road, the 71st New York came under heavy fire and panicked. But coming up were the 10th Cavalry and the Rough Riders. The troopers pushed through and deployed in a skirmish line. Some of the volunteer cavalry raised a cheer, but were quickly admonished by Colonel Roosevelt, "Don't cheer, but fight, now's the time to fight."[56]

The situation was desperate. On the left the commander of the 3rd Infantry Brigade was killed and his two successors wounded. In the center the 6th Infantry suffered twenty-five percent casualties in ten minutes. Artillery support, such as it was, had ceased, the infantry were running short of ammunition, and communications were almost nonexistent. Lawton was still heavily engaged at El Caney, and there was little hope of succor from that quarter.

The serried ranks of the Cavalry Division were swept by a scythe of fire from the heights. Remaining in position meant annihilation; they must either advance into the hail of steel or turn their backs and run. The Cavalry Division was ordered into the attack up Kettle Hill.

In the face of a galling fire the dismounted troopers of the 1st, 9th, the Rough Riders, and part of the 10th Cavalry regiments crawled up the ground. At this critical juncture a battery of three Gatling guns, "coffee grinders," recklessly galloped to the front and opened a withering fusillade on the Spanish lines; immediately, the enemy began to withdraw—now was the moment.

Conspicuously mounted and in full view of the enemy, Colonel Roosevelt took command of the forward elements of the division and ordered his bugler to sound the charge. "We were all in the spirit of the thing," he later wrote, "and greatly excited by the charge, the men cheering and running forward between shots."[57]

On the left, in front of San Juan Hill, the infantry trumpets pealed the advance and the foot troops surged forward. In the van, old, bearded, white-haired Brigadier General Hawkins sat his horse, waving his hat, "Come on! Come on!" he yelled to his men. "Yes, they were going up the hill, up the hill," wrote correspondent Stephen Crane. "It was the best moment of anybody's life." Foreign military attachés were shocked at the apparently suicidal American tactics. Echoing the French comment regarding the charge of the Light Brigade a half century before, one observer noted, "It is very gallant, but very foolish."[58]

The mowing fire of the Gatling guns kept the Spanish down, allowing the American artillery to limber up and move forward. At 1:30 P.M. the blue-clad regiments, in no formation whatever, crashed over the hill crest and into the enemy's trenches.

The Cavalry Division, having secured Kettle Hill, moved down in a flanking attack, a maneuver which, in conjunction with the main assault, drove the enemy from the heights. Roosevelt, on foot, led the attack. "Thinking that the men would all come, I jumped over the wire fence in front of us and started at the double; but, as a matter of fact, the troopers were so excited, what with shooting and being shot, and shouting and cheering, that they did not hear, or did not heed me; and after running about a hundred yards I found I had only five men along with me."[59]

But the former Assistant Secretary of the Navy and future President of the United States rallied his men. They came on at the rush and bounded into the trench line, its bottom, "filled with dead bodies in the light blue and white uniform of the Spanish regular army."[60]

By nightfall the two armies faced each other in their lines barely 800 yards apart. The Americans were in sight of Santiago, but having suffered over 1,100 casualties they were shaken, disorganized, hungry, and utterly exhausted. Shafter had committed over eighty percent of the V Corps in the battle, and there were no reserves to wrench a decisive victory.

The general was despondent, ill with fever, and the tropical heat exacted a toll on his 300 pound bulk. On July 2, the day after the battle, he wrote to Admiral Sampson, "Terrible fight yesterday . . . I urge that you make effort immediately to force the [harbor] entrance to avoid future losses among my men, which are already very heavy. You can now operate with less loss of life than I can."[61]

Up the signal halyards of the flagship *New York* soared a hoist of colorful bunting: "Disregard motions of Commander-in-Chief." Exasperated with Shafter's campaign and the general's inability to comprehend the acute dangers of taking the fleet through the minefields, Sampson steamed off for a face-to-face confrontation.

It was Sunday, July 3, and in the blockading ships age-old

routines took their place beside the grim new realities of the day. Sunday was always captain's inspection and war or no the hands made ready. In Commodore Schley's flagship, the armored cruiser *Brooklyn,* Captain Francis Cook ordered "white mustering clothes for the crew and all white for the officers. The first call for quarters had been sounded," he remembered. "I had laid out on my bunk my last laundered white coat, and was about to don it for the occasion when I heard the ringing voice of the executive officer calling 'Clear ship for action!' I knew at once from the tone that it meant business."[62]

In the battleship *Iowa,* it had just rung three bells in the forenoon watch, 9:30 A.M. In his cabin, Captain Robley Evans, "Fighting Bob," relaxed after breakfast with his naval cadet son, when the general alarm sounded throughout the ship. "My son," Evans remembered, "jumped to his feet . . .'Papa, the enemy's ships are coming out!' "[63]

From every bridge in the blockading fleet, long glasses were whipped from their beckets and trained on the harbor mouth. They saw Cervera's flagship, the *Infanta María Teresa,* smoke belching from her twin funnels, and crimson and gold Spanish battleflags snapping defiantly at her masts, steaming head-on at the *Brooklyn.* Entering gun range as they swept past El Morro, the *Vizcaya, Cristóbal Colón, Almirante Oquendo,* and the destroyers *Plutón* and *Furor* plowed forward in her wake.

On board the *María Teresa,* Captain Victor Concas was under no illusions as to the outcome of this, the death ride of the Spanish Navy. He turned to his admiral and requested permission to open fire. Throughout the doomed ship, the high, sweetly piercing notes of the bugle signaled the start of battle. "My bugles," Concas wrote, "were the last echo of those which history tells were sounded in the taking of Granada; it was the signal that the history of four centuries of greatness was ended and that Spain had passed into a nation of the fourth class. . . . 'Poor Spain,' I said to my beloved and noble admiral."[64]

In the American ships only the *Oregon* had all her boilers on line; engine telegraphs jangled, and grimy, sweaty firemen threw in their loads of coal to build up a head of steam. Within minutes all vessels were making headway.

As soon as the *María Teresa* and her consorts swung out and headed west along the coast, they came under the fire of every American gun that could bear. The Spanish warships were still fitted as for peacetime; black hulls, white upperworks, and all their woodwork lacquered, varnished, and in place. "The Spanish ships came out as gaily as brides to the altar," was how Captain Jack Philip of the *Texas* put it.[65]

They put on a brave show and they paid dearly. Fires from exploding American shells fed on the paint and oil and swept across their decks, driving the gunners from unprotected batteries. A pair of 12-inch shells slammed through the *María Teresa*'s hull, wreaking awful damage deep in her bowels.

The action soon degenerated into a wild chase, every ship on its own. Half an hour after the opening gun, the *María Teresa*, now a gutted, floating charnel house, turned ashore and ran up the beach.

One by one, the rest of Cervera's ships followed their admiral, their hulls and upperworks riddled. The *Oquendo* was next. Eight-inch shells burst under her forward barbette and in the torpedo flat, killing or wounding every man in the stations. She ran up a white flag and grounded on the beach.

The two destroyers were taken care of by the battleship *Indiana* and the armed yacht *Gloucester*. Within minutes both were out of action, the *Plutón* on the rocks, and the *Furor* sinking. According to the *New York*'s skipper, "The dramatic character of the scene was intensified . . . by the penetration of one of the *Plutón*'s boilers by a shell and the sudden rise, vertically, into the air of a vast silver-like column of steam, hundreds of feet in height; a geyser of unapproachable magnificence."[66]

Then the *Vizcaya*, flames shooting fore and aft from her decks, turned ashore. As her keel touched ground, two tremendous explosions rent her asunder.

In the end the American ships bore down on the *Colón*. But with 10-inch wooden dummies in place of her big guns she could make no effective reply. Just after 1:00 P.M. main battery shells from the *Oregon* passed over her bows and it was all over. "At 1:20 [P.M.]," noted the deck log of the *Texas*, "the chase hauled in toward shore and ran bow on beach, hauling down colors."[67]

Spain had lost her fleet and with it the war. One hundred sixty of her sailors were dead, and 1,800, including Admiral Cervera, were prisoners; only one American was killed and one wounded.

"An hour or two at Manila," said Captain Albert Barker of the navy's War Board, "an hour or two at Santiago, and the maps of the world were changed."[68]

The destruction of the Spanish fleet mooted the land campaign. Strategically it was all over; Cuba was isolated. On the morning of July 3, before the naval action had begun, Shafter sent his first ultimatum to General José Toral. If Santiago were not surrendered by the next day, a bombardment of the city would commence. Toral refused.

There was, however, a temporary truce for the exchange of wounded Spanish prisoners for the captured crew of the *Merrimac*. "Everybody drew a long breath and thanked God," said Lieutenant John Pershing (Army Chief of Staff, 1921–24) of the 10th Cavalry. "Officers and soldiers of both armies were glad, and stood in the lines facing each other with a curiosity mingled with respect."[69]

The V Corps had nearly collapsed under the rigors of tropical campaigning. Typhoid, malaria, dysentery, and the first cases of yellow fever were taking a greater toll than the Spanish Mausers. To General Shafter it was imperative that the issue be decided, lest his army melt away from sickness. After further surrender demands, all of which were refused, the truce ended on July 10. At daybreak the next morning, the artillery and the fleet resumed bombardment.

In the meantime, the army's commander, General Nelson Miles, had landed with reinforcements. Under a flag of truce, word was sent into the Spanish lines requesting a parley. At noon on July 13 Shafter, Miles, and Toral met between the trenches.

Toral informed the Americans that under Spanish law he was not permitted to surrender so long as he had ammunition and food; the honor of Spanish arms must be upheld. That, Miles noted tersely, had already been accomplished. He was given until noon the next day to communicate with his superiors and reach a decision.

When again the generals met, Toral shocked the Americans by offering up not only Santiago, but his entire command. "I was simply thunderstruck," Shafter reported, "that, of their own free will, they should give me 12,000 men that were absolutely beyond my reach."[70]

The ceremony for the capitulation was scheduled for Sunday the seventeenth, and the morning dawned bright and clear. To a large field in front of the city rode General Shafter, his divisional commanders and staffs, escorted by a troop of the 2nd Cavalry. Toral, with a company of infantry, was there to meet them. The Spanish and American troops presented arms, and the flag that had flown over the city for 382 years was pulled down and furled forever.

In column of twos, according to rank, the generals rode into Santiago. When the cathedral clock struck twelve, the flag of the United States was hoisted over the governor's palace, above the inscription that read VIVA ALFONSO XIII. In the square a battery fired a twenty-one-gun salute, the band of the 6th Cavalry struck up "Hail Columbia," and the 9th Infantry slapped their Krags and presented arms.

By late July, General Miles had landed an expedition in Puerto Rico, taken its first city, Ponce, and was in full march for San Juan. Spain knew that the time for negotiations had arrived. A note was delivered to President McKinley requesting a general armistice. This was refused and countered with a demand for preliminary peace accords with three major conditions: first, Spain must relinquish all claim of sovereignty to Cuba, and immediately evacuate the island; second, in lieu of a cash war indemnity, the outright cession to the United States of Puerto Rico plus an island in the central Pacific Ladrones (Marianas) group selected by the United States;* third, the occupation by United States forces of the city, bay, and harbor of Manila, pending the Philippine archipelago's disposition at the conclusion of a final treaty of peace.

The terms were severe. Spain sought some modification, especially for the retention of Puerto Rico, but to no avail. McKinley did, however, accede to Spain's desire for the negotiations to be held on neutral ground, and Paris was selected.

On October 1 the commissioners of peace convened in the great hall of the French Foreign Ministry. As was to be expected, there were major difficulties. Along with the abrogation of sovereignty, Spain also wished to unburden herself of Cuba's enormous internal debt. This the United States refused to assume.

The Philippines were also an obstacle. The protocol, Spain

---

*The island chosen was Guam. Her Spanish governor was completely unaware that war had broken out, and the island was captured on June 20 without a fight by the cruiser *Charleston*.

argued, spoke only of American occupation of Manila and its environs; the future of the colony must be left open to discussion. Again the United States commissioners refused to yield. Anyway, what did Spain want with the Philippines? It was constantly in rebellion, and a sap on an already empty Spanish treasury.

But now the Spanish commissioners refused to yield. They were firmly convinced of the correctness of their position, and in fact, held a tenuous strategic advantage. Despite the total American victory on land and sea, only an armistice was in place, and should negotiations be broken off, hostilities would resume. With Spain's island empire already in the enemy's possession, a renewal of the fighting might well demand an invasion of Spain itself: a European incursion wholly divorced from traditional American policy and completely beyond its present material means. To American public opinion, the fruits of war and more had already been realized; would popular support be forthcoming in a European adventure 3,000 miles away? And besides, there were the diplomatic complications of a United States offensive on the European continent that would subject the republic to the immediate meddling of the great powers. Spain might yet win the peace, if not the war.

This was not to be. In return for the cession of the Philippines, the United States offered $20 million, certain trade concessions, and the mutual relinquishment of all indemnity claims. On November 28, Spain agreed to the American terms and the treaty was signed on December 10, 1898.[71]

2:

CUBA
1899–1917

About the most unbeautiful thing in the general frame of American opinion is its contempt for small republics struggling with internal troubles.

–*Army and Navy Journal*, September 22, 1906

From the semicircle of trenches around the heights of San Juan Hill, a victorious American army looked down to its prize. It appeared a pretty town, Santiago de Cuba. On steep, hilly streets descending to the shimmering harbor, faded pastel buildings topped with red tile roofs baked in the mid-July sun. Green foliage exploded everywhere about the encircling mountains in whose bosom nestled the city and port; the whole guarded by the brooding, ancient ramparts of El Morro.

Westward, beyond the harbor mouth, beyond the view of the infantry, cavalry, and pop-gun artillery of the triumphant V Army Corps, lay the beached and blackened wrecks of the Spanish fleet; gravestones to four centuries of empire in the New World. Just offshore, riding to their anchors, sat the gravediggers—the burly, gray, coal-belching ships of the United States Navy's North Atlantic Squadron.

From the sea Santiago lay invisible, up the notch in the great fish tail that formed eastern Cuba. But from bridge and fighting top, sailors gagged on the stench wafted out by the land breeze. They watched hundreds of vultures, high overhead, as they wheeled and lumbered over what was in reality, "stewed in its misery and filth," a city of death.[1]

"The Commanding General directs you to take charge of the City of Santiago," read the scribbled order to Brigadier General

Leonard Wood (Army Chief of Staff, 1910–1914), lately of the Rough Riders and now commanding the 2nd Cavalry Brigade. On July 18, 1898, two days after the Spanish capitulation in eastern Cuba, Wood rode at the head of his staff down the narrow streets into the town. At every turn, emaciated, "ghastly-looking" people dragged aimlessly in search of a patch of shade. All about, "poisoning the air with foul exhalations," lay the rotting carcasses of dead animals piled among heaps of decomposing garbage, dung, and filth. Neighing with disgust, shying from the reek of corruption, the 2nd Brigade's horses trotted across open sewers clogged with foul water and human excrement.[2]

Leonard Wood, ex-army contract surgeon and Indian fighter, surveyed his domain. As Santiago's new governor, his task was akin to cleaning out the Augean stables. The city's normal population of about 50,000 was doubled by the concentration of two armies whose sick lists climbed by the hour. Refugees with nothing to eat but raw fruit and polluted water streamed from the countryside. There were no public funds, the municipal police and courts had ceased to function, and the city's medieval dungeons were filled alike with felons, political prisoners, and the forgotten who had long served out their sentences. By hundreds, the dead lay unburied.

Visiting the Spanish military hospital, Wood found the stench in the wards "insupportable." Heaps of infected clothing and blankets blocked the halls. In the courtyard the well was fouled with human and animal skeletons, shoes, rags, and slime a foot deep.[3]

His tasks were clear: feed the hungry, bury the dead, nurse the sick, and clean up the city.

On any given day 18,000 to 20,000 army rations were dispersed to civilians, with bacon, sugar, hardtack, and rice forming the basic diet. "All classes and all ages were represented," Wood wrote, "and the issue force worked from early in the morning until after dark, issuing and issuing, with no time to weigh things or bother about the exact amounts authorized or required. . . . Outside these stations the soldiers, with their rifles used only as bars, strove to push the crowd back, to keep order and to protect the weak . . . these were strange and very unusual sights for an American, and very unpleasant ones."[4]

Cleaning the city and disposing of the corpses—the death rate was over 200 a day—were tandem projects, and for the task Wood found a remarkable individual. "Major" George Barbour held his rank by courtesy and to match it wore a uniform sewn by a fashionable military tailor. He just seemed to show up, full of stories about Buffalo Bill and Indian fighting. He also claimed a superintendency of New York City's street cleaners; for Wood that was good enough.

Barbour was given a thousand civilians for the job. Every cart, wagon, driver, and laborer was pressed into service. All workers were given fair wages—part money, part rations. Those who refused soon learned, as Wood put it simply, "that there were things far more unpleasant than cheerful obedience."[5]

There were too many corpses for burial so they were hauled to the outskirts. On gratings of railroad iron the bodies were piled eighty high and layered with dry grass. Gallons of kerosene were poured over the pyres and the frightful heaps were torched to ashes. "It was the only thing to be done," Wood remembered, "for the dead threatened the living and a plague was at hand."[6]

Day after day the black, nauseating columns of smoke palled in a monstrous cloud over the city. On a day when rains quenched the fires, kerosene ran short. When Barbour tried to buy more, he found the price had risen to a Spanish gold dollar a gallon. Wood called the merchants to his office. "We have come to Cuba," he lectured, "at your call to relieve your distress. You are repaying our efforts by trying to make money out of us. . . . I call such conduct murder." The cost of kerosene resumed its normal level.[7]

The rubbish of centuries was hauled away, and the cobbled streets themselves ran bright with kerosene fires. But the civilian population treated Wood's measures with cynical indifference. "I do not understand you Americans," he was frequently told. "You are proud of your liberty and right to do as you please, yet here you walk into my house and tell me that I must clean my yard and sidewalk and how I must do it. Why, the Spaniards never would dare do such a thing." But Wood and Barbour were not given to debate. On more than one occasion, Barbour smashed down doors and publicly horsewhipped respectable citizens for making sewers out of the streets. By these means the death rate fell, within a month, from 200 per day to thirty-seven.[8]

Now Year's Day, 1899, dawned promisingly over Havana. Clouds of bunting hung from the porticoes of public buildings. All around, Cuban and American flags proclaimed a day of celebration. In the Plaza de Armas, the 8th and 10th in-

fantry, veterans of El Caney and San Juan Hill, were drawn up
to render honors. Crowds thronged the streets, and through them,
down to the docks, and into waiting transports, marched more
soldiers. Long, double files, whose standards bore not laconic
numbers, but the ancient, proud escutcheons of Spanish regiments.

In the palace, Cuba's last Spanish Governor-General waited
to turn the empire over to his successor. At 11:30, portly, mustached, bemedaled Major General John R. Brooke rode up at the
head of a retinue of senior officers, all resplendent in full dress.
Standing apart and almost forgotten, a small knot of Liberation
Army commanders sullenly watched the ceremony.

An interpreter read aloud the Governor-General's speech ending Spanish sovereignty of Cuba, and the custody of the island
passed into the hands of the United States. Up the staff of Havana's El Morro, the red and gold flag of Spain was hoisted for
the last time, a booming salute by the American warships echoing
about the harbor. Then the flag was slowly lowered and in its
place waved the stars and stripes.

But for the Cuban people it was a sour moment. They had
planned a grand celebration for their victorious Liberation Army:
banquets, balls, speeches, a huge public dinner. It was all to be
capped by a big parade—the Liberation Army marching into the
city as the Spanish troops marched out. But Brooke had scotched
it all. Except for their few scowling generals at the palace, there
was not an *insurrecto* to be seen in the capital.

There had been friction in Havana, particularly between the
Spanish and Cuban officers. Only weeks before, there were several
killings, and the city was very tense. Brooke, with some justification, feared a full-scale riot if both armies were permitted simultaneously in the streets. "For years we have suffered," one
prominent Havana citizen complained, "only to see, at this hour,
our emotions changed from pleasure at the departure of the Spaniards to apprehension at the arrival of the Americans."[9]

When the back of the last Spanish soldier disappeared up the
gangway, Brooke proclaimed, "To the people of Cuba." He came
before them, not as a conqueror, but as the representative of the
President of the United States. His mission was not to build a new
empire but to further the humane motives for which the United
States had intervened: "to give protection to the people, security
to person and property, to restore confidence . . . to resume the
pursuits of peace, and to afford full protection in the exercise of

all civil and religious rights." Taking his cue from "a few unofficial suggestions" cabled by President McKinley, Brooke urged upon his new charges "moderation, conciliation, and good will toward one another."[10]

Cuba was not, as its leaders and many Americans naively believed, to become immediately independent. Popular American assumptions regarding the liberation of their "little brown brothers" aside, in Washington there were no administration plans for that contingency. Indeed, Spain in the Treaty of Paris had granted sovereignty of the island to the United States. The United States Army, McKinley decided, would assume the functions of a provisional government. Then, at some unspecified time, they would deliver it to the Cuban people.

Whether complete independence was even possible in 1899 is debatable. The island was financially destitute, socially disorganized, and wracked with poverty and disease. Sixty-six percent of the population was illiterate, and there was no history whatever of real self-government.

The responsibilities of the military government, at least in its first year, mirrored Wood's herculean labors in Santiago: maintain public order, fight disease and starvation, and provide humanitarian services. Considering the chaos on the island, these tasks were best confronted by a direct command system. As such it was in form, albeit conciliatory and paternalistic, a near copy of the late Spanish regime.

"A military government is the only kind fit to cope with such conditions," wrote Colonel Hugh Scott (Army Chief of Staff, 1914–1917), Chief of Staff to the Military Governor of Havana. "There are . . . situations where the strong hand of the benevolent despot is necessary. . . . The American people are prone to believe that a race can be civilized overnight; that it is sufficient to declare a republic on paper to have one in fact. . . . You may declare a republic on paper among the mules and monkeys, but you will never get one."[11]

In the waning days of 1898 the War Department created a new entity within its administrative commands, the Military Division of Cuba, with Brooke as division commander as well as Military Governor. The island was divided into seven (later reduced to four) geographical departments, plus the city of Havana. Each department was headed by a general officer, exercising both military and civil authority.

In January 1899, within two weeks of his installation, Brooke created the framework for his civil administrative bureaucracy. Four departments were established: Justice and Public Instruction; Agriculture, Commerce, Industries, and Public Works; Finance; and State and Government. Nominally they were led by a Cuban Secretary, with a staff of army officers, and collectively comprised Brooke's advisory group, or Cuban Cabinet.

Emergencies existed in nearly every civilian sphere. Spain had totally neglected the most basic human needs and vigorous action was necessary.

When Elihu Root, the new Secretary of War, visited the island he found the conditions of the insane "particularly distressing." The unfortunates were confined in jail cells and "treated literally like wild beasts." All were taken to a central asylum in Havana and "cared for in accordance with the dictates of modern humanity."[12]

On taking up his duties the Director-General of Posts reported to Brooke, "The Spanish government . . . left no records for my guidance, and not one stamp of any denominaton, nor a cent of money." About the only thing left at the Havana post office was a mountain of undelivered mail, some of it dating back eight years.[13]

Tasker Bliss (Army Chief of Staff, 1917–1918), the owly, bespectacled chief of the Customs Service, had similarly to cope with the overwhelming Spanish neglect. The Havana customs house was located in the former convent of St. Francis, a building dating back to about 1574. As with everything else, the Spanish had taken all but the dirt. Under the rotten floor timbers, six large cesspools festered away. Bliss estimated his work gangs removed over 1,200 cubic yards "of filth and rubbish and several tons of fetid matter . . . the space was permeated with disease germs from the faulty drainage of centuries."[14]

One of the great problems facing Brooke during the early months was what to do with the Liberation Army. As an organized military force it continued under reasonably good order and discipline, and in certain remote parts of the island served as an interim political administration. But its continued existence posed serious concerns. A large, experienced, irregular army, of uncertain loyalty, and under proven leadership, was a threat to the American occupation.

Conveniently, within its ranks there was no great grumbling

or desire to continue the guerrilla war against the new occupying power. What its men most wanted was simply to be paid off and allowed to go home. But who was to open the purse, and whose purse was it to be? The Liberation Army, as with all guerrilla forces, received no regular pay. Yet, in theory, its soldiers earned a liberal monthly wage, all to come due from the Cuban government once victory was achieved. Well, the moment had arrived, and Cuba was bankrupt.

Since Cuba hadn't a peso any amount would be a windfall. Money, however, could prove a mixed blessing. A big loan to pay off the guerrillas would drive Cuba deeply in debt and might possibly even delay independence. The Liberation Army leadership opted for a minimum amount, $3 million, just enough to get the troops home.

In Oriente Province Leonard Wood, now provincial military governor, initiated his own disbandment program, trading public works jobs for guns. His nonmilitary departments were staffed largely by Liberation Army veterans, with care taken to ensure that jobs were commensurate with former rank. By mid-1899, several thousand had abandoned the insurgent ranks for civil service employment.

These and other like schemes reduced, but failed to dissolve, the Liberation Army as a military organization. As for the $3 million, General Máximo Gómez, the Commander in Chief, likened the sum to the miracle of the loaves and fishes. But he also knew it was the best deal they could get, and the return of the *insurrectos* to peaceful occupations was uppermost in his mind.

On May 27, 1899, the first mustering out was held in Havana. Every Cuban soldier who deposited his arms would receive $75 cash. With a United States infantry escort, Major Francis S. Dodge of the Army Paymaster's Department arrived in an open wagon, carrying $39,000 in gold and silver coin. On a rough wooden table Dodge set out the heavy bags of specie, while clerks fussily arranged their muster rolls. The infantry deployed in the square ready to direct the expected crowds. On hand to observe were the Cuban civil governor of Havana, groups of Liberation Army officers and the American press. Hardly a guerrilla showed his face. While the Cubans jeered, Dodge paid exactly seven men; it was a complete bust.

It transpired that a disgruntled body of Cuban officers, using threats and patriotic appeal, had organized a boycott. Most of the *insurrectos*, however, simply were not informed. But by the following day the news had circulated and the veterans, first in driblets, then by the hundreds, trooped to the pay tables.[15]

The demobilization of the Liberation Army, and its generally peaceful acquiescence to the American occupation, did away with the spectre of a continuing armed rebellion. Brooke had achieved no small victory.

But there was trouble in the American camp. Brooke, an honest, conscientious old soldier, had no time for politics or innovation. Beyond the emergencies of feeding the starving and tending the sick, he maintained no vision as to the ultimate purpose of his military administration.

Brooke, however, did give the Cubans some real responsibility and experience in civil government. But always the good soldier, he daren't move without orders, and when he did, after first asking advice from everyone, he moved very cautiously. To the army's adjutant general he wrote, "I wish to say that rapidity of action is not possible here, we are working against the habits and action of this people."[16]

The revolt against Brooke's authority came not from his Cuban charges, but from his provincial military governors, specifically Leonard Wood in Santiago and Major General James Harrison Wilson of Matanzas and Santa Clara. They were politically connected to the highest Republican Party and McKinley administration circles and both were after Brooke's job.

Wood opened the assault in the first weeks of the occupation. Prior to January 1, 1899, he had collected all customs receipts from Santiago city and province, spending the funds on local public works, health, and education projects of his choosing. But once Bliss centralized the customs service, Wood was reduced to fiscal dependence, and his programs required prior approval.

In an act of the rankest insubordination Wood expressed his views direct to the War Department. Coming from a sound military officer, and no mean colonial administrator, his recommendations were baldly self-serving and if implemented would ensure the failure of centralized command. All customs receipts, Wood urged, should be collected and disbursed by the various provincial military governors, ruling autonomously. Diverse programs would be coordinated by frequent joint conferences. From a military and administrative standpoint the plan was absurd.

Behind much of Wood's machinations lay his private agenda

of annexation. Brooke's establishment of the Cuban Cabinet and his reliance on Cuban advisors were anathema to those who wished to see Cuba absorbed into the United States. "The sentiment for our remaining here forever," Wood noted to President McKinley, "is becoming very strong in this part of Cuba." To the new governor of New York, Theodore Roosevelt, he penned his ideas for a just and equitable occupation government. All Cubans would have opportunities for civic and military advancement "and in two or three years they will insist on being part of us."[17]

The second prong in the assault on Brooke came from General Wilson, a West Point graduate who had left the army to pursue a successful railroad career. In Republican Party ranks he had risen to national committeeman from Delaware, and was on intimate terms with the sources of power.

The war brought Wilson back to the colors and he too favored annexation of Cuba. It would come through the guise of a postal and customs union with the United States where markets would be open and free to Cuban goods. A political merger would then naturally follow the economic tie. Wilson was a strong advocate of social progress through economic growth. Prosperity and stability were possible in Cuba, in contrast to other Caribbean and Central American states, because the "white race" was in the majority, and their behavior, once they grew affluent, would be responsibly conservative. "The fortunate and prosperous," he reported to Brooke, "are scarcely vicious."[18]

Agricultural reform was the crux of Wilson's rehabilitation program, and he strongly urged Brooke to sponsor agrarian reconstruction by liberal loans to smallholders and the gift of tools and animals.

But to Brooke these ideas smacked overmuch of paternalism, charity, and an inducement to pauperism. Jealousy would be aroused in those who did not receive loans or gifts in kind. To reduce the quarreling and disagreements of his departmental Diodachi, Brooke convened a headquarters conference. As an attempt to secure unity it was a dismal failure.

All present favored advancement in education and enlarging the school system. Aside from that, according to Wilson, none had definite long-range social or economic goals. Their programs went nothing beyond "clean up the towns, establish proper sanitary conditions, and build a system of country roads"; all distinctly quasi-military operations.[19]

There was also a fair amount of testiness over the annexation question, a point already mooted by the Teller Amendment. As Wilson tells it, Wood and General William Ludlow, Havana's military governor, "talked exactly as though they expected to occupy the island and remain in military command indefinitely."[20]

Wilson's enthusiasm for annexation seems to have waned, and he asked Ludlow with astonishment from whence his ideas came. Ludlow replied that they came from President McKinley himself. Wilson, if he is to be believed, took the high road with a dead-right prophecy for then and all time. The President's notions mattered not at all: "we shall be lifted out of here by the will of the American people within less than two years. *They will never consent that the President or any of his subordinates shall violate the public faith*" [italics added]. The ill-fated conference ended with neither conciliation nor result; the differences, as Brooke reported, "were irreconcilable."[21]

In the White House President McKinley was besieged with Wood's and Wilson's Congressional and influential partisans, each demanding that Brooke be sacked, and their man appointed in his place.

In the midst of the bickering, old Russell Alger, everyone's favorite scapegoat for all that had gone wrong in the Spanish-American War, was dumped from the War Department. In his place McKinley appointed a dapper New York lawyer, with close ties to the Lodge-Roosevelt Republican progressive wing, Elihu Root. For Cuba, it represented a conscious effort by the President to give the occupation some badly needed supervision.

One of the secretary's first problems was whether or not to raise a new Cuban Army. The American occupation forces, about 45,000 men, could not patrol the entire island, chase every highwayman, arrest every lawbreaker. The troops were also expensive to maintain and politically could not remain in Cuba indefinitely.

The dilemma gained new urgency with the commencement of large-scale hostilities in the Philippines. There, as in Cuba, the United States had allied itself with a revolutionary movement in the war against Spain. With the Spanish surrender, the question arose as to whether the rebel leaders would choose to submit to American occupation or continue the struggle for independence. In the Philippines, the rebels opted to fight. The Cuban parallel, with 30,000 unemployed ex–Liberation Army soldiers afoot, was too close to ignore.

Leonard Wood considered "native regiments" ideal formations for internal control, and he favored the establishment of an American-officered colonial army, on the lines of the excellent Philippine Scouts and the Puerto Rico Regiment.* The Cuban people, he wrote to Governor Roosevelt, would "more readily and gracefully submit to authority and force by their own people, than by a people of absolutely alien blood." Wood feared that any direct use of American troops in pacification duties courted disaster. If an American soldier killed a single bandit, it would be front page news in every newspaper. Some of the ex–Liberation Army had turned to brigandage, and a clash might entice others to rc-form their ranks and ignite a Philippine-style general insurrection. Finally, Wood saw a new Cuban Army as freeing large numbers of American troops for the guerrilla war in the Philippines.[22]

Root also favored the scheme. A new army, he wrote to McKinley, would "dispose of a lot of men most likely to make trouble in Cuba, turn them from possible bandits, and educate them into Americans."[23]

Brooke, however, was opposed. Raising Cuban regiments would lead the islanders to believe, truly, that the United States Army could not handle the Philippine conflict without denuding its Caribbean commitments. Further, an American-officered colonial force would "add to the distrust" of the Cuban people regarding the real intentions of the United States. His arguments prevailed, and it became a dead issue.[24]

Yet something had to be done to provide Cuba with at least a modicum of a military. The result was an unsatisfactory half-measure known as the Rural Guard. Officers and men were recruited from selected elements, the "best material," of the old Liberation Army. But when the Americans decamped, the Rural Guard was unable to sustain the new independent political order. In 1906, when Cuba rose again in revolt, the Guard proved an impotent entity.

With the autumn of 1899 the first phase of the Cuban occupation came to an end. The emergency programs had gone far toward feeding the starving and healing the sick; public works and sanitation projects were well under way; and Brooke seemingly had beaten off his rivals. But in December the axe fell.

---

*These two units were not exactly colonial, being incorporated into the Regimental List of the United States Regular Army.

With strong prodding from Roosevelt, Secretary Root entreated the President to order Brooke's relief. "I was satisfied," Root remembered, "that General Wood was the man, and he said, 'All right, go ahead.' "[25]

One week later, at sunrise, the harbor batteries of Havana woke the city with a major general's thirteen-gun salute. At noon the transfer of command took place at Brooke's headquarters and there was much resentment by the older man. Brooke, after all, was a permanent major general of the Regular Army. His upstart successor was only a brevet major general of Volunteers, whose substantive rank was still that of captain in the Army Medical Department.

To his great credit Wood did not gloat over Brooke's demise, and in a handsome gesture of peacemaking, he retained all of Brooke's staff in their positions. Immediately he began to apply the operating methods and principles that had achieved success in Santiago.

Primary education was almost nil, and because of a pernicious fee system poor children were virtually excluded from the "free" schools. The old Spanish system accommodated barely a tenth of the student population and made no attempt at teaching beyond rote memorization. What female children attended occupied their time "chiefly in embroidery."[26]

Under Wood's charge education was totally revamped and received priority in military government funds. In place of Spanish methods came a system patterned after the Ohio public schools. Pupil enrollment increased seven-fold in little over a year.

Next on the agenda came the Cuban legal process. Brooke had kept in place the old Spanish regulations. His judge advocate general deemed them adequate, but over the centuries gross venality had corrupted the system. Fee payments—bribes—were required at each step of litigation so that civil suits became financial endurance contests between the litigants.

Wood began with the premise that "the law is excellent, the procedure alone is bad." A board of pardons was established to examine prison inmates and it released those unfortunates who had never come to trial, or had been overpunished. A new law defined the crime of perjury and provided punishment. Indigent defendants were given counsel at government expense, a right decades in advance of American practice. Inefficient and corrupt judges were sacked, and court employees were put on salary.[27]

Attempts, however, to introduce the jury system and habeas corpus caused much opposition within the Cuban bar and ultimately failed. These Anglo-Saxon concepts were too alien for a people long governed under Roman law. Regarding the ancient system's wider consequences, Wood wrote to Roosevelt, "Nothing more idiotic can be imagined than the attempt to establish a liberal government under Spanish laws."[28]

Of all the American experiments in colonial government, none was more successful than the eradication of yellow fever. The disease, the most widespread of tropical killers, was commonly believed generated, like typhus, from filth. In June 1901 there arrived the Army Yellow Fever Commission, headed by Major Walter Reed of the Medical Department. Reed was drawn to the theory that the organisms were transmitted not by poor sanitation but by mosquito. Reed plunged into an exhaustive analysis. One of his, and indeed one of the world's, unsung heroes was an army contract surgeon, Dr. Jesse W. Lazear, who volunteered to be inoculated with the supposed virus and paid for progress with his life. Wood considered the research "worth the cost of the war."[29]

By the summer of 1900, six months into Wood's tenure, forces internal and external brought the occupation and the question of Cuban independence into sharp focus.

Municipal elections were conducted without incident, though Wood was disappointed in the "extreme" choice of candidates for local office. The old revolutionary National Party gained most of the seats on the town and provincial councils, and its victory was a vote for independence.

Secretary Root saw nothing but good in the outcome. "When the history of the new Cuba comes to be written," he noted to his viceroy, "the establishment of popular self-government, based on a limited suffrage, excluding so great a proportion of the elements which have brought ruin to Hayti and San Domingo will be regarded as an event of the first importance."[30]

On the far side of the world, the Philippine insurrection churned on. In China the Boxer Rebellion was in high spate, and sizable American contingents—army, navy, Marine Corps—were closely engaged in the fight. For the McKinley administration, the Congress, and the War Department it all signaled a course for early action regarding Cuba's future.

In July 1900 Wood published a civil order providing for a

Cuban constitutional convention. The election of delegates was to be held on September 3, and the session was to open in Havana on the first Monday in November.

Wood toured his fief, encouraging the "best men" to place their names on the ballot. To Root he penned, "If they send a lot of political jumping-jacks as delegates, they must not expect that their work will be received very seriously." He was not completely disappointed. For the most part the delegates were, to use the mid-century American phrase, the best and the brightest that Cuba could offer. As one Cuban historian put it, they were "generals of the wars of independence, distinguished conspirators, patriots ennobled by emigration and banishment, [and] noted specialists in Public Law."[31]

Not satisfied with merely preparing Cuba for self-government, the United States determined to continue exercising a fair amount of control over her destiny. Thus the framing of a constitution was only one matter to be dealt with by the convention. Second and equally important was the future status of Cuban-American relations. The delegates, naturally, were reluctant to agree to any arrangement that impaired complete independence but they were given little choice.

For the United States the strategic importance of Cuba lay primarily as an Atlantic bulwark to the inevitable Central American isthmian canal, and internal disruption could well provide an excuse for meddling by foreign powers. The United States Navy had lately provided the Monroe Doctrine with a set of teeth, but a more contemporary legal framework was necessary to assure peace and stability in the coming new republic. There was also the question of American and international investments, mainly the sugar plantations, mines, and Cuba's rudimentary railroads. These, too, must receive some guarantee of protection against capricious and volatile acts.

The result was an amendment to the United States Army Appropriation Bill of 1901, introduced in Congress by Senator Orville Platt of Connecticut. Article I prohibited Cuba from entering into any "treaty or other compact" with a foreign power "which will impair or tend to impair" her independence. Also prohibited were any foreign naval or military bases.

Article lll prepared the ground for future United States military interventions and in effect consigned Cuba to the status of a protectorate. It deserves to be quoted in full: "That the government of Cuba consents that the United States may exercise the right to intervene for the preservation of Cuban independence, the maintenance of a government adequate for the protection of life, property, and individual liberty, and for the discharging the obligations with respect to Cuba imposed by the Treaty of Paris [ending the Spanish-American War] on the United States, now to be assumed and undertaken by the government of Cuba."

Article VII dictated that the Cuban government sell or lease to the United States "lands necessary for coaling or naval stations at certain specified points." Eventually, the navy settled for Guantánamo Bay, a sentry box flanking the strategic Windward Passage to the Central American isthmian canal.[32]

Not surprisingly, there was a bitter struggle before the convention accepted these odious conditions. But Congress held a club: the delegates were informed that the military occupation would remain unless the articles were adopted. The delegates had no room to maneuver and the Platt Amendment was incorporated almost verbatim into the new Cuban constitution and the permanent treaty between the two nations. It remained in force until 1934.

Elihu Root was much pleased and saw in the Platt Amendment a vital safeguard to Cuban interests. The endemic revolutions that afflicted Central and South America were now, in his view, impossible on the island. For it was "known to all men that an attempt to overturn the foundations of that government will be confronted by the overwhelming power of the United States."[33]

Leonard Wood, however, saw the amendment in its true light. "There is of course," he wrote President Theodore Roosevelt, "little or no independence left Cuba under the Platt Amendment."[34]

On the last day of 1901 Cuba held a general election for the government of the soon-to-be republic. The Nationalists turned to Tomás Estrada Palma, an aging wisp, nearly seventy years old, who had spent the past quarter-century in American exile. Honest, patriotic, if a bit too friendly toward the United States, and free of factional strife, he garnered widespread support.

In Havana's great Plaza de Armas, the clocks and church bells tolled the noon of May 20, 1902. On the ancient stones the dismounted ranks of the 7th Cavalry stood to arms. Large, joyous crowds moved through the streets. Inside the Governor's Palace, in the same room where three years before Brooke had taken command in the name of the United States, stood Leonard Wood, President Tomás Estrada Palma, and the Cuban Congress and judiciary. At the last chime Wood read aloud the document of transfer. From the flagstaff overlooking the harbor and the silent wreck of the *Maine*, the stars and stripes were lowered and up went the flag of the new republic. Forty-five guns from the Cabaña Battery and the armored cruiser *Brooklyn* boomed in salute, the 7th Cavalry presented arms, and Cuba entered the consort of nations.

It was, as everyone thought, all over. Wood boarded the *Brooklyn*, the troops marched into their transports, "and were not allowed, either officers or men, to set foot again on shore." Of the occupation army only eight companies of the coast artillery—four in Havana, two at Cienfuegos, two at Santiago—remained.[35]

Tomás Estrada Palma took over a going concern. There were no debts, and the treasury was full. Yet there were other significant problems. The cane sugar market was depressed, and large numbers of unemployed agricultural workers posed a threat to public order.

The political parties formed, aligned, separated, and realigned with dizzying regularity. The Nationalists, with the support of anti-Platt Amendment factions, became the National Liberals, and then, joined by the radical faction from the Conservative Republicans, coalesced into the Liberals. The remaining Conservative Republicans re-formed as the Moderates. These labels were fairly meaningless, and the major Cuban parties were dominated by senior veterans of the Liberation Army.

Palma, who had no party affiliation, nevertheless considered the Liberals an unscrupulous bunch and, reluctantly, he placed himself at the head of the Moderate ticket for the December 1905 presidential elections.

The platform differences were not very great. The Liberal candidate, ex-General José Miguel Gómez, championed an immediate abrogation of the Platt Amendment, while Palma and the Moderates favored its eventual demise. The principal dispute seemed to be control of the "twenty millions of the treasury."[36]

The campaign was fraught, on both sides, with corruption and fraud. In April 1906 the Cuban Congress pronounced the election valid and Tomás Estrada Palma the winner. To a man, the Liberal deputies walked out. Exiting, former Liberation Army general

"Pino" Guerra shouted, "There is nothing for us to do here; we must seek justice somewhere else." The implications were clear.[37]

In the early summer the Liberals plotted revolt. The Havana police stations and the Presidential Palace would be seized; Palma and his cabinet taken prisoner. It would have to be done fast, within a matter of hours. If the revolt were prolonged, civil war at least, and American intervention at worst, would surely result.

The coup never had a chance. Hardly a secret, it was openly discussed in Havana's cafés, and the Liberal leaders were already under police surveillance. On August 16, 1906, fearing the government ready to smash the plot, Pino Guerra raised the banner of revolt. Immediately Palma arrested every Liberal politician in reach; the remainder went underground.

The revolt of 1906 was never a mass popular movement, yet within a short time, about 20,000 ill-armed and poorly disciplined rebels, mainly unemployed agricultural workers, were in the field. Against them Palma could muster only a few thousand Rural Guards, whose ability and trust were open to question.

Taking the grand name of the Constitutional Army, the rebels operated in loose, scattered columns, commanded by usually second-rate, self-appointed generals and colonels. According to Lieutenant Colonel Robert Bullard, the revolt allowed the new recruits an opportunity for "saving the country and at the same time eating meat."[38]

At first the Liberals' strategy aimed at the weakness of the Palma government and its inability to protect foreign property. But now, with the failure of the original coup, they hoped for an invocation of the Platt Amendment, an American intervention, and American-supervised elections. "The forces of Santa Clara," said one rebel leader, "will commence their offensive work against the public forces and against the properties of foreigners with the sole end that the Americans shall come as quickly as possible . . . we prefer to live under the shelter of the justice of a foreign power than submit . . . to tyranny under the flag which has cost us so much to acquire."[39]

The rebel military operations were typical of most guerrilla wars; pitched battles with government forces were usually avoided. Between intermittent attempts at disrupting communications, the rebels spent most of their time recruiting, stealing horses, accumulating supplies, and soliciting "contributions" from fearful planters.

Reports from American consuls to Jacob Sleeper, the chargé d'affaires in Havana, placed an ugly racial overtone on the revolt. "Parties of the worst class of negroes are rising up under the pretext of being revolutionists," wired the consul in Santa Clara. "[They] are robbing and sacking shops, and if this lasts much longer [they] will soon be guilty of worse offenses."[40]

By the first days of September the Constitutional Army controlled most of western Cuba. But in Havana, government officials informed Sleeper they "confidently" expected to crush the rebellion in two months. They were whistling in the dark. Palma authorized a 2,000 man increase of the Rural Guard. But only recruits of poor quality were found and they cost the government two and a half dollars in gold per day. An emergency machine gun corps, the "Foreign Legion of Artillery," was hastily formed. Composed of American, British, and German civilians, it proved of little worth.

The revolt caught the United States very much by surprise and was decidedly unwelcome. Revolts, disturbances, interventions, and minor chaos had popped up all over the Caribbean and Central America. In accord with President Theodore Roosevelt's newly conceived "Corollary" to the Monroe Doctrine, the Dominican Republic's customs service had been placed under American receivership, and the Atlantic Fleet's Santo Domingo Division patrolled her coastal waters. Chronic strife in Honduras and Haiti resulted in landings by the Marine Corps to restore temporary order.

Elihu Root, now Secretary of State, was completing a goodwill tour of Latin America and was at pains to reassure the republics of America's pacific intentions. "We wish for no territory except our own," he told an audience in Rio de Janeiro, "for no sovereignty except sovereignty over ourselves." Root feared a new intervention in Cuba would dramatically increase distrust and paranoia in the region.[41]

Roosevelt also feared a new intervention. Relations with Japan had sharply deteriorated, mostly over anti-Asian racial incidents in California. War was a real possibility. Major fleet units steamed to the western Pacific, and the strategic albatross of the Philippines already hung heavy about America's neck. What the United States did not need was a debilitating, troop-draining sideshow in its Caribbean backyard.

The initial American response to the Liberal revolt was to support Palma's government. In late August Roosevelt authorized the War Department to sell Cuba five million rounds of small arms ammunition. Other contingencies were taken in hand. Secretary of War William Howard Taft ordered the army's general staff to prepare an estimate of available troops for Cuban service.

Chief of Staff General J. Franklin Bell was under no illusions regarding the use of regular troops in irregular war and his successors would have done well, and would do well, to heed his advice. A force of 15,000 men, he informed Taft, somewhat more than a quarter of the army's strength, was available for Cuba. To increase mobility most of the units should be cavalry and mounted infantry. But a full-scale guerrilla war, Bell cautioned, would require a far greater commitment. "It is one of the most difficult operations in the world," he wrote to President Roosevelt, "to completely disarm a hostile population as skillful in the arts of concealment and deception as is the Latin Race. The heartbreaking feature of it all is that you organize an army and it goes forth with military ardor, with all the pomp and panoply of war, enthusiastically to meet and conquer the enemy, only to discover it can find nothing to fight."[42]

In Cuba, Palma's time was running out. In late August he offered an amnesty to all rebels laying down their arms; none responded. Seeing United States intervention as *his* only hope of retaining power, he pleaded with Jacob Sleeper to request American forces, if for nothing else, than to guard foreign property. Sleeper refused. He was sending regular reports to the State Department, and their response, other than approving the sale of rifle ammunition, was that the Cubans must handle this situation for themselves.

But within a fortnight came the incident that set the United States on the reluctant course of military intervention. In Pinar del Río Province Rural Guards and militia fruitlessly pursued Pino Guerra's rebels. An armored train, with militia reinforcements and the machine guns of the Foreign Legion of Artillery, rolled west from Havana.

On September 8 the train was halted and besieged by Guerra's rebels. "It was a lovely battle," an American correspondent wrote. "Unlimited ammunition to burn and nobody hurt." For hours the fight swung back and forth. The stalemate broke when a militia company hit Guerra in his flank. An exchange of ragged volleys

drove the rebels from their positions. The train, somewhat pock-
marked, returned to Havana.[43]

For embattled President Palma, the fight indicated a new rebel
willingness for battle; it was now imperative that the Americans
come. Knowing Jacob Sleeper would continue to refuse his requests for aid, Palma sought other channels.

Frank Maximilian Steinhart probably knew more about Cuba
than any American on the island. A Bavarian, he began his service
to the United States as a sergeant in the Civil War. During the
Cuban occupation he served as Leonard Wood's chief civil clerk.
Steinhart was competent, fluent in Spanish, and maintained close
ties to the Cuban business community. In 1903, on Wood's recommendation, he was appointed consul general in Havana. Most
importantly for Palma, Steinhart considered Jacob Sleeper "an
ass."

Secretly Palma approached Steinhart and made his entreaty
for American intervention. The consul general wired the State
Department, "Absolutely confidential. [Cuban] Secretary of State
. . . has requested me, in the name of President Palma, to ask
President Roosevelt send immediately two vessels; one to Habana,
other to Cienfuegos; they must come at once. Government forces
are unable to quell rebellion."[44]

Two days later, with no answer from Washington, Steinhart
sent another request.

At Oyster Bay, Long Island, President Roosevelt was spending
the last days of his summer vacation. He read Steinhart's cables
and was not amused. Cuba was America's foundling orphan. She
had been freed, fed, clothed, educated, and with high hopes cut
from the apron strings to make her own way in the world. She
was also the centerpiece of American diplomacy in the Western
Hemisphere. Cuba proved that democracy, given a firm and guiding hand from a great power, was indeed possible among a people
who had never before experienced it. Not surprisingly, Roosevelt
assumed the mien of an angry, betrayed parent whose favorite
child has gone badly astray.

Military intervention would undo all the lofty motives of the
Spanish-American War and the occupation. Elihu Root's recent
assurances to the Latin American republics would be viewed as
so much gas. "I loathe the thought of assuming any control over
[Cuba] as we have over Puerto Rico and the Philippines," wrote
the President to his old friend, Henry White, now ambassador to

Italy. The bitterness poured out. "I am so angry with that infernal little Cuban republic that I would like to wipe its people off the face of the earth. All that we have wanted from them was that they should behave themselves and be prosperous. . . . And now, lo and behold, they have started an utterly unjustifiable and pointless revolution and may get things into such a snarl that we have no alternative save to intervene—which will at once convince the suspicious idiots in South America that we do wish to interfere after all, and perhaps have some land hunger!"[45]

Reluctantly, very reluctantly, Roosevelt ordered the Navy Department to send the ships: peace cruiser* *Denver* to Havana and the gunboat *Marietta* to Cienfuegos. But he, and he alone, would define the military scope and closely control any deployment. The vessels were ordered out but under strict directives to "protect American interests" only; Palma would still have to fend for himself.

The next day, September 11, Steinhart received word from Assistant Secretary of State Robert Bacon that the ships were on the way. But Bacon warned that perhaps Steinhart did not appreciate the President's and the nation's aversion to intervention. American public opinion would not stand for it unless the Cuban government exhausted every means to quell the revolt. Until such efforts were made, "We are not prepared to consider the question of intervention at all."[46]

Informed that vessels were en route, Palma suspended civil rights in the rebel-controlled provinces and spread wide the dragnet for the Liberals still in hiding. The result was a sharp increase of insurgent activity. Palma now upped the ante. Havana, he declared, was in peril, and to avoid catastrophe, President Roosevelt must send at once two or three thousand troops. Of course, he told Steinhart, the request had to be kept secret from the public; they must never know the Cuban government had begged for intervention.[47]

This latest mendicancy reached the President at Oyster Bay and Roosevelt was faced with the unenviable task of navigating the dangerous waters between Scylla and Charybdis. Clearly there was a crisis in Cuba. To steer the course of the Platt Amendment headed the United States straight onto the rocks and whirlpools

---

*Another variation on the cruiser theme. The six ships of the *Denver* class were a compromise between a small cruiser and a large gunboat. They were well gunned but slow, unarmored, and suitable primarily for empire police duties.

of internal meddling. Yet to shrink from those hazards conjured the intolerable monster of prolonged Cuban civil war.

Roosevelt prepared for the worst. He ordered the navy to deploy additional vessels and to "have a large force of marines in Havana at the earliest possible moment on any ships able to carry them." But again, they were only for the "protection of American life and property." There was no mention whatever of an intervention to bail out the Cuban government.[48]

At 4:30 P.M., September 12, the *Denver* stood into port. Large crowds thronged the waterfront. Her skipper, Commander John Colwell, reported that "unusual interest was taken in the arrival of this ship."[49]

When the *Denver* had made fast her lines, Frank Steinhart came on board to report the situation and suggested to Colwell an informal visit, in civilian clothes, to the presidential palace.

To the naval officer, Tomás Estrada Palma appeared "very nervous, but much pleased at the presence of the *Denver* in port, and I got the impression that he regarded her presence as strengthening his administration." Nothing of substance was discussed and after half an hour's "chat," Colwell returned to his ship.[50]

Throughout the evening and night a stream of correspondents and businessmen from the international community came on board, all of whom gave Colwell their version of events. By morning he concluded that the revolt was a well-organized movement by the Liberals, whose leadership held a measure of popular support, and that the government, "always excluding Mr. Palma, of whom even the strongest opponents . . . spoke kindly but sorrowfully," was corrupt and had stolen the election. Tales of government victories were largely false; government forces were minuscule and untrustworthy, and as many as 5,000 rebels were in easy march of the city. Panic was taking hold of the population, whose great fear was a rebel attack coupled with "an uprising of the low negro and lawless elements."[51]

Colwell, this time with Jacob Sleeper, paid his formal visit to Palma the next afternoon. The chargé put the question directly to the President: "Can you guarantee protection to the lives and property of American citizens?" Palma could not. Sleeper turned to Colwell: how soon could he put a landing party ashore? He replied, "Within half an hour."[52]

Back on board the *Denver,* a landing force of 128 bluejackets and marines, two Colt machine guns, and a 3-inch field piece went ashore at the customs house. Late that evening a "gentleman of birth" came on board with a startling offer from the rebels. If Colwell could guarantee "justice and a fair hearing of their grievances" the rebels would surrender their arms and disband.[53]

Colwell presented the proposition to President Palma. There was a snag. Colwell hadn't the authority to accept or guarantee anything, but, ironically, if Palma requested the United States government to grant Colwell the power, it could be done. Palma agreed to empower Colwell to make the necessary guarantee to the rebels.

Colwell returned to the Plaza de Armas and encountered a highly agitated Jacob Sleeper; the State Department had forbidden the landing. Theodore Roosevelt had nearly gone off the deep end upon learning of it, and the blue jackets and marines must reembark at once! A presidential cable to the miserable chargé said it all: "You had no business to direct the landing of those troops without specific authority from here."[54]

Colwell, greatly irked at what he considered ignorant and contradictory actions of the State Department, refused to reembark at night. It was a dangerous maneuver militarily and might well precipitate rioting in the city. He would assume responsibility for remaining in position. The following morning, September 14, he received his orders "to take no part in troubles in Cuba. . . . You will not land force for the protection of American interests except in case of necessity." The *Denver* would be used only for "asylum in the event of necessity demanding it." Havana was quiet, the rebel leadership was actively advocating a peaceful solution, and Colwell obeyed his orders. By noon the landing force was back on board.[55]

But at the presidential palace, Tomás Estrada Palma readied the monkey wrench that would destroy any hopes for a peaceful solution and make full-scale American military intervention inevitable. Through Frank Steinhart, Palma informed the State Department that unless he received its full and unqualified support, he would resign the presidency and "deliver" Cuba to an American proconsul, "as soon as sufficient American troops are landed." Further, the Vice President and the cabinet would resign as well. Under these conditions the Cuban Congress had no proper convening authority to name a new executive. The consequences,

Steinhart cabled to Elihu Root, were a power vacuum in the capital and a "state of anarchy."[56]

Roosevelt's only remaining avenue for avoiding intervention was to go public in the hope of embarrassing the Cuban government into setting its house aright. On September 14, in a letter to the Cuban ambassador in Washington simultaneously released to Palma and the Cuban press, the President addressed the issue. "Our intervention in Cuban affairs will come only if Cuba shows that she has fallen into the insurrectionary habit, that she lacks the self-restraint necessary to secure peaceful self-government, and that her contending factions have plunged the country into anarchy." To aid the peace process, he was sending Secretary of War William Howard Taft and Assistant Secretary of State Robert Bacon to heal the schism.[57]

On publication of the letter, the parties, to Roosevelt's relief, attempted to compromise. Palma suspended military operations and certain political prisoners were released. Several of the Constitutional Army's columns likewise were called to a halt. But Palma would not treat with the Liberals while their forces were still under arms. For their part, the Liberals refused to disarm unless the disputed 1905 elections were annulled. The accommodations went nowhere.

Also, on the fourteenth, the gunboat *Marietta* anchored off the southern port of Cienfuegos. Rebel columns were very active in the area, and the managers of the big American-owned sugar plantations were fairly hysterical over being put to the torch. The rebels had made this quite plain. "The properties which we will commence to destroy by fire . . . in case we do not reach an accord with the Government," stated a rebel commander, "will be those of American citizens." They had already laid a ransom, couched as "a small obligatory war loan" on the "rich land owners" of the district. Money was not the only object. Each plantation was ordered to pony up 10,000 rounds of small arms ammunition "in the non-prorogable time of eight days."[58]

The little *Marietta* carried a crew of only 140 officers and men. Yet Commander Fullam sent nearly half ashore, with a pair of Colt machine guns, to guard the nearest plantations. So there would be no mistake as to intentions, Fullam published a "NOTICE" in the local press: "Sailors and Marines of the United States Navy have been landed under the American Flag solely for the protection of the lives and estates of American citizens. . . . Any further trespass upon [the sugar plantations], and any hostile or threatening acts towards the United States forces . . . whose mission is one of peace, can only be considered and treated as acts of war against the flag of the United States."[59]

Fullam was openly contemptuous of the rebels. "Nine-tenths of the revolutionaries are negroes," he reported to the Secretary of the Navy, "and they are not under good discipline." There was slight chance that the rebels would attack the landing parties. But with such a tiny force, prudence was required. "Be vigilant," he noted in his orders, "especially at night. Barbed wire is a splendid thing to keep off cavalry." On September 18, intervention progressed another step when two companies of marines arrived in the transport *Dixie* to augment Fullam's command.[60]

Still without any cogent policy for intervention, United States forces gathered. On September 14, two battalions of marines at Philadelphia and Norfolk received their orders "for expeditionary service in tropical waters." The special correspondent of the *Army and Navy Register* noted a new article of their equipment. "The marines sent to Cuba are well prepared to resist attacks of mosquitos, as well as attacks from Cubans. These troops have been furnished with a large supply of citronella. When this oil is applied to the person of a marine, he is immuned from attacks by mosquitos."[61]

Other, more powerful, elements collected. The new battleships *Virginia, New Jersey,* and *Louisiana* were shaking down along the east coast. Together they carried over 2,500 bluejackets and nearly 200 marines. Could not these vessels, suggested Robert Bacon to the President, be dispatched to Havana "without their departure attracting attention"? Roosevelt agreed. On September 14, escorted by the peace cruisers *Cleveland* and *Tacoma,* they were on their way. So were the cruisers *Minneapolis* and *Newark,* loaded with 700 marines and bound for Havana. "Say nothing about battleships," read the President's telegram to the Secretary of the Navy, "be indefinite about others."[62]

The next day Secretary Taft and Assistant Secretary Bacon took the train for Tampa and passage in the cruiser *Des Moines* for Havana. En route, Taft cabled his colleague Elihu Root. "The Cuban government has proved to be nothing but a house of cards. It has almost collapsed, and we have to take action at once."[63]

The emissaries met first with President Palma and then proceeded to interview everyone in reach, Moderate and Liberal alike. Taft quickly concluded that the 1905 elections were a fraud and that Palma and his administration had forfeited popular support. To his wife Helen he wrote of "the utter unfitness of these people for self-government."[64]

Taft's first concern was to keep both forces in their present positions; any further military operations, government or rebel, and he would call in the marines. A fair amount of the Atlantic Fleet plied south to Cuba; the equivalent of a battleship division, a mixed cruiser squadron, and a full regiment of marines. There would be more, much more; the big stick was poised to strike. "Everything is in readiness for a naval, military or Marine Corps occupation of Cuba," the *Army and Navy Register* informed its readers.[65]

Not surprisingly, the least enthusiastic group for intervention was the army's general staff. A protracted guerrilla war, such as they recently experienced in the Philippines, was to be avoided at all costs. Another long occupation of Cuba would soak up as many as 45,000 men, about two-thirds of the army's strength, stripping it for any other contingencies. "Officers who have had experience in the Philippines especially have no desire to take part in settling the Cuban mess by force," reported the *New York Times*. "They say that there is only one way of ending a guerilla campaign down there and that is by reconcentration." Shades of Butcher Weyler![66]

On September 24 Taft laid out his peace plan. The 1905 elections would be nullified. Tomás Estrada Palma would continue his term as President, but all national, provincial, and municipal officials come to office in 1905 would resign and stand for re-election in January 1907. The rebels would disarm and disband under a general amnesty.

Palma would have none of it. Taft's compromise was "useless" and the whole thing was "inconsistent with his dignity and honor." The 1905 election must stand; if not, he would resign. Taft cabled the news to Roosevelt. "Meantime," he noted, "we await more ships and suggest immediate mobilization of troops."[67]

In a last-ditch entreaty to Palma's patriotism, Roosevelt cabled a personal appeal. He begged Palma "to sacrifice your own feelings on the altar of your country's good." His government could not stand, and he must accept Taft's compromise. Any attempt "to dictate your own terms merely means disaster and perhaps ruin for Cuba." In a separate message, Taft was authorized to land the marines if he saw fit.[68]

At 9:00 P.M., September 28, a rump session of the Cuban Congress met for the last, pathetic act of the government of Tomás Estrada Palma. Palma, his Vice President, and the entire cabinet resigned. Cuba was now without a government. "But the old man neither wept nor spoke," noted an American correspondent. "He seemed dazed. The Cuban Republic, savagely torn by her own greedy sons, was dying before him." At midnight, the citizens of Havana listened to the bark of sergeants calling out the cadence and the measured tramp of the *Louisiana*'s marines on their way to guard the treasury. The second intervention in Cuba had begun.[69]

"To THE PEOPLE OF CUBA" headlined William Howard Taft's proclamation. As the island's new provisional governor he informed the population that the restoration of order was now under the authority of the President of the United States. Simultaneous with the posting, 2,000 marines (eventually to number nearly 3,000) organized into a Provisional Brigade, came ashore. Most boarded the trolleys of the Havana Electric Railway Company and went under canvas at Camp Columbia, Havana. Other detachments, large and small, quickly moved down the railroad into the provinces.[70]

In the United States Theodore Roosevelt ordered the general staff to "arrange for 6,000 troops to start for Cuba. . . . All troops are directed to take full supply of tentage, cots, mosquito bars and head nets." From the War Department the telegraphs clicked out the orders. With full equipment and a month's rations, two battalions each of the 5th, 11th, 17th, 27th, and 28th infantry regiments; two squadrons each of the 11th and 15th cavalry—all with machine gun platoons and regimental bands; mountain batteries from the 17th and 18th field artillery, a light battery from the 14th; the 2nd Engineer Battalion; the Signal Corps' Company I; and Companies A and B, Hospital Corps, boarded their trains for Newport News, Virginia.[71]

Originally the force was designated the First Expeditionary Brigade. On its arrival in Cuba, Taft renamed it the Army of Cuban Intervention. This was politically unwise and in mid-October it was changed to the Army of Cuban Pacification. Command was entrusted to Brigadier General Frederick Funston. An ex-volunteer with the Liberation Army, he was well acquainted with many of its senior veterans and with a goodly portion of the current rebel leadership. His tenure was curiously short-lived.

While the army mobilized, the marines were busy disarming the rebels. From Pinar del Río, Lieutenant William Upshur wrote to his father, "We went to the station to receive the rebels who came in to surrender . . . the whole thing is exactly like Richard Harding Davis' description of a revolution. We have the dirty rabble of Negroes . . . armed with every type of antiquated weapon. . . . We are living on hardtack, coffee, and canned beef (Armour's) and I think the food is excellent, the people are harmless, and you wouldn't give them another thought. If you could only see these 'spiketys,' our detachment could clear the island of them in a jiffy."[72]

In the eastern provincial capital of Camagüey, Major Albertus Catlin recorded another scene. A rebel column of 3,000 men was coming through. Twenty-five marines had the job of collecting their weapons and several hundred insurgents were quickly disarmed. "At one point," Catlin remembered, "a villainous-looking negro captain came riding up on horseback, at the head of a band of his ruffians. The sergeant in command of the three squads of marines stepped up and ordered him to dismount and disarm. By way of reply, the captain drew and cocked his revolver. The sergeant promptly clubbed his rifle and smashed the stock over the rebel's hard head, and the party threw down their arms. Captain Harllee gathered in a pile of machetes as high as his waist."[73]

But the number of confiscated guns hardly matched the number of rebels. One column of 7,000 men turned in 693 rusted pieces and no ammunition, pistols, or machetes. Hoarding was practiced; after all, this was hardly to be the last revolution in Cuba. Taft's military secretary estimated that only twelve percent of the Constitutional Army's weapons were surrendered.[74]

It was nearly harvest time and Taft considered guns less important than getting the rebels home to bring in the sugar crop. Disbandment received priority over disarmament, and by the second week of October the Constitutional Army no longer existed.

The 5th Infantry, first unit of the Army of Cuban Pacification, landed at Havana on October 6 and General Funston took command of all United States forces ashore.

Within a week he was out of a job. The reasons are somewhat murky. Taft, who fired him, gave the implausible excuse that

Funston was in temporary command only, "merely as a convenience until General Bell arrived." Also, Funston's close friendship with senior veterans of the old Liberation Army, and thus the Liberal leadership, made him an unpopular figure with the Moderates. Coupled with Taft's desire to unite the warring factions, these were the high-minded reasons for the general's ouster.[75]

But there was also another. In truth Funston presented Taft with a serious case of embarrassment. During the revolt the rebels had taken horses where they found them—"requisitioned" them for military purposes—and the owners received promises of their return. Needless to say, these promises were not kept. To speed up the disbanding of the rebel columns, Funston distributed certificates vesting temporary title to each rebel possessing a horse with "ownership to be determined later." However, either in printing or in the translation from English to Spanish, that last phrase was omitted. Funston considered it a minor point. Demobilization was the main object, and if each rebel could ride home a horse, it could only quicken the pace.[76]

Taft's views on private property verged on the religious and he was outraged. But the certificates had already gone out under his name and there was nothing he could do, save for having the new provisional government dole out a hefty indemnity to the rightful owners. But for whatever reason, Funston was out, and on October 13, Army Chief of Staff General J. Franklin Bell arrived to command in Cuba.

Taft's tenure as provisional governor was brief as well. On October 10 he proclaimed a general amnesty "covering the offenses of rebellion, sedition, or conspiracy" and the revolt was officially over. On October 12, Governor Charles Magoon came over from the recently acquired Panama Canal Zone to head the new provisional administration.[77]

Until January 28, 1909, Cuba was again under military occupation. The Army of Cuban Pacification concerned itself with five specific responsibilities: the physical occupation of the population centers and control of the railroads, ports, and communications facilities; continuous tactical marches and mock exercises to intimidate the rural population; the establishment of an island-wide intelligence network; active military participation in road-building; and most importantly, the preparation of a detailed tactical map of Cuba.

The tactical exercises began in late November 1906. To impress the Cuban people with America's armed potential, each garrison commander kept a mixed infantry-cavalry-artillery column continuously on the move. It showed "the lawless that order must be maintained and assure[d] the people that they [would] be protected from robbery and disturbances."[78]

In the United States there was some fear of the exercises. The tropical climate was considered unsuitable for white men. The *New York Times* warned that very rigorous work would soon exhaust the troops' "store of power" and cautioned against eating "native foods." That this was all nonsense was shown when a squadron of the 11th Cavalry, in heavy order, completed a forced march of 110 miles in thirty hours without losing a man or horse. An even more impressive example of the army's endurance took place in the fall of 1908. At the height of the rainy season every unit, with all its artillery, horses, mules, and transport, turned out for two consecutive twenty-one-day treks. The locals considered the operation impossible. They, like the *New York Times,* were proved wrong.[79]

The drawing of the topographical map was the job of the 2nd Engineer Battalion and when completed it was a resource beyond price. If the population was impressed with the marching prowess of the army and marines, they were awed by the mapmakers. Every hill, ravine, swamp, thicket, watercourse, and trail was precisely delineated. "The General Staff," noted the *Army and Navy Journal,* "knows the island better than all the *practicos*, or guides, in existence, and there is no maze an American officer with a map in his pocket could not thread, no camp he could not find."[80]

The provisional government under Charles Magoon was very different from the previous military government of Brooke and Wood. Roosevelt was determined to keep the occupation from becoming a political issue. On no account must the Cubans be antagonized into revolt; and in the United States there was to be no Congressional debate. In consultation with Taft and Root, Roosevelt opted to appoint a civil governor, and not a military one. To distance the occupation from the intervention and for the "temporary administration of the government of the Republic of Cuba," the island was placed in the care of the War Department's Bureau of Insular Affairs. With this formation of a civil, rather than a military occupation, the bureau took over Cuba from the general staff. It was the nearest the United States ever came to having a colonial office.[81]

For the soldiers and marines, occupation life, when they weren't marching through the countryside, had little to recommend it. Governor Magoon, on the recommendation of his chief army surgeon, prohibited saloons within a mile of Havana's Camp Columbia; those already in the dry zone were forced to close. For a time he agreed to the advice of the Surgeon General of the Army that "the sale of Coca-Cola by the post exchange be discontinued."[82]

Interservice rivalries erupted. The Army of Cuban Pacification's judge advocate general fudged his court-martial records to statistically prove that marines were more crime-prone than the army. The chief quartermaster in Havana fretted over the semimonthly supply ship, laden with $200,000 worth of stationery and blank forms in triplicate. In the regimental dispensaries, every tenth soldier and marine was treated for venereal disease.[83]

In the American-supervised elections of 1908, the Moderates swept the provincial and municipal contests. But it was ex-General José Miguel Gómez, Palma's opponent in 1902 and a leading Liberal hero of the late revolt, who won the presidency.

By 1908, the platoon- and company-sized detachments were withdrawn from the outposts and concentrated into the larger towns. In December, the marines began shipping out altogether, and by April 1, 1909, all United States forces were withdrawn. The second intervention and occupation of Cuba petered out to a quiet end. Some, however, had misgivings over the whole adventure. Notwithstanding the substantial military successes of the occupation, nothing really had been solved politically, and the eternal internecine strife endemic to Latin America between the ins and the outs would continue apace. "The U.S. will have to go back," wrote Lieutenant Colonel Robert Bullard. "It is only a question of time."

José Miguel Gómez was a president very much in the mold of Ronald Reagan. "He possesses the miracle of smiles," said one biographer. "Neither," wrote another, "can he be said to have a clear comprehension of the great social problems that stir the world." He was also a lucky president, at least until 1912. The crops were good and the world's sugar market remained stable. Graft and corruption there was, as there were huge increases and expenditures in the cost of government. But by all accounts, Gómez was extraordinarily popular.[84]

Gómez also had a regular army of 5,000 men—infantry, cavalry, artillery—and even a tiny navy. The army was a legacy of Magoon and was very much a mixed blessing. United States Army officers, who favored a more professional Rural Guard as an insular constabulary, were opposed to its establishment. After all, what did the Cubans need an army for, unless to fight other Cubans? The Moderates, and the right in general, feared an army which they knew would be a potent political force. The Liberals were averse to any armed forces not commanded by old Liberation Army veterans. In 1912 the proverbial chickens came home to roost.

It was called a race war, and white Cubans had dreaded it for a century. Of Cuba's two million people, about thirty percent, concentrated in Oriente Province, were black. During the war of independence blacks formed nearly half the enlisted and officer ranks of the Liberation Army. They had been promised political positions, public offices, social equality, and social justice. Now more than a decade after the victory they were still second-class citizens.

If anything the situation had worsened. Oriente Province was overrun with speculators. Smallholdings were gobbled up in complicated land tenure suits. Huge parcels were bought by the railroads. Sugar plantations and mining interests rapidly expanded, and the farmers and peasants quickly lost control of the land. Every piece converted to cash crop sugar meant less for subsistence agriculture. In the fields, factories, and mines, foreign workers displaced the locals. The world of the black Cubans was collapsing around them.

In the black community there was a profound sense of betrayal. In 1907 its leadership, headed by Evaristo Estanoz, an insurgent general of the late Liberal revolt, took steps toward a political realignment and formed a new movement, the Independent Party of Color. Its demands centered on race questions, specifically the increased representation of blacks in elected and appointed public office.

The movement was a direct challenge to the Liberals, who needed the black vote in order to maintain their status as Cuba's majority party. In 1910, the black Liberal leader of the Senate introduced legislation prohibiting all political parties organized on racial lines.

Estanoz would have none of it and his attitude assumed an alarming belligerency. In an interview with the Cuban press, the black leadership announced their intention to provoke American intervention and topple the Gómez government. "They want equal rights with whites," reported *La Lucha* (*The Struggle*), "or they will put an end to the republic."[85]

In Havana, the American ambassador, Arthur Beaupré, a man with considerable experience in Latin American affairs, cabled the State Department. The Independent Party of Color, he warned, "is an element of considerable danger to public order."[86]

Estanoz and his lieutenants planned for separate but coordinated uprisings throughout the island. Initially, at sunset on May 20, they would seize the Rural Guard posts in Oriente, Santa Clara, and Pinar del Río provinces. Armed bands rose and there was some skirmishing with the Guard. But the plot had leaked and some blacks were arrested. "Government is confident," Beaupré reported, "that movement is completely suppressed."[87]

In all but Oriente Province the revolt was aborted or short-lived, and to Oriente President Gómez sent his troops. About 10,000 blacks were in open revolt, and he could not absolutely guarantee protection to foreign economic interests. The American consuls, who feared for the safety of the plantations and mines, began flashing the alarm.

The uprising now took form as a peasant revolt, a popular outburst with neither leadership nor organization, and Evaristo Estanoz quickly lost control. Foreign property was attacked as a symbol of oppression but there was little loss of life. It was also very hard to separate real revolutionaries from mere armed bandits. Major Henry Davis of the Marine Corps later wrote of "small bands of men whom it appears difficult to identify as revolutionists; they are acting rather as outlaws, and I am of the opinion they are nothing but bands organized to steal."[88]

In Washington, President Taft and the State Department moved quickly. Neither wished a replay of the political collapse of 1906, and they were determined to keep Gómez in power. On May 23, the gunboats *Paducah, Nashville,* and *Petrel* were ordered to Guantánamo and Nipe bays. At League Island, Philadelphia, a brigade staff and 750 marines of the 1st Provisional Regiment boarded the transport *Prairie.* At Brooklyn, from Hampton Roads, and from the Panama Canal Zone, the 2nd Marine Provisional Regiment was hastily assembled out of diverse detachments and sailed in the fleet for Key West, Guantánamo, and Havana. Colonel Lincoln Karmany, a tough, old campaigner, was picked to command the brigade. Though it's perhaps apocryphal, Karmany is credited with the motto "There may be a few good men who don't drink, but they've got to prove it." Should the need arise for extra muscle, the 3rd and 4th divisions of the Atlantic Fleet, nine battleships, dropped anchor at Key West.[89]

When all had been mobilized and bound for their destinations, Ambassador Beaupré presented the State Department's views to the Cuban government. If Gómez and his army proved unable to protect American lives and property, the United States, "pursuant to its uniform custom in such cases, will land forces to accord necessary protection. This," he hastened to assure his audience, "is not intervention."[90]

Gómez privately welcomed this nonintervention intervention. To Beaupré he expressed himself as "gratified," but it was hardly politic to go public.

On May 29 events turned ugly. At the embassy Beaupré received a disturbing report from the President of the Guantánamo and Western Railway. The company store had been robbed by a band of insurgents. Their illiterate chief, giving what he thought was a receipt for the stolen goods, instead presented what purported to be an original order from Evaristo Estanoz: "If by June 1, the . . . law [prohibiting black political parties] is not repealed, you will at once start to destroy all railroad bridges, telegraph and telephone lines, and other property of American ownership, and if this does not accomplish our purpose . . . within 15 days hereafter, you will start killing white men not of our color irrespective of nationality." The order, never positively authenticated, sent a chill through the island.[91]

On June 2 the rebels put the torch to the town of La Maya. Three days later, Gómez suspended all constitutional guarantees in Oriente Province. That same day, in response to repeated and loud demands by American planters and miners, the marines from the *Prairie* went ashore at Guantánamo Bay. Other detachments from the fleet landed at various points on the provincial coast. From Key West steamed the four battleships of the 4th Division.

Fanning out into the interior, platoon- and company-sized units of marines mounted guard over the mines, mills, plantations, and railroads. There was some random shooting, but no general action. Young Lieutenant Alexander Vandegrift (Commandant of the Marine Corps, 1944–1948) later wrote, "At El Cuero we protected a valuable American-owned manganese mine, a mission since familiar as guarding 'the lives and property of American citizens'.... Except for one night when we were fired upon, the mission proved somewhat boring."[92]

The landing of United States forces freed the Cuban Army from their responsibility for protecting installations. They took to the field with a vengeance and there was widespread and indiscriminate killing. Large numbers of black prisoners were shot "while trying to escape." American civilians reported the Cuban Army "cutting off [the] heads, pretty much without discrimination, of all negroes found outside the town limits." The skipper of the gunboat *Petrel* wired the Secretary of the Navy, "Since the withdrawal of constitutional guarantees several negroes ... have been hanged, presumably by the soldiers, but no one believes that these negroes were really rebels. As a rule, the bodies are left hanging to the trees, or left by the roadside, no effort being made to bury them or to fix the responsibility for the executions." In the end, more than 6,000 blacks were exterminated by the Cuban Army, and Oriente Province was hideously pocked with mass, nameless graves.[93]

On June 26 Evaristo Estanoz was killed near Nipe Bay, on Oriente's north coast. Brought to Santiago by Cuban troops for positive identification, the body was placed on public display, "for the benefit," one Marine Corps historian later put it, "of all rebel sympathizers."[94]

The rebellion, formless and forlorn, disintegrated. In mid-July, the marine guard units were withdrawn to Guantánamo Bay, and by stages returned to their regular stations.

The singular brutality by which the new Cuban Army crushed the black revolt calls into question Taft and Knox's policy of a "non-intervention" intervention. The Platt Amendment, odious on its face, could well have been used to save countless lives as well as protect American interests. Later, in Haiti, where American investments were comparatively minor, humanitarian motives, rather than economic, became the stated cause of intervention.

The last United States military incursion in Cuba was the sugar intervention of 1917. Superficially it was little different from the 1906 revolt against Tomás Estrada Palma: an election stolen by the right, followed by an insurrection of the left, culminating in the landing of United States forces. There, however, the similarities end.

The elections of 1912 saw the decline of the Liberals, and replacing the Moderates, a new Conservative party, led by ex-General Mario García Menocal, assumed the reins of power. A battle-proven veteran of the old Liberation Army, he was hailed in both Cuba and the United States as a refreshing change from the corruption and venality that had insidiously pervaded Cuban politics.

In 1912 that might well have been, but too much had been promised to too many, and Menocal's large and extended family supped well at the government table. Four years later, reneging on a pledge not to seek reelection, he began turning the machinery to assure victory at the polls. Revolt was inevitable.

During the fall campaign violence swept across the Pearl of the Antilles. Neither party could play the role of blameless innocent, and Menocal was forced to appoint military supervisors to police the voting. This naturally led to further acrimony, the Liberals charging the army as more concerned with Menocal's election than with ensuring fairness.

Both parties, Conservative and Liberal, did their share of ballot stuffing. The results were very close, and it was assumed by all, Menocal included, that the Liberals had won. On the night of November 1, he was prepared to concede defeat. The legend in Cuba has it, however, that several female members of the President's family refused to accept the outcome and prevailed, with "feminine passion," in forcing Menocal to falsify the results. With the new count, not published until late December, the supposed Liberal victory vanished.

In January 1917, the Liberals petitioned the Supreme Court of Cuba. Wary and distrustful, because the bench was packed with Menocal supporters, they were jubilant at the decision. New elections were ordered for critical precincts in Oriente and Santa Clara provinces. As the Liberals were the legitimate majority party, their victory was a foregone conclusion—if the elections were held fairly. As a guarantee some of the Liberal leadership considered an appeal to the United States to supervise the vote, but no invitation was made.

But the United States was not a disinterested spectator. As its relations with Germany deteriorated by the day, leading to a diplomatic break on February 3, 1917, peace and stability in Cuba assumed pressing importance. The Marine Corps and sizable contingents of the Atlantic Fleet were heavily engaged in pacification and occupation duties in Haiti and the Dominican Republic. In Mexico General Pershing, with 6,000 cavalry, fruitlessly chased Pancho Villa in the mountains south of the Rio Grande, and not for the last time, a real war with Mexico assumed distinct proportions. A revolution in Cuba, with the possibility, if not probability, of American military intervention was a drain on resources the United States could ill afford.

In early February, the first precautionary deployments were ordered out, and Battleship Division 5, *Connecticut, Michigan, South Carolina,* dropped their anchors in Guantánamo Bay.

By mid-month it was apparent in Washington that hostilities were not far off. In the first of a series of notes passed to the Cuban government, Secretary of State Robert Lansing cabled his ambassador, William Gonzales.* The Cuban parties, Lansing naively hoped, would resolve their grievances peacefully. Such a settlement would "undoubtedly stand as a fine example before the world as a case where misunderstandings were being adjusted by law instead of by arms." The plea fell on deaf ears.[95]

In fact, the Liberals already had their plan in motion. Ex-President José Miguel Gómez, slated to head the revolt in Santa Clara, put to sea in his yacht, ostensibly for a fishing trip. Once the banner was raised, his troops would move up the railroad to Havana, three to four days' march, and force Menocal's abdication. Other Liberal leaders, Pino Guerra of 1906 fame, and Baldomero Acosta, a former major league ballplayer for the Washington Senators, took the field in the west.**

On the night of February 11 the storm broke. At Camp Columbia, Havana, the whole garrison was slated to rise, join with the city police, and in a *coup de main,* topple Menocal from power. The firing of a signal gun threw the base into an uproar. But only a handful of soldiers took arms against the government, and the ringleaders of the mutiny were forced to flee. In the east, the Liberals had better luck, Camagüey, Santiago, and Guantánamo City were seized by rebellious soldiery.

Throughout Cuba, in Pinar del Río, in Havana, in Matanzas, Camagüey, Santa Clara, and Oriente, the revolt flashed through the provinces. Numbers of the Rural Guard, as well as whole units

---

*The son of an expatriate Cuban father, Gonzales was nonetheless thoroughly American, a South Carolina publisher who hardly spoke a word of Spanish.

**It is interesting to note that Fidel Castro was a promising minor league pitcher in the Senators' organization.

of the Cuban Army, joined the insurgent colors. The government forces were in disarray, and a quick move on Havana would probably have been successful. But Mario Menocal was made of sterner stuff than Tomás Estrada Palma. The railroads leading east from Havana were the crucial arteries for the rebel advance. Menocal ordered the bridges blown, and the Liberals were halted literally in their tracks. Menocal was granted some precious time to concentrate and organize his forces.

In the offing came cries from the American sugar plantations for immediate protection. On February 12 the gunboat *Paducah* landed her bluejackets on the southwest coast of Santa Clara.

Two days later, Ambassador Gonzales received a second note from Secretary Lansing for passage to Cuban government and press. The United States viewed the situation with the "greatest apprehension." If the Liberals harbored any idea of a favorable reception, their hopes were dashed. Washington, the State Department warned, would give its "confidence and support" to constitutionally established governments only.[96]

The day was a busy one in Oriente. There were rumors that Menocal's troops were shooting prisoners. In response the rebel commander in Santiago threatened to reciprocate in kind, bringing a warning from Ambassador Gonzales against acts of "barbarism." The rebel leader was quick to respond, "I shall ingenuously confess to you that my threat of reprisals was a simulated act of barbarism."[97]

At the United States Navy's Guantánamo Bay station, a trio of Cuban gunboats arrived unexpectedly and dropped anchor. Paying a call, Commander Dudley Knox, the base commander, learned that the three tiny craft had just managed to escape from Santiago and considered themselves very lucky to have run a silent gauntlet of rebel batteries. Back on shore Knox received a radiogram from the American consul. The situation in Santiago had reached flash point. The rebels had seized all telegraph, telephone, and radio communications. Worse, the rebel commander was even now mining the harbor; an American warship was required at once.

The only available men-of-war were the armored cruiser *Montana* and the ancient gunboat *Petrel*, a veteran of Dewey's Squadron at Manila Bay. The *Montana* was far too valuable a risk if indeed there were mines in the fairway. The *Petrel*, on the other hand, had been condemned by the Board of Inspection and Survey, and now rusted her days away as the station ship, tied to the pier. Her bottom was badly pitted and in danger of collapse, half her gun mounts were empty, and departmental orders forbade taking her into deep water. Yet within three hours of receiving the consul's message, she was at sea, Knox on her bridge, wooden dummies in her gun mounts, bound for Santiago.

Before dawn, February 15, her hands at general quarters, including men at the dummy guns, the *Petrel* arrived off Santiago. Coming on board were the collector of customs and a rebel officer. Both expressed their fear of the government gunboats. This to Knox presented a somewhat ludicrous situation, as the Cuban warships were equally afraid of the rebel shore batteries. Could not Knox and the *Petrel*, they asked, prevent the government craft from entering the bay? Knox declined, as it posed an unwarranted interference with Cuban sovereignty. This being the case, the rebel officer claimed he had no choice but to mine the harbor and sink blockships in the channel.

Shortly after, the steamer *Julia* was spotted; she was under tow, showed no lights, and was making for the harbor entrance. She was doubtless a blockship, and rebel troops could be seen on her upper deck; the *Petrel* gave chase. The old gunboat's crew were all in various states of undress; rifle-armed sailors at the hammock nettings "completed a picture," Knox wrote, "strongly suggestive of old-time pirate days."[98]

The *Julia* was overhauled and from her skipper Knox learned that two other blockships laden with dynamite were already in place and only awaiting orders to be sunk. Against these it was impossible to take any action, but the *Julia* was sent back into port under her tow.

Right after morning colors, the *Petrel* received Colonel de Mola, commander of the rebel forces in Santiago. He was described by Knox as "clean-cut, alert, well-bred, perfectly poised . . . and a most capable leader." De Mola reiterated the military necessity of mining and blocking the harbor. If he were prevented and government warships forced the entrance, he was prepared to torch the city and dynamite the public buildings. Knox's strong protests met with a strangely cheerful compliance. A deal was struck. Knox promised to keep the gunboats out and de Mola agreed to keep the channel clear. Knox knew well there was only the remotest possibility of the Cuban vessels even attempting to enter the harbor.[99]

All went well until the next night when the *Petrel*'s radio operator picked up a message from Admiral Henry Mayo, commander of the Atlantic Fleet, regarding Knox's deal with de Mola. "Not authorized to give such guarantees," was his admonition to Knox. Yet paradoxically Knox was ordered to use every measure "short of actual force" to prevent the blocking of the channel. Reinforcements were on the way. The old cruiser *San Francisco* was due to arrive on the eighteenth. Officially rebuked in his efforts, Knox sent word to de Mola terminating their mutual arrangement.[100]

The situation was now in great flux. Reports of government steamers loaded with troops and bound out from Havana filtered into Santiago. In the city, the American consul feared that even a false alarm could precipitate the rebel threats of destruction.

Knox was left with no choice but further parley. The rebel commander again agreed to lay no mines and to take special precautions against damaging neutral shipping. But should he be forced to evacuate, his threat to fire and dynamite the town still held. Somehow Knox again convinced de Mola to leave the entire matter in abeyance pending the arrival of the *San Francisco*. Knox knew de Mola's threat might all be a rebel bluff, but circumstances were serious enough for him to report it directly to the Navy Department. On the night of February 19 he received his reply. The *Petrel* and *San Francisco* were to prevent all government ships from entering the harbor of Santiago de Cuba. "Washington," Knox wryly noted, "had caught up with the situation, just as the situation had ended."[101]

On February 19 Secretary Lansing sent his third note to Ambassador Gonzales for presentation to the Cuban government and press. The Liberal revolt was deemed by the United States "lawless and unconstitutional . . . not to be countenanced." The United States would hold the rebel leadership responsible for all damages and injuries to foreigners and their property. The revolution was doomed.[102]

In the hinterland surrounding the base at Guantánamo Bay, rebels were hard at work burning the cane fields, which placed the station's water supply in jeopardy. Back at his post ashore, Commander Knox ordered out his marine detachment reinforced by the *Montana*'s marines, 220 strong in all, north into Guantánamo City.

The same day, February 25, a provisional marine battalion of

200 men landed from Battleship Division 5 to protect the sugar plantations on the western hook of Oriente Province. During the first week of March, six companies of marines were diverted from occupation duties in Haiti and moved into the hinterland around Guantánamo Bay.

On March 7, in Santa Clara, government forces roundly defeated the insurgents, capturing Gómez and almost his entire command in the process. For all intents and purposes, the battle, along with the hostile attitude of the United States, effectively ended the sugar revolt of 1917.

But in Camagüey and Oriente sporadic fighting continued. The Liberals still cherished a hope that depredations against foreign economic interests, carried on long enough, would ensure a total American intervention and with it the supervision of fair elections.

But for the rebels, the situation steadily deteriorated. Government forces, by land and sea, advanced on Santiago. To avert a possible bloodbath, the rebel military and civil leadership appealed to the *San Francisco*'s skipper to take over the city. He accepted on condition that all insurgent troops evacuate, and should they return, surrender their weapons to the Americans. The rebels agreed. On March 8, landing parties from the *San Francisco, Olympia*, and gunboat *Machias*, reinforced by two companies of marines from Haiti, went ashore. By midnight, the city was clear of all rebels. "Marines protecting the city," cabled the American consul to Secretary Lansing. "The people excited but all quiet."[103]

On March 18, at the urging of the United States, Menocal promulgated a bill providing amnesty for all rebels giving up the fight.

On April 6 the United States declared war on Germany. Cuba followed suit the next day, offering up her soldiers for the cause. The United States declined; it was far more important that the Cuban Army protect Cuban mines and sugar plantations, which were an important war resource for the U.S. The war also brought added pressure from the United States on the remaining rebels in the field. In some American circles the whole 1917 sugar revolt was seen as an insidious German plot to destabilize the Caribbean and tie down a sizable element of the American military. There was no basis for the assumption, at least not in Cuba; nevertheless Lansing informed Ambassador Gonzales "that unless all those under arms against the Government of Cuba return immediately to their allegiance it may become necessary for the United States to regard them as its enemies and to deal with them accordingly."[104]

In mid-May the overriding needs of the war in Europe led to the withdrawal of all marines from Cuba—save the permanent garrison at Guantánamo Bay. But so crucial to the war effort was Cuban sugar production that the United States planned to send a regiment of cavalry as a backup stiffener to the Cuban Army. It was later decided at a White House conference that the horse soldiers could not be spared. Instead, in August and December, at League Island, Philadelphia, and Quantico, Virginia, the 7th and 9th marine regiments were formed and shipped to Guantánamo Bay. Together they comprised the 3rd Marine Brigade, the nucleus of the newly conceived Advanced Base Force. Organized and trained to seize and hold forward bases for the fleet, they formed the kernel of the six marine divisions that swept the Pacific in World War II.

In November 1918, with war's end in Europe, the brigade was reinforced with the 1st Marines. For Cuba, in peacetime, three full marine regiments could hardly be sustained. Postwar parsimony in Congress, and other area commitments, saw a gradual reduction of U.S. troops in Cuba. By late summer 1919, the 1st Marines had been withdrawn. Two companies of the brigade were stationed in Camagüey, while the remainder trained at Guantánamo Bay. On January 6, 1922, the American military presence in Cuba came to an end. All, that is, except for Guantánamo Bay, where major base facilities are still maintained under a perpetual lease.

3:

PANAMA
1885–1904

I took the Canal Zone and let Congress debate.

–Theodore Roosevelt

On February 16, 1898, the day following the *Maine* catastrophe, across the hemisphere in the pine damp and mist shrouds of the Pacific northwest, the battleship *Oregon* completed her first refit and floated out of drydock. As relations with Spain deteriorated and the navy mobilized for war, her orders arrived. "The situation is getting worse . . . go to San Francisco as soon as possible and get ammunition." On March 7, she pointed her ram-snouted bow to sea and steamed out of Puget Sound.[1]

For ten days in San Francisco, she filled her magazines and bunkers and made good the deficiencies in her officers and crew. On the seventeenth, her skipper was "condemned by medical survey" and Captain Charles Clark took command. Two days later she passed out the Golden Gate bound for Callao, Peru.[2]

At eleven knots, the *Oregon* plowed ever southward. In her stokeholds and engine spaces temperatures reached 160 degrees, but for the engineers, firemen, and coal passers there was no respite. Even a cool drink of fresh water was a luxury; most of that elixir went straight into the insatiable bowels of her double-ended firetube boilers.

When the anchor dropped at Callao she had broken her first record, steaming 5,175 miles nonstop; no battleship had ever come close to this. Coaling and minor repairs completed, the *Oregon* left Callao on April 7 for the Strait of Magellan. "The belief was

79

general," wrote one of her engineering officers, "that war with Spain was inevitable." In the wet, hideously suffocating snipe marsh of her engineering spaces, speed was increased to thirteen knots.[3]

At the entrance to the strait, the ship was struck by a violent gale which soon changed to heavy, driving snows. "With sheer cliffs on either hand," Captain Clark noted, "and fathomless depths below, there could be no pause or hesitation in this exciting race, and I think there was no man on board that did not feel the thrill of it."[4]

At Argentina's Punta Arenas the coal hulk tied up alongside. But the black diamonds lay under cargo, and to begin the unspeakably filthy work of coaling ship the crew had first to shift several tons of greasy, lanolin-soaked raw wool.

Here the *Oregon* was joined by the little gunboat *Marietta*. Reports were received of the lone Spanish torpedo gunboat *Temerario* lying in wait across their path. Indeed, the American press noted daily the progress of the Spanish vessel, and her complement of two torpedo tubes seemed in that era to predict a pending battle on equal terms. "It is possible," Minnesota's *Saint Paul Pioneer Press* informed its readers, that "the *Temerario* may have started to disable the battleship." Fortunately for the Spanish craft, which would have been blown out of the water by the *Oregon*'s broadsides, this was no more than a sensational rumor.[5]

As the ships steamed north, the *Marietta* scouted ahead, tossing barrels over the side which the *Oregon* used for target. The battleship's crew worked like galley slaves. Captain Clark reported on "the engineer officers . . . voluntarily doubling their watches . . . [and] the attempt of men to return to the fire room after being carried out of it insensible." They arrived at Rio de Janeiro on April 30.[6]

"War has been declared between the United States and Spain from April 21," read the cable from Secretary Long. The next day came further news: "Four Spanish armored cruisers, heavy and fast, three torpedo boat destroyers, sailed from Cape Verde to the west, destination unknown." Fearful lest the *Oregon* fall in with a supposedly superior force, Long initially ordered the ship to remain at Rio. Fortunately he countermanded the directive and permitted Clark to act on his initiative.[7]

At Rio the *Oregon* shed her peacetime white and buff for the gray "war color." To avoid an open contravention of international law forbidding military preparations in a neutral port, the painting was done at night in virtual secret. Here the two ships were joined by one of the navy's foreign purchases, the auxiliary cruiser *Nictheroy* (USS *Buffalo*). But neither she nor the *Marietta* could keep speed with the *Oregon*, forcing Clark to leave these ships to their own devices; he ordered them to "beach if necessary to avoid capture."[8]

Steaming north, Clark pondered the tactical situation. Should the *Oregon* encounter the enemy cruiser squadron, the battleship, he noted, "might beat off and even cripple the Spanish fleet." With Admiral Cervera steaming about the Caribbean searching for, above all else, a safe harbor, there was no real threat of meeting the enemy, but Clark couldn't know that, and he put the worst-case scenario to the crew. One sailor wrote in his diary, "After telling us about the fleet that was going to whip the socks off us . . . he said . . . it was his duty to the Government to get the ship around . . . and stear clear of the fleet if possible. But in case he did meet the fleet he was sure Spain's fighting efficiency on the sea would be demineshed. So we all gave him three rousen cheers and the old man Blushed, but he is dandy Just the same."[9]

For days on end, while the *Oregon* was "lost from communications," the American public waited in mounting tension. Off the mouth of the Amazon the battleship crossed paths with the tiny yawl *Spray*, sailed by one man, Joshua Slocum of New Bedford, Massachusetts. Slocum was completing the first solo circumnavigation of the globe, and on learning of the war with Spain, hoisted the signal "Let us keep together for mutual protection."[10]

On May 18 the *Oregon* coaled at Barbados, then steamed through the Lesser Antilles and the Bahamas. On May 24, just north of Palm Beach, Florida, Captain Clark wrote, "The rays of Jupiter [inlet] Light [house], streamed out to the *Oregon* like the fingers of some friendly hand extended to welcome her home."[11]

Militarily she had accomplished an astounding feat. In sixty-six days the ship had steamed over 15,000 miles, arriving at the seat of war in excellent fighting trim. It was a magnificent tribute to her builders, her officers, and crew. But politically and strategically the voyage brought home to the navy and the nation, as nothing else could, the absolute necessity for a trans-isthmian ocean canal. The Spanish-American War was the United States' first global conflict, and anyone who followed the voyage and could read a map instantly recognized the value of rapid mobilization of the fleet on either coast. Had the canal been in place in 1898, the *Oregon* would have cut her time by two-thirds.

At war's end, the Central American isthmus was distantly guarded in the Pacific by newly acquired Hawaii, and closely in the Atlantic by new bases flanking the Windward and Mona passages at Guantánamo Bay and Puerto Rico. It only remained to choose the canal route and negotiate the lease.

Indeed, the need had existed for nigh on 400 years, from the day in 1513 when Vasco Núñez de Balboa crossed the isthmus, set his eyes upon the Pacific Ocean and claimed it and all its shores for the King of Spain. Soon thereafter, the first stones were laid for a post road joining the oceans. In 1519, after enormous difficulties, a cobbled track wide enough for a pair of pack mules opened as the great highway of the Spanish empire in the New World. By 1534 there were already major improvements. The serpentine Chagres River,* whose mouth empties into the Atlantic about six miles west of the entrance to the present-day Panama Canal, was dredged for shallow-draft vessels, allowing waterborne trade for about two-thirds the distance between the oceans. But for the last fifteen miles to the Pacific it was still by pack mule. With hardly a change, the path across the strategic choke point of the Western Hemisphere remained unaltered for over 300 years.

In 1819, following a successful revolution led by Simón Bolívar, the Granadan Federation—present-day Colombia, Ecuador, and Venezuela—was formed. Two years later, Panama was absorbed into the greater nationhood. In 1831 the federation divided into its component states, Panama forming the northern panhandle of New Granada, which in mid-century changed its name to the United States of Colombia. The Panamanian people, however, as a result of the region's geography, never fully absorbed themselves into the Colombian polity, and Panamanian nationalism and separatist tendencies remained strong.

In the United States of America, victory in the Mexican War and the discovery of gold in California stretched

---

*The Chagres was mostly eliminated during the construction of the Panama Canal, most of its watershed now being occupied by Gatún Lake, the world's largest manmade body of water.

the national domain unbroken across the continent. It was the high spate of Manifest Destiny, the dream of casting American hegemony from pole to pole and sea to sea. There was not yet a transcontinental railroad, and the highways west of the Mississippi were little more than wheel ruts in the virgin prairie. The overland trek was miserably slow, with travel from St. Louis to Oregon often taking six months. But by ship from New York, south into the Caribbean and then west, across the isthmus by flatboat and muleback, and then by ship again to San Francisco took less than two. The sea trade was lucrative, and Panama, by accident of geography, provided the crucial linchpin in the chain of Manifest Destiny.

The American ambassador in the New Granadan capital of Bogotá, Benjamin A. Bidlack, seized the opportunity to firmly establish a United States influence in the isthmus of Panama. With foreign minister Manuel María Mallarino, he negotiated the cornerstone treaty between the two nations.

Ratified in 1848, the treaty guaranteed that "the right of way or transit across the Isthmus of Panama, upon any modes of communication that now exist, or that may be . . . constructed, shall be open and free to the Government and citizens of the United States." In return the United States pledged to defend "the perfect neutrality of the . . . Isthmus . . . that the free transit from one to the other sea, may not be interrupted or embarrassed in any future time . . . and . . . also guarantees . . . the rights of sovereignty and property which New Granada has and possesses over said territory."[12]

The treaty, which remained in effect until 1903, served upon the United States the right and duty to maintain the security of isthmian transit, whatever it might be and without regard to ownership. The call would not be long in coming.

The advancing technology of steam engineering soon brought the railroad men to Panama. In 1849 New Granada transferred a ninety-nine-year concession to the American-owned Panama Railroad Company to build and operate an isthmian railway. The line opened for business in 1855 with its Atlantic terminus at the new ramshackle town of Aspinwall (renamed Colón in 1890), and its Pacific station at the departmental capital, Panama City.

The one-track line, forty-eight miles long, was the world's first transcontinental railroad, and the three-hour, one-way passage cost twenty-five dollars in gold. This monumental construction feat brought thousands of Central American and Caribbean laborers to the isthmus. The line of transit became a natural habitat for miscreants, and the local authorities were powerless in maintaining order, particularly during the six-month rainy season. With little to occupy themselves, the unemployed provided a powder keg of instability ever ready to explode and trigger an American military intervention.

Panama City was a boomtown and literally packed to the rafters. Navy Lieutenant Daniel Ammen "found not a place where to rest our heads. We visited house after house in which bunks were built in the rooms three or four over one another, and yet not even under such conditions was a resting-place to be found."[13]

In 1856 large-scale rioting by unemployed laborers and local "disorderly elements" resulted in the death of fifteen Americans and the wounding of fifty others. The turmoil continued until the arrival of the United States Navy sloop-of-war *St. Mary's*. But with a crew of less than 200 men, and the New Granadan authorities refusing to act, Commander Theodorus Bailey could do little by himself to quell the situation. But he had been warned by the Secretary of the Navy that in any attempt "made to assail and plunder our citizens, you will defend and protect them and resort to force if necessary." Bailey ordered the ship cleared for action, and every gawking ruffian on the waterfront watched her ports open and the guns run out. For a time, a measure of control was established.[14]

Some months later when rioting broke out anew, the *St. Mary's* and the big 54-gun frigate, *Independence*, flagship of Commodore William Mervine's Pacific Squadron, lay at anchor in the steamy port. Mervine ordered ashore a landing force of 160 bluejackets and marines, dragging with them a pair of smoothbore howitzers. With muskets at the slope, and heavy cutlasses hanging low on their belts, the blue-clad "battalion" marched to the Panama Railroad station. After clearing the rioters from the terminal grounds, they made camp and, in accord with the terms of the Bidlack-Mallarino Treaty, prepared to defend the line of transit against attack. The landing force was outnumbered by the rioters by at least five to one. But after conducting some convincing demonstrations of volley firing and battery drill, the troubles subsided and the landing force was withdrawn.

Over the following twenty-odd years, the navy conducted several small-scale landings with similar result. But in the United

States, the impulse to Manifest Destiny waned. The Civil War, Reconstruction, and the settling of the west absorbed the country's energies, and the navy plunged into a precipitous postwar decline. America turned her face inward.

Meanwhile in Panama there arrived a brilliant French entrepreneur, Ferdinand de Lesseps, builder of the Suez Canal. In 1882 he attempted the dream of centuries and scooped the first tons of earth from the mountains at Culebra.

Colombian politics and revolution intervened with de Lesseps' progress. Following the Conservative victory in the presidential elections of 1884, a general insurrection by the Liberal* outs swept the country. By December, communications from Bogotá were virtually cut. "In the present disordered condition of society," Ambassador Scruggs noted to the State Department, "we may reasonably anticipate the usual disregard of the rights of foreigners . . . on the Isthmus."[15]

De Lesseps' canal work gangs had swelled the population and "thousands of desperate and vicious characters" collected at Panama City. Moreover, the Bogotá government had created a power vacuum when it shifted about 500 troops from the Panama garrison to areas of insurrection; revolt on the isthmus was imminent. On March 11, 1885, anticipating trouble, Commander Theodore Kane brought the screw sloop *Galena* to anchor off Colón.[16]

Five days later in Panama City, General Rafael Aizpuru, one-time departmental governor of Panama and a "disreputable revolutionist" according to Colombian authorities, and 250 men attacked the depleted government garrison. After a heavy fight the rebels captured the town and Aizpuru declared himself President of Panama. No sooner was the new administration in place than Aizpuru's men went on a rampage. Railroad cars were pillaged, switches destroyed, the telegraph wires cut, and railroad employees taken prisoner; the railroad ground to a halt.

Across the isthmus in Colón, some recently arrived Colombian troops, estimated at 150 to 200 men, boarded a special and chugged down the line to retake the capital. Their departure left Colón bereft of government forces, and Commander Kane deemed it prudent to put ashore sixteen marines and a dozen

---

*The Liberals were generally of the poorer, less educated classes, often joined in Panama by bodies of regional workers seeking plunder in the chronic disorder. The Conservatives constituted the "better," more educated classes, including most of the large landowners.

bluejackets to safeguard American property. They were a token that could hardly be expected to do more than hold the docks.

Another minuscule band now appeared in Colón; no more than a dozen men, ragged, barefoot, and armed with machetes. This was the "army" of Pedro Prestan, a charismatic, xenophobic Haitian ex-patriot, who reserved his particular hatred for white North Americans. Politically, he was recognized as a leader of the Colombian Liberals' radical wing.

With no government troops in the town, Prestan's men began a campaign of extortion against the local merchants. Railroad property was seized, tracks were torn up, and telegraph poles ripped down. For nearly two weeks Prestan's gang held sway in Colón. To the chagrin of the merchants and French canal officials, Commander Kane held closely to his orders to protect American lives and property. He also considered his strength insufficient for anything but guarding the wharf, and as a result the *Galena*'s landing party did nothing to stop the depredations.

On March 29 there arrived in the harbor a Pacific Mail steamer packed with a cargo of contraband arms. Prestan demanded the weapons, but was refused them by the local Pacific Mail superintendent. Prestan then took him, three other American civilians, and two of the *Galena*'s officers as hostages. One of the latter was sent to Commander Kane with the message that none would be released until the arms were turned over. Further, should the *Galena* interfere, the hostages and every American in Colón would die. Alarmed at the rapidly degenerating situation and believing Prestan would carry out his threat, the United States consul ordered the steamer to surrender her cargo. Prestan was true to his word, and on learning of the consul's action, he released his prisoners.

Theodore Kane, however, refused to be a party to the negotiations or to treat with rebels, and before a single rifle could be unloaded, the *Galena* stood into the harbor. A boarding party clambered up the steamer's side and quickly made fast a towing cable. With bare steerage way, and clouds of greasy black smoke, the *Galena* towed her charge into the open harbor. Prestan was outraged, and three Americans were retaken as hostages.

At dawn the next day, March 30, Commander Kane reinforced his tiny dock picket with every available officer and enlisted man, 112 in all, fully half the ship's company. But to the consternation of the foreign community, he refused to apprehend Prestan, or take any action to halt his campaign of extortion.

Feeling he could act with impunity, Prestan actively recruited from among the work gangs. He soon increased his band ten-fold and now constituted the major threat to Colombian sovereignty on the isthmus. From Panama City government reinforcements moved north up the line toward Colón. To avoid a pitched battle in the streets, the railroad's general superintendent halted their train just to the south of the town at Monkey Hill.

On the morning of April 1 the forces collided, and a sharp fight surged back and forth across the tracks. After an hour, during which the hostages managed their escape, Prestan's band cracked and fell back on Colón. In defeat, two of his lieutenants, Haitian "General" Pautrizelle, and West Indian George Davis, alias Cocobolo, torched the town. There was no fire brigade, and Colón burned to the ground. At dockside, the *Galena*'s crew managed to restore some semblance of order, and those men who could be spared fought the fires around the railroad depot. But all that remained of the city were the stone buildings of the Panama Railroad Company, the shipping lines, and a stone church. Colón's destitute civilians were, as well as possible, fed from the *Galena*'s stores, and her decks were crowded with refugees.

Pautrizelle and Cocobolo were captured by one of the *Galena*'s lieutenants. They were taken on board in double irons and later hanged by the Colombian authorities. "These two beauties," commented a marine officer who was shortly to arrive, "were the first men on the Isthmus to die by hanging. They had heretofore shot their offenders. This double execution changed the fashions in capital punishment in the Central American countries, for the time-honored activities of the firing squad were thrown into the discard through the restraining influences of the expeditionary force, and hanging was introduced to the Isthmus customs."[17]

While the fires raged in Colón, across the isthmus in Panama City, Rafael Aizpuru came out of hiding, and with a sizable force attacked the *cuartel* (police barracks) where some 100 government troops had barricaded themselves. Their defense was stout, but when the rebels threatened to dynamite the building they surrendered. Aizpuru again declared himself President of Panama, and this time he swore to kill every American on the isthmus.

The telegraph cables to Washington were abuzz. From Colón, Consul Wright, whom Prestan promised "death on sight," pleaded with the State Department for "more force here or Americans must abandon [the] Isthmus."[18]

In the Navy Department, Secretary William C. Whitney,

hounded by American commercial interests to save their property, ordered the screw sloop *Alliance* to Colón "with all practicable dispatch." Whitney also cabled a strong nudge to Commander Kane. The *Galena*'s skipper was reminded that he had been sent to Colón "to protect American interests and the lives and property of American citizens and all that is implied in these orders is expected to be done by you to the extent of the forces under your command." At Key West, Rear Admiral James Edward Jouett, commander of the North Atlantic Squadron, coaled his flagship, the screw frigate *Tennessee*, and with the screw sloop *Swatara* he made ready for sea.[19]

On April 1, 1885, Whitney committed the United States to full-scale intervention. It was America's largest foreign military operation between the Mexican War, which ended in 1847, and the Spanish-American War of 1898; it was as well the last gasp of the Old Navy. Jouett got his orders to sail immediately and was informed that an expeditionary force comprising "all available officers and men, Marines and bluejackets," would soon follow.

From the Navy's Bureau of Navigation, Commander Bowman Hendry McCalla was dispatched to take command. McCalla arrived at the Brooklyn Navy Yard on April 3 and lost no time putting his scant brigade together. The 460 marines and 280 bluejackets, stripped from every east coast yard and receiving ship, were formed into four thin battalions. Six 3-inch field guns and three Gatlings comprised the artillery. So meager was the plate that was the legacy of the Old Navy that McCalla was forced to entreat the army for a loan of 100 entrenching tools and 800 rubber ground sheets.[20]

Brevet Lieutenant Colonel Charles Heywood (Commandant of the Marine Corps, 1891–1903) and his 1st Battalion of marines sailed from Brooklyn in the *City of Para* on April 3. On the seventh, McCalla, his staff, the remaining three battalions, and the artillery train were ferried into New York's East River by the yard tugs and boarded the steamer *Acapulco*.* "A daily routine was established," McCalla noted to Secretary Whitney. "Opportunities were afforded all for target practice at floating targets, and Passed Assistant Surgeon Whiting instructed officers and men in the general principles of anatomy, the use of bandages and tourniquets,

---

*The navy's resources were then so lean that there were no transports in commission and passage was paid by the government for the troops sailing in the civilian vessels. Had the navy wished to charter a vessel, the cost could have reached a prohibitive $2,500 per day.

[and] recommended certain sanitary precautions to be adopted in the climate about to be encountered. There was some confusion the first evening out, but the steamer's accommodations were excellent, the fare good."[21]

The businessmen badgering the Navy Department for protection against the rebels were ecstatic. J.B. Houston, president of the Pacific Mail Steamship Company, magnanimously donated free passage for another 200 men. He was careful though, to make the gesture after the expedition had sailed, and after Whitney had already refused requests for artillery reinforcements. "Can I serve you in any other way?" he begged the Secretary.[22]

On April 8 the screw sloop *Shenandoah* landed 125 bluejackets and marines at Panama City who set up a defensive perimeter around the railroad depot. The position denied the terminus to Aizpuru's rebels controlling the line of transit. But Aizpuru had loftier goals. According to Consul General Thomas Adamson, to whom the rebel made repeated requests for an audience, Aizpuru sought an opportunity to "declare the secession of the 'sovereign' State of Panama from the [Colombian] union and place it under the protection of the United States of America." Cautious of compromising America's isthmian policy, which at this point, in accordance with the Bidlack-Mallarino Treaty, sought only to restore order and preserve Colombian authority along the line of transit, Adamson stalled and awaited the ships.[23]

In mid-morning, April 10, the political wish lists of the Panamanian revolutionaries were mooted; the United States, they soon learned, would not acquiesce to the notion of an independent Panama, at least not yet. On the Colón waterfront, refugees, citizens, and troops watched the *Tennessee* and *Swatara* stand into port. Jouett, according to protocol, had first to secure landing clearance from the nominal Colombian commander. It was, after all, Colombian territory on which the United States was about to commit its forces.

From the *Tennessee* the admiral's flag lieutenant, bearing Jouett's missive, was swiftly rowed to the railroad pier. For the Colombians, it was a galling experience. By acceding to Jouett's request they were forced to admit their impotence in maintaining stability on the isthmus. Not that they had any real choice. The bullet-headed admiral, so far as it suited him, observed the diplomatic niceties. But as he later told Secretary Whitney, "any refusal could not be allowed to delay the landing."

The government officer cabled Bogotá for instructions. To salve its national pride, the Colombian government found the expediency of Colón's appalling conditions reason enough to permit the landing. The American fleet could be considered a relief mission to alleviate the suffering. The next day Jouett received "permission" to land for "sanitary motives." Immediately, 175 bluejackets and marines with four 3-inch field guns were put ashore.[24]

Sanitary conditions in Colón were, in fact, deplorable. Navy surgeon Herndon reported to the Surgeon General of the Navy, "A few hours after our arrival I visited the town, and learned that yellow fever existed to a considerable extent. The place is very much overcrowded, and in an extremely filthy condition. . . . All persons in the city that I have been able to interview say that Colón is now an unhealthy place, and that malarial fevers of a very severe type as well as a fatal form of dysentery now prevails in the city."[25]

But Admiral Jouett's first order of business was to clear the line of transit and get the trains moving. "The whole country through which ran the Panama Railroad," he noted, "was utterly destitute of any government or authority whatever, civil or military. In view of this, and of the well-known fact that among the fifteen or twenty thousand people living along the line of transit, there were many dispersed revolutionists and desperados from all parts of the world, [I] decided to make the moving force so strong that not only could any offered opposition be easily overcome, but the lookers-on would be impressed with the folly of any attempt in that direction."[26]

On the eleventh the *City of Para* came to anchor, and Colonel Heywood's marines, wearing their Prussian-style spiked helmets, landed at the railroad pier.

In the trainyard work gangs of bluejackets toiled, fashioning a pair of makeshift armored flatcars; to each were mounted a 1-pounder Hotchkiss revolving cannon and a 12-pounder smooth-bore howitzer. For protection of the thirty-man gun crews and their escorting riflemen, a four-foot shield of boiler iron was bolted all around. The task took nearly six hours and was accomplished, according to Admiral Jouett, "in a very satisfactory manner."

By afternoon the admiral was ready to reopen the line of transit. At 2:00 P.M. the armored cars were coupled, Heywood's battalion and the civilian passengers from the *City of Para* found their seats in the coaches, and the first train to leave Colón in nearly six weeks chugged down the line. Just past the midway point, at the Matachin bridge, ninety marines and bluejackets, backed by a pair of 3-inch field guns, were offloaded and posted as a garrison.

"The forests and jungle that crowded in on the narrow cleared strip of the right of way had hardly felt the presence of civilization," wrote First Lieutenant George Elliott (Commandant of the Marine Corps, 1903–1911), "and were thickly populated with jaguars, deer, pecaries, monkeys, pythons, and a fine variety of smaller reptiles." Scarcely three hours after leaving Colón, the train, "without molestation," pulled into Panama City. By sundown, April 11, the expeditionary forces controlled the line of transit "and were prepared," wrote Jouett to Secretary Whitney, "to protect life and property."[27]

On April 14, bowing to the *fait accompli*, Colombia formally requested a United States military presence under the terms of the 1848 Bidlack-Mallarino Treaty.

The next day at Colón, the *Acapulco* stood in. Commander McCalla landed with his battalions and assumed command of all United States forces ashore. In this most unhealthy of climates he took care to preserve the health of his troops. "Be pleased to prohibit the use of all wines, spiritous and malt liquors," he cabled to Lieutenant Colonel Heywood. "Avoid as far as possible, ceremonies and parades. . . . Tea is better for all than coffee; use the latter but once a day; of the former you can have all that you desire." Further sanitary regulations posted in the standing orders dictated that quinine be taken before breakfast, meals eaten at regular hours, and to "Keep bowels open. . . . Keep out of night air as much as possible. . . . Wear flannel next to skin at night."[28]

On April 21 McCalla moved his command post and two additional companies of marines to the depot grounds in Panama City, temporarily renamed Camp Jouett. Except for this enclave, the city was controlled by forces loyal to Rafael Aizpuru, "in whose ranks," McCalla noted, "were some of Prestan's men who had taken part in the burning of Colón." He estimated the rebels at about 500, many of whom had taken up a strong defensive position behind the thick, loopholed walls of the old monastery on the Plaza San Francisco.[29]

McCalla feared that when sufficient Colombian forces arrived to quash the revolt, the rebels, in an act of vengeance, would torch the city. There was no fire brigade, nor any central water supply. "The prospect of plunder," he reported, was also an incentive to the rebels. "My chief anxiety was that I should not be able to prevent the destruction of the city."[30]

On the morning of April 24 Aizpuru began erecting barricades that severed communications between Camp Jouett and the telegraph office. Then and there McCalla resolved to fully occupy Panama City. The *Shenandoah*, at anchor in the harbor, landed all her available men. McCalla notified Admiral Jouett by telephone, and requested the entire landing force "with all the guns to Panama [City], using the utmost dispatch." Railroad General Superintendent George Burt ordered a special coupled up, and the reinforcements were on the way.

It was discovered that an old underground passage led from Aizpuru's monastery strongpoint in the Plaza San Francisco to the cathedral on the Plaza Santa Ana. This exit, McCalla noted, "was the center of the part of the city occupied by the worst classes." To prevent its use by the rebels, the forty-nine marines of Company D, 1st Battalion, were dispatched from Camp Jouett to occupy the church, "the keys of which were cheerfully turned over by the priests in charge. Care was taken that no injury was done to the churches."[31]

By 1:00 P.M., McCalla's 824 marines and bluejackets were in position. Three marching columns, reinforced by artillery and the Gatling guns, would make the direct assault. Taking the rebels along the seawall flank was given to the *Shenandoah* landing force. That ship had also landed a "Farmer's dynamo machine,"* along with wire, fuses, and tanks of gunpowder, "to be used, if necessary to blow up buildings."[32]

The occupation went off like a textbook exercise in battalion drill. McCalla posted himself with the center column, "which will carry the colors of the First Battalion of Marines," and ordered his bugler to sound the advance. "The several columns advanced without music," he noted to Admiral Jouett, "the marines in two lines deployed for street fighting, the Gatlings and field pieces between the lines."[33]

The marines came up to Aizpuru's first barricade, heavy wooden posts set in the ground, connected by boards, and packed

---

*A hand-cranked, electrical-generating device invented by Moses Farmer.

with earth. There was no resistance and down it came. The sand-bag barricade near the main *cuartel* was also dismantled without incident and a Gatling gun soon occupied the position.

By 5:00 P.M., the 2nd Battalion's C and E companies, with a pair each of Gatlings and 3-inch guns, arrived from Colón. In the whole operation, hardly a round was fired. The only altercation came in the evening between "some citizens in the Cathedral Square, during which several shots were exchanged." A Gatling gun was "sufficiently elevated to clear the tops of the houses, [and] was fired across the plaza, clearing it in a few seconds."[34]

In a "NOTICE TO THE PUBLIC," McCalla proclaimed the following in the evening edition of the *Panama Star and Herald*: "I have entered the city peacefully, in order to take measures to prevent injury to American interests. All law-abiding citizens will be protected. All saloons and liquor shops must be closed. The city will be policed by the forces under my command, and no one will be permitted to enter the city by land or sea."[35]

Near the American consulate, the marines caught up with Rafael Aizpuru. With his secretaries of war and state, he was placed under arrest. At a cordial meeting in the consulate, McCalla informed the rebel that he had no desire to interfere with the existing government. But until Aizpuru could provide "definite assurance" that American citizens and their property would come to no harm, McCalla was "compelled to detain" him. Aizpuru, however, was given the option of taking confinement at his head-quarters or, at the invitation of its proprietor, at the more con-genial Grand Central Hotel. He chose the latter, and with a platoon of marine guards as escort, submitted to arrest.[36]

After making secure their new positions, the marines took time to study their latest prize. "The city of Panama," wrote Lieutenant Elliott, "was then filthy, odorous, and neglected. The streets were narrow, very poorly lighted and never clean. When the tide was out and left the flats in front of the city exposed to the sun, there arose therefrom a terrible stench. . . . Dens of all kinds of vice ran openly, and gambling devices invaded the sidewalks which were crowded during the whole twenty-four hours with adventurers and adventuresses from all quarters of the globe."[37]

The American occupation of Panama City was short-lived. The next morning, April 25, McCalla secured Aizpuru's promise "to fulfill the duty of thoroughly protecting the lives and interests of the American citizens and foreigners." McCalla, in return, promised to take "no part in any political contest," and withdrew his forces to Camp Jouett.[38]

But from the camp and the environs of the solid brick railroad depot, the marines and bluejackets still exercised military domination. All landward approaches to the city were patrolled, and heavy guards were posted on the railroad bridges. "See that each [sentry] gets a cup of coffee and a piece of hard bread," McCalla noted in his orders, "and that he has his poncho."[39]

On April 28 a motley flotilla of tugs, hulks, and whaleboats brought 600 Colombian troops into port. Hoping to prevent a clash between these and Aizpuru's forces, McCalla dispatched his aide-de-camp "to present my compliments" to the Colombian commander. "May I beg leave to request," he penned, "that the national force under your command may be directed not to land within my lines?" Since the American positions generally faced the sea, McCalla was placing a fine diplomatic point in preventing the Colombians from entering their own territory; it would not be the last time.[40]

That day, too, the State Department received a note from the Colombian ambassador. "Peace in Colombia. Prestan hanged today in Colón." One witness to the event was Passed Midshipman Robert Coontz (Chief of Naval Operations, 1919–1922). "The method of hanging was as follows: a cable was stretched between two telegraph poles across the railroad tracks; the hangman's rope was attached to the center of the cable; Prestan was placed on the roof of a freight car which was hauled under the cable; the loose end of the rope was tied around the man's neck, and the freight car was moved. Vast crowds were allowed to witness the execution, and the effect was that for a time a condition of peace prevailed."[41]

On April 29 Admiral Jouett took the train to Panama City, and in the railroad offices he convened a peace conference. Aizpuru had no choice but to surrender again and his revolutionary movement collapsed. The next day Colombian troops marched in. To render appropriate honors, two companies of marines with a Gatling gun and a 3-inch landing piece were drawn up in front of the depot. The Colombian flag was hoisted over Camp Jouett and the American men-of-war in the harbor fired a twenty-one-gun national salute. On May 1 the various ships' detachments returned to their vessels. Admiral Jouett and the North Atlantic Squadron remained on station at Colón until July 15, when, leaving one ship behind, he steamed home to American waters.

Militarily, the intervention went very well. However, McCalla in his report to the Secretary of the Navy noted many serious systemic deficiencies requiring immediate attention. "While the Marine Corps is highly efficient and admirably disciplined," he noted, "their tactics are of a by-gone day. 'Heavy infantry' disappeared with the introduction of the long-range breech-loader. Unless officers and men are instructed in the principles of modern tactics and are taught to avail themselves of cover in advancing to an attack, they will only discover its advantages by fatal experience."[42]

On the matter of realistic training for the naval service in future operations, McCalla was emphatic. Ship's landing parties should perform assault techniques at least once a week. "The need for them must now be apparent to the most conservative [naval officers]. . . . Dress parades should be abolished, and only those maneuvers likely to be of use in actual service should be practiced."[43]

The most interesting of McCalla's observations went straight to the heart of the antiquated administration of the navy—the complete absence of a centralized military command structure. McCalla strongly advocated to Secretary Whitney the establishment of "a central office in the Navy Department, the chief of which . . . should be held responsible for the technical details necessary to fit out an expedition. . . . Under the present system the chiefs of half a dozen bureaus may overwhelm the commanding officer of an expedition . . . thereby causing delay or possible failure." But McCalla would be five years in his grave before the office of the Chief of Naval Operations was established in 1915.[44]

Still, the creaky bureaucratic machinery, not yet wakened from the somnolent years of the Old Navy, functioned better than would reasonably have been expected. Fully one-third of the Marine Corps had been quickly assembled, albeit with woefully insufficient equipment and civilian transport, and sent overseas. Senior officers on the spot assumed wide-ranging latitude in the conduct of political affairs, which would result in virtually vice-regal powers in the decades to come.

The Panama expedition of 1885 was to become a model for future United States military interventions on the isthmus, whereby a cycle of rumor, agitation, and revolt would lead to a rapid concentration of naval forces and the dispatch of troops to restore local lines of transit. The price Colombia would pay for United States—imposed stability would be very great indeed.

In 1889, with about ten percent of the work done, Ferdinand de Lesseps' Panama canal-building efforts collapsed in bankruptcy, mismanagement, and disease. The French government, remembering its Mexican debacle of mid-century and casting a keen eye to an America resurgent, refused any financial support to the venture. As a further deterrence, the United States Congress flexed its growing Monroe Doctrine muscles and passed a joint, bipartisan resolution which expressed "serious concern and disapproval" of any European government's connection with a canal project.

The United States opposed any foreign government's hegemony over the future Central American canal, wherever it might be (Panama was not the only contender) and had since mid-century. In 1850 the United States and Great Britain had entered into the Clayton-Bulwer Treaty, the signatories pledging never to "obtain or maintain for itself any exclusive control" over an isthmian waterway. Fortifications, military occupation, and colonization were equally prohibited. The parties would act in concert to preserve the canal's neutrality and encourage private capital to undertake construction.[45]

For half a century the Clayton-Bulwer Treaty, with its implications of British partnership in any future canal, stuck like a fishbone in the craws of America's new expansionists. In 1894, as a result of Democratic President Grover Cleveland's policy of restraint in securing an overseas empire, the young Theodore Roosevelt wrote to Senator Henry Cabot Lodge, "I do wish our Republicans would go in avowedly . . . and build an oceanic canal with the money of Uncle Sam."[46]

The late nineteenth century surge for American expansion was fueled in large part by a brainy naval officer, Captain Alfred Thayer Mahan. A highly gifted theoretician, historian, and leading proponent of naval reform, he had been appointed the second president of the Naval War College. In 1890 a collection of his lectures titled *The Influence of Seapower Upon History* was published in Boston. The book struck the world's naval and geopolitical thinkers like a battleship's broadside.

Using the analogy of Britain's control of the Mediterranean by means of holding Gibraltar and the Suez Canal, Mahan forcefully propounded the construction of an isthmian canal as absolutely necessary to America's standing as a world power. "If [a canal] be made, and fulfill the hopes of its builders," he wrote, "the Caribbean will be changed from a terminus . . . into one of the great highways of the world. Along this path a great commerce will travel, bringing the interests of the other great nations . . . close along our shores, as they have never been before. With this it will not be so easy as heretofore [for the United States] to stand aloof from international complications. . . . Whether they will or no, Americans must now begin to look outward."[47]

The Spanish-American War, and particularly the great voyage of the *Oregon*, brought that message into sharp clarity. By war's end in August 1898 the victorious United States held an empire stretching from Samoa and the Philippines, through Guam, Wake, Midway, and Hawaii,* then across sea and isthmus to Guantánamo Bay, Cuba, and Puerto Rico. The latter two were the sentry boxes guarding the critical Windward and Mona passages, the principal Atlantic gateways to any isthmian canal.

The British, with a view to breaking out of their diplomatic isolationism, were quick to recognize the new colossus across the sea. "When one half of the Anglo-Saxon race holds the waterway between the Mediterranean and the Indian Ocean," noted the London *Spectator*, "what could be more appropriate than that the other half should hold that between the Atlantic and the Pacific? . . . It is not for us to delay but to hasten that auspicious hour."[48]

Yet the Clayton-Bulwer Treaty remained a stumbling block to any unilateral American enterprise. "As for treaties," wrote New York's new governor Theodore Roosevelt in 1899, "I do not admit the 'dead hand' of the treaty making power of the past. A treaty can always be honorably abrogated."[49]

And so it was. In late 1899 Britain's embroilment in the Boer War signaled the death of Clayton-Bulwer. The new agreement, without even a nod to Central American sovereignty, was negotiated by Secretary of State John Hay and Ambassador Lord Julian Pauncefote. It permitted the United States government to con-

---

*American Samoa and Wake were annexed in 1899; Midway in 1867; and several islets between Hawaii and Samoa: Palmyra in 1898; and Johnston, Jarvis, and Howland in the 1850's.

struct, and the "exclusive right" to regulate and manage, a neutral, unfortified isthmian waterway.[50]

When the Hay-Pauncefote Treaty was sent to the United States Senate for ratification in February 1900 it received a chilly reception. The new life artery of the United States Navy could not lay naked to attack, and the neutrality and antifortification clauses were condemned by Republicans and Democrats alike. Governor Roosevelt beseeched John Hay and the President to "drop the treaty and push through a bill to build and fortify our own canal." The normally anti-imperialist Democrats at their national convention in Kansas City adopted a plank denouncing the treaty "as a surrender of American rights and interests not to be tolerated by the American people." The treaty was rejected.[51]

The Senate received a revised document in November 1901. The canal was still held to be a neutral waterway, but gone were the clauses prohibiting fortification. In their place was inserted the weaker assertion that "the United States . . . shall be at liberty to maintain such military police along the canal as may be necessary to protect it against lawlessness and disorder." In December the treaty was ratified and sent to President Theodore Roosevelt for his signature.*[52]

These negotiations were hardly conducted in a political vacuum. Since 1899 Colombia had been rocked by civil war between the Conservative ins and the Liberal outs. It was the worst conflict in her history, costing over 100,000 lives until peace was restored in 1902. Yet in Colombia's Department of Panama, the strife had yet to reach the line of transit, and until it did, the United States remained a disinterested spectator.

But as the conflict worsened in the summer of 1901 the navy's General Board** and the Navy War College began a confidential strategic study of the isthmus. Landings, interior trails, critical locations along the railroad, places "such as we would be compelled to occupy in case of disturbances," were included into operational plans and distributed to the North Atlantic and Pacific

---

*Roosevelt was elected McKinley's vice president in 1900, and assumed the presidency upon McKinley's assassination in September 1901.
**The General Board, formed in 1900 by Navy Secretary John D. Long and chaired by Admiral Dewey, was a precursor to the Office of the Chief of Naval Operations. Its mission was to "insure efficient preparation of the fleet in case of war and for the naval defense of the coast."

fleets. In mid-August the battleship *Iowa* was dispatched to Panama City, where her skipper, Captain Thomas Perry, investigated potential landing sites and interior communications. In September he reported to the Secretary of the Navy "profound peace prevailing . . . but for the accounts in the New York papers still arriving, no one here present would suspect there was any impending trouble. . . . No soldiers are seen in the city except the drowsy sentry at the door of the cuartel."[53]

On the Atlantic side at Colón conditions were much the same. "Of the American interests in danger," noted the outgoing commander of the gunboat *Machias*, "the most conspicuous is that of this ship's company which, after a long siege of the tropics and but a few weeks change of climate, has by force of circumstances been sent here in the wet and most unhealthy season of the year."[54]

But within a week Lieutenant Commander Henry McCrea, the gunboat's new skipper, noticed some ominous portents. On October 1 he reported to Secretary Long strong undercurrents of discontent in Colón: "Times are hard and the government is blamed by all the citizens." Prominent Liberals were cast in jail and "the prisons kept full both here and in Panama [City.]"[55]

By mid-November a Liberal army of several hundred well-armed troops was making its presence felt along the railroad. The telegraph lines were cut, track was torn up, and repair gangs harassed. On November 20 United States Consul General Hezekiah Gudger and Captain Perry of the *Iowa* paid a call on the governor to impress upon him the seriousness of the situation. During the meeting came some astounding news; the Liberals had just captured Colón! With their victory came a pledge to cease disrupting the line of transit. Communications were restored and the trains ran on schedule. "Things began to take a brighter aspect," noted Gudger to the State Department. For the moment there was no need to commit a landing force.[56]

But the fall of Colón to the Liberals brought with it a Colombian request for United States intervention. American officials on the isthmus and in Washington demurred. Captain Perry, strictly interpreting the clauses of the Bidlack-Mallarino Treaty, felt that any undertaking on the part of the United States should arise only after the Colombian government "has exhausted its [own] means to maintain transit. . . . As the Colombian government has made no effort to do these things, it cannot be said that the obligation is the United States'." Besides, once Colón passed to Lib-

eral control the railroad's repair gangs were no longer impeded
and telegraph and train service was back on schedule. It made no
difference to the United States which faction controlled the isthmus, so long as the line of transit remained free. "Just as soon as
there is any interference with the free transit of the Isthmus,"
Perry noted to the consul general, "[I will] occupy the line with
the force under my command and supervise it."[57]

"Situation quite satisfactory," Perry reported on November 22.
"Liberals along the line inclined to protect rather than interfere.
All trains moving."[58]

The next day the signals changed. "Land force," cabled Navy
Secretary Long, "[be] prepared to forestall interruption [of]
transit. This is necessary to forestall possible action by other powers."[59]

These "other powers," the cruisers HMS *Tribune* and the
French Navy's plow-snouted *Suchet,* had dropped their anchors
in Colón. The gunboat *Marietta* had also just arrived, and with
the *Machias* she put ashore 133 bluejackets and marines; strong
guards were mounted on all trains as far as Matachin.

From Panama City Perry reported, "There was an impression
that a decisive battle was impending between [the Liberals and
the Government] . . . there was an air in the streets of expectancy,
anxiety, and possible disaster, but no news."[60]

Later that November 23, at a meeting in Colón attended by
the commanding officers of the four men-of-war in the harbor
plus the American, British, and French consuls, it was learned the
government armed steamer *Pinzon,* loaded with troops, was en
route to wrest the place from the Liberals. The conferees determined she must give ninety-six hours notice for the evacuation
of noncombatants or else be denied permission to bombard the
town, "which is unfortified and almost exclusively occupied by
foreigners."[61]

At 9:00 A.M., November 24, the *Pinzon* stood into port. The
Machias signaled the Liberals ashore not to open fire on the government vessel and Lieutenant Commander McCrea chuffed off
in his gig for the steamer. He found about 600 troops in the *Pinzon.*
The ship was "the most densely crowded vessel I have ever seen."
McCrea handed the Colombian commander the ninety-six-hour
bombardment notice "resolution." The general would "consider
it" but could probably grant no more than twenty-four hours, as
he had on board only two days' rations for his troops.[62]

Ashore McCrea cabled the Navy Department for instructions. "Shall landing [of Government forces] with incidental firing be permitted at American wharves?" The response was equivocal. "Our duty is to preserve free transit," answered Secretary Long. McCrea was told to exercise his discretion. It was a tall order of responsibility for a lieutenant commander.[63]

There was no question that McCrea, backed by the fourteen 4-inch guns of the *Machias* and *Marietta,* could dictate to the Colombians any terms he wished. But to do so would create political repercussions, and he was specifically enjoined from aiding either party. To compound his dilemma, McCrea was then approached by the American consul, Oscar Malmros, who told him that the Colombian commander had rejected the ninety-six-hour resolution and would open fire on Colón in twenty-four hours. What, the consul wanted to know, was McCrea going to do about it? "Stop it if possible," he replied. All American citizens were directed to take refuge in the warships.[64]

Late that afternoon, in a final attempt at diplomacy, a parley with the government and Liberal officers was convened on board HMS *Tribune.* To the relief of all, the combatants agreed not to fire on each other. The *Pinzon* promptly upped anchor and steamed out of harbor. In McCrea's opinion, this precipitous government withdrawal was due solely to short rations.

The day was a full one as well across the isthmus in Panama City. At 8:00 A.M., Consul General Hezekiah Gudger boarded the No. 2 "passenger and express" train for Colón. Ten miles out of the station, it was stopped by about thirty armed Liberals. Ignoring Gudger's assurance that no government troops were aboard and his admonition against the halting of transport, the Liberals searched the train. It was a procedure they repeated every few miles. "During all the way [to Matachin]," Gudger noted, "we passed the [Liberal] soldiers with guns cocked and presented directly toward the passengers. From Culebra the menace was constant and alarming and one fire, even accidental, would have caused the death of every passenger and railroad official on the train. . . . It looked like a disorganized mob, in which every man felt himself in command."[65]

From Matachin Gudger telegraphed the situation to Perry at Panama City. The consul general's return journey was only slightly less anxious. "We passed the Government soldiers," he cabled the State Department. "While not so bad, [they] went through the same presentation of cocked guns. The conditions as I saw them, convince me that life is not safe on the trains . . . and that however much we may regret to do so, the awful moment has arrived when we should take a firm and decided stand."[66]

The *Iowa*'s landing force of 248 bluejackets and marines was ready, and on receipt of Gudger's cable Perry ordered them ashore to occupy the railroad depot. The Colombian government at last stirred itself. General Alban, Governor of Panama, arrived with 600 troops, and in a bloody engagement along the tracks he drove the Liberals halfway back to Colón.

During the night the *Iowa*'s shipfitters mounted a pair of Colt machine guns on an improvised armored flatcar. The next morning, November 25, flying the American flag, the car was coupled to the front of the engine. Perry loaded 150 men aboard the No. 2 "to take train through [to Colón], clear the line, and restore transit." At Río Grande Superior lay the debris of the Colombian battle. "Ghastly sight of dead bodies lying along track," noted Perry in his report; "most inhuman and revolting."[67]

At Matachin station, around which the government troops were encamped, Perry was confronted by General Alban. The governor vehemently protested that his forces alone were sufficient to protect and restore the line of transit and demanded his troops be permitted to board the No. 2 for Colón. Perry refused, citing the Colombian government's request for American intervention. American commanders would treat both sides, Liberal and government, with the same edge of the sword, and Alban could not expect military transportation "except as I permitted. . . . He seemed bitterly disappointed." Keeping to its schedule, the No. 2 steamed out of Matachin. General Alban's troops hoisted their gear and marched along the tracks to the next Liberal stronghold athwart the Chagres River at the vital Barbacoas Bridge.[68]

Perry and the No. 2 pulled into Colón in late morning. For the safety of subsequent trains, all would fly the American flag and travel with an armed bluejacket and marine escort of forty men. In this manner Perry and the bulk of the *Iowa*'s landing force returned to Panama City. "On the way back," he noted, "the greatest respect was shown and no objectionable act was committed by either Conservative [government] or Liberal soldiers." With the United States sticking to the letter of its obligations, namely to keep the line of transit secure, the Colombian factions had free rein to cut each other to pieces.[69]

The battle for the Barbacoas Bridge was a costly government victory, and the Liberal forces retreated up the line to await the next attack. The wounded of both sides were loaded aboard the trains for Panama City, and were equally tended by the *Iowa*'s surgeons.

On a rainy November 27 General Alban's army stormed the Liberal positions at Buena Vista. The battle was fought right along the tracks. With the exception of one incident where the government troops used a train to mask their movements, both sides held fire to allow unhindered passage.

In Colón the Liberal General de la Rosa saw his position as untenable. With or without rail transport the government forces were advancing, and the arrival, again, of the *Pinzon,* had turned his seaward flank. De la Rosa approached Captain Galloway of HMS *Tribune* with an offer to surrender the town.

In early morning, November 28, Perry and Galloway met in a freight car with General Alban to discuss the terms of capitulation. Alban agreed to parley with the Liberals, offering a grant of life and liberty to all who laid down their arms.

The parties—Colombians, Americans, British, French, plus interpreters—met in the tiny wardroom of the *Marietta.* It was agreed that de la Rosa would cede Colón to the temporary charge of the commanding officers of the warships anchored in the harbor. These naval officers would then in turn effect the transfer to General Alban when his troops arrived later in the day.

The skippers considered a landing force of 300 men adequate to garrison the town during the political vacuum, each vessel protecting its own national interests and property. The United States contingent, which alone numbered 300 bluejackets and marines, exercised general responsibility for the town and railroad.

In late morning, November 28, the transfer of Colón to the multinational force took place in front of the *cuartel.* At its gates were drawn up the landing parties of the United States Navy and Marine Corps. Across the mud street, General de la Rosa stood before his Liberal army and formally handed the town over to the naval officers. The Liberals piled arms and their flag was hauled down. "Much feeling was shown at this time by the whole Liberal command," Perry noted, "a large majority of them being in tears."[70]

General Alban was met at the outskirts by the naval commanders and the United States battalion. At the gates of the *cuartel,*

Perry, on behalf of his naval colleagues, transferred the sovereignty of Colón back to the Colombian Government. The *Pinzon*
finally landed her troops and United States forces were withdrawn. "That Friday night passed quietly," Perry reported to the
Navy Department, "and there was no disturbance whatever, peace
being restored."[71]

By the second week in December, conditions along the railroad
were "perfectly normal." On the ninth, Perry ordered all remaining bluejackets and marines back to their ships. "The integrity of
the transit on the Isthmus," he noted, was secure "for a long time
in the future, possibly for years."[72]

In Washington the legislative and diplomatic
process regarding construction of an isthmian canal ground on.
Prior to 1902 it was generally assumed that any transcontinental
waterway under United States control would be built in southern
Nicaragua. Here, as opposed to mountainous Panama, the continental divide was quite low, and the San Juan River and the
great Lake Nicaragua provided a natural waterway to within a
few miles of the Pacific Ocean. This so-called American route was
contrasted with the discredited French effort in Panama.

In 1899, following the Spanish-American War, President
McKinley appointed Rear Admiral John G. Walker, ex–Chief of
the Bureau of Navigation, to chair an Isthmian Canal Commission
to determine the "most practical and feasible route." On November 16, 1901, their report was presented to President Roosevelt.
Each route—Nicaraguan and Panamanian—offered distinct advantages. Nicaragua was closer to United States ports by nearly
600 miles, her health conditions were somewhat better, and there
was greater probability of economic development along the canal
route. Additionally, the low rise of the continental divide meant
easier construction if enough labor could be gotten to the site.

A canal in Panama, however, would cut 134 miles off the
waterway, necessitating fewer locks and turns. There was a large
and readily available labor supply in Panama, and thanks to
French surveys of the region, more was known of its topography.
There were already established ports—Colón and Panama City
—at either end of the proposed canal, which would permit construction to begin a year earlier in Panama than in Nicaragua.
Finally there was the cost. A Panamanian project, at upward of
$144 million, was $58 million cheaper.

The Walker Commission originally opted for Panama. But an agreement had first to be concluded with the French shareholders whose New Panama Canal Company had assumed the burden from the original bankrupt venture. Its substantial assets included the builder's concession from the Colombian government, maps, surveys, records, and nearly all the shares of the Panama Railroad Company. The commission deemed $40 million a reasonable price for these holdings. With the French counteroffer of over $109 million, the Walker Commission reversed its decision. Nicaragua, the admiral now reported to President Roosevelt, was "the most practicable and feasible route."[73]

The State Department instructed its ambassador to open negotiations with the Nicaraguan president, General José Santós Zelaya. Up front Zelaya demanded a cash payment of $6 million, and a protocol was drawn up as the basis of a canal treaty. But the State Department found the protocol unsatisfactory, in the main because Zelaya refused to permit United States courts in any Nicaraguan canal zone. Negotiations continued in Washington.

The House of Representatives had meanwhile passed the Hepburn Bill appropriating funds for a Nicaraguan canal. But before the bill went to the Senate, the New Panama Canal Company altered its position and offered to sell its assets to the United States at the recommended $40 million. President Roosevelt hastily reconvened the Walker Commission and obtained a unanimous decision in favor of Panama. In the Senate John Spooner of Wisconsin offered an amendment. If valid title for the builder's concession could be obtained from the New Panama Canal Company and an acceptable treaty concluded with Colombia, the canal would be built in Panama. If these prerequisites could not be obtained in reasonable time, President Roosevelt was to proceed with the Nicaragua plan. After a hard fight on the Senate floor, the Spooner Amendment became law on June 28, 1902.

Much of the credit for this turnabout belonged to a remarkable Frenchman, Philippe Bunau-Varilla. By trade a military engineer, he arrived in Panama in 1884, taking charge of de Lesseps' excavations at Culebra. One year later, at age twenty-six, he was appointed engineer in chief of the entire Panama canal project.

Although de Lesseps' endeavor went bust in 1888, Bunau-Varilla remained committed to the task, and when the New Panama Canal Company was formed he became one of its major

stockholders. A brilliant and persuasive advocate for the Panama
route, Bunau-Varilla tirelessly lobbied members of Congress and
the administration. Peripatetic by nature, he crisscrossed the
United States spreading the gospel of Panama to America's bankers and industrialists. During the debate on the Spooner Amendment, he achieved, up to that point, his greatest coup.

As an engineer Bunau-Varilla based his arguments on the
physical disparities of the sites. The Panama route, he maintained,
had "no winds, no currents (except on rare occasions), no sharp
curves, no sediments, no bad harbors, no volcanoes." For Nicaragua, he presented a record of geologic instability based on "four
centuries of undisputable proof. . . . Look at the coat of arms of
the Republic of Nicaragua," he preached, "look at the Nicaraguan
postage stamps. . . . What have the Nicaraguans chosen to char-
acterize their country on their coat of arms, on their postage
stamps? Volcanoes!" To all members of Congress, Bunau-Varilla
distributed a collection of Nicaraguan stamps, replete with belching volcanoes. Enough minds and votes were changed to enable
passage of the amendment.[74]

The Spooner Amendment presented the Colombian government with a difficult dilemma. The government's most vital interest was in seeing the canal built in its Department of Panama.
The isthmus was virtually the only strategic asset Colombia possessed and if the canal were built in Nicaragua this panhandle
would dwindle into little more than a provincial backwater. The
canal was of paramount importance to the economic well-being
of the people of Panama. Already there were factions that spoke
of secession if the Bogotá government failed to reach an agreement with the United States. And the money was no small item.
Colombia, as a result of her crippling civil war, was bankrupt;
United States capital would provide desperately needed funds.
But negotiations bogged down concerning the extent of United
States control over a canal zone that would remain, de jure, Colombian territory.

The Conservative Colombian president, elderly, scholarly José
Manuel Marroquín, shied away from personal responsibility for
painful decisions regarding national sovereignty in the canal zone.
But he did not want to be accused of losing the canal by failing
to reach an agreement with the United States. The whole question,
he maintained, must be submitted to the Colombian Congress.
That body would not meet until the fall, and the United States

would not countenance such a delay. Any further demur, cautioned American Ambassador Charles Burdett Hart, meant the canal would go to Nicaragua.

Marroquín was a realist, and so to his ambassador in Washington, Vicente José Concha, he mailed instructions to sign the best deal the United States offered.

Simultaneously the Panamanian line of transit was again threatened. On September 8, from Panama City, the skipper of the ancient screw sloop *Ranger* cabled the Navy Department that 2,000 ragged, poorly equipped government troops had just surrendered to the Liberals. Large numbers of the soldiery, on both sides, were hardly even teenagers, a result of the war's depletion of the male population. The capitulation had taken place at Aguadulce, about eighty miles away to the west. "The revolutionists," he noted, "are reported to be advancing on Panama [City]."[75]

With the Liberal victory the Colombian government removed all train guards and evacuated its civil officials from the line of transit. To meet the suspected Liberal advance, the army concentrated at Colón's Monkey Hill and in positions around Panama City. Government troops placed obstructions on the tracks, halted the trains, and arrested any passenger thought to harbor Liberal sympathies.

The *Ranger*'s report set off the alarms at the State and Navy departments. With delicate negotiations for the canal treaty in progress and communications with Bogotá at a near standstill, the machinery for intervention was set in motion. "The Department believes it wise," penned Navy Secretary Moody to President Roosevelt, "to have United States forces at hand [on the isthmus] . . . to protect the interests of the United States in the event of military leaders of either party being unable to control their forces." The President agreed.[76]

On September 11 the cruiser *Cincinnati* was dispatched to Colón. At the navy yard in Bremerton, Washington, Rear Admiral Silas Casey, commanding the Pacific Squadron, steamed in the battleship *Wisconsin* to Panama City.

From Headquarters Marine Corps, Commandant Charles Heywood penned his instructions. "[O]n account of the possible injury to Americans and American interests and property on the Isthmus of Panama," four companies—342 officers and men, and

two Colt machine guns—boarded the transport *Panther* at Philadelphia.[77]

While orders were being issued the Colombian government
was making discreet overtures requesting United States interces-
sion in the civil war, "especially on the Isthmus where the revolution is strong." Colombia had but one card to play, the canal
treaty. "Not only is the question of humanity involved," Ambassador Hart noted in his cable, but while the war continued there
would be no sessions of the Colombian Congress, and thus no
decision on the canal treaty.[78]

News of the impasse was taken to President Roosevelt, who
agreed that the navy would assume the role of honest broker.
Rear Admiral Casey was still en route on the *Wisconsin*, so the task
initially fell to the relatively junior skipper of the *Cincinnati*, Commander Thomas McLean.

The *Cincinnati* anchored in Colón on the afternoon of September 15 and McLean took the train to Panama City. He confronted the governor directly, demanding unimpeded passage
along the line of transit and was assured depredations would cease.
The next morning, however, on his return to Colón, the train had
to halt before blocked tracks.

The *Cincinnati*'s landing force was ordered ashore. To the
government and Liberal commanders McLean sent identical mes-
sages that "United States naval forces are guarding the railway
trains and the line of transit . . . from sea to sea . . . no persons
whatever will be allowed to obstruct, embarrass, or interfere. . . .
No armed men except forces of the United States will be allowed
to come on or use the line. All of this is without prejudice or any
desire to interfere in domestic contentions of the Colombians."[79]

McLean soon softened the diktat. Unarmed Colombian government troops, their weapons carried in the baggage cars of
separate trains, were permitted passage from both coasts. The
authorities were informed that this should not be taken as a prec-
edent, and each request for military passage was to be considered
on its own merits.

On September 20 further orders emanated from Headquarters Marine Corps. A second battalion, 648 officers and men, two
3-inch field guns, four Colts, "and the necessary color guard" were
scoured from the east coast navy yards and receiving ships. From
their diverse stations the marines entrained for Norfolk, and
within four days were ready to sail in the transport *Prairie*.

On September 23 the *Panther*, carrying the first contingent, dropped anchor in Colón, and Lieutenant Colonel Ben Russell's battalion came ashore. Losing not a moment, the headquarters and three companies boarded a special for Panama City, while the remaining company, under Major George Barnett (Commandant of the Marine Corps, 1914–1920) "very comfortably" established their camp on Colón's Pacific Mail steamer wharf. Potable water for both garrisons was provided by the distillation plant in the *Panther*. This was very much a necessity, as yellow fever and dysentery were reaching epidemic proportions among the Colombian government forces.[80]

The next day detachments of thirty-five to forty men mounted guard on the trains. A second-class carriage was provided for the marines, and their Colt machine gun was carried in the baggage car. "Very little, if any, trouble was experienced in properly guarding the trains," an officer reported, "but there were numerous places where a determined, resolute party of an enemy . . . could have stopped the train by obstructions on the track and practically annihilated the guard."[81]

There was an incident on September 24, but it resulted only in a cracked jaw and some wounded pride. At Empire (Emperador) Station on the line between Panama City and Matachin, the marine guard was rushed by about 250 Liberal troops seeking to remove a government officer from the train. According to the special correspondent of the *Army and Navy Register*, "Immediately the automatic gun was turned on the insurgents, the marines opened magazines and aimed rifles . . . but there were several [Liberals] who were bold and attempted to board . . . [and were] promptly thrown off by the men. One ambitious insurgent tried to force his way. . . . A private of Company C 'clubbed' his rifle and brought it up under the insurgent's jaw, knocking him off and bruised his face so that a small quantity of blood oozed out of the scratch."[82]

History records few instances where a majority of the population welcomes an occupying army. But Panama, wracked by civil war, desperately needed an element of stability which the Colombian government was unable to provide. As Commander McLean reported to the Navy Department, "I believe that most of the respectable people in this district who have some other occupation than continual fratricidal strife welcome the presence of the United States forces, though most of them do not venture to say so."[83]

On September 30 the *Wisconsin*, all white, buff, and gilt,

dropped anchor off Panama City. Rear Admiral Casey assumed command ashore and entrained for Colón. At Empire Station, he came upon a train, "with 90 or 100 soldiers on board, quartered in a car promiscuously [i.e. indiscriminately] with men, women, and children passengers." The commander of the marine guard informed the admiral that many of the Colombian troops were sick, some with yellow fever, "and that the stench coming from the car was unbearable. If there had been no other reason," Casey reported to the Navy Department, "this alone would have been sufficient to stop further transport of Government troops without sanitary inspection." Thereafter, only government officers having special permission and unarmed discharged soldiers were permitted military rail transport.[84]

On October 8 Casey dispatched letters to the government and Liberal commanders regarding peace talks to be held on board the *Wisconsin*. The local officials readily agreed. The government situation on the isthmus was in imminent danger of collapse, and unless some sort of truce was arranged, the whole Department of Panama might well fall to the Liberals. "It is my opinion," Casey reported, "that if it were not for the restraining influence of our naval force here, Panama would fall an easy victim to the combined land forces and gunboats of the insurgents."[85]

But Liberal opportunities were fast evaporating. In mid-month a steamer arrived at Colón with word of major government victories in the Colombian hinterland. The tide of war had turned, and it was only a matter of time before sufficient government reinforcements were sent to Panama to quell the revolution.

The first of these reinforcements, in the person of General Nicholas Perdomo, who according to Silas Casey was "said to be clothed with ministerial powers," landed at Colón on October 16. Casey offered the general transportation to Panama City. Perdomo accepted, and with a numerous staff, heavily guarded by the marines, he boarded a first-class carriage to cross the isthmus.

General Perdomo was received with full military honors on board the *Wisconsin*. The Colombian flag was broken out at the foremast, six sideboys manned the quarterdeck, and a salute of thirteen guns boomed in the harbor. Nothing was resolved. "Great things were expected on Perdomo's arrival," Casey reported, "but as he came attended only by numerous generals, of which there were apparently a surfeit in the city, I fail to see how he can accomplish much."[86]

The health of his command, coupled with a seeping lethargy in unhealthy Panama, also weighed heavily on the admiral's mind. "The [marines] are cooped up on a railroad wharf, practically prisoners, with no diversion or means of amusement. As they become weakened by climatic influences they naturally in time become restless and depressed. Guarding trains affords relaxation and a change from the close confinements to quarters, but that too . . . becomes monotonous. A change to a northern climate after six weeks or two months service would be greatly desired."[87]

The sailors didn't even have the diversion of guarding trains and were confined to the suffocating heat of their steel ships. Portions of the *Wisconsin*'s berth deck became uninhabitable. All the battleship's junior and warrant officers, and many enlisted men, were forced to sling hammocks on the upper deck, only to snatch them up and scurry below with the frequent heavy rains. In the dynamo room the temperature reached 140 degrees. Yet engineers and electricians stood their watches. "Owing to the unsanitary conditions of the city," Casey continued, "no liberty is allowed. . . . When we consider that a large number of the crews are composed of young country lads serving their first enlistment, such long confinement on shipboard has a most discouraging influence."[88]

On October 29, with no end in sight to the isthmian conflict, the marines and Colombian troops came very near to a firefight. Near mid-morning, the Panama Railroad, without seeking Admiral Casey's permission, brought over three boxcars of government ammunition from Colón to Panama City. Captain Dion Williams was ordered to seize the cars. Taking thirty-two marines, he marched to the station and found it occupied by about sixty government troops, with guards atop the boxcars. Along the track, a line of mule carts and laborers stood ready to unload.

"I directed the officer in charge of the Colombian soldiers to withdraw his troops from the station and platform and his guards from the cars," Williams reported. "This he positively refused to do, and I directed a sergeant and 12 men to remove the Colombian guards from the cars and station. This was quickly and effectively done without confusion or the use of unnecessary force."

Humiliated by the power of a numerically inferior force, the Colombian commander drew up his company in the street and ordered them to load their rifles. "Through an interpreter," Williams continued, "I informed him that in case he loaded his pieces I might be compelled to fire upon his men in self defense. He then desisted and marched his men to the barracks opposite the station."

Williams shunted the cars to the safety of "Camp Casey" on the American wharf. This the Colombians found infuriating. "Several highly excited Colombians, claiming to be high officers, violently protested my action, and one of them shook his fist in a threatening manner, whereupon I had them removed from the station also."[89]

On October 31 the long-awaited Colombian reinforcements landed at both sides of the isthmus. General Perdomo requested permission to transport his forces inland and Casey assented. Where before the government garrisons feared to venture beyond the outworks of Colón and Panama City, the inland movement of these 2,500 troops now squeezed the Liberal army off the line of transit. By the first week in October none were to be seen. Further Liberal defeats occurred in Colombia proper. "It seems probable," Admiral Casey noted, "that the surrender [in the hinterland] . . . will have a disheartening influence on the insurgent forces in this district."[90]

By mid-November Colombia had 8,000 troops on the isthmus and Casey considered them sufficient to maintain uninterrupted traffic. Orders were issued to remove all marine guards from the trains and to reembark the entire battalion in the *Panther*.

On November 19, a day after the marines left the isthmus, the railroad tug *Bolívar* arrived at Panama City, bearing the commander of the revolutionary forces. For two days on board the *Wisconsin*, government and rebel forces hacked out a peace treaty ending the civil war in Panama. Of the fourteen articles, with their provisions of amnesty for Liberals laying down their arms, and their retention of swords and flags, the parties pledged themselves to "carry to a happy terminus the negotiation upon the Panama Canal."[91]

For the first time in two years bands played in the public squares, and the people of Panama City and Colón were permitted in the streets at any hour. "The Government forces are being slowly disbanded," noted the skipper of the gunboat *Bancroft*. "Forty percent of them are boys from 9 to 15 years of age. They are filthy in person and dress and poorly clad, and appear like a rabble of children."[92]

In Washington, in spite of the Spooner Amendment and the platitudes so recently expressed on board the *Wisconsin*, treaty negotiations with Colombia came to a virtual halt. Much of the problem was due to false perceptions. Unlike some Caribbean and Latin American governments, Colombia's was relatively responsible. Its politicians were generally high-minded and maintained, at least up to this time, a fair regard for the United States and its political and social ideals.

Theodore Roosevelt saw it differently. "To talk of Colombia as a responsible Power to be dealt with as we would deal with Holland or Denmark ... is a mere absurdity," he later said. "The analogy is with a group of Sicilian ... bandits. You could no more make an agreement with the Colombian rulers than you could nail currant jelly to a wall." President Marroquín he wrongly considered to be a corrupt despot holding out for a better bargain.[93]

As part of the proposed canal treaty, the United States had lately offered Colombia a cash payment of $7 million, plus an annuity of $100,000, to compensate for lost Panama Railroad revenues. This was hardly fair compensation. In 1902, even with the strife on the isthmus, Colombia's yearly income from the railroad, customs houses, and lighthouse fees were well over half a million dollars; and the annuity would not begin until fourteen years had elapsed.

After initial agreement, Colombia's ambassador to Washington, José Vicente Concha retracted and deemed this insufficient. Meanwhile at the State Department and the White House, it was assumed that Marroquín and his cronies would eventually take their "share" of the 7 million and abscond.

The press took up the cudgel. "The fact is not to be disguised," noted the *New York Times* on November 15, 1902, in what was the prevailing view of the Roosevelt administration, "that any attempt on the part of Colombia to hold up the United States for the payment of an additional sum for the right of way exceeding the bounds of reason is to be resisted by this Government to the limit." The article continued, introducing a new concept into the current understanding of international law. "It is distinctly recognized that the canal is a world project. The *international right of eminent domain* [emphasis added] is considered with the canal, and the obstructive course of Colombia will not be tolerated a moment beyond the ordinary limits of polite diplomatic intercourse."[94]

This was an astounding principle. The dismayed Colombian consul in New York notified his embassy in Washington, "In plain words . . . 'international right of eminent domain' . . . means that if the U.S. cannot agree with Colombia there is a notion of *taking* control of the Isthmus and paying a proper amount afterward. This [is] a question the possibility of which ought to be seriously (though quietly) considered."[95] Unfortunately for Colombia, Ambassador Concha ignored the warning.

In Congress Senator Shelby Cullom of Illinois paralleled the views of the *Times* and the administration. If Colombia could not come to a satisfactory agreement, the United States would treat directly with the New Panama Canal Company, icing Colombia from any part in the negotiations; compensation for her would be determined later. In justifying the transfer of sovereign rights by second and third parties, Cullom argued that an isthmian canal, like the world's oceans, was considered a "universal public utility."[96]

Feeling that his country's sovereignty was being given short, if any, shrift, Concha resigned. The treaty task was taken up by the embassy's chargé d'affaires, Dr. Tomás Herrán.

The United States had just upped the Colombian cash payment to $10 million in gold coin, which the Roosevelt administration considered little short of extortion on the part of the Bogotá government. But on the matter of the annuity, Secretary of State John Hay would not budge. With negotiations deadlocked there entered again into the play Philippe Bunau-Varilla. In December 1902 he arrived in Washington, determined at all costs to prevent the building of a Nicaragua canal. Bunau-Varilla considered the American offer of $10 million a fair price and then calculated a compromise annuity of $250,000 to begin in nine years. He sent the figures to Marroquín and Herrán, and through Senate intermediaries to President Roosevelt.

Before returning to Europe, Bunau-Varilla presented his proposals to the powerful Republican Senator from Ohio, Mark Hanna, imploring him to assist in the negotiations. Hanna agreed, informing President Roosevelt that he had positive information that Dr. Herrán, given the new figures, would sign the treaty.

A new document with Bunau-Varilla's numbers was drafted by the State Department. But Herrán, receiving contrary instructions from his government, refused to sign. John Hay threatened an ultimatum, and on January 22, 1903, it was delivered into Herrán's hands. "I am commanded by the President," Hay warned, "to say to you that the reasonable time . . . for the conclusion of negotiations . . . has expired, and that he has authorized me to sign with you the treaty . . . with the modification that the sum of $100,000, fixed . . . as the annual payment, be increased to $250,000. I am not authorized to consider or discuss any other change."[97]

At the end of his tether, Herrán agreed. That same evening he went to the home of Secretary Hay. "Then and there," declared the chargé, he would affix his name to the ill-fated document, known as the Hay-Herrán Treaty. It gave the United States exclusive rights to construct, operate, and defend the canal, along with a ten-kilometer-wide "canal zone." On March 17, 1903, after a stiff fight by pro-Nicaragua Senators, it was ratified by the United States Senate.

In Colombia a new Congress had been elected, and one of its first orders of business was the ratification of the Hay-Herrán Treaty. President Marroquín equivocated. He informed his countrymen that he did not expect them to react with great joy over its provisions, and again placed full responsibility for ratification on the Colombian Congress. His attitude seemed to invite rejection.

To this very real possibility, Dr. Herrán warned his government of the consequences. "Should this treaty unfortunately fail of approval by the [Colombian] Congress, one of two results must follow. Either the United States in accordance with [the Spooner Amendment] will enter into treaties with Nicaragua . . . and proceed to construct the Nicaragua Canal or . . . they will seize upon the Isthmus by force and make their own terms for the retention of it."[98]

Dr. Herrán, now elevated to ambassadorial rank, seemed to have a mental crystal ball. Although it didn't take a great leap in assumptions to predict the worst-case scenario, his next warning resolved into the facts of history. On April 3 he wrote to a friend, "Another danger even more grave presents itself; and that is, that the 'Republic of Panama' may declare itself independent and that the [canal] treaty may be made with it."[99]

The treaty was in trouble. Arthur Beaupré, the new and capable United States ambassador, cabled from Bogotá, "Without

question, public opinion [in Colombia] is strongly against its ratification." Far from aiding matters, Marroquín's government
seemed intent on antagonizing the United States. Representations
from Bogotá were made to the British, German, and French governments to enter into competitive bidding for canal rights, but
they would have none of it, Germany being particularly vociferous
in her refusal.[100]

The final Colombian obstacle Roosevelt and Hay considered
nothing short of blackmail. By the terms of the treaty, the New
Panama Canal Company was authorized to sell its shares and assets
to the United States for $40 million. It was the biggest real estate
deal in history up to that time. Colombia now approached the
company's representative in Bogotá. If the New Panama Canal
Company were willing to pay Colombia $10 million from the sale,
the treaty might be ratified.

Bilateral deals between Colombia and the company had been
vetoed by Hay, and he considered their reintroduction a "breach
of faith."[101]

President Roosevelt, an ardent supporter of the Panama route,
was chagrined by the Colombian maneuvers. "Those contemptible
little creatures in Bogotá," he wrote to John Hay, "ought to understand how much they are jeopardizing things and imperiling
their own future."[102]

Within days, the New Panama Canal Company's general counsel, William Nelson Cromwell, planted a remarkable piece in the
New York World. "Information also has reached [Washington D.C.]
that the State of Panama . . . stands ready to secede from Colombia
and enter into a canal treaty with the United States. . . . The citizens of Panama propose . . . giving this Government the equivalent of absolute sovereignty over the Canal Zone. . . . In return
the President of the United States would promptly recognize the
new Government . . . and would at once appoint a minister to
negotiate and sign a canal treaty." There were no denials from
the White House.[103]

Panama's future as part of Colombia hung by
a rapidly unraveling rope. In late July, 1903, an extraordinary
luncheon meeting, in all probability convened at long distance by
William Nelson Cromwell, was held at a country estate outside
Panama City. The guests included some of the most important
personages of the department, among them the Colombian sen-

ator who also served as the attorney, land agent, and chief lobbyist for the Panama Railroad; railroad Assistant Superintendent Herbert Prescott; United States Consul General Hezekiah Gudger; Major William Murray Black of the United States Army*; and General Rubén Varón of the Colombian sea forces.

The purpose of the lunch was nothing less than the initial planning session for the creation of the Republic of Panama. According to Consul General Gudger, "Plans for the revolution were freely discussed."[104]

On August 12 it became a certainty. In Bogotá the Colombian Senate, by a unanimous vote, rejected the Hay-Herrán Treaty. Ambassador Beaupré immediately notified the State Department of "an almost hysterical condition of alarm and uncertainty . . . as to the future action of the United States." That they had cause to fear was evident by President Roosevelt's note to Hay, "We may have to give a lesson to those jack rabbits."[105]

Roosevelt's big stick was poised to strike. A United States–backed Panamanian revolution would indeed solve the canal dilemma, but there were those in the State Department who advised prudence. "Such a scheme could, of course, have no countenance from us," noted Assistant Secretary of State Alvey Adee to his chief. "Our policy before the world should stand, like Mrs. Caesar, without suspicion."[106]

On August 26 the revolutionary junta dispatched to the United States Dr. Manuel Amador, a physician and Panamanian patriot of "unblemished character," to secure private funds and arms for the revolt as well as possible support from the American government.

Dr. Amador was given little money to defray his expenses, so aboard the steamer he resorted to playing poker to finance his mission. One of the passengers from whom he won a substantial amount was J. Gabriel Duque, a Cuban of United States citizenry and owner of the Panama *Star & Herald*. Duque was not part of the conspiracy, though some accounts place him at the luncheon meeting, but he was well informed of its intentions.

On September 1 the steamer docked in New York, Amador went off to find a cheap hotel, and J. Gabriel Duque sped to Wall Street and the offices of William Nelson Cromwell. Duque's motives are unclear. What is known, however, is that in exchange for

*In Panama as part of his duties with the Walker Isthmian Canal Commission.

a $100,000 contribution to the revolution, Cromwell promised J. Gabriel Duque the presidency of the new Republic of Panama. A meeting with Secretary Hay to discuss possible American aid to the insurrection was scheduled for two days hence.

On September 2 Dr. Amador trooped down to Wall Street for his own audience with Cromwell. To the elderly physician, Cromwell was effusive with charm and promises. There was no doubt of United States support for the revolution, and a meeting between Amador and Hay was on the agenda. That same day a curious article appeared in the *Washington Post,* and whoever planted it was certainly no friend of the plotters. "H. [sic.] G. Duque, editor and proprietor of the Panama *Star & Herald* . . . who arrived to-day in New York, declared that if the canal treaty fell through a revolution would be likely to follow."[107]

The next day at the State Department, J. Gabriel Duque was ushered into Hay's office. The secretary was courteous and sympathetic, but would give no assurances of United States aid to the conspiracy. He did declare, however, that the United States was determined to build the canal, and would not permit Colombia to thwart the project. The meeting concluded with Hay allegedly claiming that should the revolutionaries take possession of Colón and Panama City, they could depend on the United States to prevent the landing of Colombian troops. This action, the secretary stated, was merely the guarantee in the old Bidlack-Mallarino Treaty of "free and uninterrupted transit" which the United States was duty-bound to protect.[108]

J. Gabriel Duque now showed his colors, and a varied lot they were. Immediately upon leaving the State Department, he went straight to the Colombian embassy and revealed *everything*—his poker-playing conversations with Amador, Cromwell's offer of the presidency of Panama, the meeting with Hay—to Tomás Herrán. The ambassador cabled this priceless intelligence to his government, "Revolutionary agents of Panama here. . . . If treaty is not approved by September 22 it is probable that there will be a revolution with American support."[109]

Herrán hired private detectives to shadow Dr. Amador. He also cabled Cromwell a warning that the New Panama Canal Company would be held liable, and its concession confiscated by the Colombian government, for any revolt in Panama. Cromwell panicked. The enormous brokerage and attorney's fees he would amass on the sale of the canal concession were the only reason he was committed to Panamanian independence. He publicly disassociated himself from the revolutionaries, and when Dr. Amador inquired as to the progress of obtaining American support, he was rudely rebuffed.

Feeling his mission a complete failure Amador wired the junta in code, "Disappointed," and prepared to sail home on the next steamer. Virtually as he was buckling shut his suitcase, a message came from a New York–based Panamanian banker advising Amador to forget the slippery Cromwell. If the doctor remained quietly in New York, "help from another quarter" would come. Two weeks later, Philippe Bunau-Varilla arrived from Paris and booked a room at the Waldorf-Astoria.[110]

While the globe-trotting Frenchman was still at sea, John Hay presented several options on the canal dilemma to President Roosevelt. Essentially, they were: (1) stand fast and brook no further compromise on the Hay-Herrán Treaty; (2) await the result of the Panamanian secessionist movement "against that government of folly and graft that now rules at Bogotá"; (3) "take a hand in rescuing the Isthmus from anarchy.... Something we shall be forced to do in the case of a serious insurrectionary movement.... Our intervention should not ... be to the profit, as heretofore, of Bogotá"; (4) scrap the treaty and reopen serious negotiations with Nicaragua.[111]

It was the third option that President Roosevelt found most appealing. On September 15 he queried Hay as to whether in the event of a revolt, the United States could "in some shape or way ... interfere when it becomes necessary so as to secure the Panama route without further dealing with the foolish and homicidal corruptionists in Bogotá."[112]

On September 24 Amador met for the first time with Bunau-Varilla in the Waldorf's Room 1162, "the cradle of the Panama Republic." Cromwell, Bunau-Varilla maintained, was a charlatan, and Amador had shown "unpardonable folly" in believing his "empty talk." Bunau-Varilla himself would go to Washington to meet with Hay and the President. To his colleagues of the junta, Amador sent another one-word message: "Hopes."[113]

The meeting, arranged by Assistant Secretary of State Francis Loomis, another of Bunau-Varilla's army of "personal friends," took place on October 10 in the White House. There is no official record, and later accounts by the principals are somewhat defensive and self-serving. Bunau-Varilla was introduced as the publisher of *Le Matin,* in which he had just purchased a proprietary interest. The paper had championed Captain Alfred Dreyfus during the recent and infamous *affaire,* and the conversation began with a discussion of that wrongly disgraced officer. "The bridge was found," Bunau-Varilla wrote, and "I crossed it. 'Mr. President,' I said, 'Captain Dreyfus has not been the only victim of detestable political passions. Panama is another.' "

To this, according to Bunau-Varilla, Roosevelt exclaimed, "Oh yes. . . . Well, what do you think is going to be the outcome of the present situation?" After a moment of silence to collect his thoughts, Bunau-Varilla slowly and emphatically replied, " 'Mr. President, a Revolution'. . . . The features of the President," he later recorded, "manifested profound surprise, 'A Revolution! . . . Would it be possible?' "[114]

Bunau-Varilla came away feeling he had exactly gauged Roosevelt's mood. No one will ever know. Some months later Assistant Secretary Loomis wrote, "Nothing was said that could be in any way construed as advising, instigating, suggesting, or encouraging a revolutionary movement."[115]

Bunau-Varilla was back in New York and on October 13 met again with Dr. Amador at the Waldorf. His fertile mind had already devised a scenario whereby the United States would intervene forty-eight hours after the junta declared Panama independent. The Frenchman needed no powers of divination. An analysis of the previous interventions made plain the proper strategy. If a revolution were to erupt within cannon shot of the line of transit, which included Colón and Panama City, the United States could automatically, by right of treaty, and without prior motive, intervene.

He handed Amador a revolutionary kit containing the junta's military operations, cable codes, a declaration of independence, the framework for a constitution (based on the American-inspired Cuban model), and a new flag designed and sewn by Mme. Bunau-Varilla.* To finance the revolt, he personally negotiated a $100,000 loan from a consortium of European banks.

The real battle, he told Amador, would be in Washington, especially during the "delicate period, that of the complete recognition of the new Republic." This fight Bunau-Varilla claimed as his own. And to assure victory, he demanded that the junta

---

*The declaration of independence, constitution, and flag were rejected by the junta and replaced with documents and a banner of Panamanian origin.

appoint him Panama's ambassador to the United States. Dr. Amador was greatly perturbed. He had expected much more, and not only in dollars. There was nothing concrete from the American government, and the only assurance he received was Bunau-Varilla's word. They departed "coldly." After a sleepless night Amador returned to the Waldorf and consented to Bunau-Varilla's propositions.[116]

Bunau-Varilla was off again to Washington, this time for a meeting with John Hay. To the Secretary's query, "These events [in Panama] what do you think they will be?" Bunau-Varilla responded, "The whole thing will end in a revolution. You must take your measures, if you do not want to be taken yourself by surprise." To Bunau-Varilla's surprise, the Secretary denied any possibility of that. "Yes," Hay is recorded to have ventured, "but we shall not be caught napping. Orders have been given to naval forces on the Pacific to sail towards the Isthmus."[117]

Indeed, these orders had been issued to Rear Admiral Henry Glass, commanding the Pacific Squadron. On its face, they were innocuous enough, the squadron merely being directed to sail from San Francisco "about [October] twenty-second . . . on exercise cruise to Acapulco." The fact that Hay and the State Department were fully informed of what was ostensibly workaday fleet training is quite significant.[118]

An army intelligence mission to Central America and the Caribbean had just returned to the United States. The chief of staff reported that Captain Chauncey Humphrey and Second Lieutenant Grayson Murphy, "while on the Isthmus became satisfied beyond question that, owing largely to . . . the failure of Colombia to ratify the Hay-Herrán treaty, a revolutionary party was in course of organization having for its object the separation of the State of Panama from Colombia."[119]

On the Colón docks they had seen substantial amounts of small arms and ammunition smuggled in piano boxes and merchandise crates. In Panama City the fire brigade (organized and funded by none other than J. Gabriel Duque) was "really intended for a revolutionary military organization," as were the departmental police. Humphrey and Murphy expected the revolution to erupt anytime after October, "immediately upon the adjournment of the Colombian Congress." On October 16, at the behest of the chief of staff, they were received in the White House by President Roosevelt.[120]

The President cautioned the officers to say nothing regarding the interview, or that it even took place. They were questioned exhaustively and were astonished at Roosevelt's knowledge of Panamanian topography. Although the President said nothing of his future plans regarding the isthmus, the officers came away with the distinct feeling that Theodore Roosevelt was not going to sit by and allow events to take their course.

No doubt remained in the minds of Roosevelt and Hay that a Panamanian uprising was imminent. In retrospect it is clear that neither—as has been claimed—initiated the movement to grab the canal zone from Colombia. But without a doubt they welcomed the revolution, and both men fully realized that the conspirators were counting on the United States Navy to prevent Colombian interference. To Roosevelt, a revolution in Panama was the easiest and surest path to the goal of an isthmian canal. It was far more certain—if handled correctly—than any plan that might be given to debate by the United States Congress, and he determined not to allow this opportunity to vanish through the application of half measures. On October 19 he ordered fleet units to assemble within striking distance of the isthmus.

From San Francisco Admiral Glass dispatched the cruiser *Boston*, "with all speed," to San Juan del Sur, Nicaragua. "Secret and confidential," noted an addendum; "her ostensible destination Acapulco only." At League Island, Philadelphia, the transport *Dixie* embarked a battalion of marines, ready to sail for an unknown destination by the twenty-third.[121]

On October 19 Amador met with Bunau-Varilla for the last time in New York. The revolution, Bunau-Varilla declared, must take place on November 3, election day in the United States. America's newspapers would be filled with domestic events and small notice paid to an isthmian revolt or to the timely arrival of United States warships in Panamanian waters. The next day Amador boarded the steamer *Yucatan* for passage to Colón. Ironically, she was the same vessel that had carried Roosevelt and the Rough Riders to Cuba in 1898.

While Amador sailed home, the *Dixie* completed loading at League Island. On October 24 a full battalion, 393 marines, commanded by Major John A. Lejeune (Commandant of the Marine Corps, 1920–1929), marched up the brow. "As late as four o'clock in the afternoon, no one on board had any knowledge of the destination of the ship," Lejeune wrote. "At that hour, Captain

Delano went to the [navy yard] Commandant's Office and reported that the ship was ready to sail . . . but that he couldn't very well do so until a destination was assigned . . . all kinds of rumors were rife among the officers and men, and a correspondent of the New York *Herald* who was on board, stated to me . . . that he was positive that the *Dixie*'s destination was the Isthmus of Panama. We guyed him when the Captain returned on board and announced that we would sail . . . for Guantánamo Bay." In mid-afternoon the *Dixie* cast off her moorings and set a course for the Cuban base, from whence the gunboat *Nashville* steamed for Kingston, Jamaica, one step closer to the isthmus.[122]

In Panama City the junta was busily engaged in neutralizing the Colombian garrison. With promises of money and position in the new republic, Colonel Esteban Huertas, the diminutive commander of the *Colombia* Battalion, was won over to the cause—contingent, of course, upon United States support. He, in turn, convinced most of his officers and men to follow suit. Of the minuscule Colombian sea forces, General Rubén Varón, of the gunboat *Padilla*, was bought off with a promise of $35,000 in silver. To denude the line of transit of remaining loyal government forces, the newly appointed governor, José de Obaldía, a native Panamanian with separatist sympathies, put in motion an ingenious scheme.

In late October he concocted a false Nicaraguan attack on Panama's western territory. To deal with the "threat," Obaldía dispatched into the interior about 250 troops, commanded by a loyal officer. News of the "invasion" was cabled to Bogotá. The Colombian government acted quickly, so quickly in fact that they nearly wrecked the revolution. At the mainland port of Cartagena, General Juan Tobar loaded his veteran *Tiradores* (Sharpshooter) Battalion and steamed for Colón. The gunboats *Bogotá* and *Padilla*, at anchor in Panama City, were ordered to fill with coal, steam for a mainland port, and return to Panama with further reinforcements. As their plans unraveled, the junta began losing heart.

On October 27 Dr. Amador arrived at Colón, and that evening met with the conspirators at Panama City. If anything, his coming further deepened the gloom. He brought with him no money, no secret treaty of alliance with the United States, and only vague, wholly unofficial, assurances from Bunau-Varilla. Two days later, Amador met with Governor Obaldía and learned of the dispatch of Colombian reinforcements. In a garbled version of their prearranged cable code, the doctor wired Bunau-Varilla of the deteriorating situation: "Fate news bad powerful tiger. Urge vapor Colón"; translation: "Colombian troops arriving. Atlantic. Five days. More than 200."[123]

For once, Bunau-Varilla nearly lost his composure. He must, barring all else, guarantee a United States warship in Panamanian waters on November 3. "If I succeeded in this task," he wrote, "the Canal was saved. If I failed it was lost. . . . It remained for me to set the machine in motion." He left the Waldorf and boarded the next train to Washington.[124]

Bunau-Varilla met twice with Assistant Secretary Loomis. He retold the story of the 1885 intervention, and the rebuke that had fallen on the head of the *Galena*'s commander, who "did not manage to interfere in time." But Loomis would neither commit himself nor the government to any venture, and the meeting ended on an inconclusive note.[125]

The next day, October 30, the two met, according to Bunau-Varilla quite by accident, in Lafayette Park. The assistant secretary was cryptically vague. "This situation," he opined, "is really fraught with peril for the town of Colón. It would be deplorable if the catastrophe of 1885 were to be renewed today." To this statement, Bunau-Varilla could attach "but one interpretation: 'A cruiser has been sent to Colón.' "[126]

The newspapers had already reported the *Dixie* at Guantánamo and the *Nashville* at Kingston. Guessing, if indeed it was a guess, that it had to be the latter ship, Bunau-Varilla estimated she could steam the 600 miles to Colón in two days. As a safety measure, he added twelve hours. Confident now of American intervention, he cabled Amador: "All right will reach two days and half."[127]

Detective historians searching for a smoking gun will hunt in vain. Bunau-Varilla was inclined to inflate his own importance, and whether the final decision to intervene resulted from his meetings with Loomis remains a mystery. Enough rumors and newspaper accounts, to say nothing of J. Gabriel Duque's treachery, had already convinced the policymakers in Washington and Bogotá that the balloon was about to go up in Panama. Whether Bunau-Varilla actually engineered the final American naval movements is academic. But the coincidence, nonetheless, is remarkable.

Within hours of the telegram to Amador, the *Nashville*'s skipper, Commander John Hubbard, received his orders. The first portion of the message was in plain language, "Hold vessel in readiness to return to Guantánamo." The remainder, however, was sent in code and marked " 'SECRET'. . . . Proceed at once to Colón. . . . Your destination is secret."[128]

On the isthmus Bunau-Varilla's cable stiffened the junta's flagging spirits. At Colón the conspirators managed to recruit Porfirio Meléndez, the town's police chief and part-time railroad straw boss. Under the guise of higher-paying United Fruit Company jobs he mustered about 300 section hands, holding them ready to overcome the police garrison.

Critically important support now came from the Panama Railroad. If the revolution were to succeed, the Colombian reinforcements must be denied its use. Colonel James Shaler, the railroad's general superintendent, ordered all idle rolling stock at Colón to be shunted south to Panama City; there would be no trains for General Tobar and the *Tiradores*.

In the meantime Governor Obaldía's orders from Bogotá to coal and dispatch the gunboats were met with creative obstructionism. To allay suspicions a small amount of coal was bunkered in the *Padilla*, whose commanding officer had already turned his coat. The railroad, which owned the coal yards along the line of transit, then "informed" Obaldía that all remaining stocks in Panama City had been contracted for by the shipping lines; patently false. As for the coal yards in Colón, the railroad "refused" to accept Obaldía's requisition; cash on the barrelhead was required.

Obaldía dutifully wired his government a most extraordinary message. "Have cabled San Francisco to get coal from the Pacific Mail [steamship company]. . . . Railroad refuses to give it. *Padilla* ready. . . . There is no invasion [from Nicaragua]." The San Francisco ploy was a lie; there would be no coal for the Colombian government from that quarter either, and Obaldía knew it. The steamer line's general counsel, William Nelson Cromwell, had already made secret arrangements to block any transfer.[129]

As for the phantom Nicaraguan invasion, Obaldía's seemingly casual mention was a desperate last-minute ploy to prevent the arrival of Colombian reinforcements. It was in vain. The gunboat *Cartagena*, with the *Tiradores* embarked, was already at sea. Obaldía's plan to rid the line of transit of government forces had backfired. Of this the junta knew nothing. In all Panama, only

Obaldía, Amador, his wife María (whom William Howard Taft described as a woman "of courage and snap"), and the railroad officials knew that the revolution hung by a thread.

But the United States Navy was on the move. On November 2 Rear Admiral Glass, at Acapulco with the cruiser *Marblehead*, gunboat *Concord*, and the monitor *Wyoming*, got his orders: "Proceed with all possible dispatch to Panama. . . . Maintain free and uninterrupted transit. If interruption is threatened by armed force occupy the line of railroad. Prevent landing of any armed force, either Government or insurgent . . . if in your judgment landing would precipitate a conflict." Identical orders were sent to the *Nashville* in care of the United States consul at Colón, and to the *Dixie* at Kingston.[130]

At mid-afternoon, November 2, just as Bunau-Varilla had predicted, the *Nashville* was first on the scene. "At 3:05 [P.M.] sighted land," penned her officer of the deck in the log, "at 5:25 standing into Colón Harbor, sounded to quarters." From the railroad offices General Superintendent Shaler cabled his assistant in Panama City, "*Nashville* has been sighted. This I presume, settles the question."[131]

In Colón, as indeed in all of Panama, there was quiet. Commander Hubbard, not yet in receipt of the Navy Department's cable regarding the line of transit, was ignorant of the pending revolution.* At ten minutes before midnight the *Nashville*'s lookouts sighted the *Cartagena*, ablaze with lights, as she rounded Manzanillo Point, and stood into harbor.

With the dawn of November 3 Hubbard took his gig to the Colombian vessel, and was informed that the *Tiradores*, nearly 500 strong, were ready to land. Without orders to the contrary, and seeing no signs of any disturbance along the line of transit, Hubbard posed no objections.

The arrival of the *Cartagena*, coupled with the landing of General Tobar and the *Tiradores*, completely unnerved the junta. One by one, they began slipping home, until only Dr. Amador and his indefatigable wife María remained committed to the revolution. The doctor, in fact, was nearly ready to cash it in as well. But Doña María was adamant. It was too late to back down. The United States Navy, just as Bunau-Varilla had promised, was already at Colón; and troops or no troops, the junta must fight. At a rump

---

*Rudimentary radios were not installed in United States naval ships until 1905.

session of its stronger-hearted members, stiffened with the presence of Assistant Railroad Superintendent Herbert Prescott, it was agreed that the revolt would go forward at 5:00 P.M. that day.

Of supreme importance was the neutralization of the *Tiradores*. According to legend, it was Doña María who devised the plan of separating General Tobar from his command, leaving both impotent at the moment of crisis. The plot was telegraphed to Colonel Shaler at Colón, who had the major part to play.

At Colón General Tobar and his troops were met by Colonel Shaler, who graciously offered the general and his staff a special of an engine and car for the ride to Panama City. Unfortunately, Shaler informed the general, there was no rolling stock for the troops; they would have to wait another four hours, until 1:00 P.M. Tobar refused the hospitality. As he later testified, "Mr. Shaler invited me at once to take a seat in a special car, which by order of . . . Obaldía he had in readiness for me, and he even insisted that I should do so, telling me that the hour fixed for . . . departure had already passed. . . . I pointed out to him that it was not possible for me to accept . . . because I wished to take [the *Tiradores*] with me to Panama."[132]

But Shaler was persistent and finally persuaded the reluctant general to board the train. "As he insisted in his efforts," Tobar continued, "and I was able to satisfy myself . . . that the troops . . . would go over in a special train to be dispatched at 1:00 P.M., I found no justifiable reason to persist in my refusal. . . . I had not the slightest idea that a barrack uprising was planned."[133]

Leaving the *Tiradores,* Tobar and his staff, escorted by Colonel Shaler, boarded the special. But not everyone was convinced. One of the staff officers, General Ramón Amaya was uneasy, there was something not right. Acting on the impulse, he elbowed his way through and tried to leave the train—too late. Shaler had spotted him and reached for the whistle cord. The engine puffed, and the special began to roll out of Colón. With that, Shaler hopped off the platform and with a jovial wave wished General Tobar a pleasant journey. Doña María's plan had worked perfectly.

Shaler cabled Herbert Prescott in Panama City to expect Tobar in about two hours, 11:00 A.M. He would try to delay the *Tiradores* in Colón for as long as possible.

Prescott passed the message to Dr. Amador, who made his way to the Chiriqui Barracks and Colonel Esteban Huertas. Amador had to be certain of his cooperation in the revolt; if Huertas remained loyal to the Bogotá government, they would probably all hang as traitors. According to one of the soldiers, Amador told the colonel, "Huertas, what you are today you owe to Panama. From Bogotá you can hope for nothing. . . . If you will aid us, we shall reach to immortality in the history of the new Republic. Here [in Panama City] you will have four American warships. There will be the same number in Colón.* You and your battalion [if they remain loyal] can accomplish nothing against the superior force of the cruisers. . . . Choose here, glory and riches; in Bogotá, misery and ingratitude." Huertas remained silent. Then, looking up to Amador, he held out his hand. "I accept," he said.[134]

At Colón the special's coal smoke had hardly disappeared when Commander Hubbard on the *Nashville* finally received the department's order to prevent the landing of armed forces on the line of transit. He immediately went ashore and wired the Navy Department.

The *Nashville,* Hubbard noted, had been at anchor in Colón nearly half a day, and no orders had been received. Such being the case, there was no reason to prevent the *Tiradores* from landing. Further, there was no revolution on the isthmus and no disturbances either. But unofficially, he must have received some information. "It is possible," Hubbard concluded, "that movement may be made tonight at Panama [City] to declare independence, in which event I will [original message mutilated] here. Situation is most critical if revolutionary leaders act."[135]

At 10:30 A.M., in Panama City, Colonel Huertas marched at the head of the *Colombia* Battalion to the railroad station to receive General Tobar. The special pulled in an hour later, and if any suspicions were left in the general's mind, they were soon eased. Governor Obaldía laid on a first-class reception. The troops were drawn up in review order, as were a strong detachment of the municipal police. A deputation of Panama City's most prominent citizens, including the distinguished Dr. Manuel Amador arrived with the governor. General Tobar, after taking the salute, climbed into the first of a long line of carriages for the drive to the governor's residence. "There was nothing," he recalled, "that did not show the most complete assurance that peace reigned throughout the department."[136]

But at lunch Tobar began to sniff the wind. A Colombian

---

*An exact estimate as it turned out.

loyalist whispered that a mass meeting of citizens was planned for the evening, and that the arrival of the *Tiradores* had caused great consternation among the civic leaders. When a calling card was handed him, bearing a warning note to trust no one, Tobar's fears were at last aroused.

The general left the meal unfinished and sent an officer to Governor Obaldía requesting immediate dispatch of the *Tiradores* from Colón. Then, with his aides, Tobar went to the barracks of the *Colombia* Battalion to inspect the troops. Following that exercise, Tobar, accompanied by Huertas, went down to the seawall to give instructions for the city's defense. Here he was informed by Obaldía's secretary that the railroad "was placing difficulties" in the *Tiradores*' path. Because "certain sums of money" were owed to the railroad, Colonel Shaler refused to ship the battalion unless Obaldía paid cash in advance for the tickets!

With that Tobar went himself to confront the governor. Obaldía expressed great surprise that his orders for the train had been ignored. As General Tobar remembered it, "I could see that the governor's mind was not at ease, and I made clear to him the necessity of bringing over the troops, offering him . . . the money necessary to pay for the trains. Governor Obaldía protested to me that there was no need of that, that the orders had been given, and that it was certain that the battalion would be sent over at 5:00 P.M."[137]

Tobar was hardly mollified and any lingering doubts regarding a revolt vanished. At the Chiriqui Barracks a treasury official informed the general that large-scale disturbances would begin shortly; that Governor Obaldía was sitting on his hands, and had issued no orders for the dispatch of the *Tiradores*. Further, that Colonel Huertas and the departmental police had been turned, and were now in the pay of the junta.

It was about 3:00 P.M. On benches near the barracks' seawall gate Tobar found Colonel Huertas sitting with several officers. The general took Huertas aside, explained the "critical" situation to him and, placing a fatal amount of faith in Huertas' loyalty, gave orders to prepare the barracks for defense against a large demonstration. A fully armed company was to muster and patrol the streets.

By now groups of "rioters" were reported massing opposite the barracks, and Huertas received permission to send out the first patrol. The colonel sought out Captain Marco Salazar. Arm yourself and a company, Salazar was told, then "Go and place under arrest all those sitting on the benches." "Who? The generals?" queried the puzzled captain.

"Yes," Huertas replied. "Take them to the police station and turn them over to [the] Commandant."[138]

With fixed bayonets Captain Salazar marched his company out the seawall gate, stepping as though to pass in review of General Tobar. The company then opened into two files, one passing in front of the general and the other behind. At a shouted word of command, the troops came to the "on guard"; down came the bayonets, pointed straight at Tobar's heart.

"Generals," said Captain Salazar, "you are my prisoners."

But "I am the Commander in Chief!" exploded a stunned General Tobar.

"You and your aides," Salazar continued.

Tobar was dumbstruck. "By whose orders?"

"[Colonel] Huertas," came the nonplussed reply.[139]

Seeing that none of his staff had drawn their swords or pistols in defense Tobar futilely lunged through the bayonet cordon. An appeal to the patriotism of Captain Salazar and the troops was met with jeers. He called for Huertas, and for General Castro, the nominal government commander on the isthmus; neither showed their face.

The mob which had gathered opposite the barracks grew large, and through the mass, amidst shouts for "*el Presidente Amador!*" and "*el Istmo Libre!*" General Tobar and his staff were taken off to the *calabozo.*

Immediately after Tobar had been taken prisoner, Dr. Amador declared the revolution to American Consul General Felix Ehrman, who cabled the news to Washington. At 9:50 P.M., Secretary Hay received the message, "Uprising occurred tonight . . . no bloodshed. Army . . . officers taken prisoners. Government will be organized tonight. . . . Soldiers changed. Supposed same movement will be effected in Colón. Order prevails so far. Situation serious. Four hundred [Colombian] soldiers landed Colón today."[140]

All day at Colón the *Tiradores'* commander, Colonel Torres, made every effort to get his battalion across the isthmus to Panama City. The 1:00 P.M. train Shaler had promised was now unavailable. He told Torres it was against company regulations to transport his troops unless their fares were paid in advance. Torres hadn't any funds so he demanded a train on the credit account of the Colombian government. This could not legally be refused. But the general superintendent noted in a fine point that all requisitions of that sort had to be signed by the departmental governor, and Obaldía had done no such thing.

At 11:00 P.M. that night of November 3, Shaler notified Commander Hubbard of Tobar's arrest and of the situation then obtaining in Panama City. Hubbard's response sealed any hope of the *Tiradores* ever getting across the isthmus and quashing the revolution. "The condition of affairs at Panama," he wrote the superintendent, "being such that any movement of troops . . . must inevitably produce a conflict and interrupt the transit . . . I am obliged to prohibit the carrying of troops of either party . . . by your railroad, and hereby notify you that I do so prohibit it."[141]

While Hubbard composed his diktat, there occurred in Panama City the only direct and immediate Colombian military response to the revolution. Upon being informed of General Tobar's arrest the senior officer of the gunboat *Bogotá* sent an ultimatum to the junta: release the generals within two hours or the city would suffer bombardment. There were as yet no United States warships at Panama City to prevent him, and at 11:00 P.M. the Colombian made good his threat. In the space of half an hour, about half a dozen shells fell in the city. The casualties were one Chinese merchant killed in his shop, and the mortal wounding of a donkey in the slaughterhouse.[142]

With the dawn of the fourth Colonel Torres at Colón again demanded a train, and was again refused by Superintendent Shaler, this time citing Hubbard's decree. Colonel Torres hadn't a notion of what had transpired in Panama City, and was told of the arrest and revolution only later that morning. Over a drink at the Astor House bar, Police Chief Melendez apprised the colonel of events: the arrest, the revolution, the arrival of United States forces. He concluded with an offer of $8,000 in gold if Torres would reembark the *Tiradores* in the *Cartagena* and return to Colombia.

Flabbergasted, Torres refused to believe it. But the news was soon confirmed and Torres flew into a "violent passion," swearing to kill every American in Colón unless General Tobar and the others were immediately released. To compound his rage Torres received a personal copy of Hubbard's order prohibiting military use of the railroad. It concluded, "Trusting that this action on my [Hubbard's] part will meet with your cordial acquiescence."[143]

It did hardly that. Taking himself to the town's prefect, Torres ordered the man to inform the American consul that the *Tiradores* would put Colón to the torch and kill every American unless General Tobar was released by 2:00 P.M. The prefect begged Torres to take the money and depart, then went to inform Shaler of the threat.

Just before 11:00 A.M. Hubbard was summoned ashore by the prearranged signal of hoisting the United States flag over the railroad depot. After a hurried conference, Hubbard ordered all American male citizens to muster in the railroad's stone depot; which as he noted was "susceptible of being put in good shape for defense." The women and children were taken on board two commercial steamers, "both ready to haul out from dock if necessary."[144]

A curious reinforcement now showed itself: Major William Murray Black, United States Army Corps of Engineers, the same officer who had been in attendance at the junta's July secessionist lunch. He was given command of the armed civilians, who adopted the name Black's Legion.

Hubbard returned to the *Nashville*. "Called away landing parties," penned the officer of the deck, "lowered the waist boats." Ten minutes later, "lightly equipped with one day's rations," plus extra arms for the civilians, forty-two bluejackets and marines under the ship's executive officer, Lieutenant Commander Witzel, went over the side and into the cutters. The *Nashville* got up steam, cleared for action, and headed close inshore. She carried eight 4-inch guns, and for half of these the powder division brought up shrapnel, the better to deal with infantry targets. The remaining gun crews loaded high explosive shell and trained their barrels on the *Cartagena*.[145]

Then came a big surprise. No sooner were the cutters heading for the beach than the *Cartagena* hoisted her anchor and abruptly steamed off. "I did not deem it expedient to detain her," Hubbard reported. But the *Tiradores* were now trapped in Colón.[146]

Ashore the *Tiradores* surrounded the railroad depot. For a time, "their attitude was most threatening," Hubbard noted, "it being seemingly their purpose to provoke an attack. Happily, our men were cool and steady and, while the tension was very great, no shot was fired."[147]

To Colonel Torres, his hopeless position was plain. In mid-afternoon he presented himself at the depot and demanded to meet with the senior American officer. Hubbard was on board *Nashville*, so he was received by Lieutenant Commander Witzel, with Shaler, Consul Malmros, and Police Chief Meléndez in attendance. Torres denied making any bloody threats against Americans, who were obviously under a "misapprehension" as to his intentions. Would it be possible, he inquired, to send a pair of officers to Panama City and seek instructions from General Tobar? In the meantime, if the *Nashville*'s landing force were to reembark, and the town left in the care of Meléndez' municipal police, he would withdraw the *Tiradores* to the outskirts at Monkey Hill. Witzel immediately wrote a safe-conduct pass, and Shaler furnished a special for the envoys. Hubbard, informed of Torres' probable "good faith," ordered the landing force back to the ship.

With the withdrawal of both forces, Colón settled down for a quiet night. However, the dawn of November 5 brought trouble anew. From the *Nashville*'s bridge Hubbard saw the *Tiradores* not on Monkey Hill but camped in buildings on the edge of town. Following a sharp inquiry, Torres stated his men had been driven back into town by ravenous mosquitoes—which was probably true enough, and would have sufficed to mollify Hubbard had not Torres pressed the issue. He pointedly noted that unless the envoys, who were due back on the 10:45 A.M. train, brought orders from General Tobar to quit Colón, he would reoccupy the town, "determined to resist any attack rather than be traitors."[148]

Witzel and the landing force, this time with a pair of 1-pounder rapid-fire guns, reentered their positions in the barricaded railroad depot. Right on time, the No. 2 passenger and express rumbled into the station; the envoys had brought no orders from General Tobar to evacuate Colón. As the general later testified, "my duty and the duty of the army I commanded was sufficiently clear, and that in consequence no human force could drag from me the order desired." On the *Nashville*, the decks were cleared for action, and she stood close inshore to cover the wharves and depot with gunfire.[149]

The *Tiradores*, seasoned veterans of the late civil war, outnumbered the landing force ten to one, yet Hubbard had the equalizer in the *Nashville*'s broadside. In American frontier parlance it was a Mexican standoff.

Once again Police Chief Meléndez approached Torres with

the $8,000 offer, this time adding an unspecified "substantial indemnity." A British steamer was in port, and she, Meléndez continued, would take the *Tiradores* back to Colombia. Loyal officer that he was, Torres refused. Even if General Tobar had given him permission to evacuate the town, he would not leave unless the general was released and given safe conduct to Colón. In essence, he told Meléndez to go to hell.

Word of Torres' intransigence reached Panama City by telephone. It seemed the only way to avert bloodshed in Colón was to release General Tobar and the staff. There was, however, a quandary. Hubbard's order prohibiting military forces from the railroad meant that Tobar must travel without armed guards. The junta demanded Tobar's word that he would attempt no escape, and this Tobar refused. They could either transport him as a prisoner, in which case it was his duty as a soldier to escape, or they could send him back to jail. Hubbard broke the impasse. He had no objection to an armed escort of civilians, and Tobar and his staff were put on the next train for Colón.

But it was all anticlimactic. At 6:20 P.M., the *Nashville*'s officer of the deck penned in the log, "sighted USS *Dixie*." This settled the whole question of the Panama revolution. With it disappeared Colombian sovereignty on the isthmus and began a near century of United States occupation of the Canal Zone.

Within the hour, the ships were in hailing distance. From the *Nashville*'s bridge, Hubbard shouted through a megaphone to the *Dixie*'s skipper, "Situation ashore very grave; you should have your battalion ready to land immediately. . . . I will show you where to go and follow you in." In the *Dixie*, all boats were lowered, and two companies of marines, with Major Lejeune at their head, clambered in. Under tow of the steam launches, the reinforcements headed toward the fleet landing at the railroad wharf.[150]

"Colón harbor was then an open roadstead," Lejeune wrote, "and a heavy sea was running, making it necessary to proceed with great care, especially as the night was inky black owing to the dense, low-hanging clouds from which there began to fall one of the hardest downpours I ever experienced. . . . On reaching [the wharf], we were informed that the Colombian troops, on learning that the *Dixie* with a battalion of marines was in the offing, had decided to return home on board the Royal Mail steamer which sailed for Cartagena as we landed on the dock."[151]

So it was. On learning of Tobar's release Colonel Torres accepted Meléndez' offer, and as the marines advanced in open order up the mud streets, the *Tiradores* marched up the brows of the merchantman and steamed off. Ironically, the special that brought General Tobar arrived too late to catch her, and he remained in Colón until November 12.

Once the marines secured the railroad depot and established patrols in the town, the *Nashville*'s weary landing force returned to their ship.

"All quiet ashore," Lejeune signaled with the first light of Friday, November 6. An hour later came the welcome launch from the *Dixie* with a hot breakfast. In mid-morning Lejeune took himself to the prefecture. A public meeting was advertised, "at which important action would be taken. . . . A great concourse of people had assembled. I was courteously escorted through the crowd . . . into the hall where I found a seat reserved next to the American Consul. Señor Meléndez . . . read very dramatically a paper declaring that the State of Colón was . . . a free and independent state, and that it forthwith united itself with the State of Panama to form the Republic of Panama."[152]

When the shouting ceased, Meléndez announced the new flag of the republic would be hoisted above the prefecture. Both Lejeune and Consul Malmros were invited to participate; "Both of us declined on the ground that we were present in the capacity of observers only." Meléndez then handed the flag to Major William Murray Black, who, wearing the uniform of the United States Army, hoisted it to the top of the pole. *"Viva la Republica!"* shouted the crowd, *"Vivan los Americanos!"*[153]

On that November 6, 1903, a busy day for all, the United States granted political recognition to the new republic. In Bogotá the reaction was violent, martial law was declared, and a heavy guard was placed around the American embassy. In a pathetic gesture, and blind to the *fait accompli*, the Colombian government requested United States military intervention to preserve order on the isthmus. Desperately Marroquín offered to call a special session of the Colombian Congress to ratify the Hay-Herrán Treaty. But it was all for nothing.

To Ambassador Arthur Beaupré in Bogotá, Hay cabled the death knell, "Panama . . . having adopted a government of their own . . . with which the Government of the United States has entered into relations, the President of the United States . . . holds that he is bound, not merely by treaty obligations, but by the interests of civilization, to see that the peaceable traffic of the world across the Isthmus of Panama shall not longer be disturbed by a constant succession of unnecessary and wasteful civil wars."[154]

On November 7 the *Boston* dropped anchor off Panama City. On the tenth, the *Marblehead*, flying the flag of Rear Admiral Henry Glass, stood in. "A regular government had been established and perfect order prevailed," he noted in his report.

A treaty was drafted in near-record time, and on November 18 at John Hay's home the Secretary and Panama's new Minister Plenipotentiary put their names to what history calls the Hay–Bunau-Varilla Treaty. Its second article was the most significant: "The Republic of Panama grants to the United States in perpetuity the use, occupation and control of a zone of land . . . for the construction, maintenance, operation, sanitation and protection of said Canal of the width of ten miles . . . on each side of the center line of the route of the Canal to be constructed."[155]

On February 20, 1904, in Panama City's Cathedral Plaza, Dr. Manuel Amador was inaugurated as the first President of the Republic of Panama.

4:

NICARAGUA I
1912

Revolution was on again, and we Marines were off again.

—Major General Smedley D. Butler, USMC

José Santós Zelaya, the Liberal* president who ruled Nicaragua at the turn of the century, occupies a prominent niche in the American government's gallery of historical villains.

Zelaya assumed the presidency in 1893 as a result of revolution and moved rapidly to assure Nicaragua's primacy in Central America. Foreign capital and industry were welcomed, the treasury was fairly solvent, and debts were rarely in default. Zelaya, however, was a corruption-ridden despot who auctioned Nicaragua's substantial natural resources and economic concessions to the highest bidder. Kickbacks and monopolies granted to favorites became the normal order of business, with Zelaya and his cronies greatly enriching themselves. It was a government of the "kleptocracy," as one senior American officer recently said. Zelaya was loathed in Washington. Huntington Wilson, the number-two man at the State Department, considered him "guilty of murder and rape, as well as robbing his countrymen by graft to the extent of making himself a multi-millionaire." President Taft refused even "to tolerate and deal with such medieval despots as . . . Zelaya."[1]

Zelaya's obnoxious nationalism did nothing to garner external

---

*In Nicaragua, Liberal and Conservative originally connoted anti- and pro-clericalism respectively. By the early twentieth century, the labels signified little more than variations of a debilitating, hereditary regionalism, or *localismo*. In their ideas on hemispheric relations, the Conservatives were, on balance, less anti-American than their Liberal enemies.

137

friendship. "Appeal by all means!" he told a Peruvian facing deportation. "When I ridicule the United States, laugh at Germany, and spit on England, what do you suppose I care for your beggarly little Peru?"[2]

His foreign policy centered upon the reestablishment, with Nicaraguan hegemony, of the old Central American Union, the short-lived isthmian confederation that was created immediately following independence from Spain in 1823. In pursuit of this goal Zelaya was a constant destabilizing factor in the region. In 1907 he encouraged revolt in Honduras. The rebels were driven back into Nicaragua and Zelaya threatened war. An attempted mediation by Elihu Root collapsed amidst Zelaya's obstructionism, and on March 18 the Nicaraguan army swept over the border. At Namasigüe they met a combined Honduran-Salvadoran force, and for the first time machine guns were used in a Central American war; the casualties were horrendous, and Zelaya's army marched into the Honduran capital.

In December, at Root's urging, Theodore Roosevelt convened a plenary conference of the Central American republics in an attempt to negotiate regional peace. In a major diplomatic triumph the conferees signed a General Treaty of Peace and Amity, agreeing to take all future disputes to a Permanent Central American Court of Justice. Zelaya, however, had no intention of abiding by the terms. In March 1909 Philander Knox assumed the office of Secretary of State in the new Taft administration. As a check to Nicaraguan adventurism his department immediately notified the navy that it would be "politically expedient to keep for the present two naval vessels in Nicaraguan waters."[3]

Zelaya had been in power for sixteen years in 1909 and his grip seemed firm as ever. But the Conservative outs as well as certain Liberal politicos in eastern Nicaragua, where monopolies and foreign concessions flourished, plotted revolution. At Bluefields, the chief eastern port and regional economic center, the estranged Liberal governor, General Juan Estrada, cast his lot and leadership with the Conservative rebels. In return for a promise of the presidency, Estrada declared the town and coast in revolt. Funds for the insurrection were obtained from local Americans and their associates in the United States. But a request for official United States support, or at least sympathetic neutrality, was refused.

Zelaya gathered his forces and marched. In the wilds of central

Nicaragua he crushed the incipient rebellion by arresting the Conservative leadership and seemed fair to reestablishing his authority. Then, as the cliché has it, he snatched defeat from the jaws of victory. Two American mercenaries in the pay of the rebels, Lee Roy Cannon and Leonard Groce, were captured while laying dynamite in the San Juan River. Zelaya foolishly ordered their execution.

The State Department, though denouncing their participation, considered the dead men officers in the rebel army entitled to treatment as prisoners of war. Secretary Knox condemned Zelaya as "a blot upon the history of Nicaragua" and severed diplomatic relations. Senior department officials advocated seizing Corinto, the capital's Pacific port of entry, and possibly Managua itself. Knox, however, opted for a subtler approach. Both factions would be held strictly accountable for the protection of American lives and property, but if Zelaya and the Liberals continued in office, Nicaragua faced the levy of extremely heavy punitive damages for the deaths of Cannon and Groce. Though technically neutral, Knox's position was a thinly veiled gesture of support to Estrada and the Conservative rebels.[4]

Diplomatically trapped, Zelaya could do little but hurl a barrage of vilification at the United States. He then resigned the presidency in favor of José Madriz and left the country. Madriz, a generally respected Liberal and lately Nicaragua's legate to the Central American Court of Justice, was equally unsatisfactory to the State Department. Knox would have no truck with any *Zelayista*, no matter how moderate, and with benign encouragement to the rebels he refused recognition to the new government.

But Knox grew frustrated with indirect efforts to topple the Liberals, and indeed with the diplomatic means at hand for keeping regional tranquility. The peace accords of the 1907 Washington conference were ineffective. Strife in Central America was endemic, and the State Department was continually bedeviled by its case-by-case search for clear, legal rights of intervention. The Platt Amendment served this purpose for Cuba. The Hay–Bunau-Varilla Treaty did the same for Panama. And since 1906 rights of intervention were granted to the United States by the Dominican Republic in her customs receivership agreement. But it was a patchwork, nothing comprehensive. In frustration, Knox noted to President Taft, "There should be some conventional right to intervene in Central American affairs promptly, without waiting for outbreaks and with a view to averting rather than quelling disturbances."[5]

With as yet no commitment to intervention, on December 1 Rear Admiral William Kimball hoisted his flag in the cruiser *Albany*, steamed to Corinto, and took command of the hastily formed Nicaraguan Expeditionary Force. At League Island, Philadelphia, a 750-man provisional marine regiment boarded its transports. Via Panama Railroad they crossed the isthmus and took ship for Corinto. The Marine Corps' permanent Panama battalion, commanded by Major Smedley D. Butler, also loaded its gear into the *Buffalo* and headed north. Butler, a controversial, hatchet-faced, bantam rooster of a soldier destined to play major roles in the Banana Wars, later called the expedition the "First Punic War."

Corinto, Butler noted, "is the hottest place this side of hell. Even with the fan going, it was 110 degrees in my cabin." For three months, "packed like sardines," he and his men sat, sweated, and waited.[6]

In mid-February 1910 Estrada's rebels advanced inland from Bluefields and inflicted a stinging defeat on the government army. But a hoped-for general uprising did not materialize. Madriz reorganized his forces, counterattacked, and threw the rebels back to the east coast. With the revolution stalled and seemingly broken, and the State Department still refusing recognition to Madriz, Admiral Kimball suggested that his squadron officers establish a temporary government. To the Secretary of the Navy he penned, "Though in theory Nicaraguans hate Americans, they actually have a child-like faith in our kindness, helpfulness, and innate fairness."[7]

The suggestion died on the Secretary's desk. The Nicaraguan Expeditionary Force was gradually reduced, and by mid-March the marine-laden transports returned to Panama.

Two months later the action flared up again at Bluefields. Government forces had closed in and threatened to bombard the town by land and sea unless Estrada evacuate the customs house in twenty-four hours. The gunboats *Dubuque* and *Paducah* were on station and their landing parties went ashore to establish a neutral zone. The senior naval officer, Commander Gilmer, equally prohibited either side from engaging in any hostilities within the town limits. Vainly Madriz complained that Gilmer's actions prevented the defeat of the rebels.

The government army then landed on the customs house

bluff, cut Estrada's seaborne supply route, and began searching all vessels entering the port for rebel contraband. More than one ship's hold was found carrying rifles and ammunition. But the State and Navy departments ordered U.S. officers to prohibit future searches on grounds that it interfered with neutral commerce.

In late May Smedley Butler and his Panama battalion landed at Bluefields, "the jumping off place of the world." Cynical and astute he quickly assessed the situation. Estrada with 350 men was bottled up in town, the government army, outnumbering the rebels four-fold, was camped outside. "Unless something drastic was done at once," he later wrote, "the revolution would fail. It didn't take a ton of bricks to make me see daylight. It was plain that Washington would like to see the revolutionists come out on top."[8]

Butler sent a letter to the government commanders. The United States, he said, had no objection to their taking the town. But as the marines and bluejackets were there to protect American lives and property, the government troops must assault unarmed, "because their soldiers were poor marksmen and might accidently hit American citizens." Politely, Butler offered the services of his marines as gun checkers. The government officers were apoplectic. "How are we to take the town if we can't shoot?" they asked. "And won't you also disarm the revolutionists defending the town?" Butler was nonplussed. There was no danger from the rebels because they would shoot *outward,* "but your soldiers," he told the officers, "would be firing *toward* us." Checkmated and frustrated, the government army withdrew, pursued at a safe distance by the rebels.[9]

Butler was now confronted with another situation that he dealt with in his customary manner. The revolution had attracted, as Nicaragua always seems to, a number of American mercenaries. There were about fifty of them in Bluefields led by "General Vic" Gordon. To Butler they were nothing but "tramps" and "beachcombers." All held at least a colonelcy in the rebel army, "but they didn't have any regiments and they never saw a battlefield. All they did was live on the fat of the land and bask like lazy lizards in the sun."[10]

The adventurers lived at Bluefields' El Tropicale Hotel, which Butler and his men "dubbed the 'war college' because it was the headquarters of these high-ranking bums." Rebel leaders pleaded with Butler to rid the town of the parasites, and arrangements

were made with a schooner to dump them in Costa Rica. The
mercenaries refused the offer. The following morning the marines entered the "war college." A corporal pulled General Vic
out of a barber's chair, and "by an unwilling ear" dragged him to
the docks. After a chase through town the remainder were clapped
below hatches and the schooner sailed off. Costa Rica, and Panama
as well, refused to accept them, and they were unceremoniously
dumped on a semidesert island. All would have died had they not
been rescued by a passing freighter.[11]

Throughout the summer of 1910, encouraged by the United
States' "neutral" stand, scattered revolts taxed and winnowed away
the stamina of the government and its army. In mid-August the
rebels won decisive victories on the eastern shores of Lake Managua, a scarce twenty miles from the capital, and at Granada,
the traditional Conservative stronghold to the south. The Liberal
government collapsed, and on August 28 the Conservative rebels
marched into Managua. Juan Estrada was declared the new president, and Adolfo Díaz, "our Nicaraguan" and, according to Butler, "the efficiency manager of the revolution," assumed the vice
presidency.[12]

Immediately Estrada appealed for United States recognition
and declared his intent to hold elections and restructure the economy. For Taft and Knox these were glad tidings. Their program
of dollar diplomacy, or as Knox called it, "dollars instead of
bullets," would enable the United States to achieve a stable Latin
America without resorting to military intervention. They also envisioned a similar customs receivership relation as maintained with
the Dominican Republic. When Estrada requested assistance in
securing a loan from American banks, Knox was ready to oblige.[13]

Thomas Dawson, the highest-ranking black in the U.S. diplomatic service and the first chief of the State Department's Latin
American Division, was dispatched to Nicaragua. The resulting
"Dawson Agreements," which the envoy compelled Estrada and
the entire Conservative leadership to sign, broke the Zelaya monopolies. They also established a claims commission to compensate
foreigners for losses incurred in the civil war, guaranteed punishment for the execution of Cannon and Groce, and provided
for a customs receivership on the Dominican model.

On January 1, 1911, the United States formally recognized
the Estrada-Díaz government. But there was much opposition to
the accords within Nicaragua. Elliott Northcott, the new Amer-

ican ambassador, found "an overwhelming majority of Nic-araguans . . . antagonistic to the United States." The proposed customs receivership, which would in effect make the United States Nicaragua's tax collector at her ports of entry, was consid-ered especially obnoxious. Estrada's courting of American support carried with it a heavy political price, and his domestic popularity, such as it was, plummeted. The Dawson Agreements collapsed, and a new revolt simmered.

Its chief initiator was General Luís Mena, Minister of War, whom Butler described as "an ox driver, a rough giant of a man." On May 8 Estrada ordered his arrest on grounds of "contemplated treason." Though leader of a Conservative government, Estrada had never shed his Liberal cloak, and "in a fit of drunken insanity," Northcott reported, he summoned a number of his former Liberal compatriots to the capital's military quarter, the Campo de Marte. The garrison officers, Conservative Mena loyalists, refused to pro-vide them arms, and instead turned their guns, literally, on the president's house and demanded Estrada's resignation.[14]

The next day he abdicated in favor of Vice President Díaz, and General Mena resumed his office in the War Ministry.

Díaz came to office with a sincere belief that Nicaragua could benefit from a close relationship with the United States. But with Mena in firm control of the army he was compelled to gain the general's support by promising him the presidency in the next term.

In the National Assembly a new constitution providing for a Mena presidency was under debate. Requests from the United States State Department that it not be promulgated until the ar-rival of the new American ambassador went, amidst vociferous anti-American rhetoric, unheeded. Domestic support for Díaz rapidly declined, and he desperately appealed for United States assistance. "The [Nicaraguan] Government," cabled the American chargé, "is not in a position to withstand, unaided, even a feeble uprising."[15]

In March Secretary Knox arrived in Managua to bolster the Díaz administration. Díaz responded by jailing anti-American demonstrators and censoring the anti-American press. The plat-itude-strewn visit had little effect. Mena prepared for revolution and moved substantial amounts of munitions south to the arsenal at Granada. He also recruited troops, equipping them with di-verted government funds.

But it was the Liberals who precipitated events. On May 31, in an act independent of Mena's plotting, they blew up Managua's Fort La Loma, killing sixty government troops. The incident was followed by several small, ineffectual attacks around the capital by Conservative Mena loyalists.

The crisis came on July 29 when Mena brought up some 100 soldiers and attempted to occupy La Loma. The 35-man garrison, loyal to the Díaz government, opened fire with machine guns, and Mena's troops were cut down. They fled to the general's home from where Mena escaped through a secret passage to a barracks in the Campo de Marte.

The Mena rebels were trapped and a general firefight was in progress. In late afternoon President Díaz arrived at the American embassy to see George Weitzel, the new ambassador. Díaz assured him that it was only a matter of time before the rebels were annihilated, and pleaded that Weitzel arrange a settlement "for the purpose of avoiding useless bloodshed." In the midst of pouring rains and at no small danger, Weitzel walked to the Campo. "I waited for a few minutes," he cabled, "in the hope that the combatants would cease firing to let me cross in safety." The fire slackened and Weitzel crossed over to Mena's barracks. "He was considerably excited," but after receiving Weitzel's promise of safety for his wife, he gave up the fight. Taking most of the municipal police Mena withdrew south to the Masaya and Granada area, shutting off the capital's electricity on his way out.[16]

Weitzel was immediately beset by demands from the American and foreign colonies for protection from both the Liberals and Mena's factional Conservative revolution. When he formally asked Díaz for assurances that property would be protected, the president responded with an appeal for American intervention. At Weitzel's request, the gunboat *Annapolis* landed 100 bluejackets at Corinto, where they entrained for Managua and duty as legation guards. The capital, for the moment, was quiet. But Weitzel saw that the calm would be temporary. The sailors were no more than a token, and it was plain that the government could not simultaneously put down the revolt and protect foreign citizens and property; more forces were required. On August 5 President Taft penned a terse note regarding United States intervention: "The authority requested herein is hereby given."[17]

The next day the peace cruiser *Tacoma* put her landing party ashore at Bluefields. On the tenth, Smedley Butler's Panama battalion, 361 officers and men, embarked for Corinto. That same day at Managua, the Liberal rebel general, Benjamin Zeledón, notified the diplomatic corps of his intention to bombard the city in twelve hours. A two-day armistice was supposedly in place, and Weitzel considered the threat an "inexcusable breach of faith." Zeledón and the *insurrectos*, he reported, were "beyond the pale of civilization and should be treated not as rebels, but as savages who have violated all rules of warfare."[18]

The rebel guns opened fire in the early morning of August 11, and continued intermittently for three days. Most of the shells fell in the residential sections, forcing thousands of citizens to flee into the countryside. Tragically, 132 women and children were killed or wounded, and not one man. On the fourteenth, the Liberal rebels withdrew south to Masaya and linked up with Mena's Conservative army.

In the midst of the shelling, Butler's battalion landed at Corinto. Informed of the situation by telephone, Butler entrained his troops and arrived at Managua the day after the rebels withdrew. He was given, as Weitzel noted, "a warm welcome by natives and foreigners alike."[19]

But behind him, the rebels had cut all communications: rail, telegraph, and telephone to the coast. They continued sporadic operations in the Managua area, but the real action had moved north to the Liberal stronghold at León. The government forces were badly beaten, and they streamed away in retreat. "Prospects," Butler noted, "looked bleak for the regime of Adolfo Díaz, our protégé."[20]

With Butler's battalion in Managua, it was no longer necessary for the entire *Annapolis* contingent to remain, so on August 20 Commander Terhune, with fifty bluejackets and twenty-five marines, boarded the train for Corinto. In his autobiography, Butler writes that Terhune initially delayed the journey. As Terhune was "not at all anxious to exchange the comparative safety of Managua for a trip through the rebel country, he waited for ice, Apollinaris water and other vital military supplies" before proceeding.[21]

On the morning of August 21, Butler received a telephone call from Terhune, about twenty-five miles up the line. "I could feel that he was trembling with fright." Terhune, though Butler's senior in rank, requested the marine's permission to return to Managua on the local firewood train. "I had a terrible experience in León—terrible," he exclaimed. Butler, assuming there had been a fight and that several men were wounded, met Terhune at the station with an ambulance. The naval officer's once white uniform was filthy, "and his head was grotesquely swallowed up by a large brimmed native straw hat."

Butler inquired about the wounded.

"There are no wounded," Terhune replied.

"What happened to your train then?"

"I had to leave it at León."

"Didn't you have a fight?"

"No."

Butler was mystified. "How did you get from León the thirty miles to that station where you telephoned me?"

"We walked," said the crestfallen sailor.

Butler couldn't believe it. "And you didn't even put up a fight for the train?"

"Oh," agonized Terhune, "you don't know that crowd. They're bloodthirsty. Even the women spit in your face. . . . I'm going to bed."

From the enlisted men, Butler received another account. The train had been stopped at León by an excited crowd, whose threats verily panicked Commander Terhune. He bolted from the train, and the enlisted men, lacking any orders, followed. "They felt miserably humiliated," Butler wrote, "and came to me boiling over with indignation." They gave Terhune the nickname "General Walkemback."

Butler confronted Terhune in his bedroom at the embassy. The naval officer was dressed "in a suit of blue silk pajamas [and was] sitting up in bed, with a bottle of Scotch and mineral water beside him." They must, he informed Terhune, retake the train, open the railroad and establish communications with the coast. Terhune refused. Butler requested permission to go it alone with the marines.

Again, Terhune refused. "No, it's too dangerous."

"I was disgusted," Butler wrote, "and left him with his Scotch."

Whether or not Butler really meant it at the time is not known, but his adjutant delivered Terhune an ultimatum. For the reputation of the naval service as well as the safety of Managua, the railroad must be reopened to Corinto. If Terhune refused, Butler would resign from the Marine Corps, citing Terhune's cowardice in recovering the train as the reason. Terhune finally assented to go along.

Butler, Terhune, and 100 bluejackets and marines took the wood train and headed north for León. It was very slow going, a few yards at a time, repairing broken track and damaged culverts. Approaching the bridge before town, the train was halted by a band of jeering rebels entrenched behind a barricade of adobe stone. Butler bluffed his way through, but at the other end of the bridge was another barricade and "at least a thousand excited little soldiers, armed with every kind of weapon from rifle to razor. . . . The rebels jumped up and down like maniacs," Butler remembered, "yelling blood-curdling threats and Central American insults at the top of their lungs."

Butler halted the train to take on fuel and water when a rebel general approached and shoved a pistol into his stomach. "If the train moves, I shoot," he said. Butler disarmed the *insurrecto* and took him hostage. The wood train rumbled into León, and there Terhune's train was returned.

They continued on to Corinto, repairing track all the way. There were rumors that the rebels had mined the tracks, Lieutenant Alexander Vandegrift remembered. Butler ordered Vandegrift to "take a corporal, get up on the front end of this train and look for mines." When the corporal inquired what he should do if he indeed saw a mine, the future victor of Guadalcanal had a simple answer. "You see a mine, you yell '*mine*' as loud as you can and jump as far as you can."[22]

At Corinto, units of the Pacific Fleet were at anchor, commanded by Rear Admiral William Southerland in the armored cruiser *California*. For the return trip to Managua, Butler loaded up another 200 bluejackets. The rebels had torn up the track again and repairs were made all the way back to the capital. At León, Butler left a strong detachment to keep the bridge and line clear and continued south. The rickety wood train had bad brakes, no whistle, and only a single lantern for light. A hapless cow was run down as was a flock of sheep. With slipping brakes, the train shot past the government outposts at Managua "like a toboggan on ice." The government troops, thinking the train was full of rebels, opened fire. The train raced past the station, smashing through the gates, and only halted when it hit an upgrade.[23]

Managua, however, was still cut off from the world and the rebels controlled all routes to the capital, north, south, and east. The morale of the government forces in the capital, about 4,000, hit bottom, and numbers began to melt away. Butler took unofficial command. "I had absolutely no authority for this step," he wrote, "but the government could not win without our support, and I knew which way the wind blew."[24]

Further support was well on its way. At League Island, "Uncle Joe" Pendleton's 800-man provisional marine regiment embarked for Panama. The *California* and *Denver* landing forces were already ashore at Corinto and the railroad towns along the line. The armored cruiser hove off for Balboa and returned on September 4 with Pendleton's marines. The store ship *Glacier* steamed into Corinto with provisions, and colliers *Prometheus* and *Saturn* with coal for the fleet. The armored cruiser *Colorado* and the peace cruiser *Cleveland* were en route. There would be nearly 2,500 men ashore when all arrived.

Southerland planned initially to reopen communications between Managua and the coast, and then to push down the line clearing the railroad to Granada. He ordered Pendleton's regiment to the capital, "peaceably if possible but using force if opposed." At León, "the hotbed of *insurrecto* feeling along your route," Pendleton was to pick up two companies of *California* bluejackets as reinforcements.[25]

"In your conversations with the better elements of this country," the admiral noted to his marine commanders, "make clear to them the most essential principles governing the rules of civilized warfare and the fact that you will neither permit the bombardment of unfortified towns nor inhuman or brutal practices."[26]

These were no hollow phrases. At León the site of a recent massacre, Pendleton sliced off Charles G. "Squeegee" Long's 300 man battalion, which was armed with a pair of Colts and 3-inch guns to monitor events and storm the town if necessary. Some three weeks before, the locals had inflicted on Díaz's army a terrible retribution there. Seven hundred government troops, about half of them Honduran mercenaries, under the Honduran General Duron, moved north from Managua to crush the rebellion in the center of Nicaraguan Liberalism. Of Duron's officers, two were a pair of "bilgers"—failures—from West Point, holding government commissions.

Duron had marched into the town and his troops went completely out of control, raping, looting, murdering at random and will. The townsfolk took to arms and struck back. As Butler later wrote, Duron's men "scurried like sheep" to a nearby hacienda. In the melee the bilgers were badly wounded. Surrounded in the walled estate, Duron opted to cut his way out. He formed his troops in column and crashed through the gate. But the locals had taken to the roofs, and "picked them off like clay ducks in a shooting gallery." The 700 men were virtually wiped out. The bilgers, however, did not participate in the sortie. Wounded and drunk, they were found hiding under beds and killed with the bayonet.

Duron and his army were buried in a mass grave. Later the father of one of the bilgers appealed to the United States and Nicaraguan governments for the return of his son's body. "Our Marines," Butler wrote, "subsequently had to spend a couple of weeks digging among the six-week-old corpses before they found the boys, who were identified by their West Point cadet buttons."[27]

Pendleton arrived in Managua on September 6 and Admiral Southerland set about restoring rail service to the coast. He hoped to have some trains running within a week, but saw there would be no regular schedule, as "the railroad people seem very dilatory." Still, he was pleased. "The situation now completely quiet," he reported, "and absolutely under the control of myself from Corinto [to] Managua, and it is reduced to the status [of an] ordinary Central American revolution."[28]

Southerland's next agenda was to push south and open the railroad to Granada. "This action," he noted, "should mark the beginning of the end . . . and thus stop further revolutionary movements in this country for all times." The town, bastion of Nicaraguan Conservatism, held about 25,000 people, and as Ambassador Weitzel noted to the State Department, "claims to represent the intelligence, wealth and purest Spanish blood of Nicaragua." It was being held in a state of terror by Mena's son Daniel, whom Weitzel characterized as "an irresponsible negroid Indian."[29]

In late July, on the day of Mena's attempted coup, Daniel had arrested the town's prominent citizenry and locked them in small, filthy cells, without toilets, food, or water. After several days, food was offered at 1,000 pesos a plate. The town's food stocks were confiscated, and his soldiers ran wild in a spree of looting. Mass starvation had already taken hold, among children particularly. Atrocities were committed, women terrorized, and as Weitzel reported, Daniel's soldiers entered a girls' school dormitory on "the pretext of looking for Government [troops] disguised as women, [and] compelled the occupants of the beds to prove their sex."

Appeals were sent to Mena for the evacuation of the women and children. He refused and issued orders that in the event Granada were attacked, women and children "of Government sympathy," would be banked as shields around his San Francisco church-arsenal stronghold.[30]

On September 15 Butler mustered 400 marines and blue-jackets, a pair of Colts and 3-inch guns, and loaded all on board a train packed with Red Cross supplies for Granada. The incline grade was steep, a condition the rebels had greatly exacerbated by greasing the tracks with milkweed. Steel spun futilely on steel and wheels refused to grip, "which forced us," Archy Vandegrift wrote, "to dismount frequently to push the train over the hills."[31]

Approaching Masaya, fifteen miles south of Managua, Butler's train had to pass between two small mountains, Coyotepe and Barranca, that commanded the valley and approach. Atop, in crude forts with a couple of field guns, were General Zeledón's Liberal rebels. Without warning, artillery fire fell about the train. A vigorously waved American flag had no effect. Butler reversed to a safe distance and with two aides went forward on foot. At a barbed wire barricade he demanded the rebel pickets take him to the rebel commander.

Blindfolded, the marines were taken inside the rebel lines, and there confronted General Zeledón, "a short plump man with a dark mustache." Butler demanded he remove himself from the heights, "and take your revolution elsewhere." Zeledón was ready to comply until he realized that Butler was a "mere" major of marines, and there were more exalted Americans near at hand. "I can't surrender the hills without talking to the Admiral," he said. Butler knew this would mean insufferable delay. "All admirals," he wrote, "like diplomats, love conferences."[32]

Butler was reinforced with an additional battalion and a battery of artillery, and the negotiations commenced. When Zeledón balked, Uncle Joe Pendleton, by nature a kindly man and much beloved by his men, brooked no further delay. "Unless by daylight tomorrow morning, September 19th, 1912," he wrote to the rebel, "you have completely evacuated all your positions threatening the railroad . . . and unless white flags are conspicuously displayed, indicating this complete evacuation, I shall attack you with all my guns and men, and drive you out."[33]

In high dudgeon, Zeledón vehemently protested the American

actions "in extenso." As for Pendleton's threat, he laid on Southerland's head all responsibility "that shall derive from [that] act of violence."[34]

The marines prepared for battle. "At four in the morning," remembered Butler, "we marched into position, ready to attack the two hills. Exactly at six o'clock the white flag went up. We were all disappointed because we knew we would have to come back sooner or later and put up a fight for those hills."[35]

In the early evening of the nineteenth, Butler loaded his battalion, bayonets fixed, in the Red Cross train and chugged south through Masaya. As a usual precaution, a flatcar had been coupled forward of the engine, and Butler sat up front, legs dangling. When nearly past the town, at Nindiri Station, two mounted men approached and opened fire. A shot struck the marine at Butler's side. "It is my opinion," Butler reported, "that [the Nicaraguan] was drunk, and ugly over our passage." Butler halted the train and cautioned his men to keep still and not return fire. The inebriated local continued with his pistol, and was soon joined by half a dozen others who commenced potting the boxcars. "It appeared to me," Butler continued, "that a 'row' was about to occur."[36]

As the train moved slowly forward, massed snipers in the houses that lined the streets on either side of the tracks opened a heavy fire. "We were," Butler noted, "in a damn nasty position." The marine machine gunners atop the boxcars returned fire. "By this time firing from the train and the streets . . . became general, everybody shooting in every direction . . . for about five minutes . . . then it gradually died out."[37]

The train moved forward; in its wake lay fifty-six dead rebels and seventy wounded, of whom twelve later died. In the first hours of September 20 General Zeledón's emissary arrived with profuse apologies. The attack was "unauthorized" and precipitated by persons over whom he exercised no control. Butler sent the aide back with a warning holding the rebel chief responsible for all "such breaks of faith." It was soon discovered, however, that the ambush was indeed premeditated, in fact, "carefully planned," and as Southerland noted, "an act of treachery on the part of General Zeledón."[38]

Repairing track all the way, Butler continued slowly on to Granada. Late on the twentieth, he arrived at the outskirts. The next morning he sent a message into the town demanding Mena's surrender, and then proceeded to construct an elaborate ruse.

Down the muzzles of his 3-inch field pieces he thrust long poles, covering the whole with tent flies. "They looked as long and as deadly as 14-inch guns." Mena's delegates were conducted blindfolded into the presence and were confronted by Butler's 400 troops, massed in such a way as to appear a much larger body. Butler demanded Mena surrender the railroad and town without a fight and remove his soldiers from the line of transit. If he refused, Butler threatened to "attack Granada with my big guns and all my regiments."[39]

With no response at the next dawn, Butler deployed his command, and marching down the track, advanced on the town. At the station he was met by Mena's legates bearing a white flag and the erstwhile war minister's surrender. Southerland and Pendleton arrived two days later and took the formal capitulation. All rebel soldiers were disarmed, and Mena, accompanied by the admiral, entrained for Corinto and exile in Panama.

The citizens of Granada were a pathetic sight and could not have lasted much longer. "On the day of the arrival of the marines," Weitzel noted, "a woman with five young children was planning to take them in a boat on the lake to drown them all in preference to the lingering death of starvation."[40]

The back of the revolution was broken, but Zeledón was still firmly entrenched in the hills about Masaya and showed no signs of giving up the fight. Pendleton concentrated his forces. The rebel positions were formidable. Coyotepe rose some 500 feet with steep slopes on all sides. Barranca, a thousand yards away, was half as high. Two thousand rebels, strongly entrenched with machine guns behind barbed wire, defended the heights.

To Pendleton's surrender demand, Zeledón disdainfully replied, "I have been reluctant to believe that it is signed by one trained in military matters who serves under the flag of the great American Nation that prides itself on being the guiding spirit of the Democratic Republics of the American Continent."[41]

On the morning of October 3 Pendleton's guns opened the bombardment. "Remembering our last experience with Zeledón," Butler wrote, "we were afraid the white flags would be displayed to cheat us out of a scrap again." There were no flags, and the guns continued all day. That night Uncle Joe's 850 marines and bluejackets moved into position, "as secretly as possible . . . and as near the summit [of Coyotepe] as possible without discovery." Butler would begin the attack before dawn the fourth, assaulting from the left. The center and right would be attacked simultaneously by the Americans and Nicaraguan government troops. "Hoping to see you on Coyotepe," Uncle Joe penned to Butler.[42]

All day the rebels stayed hidden and did not return fire. With the dark, Butler's men attempted some sleep on the cement drying floors of a coffee plantation. Before dawn, with no breakfast, the troops moved to the line of departure. "No one smoked," he remembered, "no one spoke. We marched forward in two lines, holding hands to keep from losing one another." The barbed wire in the rebels' outer perimeter was cut, the companies passed through the gaps and rapidly deployed.[43]

"While the foot of the hill was still wrapped in the misty shadows of the early morning," Pendleton recalled, "the crest was clearly outlined against the brightening sky. 'Advance' was the command given the battalion commanders, and 'Advance' was the command passed by them to the shadowy lines and passed in quiet undertones by the company officers, and the line moved toward the bottom of the slope."[44]

When twenty paces beyond the wire, a shot rang from the top of the hill, and rebel heads popped over the trench lips. The marine skirmish line opened fire and the rebels disappeared. Through his field glasses, Pendleton watched "the dust in little spurts rising from the edge of the parapet as the Springfield bullets clipped it . . . skimming the edge with wonderful accuracy."[45]

As the marines and bluejackets advanced in alternate company rushes, the rebels opened a heavy rifle and machine gun fire and men began to fall. The assault pressed on. Pendleton watched one marine, Durham, who was killed during the action, "standing erect in the face of the scorching fire as calmly as if on drill, as if he were showing how such a job should be done, he cut his way through the last of the barbed-wire entanglements."[46]

Bayonets fixed, the marines and bluejackets charged the final yards. The government troops, however, hung back. As Butler noted, "They discreetly waited to find out first what was going to happen to us." In less than an hour it was over. Three marines and twenty-seven rebels lay dead, nine rebels were taken prisoner, and the remainder fled. The marines then turned the rebel guns on Coyotepe at the Barranca fort, and its garrison joined their comrades in flight to Masaya. General Zeledón was probably killed by his own men while attempting escape; that at least is the accepted story. A letter from Butler to Southerland, however, suggests a different outcome. "Government forces have captured Ze-ledón," Butler reported, "and have asked me if we want him. Am sending force to Masaya at once to preserve order so if you direct I can have Zeledón sent back here under guard or protected by my men in Masaya. Personally would suggest that through some inaction on our part some one might hang him."*[47]

Once the hills were taken the hitherto inactive government troops attacked Masaya. The Liberal rebels, taking refuge in the cathedral, fought back savagely. As Butler passed through, he watched "native soldiers, half naked, parading in [looted] silk hats and women's underclothes. Everybody was reeling in circles, drunk and hilarious. A few were playfully shooting their own comrades. Otherwise there was no violence."[48]

The final significant operation of the 1912 intervention was the occupation of León, whose Liberal garrison still posed a threat to the railroad. But since their recent defeats, the León Liberals had become much discouraged and were actively seeking terms of surrender. Surrender, to the Americans, that is, as they had no wish to subject their city to the gentle ministrations of the government army.

On October 5 Squeegee Long received substantial reinforcements until his command aggregated 1,300 marines and blue-jackets. Along with his demand that the rebels evacuate the town came a grant of amnesty from President Díaz for common soldiers, but not for officers. "If your demands are refused," read Pendleton's instructions to Long, "and you can quietly capture any of the leaders, do so, and hold them hostages."[49]

Conditions in the city rapidly deteriorated. Long doubted the rebel leaders' ability to keep their soldiers in hand "in case of any drunkenness." On the night of the fifth there was considerable discharging of rifles in the streets.

Long deployed his troops. He planned to enter the city from the east with his main body, the regiment's 1st and 2nd battalions. The railroad station, at the north end, was already held by the armored cruisers' marine detachments. The *Colorado*'s bluejackets would advance on the south and occupy the key churches which were used by the rebels as fortified positions. The *California*'s bluejackets were assigned the pumping station and reservoir. Long's 3-inch guns sighted in on the cathedral.

On the morning of the sixth, Liberal legates arrived at Long's

---

*The admiral's response, if any, was not found by the author.

command post to negotiate the capitulation. By noon, however, they had lost control. The rebel soldiers were already engaged in a drunken looting spree and several fires were reported. By midafternoon Long, "decided that an immediate occupation of the city was necessary."[50]

What resistance there was "from unorganized and mostly drunk rebels" fell upon the *Colorado*'s bluejackets. They were 193 officers and men with a Colt machine gun and two 3-inch landing pieces. Their advance began on the town's south edge, and they immediately began taking fire from snipers in the outlying brush. Unscathed, the column entered the Avenida Central, where the advance guard 1st Company drove in the opposition and took position behind the abandoned rebel barricade.

Heavy firing erupted from ahead and from houses flanking the avenue. The Colt was brought up and stuttered into action. But after 125 rounds it jammed and went out of commission. The bluejackets worked around the barricade and up the street smashing in doors, and a number of civilians were taken prisoner. Rebel firing continued from the front and two sailors were killed. A 3-inch gun was manhandled into position and after four shots resistance on the Avenida ceased.

But the *Colorado*'s advance guard 1st Company had overreached, and was cut off far ahead of the skirmish line. Part of the 3rd Company advanced to regain contact. "Owing to the excessive heat and the poor condition of the roads," reported the bluejacket skipper, "it was impossible to keep up with the firing line with the 3-inch piece and the firing line failed to keep touch with the main body . . . many were if anything too impetuous in their advance." A second skirmish line formed and moved forward. Resistance slackened, and the *Colorado* battalion occupied its assigned objectives.[51]

"It is worthy of note," continued the naval officer, "that the natives frequently used the white flag as a means of safety during the advance of our men, and later on, from house or [garbled], would open fire." One of the ship's two casualties had been "considerably mutilated by machetes," and his shoes were stripped before the bluejackets could return and remove the corpse.[52]

"Things quiet in the city," reported Squeegee Long later. "We killed about fifty. . . . The sale of alcoholic liquors was prohibited and other regulations issued for the proper guidance of the inhabitants."[53]

The occupation of León ended the bipolar revolution, but to

insure that the peace would continue, Southerland sent a number of small mounted columns into the interior. Pendleton, with Butler as second in command, led the expedition to Matagalpa, sixty miles northeast of the capital. "I think nearly everybody," Uncle Joe reported, "on whatever political side they stand, was glad to see us, and I think they were impressed with the idea that the United States means that revolutions in Nicaragua are done with."[54]

By late November 1912, the bulk of the American forces were withdrawn. One company of marines remained at Managua as a legation guard, and for a time Squeegee Long's battalion garrisoned León. Before Christmas he reported of the city, "Today ends a week of religious festivities, during which there were no disturbances."[55]

5:

HAITI
1915–1934

We took over the guardianship, I guess you could call it, of the republic.

–Major General Walter Greatsinger Farrell,
 USMC, Ret.

It was a typically filthy day, but the sailors expected nothing else in mid-January off Cape Hatteras. On the wings of the open bridge, officers and bluejackets hunkered deeper into the folds of their sou'westers in a vain effort at keeping out the driving sleet. Driving through the nauseating Hatteras rollers, the big armored cruiser *Washington*'s knife-like bow clove the dirty green-black seas, sending a lash of salt spray and misery to the watch standers on deck.

The ship, with the marines' 12th Company embarked, was on her way to the welcome currents of the Gulf Stream and the Caribbean. From her mainmast whipped the blue, two-starred flag of Rear Admiral William Caperton, Commander, Cruiser Squadron, Atlantic Fleet. But there were no other vessels in stately line astern of the flagship. For it was a troubled world in 1915, and the Cruiser Squadron was spread over the oceans from the Caribbean to the eastern Mediterranean. The *Washington*'s first stop was scheduled at Santo Domingo, capital of the Dominican Republic, where the United States maintained customs house receivership.

In the relative comfort of the cruiser's radio room, a sailor tapped his key in acknowledgment and handed the message pad to the watch officer for decoding. In a few minutes it was on its way to "flag country." Admiral Caperton read the yellow form; it was from Secretary of the Navy Josephus Daniels and very urgent: "Proceed Cape Haïtien without delay."[1]

Cap Haïtien, Haiti's second city, sits on the northern pincer of the crab claw–shaped island of Hispaniola (which Haiti shares with the Dominican Republic), so there was no need to change course until the final leg. In the stoke holds, deep within the ship's bowels, engine order repeaters jangled and blackened firemen shoveled more coal under the *Washington*'s boilers. Pounding south the weather improved by the hour. Through the warm seas of the Silver Bank Passage, and west along Hispaniola's north coast, four heavy plumes of coal smoke marked her way. On January 23 the anchor roared out the hawsepipe.

The admiral's barge was smartly hoisted out, and was soon puffing for the jetty. With Admiral Caperton was Captain Edward L. Beach, in his dual role as the *Washington*'s skipper and the Cruiser Squadron's chief of staff. To Ned Beach, Cap Haïtien, a city of 25,000 souls, "presented the appearance of a ruined town. Business was at a standstill. The streets, still paved with cobblestones placed there by the French, one hundred and fifty years ago, were uncared-for. Walls of buildings were cracked and crumbling and in disrepair. But one thing was flourishing, and that was revolution."[2]

And that was a fact of life in Haiti. A land of black African slaves with a minority of mixed-blood mulattoes, she had, following a bloody uprising, declared her independence from France in 1804. The revolt ended with the death or expulsion of every white European and the birth of the world's first black republic; a pariah among the nations.

There came civil war, partition, rejoining, and then, in Haitian terms, relative stability, the state being ruled successively by one king, one emperor, one president, and three presidents-for-life. Near mid-century, even this measure of stability came to an end; for the next seventy-two years, until the United States intervention in 1915, Haiti suffered through 102 civil wars, revolutions, and palace revolts. Of the twenty-two heads of state during this time —seven between 1912 and 1915—only one served out his term in office. Twenty-eight times the United States Navy sent its ships into Haitian waters to protect American and foreign nationals. Indeed, since 1914, the Cruiser Squadron had been on almost constant patrol off the ports of the unhappy republic.

Beginning with the establishment of the Panama Canal Zone

in 1903, the United States took a far greater interest in Haiti than heretofore. Haiti's ports bordering the Windward Passage were coveted as coaling stations by several European powers, a hemispheric incursion the United States was determined to prevent.

In 1915 Haiti maintained a population of about two million —ninety percent of whom were Creole-speaking blacks, the large majority of them illiterate. The remaining ten percent, the *élite*, were mixed-race, Franco-black mulattoes. Their language was French; for the most part they were educated in France and formed the professional and governing class. The *élite* grew fat and rich off government jobs, contracts, and an enormous amount of graft. The two classes had nothing but contempt for each other.

The national treasury was nearly always broke, and huge loans on foreign banks saddled the economy with insurmountable debts. These rapidly increased as successive regimes sought to pay off short-term bonds floated to finance the revolutions that placed them in power. By 1912 practically all sources of revenue were pledged to interest payment, and the government was totally without funds for the day-to-day running of the country. Only a fixed amount, advanced monthly by the U.S.- and French-controlled National Bank, kept the state from complete insolvency.

Less than two months before Admiral Caperton received his orders to steam for Cap Haïtien, the economy collapsed. To pay off its mercenary retainers—the *cacos*—the government of President Davilmar Théodore printed millions of *gourdes*—the unit of currency, worth about twenty cents—on ordinary newsprint. They were worthless, but merchants were nonetheless extorted by the *cacos* to accept them at gun- and knifepoint.*

In the United States there was real fear of the *cacos* seizing the gold reserves of the National Bank. In response, Secretary of State William Jennings Bryan (whose view of Haiti can be summarized by his statement, "Dear me, think of it, Niggers speaking French") requested that the Navy Department send a vessel and remove the gold.[3]

On December 17, 1914, the gunboat *Machias* tied up in the harbor of the capital, Port-au-Prince. While all in the city were taking their noon rest, fifty marines marched to the bank, piled the gold onto mule carts and into the *Machias'* hold for safe trans-

*In the spring of 1990, as this book goes to press, the Haitian government is paying its army in cement and flour, to be sold on the black market for cash.

fer to the vaults of the National City Bank in New York. Haiti was outraged. Her ambassador in Washington angrily rounded on Secretary Bryan, calling the affair "a flagrant invasion of the sovereignty and independence of the Republic of Haiti."[4]

That was unquestionable, but so was the fear of the *cacos*— the perpetual wild card in the deadly game of Haitian politics. The *cacos*, whose name derived from the "kaa-ko" call of a local bird of prey, were descended from runaway slaves and generally lived in quasi-military bands in the north and central mountains. In times of relative peace, the *cacos* lived by pure banditry: preying on farmers, extorting whole villages, and robbing travelers on Haiti's few miles of bad road. The *cacos* took money from any revolutionary faction seeking the National Palace, serving as the insurgent force until their candidate achieved the presidency. If he lost, they retreated back into their mountain forts, or slipped over the border into the Dominican Republic. But if the revolution was successful, the *cacos* could expect their fair share of the national treasury. A president remained in office only so long as he paid. Once the money stopped, the *cacos* changed sides and supported the next contender.

This happened three times in 1914 alone. In October President Charles Zamor requested United States military intervention to prevent his ouster. Accordingly Secretary Bryan issued instructions, which arrived on the desk of Marine Corps Commandant George Barnett, "to take charge of . . . Port-au-Prince . . . and restore Charles Zamor." At Guantánamo Bay the transport *Hancock* embarked the 5th Marine Regiment and steamed for Port-au-Prince, but was too late. Zamor was out and the new president, Davilmar Théodore of the newsprint banknotes, assumed the mantle.[5]

The *Hancock* was hardly back at her moorings at Guantánamo Bay when the next revolution began brewing up. As always, it began in the north. "The first battle invariably was fought at Kilometer Post 17, on the railroad to Grande Rivière," noted Major Smedley Butler. If the rebels triumphed, "they marched south to Port-au-Prince, and if the President was wise, he bolted with the treasury before the rebel army reached the outskirts of town."[6]

This latest interruption was the work of General Vilbrun Guillaume Sam, a black whom President Théodore had just appointed to command the government's forces in the Department of the North. Swarms of destitute *cacos*, their newsprint currency spent, pillaged their way home and were enlisted by General Sam. From Cap Haïtien, the departmental seat, United States Consul Lemuel Livingston kept the State Department apprised of events.*

At the White House Woodrow Wilson fumed. In a memorandum to Secretary Bryan, he noted, "The more I think about the situation, the more I am convinced that it is our duty to take immediate action. . . . I mean to send a commissioner there . . . and to say to them as firmly and definitely as is consistent with courtesy and kindness that the United States cannot consent to stand by and permit revolutionary conditions to constantly exist." But the mission resulted in complete failure. In a glaring error of omission, Bryan neglected to provide the envoys with credentials. They were rebuffed at every office, and quit Haiti within a week of their arrival.[7]

On January 15 Vilbrun Guillaume Sam, still playing the charade of holding the government's commission in the north, gathered the leading citizens of Cap Haïtien and announced his presidential candidacy. Under the circumstances, he told his audience, it was the only course now open. The *cacos* were advancing on the town, and Davilmar Théodore had given him no means to resist. Then, with masterful stage management, a thousand *cacos*, under "General" Metellus, complete with several pieces of artillery, paraded down the Cap's main street. For once, there was no looting, extortions, or random shootings. "This," cabled Lemuel Livingston, "is entirely exceptional as a revolutionary incident."[8]

On January 19 Metellus' artillery banged out a seventeen-gun salute, and Sam proclaimed himself *Chef du Pouvoir Exécutif* (Chief of Executive Power). "Vilbrun Guillaume Sam is now considered the future president of Haiti," Livingston wired. "He will march to Port-au-Prince without any opposition, and the Government of [Davilmar] Théodore will fall without the firing of a single shot." Within hours of the telegram's arrival at the State Department, the navy's powerful transmitters clicked out the orders to Admiral Caperton: "Proceed Cape Haïtien without delay."[9]

Livingston was at quayside when Admiral Caperton came ashore at the Cap and suggested a call on Guillaume Sam as soon as it could be arranged. It occurred two days hence,

---

*Lemuel Livingston was an American black who had married into a prominent Cap Haïtien family. His political acumen was excellent, and his advice invariably correct.

on January 25, and was a scene right out of a comic opera. Admiral Caperton remembered, "We were met at the door by a tatterde-malion soldiery, while inside a very gorgeous black gentleman, arrayed like a head bellhop at the Waldorf, directed us through a room and then up a pair of steps . . . where he took our caps and gloves . . . saying the General would be pleased to see us in a moment. . . . Once upstairs in the reception room, a large por-trait caught my eye. It seemed to be of some familiar face. In a moment General Guillaume Sam appeared. Greatly to my sur-prise, I recognized him as the bellhop; only this time he had discarded his coat for another, but more elaborate one, and an enormous sword clanked around his heels. A glance at the portrait on the wall convinced me. It was also Guillaume Sam."[10]

The dapper, ramrod straight admiral from Tennessee proved a consummate diplomat and took no outward notice of Sam's play-acting. For his part, Sam was the perfect host, and the meeting came off well. Sam pledged he would neither "loot, or burn down cities, or fire in the cities"; a singular commitment from the com-mander of a *caco*-backed revolution. And Sam kept his word, though perhaps the reason for this was the admiral's decision to "escort" the revolution during its traditional southward march.[11]

For this work the burly *Washington* was ill-suited and the peace cruiser *Des Moines* and gunboat *Wheeling* arrived, and at every port on Sam's trek south there awaited a United States warship. He took it all in good humor. "I met him at each town," Caperton recalled, "and so he finally laughingly said to me, 'Every time I enter a city I find your representatives outside . . . asking me to behave myself.' . . . and upon the whole [he] did very well, con-sidering everything."[12]

On February 5 Sam entered Gonaïves, Haiti's third city, just short of the halfway mark to the capital. The government of Davilmar Théodore reacted feebly, according to Ned Beach, "gathering volunteers with clubs and sending them north tied together with ropes." Two weeks later Sam's forces, joined by additional *caco* bands, surrounded Port-au-Prince and cut the water supply.[13]

At noon, February 22, the guns of Fort Nationale and Battery St. Claire boomed out to the capital that yet another president was bound for exile.

Three days later, in the midst of a triumphal procession, Vil-brun Guillaume Sam entered Port-au-Prince, and immediately spread around $50,000 in gold to the *caco* chiefs who proclaimed him *Chef du Pouvoir Exécutif*. In a week, the National Assembly made it official. Admiral Caperton's mission to Haiti ended for the time being, the *Washington* steamed for Mexican waters.

For a couple of weeks things went quite well for Vilbrun Guillaume Sam. The gold kept the *caco* chiefs quiescent, and they paid their soldiers in what remained of Davilmar Théodore's newsprint banknotes—still negotiable at a discount rate. Additionally, a portion of the revenue from the customs houses was actually budgeted for legitimate government expenses.

But neither the gold, the money, nor the deceptive calm that heralded Sam's regime could last. The treasury was soon depleted as Sam doled out about $24,000 each week to finance his revolutionary debts, and by late March a new revolution, led by *élite* Dr. Rosalvo Bobo, was already festering in the north. A month later Bobo's *caco* army captured Cap Haïtien and looted the customs house. Sam's supporters and appointees fled for their lives into the foreign consulates. The *cacos'* depredations on behalf of Dr. Bobo took on grisly proportions. Two village leaders were beheaded and others shot out of hand for not submitting to their extortions. From his consular balcony, Lemuel Livingston watched the lopped heads paraded through the streets. On May 19 a general massacre in the consulates was prevented only when the French cruiser *Descartes* put ashore her landing force.

Sam's reaction in Port-au-Prince was typical of an about-to-be-deposed Haitian president. His press-gangs combed the streets and outlying villages, clubbing old men and boys into ragged formations, and then, binding them with ropes, forced them to stumble north to fight. As an insurance policy, Sam's police arrested about 200 of the mulatto *élite*, thought to be supporters of Dr. Bobo, and cast them into the capital's penitentiary.

Woodrow Wilson dispatched yet another commission, this time with credentials, headed by New York attorney Paul Fuller. "Only an honest and efficient government deserves support," the President wrote. "The Government of the United States [cannot] justify the expenditure of money or the sacrifice of American lives in support of any other kind."[14]

In Port-au-Prince, Fuller presented the American demands, which were essentially the gist of the Roosevelt Corollary to the Monroe Doctrine: Haiti must accept a binding United States role in her political and economic affairs; absolutely no concessions granted to foreign powers of naval bases or coaling stations; submission to immediate arbitration of outstanding external debts; and the right of American military intervention should conditions so warrant. Hardly unexpectedly, though Woodrow Wilson was sufficiently naive to be surprised by the reaction, the Haitians rejected the terms outright. They refused even to negotiate, or to accept any American aid for the restoration of order.

Fuller took leave of Haiti on June 27 and submitted his report. The Haitian government, he felt, was incapable of negotiating in good faith, and the chaotic conditions were far beyond its means to control. He advised the President to land the marines and exact a treaty placing Haiti in virtual protective custody of the United States. Woodrow Wilson agreed. "Action is evidently necessary and no doubt it would be a mistake to postpone it long."[15]

The first steps were already taken. In response to the collapse of government authority in the north and the politically uncomfortable presence of the *Descartes*, Admiral Caperton again received orders to steam for Cap Haïtien. With the *Washington* and the armed yacht *Eagle*, he arrived with a maximum of salutes and ceremony on July 1, informing the French captain that the United States Navy would now take over the peacekeeping in the town.

While the *Washington* swung to her hook in the roads, the handy *Eagle* was sent inshore, the better for her pair of 6-pounder guns to cover the bridge over the Grande Rivière. A marine landing party occupied the United States consulate and set up a field radio enabling uninterrupted communications between ships and shore.

Ned Beach, Livingston, and a squad of eight marines marched inland in hopes of contacting both the local government commander and Dr. Rosalvo Bobo. To each of these men, the message was unequivocal: all further fighting must take place east of the Grande Rivière, well clear of the town. Dr. Bobo proved elusive, but they managed to locate one of the doctor's "cabinet ministers" by a deserted village. There was an eerie feeling to the place. "The only thing living in it was a donkey," Ned Beach remembered.[16]

But a few miles beyond, through houseless scrub and jungle, the party came to a clearing that swarmed with *cacos*. "A more villainous appearing set of men were never gathered together," Ned Beach wrote. "All were but slightly clad, and each was armed with a musket, a pistol, a sword, and a long, vicious knife. . . . Each man looked to be a diabolical devil." The admiral's message was delivered. Beach, Livingston, and the marines were treated to a meal of coffee, green oranges, and "a great, fat, beautiful dressed turkey," and then they returned to the Cap. The warning had its effect, and save for some desultory sniping across the Grande Rivière, Cap Haïtien remained quiet.[17]

Then, in the predawn hours of July 27, Haiti exploded in blood. In Port-au-Prince, Charles de Delva, ex–police chief in the government of ex-President Oreste Zamor, left his asylum in the Portuguese legation. With thirty-six followers he surrounded the National Palace, torched the outbuildings with lamp oil, and opened fire. Vilbrun Guillaume Sam, his family, and a few retainers, held out until daybreak. Alone, and wounded in the leg, he managed an escape to the French legation.

The events that followed were all too common to Haitian politics. Rifle-firing mobs thronged the capital's streets. A Committee of Safety was organized as a provisional government, and a crowd surged to the penitentiary to liberate Sam's insurance policy hostages. They were met by consummate horror. On the orders of police chief General Charles-Oscar Etienne, nicknamed "the Terrible," the prison guards were directed "to shoot all [political] prisoners!" Compared to what occurred, ordinary shooting would have been a merciful death.

"The prisoners," commented Marine Corps Major General Walter Greatsinger Farrell, "were held in these two rows of 'lion cages,' sort of like you would see in a zoo. He had the gendarmes go down the fronts of the cages, and starting in the first cage on both sides, they began shooting the prisoners."[18]

A member of one of Haiti's most prominent *élite* families survived. "A flash of red light entered our cell, my comrades were slaughtered, disemboweled, reduced to a mass of flesh. . . . Prisoners trying to escape through a curtain of bullets fell to earth squirming and gutted, or were caught and bayoneted."[19]

For hours the butchery continued. "Terrific firing in the town," reported R. Beale Davis, Jr., the young American chargé d'affaires. Investigating for himself Davis made his way to the prison. "Bodies lay piled together just as they had fallen, and from their appearance, it looked as if every sort of weapon had been used." Ned Beach considered it "the most horrible atrocity of Haiti's history."[20]

The British ambassador cabled the Foreign Office: "They were found shot, hacked, mutilated, and disemboweled—the walls and floors of the prison were spattered with their blood, their brains, and their entrails." The exact number slaughtered is unknown; Beale Davis estimated "nearly 200." General Charles-Oscar Etienne fled to the Dominican legation.[21]

"Before long," Major General Farrell continued, "there were enough of these people, bleeding and dead, so that the blood was running down and out under the penitentiary wall, into the outside gutters. A mob started to form. They got some great big sugar kettles, real big ones, like a hog-dipping kettle, and stuck them under the outflow to catch the blood—there is plenty of room, about four or five feet. Then they brought these jeroboams of rum, looted a hardware store for tin cups, and poured the rum into the kettles. They mixed the blood and the rum up and started passing it out. The mob got drunk on the combination."[22]

Dressed in morning coat, striped trousers, silk topper, and gloves, the father of three sons butchered in the prison yard presented himself at the Dominican legation doors. He sent in his calling card to Charles-Oscar Etienne, and when that worthy appeared, put three bullets into his chest. The mob broke through the gates, and Etienne's body was dragged into the street. The British ambassador informed his superiors, "It was shot at, hacked at, and defiled by every passer-by. . . . By evening [it] had become an unrecognizable pulp of flesh." The next morning, the offal was doused with cooking oil and set alight, cleansing the gutter of whatever the city's pariah dogs had left.[23]

A mob of 100 armed men, mostly relatives of the slain hostages, attempted to storm the French legation. Beale Davis was within. "[Sam] was in a perfect frenzy of fear, creeping about the house like a hunted animal, or terror stricken that when passing an open window he would crawl on all fours for fear someone on the outside would see him." Five times before dusk Ambassador and Mme. Girard, aided by the diplomatic corps, held the revenge-crazed mob at the gates.[24]

All during the day at Cap Haïtien, scraps of information reached the various consulates. By early evening a cable from Beale Davis confirmed that a revolution had overthrown Vilbrun Guillaume Sam. Several legations at the capital were under siege, and warships were required at once. Immediately Admiral Caperton radioed the Navy Department, "Situation very grave . . . am proceeding with *Washington* to Port-au-

Prince. . . . Have requested company of marines at Guantánamo Bay to embark [in] *Jason* for expeditionary service in Haiti."[25]

"7:00 P.M.," penned the *Washington*'s officer of the deck in the log. "Commenced heaving short, making all preparations for getting under way." It was a terse notation, "boiler plate" some would call it, a standard entry in any deck log. None could foresee that it presaged nineteen years of United States military occupation of Haiti; a scrub brush, as Assistant Secretary of State Alvey Adee put it, to scour the "public nuisance at our doors."

In Port-au-Prince the morning of July 28 gave over to long, wailing processions bearing the coffins of the slain prisoners. From dawn to noon the church bells tolled. The dead were barely in the ground when a group of about eighty mourners smashed through the French legation doors in a mad search for Vilbrun Guillaume Sam. Nothing and no place was spared, and the building was ransacked before Sam was found cowering in Ambassador Girard's lavatory. Knives plunged and hacked away at his form. Then, still alive, Sam was impaled on the legation's iron gate posts. From these lances the body was thrown to the gravel drive where a machete-wielding mob chopped it to bits. The head was stuck on a pole, and the torso, bound with ropes, was dragged through the streets.

"11:40 A.M.," noted the *Washington*'s officer of the deck. "Anchored in Port-au-Prince, Haiti." They were a mile from shore, and from the bridge wing, Admiral Caperton and Captain Beach stared through their glasses at the hideous scenes being played out on the waterfront.

The gig was hoisted out, and with an armed crew Ned Beach headed for shore. Vainly he searched for anyone in civil or military authority. He remembered the chaos, "Crowds of citizens were rushing about, some shooting weapons pointed upwards. Soldiers were running up and down, also shooting. Officers on small horses were dashing aimlessly through the streets." At the American legation Beach met with Beale Davis who confirmed the situation in the capital had reached social and political collapse. His British and French colleagues agreed, and all returned in the gig to the *Washington.*

"The diplomats pleaded with me to land forces," Admiral Caperton remembered, "and to do it as quickly as possible, as they had no idea what might or might not happen."[26]

At the State Department, the new Secretary, Robert Lansing,

read the incoming cables. At 3:00 P.M., just the time of the ambassadorial conference on board *Washington*, the navy's transmitters were keyed, and the United States committed itself irrevocably to intervention. To Admiral Caperton went the order, "State Department desires American forces to be landed Port-au-Prince and American and foreign interests protected."[27]

But Caperton had already decided. "This force," he dictated to his flag secretary, "will occupy Port-au-Prince for the purpose of protecting life and property and preserving order." Marine Captain George van Orden would command the landing force. In addition to the *Washington*'s marine detachment and the embarked 12th Expeditionary Company, 173 bluejackets were mustered. In all there were 340 officers and men, hardly enough to march into, let alone pacify, a riot-thralled city of 100,000 inhabitants.[28]

Throughout the ship, preparations were gotten in hand. The men donned light marching order, with bedroll, rifle, fifty rounds of ammunition, and one day's rations and water. While they assembled on the forecastle, 1-pounder guns were mounted in the boats for direct landing support.

The landing site posed a problem. The nearest approach, from the wharf directly in front of the city, was considered too hazardous. There was no way of gauging initial resistance, and to advance frontally in the night, through narrow streets with green troops invited catastrophe. Van Orden opted to come ashore at Bizoton, the Haitian navy yard two miles west of the capital. Its distance from the city gave the force some time to sort themselves out, and the march could proceed along what passed for a decent road. Further, van Orden's left flank, hugging the bay, would be covered by the *Washington*'s armed boats.

By 4:45 P.M., all was ready. The steam launches, with cutters in tow, puffed alongside, and from the bridge came the thin wail of a boatswain's pipe, "Land the landing force!"

In less than an hour the last squad splashed over the gunwales and trotted up the beach. Working fast, van Orden divided his troops into three echelons. Captain Giles Bishop's 12th Company formed the advance guard. Van Orden commanded the main body in the center, and half the bluejackets guarded the rear at Bizoton. To cover the right, landward flank, two-man patrols were sent east of the Bizoton–Port-au-Prince road. In ten minutes van Orden gave the order to march.

In open columns, well spaced, Giles Bishop brought the advance guard to the southern end of Port-au-Prince, the broken walls of Fort Lerebours. The main body closed up and took station to the right—landward—flank. Patrols were sent up the capital's five main north-south streets. The deployment covered a goodly portion of the "native district," where any resistance was sure to come. But except for the muffled crack of the odd rifle somewhere in the city, all was quiet.

During the landing force's march to Fort Lerebours, Ned Beach entered the National Palace where he found General Ermane Robin, the titular commander of the Port-au-Prince garrison. Beach pleaded with him to order his troops back into barracks. But there was no longer a chain of command through which the order could pass, and large bodies of soldiers continued to roam the streets. Beach requested the general accompany him to the southern suburbs to meet the advancing columns and guide them into the city. Robin agreed, and the two men set off on foot. At Fort Lerebours they met one of Bishop's points moving up the street.

As day faded to dusk, random sniping popped along the front and the patrols reported mobs of disorganized soldiers. Yet so disciplined was the landing force, and remarkably so for largely untried troops, that not a single man fired his rifle in a wasted response.

Van Orden ordered the advance to continue. Slowly, keeping their intervals so as not to present bunched targets, the marines and bluejackets cautiously moved through the darkening streets. From the alleys and the occasional upper window, Haitian soldiers, joined by some civilians, kept up a desultory fire. These snipers were quickly silenced as Bishop sliced off sections and squads to flush out their nests. Two Haitians were killed and ten wounded in the process. But most of the Haitian soldiery were more than glad to be out of it and large groups willingly surrendered their arms without incident.

Shortly after 6:00 P.M., the columns reached the Rue des Casernes, Port-au-Prince's central east-west artery. Van Orden brought the main body to the gates of the National Palace and was met by a large and noisy mob of soldiers and civilians. The Haitians loosed a few shots, but were quickly disarmed and all initial resistance ceased.

Night settled on Port-au-Prince, and van Orden made his deployments. Giles Bishop and the 12th Expeditionary Company patrolled the legations and foreign quarter. The *Washington*'s marines marched up to the Vallière market square astride the railroad to prevent armed bands from infiltrating the city from the north. At the Champ de Mars, the huge square separating the legations and foreign sections from the rest of the capital, van Orden bivouacked the main body.

With its imposing name, the cobbled square was laid out in the grand French manner. Ideal for military spectacles, and fronting the National Palace, it was the logical ground to concentrate the landing force. However, before the marines and bluejackets bedded down, there was much work to be done, and they set to in the classic labor of policing the area.

Surgeon Cuthbertson found the Champ de Mars appalling. "The filthiest and most unsanitary place in the city," he wrote, "covered with filth, triturated dried human excrement, dust fouled with spit, fruit skins, banana stems, and in one place, a shallow pool of foul smelling water. . . . The whole was pervaded with a heavy odor, worse than a stable, and more like an open air privy."[29]

While his men stood their watches or shoveled muck, van Orden with General Robin at his side toured the city, quieting the Haitian soldiery and preventing further disorder. For the first time in weeks, Port-au-Prince settled into an uneasy calm.

The next morning, July 29, Admiral Caperton directed Ned Beach to assume military command on shore, and if the situation warranted, civil authority as well: "Take up your quarters in the [American] Legation. Give what orders you deem necessary. . . . Under no circumstances whatever, haul down any Haitian flag. . . . Find out where the government money is kept. Take any necessary measures to protect it. Find out what weapons and ammunition are in the city, and where they are."[30]

Marine patrols combed the city. All citizens found carrying arms had them confiscated and were sent about their business. Astride the railroad to the north and south, small command posts were established to disarm any *cacos* entering the capital. In late afternoon, the collier *Jason* steamed in from Guantánamo Bay with the 24th Company.

Just as these marines were coming ashore, word was received of an impending *caco* attack from the south. Leaving detachments to maintain order in the city's center, van Orden deployed in the

ruins of Fort Lerebours. In the *Washington,* the starboard batteries
were loaded and trained on the beach. At 8:00 P.M., the *cacos*
attacked, opening a heavy harassing fire from the overgrown
brush beyond the city's last houses. Most of this shooting fell on
the naval companies, their white uniforms presenting a fine target.
But the *cacos* were no match for the disciplined, well-aimed fire
of the marines. Aided by the *Washington's* powerful searchlights,
the *cacos* were driven from cover and, leaving six dead and two
wounded, retreated into the hills. Two sailors were killed, one of
whom was Seaman William Gompers, nephew of labor leader
Samuel Gompers.

On board the *Washington* Admiral Caperton
pondered the immediate future. As yet he had not an inkling of
what the State and Navy departments planned for his fiefdom.
The landing force had only the most tenuous grip on Port-au-
Prince, and the place was still infested with about 1,500 *cacos,* as
well as the ragtags and remnants of the Haitian Army. Further
complicating matters were reports from Cap Haïtien of new violence and revolutionary activity fomented by Dr. Rosalvo Bobo.
If his superiors expected him to hold the capital, and pacify the
countryside as well, then substantial reinforcements were required. Caperton radioed his concerns to Navy Secretary Daniels:
"No cause for alarm, but absolutely necessary I have sufficient
force to handle situation. . . . At least one regiment of marines
. . . at Port-au-Prince at once. . . . What action [Haitian government and insurgent] army in north will take when news reaches
them of American occupation not known. They can reach Port-
au-Prince in one week."[31]

In Washington, Robert Lansing put the "distressing and very
perplexing" Haitian situation to Woodrow Wilson. The President
passionately believed in constitutional government, to be imposed
at bayonet point if need be, and to Lansing he was unequivocal:
"There is nothing to do but to take the bull by the horns and
restore order . . . and put an end to revolution. . . . In other words,
we consider it our duty to insist on constitutional government
there, and will, if necessary, if they force us to it as the only way,
take charge of elections and see that a real government is erected
which we can support."[32]

With Wilson's solid backing, Caperton's request for reinforcements was handled swiftly. On July 30 the machinery of the naval

service cranked into high gear. Five companies of the 2nd Marine Regiment at League Island, Philadelphia, "fully equipped for shore service in the tropics," were ordered to embark in the battleship *Connecticut*. An additional 126 men, new recruits from the Marine Barracks, Norfolk, would board as the ship swept past the Virginia capes. Colonel Eli Cole, one of the Marine Corps' brainier officers, was called from Annapolis to assume command.

At League Island, the sailors and marines labored through the night preparing their expeditionary gear and loading ship. Colonel Cole arrived at 8:00 A.M. on July 31. At pierside, he found the regiment already formed in column of companies, "completely equipped and ready to march on board the vessel." An hour later, the *Connecticut*'s boatswain's mate of the watch put his call to his lips, "Shift colors; the ship is underway!" It had all been done in less than twenty-four hours.[33]

The military situation, for the moment, had stabilized, giving Caperton and Beach an opportunity to deal with the political vacuum. "The State Department from dispatches received today," the admiral radioed to Secretary Daniels, "evidently thinks that a de facto government exists at Port-au-Prince. No de facto government exists here. All government functions are at present carried on by a committee of citizens practically under my direction."[34]

This was somewhat stretching the point. A Revolutionary Committee was formed almost as soon as the first knife was plunged into Guillaume Sam's chest. Each morning Ned Beach met with its members, who were invariably polite, but offered no assistance in bringing about a free election. "The chief interest of this Committee," Beach said, "was to convince me that [Sam] had been eliminated for the purpose of having Dr. Bobo made president, and we Americans were in honor bound not to interfere."[35]

Within days of the landing, the committee tested its strength by throwing opponents in jail. This Caperton refused to tolerate, and he demanded and received their release. Stopping at nothing, the committee commandeered the telegraph office for its exclusive use and flooded the country with pro-Bobo propaganda. In this, too, Caperton intervened, ordering the marines to kick the committee out and restore general service.

But the committee was not yet done with mischief. It tapped hidden government vaults and distributed the funds to members and supporters. Caperton ordered the marines to seize every last *gourde*. They were deposited into a special restricted account in the National Bank, with the *Washington*'s paymaster exercising sole fiduciary power. This had unfortunate peripheral consequences. The deposit was labeled "Admiral Caperton Account" and it prompted irresponsible elements to declare, "Admiral Caperton has already placed to his personal credit the sum of $216,000 as his share of the pillage of the Treasury."[36]

Feeding Port-au-Prince was a major problem. The *cacos* were tearing up the few miles of ramshackle railroads and only a trickle of food made its way to market. "Provisions greatly increased in price," Caperton reported to Secretary Daniels. "Poorer classes without food, and many suffering greatly." As an emergency measure, navy rations were given to the local clergy for disbursement. But it was a temporary solution at best. Until the *cacos* were smashed, their power and influence destroyed, no stability could ever be achieved.[37]

In the capital alone the *cacos* outnumbered the landing force by almost four to one. They had weapons hidden in every hole and corner of the city, and were demanding the election of Rosalvo Bobo as president. In the north the *Eagle* reported heavy firing at the outskirts of Cap Haïtien, and large *caco* bands advancing on the town. The situation was alarming. "Arrival of [another] regiment of marines is demanded . . . with least possible delay," the admiral radioed to Secretary Daniels. The armored cruiser *Tennessee* tied up at League Island to await further developments. At Headquarters Marine Corps plans were set in motion to ship the 1st Regiment and activate the staff of the 1st Marine Expeditionary Brigade.[38]

Admiral Caperton also had his hands full with the several thousand Haitian troops in Port-au-Prince. Virtually all had been press-ganged into service by various regimes, and they wandered leaderless and penniless in the capital's streets. On August 3 Secretary Daniels was informed, "Last night found squads of native soldiers . . . posted all over the city. [They] challenged everybody and demanded countersign. This gave rise to uneasiness." Who ordered the troops out is unclear, though all evidence pointed to the Revolutionary Committee.[39]

It was plain they were conspiring to grab power in the city, either for their own ends, or to foster the candidacy of Rosalvo

Bobo, and the Port-au-Prince garrison provided a handy tool. But on the morning of August 4 the *Connecticut* steamed into port, and the committee's plans became moot. Colonel Cole reported on board the *Washington* and received his orders: take command of all United States forces ashore and disband the Haitian Army.

The move took the Revolutionary Committee totally by surprise. During Ned Beach's daily ritual of presiding over their meeting, the marines fanned out and marched with fixed bayonets into the Haitian barracks, the arsenal, and every military facility in the capital. Three thousand modern rifles, four million rounds of small arms ammunition, a number of machine guns, and the breech blocks of a dozen field pieces were seized.

The Haitian soldiers were formed in ranks, given a ten-*gourde* note (about two dollars), told they were no longer in the army, and marched out of town. They went wild in their elation. Ned Beach watched them, "tearing from their clothes the red tape that had meant they were soldiers. But when they knew they were to receive what they considered to be the huge sum of ten *gourdes*, pandemonium broke loose. They shouted and howled and yelled, danced and ran about."[40]

The committee was livid. "Each Committeeman jumped to his feet," Beach remembered. "Wild, indignant protestations were shouted. The ground under them was being torn away. Their power had vanished."[41]

In the north, the running sore of rebellion oozed around Cap Haïtien. On the day the Port-au-Prince garrison was disbanded, Dr. Bobo's *cacos* attempted a march into the town. It came to naught when the *Eagle*'s gunners lobbed some well-placed 6-pounder shells just to their front, chasing the bandits back into the jungle. The skipper informed the *caco* chiefs that if they tried it again, his gunners would adjust their aim accordingly. The promise was bolstered when the old gunboat *Nashville* chugged into the Cap and her bluejacket landing force dug in astride the Grande Rivière bridge.

Tensions were relieved the next day when the last of Vilbrun Guillaume Sam's army, about 450 hungry and very scared soldiers, gave up their arms to *Nashville*'s bluejackets and fled for their lives to the bishop's palace. Then, in what seemed to be the hidden hand of a master stage manager, about 2,000 *cacos* magically appeared at the Grande Rivière bridge, surrendered their rifles, and marched into the town.

With every vestige of Sam's regime toppled, the Cap's leading citizens formed a Committee of Safety and pledged their allegiance to Rosalvo Bobo. He was now definitely a man to be reckoned with; firmly established in Haiti's second city, nearly every *caco* chief rallied to his cause. Worse, the wily *cacos*, though ostensibly disarmed, had cached arms and ammunition all over the Cap. Livingston estimated that thousands of the bandits could arrive at Port-au-Prince's gates in ten days.

To forestall that calamity Admiral Caperton organized a commission of prominent Port-au-Prince citizens. Accompanied by Caperton's French-speaking aide, Lieutenant Coffey, they sailed in the *Jason* with orders to bring Dr. Bobo to the capital. Both to augment the commission's authority and in response to Livingston's message, "United States forces insufficient to maintain peace and patrol city," the *Connecticut* was dispatched as well.

When the ships arrived at Cap Haïtien, Lieutenant Coffey got Sam's soldiers out of the bishop's palace and sent them home. He also deemed it prudent to evacuate the St. Joseph Convent, and its nuns took up quarters in the coal-grimy *Jason*. But Coffey's great coup was in convincing Dr. Bobo to take passage to Port-au-Prince. The doctor boarded the collier with a staff of twenty-six "generals" and talked nonstop to everyone of his plans for Haiti's regeneration. Coffey, after listening to incessant monologues, considered Bobo mentally unbalanced and a dangerous adversary.

"Some unrest and agitation in Port-au-Prince," radioed Caperton on August 5 to Secretary Daniels. "Am taking extra precautions tonight." Three companies were ordered out. They marched into Fort Nationale and seized "14 cannon of various kinds," 450 rifles, and a million rounds of ammunition. Trouble also threatened at Gonaïves. With neither troops nor ships to spare, Caperton had some machine guns mounted in the navy tug *Osceola*, and sent her chugging north.[42]

A legislative presidential election was scheduled for Sunday, August 8.* This Caperton considered "inopportune." Bobo was still in transit, and a candidate more amenable to the United States point of view was preferred. The Haitian Congress agreed to the admiral's "request" and the election was postponed.

---

*The presidents were elected indirectly through legislative rather than popular votes.

The most desirable candidate was Solon Ménos, Haiti's ambassador in Washington; but he was too valuable in that post to risk his recall. "In his absence," Caperton noted to Daniels, "I have been informed that [Philippe Sudre] Dartiguenave, President of the Senate, is the candidate likely to be elected. He, I have learned from my sources, is a man of personal honor, patriotism, and ability." Even better, he had never been connected with revolutionary movements, had no use for the *cacos*, and supported political and economic agreements with the United States. "Should he be elected," Caperton continued, "he must be sustained by the protection of the United States. . . . Only fear of *cacos* would elect Bobo, and if he were elected, a revolution against him would undoubtedly break out unless the United States prevented it."[43]

On August 6 the *Jason* returned to Port-au-Prince. Down her accommodation ladder and into a launch stepped Rosalvo Bobo, carrying a suitcase printed with large white letters, "Dr. Rosalvo Bobo, *Chef de Pouvoir Exécutif*." Awaiting his arrival in the *Washington*, Ned Beach watched "while Dr. Bobo mounted the gangway . . . with a rather slow stride, intended perhaps, to be stately and majestic. . . . On reaching the quarterdeck, with a grand air he removed his silk hat and held it extended, after the manner of potentates; and then he stood there, in his Prince Albert coat, awaiting the salute of guns, and the beating of drums, the blowing of bugles, the presenting of arms; courtesies and honors always accorded a visiting head of state." The doctor waited in vain. There were no sideboys, no marines drawn up, no men at the saluting guns, no signalman to break out a presidential flag at the masthead. There was only a ship's officer. "Howdy do, Doctor," he said, putting out his hand, "glad to see you, come below."[44]

In the flag cabin Caperton remained out of sight and the interview was conducted by Ned Beach. He wasted no time in putting the obvious questions: was Dr. Bobo a candidate for the presidency? The doctor exploded, "Sir, I am more than a candidate, I am Chief of the Executive Power; I command an Army in the North of Haiti which is now unopposed. . . . The Haitian presidency is already mine; the election is a mere formality."[45]

As far as the United States was concerned, Rosalvo Bobo had just sounded his own political death knell. Ned Beach shot back, "You are not a candidate because the United States forbids [it]." As if that weren't bad enough, Beach insulted Bobo to his face,

"You are not a patriot, you are a menace and a curse to your country. . . . There is to be no more revolution, ever, in Haiti, no more presidents made by force."[46]

Bobo flew into tantrums of passion and bitterness, but only for a moment. He was too canny a politician not to know the rules had changed. Then and there he resigned any pretensions to the title *Chef de Pouvoir Exécutif*, signed cables officially disbanding his *caco* army, and went ashore a "private citizen." At dockside he was greeted by a large crowd of the city's rabble and given a triumphal parade.

On Sunday, August 8, Ned Beach convened a meeting with Dartiguenave and Bobo at the American embassy. To each man he put the question, "Are there any other Haitians as well qualified as you to be President of Haiti?" In what sounds very much like a coached response, Philippe Dartiguenave humbly answered first. Yes there were; he himself did not seek the office, "but I will not avoid it." Bobo replied—probably just as expected—with a resounding "NO! I alone have sufficient honor and patriotism and intelligence. And I alone of all Haitians, enjoy the love and confidence of my people. There is no other!"[47]

Keeping his anger in check, Beach asked his second question to Dartiguenave, "Should Dr. Bobo be elected, will you promise to help him loyally in his efforts to secure the welfare of Haiti?" Again Dartiguenave answered affirmatively. Bobo, in a complete lather, leapt from the table. "NEVER!" he shouted. "If I am not elected, it will be because the presidency has been stolen from me! By rights I am already President! . . . I will not help him! If I am cheated of my rights, I will leave the country. . . . She can never survive without me!"[48]

Caperton radioed the gist of the conference to the Navy Department. Secretary Daniels was away from Washington, and the government's policy was drafted by the relatively unknown assistant secretary. "The election of Dartiguenave," replied young Franklin Delano Roosevelt, "is preferred by the United States." Caperton set the date for August 12.[49]

At League Island preparations for outfitting the *Tennessee* and embarking the reinforced 1st Marine Regiment went on around the clock. Seven rifle companies, a signal company, and a brigade headquarters—850 officers and men, with thirty-five machine guns—made ready to board. When united

with the 2nd Marines in Haiti the regiments would form the 1st
Marine Expeditionary Brigade. Selected for overall command was
the 1st Marines' skipper, Colonel Littleton W.T. Waller.

Fifty-nine years old, well girthed and mustached, Waller was
one of the Marine Corps' most experienced field officers. In an
era abounding with legendary marines, Waller was a Zeus among
lesser gods. His expeditionary service covered the globe across
Egypt, China, the Philippines, Panama, Cuba, and Mexico. At the
high point of American empire he was the best colonial soldier
in the lists.

On August 10 the *Tennessee* cast off her lines, and Captain
Frederic "Dopey" Wise, commander of the 6th Company, noted,
she steamed off "to straighten out affairs in Haiti."[50]

There tensions ran high as election day neared. The *cacos* tore
up the railroad in the north, and ex-soldiers of Vilbrun Sam, now
nothing more than bandits, pillaged between Port-au-Prince and
Gonaïves. In the capital the streets erupted into violent nights of
assault, robbery, and roving gangs of *cacos*. On the morning of
the eleventh, one day before the election, the city awoke to find
its walls plastered with a decree by the Revolutionary Committee
dissolving the Haitian Congress. They proclaimed a provisional
government and ordered the doors sealed to the Chamber of
Deputies. At the American embassy, Ned Beach's informants told
of Bobo's plans to halt the election by staging a major riot.

Beach ordered the marines to tear down every committee
proclamation in the city and summoned the committee and Dr.
Bobo to the embassy. Because most leading Haitians carried concealed weapons, Beach stationed two marines, expert pistol shots,
in the room, and the furniture was arranged to give these men a
clear field of fire. When Bobo and the participants took their seats,
Ned Beach, to their stunned silence, dissolved the committee. If
ex-members, individually or in concert, attempted to give orders,
they would be branded as public enemies of the United States.

Should they attempt the proposed riot, every Haitian in the
room would die. "You are informed that the first shot fired tomorrow will be an order for the summary and instant execution
of each of you. You will all be immediately shot." With that Beach
dismissed the committee, warning that if they valued their lives
they "had better endeavor to make sure that tomorrow is the most
peaceful day in Haitian history." Amidst the shock, one man, the
ex–police chief Charles de Delva, laughed out loud, saying it was
all a continuing game. "You win," he chuckled to Ned Beach.[51]

If August 12, 1915, election day, wasn't the most peaceful in Haitian history, it came close. Eli Cole deployed his regiment in a *cordon sanitaire* covering a two-block radius around the Chamber of Deputies. Sandbagged machine gun positions sprouted in every major intersection, and bluejacket gunners surveyed the critical approaches from the sights of a pair of 3-inch guns.

At their request Caperton permitted the Haitian congressmen to carry pistols into the chamber "with the understanding that they would be free to shoot themselves while in session, but not others." Permission to carry arms did not extend to friends and observers. Access to the visitors' gallery was strictly limited to those with signed passes from Eli Cole. Everyone was politely frisked, netting the marines another wagonload of handguns. As a final measure that all would be properly done, marines with fixed bayonets stood at parade rest in the aisles. "It must have been a pleasant sensation," Admiral Caperton mused, "to cast a ballot under such circumstances."[52]

On the floor Ned Beach wheeled and dealed like a seasoned political campaigner, gathering in the votes and political IOUs. The results were predictable. Of 115 votes, Philippe Sudre Dartiguenave received ninety-four. Dr. Rosalvo Bobo went down to crushing defeat with three votes.*

On the election of a president it was traditional to fire a twenty-one-gun salute from Fort Nationale. Dartiguenave was accorded the honor. But it was already past noon, and not a sound or puff of smoke had emanated from the fort. At the presidential reception, amidst the drinking of warm champagne, the guests grew restive and whispered nervously of a coup.

Ned Beach, concerned over what was happening, or rather, what was not happening, sent Lieutenant Oberlin of the Cruiser Squadron staff, together with a gunner's mate and a couple of hands, to investigate the disquieting silence.

It was all very simple; there was no salute because there was no ammunition or firing locks for the guns; they had all been seized by the marines the week before. Willing to try anything to fire the salute, the men set to work. In a corner of the fort they unearthed some black powder, and rummaging through the garbage they managed to extricate several empty shell cases. Oberlin and the gunner fashioned enough saluting charges, and with mud

---

*True to his word, Bobo boarded the Santo Domingo steamer and began an odyssey of exile that ended with his death in Paris in 1929.

wads the first was rammed down a gun bore. Properly done with a battery of six guns and fifty men, the salute should have taken about five minutes. But with a single piece, each round touched off with a cigarette, it was two hours before the last booming puff heralded the presidency of Philippe Sudre Dartiguenave. "Day passed without disorder in Port-au-Prince," radioed Admiral Caperton to the Navy Department.[53]

In the United States there was general approval of the turn of events. *The Outlook* stressed to its readers, "how much this country must at times depend upon the judgment, discretion, and administrative ability of its naval officers." The *New York Sun* was fulsome in its praise of Admiral Caperton. He had "restored order, conciliated the revolutionists, and won the confidence of the politicians as if by magic . . . it was his mission to abolish war . . . and provide work by cleaning house in fetid Port-au-Prince . . . hostility vanished and the American occupation became popular."[54]

In Haiti that popularity was hardly universal. No sooner had Dartiguenave taken his oath, than the nationalist-minded burghers of Port-de-Paix, forty miles west of Cap Haïtien, refused to accept an American puppet government and threw their support to the *cacos*. Riots, arson, and looting erupted in the larger towns.

On August 13 rooftop watchers in Port-au-Prince saw the tall cage masts of the *Tennessee* peek over the horizon, and an hour later the armored cruiser anchored in the roadstead. In lighters the 1st Marines went ashore, taking up their quarters in the unoccupied *Caserne*. Dopey Wise of the 6th Company observed, "Martial law was in effect. No Haitian was allowed to carry arms. All arms found were confiscated. Squads of marines patrolled the city to prevent any disorder. We went on patrol as soon as we got there."[55]

Private Faustin Wirkus of the 22nd Company also noted his impressions. "We marched over the long railroad pier until we were beyond the sheds and warehouses and in the waterfront street. It hurt. It stunk. Fairyland had turned into a pigsty. More than that, we were not welcome. We could feel it as distinctly as we could smell the rot along the gutters."[56]

Tony Waller took charge of all American forces ashore. In Ned Beach's opinion, he was "the personification of those qualities that have made the Marine Corps famous, and just the man to bring some measure of peace to the troubled land." But first there needed some command shuffling. To relieve Waller of the double burden of the brigade and the 1st Marines, Eli Cole assumed command of the latter, and Colonel Theodore Kane took the 2nd Marines. On August 16 Cole sailed with his headquarters and 1st Battalion for Cap Haïtien.

The State and Navy departments considered the time opportune to place the Haitian infrastructure under American "guidance." In mid-August Beale Davis submitted a preliminary treaty draft to President Dartiguenave. Its salient points provided for direct United States control of the customs service; advisory supervision of all government finances; the formation of an American-officered, nonpartisan, national constabulary as the sole military force of the Haitian government; and finally, the right of United States armed intervention to suppress revolution and enforce the provisions of the treaty. For all intents and purposes it transformed Haiti into an American colony.

Secretary Lansing tactlessly demanded "acceptance without modification" in a week's time. As should have been expected, Dartiguenave, his cabinet, and the Haitian Congress rejected the treaty. For the first time since the landing, there occurred direct anti-American demonstrations in Port-au-Prince. A newspaper editor, virulent in his attacks on American policy, was arrested by the marines, setting off a near riot. He was finally released, but only after Caperton received an official protest from the Haitian government.

Robert Lansing's patience with Dartiguenave was stretched to the limit, and he suggested to Caperton that a more pliant regime would be satisfactory to the State Department. To this, however, the admiral was opposed. Any candidate sufficiently weak to succumb completely to American pressure would lack any popular support and his elevation would only presage another revolution. In Caperton's opinion the United States had made its choice and must give Dartiguenave time and room to govern. Additionally, he noted to Navy Secretary Daniels, "It is to be remembered that there are practically no patriotic people in Haiti, in the sense of people willing to unselfishly sacrifice their own personal interests for the good of the country . . . who will not . . . dissociate themselves from the faction leaders, their *cacos,* and the revolutionary methods. . . . It would be detrimental to their own political fortunes."[57]

But Dartiguenave found a path through the impasse, and

allowing a few weeks to lapse he privately visited Beale Davis. The treaty, he maintained, must appear a product of real negotiations between the United States and Haiti, and not a State Department diktat rammed down the throat of a prostrate nation. If Washington would permit him to make some changes in the wording of the text, leaving the basic premise intact, it was possible to carry the thing through ratification. Davis agreed and cabled Lansing the proposal.

There were yet more pressing matters at hand. The legal niceties of armored cruiser diplomacy put no food on Haiti's table. Due to the bankruptcy of the treasury and the general disruption of shipping and external trade caused by the world war, malnutrition had reached epidemic proportions. In Port-au-Prince hundreds, if not thousands, of women and children had no food whatever. As a stopgap solution the leftovers from the *Washington*'s messdecks and wardroom were collected, mixed with rice, and served twice daily to 800 women and children. When a marine patrol found a nursing mother dead in the street, her infant still at her breast, Admiral Caperton demanded that the American government relieve the suffering. After several pleadings he finally received orders from Secretary Daniels to take charge of Haiti's corruption-ridden customs houses. "You will use the funds that are collected," the Secretary informed his admiral-proconsul, "for organizing and maintaining an efficient constabulary, for conducting such temporary public works, as well as affording immediate relief to the discharged soldiers and starving populace by giving them employment, and finally for the support of the Dartiguenave government." The customs house order gave the United States near total control over Haiti's revenues, a major clause of the as-yet-unsigned treaty.[58]

In addition to the main facility at Port-au-Prince, the customs houses at Cap Haïtien, Port de Paix, Gonaïves, Jacmel, Les Cayes, Jérémie, Petit Goâve, and St. Marc would be taken over. To each, with the exception of the capital and Cap Haïtien, which already maintained sizable American garrisons, were sent a gunboat and a company of marines with one or two machine guns. The actual administration of the customs service and collection of the duties was placed in the capable hands of navy paymasters.

With a detachment of the 12th Company, Assistant Paymaster Fred McMillen boarded the armed tug *Osceola* for Petit Goâve, a town of about 6,000 people forty-five miles west of Port-au-Prince. It was once a thriving coffee export center and until 1902 it had boasted a modern steel and concrete wharf, complete with narrow-gauge railway for moving goods.[59]

But these facilities, along with the customs house itself, and most of the town, had been torched, as McMillen noted, in "one of the seasonal revolutions." The big commodities warehouse was spared these human depredations, only to have its roof torn away by a recent hurricane. Thousands of tons of coffee moldered away within its walls. McMillen's heart sagged when he inspected the most essential customs house equipment, the two huge balance scales for weighing goods in bulk. They sat in the open, uncovered to the weather, and had been in use since the days of French colonization—at least 114 years. Their wooden frames and weighing platforms were rotted away, and most of the original weights had long ago been stolen by local fishermen for anchors. As replacements there were chunks of scrap iron and heavy stones. In rainy weather, which was often, the balances were surrounded by a sea of mud.

In good times Petit Goâve could ship 2,000 tons of coffee a month and if it were to approach anywhere near that figure, the entire physical plant would have to be rebuilt, almost from scratch. For Paymaster McMillen it was a task akin to the Hebrews making bricks without straw. There were no building materials in the town, no tools or hardware, and no mechanics nearer than Port-au-Prince. McMillen managed to find an ancient, crippled Jamaican carpenter, who after much cajoling, agreed to supervise repair of the warehouse roof and cobbling the street around the balances. McMillen scrounged some corrugated sheet iron and yellow pine to begin the task.

The wharf was an even bigger problem, and its repair was more suited to an officer of the Civil Engineering Corps. But McMillen, after repeated pleas over the marines' radio, winkled out a coaster from Port-au-Prince with enough materials, and "a modest assortment of hand tools," to make a start. Using scantlings from an abandoned shed and parts of an old hand windlass, he constructed a pile driver. After many delays, labor problems, "carnival days, and the devastating fevers, mostly typhoid," the wharf was repaired just enough to handle "emergency jobs."

Petit Goâve Bay lacked the simplest aids to navigation, a situation McMillen attempted to rectify by painting empty gasoline drums and planting them about the rocks and sandbars. But within days the drums were stolen, and he "abandoned any further hydrographic work in Haiti." Finally the paymaster put his hand to simplifying the bureaucracy and the unbelievable amount of paper passing that Haitian law deemed necessary for export commodities. Instead of taking a month, invoices now cleared the customs house in three days. Within a year McMillen's reforms nearly doubled the town's export of coffee and income from customs receipts.

On an August day Dopey Wise marched his 6th Company into the gunboat *Marietta* and steamed west along Haiti's southern crab claw to Jérémie. He had with him two officers, 100 marines, and a navy hospital corpsman. His orders from Eli Cole were succinct: "Disarm all Haitian soldiers found there. Take control of the customs . . . continue the existing civil government."[60]

From the gunboat's tiny quarterdeck Wise inspected his new domain. "It was a typical French colonial settlement. Old buildings, two or three storeys high crowded around the waterfront and barricaded the narrow streets which gradually rose towards the mountains, giving the town the appearance of looking down on you. The outskirts simmered down to all sorts of nondescript shacks huddled together—a hell of a place to land men, if there were to be any resistance."

Captain Wise's nickname belied a high order of intelligence. He had been through some very hard fighting in China during the Boxer Rebellion, and he was under no illusion regarding the pitfalls of foreign occupation. A lapse in discipline by one man, any breach of tact or a moment of insensitivity to local custom, any arbitrary or unnecessary show of force, he knew, could quickly escalate into acts of terror by the civilian population and the consequent retaliation by the occupation forces.

"I had already figured out that these Haitians had a devil of a time," he wrote. "They had years of revolutions, to be climaxed now by the arrival of foreign troops [and] the wildest rumors were being circulated as to our intentions. . . . They were a proud, sensitive outfit, exceedingly emotional. . . . God knows up to that date there had been plenty to develop their emotions . . . they were terrified and dumbly on the defensive."

Wise and the gunboat's skipper, both unarmed, "without even

a ceremonial sword, so that there could be no misinterpretation," went ashore to prepare the way. A large, silent crowd had gathered on the wharf. Most "were ragged and half-clothed . . . a number of soldiers carrying new rifles, and three or four well-dressed civilians."

At the American consulate they received a pleasant surprise. "We found the [consular] agent, a fine-appearing [Haitian] mulatto [who] told us that he was a proud graduate of Fordham University, New York, and that he was delighted to assist the Americans." With the agent the officers visited the town *chef*. He too was glad to welcome the Americans, "and with a sparkle in his eye, said that personally he would be enchanted to see the last of those Haitian soldiers in Jérémie . . . that they were from Port-au-Prince and a set of thieves."

The officers returned to the waterfront and rented a large warehouse to billet the company, who were only then ordered ashore. The first night in town, Wise selected a French-speaking marine, a Canadian, to walk the streets, mingling with the people. He came to no harm and reported all well, though there was much speculation over what the marines would actually do. But as Dopey Wise discerned, "No matter what we did, nothing could be worse than their old regime."

The captain's primary task for the morrow was a most delicate one, disarming the Jérémie garrison, about 100 ragged-shirted, barefoot soldiers. But, Wise noted, "they carried excellent rifles. It was my job to get those rifles. I knew if I demanded the immediate surrender of those guns, I'd never get all of them. I knew they'd disappear." Accompanied by the Fordham-educated consular agent, one lieutenant, and a squad of eight armed marines, Wise marched to the barracks and requested, not ordered, the Haitian captain to parade his men. Their tattered and shoeless turnout notwithstanding, Wise's keen eye saw "they were a well-disciplined outfit. I had their captain give the order to 'stack arms.'" At that, the marines grabbed the rifles. "That Haitian officer was too flabbergasted to think, so I ordered him to take his men into the barracks. We saluted, and he obeyed."

Jérémie was quiet enough to warrant no roving patrols, and the only armed men in evidence were two squads of marines on duty at the customs house. Here Wise established his headquarters, and each morning received the people for redress of grievances.

About a month after the landing there occurred the ugly incident Wise so fervently hoped to avoid and which, were it not for the near perfect discipline of the marines, would have spun the wheel of blood and retribution.

The marines off duty had taken to afternoon swimming in a large stream and one of them had just drowned. Receiving word at the customs house Wise ordered his executive officer, Lieutenant Coyle, to investigate. Coyle mounted his pony and galloped off. At the stream, in Wise's words, Coyle "found a crowd of ragged natives had collected, as they do by magic in Haiti where ever there is excitement." The lieutenant ordered the townsfolk to fall back and all obeyed, except "one huge, half-naked ruffian, who crazed with excitement was arguing, gesticulating, and beckoning the others to come up again." Coyle rounded on the instigator and knocked him flat with a punch to the jaw. At this display of judicious force, the Haitians backed further off, and "howled with delight at this unexpected entertainment." When a citizen offered a mule cart for the drowned marine, the situation seemed to have diffused.

In a taggle, as they were off duty, and unarmed, in accord with Wise's orders, the swimmers followed the cart to the customs house. Suddenly the man Lieutenant Coyle had bested leaped out of the throng and "practically cut [Sergeant] Thompson's head off with one blow of a cane knife; jumped back into the crowd and disappeared."

With a wild, undisciplined rush, the marines tore into the crowd; all except Sergeant Neilson, an old campaigner, who immediately took command. "Halt!" he bellowed, and the marines stopped in their tracks. "Silence!" Neilson rapped out as if on a drill field. "Private Jones, double back to the customs house, tell the sergeant I want his guard. Form a screen around Thompson's body. Silence!"

In three minutes the two squads of the customs house guard arrived at the double. Through Neilson's quick reactions no harm came to any Haitian, few even had the chance to see the mutilated body. Once the mule cart moved off, there was nothing for the crowd to do, and "shrugging their shoulders, they slipped away to their own affairs."

At the customs house the consular agent identified the murderer as "a notorious roustabout, vicious to a degree, a bully who had a small following." Lieutenant Coyle was his intended victim, but the assassin's rifle had misfired, and drawing his machete, he sprang at the first marine in reach. The consular agent explained the impossibility of capturing the man, as he was now doubtless deep in the jungle.

The next morning Wise received a deputation of Jérémie's leading citizens. Their regret at the incident was evident and they pleaded with him to understand that the murder did not reflect on the town, but was the sole act of a criminal. Wise gave his assurance. "We had already decided the night before," he wrote, "that a community should not be punished for the act of an individual. It would have taken but one wrong move on our part to have made a wildly excited mob out of a quiet, curious crowd. We were exceedingly proud of the discipline that existed in our command."

Jérémie settled down "to the quiet, wholesome life of a busy small town, lightly garrisoned." Funds for municipal improvements were disbursed from the senior paymaster's office in Port-au-Prince, and Wise put large numbers of townspeople to work cleaning up the community and repairing public buildings.

One of his biggest projects was Jérémie's prison. "A big stone building," Wise noted, "and it was a cesspool." The Haitian penal system had few equals in barbarity. Once a man was within the walls the authorities considered their responsibility ended. There was literally no food, and unless a prisoner received some by a relative or friend, he starved. The inmates were in a pitiful condition, and Wise set them to work in a thorough housecleaning, the first ever. Wise soon found himself in the predicament of a "chronic surplus" of prisoners, though not all were malefactors. Each time a convict work detail marched back inside the walls, the marines counted among them free men glad to serve time for three meals and a straw mattress. On discharge the prisoners were permitted to keep their tin can mess kits.

"We were all beginning to settle down," Dopey Wise remembered, "then stories began to drift in to all of us that the American occupation in the north was meeting with resistance."

The *cacos* were on the move. By mid-August an emboldened chief named Dejean, "a murderer of the most fiendish variety" whose specialty was cutting out the tongues of his victims and drinking their blood, pushed down the railroad to within eight miles of Port-au-Prince. The marines took to the offensive. A platoon started northeast from the capital and after a brief firefight captured Dejean. The bandit was clapped in irons and put on the train, while from the right-of-way hundreds of peasants cheered.[61]

From Port-de-Paix on the north coast came signals from the *Nashville* of the collapse of civil authority. The town was strongly pro-Bobo and anti-American, and a large band of *cacos* lurked in the vicinity. To prevent their advance, a company of marines sailed from Cap Haïtien to secure the town and customs house. On August 23, while the marines were still at sea, the *cacos* moved in. They extorted money from the merchants, declaimed in loud defiance their hatred for the United States, and summoned all Haitians to a patriotic revolt. But when the marines landed the next day, the bandits disappeared into the hinterland.

Cap Haïtien was the thorn in the side of the occupation. Since mid-August it was under martial law with Commander Percy Olmstead, skipper of the *Nashville*, serving as military and civil governor. In the surrounding countryside the *cacos* roamed and pillaged, following their age-old vocation. The senior officer at the Cap, Captain E.H. Durell of the *Connecticut*, repeatedly proffered amnesty in return for guns; all tenders were ignored.

Through an intermediary Durell then offered 100 *gourdes* to each chief and fifteen for each ordinary *caco* who surrendered his rifle. The broker countered with a demand for 600,000 *gourdes*, nearly $120,000! Durell considered this preposterous and a meeting was arranged with "General" Antoine Morenci, a senior *caco* chief. The decorum of the long parley was courteous, but the *cacos* refused any cooperation. They detested the American puppet Philippe Dartiguenave and pronounced Dr. Bobo the rightful president of Haiti. They would keep their guns, they told Durell, and withdraw into their hill fortresses. With that, Morenci and his retinue mounted their ponies, gave a loud cheer for Rosalvo Bobo and rode off.

If they were to remain, the senior American commanders saw no other choice than a major campaign to crush the *cacos*. Caperton radioed the Navy Department for the necessary reinforcements to begin the First Caco War. On August 21 orders were cut for the recently formed marine artillery battalion at Annapolis "to embark . . . fully armed and equipped both as artillery and as infantry, on board the USS *Tennessee* for passage to Port-au-Prince, Haiti." The battalion, nucleus of the eventual 10th Marine Regiment, counted 325 officers and men in the 1st, 9th, and 13th companies, equipped with twelve army pattern 3-inch field guns and a pair of heavy, truck-towed 4.7-inch pieces. On the last day of August the 13th Company landed at the Cap, the remainder sailing on to Port-au-Prince.[62]

The 1st Marine Expeditionary Brigade was complete. Its order of battle comprised the 1st and 2nd regiments, the artillery battalion, the 29th (signal) Company, plus the marine detachments from the *Connecticut, Washington,* and *Tennessee*: eighty-eight officers, 1,941 rank and file.

While Caperton and Waller made plans for the general offensive, the *cacos* probed for weak spots among the penny-packet detachments of marines and bluejackets dispersed in the coastal towns. In early September Dr. Bobo's self-styled "war minister," Septimus Rameau, moved within striking distance of Gonaïves, halted the trade into the town, and planted himself firmly astride the railroad. "Very little food comes into Gonaïves," Caperton reported, and the inhabitants were "uneasy."[63]

The 7th Company, with a small bluejacket force from the *Castine,* made up the garrison with 109 men. In their first clash with Rameau's *cacos,* a mounted squad was cut off and outnumbered eight-fold on a jungle trail. The marines fired a few shots into the bush, and the *cacos* disappeared with no casualties to either side. Rameau, however, tightened his grip and fairly laid Gonaïves to siege.

The situation demanded superior leadership, and Smedley Butler sailed down from the Cap to take command. He found the troops barricaded in their quarters "and the rebels squatting in the bushes firing for all they were worth." Brazenly Butler demanded the *cacos* lay down their arms, and when they ignored the offer, Butler and his men "made a grand rush and drove the whole crowd out of town."[64]

Dusk came, and with it a hot, humid shroud settled on Gonaïves. On the top floor of their two-story headquarters, the marines, bellies full of canned corned beef and ship's bread, threw off their clothing and fell on their bedrolls. Downstairs, Butler and his officers were "sitting down to a well earned supper," when the tinny ring of the field telephone interrupted the meal. It was one of the outposts, and it reported Rameau's *cacos* burning up the railroad. Food instantly forgotten, Butler ordered his bugler to sound the call to arms, and began one of the strangest little battles in the history of the Corps. "Who wants a fight!" he yelled. Without stopping to dress, the marines snatched up their Springfields and buckled on their cartridge belts. "We flew up the street," Butler recalled, "streaked along the railroad track and plunged head-long into the rebels. . . . It was the funniest fight I ever saw." Baying and whooping like a pack of hounds, the marines, some naked, others clad only in skivvies, banged away at the retreating *cacos*. Futilely Butler blew his whistle, and the bugler sounded "to the rear" and "cease firing." "Those undressed marines went right on shooting. . . . 'Here comes one'—BANG BANG—I'd hear . . . 'and hell! Here's another'—BANG BANG. But the men were in their element and nothing could stop them. . . . It was something of a shock to the rebels to have marines in underwear suddenly pounce on them with blood curdling yells. The *cacos* fully expected us to wait around and call a conference over the burning of the railroad."[65]

The next morning Butler set off at the head of a fifty-man mounted patrol to flush Rameau into the open. At the hamlet of Poteau they came up with the *cacos'* rear guard. The marine point men set up a shout for the general and presently he stopped his horse and waited. Butler, with two privates, approached. Rameau was a "weazoned, sour-looking little devil and he screwed up his face maliciously as he looked down at me." Butler demanded the *caco* chief dismount, "and stand on the ground as I'm doing." The *cacos* outnumbered the marines by at least ten to one and Rameau felt no compunction to obey. Butler sprang at his bridle and jerked Rameau out of the saddle. "This," the marine major noted, "was more humiliating to him than defeat in battle." After extracting a promise to cease interference with Gonaïves' food and water, the patrol trotted back to town.[66]

The next day Butler moved out with his mounted detachment escorting the work gangs repairing the tracks. As could have been expected, he came upon the *cacos*, who were setting fire to a bridge. Rameau was captured, and packed off in irons to Port-au-Prince.

But the *cacos* were like sparks, driven by the wind. Their principal locus of activity was in the hinterland around Cap Haïtien. By late September they had cut off the city from its food sources. To open the railroad, Eli Cole sent south a strong patrol to the railhead town of Grande Rivière. The move greatly upset the *cacos*, but they chose not to interfere. Perceiving this a sign of weakness and discord, Cole offered the chiefs the standard deal of money and amnesty for guns; his offer came to nothing.

Attempting to impress the *cacos* with a show of force, Cole stepped up his patrols with short marches through the *cacos'* outposts into the interior. The first was sent to Haut-du-Cap, about four miles inland. "It is desired," Cole noted in his orders, "that our forces do not start an attack; any *caco* forces encountered should be informed that we do not propose to attack them unless they interfere with and attack our forces, in which case, force will be used." The patrol reached Haut-du-Cap without incident and turned about for the return march. As the rear guard exited, the townspeople set up a great warning shout. The marines halted and across their front materialized the *caco* outpost riders. At first they refused the marines passage, but after a heated argument the patrol continued on. When word of the outpost commander's pliability reached the local chief he ordered his subordinate's head lopped off with a machete.[67]

This lesson in *caco* discipline showed to good effect, as the marines were soon to learn. On September 27 Cole sent two strong patrols on a reconnaissance of the Cap's southern approaches. The first, five squads of the *Connecticut's* marines—forty men under Captain Frederick Barker—moved off at daylight. Their planned route passed through Haut-du-Cap, then south to Plaine-du-Nord. There Barker was to halt until 2:00 P.M., reverse march back to Haut-du-Cap and await a rendezvous with the second patrol.

The second patrol formed six squads, forty-eight marine gunners of the Captain Chandler Campbell's 13th Company. His orders were to march through Haut-du-Cap, swing east to the hamlets beyond, then return to the village and await Barker. When the patrols mustered at dawn information arrived at Cole's command post that resistance could be expected. Barker and Campbell were told to "go ahead," but to hold fire unless the *cacos* shot first.

Barker's column didn't have long to wait. They were surrounded midway on the trail to Haut-du-Cap, and the point and flanks came under heavy fire. But the *cacos* were poor marksmen, and the *Connecticut's* marines fought their way into the village. The shooting could be distinctly heard at Cap Haïtien and twenty-five men were sent down the trail as reinforcements. They, too, came under heavy fire and two men were wounded.

It was obvious to Cole that a vicious little firefight had developed and taking the remainder of the *Connecticut's* marines—another twenty-five men—he marched to the relief. On Cole's arrival at Haut-du-Cap Barker's column again set off on patrol.

But they were almost immediately enveloped and forced back. For nearly an hour the marines poured a deadly fusillade of rifle fire against five times their number of *cacos,* who swarmed around the shacks and walls of the village.

The siege of Haut-du-Cap ended just before noon, when Campbell's gunners broke through from the east setting the bandits in flight. The *cacos* had received a severe drubbing. At the cost of two marines killed and eight wounded, sixty *cacos* lay dead. "Have cleaned out village of Haut-du-Cap," Cole reported to Admiral Caperton, "respecting all private property . . . will continue operations tomorrow."[68]

Some of Eli Cole's contemporaries, notably Butler and Waller, often faulted the colonel as overly cautious and deliberate, but "tomorrow" proved no hollow word to embellish a report. On September 27 Cole issued Field Order No. 8 for the capture of Quartier Morin, a *caco* base five miles east along the coast. Near mid-morning the advance guard 11th Company marched out of the Cap. They were followed by the main body: the 5th, 13th, and 23rd companies. Last came the *Connecticut*'s marines forming the rear guard. In less than two hours, with only a single shot fired from the bush, the points entered the town. It was full of its women and children, but only one man seemed to be in residence, Dr. Fouché, the *cacos*' "surgeon general." According to Eli Cole, the doctor "said the war was over; that they wanted to be good . . . that the day before had been a very severe lesson to them, and they realized it would not pay to attack us again." For the moment, it held true.[69]

On October 1 the *Osceola* chugged into Cap Haïtien, bringing with her Colonel Waller to personally assume operational command in the north. Beneath a veneer of civility between the senior American officers, there was a goodly amount of interservice backstabbing. For years a controversy had simmered, blowing wide open in a Congressional debate in 1909, over the role of the Marine Corps in the naval service. It wasn't the first, and would not be the last time the Corps had to politically fight for its life and keep from amalgamation into the army. The marines won the latest battle but the skirmishing continued. Waller's orders to command all forces ashore—navy and Marine Corps alike—came direct from Secretary Daniels. Captain Durell, skipper of the *Connecticut,* a man Waller charged with "timidity," was now relieved of this duty. Irked, Durell imposed upon Admiral Caperton to change the Secretary's orders, "so," as Waller wrote to his son, "I would not have command. . . . Cole was aiding them in this so that he would not be under me."[70]

Caperton bent under the pressure and issued contravening orders. Amidst the backbiting, offensive operations came to a halt. "Well," Waller continued, "they were so timid that they would not do anything and nearly killed the men with guard duty." Waller confronted the admiral directly, "I told him the Secretary had put me in command of the troops . . . and I was going to command them." Caperton conceded the point; "a mistake" had been made in reading the orders and new ones, confirming Waller in command, were issued. The marines "were delighted when I had knocked the weak-kneed bunch out of the box."[71]

Waller did not sulk. Wasting not an hour, Waller arranged a parley with General Morenci and his subchiefs at Quartier Morin. To the great surprise of all, Morenci agreed to give up his arms in return for fifteen *gourdes* per rifle, and complete amnesty from the Haitian government. After October 5 any armed *caco* would be considered and treated as a bandit. Morenci was probably sincere when he put his pen to the agreement, but most of the bands would have none of it. Nonetheless, several hundred *cacos* came forth to pile arms and receive their reward and amnesty.

Tony Waller's strategy for bringing the unrepentant *cacos* to battle was a classic of anti-insurgent warfare. He would throw a net, albeit a thin one, around the entire *caco* region of northeast Haiti. Then drawing it tight, flush the *cacos* into the plains, or bottle them up in their mountain forts. His first cast of the net sealed the border with the Dominican Republic at Ouanaminthe on the Massacre River, one of the traditional starting gates for Haitian revolutions.

The town was garrisoned by 400 ragged, poorly armed government soldiers, nearly dead from starvation. On October 4 Waller with the 11th Company boarded the *Nashville* for Fort Liberté. Leaving half the company at the fort to protect his rear, Waller marched overland to Ouanaminthe. The Haitian soldiers received them with joy and eagerly surrendered their arms in return for transportation home. Fifteen *gourdes* was the agreed sum for a demobilized private. But most claimed the rank of *general de brigade*, the highest in the Haitian service, and were so paid.

Having plugged the bolt hole in the east, Waller cast his net to the west. On October 20 four squads of the 13th Company pushed down from the Cap twenty miles deep into *caco* country and occupied the hamlet of Bahon, at the critical narrows of the Grande Rivière. Two days later Eli Cole with the 23rd Company bisected this line and marched into the big railhead river town of Grande-Rivière-du-Nord.

The *cacos* were now trapped in a roughly teapot-shaped region of about 400 square miles, very broken country with only the barest of jungle tracks and dotted with ancient French stone and masonry forts. Into these redoubts the *cacos* fled. "It was very difficult to find out [their] exact location," Waller noted, "so I ordered a reconnaissance made, which covered between 300 and 400 miles around." To lead the mission, Waller picked his best man, Smedley Butler. As with so many of his legendary exploits, Butler's jungle march has been enshrined as a minor Marine Corps epic.[72]

On October 22, in Butler's words, "Twenty-seven of us—all old timers,"* mounted on ponies, with a dozen pack animals, and one Colt machine gun, set out from Fort Liberté on their clockwise trek through *caco* country. It was soon clear that the donkeys were overloaded, and it was necessary to recruit bearers from various hamlets. "The carriers," Butler noted, "were well fed, and we paid them ten cents a day. They exulted in being on the winning side; for they all had grudges to settle against the *cacos*."[73]

The going was slow; every few miles the marines were forced to dismount and flush out nests of *cacos* who crouched in ambush among the tangle of scrub. Tracking the *cacos* was fairly easy. "We always knew which way the bandits were going by the orange peels. They left one continuous peeling along their trail." If the first peels were moist, and the next were dry, they knew the *cacos* had approached and turned away. "We got so expert we could almost smell the rascals. But we couldn't seem to root them all out." Through conversations with the locals, Butler learned of a major *caco* position at a place called Fort Capois. "If we were to restore peace to the countryside, we had to find the fort and destroy the band."

Fort Capois was sited on the east bank of the Grande Rivière, about halfway between Grande-Rivière-du-Nord and Bahon; "but for once," Butler continued, "the orange peel trail was missing."

---

*The number twenty-seven is at variance with official records, which place the strength of the patrol at forty.

Not a white man had passed this way since the French had left in 1804. Butler's map, though he didn't realize it until later, was worthless, and he led his little force through more than 100 miles of near trackless ground. Luck came on the third day. "As we were jogging along a river bank, we met a hideous, ungainly brute. He must have been the ugliest man in Haiti." Butler offered the man twenty-five *gourdes* to guide the patrol to Fort Capois. "And if you don't," Butler warned, "I'll shoot you." The Haitian agreed and the marines doubled back on their trail, until Butler saw, through a gap, "a mountain peak about a mile away, towering one thousand feet above us." The peak was girded with stone walls and trenches, and through his field glasses Butler watched swarms of *cacos* crawling over the ramparts.

In numbers the marines were no match for the *cacos* in their dug-in position. Also Butler was suspicious of his guide, who he was certain had given the *cacos* a signal. It was time to get out. On his map the hamlet of Vallière showed about five miles off (it was actually forty miles east). Once there, the marines could barricade themselves in the stone church if necessary.

An annoying drizzle soon became a tropical deluge that all but obliterated the jungle track. "It was pitch dark," Butler remembered. "We had to feel our way, slipping and sliding along the trail. The roar of the river two hundred feet below was scarcely music to our ears." The spate, swift-flowing and swollen by the rains, had to be crossed. Each man leading his horse and grasping the tail of the one in front, they plunged in. When about half had crossed, one man lost his grip and the column broke.

The timing couldn't have been worse, for at that moment "the *cacos* jumped us. Rifles seemed to crack out from the sky, from below, from all sides." In the teeming river horses plunged and reared in agony, and a dozen were swept away as *caco* bullets found their marks.

The marines escaped the hail of lead and in the relative safety of the opposite bank managed to form up on high ground. "We were in a nasty mess," said Butler, "but for some reason I felt strangely exhilarated. I turned to Dr. Borden, who had just crawled up the bank and said, 'Isn't this great!' "

Placing their remaining animals in the center (there is no mention in Butler's account of the Haitian bearers, and the assumption is they were no longer with the patrol), the marines formed a defensive perimeter to await daylight or a wild *caco* charge. It was then that Sergeant Dan Daly (along with Butler, the only marine ever awarded two Congressional Medals of Honor) realized the machine gun had been lost in the river. In an act of incredible bravery, he volunteered to retrieve it.

"With bandits continually shooting at him," Butler recalled, "he swam in the river until he found the machine gun on a dead horse near the bank. He coolly and deliberately strapped the gun on his back, picked up the ammunition and climbed up to rejoin us. I wouldn't have had the courage to do it. . . . For this amazing stunt I recommended him for the Medal of Honor."

By the volume of their fire Butler estimated he was surrounded by about 500 *cacos*. "I knew it was safer to keep moving than to remain in one spot. But hardly would I swing my little detachment a few yards, when a howling mass of natives would dash by us and slash through the bushes with knives and bayonets. It was a hell of a night." Using psychological warfare tactics the marines would encounter a quarter century later with the Japanese on Guadalcanal, the *cacos* blew incessantly on their conch shells. "They called out to us and our interpreter explained that they intended to chop us into small pieces when they caught us. Everybody's hands were cold and clammy. I reached out in the dark for the nearest hand to give and receive a little courage."

Mercifully the night neared its end and Butler took a moment to assess his plight. To remain in position or attempt a withdrawal meant slow death by attrition, if not by horrible mutilation; to Butler there was but one course left: attack. Deploying his men into three squads under Captain Upshur, Lieutenant Ostermann, and Sergeant Daly, Butler's orders were brief: "Just go for those devils as soon as it's light. Move straight forward and shoot everyone in sight."

The *cacos* had pulled back somewhat and were entrenched about 350 yards to the marines' front in an outwork of Fort Capois, Fort Dipitié. Butler blew his whistle and the marines, bayonets fixed, bounded forward in a mad rush. "We knocked hell out of them. We carried the fort at a run. You never heard such a damn racket. We killed about seventy-five *cacos* and the rest took to the bushes. But the marines went wild after their devilish night and hunted the *cacos* down like pigs."

Fort Dipitié was demolished, and all the surrounding huts were put to the torch. "Swept clear the district within one mile of all *cacos*," Butler noted in his report. Unbelievably, only one marine had received a wound in the entire action.

The bedraggled and exhausted patrol began its march eastward to Vallière. On empty stomachs—they had eaten but two meals in three days—the marines hacked their way over jungle hill paths into the deserted hamlet of Gros Roche. They pushed along the riverbank, halting only when torrential rains caused the waters to rise twelve feet in half an hour. Two more precious horses and two donkeys were swept away by the deluge. In the afternoon of October 26 Butler led his men into Vallière. The next morning, barely rested and watered, they marched the final thirty miles north to Fort Liberté.

The marked success of the reconnaissance was due to its near perfect use of small-unit tactics. The marines had located Fort Capois, destroyed Fort Dipitié, and inflicted a major defeat to an overwhelmingly superior force. Upshur, Ostermann, and Daly each received the Medal of Honor.

"Request that I be given opportunity to take command of operations against *cacos* in district," Butler wrote to Waller; he would not be disappointed.[74]

To coordinate operations, Waller established his field headquarters at Le Trou, a village roughly between Fort Liberté and Grande-Rivière-du-Nord. Boldly on the hot, black night of November 2, the *cacos* crept down from the hills and attacked. "Hell broke loose," wrote the naval officer commanding a company of the *Connecticut*'s bluejackets. "The devils had gotten well into town and opened up at about 50 yards range. . . . Everybody got underway quickly and soon pushed the beggars back a bit. . . . Rotten shooting all around. Took a crack at one myself about 200 yards off but didn't come within a mile of him. . . . Bluejackets are anxious and shooting wild. *Cacos* call machine guns 'devil guns.' "[75]

It was a furious fight. His portly bulk defying *caco* bullets, Waller stood in the thick of it, banging away with his pistol and personally directing the defense. In twenty minutes it was over. Dragging their wounded, the *cacos* retreated back into the hills, but thirty-eight of them lay dead in the Le Trou mud. "The *cacos* claim that they defeated us yesterday," wrote the bluejacket officer. "They have told the niggers in the hills that three of the Chiefs caught Colonel Waller on a horse, pulled him off and chopped his head off. Some story. I trust that their further victories are on the same order."[76]

Waller, in a letter to his son, mentions the same rumor; "people from the country said that the *cacos* said they had defeated us and had cut my head off with three blows of a machete as I was running away on my mule. This is the last I hope. I have been beheaded too often now. First I am reported as actually beheaded and then I get [it] in the neck from Washington."[77]

Waller gave the *cacos* no time to regroup, and with the new day the staff set to planning the capture of Fort Capois. The attacking force comprised elements of the 13th, 19th, and 23rd companies, the *Connecticut*'s marines, and her landing company of bluejackets.

On the morning of the fifth, the 13th Company led the attack. Its skipper, Chandler Campbell, wrote, "We were fired on when about 1,500 yards from the fort, and had to clear several hills. . . . Progress was difficult as trails were very steep and we were under fire from both fort and outposts." The outworks were driven in, and when 200 yards from the walls the main assault went forward. Just as Campbell gave the order to charge with the bayonet, "We saw about 50 [*cacos*] coming over the hills; our rearguard was in good position and easily took care of these."[78]

The late arrivals were driven into Campbell's rear by Butler, leading three companies down from the north, and Campbell waited until they enveloped the fort before continuing the assault. "The fort opened a heavy fire," Campbell continued, "and I saw a *caco* jump [the] parapet, followed by another man." The bandits were escaping and he could tarry no longer. "Charged immediately, but a heavy fog rolled in obstructing our view in all directions." When the marines entered the fort, not a *caco* remained. There was much blood, but neither dead nor wounded were found.[79]

Three days later Butler with the 15th Company captured Forts Selon and Berthol without firing a shot. At the sight of the marines, the *cacos* bolted. "All houses in *caco* country now displaying white flags," Waller reported, "and people say they have had enough; no ammunition and leaders have fled. . . . Satisfied that the movement crushed was more than aggregation of ordinary brigands."[80]

There now remained only Fort Rivière, the last *caco* stronghold in Haiti. Built by the French in the latter part of the eighteenth century, four miles west of the Grande Rivière narrows, and 4,000 feet up a mountain peak, it was an old brick-and-stone-bastioned work. On three sides the masonry walls joined the rock of the mountain, forming a steep precipice into the valley. On the fourth side, a natural glacis led up to the sally port.

Eli Cole and his regimental staff considered it well nigh impregnable. At a council of war, the staff aired their view that taking the fort required the whole 1st Marine Regiment, supported by at least one battery of artillery. Butler considered the estimate ridiculous. "Colonel," he broke in, "if you let me pick one hundred men from the eight hundred you have here, I feel we can capture the place at once without wasting more words."[81]

The two men had never been on the best of terms. Butler, a self-described "bushwhacker," had little time and no patience for the colonel's conservative, staff-college solutions. "Cole was a fine officer," he later wrote, "but inclined to be over-educated. If you have too much education, you are acutely conscious of the risks you run and are afraid to act." The colonel, however, recognized Butler's outline as an audacious but conceptually sound operation. "And this time," Butler smilingly noted, "he decided he'd let me have my way."[82]

From the 5th and 13th companies, the machine gun sections of the 23rd, the *Connecticut*'s marines and bluejackets, Butler picked 100 men whom he considered "the cream of the Corps, and the sailors were a splendid crowd. They had been serving with the marines for two months and . . . had learned a lot of tricks of bush warfare." One quickly adopted was the casting off of their bullet-catching whites for khaki marine shirts and breeches. Even better from Butler's viewpoint, "They'd stopped shooting each other . . . also they had no senior 'know it all' naval officer playing soldier."[83]

At dusk, November 16, the column started along the jungle paths for the nightlong climb up the mountain crest. By daybreak the *caco* outposts were driven in, and the troops deployed for a three-pronged attack.

Barker's *Connecticut* marines, with the 23rd Company's machine gunners, faced the south wall to lay the base of fire. Once the *cacos* were swept from the ramparts, Campbell's 13th, and Butler with the 5th Company, would storm the east and west walls. To forestall any *caco* escape the *Connecticut*'s bluejackets planted themselves firmly astride the fort's northern approaches. The men soon learned this was to be no repeat of the cut-and-run *caco* tactics shown at Fort Capois, for with the sun several women were seen coming down the trail from the fort—a sure sign their men intended to fight where they stood.

At 7:30 A.M. Butler blew his whistle and the companies advanced to the attack. The ground before them, save for some scattered rocks, was devoid of cover. Worse yet, the eastern approaches were nearly perpendicular, and Campbell's 13th Company was immediately pinned down by heavy fire. "The original loopholes," Butler observed, were blocked up, "but the embrazures indenting the rim of the walls offered perfect lookouts from which to riddle an invading force." Taking what scant cover came in reach, the 13th flattened out, and with their Benet-Mercie machine guns commenced potting the *cacos* from the walls.

Butler, on the west slope, realized he must assault with the 5th Company alone. Quickly he divided his twenty-seven-strong detachment in half. The first, with a pair of Colts, took cover in some rocks and swept the embrasures with fire; the second—in classic military terms known as the "forlorn hope"—leapfrogged ahead to storm the sally port. With thirteen men, Butler led the rush up the stony glacis. "The last spurt up the rocks was exciting," he remembered. "The *caco* bullets rattled all around us." Out of breath and hearts pounding, they reached the thirty-foot wall, squeezing against the ancient stone to avoid plunging fire from above.

To their horror Butler's men discovered the sally port sealed with boulders and bricks. Clinging to the wall like limpets, they inched along in a desperate attempt at finding a passageway. "Then we found the *caco* entrance—a drain four feet wide and three feet high, extending back for fifteen feet into the interior." It, too, was partially bricked up at its inner face, behind which a *caco* rifleman squeezed off a few ineffective shots; again the marines gripped the wall for their lives.

With the machine guns scything the *cacos* above, the marines were in no immediate danger. "We were quite safe where we were," Butler noted, "but we couldn't remain in that position for ever. I was sticking tight as glue to the wall on one side of the drain opening. Across from me on the other side of the drain was Sergeant Iams, with my orderly [Private] Samuel Gross next to him. I knew that the only way to get into that fort was through that hole. I it was who had brought the crowd up there. I it was who had bragged how easy it would be to take the fort. So now it was up to me to lead the procession. A stream of bullets was crashing through the passage. I simply didn't have the courage to poke my head into the drain. . . . I was writhing inside with indecision. I glanced across at Iams . . . helpless pleading must have been written all over my face. Iams took one look at me and then said, 'Oh Hell, I'm going through.'"

It was an act of extraordinary bravery. Butler, feeling he could no longer hang back, attempted to follow, but was shoved aside by his orderly, Private Gross. Butler then plunged in, the three men on hands and knees crawling furiously through what could well prove a tunnel of death. The *caco* rifleman loosed a round right in their faces; miraculously he missed. Before the *caco* could reload, Iams was through and shot the bandit dead. On the sergeant's heels Gross and Butler tumbled out of the drain into the courtyard, where about seventy-five "half naked madmen, howling and leaping, pounced down on us."

Iams and Gross quickly dispatched a pair of chiefs, while Butler fired his .45 into the crowd. His shots missed, and a huge *caco* "made a frenzied rush at me. . . . Just as he was bringing down a heavy club on my head, Gross aimed his rifle and finished him." To the three marines it must have seemed an eternity, but it was only seconds before the rest of the storming party and the 5th Company "began to pop out of the hole like corks out of bottles."

There was savage hand-to-hand combat as the marines, their blood up and outnumbered three to one, cut and thrust their way across the courtyard. "The bandits in their panic," Butler later wrote, "reverted to the primitive. They threw away their loaded guns and grabbed swords and clubs, rocks and bricks, which were no match for bullets and bayonets."

Heavy automatic fire had driven the *cacos* from the embrasures, allowing Campbell and Barker to scramble their companies over the walls. They debouched into the vaults and casemates, flushing the *cacos* into the courtyard killing ground. Any who managed to reach, let alone escape, over the north wall were gunned down or taken prisoner by the *Connecticut*'s bluejackets.

Ten minutes after Sergeant Iams leapt out of the drain it was all over. Fifty *cacos* lay dead in the yard; the rest prisoners at the point of a bayonet.

The capture of Fort Rivière was an astounding little victory. Not a marine or sailor was wounded, and with it ended all organized *cacos* activity. To prevent its use evermore, Butler brought in a ton of dynamite and blasted the fort to rubble. For their part in the battle, Butler, Iams, and Gross were all awarded Medals of Honor. Each received a promotion, and for Iams and Gross, "a gratuity of $100 to each."

So ended the First Caco War and the initial phase of the Haitian occupation. The *cacos* would rise up again soon enough, but for the present, Admiral Caperton reported to Secretary Daniels, "This area is now patrolled throughout by our forces, is now peaceful, and country people are busy with their crops."[84]

Certain provisions of the treaty forced upon the Haitian government, though they were not ratified by the United States until the spring of 1916, had already gone into effect. "The Haitian Government," according to Article X, "obligates itself . . . to create without delay an efficient constabulary . . . composed of native Haitians. This constabulary shall be organized and officered by Americans, appointed by the President of Haiti, upon the nomination by the President of the United States."[85]

It was a desperately needed reform. The old Haitian Army disbanded by Admiral Caperton in the first weeks of the occupation was a top-heavy, inefficient, and thoroughly corrupt organization. Its paper strength counted thirty-eight infantry and four artillery regiments, four regiments of the presidential guard, and forty-three *gendarmerie* companies. In fact, about 1,000 privates, officered by 308 generals and fifty colonels, answered to the roll. Recruitment was by press-gang, and any man who could tender a bribe of ten *gourdes*, about two dollars, bought his release. The sons of the *élite* were generally exempt, being allowed to enlist in the fire brigades or the parade companies of the presidential guard.

Theoretically a Haitian private received twenty cents a month, plus a ration allowance of eighty cents. In reality, he was paid nothing. Unfailingly the Haitian Congress appropriated the funds. But it was first divided up among the generals, then the various staffs got their cut, and whatever fraction remained went to the troops. Payday, if it was announced, was usually delayed until most of the men were out of barracks. Pay call then sounded, and the pittance, if any, was divided among the privates lucky enough to be present.

In September 1915 recruitment began for the new force, the *Gendarmerie d'Haiti*. Its initial strength was low, 336 men, mostly privates. The leadership cadre composed French-speaking officers and sergeants, seconded for duty from the marine brigade. These marines were bumped a rank or two, so that a lieutenant found himself a captain or major in the Haitian service, a sergeant became a lieutenant, and privates were elevated to noncommissioned officer status. From June 1916, by act of the United States

Congress, the marine cadre, in addition to their regular pay, drew a salary from the Haitian government commensurate with their *gendarmerie* rank. In December 1915 Lieutenant Colonel Smedley Butler pinned on the stars of a major general of the Republic of Haiti and took command.

Recruitment was mixed. While there was no dearth of volunteers, their quality, at first, left much to be desired. Many ex-*cacos*, lured by the promise of food and regular pay, came down from the hills to join up. On medical examination, ninety-five percent of the recruits were diagnosed as having malaria, syphilis, or yaws, and eighty-five percent carried intestinal parasites. Good men were not attracted. The Haitians knew only one kind of soldier or policeman; the Haitian kind—press-ganged, corrupt, and neglected.

One of the great novelties for the new *gendarmes* was the queer American practice of regular pay. At the end of the first month's service, they were incredulous to find they were paid in full and were not required to divide it among the marine officers. This, perhaps more than anything else, served to attract a better class of men into the ranks.

At first, the *gendarmerie* were equipped with old Marine Corps uniforms and Krag-Jorgensen rifles of Spanish-American War vintage. Drill was in English, by rote, and straight from the manual, a practice continued to the end of the occupation two decades hence. When Sergeant Lewis Puller arrived in Port-au-Prince in 1919 to take a lieutenant's commission in the *gendarmerie*, he watched a battalion at close order drill. Haitian sergeants, armed with two-and-a-half-foot-long hardwood sticks, cracked heads at the least sign of inattention. The *gendarmes* wheeled and formed with the precision of Parris Island recruits. But when the formation marched off, Puller saw half a dozen bodies on the ground and hastened to inform his new skipper. "Mister," rejoined the commanding officer, "do you think I'm blind? They'll soon be back. It happens every day. Just a touch of the heat."[86]

Lieutenant Alexander Vandegrift, holding a *gendarmerie* commission as a major, recruited, trained, and equipped two companies at Cap Haïtien. On their first march into the hinterland, Vandegrift noticed his men were barefoot. As they had just been issued new Marine Corps shoes, he ordered his Haitian sergeant to have the men put them on. The march visibly slowed. On coming to a river, the *gendarmes* requested permission to remove their shoes. "This time I let them remain barefooted. The march again quickened. Whenever we came to a town we stopped, the men put on their shoes, we marched through the town smartly, then outside off came the shoes. This became a standard operating procedure in Haiti for years."[87]

The first direct uprising against the occupation, the Pierre-Paul revolt, broke out on the night of January 5, 1916. Fomented by Antoine Pierre-Paul, a leading member in a former administration, it was a pathetic affair and doomed from the start.

Pierre-Paul was almost certainly in the pay of the German foreign office with funds disbursed through German merchants in Port-au-Prince. It was another in a series of real and imagined German attempts at distracting the United States from the European war by miring it in backyard Caribbean brushfires. At the Haitian end, the plotters aimed at the assassination of President Dartiguenave. Arms were cached, the requisite *cacos* were hired, and a prominent chief, Mizaël Codio, was entrusted with military command.

It was no secret. Admiral Caperton was well informed, and for weeks was beseeched by Dartiguenave to place Pierre-Paul under arrest. The admiral demurred, wishing, as he noted to the Secretary of the Navy, "to ascertain more fully just how far the German colony were concerned in it."[88]

In the first hours of January 5 the *cacos* opened fire on the National Palace, the marine barracks, and the provost marshal's office. The latter was held by two marines and forty *gendarmes* equipped only with clubs. The marines had but two pistols and a Springfield rifle.

The attack failed miserably. Private Wirkus of the 22nd Company remembered, "A black man with a red hatband came up under the balcony, unobserved, and shot Wedor through the foot. Another Negro, a giant of a fellow, with a red turban wrapped around his head, charged up the steps to the aid of the man who had shot Wedor. 'One-two' Kenny shot the second man as he rushed up the steps. 'One-two' got his name from the fussy way in which he called off the numbers in infantry drill. . . . 'One-two' was just that way about killing the man who shot Wedor through the foot."[89]

In the streets, men rushed about yelling *"Vivent les cacos."* In the pitch blackness, the sentries at the marine barracks held their fire, cracking out a shot only when a target came into their sights. Five *cacos* were killed or wounded before the perpetrators scattered to the winds. It was over in less than an hour. According to the official report, "Sixteen Haitian leaders and men of bad character" were arrested, and fair amount of rifles confiscated.[90]

Pierre-Paul's house was surrounded, but he managed his escape, as Caperton reported, "with the assistance, and through the house of a German." With Codio at their head, the main body of *cacos* fled east to the Dominican border. Codio, however, was soon captured and thrown into lockup at the Port-au-Prince penitentiary.[91]

The Pierre-Paul uprising had an interesting epilogue. On May 30, timed to coincide with the marines' celebration of Decoration Day, Codio led a mass escape of 150 *cacos*.

Supplied with arms by the *caco* "General" Metellus, and through, Waller noted, "the connivance of some *gendarmes,* and the fright of others," Codio and his fellow inmates crashed the gate. For hours they rampaged through the city, looting and setting fires. Hotly pursued to the eastern outskirts by somewhat disorganized marine and *gendarmerie* patrols, Codio, joined by Metellus, shot his way east into Croix-des-Bouquets. The place was garrisoned by two marines and probably no more than twenty *gendarmes.* All but five bolted, leaving the remainder to fight alone. The marines and their little handful killed twelve *cacos* before retreating to avoid capture.[92]

Waller ordered out a mounted column, and at a Dominican frontier hamlet found Codio, Metellus, and a dozen *cacos* "practically surrounded" by the townsfolk. The marines relieved the Haitians of their charges and began the march back to Port-au-Prince. En route, while crossing a stream, the *cacos* asked permission to wash. It was granted, and the *cacos* tore into the bush. It was a big mistake. All were shot down. "General Codio was shot attempting to escape from a Marine guard," noted a Port-au-Prince obituary. "The people of the country side," Waller wrote to Secretary Daniels, "were overjoyed when they learned the fate of these men." "Really," Private Faustin Wirkus mused, "all pacifists and professional sympathizers with the oppressed to the contrary, it was the only way."[93]

Indeed it was. As if the United States did not have enough on its plate, in May 1916 a revolution across the border in the Dominican Republic, leading to a full-scale American occupation, stripped half the marine brigade; and meanwhile in Haiti the *cacos* were again on the move.

By early 1916 the *gendarmerie* mustered 1,500 troops, scattered in penny-packet detachments among 117 posts, and presented easy prey. All through the spring the tiny posts came under intermittent attack. But training, discipline, and a full supply of Krag rifles, with plenty of ammunition, eventually made their mark, and by summertime the *gendarmerie* were almost able to hold their own.

On the diplomatic front, the ratification of the Haitian-American treaty enabled the occupation authorities to proceed with necessary reforms, and to establish the machinery under which Haiti would be governed for the next eighteen years. A centrally directed colonial office, or at least a transfer of the United States Army's Bureau of Insular Affairs from the War Department to State, was necessary to most effectively govern Haiti. But instead of coordinating policy, Washington divided the imperial pie.

For Haiti this meant the creation of five "treaty services," whose heads were officially named by the President of Haiti upon a nomination by the President of the United States. It was, of course, a polite sham. The financial advisor and receiver-general of customs were appointed by the State Department, while the *Chef de Gendarmerie* and chiefs of public works and public health held their commissions by grace of the Secretary of the Navy.

It might be presumed that the American ambassador, Arthur Bailly-Blanchard, would have assumed some sort of control. But he was completely ineffective and barely deigned even to report to the State Department on the progress of events. Therefore, the single most responsible policy formulator, and thus the seat of American power in Haiti, remained the military commander; until July 1916 this was Admiral Caperton.

But in the summer of 1916 Admiral Caperton left to command the Pacific Fleet. Ned Beach, in effect his prime minister, shifted to Dominican waters. Rear Admiral Harry Knapp now commanded the Cruiser Squadron, and as such assumed authority as senior military officer on Hispaniola. But by autumn, with the Dominican intervention in high gear, he had little time to spare for Haiti.

Haitians fostered a hope that the establishment of the treaty services would bring with it a relaxation of military control. Far from it. The State Department requested that the navy continue martial law, at least until the *gendarmerie* proved its efficiency and until the other treaty services effectively organized. In Washington, Navy Secretary Daniels, uncomfortable with the entire question of the occupation, opted for a hands-off approach. As long as the marines kept Haiti quiet, he would not interfere.

In effect Haiti's new rulers were now Waller, Cole, who assumed command of the brigade in November 1916, and Butler, and none of these possessed, or in fact desired, the diplomatic skills of the departing naval officers. There would be no patience with traditional political mores.

Beach wrote of the "refinement and culture that marks the Haitian highest class." But Waller scorned the *élite* and considered Haitian politicians a bunch of grafters. The general, addressing Dartiguenave after the president had the temerity to complain of Marine Corps activities, stated the facts plainly: "You are president because we Americans are in Haiti. If you continue to denounce me, I'll have my government recall its troops for twenty-four hours and by the time we pass Gonâve [Island], you'll be chased out of the Presidential Palace."[94]

"I see nothing to be done," wrote Eli Cole to Admiral Knapp, "but to let them demonstrate to their capacity, if such they have, or let them hang themselves so that a military government becomes necessary."[95]

Imperialist or not, the occupation brought to Haiti the enormous and much needed benefits of the navy's expertise in public health. In 1917 ten navy doctors, a dentist, and forty enlisted hospital corpsmen were on duty. "The sanitary condition of the whole island is indescribably bad," noted the navy's surgeon general to Secretary Daniels, "and that cannot be brought up to a modern standard for many years to come, as it is only by educating the native population that permanent changes for the better can be effected, and this takes time."[96]

From Jacmel on the south coast Assistant Surgeon L.F. Drum reported, "*Gendarmes* are on duty in the market place to prevent the infraction of recently enacted sanitary laws, which aim to suppress the general practice of urination and defecation in public, provide for the collection of refuse from the streets, and for the corraling of stray hogs, goats, and dogs."[97]

Nursing mothers received the particular attention of Assistant Surgeon Michael at Port-de-Paix. "Puerperal infection plays a considerable role in the mortality of the women," he reported. "They nurse their children for from one-and-one-half to two years, a practice partly justified by the difficulty of obtaining suitable food for children." Michael traced part of the problem to the watered-down milk sold at the markets. He had all cow's and goat's milk inspected, and milk "whose specific gravity indicates dilution is thrown out." The markets themselves, great breeders of disease, he ordered to be thoroughly scrubbed, with "a special cleaning given Sunday morning by prison labor. Efforts are made to keep beggars with open sores out of the market."[98]

Some women also received a new, and for Haiti, a desperately needed career opportunity. At the request of the navy's senior medical officer in Port-au-Prince, members of the Navy Nurse Corps arrived to instruct the Catholic sisters in the organization of a school of nursing for native women.

One of the great successes of the occupation, concomitant with its single greatest systemic abuse, was the vast improvement of Haiti's roads. The French, during their colonial period, had built an adequate net connecting the major towns. But by 1916 only relics remained. Some of the French roads were so overgrown with vegetation that all trace had disappeared. No wheeled transport could pass from one town to the next. Overland, the 180 miles between Port-au-Prince and Cap Haïtien took up to three weeks.

The lack not only stifled economic development but was a serious military obstacle as well, prohibiting the rapid deployment of troops into the interior. Massive public works require massive public monies, and the Haitian government, even with revenues and disbursement under American auspices, had none. An accounting showed an estimated $8,000 per month could be spared. Yet this was hardly enough for labor, to say nothing of materials and tools. According to historians Robert and Nancy Heinl, it was a Haitian cabinet minister who pointed the Americans to an 1865 law, Article 54 of the Rural Code of the Republic of Haiti: "Public highways and communications will be maintained and repaired by the inhabitants, in rotation, in each section through which these roads pass and each time repairs are necessary."[99]

It was the ancient French feudal practice of the *corvée*, and strikingly similar to the old American road tax law. Citizens were required to either pay a public works tax, or in lieu, donate their labor. The Haitian code placed enforcement and supervision of the *corvée* with the rural police. As the *gendarmerie* were now Haiti's police, and the public works treaty service not yet functioning, Butler suggested he take charge.

Camps for the labor gangs were built and provided with food and nightly entertainment. At first, local reaction was highly favorable. Drawn by regular rations, lodging, and work, men lined up for the *corvée*. The lists of able-bodied workers were set by local magistrates and mayors, who turned them over to the *gendarmerie* for muster. Once on the list, a man either had to pay the tax or report for up to three weeks' work. "Nobody had any money," Butler remembered, "so they reported for work. I was well aware that this thing was capable of tremendous abuse, and had been abused by Haitians previously."[100]

The system was indeed ripe for corruption, and none took more advantage than the local Haitian civil servants. Eventually, any amount was accepted, not just the proper tax, as a bribe to avoid the list. If a peasant had no money, and very few did, he was kept on the *corvée* until he could buy his way out. A number of *gendarmes*, lacking direct marine officer supervision, reverted to their old *caco* ways and likewise turned to extortion, in some cases pocketing the ration allowances as well. Popular enthusiasm turned to discontent and eventually abhorrence.

Butler, however, whatever his diplomatic shortcomings, ran as clean an organization as possible, and the worst offenses did not occur until he left for the Great War in 1918. Under his command there was rapid progress. In about five months 112 miles of motor transport road bridged the coastal plain from Port-au-Prince to Gonaïves. One marine lieutenant, who put his work gangs on ten-hour shifts and supplied regular rations with meat each day, had 800 volunteers for renewed *corvée* service. With additional funds and 4,000 laborers, the road was completed through the heart of *caco* country, all the way to Cap Haïtien.

On January 1, 1918, Butler took President Dartiguenave and the cabinet on a motor trip to the Cap. The journey that once took three weeks was now traveled in less than fourteen hours. The general remembered, "We had two automobiles . . . a Ford roadster and a truck. The President sat beside me in the roadster and his Cabinet followed behind us in the truck. As we traveled in state along the road, all the workmen who had been carefully coached beforehand, lined up to present their picks and shovels, just as soldiers present arms."[101]

The war in Europe was a significant factor in the abuse and corruption of the *corvée* system. Beginning in the spring of 1917 with the United States declaration of war against Germany, every marine in Haiti (*and* the Dominican Republic, *and* every American empire outpost) clamored for reassignment to the regiments being shipped to France. Young Lieutenant Alexander Vandegrift, who was destined to remain on Hispaniola, was bitter. The future victor of Guadalcanal recalled years later, "The next twenty months constituted the most frustrating period of my life, nor was I alone in my attitude. Regular soldiers all, we had spent our adult lives working and studying and training for this supreme moment and now it became increasingly obvious that we were shunted aside despite the most ingenious attempts and pathetic appeals directly to the Commandant to send us over there. . . . We naturally carried on our duties, but with no great grace."[102]

Many, however, were sent and the thinned, grumbling ranks of the brigade were filled with recent stateside recruits. On Butler's relief in the spring of 1918 the *corvée* degenerated into virtual peonage. As in the old Haitian Army, laborers were press-ganged by the *gendarmerie*, and, often manacled, marched several days to districts far from their homes. In a vain attempt to combat the abuse of continual service, cards were issued to all discharged workers. But in practice, the local mayors and magistrates selected anyone they wished, even destroying the cards showing that men had done their share. And it was not uncommon to find *corvée* labor improving private holdings.

"The trouble was," recalled Major General Walter Greatsinger Farrell, who had been sent to Haiti from France, "when a man had done his tour, they got a bunch of them together for discharge and brought another group in. As these people were leaving the road, way the hell in the back country, maybe two or three days march from home, they'd run into the *gendarme* press-gang. They'd gather them up and take them to another place on the road, and put them back to work. Well, you only need to do that a couple of times before they got pretty well fed up with it. They thought they were now fugitives, and they took to the hills."[103]

Under lax American supervision, the abuses continued. Revulsion among the peasantry reached flash point. *Gendarmerie* press-gangs were attacked, and a *gendarme* killed near Jacmel. One insidious feature of the *corvée* was the opportunity it gave unscrupulous leaders to accuse the Americans of attempting to reintroduce slavery.

By late 1918 Colonel Alexander Williams, Butler's successor as *Chef de Gendarmerie* and the man who received a good part of the opprobrium, "recommended" to the president that the *corvée* be disbanded. On October 1, it ceased operations in all but the remote eastern region around Hinche, where it continued to function illegally, with the worst abuses, and ultimately a scandal that would rock the Marine Corps.

"Over there," in France, the 4th Marine Brigade was covering itself in blood and glory. In the newspapers and on every streetcorner in the United States, the names Château-Thierry and Belleau Wood reverberated with the great deeds of the Corps. For the 1st Marine Brigade in Haiti (and the 2nd Marine Brigade in the Dominican Republic), nobody, it seemed, gave a damn. The trickle of stateside enlistees hardly served to flesh out the depleted ranks. "The number of white troops at present in this country is entirely inadequate in case anything goes wrong," Eli Cole reported, "and while I hope everything will go well, it is neither advisable or safe to reduce our forces as has been done."[104]

Equally dire was the quality of the replacements. Most were brand-new enlistees, joined to fight Germans, and they were hardly overjoyed at being shipped to Haiti (or the Dominican Republic). Officer replacements were not much better. The rapid expansion of the Corps, increasing over seven-fold from 1916 to 1918, brought new and ofttimes unfit officers to the island. With no experience, they were thrust into positions of responsibility, with the inevitable result of a decided slackening of discipline and standards.

The *gendarmerie*, dissipated in overseeing the *corvée*, was neither fully trained, wholly dependable, nor yet ready for protracted field service. Its marksmanship was atrocious, and ranges for executions had to be reduced from thirty to fifteen feet.

It was a situation ripe for a rebellion. "All they needed was a good leader," the soon-to-return Dopey Wise later wrote. "In Charlemagne they found a damn good one."[105]

Charlemagne Masséna Péralte was "a man large in spirit, pride, intelligence, and ambition," wrote the historian Robert Heinl, "in short, a *gros nègre*."[106] Charlemagne was a native of Hinche, graduate of an exclusive French *lycée*, an ex-general of the old Haitian Army, and brother-in-law of ex-President Oreste Zamor. He was also a sworn enemy of Philippe Sudre Dartiguenave, and a stalking horse for Rosalvo Bobo, now closely following affairs from Kingston, Jamaica.

Long under suspicion for revolutionary activities, Charlemagne was convicted in early 1918 of complicity in a botched midnight raid on the Hinche *gendarmerie* payroll. Caught before he could slip over the border, he was sentenced to five years' hard labor in the prison at Cap Haïtien. On September 3, with a single *gendarme* guard, Charlemagne found himself on a work detail cleaning the streets. "A member of the Yale faculty," Dopey Wise noted, "cleaning streets under armed guard in New Haven would not cause a greater sensation. It was a disgrace worse than death."[107]

By appealing to his guard's patriotism, Charlemagne induced the *gendarme* to join him in escape. With a single Krag-Jorgensen rifle and the ability to exploit the general hatred of the *corvée*, he launched the great *caco* rebellion "to drive the invaders into the sea and free Haiti."

Charlemagne aimed his first offensives at the small, scattered *gendarmerie* posts—the glaring symbols of the puppet Haitian government and the hated *corvée*. These raids served the dual purpose of discrediting the effectiveness of the occupation and acquiring a number of relatively modern weapons.

The first big attack came on October 17, 1918, and was aimed at the *gendarmerie* barracks at Hinche. For Charlemagne it was a tactical fiasco but something of a strategic victory. Before midnight, about 100 *cacos* swarmed up to the town. The two marines and the little *gendarme* garrison met the howling assault with disciplined rifle fire. Before half an hour passed, thirty-five dead *cacos* lay scattered about the streets. In a rare miscalculation, Colonel John Russell, the normally astute brigade commander who had taken over from Eli Cole, reported, "This affair has no political or military significance whatsoever."[108]

Charlemagne struck again on November 10. This time it was

Maissade, just upriver from Hinche, and there were no marines to stiffen the *gendarmes*. The town was sacked, the barracks burned, and the garrison routed. Over the next four months, the *cacos* mounted a score of attacks but without great success. Their victory at Maissade remained their only one, as the *gendarmerie*, at times outnumbered twenty or thirty to one, put up stout resistance and held the towns.

The rebellion, however, was gaining strength, and by the spring of 1919 Charlemagne had about 5,000 *cacos* in the field and at least twice that number of civilians in a network of active supporters. In March Colonel Alexander Williams, the *Chef de Gendarmerie*, at last realized he had a full scale revolution to contend with. The *gendarmerie* was unable to crush it, and he belatedly requested the assistance of the marine brigade.

Brigadier General Albertus Catlin, a badly shot-up veteran of Belleau Wood, had taken command. The brigade mustered less than a thousand men, and Catlin ordered five companies, fully half his force, to the troubled regions around Hinche and the Dominican frontier. The marines occupied the towns, while the *gendarmerie* took to the field for much needed operational experience. Welcome reinforcements arrived. Four companies of the 7th Marines were shipped in from Guantánamo Bay. On March 31 there landed at Bizoton the thirteen aircraft—seven HS-2 flying boats, six Curtis Jennys—of the Marine Corps' Squadron E.

The anti-insurgent campaign was now carried on with considerable aggressiveness but showed little success. Armed clashes increased by the month, until there were over eighty between July and September. Nearly 500 *cacos* were killed, prompting a senior naval officer to announce that the war was going "well." Much like the Vietnam body counts of fifty years later, enumerating enemy corpses as a standard of victory was a big mistake.

In May 1919 Dopey Wise, now a lieutenant colonel, returned from the battlefields of France to become the new *Chef de Gendarmerie*. He found the military climate alarming. "You couldn't go out of any of the towns," he remembered, "without a *caco* taking a shot at you, though he wouldn't hit you." The *gendarmerie* was in very poor shape, and Catlin, he saw, was in no way pleased with its condition or efficiency.[109]

In the *gendarmes* in Port-au-Prince, Wise found an organization well uniformed, drilled, and armed. But they were show troops, in no way indicative of the whole. In the hinterland "they were in bad shape. Their rifles," Wise noted, "were a joke. They were discarded Krags, most of them with the sights knocked off. If they hit a house at point-blank range with these weapons, they were doing well." Quarters were tumbledown affairs, and morale very low. "The *cacos* seemed to have them bluffed."[110]

Wise chose as his first task the restoration of morale. "I knew that nothing appeals to the African mind as much as being well dressed." From the treaty service financial advisor, he obtained sufficient funds and bought new uniforms and shoes. Work gangs were turned to, repairing the barracks. From the brigade, he borrowed modern Springfield rifles. Both Butler and Williams had discouraged marksmanship on the theory that it was dangerous to teach the Haitians how to shoot; they might someday turn their coats. Wise issued orders to begin target practice at once. The Marine Corps close-order drill, which had only been applied to the Port-au-Prince *gendarmes*, was made a standard for the organization. The reforms took effect. "I grinned to myself," Wise wrote, "as I saw them begin to walk through the streets with a touch of swagger."[111]

In very certain terms Wise ordered his officers to impress upon their men that they were better than the *cacos*: better armed, better disciplined, and they had plenty of ammunition. When they met a *caco* band, instead of running away, they were to attack and pursue. "I told [the brigade officers] it was all damned foolishness to say that black troops couldn't fight. That I had seen the Senegalese in France, and they had fought as well as any white troops in the world."[112]

With his senior commanders, Wise discussed the revolution. "I impressed it on them that there was no use killing a lot of Haitians who would eventually make good laborers. That the thing to do was to get the leaders. We all knew that there was one *caco* leader who stood head and shoulders above all the others. His name was Charlemagne Péralte."[113]

By the summer of 1919 the short-term, war-duration marine enlistees and officers were in large part replaced by long-service regulars. First Lieutenant Walter Greatsinger Farrell (who would later command the 53rd Company), arrived from France. Ordered to Hinche, he soon made his first patrol into the bush. The retired marine major general remembered, "I'd been there about four or five days when I was sent out on a night patrol as an observer. We got a couple of hours out of camp, going along this trail, and suddenly off a little ways a *bourrique* [burro] started to sing—'Yee wonka yee wonka.' Well, I'd never heard that! I thought it was a *caco* war cry or something. I flipped my pistol out and dived into the brush, got a little ways in there and ran into this animal. Of course, everybody in the patrol had a good laugh."[114]

Any complacency the Americans felt over progress in quelling the rebellion was shattered during the night of October 5–6. With 300 *cacos*, Charlemagne moved to the northern gates of Port-au-Prince. Because he had grandiosely and foolishly sent an advance warning to the British embassy, requesting the chargé "to settle the situation and submit your reply before I am forced to change my mind," the marines and *gendarmes* were well alerted.[115]

Before dawn on October 6 Charlemagne's forces, joined by a number of Port-au-Prince sympathizers, burst screaming into the city. Immediately they were met by withering rifle and machine gun fire. Squads of marines and *gendarmes* rushed to the counterattack. Inside of two minutes the raid collapsed into a disorganized rout. With the sun, patrols fanned north and east. Charlemagne's base camp was overrun; thirty dead *cacos* lay strewn about, and twenty horses, a number of rifles and swords, and Charlemagne's prized and only field gun were captured. The charismatic leader, however, escaped.

An elaborate ruse was formulated to capture Charlemagne Péralte. "It was a pretty big order," Wise remembered. "It meant running down one Haitian out of several millions. . . . And that one Haitian was surrounded by his friends, operating in a country almost entirely sympathetic to him. [He] was protected by a fanatical body-guard, never slept two nights in the same place, and must be run down in a tangled maze of mountains and valleys and jungles, of which there were no accurate maps."[116]

Neither could the elusive Charlemagne be taken by a strong column, or in the fighting around the towns. He never participated in the raids, remaining miles behind the action, directing operations. But Sergeant Herman Hanneken* had a plan. Hanneken, who held a captain's commission in the *gendarmerie*, had cultivated a valuable ally, a former *caco* general, Jean-Baptiste

---

*Hanneken led a battalion under Vandegrift on Guadalcanal, rose to command the 7th Marines, and retired in the rank of brigadier general.

Conze. For $2,000 Conze offered to lead the *gendarmes* to Charlemagne's camp.

First he would have to raise his own *caco* band as a cover. The plan was taken to Dopey Wise and he immediately agreed. Funded with a stack of *gourdes*, Conze loudly and publicly aired his grievances against the Americans, pronouncing "Haiti for the Haitians" to all who listened. He revealed a stock of arms, a copious amount of rum, and in no time had a band of eager *cacos* under command.

Charlemagne maintained an intelligence service that stretched into every hamlet, and was soon aware of this new soldier of the revolution; yet he was suspicious. One night, while Conze and his *cacos* sat around their fires, Charlemagne, surrounded by his bodyguard, stepped out of the jungle and put a pistol to Conze's head: "Conze, you are not a true *caco*. You are nothing but a spy in the pay of those accursed Americans." Conze, a whisker away from death, continued to play the part. "If you believe that, the best thing you can do is kill me now." It worked. Charlemagne holstered his pistol and gave Conze the chance to prove his loyalty.[117]

Charlemagne badly needed a victory after his recent repulse from Port-au-Prince, and the capture of a major town would provide an irresistible impetus for the revolution. Conze might well be worth the risk.

For his coup, Conze chose Grande-Rivière-du-Nord, Hanneken's base, in the heart of the old *caco* country. Hanneken's sixty *gendarmes* in the town were heavily reinforced, and marine machine gunners took position on the roofs. When Conze's *cacos* attacked, the *gendarmes* would feign a withdrawal, and when Charlemagne rode in to take possession, he would be cut down by the marines' automatic fire. North and south of the town, from Cap Haïtien, all the way to Hinche, marine units established blocking positions to cut Charlemagne's line of retreat.

On October 26 Charlemagne, his staff, and 1,200 *cacos* moved into the rubble of Fort Capois. To give more credence to his ruse, Hanneken led a carefully staged "attack" on Conze's band, resulting in a conspicuous "failure" for the *gendarmerie*. Hanneken sulked about Grande Rivière, his arm in a sling, "blooded" by issue red ink. The story of the "rout" quickly spread, Conze was credited with Hanneken's wound, and his stock rose dramatically.

On the night of October 30 Conze and his *cacos*, "yelling like fiends, full of rum, blazing away with everything they had," burst into Grande Rivière. As planned, while the machine gunners on the roofs stayed well hidden, the *gendarmes* bolted. Conze sent word to Charlemagne that he could now march in triumph into the town. But Charlemagne was still suspicious and refused. By runner he ordered Conze to bring an honor guard up to the camp; only then would he consider coming in.[118]

Hanneken devised a brilliant improvisation; the *gendarmerie* would provide the honor guard. Taking his second in command, Lieutenant William Button (corporal, USMC), and sixteen picked *gendarmes* dressed in rags, the two marines painted their bodies with burnt cork and followed Conze into the hills.

Hanneken and Button had to pass as blacks among blacks, and, though both spoke fluent Creole, it was ticklish business. They passed six *caco* outposts before arriving at Charlemagne's camp. At each outpost they were stopped and questioned, but Conze gave the proper password and they were allowed to proceed. At the last checkpoint, on the very edge of the camp, the game was nearly given away.

There are several versions of what happened. "The leader there," Hanneken remembered, "was on the job." He spied Button's Browning automatic rifle, and looking the marine square in the face demanded, "Where did you get that gun?" "It's a white man's gun," Button replied. The *caco* caught Button's accent, grabbed for the BAR, and shouted the alarm. Button kept his head, "Let me go!" he yelled, "Don't you see my [chief, Conze] is getting out of sight."[119]

According to Dopey Wise, at that moment a woman in the camp threw a handful of brush onto the fire. As it flared up, Hanneken spotted Charlemagne somewhere between fifteen and forty feet away. He drew his .45 and put two bullets into Charlemagne's heart.

Major General Walter Greatsinger Farrell's version is quite different. He recalls Conze entering Charlemagne's tent and presenting him with a .38 caliber pearl-handled Smith & Wesson revolver. "Two men then walked out of the tent, dressed identically alike, same mustache, everything. They looked alike as two peas in a pod. The other man was [Charlemagne's] half-brother. When the two men stood across the fire from Hanneken, he knew by the pearl-handled pistol, who was who. He brought his .45 out, and drilled two bullets into his heart."[120]

Firing erupted from all sides. Button unslung his BAR and emptied the magazine into the frenzied bodyguards. Throughout the night they held off repeated attacks by as many as 250 *cacos*. At dawn, strapping Charlemagne's body onto a mule, Hanneken led his men, all the while fighting a rear-guard action, back to Grande-Rivìere. "If I remember the figures right," General Farrell noted nearly seventy years later, "they counted 163 dead on that road." The body was then taken by rail to Cap Haïtien, where it was identified by the local *abbé*, who administered last rites.[121]

To convince all that Charlemagne was dead, the corpse was put on public display and hundreds came to see it. The body was then laid out on a door, photographed, and the pictures distributed, many by air drop, throughout Haiti.

For the action Hanneken and Button received the Congressional Medal of Honor, and Hanneken obtained a regular commission as a second lieutenant in the Marine Corps as well.

In the week following Charlemagne's death, the cordon of marine and *gendarmerie* trail blocks and ambushes prevented large numbers of *cacos* from crossing the mountains into the central plateau. Over 300 *cacos* were captured, though most were soon released on their promise of good behavior, and permitted to return to their villages.

Lieutenant Farrell led one of these trail-blocking patrols. "They figured [Charlemagne's] army would disperse, make through the passes and head south, and we would pick them off when they came through. We were on our way to Gros Roche. The trail kept branching off until I saw a small habitation—four or five huts, a big mango tree with a table, some chairs, and three men. One thing I noticed was that one man was well dressed and he had a Krag-Jorgensen rifle leaning against the table. I figured the man was a *gendarme* vigilante,* so I kept walking on in. He looked up, saw me, and sort of froze. He waited until I got about twenty paces. Then smiled, nodded his head, and slowly got up, took the rifle and executed a French present arms. When I got a little closer, something went over his face, he flickered, brought his rifle up and fired. But before he got the round off, I got one into him. I hit him in the belly, and his round went over my head. Then all hell broke loose. They fired at me from a couple of different places, and the excitement was pretty tight for a minute or two. I had my .45 out pulling the trigger to beat hell. One of the *cacos* was mounting a horse and he turned around and took

---

*A trustworthy civilian in the pay of the *gendarmerie*.

a shot at me. So I zinged one down on him, and he went over, leaving the horse. The patrol, hearing the firing, came charging through, and we killed and wounded several. The guy who I thought was a *gendarme* vigilante turned out to be 'General' Henri Philippe Delezon, secretary of forestry and agriculture of the revolutionary government. Well, we fixed up their wounded as best we could, and went on."[122]

With the death of Charlemagne, north Haiti entered a period of prolonged peace. The action moved south and command of the revolution devolved upon Charlemagne's chief lieutenant, Benoît Batraville. Colonel John Russell, again in command of the brigade, described him as "a much more aggressive man than Charlemagne, but lacking in intelligence and leadership."[123]

The marine brigade now mustered 1,346 men, and included the newly raised 8th Marines under Louis McCarty Little in overall command of operations. The *gendarmerie*, now a battle-tested force of 2,700, had recovered from its malaise and was ready to give a good accounting. To prepare for an all-out campaign to crush the *cacos* in central and south Haiti, the country was divided into tactical zones of operations, and sufficient troops were assigned to each. Active, intense patrolling commenced. One marine officer remembered, "Little really drove us. We would come in from a fifteen-day patrol at daybreak, exchange our enlisted men and be off by dark."[124]

The offensive kicked off on New Year's day, 1920. Batraville had about 2,500 *cacos* spread in camps throughout the region south of Hinche. Lieutenant Farrell remembered the operations. "I went out on a platoon-sized patrol; points out in front, and a senior noncom bringing up the rear. Well, we didn't get into a fight. I made another patrol, and we still didn't get into a fight; nothing much happened, a few long-range shots. These gooks, I said, are here in large numbers, they ought to be able to smother our outfits by making a massed attack and getting out again. The only solution I see to this thing is to make them attack. You go out with a small enough outfit so that we say, here's our candy, come and get it! With our superior marksmanship and plenty of ammunition we can drive them off. So we decided to try it. We took out a patrol of about ten men and got a reaction. The *cacos* made a half-assed attack and we drove them off. We tried to take off after them, but they scattered. So we reduced our number again to about seven, and then we started getting fights. That's what broke that thing up. We were getting their casualties, and weren't taking any ourselves."[125]

But for Farrell, even a seven-man patrol seemed too large. "We got word that Batraville was going to hold a voodoo ceremony in Chapelle St. Martin, way back in the mountains. He was supposed to have only his bodyguard troops, about 500, so we figured a four-man patrol would be about right.

"Little called for volunteers, there were dozens, so he said, 'Okay, Farrell, I'll take you. Who do you want.' I picked Sergeant Chapman and Privates Seely and McKay as my automatic riflemen. We had two BARs, Chapman had a rifle, I had a shotgun and a .45.

"We got to Chapelle St. Martin and the place was empty. We pulled on top of a hill, dug in, and barricaded our position with thorn brush. We laid there for two days. On the third night, we saw some torches along the hills, a long line of torches, moving toward the *chapelle*. We knew this was the start of the voodoo ceremony, and got ready. But instead of going to the *chapelle*, they got around back of us. 'What the hell is going on here?' I said.

"We found out pretty quick what was going on. Because on command, the whole bunch of them threw their torches into the dry grass. They knew we were there. Well, we gave them a spray of Browning and got to work setting a back fire. The next morning we packed up to go.

"A couple of miles down the line we saw a man with a rifle around his shoulder, walking post; could be a *caco*, could be a *gendarme*, could be a vigilante. We went down to see and ran into a few men behind a stone outcropping. They opened fire, and we opened up on them. They left, we went forward and came up against a rough rock wall. There were a dozen of them behind that. As soon as we started work on them, they shoved off. Another bunch tried to work around us. They came down an open slope, we spotted them, and opened fire within shotgun range. We pushed on and came up against another rock wall about a hundred yards away. Three *cacos* started to run, and we opened up and cut them down.

"Then we heard the count, 'one, two, three,' in French, and the whole edge of this rock wall turned black with men. They all stuck their guns over and started firing; probably not aiming, because I can't see how they could have missed us. We gave them a burst of Browning, they ducked down again, and we got ready. We put the BARs on semiautomatic, every shot had to be an aimed shot, because there were a hell of a lot of them—somewhere about two hundred—and only four of us.

"We kept working on them; they kept firing volleys, and started to pull out. We followed them and found their camp and corral, way up on a rock, with finger and toe holds. I left Seely and McKay down below and started up with Chapman. I heard a shot behind me and cussed out my men below. 'What the hell are you shooting at?' 'That wasn't us, Lieutenant, there's a gook up there that took a shot at you.' I climbed up, and there was a little palm hut there; I looked into it, and this guy put a round between the edge of my hat and the side of my head. I could feel the breeze. He had been lying behind a log, got up and ran into the brush. I could see where he was going. So when he pulled into an open space, I pulled the trigger and he went down.

"We climbed back down, took four horses out of their corral and headed back to Hinche. Well, that was the biggest fight I had. I reported three dead to Colonel Little, and he accused me of filing a false report. A local Marist priest had counted forty-seven dead *cacos* which he buried in three mass graves around Chapelle St. Martin."[126]

In the predawn of January 15, 1920, Batraville and more than 300 *cacos* launched a suicidal attack on Port-au-Prince. Russell's intelligence section provided advance warning, and the marines and *gendarmerie* were ready. According to Russell's son-in-law, "The *cacos* advanc[ed] into town in columns and with flags and conch horns blowing." They were met with massed BAR and machine gun fire, scattering their ranks. One group made for the slums, and set a block afire, lighting up the entire surrounding countryside.[127]

Patrols swiftly combed the city. One, led by Lieutenant Gerald Thomas, collided head on with the *cacos* on the waterfront, running for the National Bank. "Near the Iron Market," he recalled, "we saw a large number of *cacos* coming down the street. We detrucked and opened fire. I had one man killed and six wounded in five minutes, but we mowed the *cacos* down."[128]

Fully a fifth of the raiders were wiped out in the streets, and surviving *cacos* forevermore referred to the night as *"la débâcle."*

At daylight, patrols moved east and north of the city, and more than fifty additional *cacos* were killed.

Caco chiefs began to surrender in numbers. In return for a good behavior pass, Russell required them to go into the countryside and induce others to lay down their arms. "They must at once," he reported, "go out with one of our patrols, thus identifying themselves with the occupation." By March, over 10,000 passes were issued, and Batraville's days were numbered.[129]

But he still held sway over a considerable force, and in January, just after *la débâcle,* he was elected president of Haiti by his subchiefs. "It is important," Russell noted, "that he should be taken, from both a military and political standpoint." A reward of 5,000 *gourdes* was offered to anyone giving information of his whereabouts.[130]

Batraville gained his last "victory" in a horrible episode on April 4. At daylight, near the bordertown of Las Cahobas, a small patrol of four marines, led by *gendarmerie* Lieutenant Lawrence Muth (sergeant, USMC), topped a rise and opened fire on a small group of armed *cacos.* They were bait: the patrol had blundered into an ambush.

Heavy fire came from the flanks and rear, and Muth was hit immediately in the head and stomach. The next senior man, Private Stone, received a shot in the neck. The bullet struck the receiver of his rifle, which blew up on discharge and blinded him. Stone and the remaining two marines retreated back to Las Cahobas, killing about ten *cacos* in the withdrawal. Muth was left for dead on the trail.

From Mirebalais and Las Cahobas, twenty-one marine and *gendarmerie* patrols were sent scouring the hills. That afternoon they found Muth's body. According to Russell's report, it was naked; "the head and heart had been taken away and the latter probably eaten."[131]

Muth had not died on the trail. Alive, he was dragged into the bush. Under interrogation, a *caco* revealed that Muth, too weak to stand, was revived and propped up while Batraville made a speech, he then raised a machete and cut off Muth's head. According to the *caco,* they smeared bits of Muth's brains on their bullets, "so that when we fire at Marines we do not miss." Lieutenant Colonel Richard Hooker later stated before a United States Senate committee, "They cut off his private parts, took out his heart and liver, opened his stomach, and took out his intestines, and took large strips of flesh from his thighs. His heart and liver were eaten."[132]

At Las Cahobas on May 18 Captain Jesse Perkins learned from a peasant that a large *caco* band, perhaps 200 men, was within four hours' march. At dawn the next morning, his eighteen-man patrol drove in the first outposts. Perkins pursued at high speed. As they approached the camp, situated in very rough country, with innumerable large boulders all around, the marines came under heavy fire. Perkins sent the main body of the patrol to cut off any escape from the rear. With three men, and a BAR spraying fire, he rushed the entrance. Ten feet inside stood Benôit Batraville. He raised his rifle, and, as Perkins reported, "was immediately shot down by Sergt. Passmore."[133]

There were no other *cacos* in sight, but rifles still popped from among the rocks. The main body of the patrol burst in, and the *cacos*, realizing Batraville was dead, vanished into the hills. "Then," Perkins noted, "we turned to examine Benoît's person and he was in the act of rising and reaching for his revolver. Hence it was necessary for Sergt. Taubert to finish killing him. . . . He was barefooted, wore a straw hat and ordinary blue clothes." They found on the body Muth's rifle and Colt revolver.[134]

The death of Benoît Batraville ended the Second Caco War and all armed resistance to the occupation came to an end. But in the United States, an avalanche of scandal was about to shake the Marine Corps to its very foundations.

Hinche, a town of about 5,000 people, lies atop the central plateau of eastern Haiti, roughly between Port-au-Prince and Cap Haïtien. It is in remote, wild, and forbidding country, and until the *corvée* road was built, it was completely isolated from either city. In the sixteenth century, before the arrival of the French and during the very early days of Spanish rule, it was dubbed Hinche the Accursed.

In January 1919 reports came to brigade command that the *corvée*, officially halted the previous October, was still going strong. Worse, there were substantiated rumors that *caco* prisoners working on the roads were being shot out of hand, by members of the *gendarmerie*, and that others were disappearing without a trace.

On reading the reports, General Catlin sent his trusted deputy, Richard Hooker, to investigate. At Hinche, Hooker was met by the *gendarmerie* district commander, Major Clarke Wells, who stated the charges were baseless.

Hooker remained suspicious, however, and rightfully so. He found the *corvée* active at both Hinche and Maissade. As he told Catlin, "The *gendarmes* used the natives so brutally that many had left their gardens and either joined the bandits or had come into the towns for safety."[135]

Catlin went to investigate. He spoke with everyone: local French priests, town magistrates, and frightened peasants alike. There was little doubt of the truth. With Wells' sanction, the *corvée* was in full operation, even to the working of the Maissade magistrate's farm, which was guarded by the *gendarmerie*. *Caco* prisoners were routinely shot, "escaping" the usual excuse given by the *gendarmes*.

Charlemagne Péralte's revolt was in full fire at the time these abuses and atrocities were committed, and the Hinche region provided fertile ground for rebel recruits. Yet instead of detailing conditions truthfully, Wells ordered his subordinate *gendarmerie* commanders to falsify their reports; "everything quiet," read the accounts coming from Hinche. He also made it quite clear to his officers that he wanted neither to see the prisoners nor to hear about their treatment.[136]

Catlin relieved Wells of his command, calling him a murderer, liar, and unfit to wear the uniform of the Marine Corps. A general court-martial was in order, and proceedings were initiated. But Catlin believed the evidence against Wells would not stand. The charges were withdrawn, and Wells was transferred, along with the rest of his officers, "for the good of the Corps," back to the United States. Catlin and his new *Chef de Gendarmerie*, Dopey Wise, issued a general order prohibiting the summary execution and oppression of Haitians. It was published and read to every member of the brigade.[137]

Nearly seventy years later, Major General Walter Greatsinger Farrell commented, "I heard that Captain Becker, who had command of the company in Maissade, had been accused of shooting up pack trains of women. It seems he stopped a pack train one time, and found that the women had rifles hidden in their *macoutes* [saddlebags]. A couple of the women turned out to have balls. Therefore he was pretty careless about opening up on pack trains. But Becker was loony as a bug, and later they sent him to an asylum."[138]

When Dopey Wise returned to Haiti in the summer of 1919, he was ordered to investigate a double murder in the Port-au-Prince suburb of Croix de Bouquets. "Two Haitians," he was told, "were shot there by the *gendarmerie* the other night." At the post he found Lieutenant Louis Brokaw (sergeant, USMC) and about twenty *gendarmes*. Wise put it to the lieutenant, "What do you know about it?" "Nothing," Brokaw responded. Wise interviewed the French priest and the town's white storekeeper; neither would talk.[139]

At the telephone exchange were three marine wiremen who also denied any knowledge of executions. But Wise felt they had denied overmuch. A "No, Sir" would have sufficed; these men, however, were quite voluble as to their ignorance. "You can't deal with men at close range for years," Wise later wrote, "without developing a hunch that tells you whether they're lying or telling the truth."[140]

Wise returned to the storekeeper and wheedled out one version of the story. Brokaw, two of the wiremen, Privates Walter Johnson and John McQuilkin, and a local Haitian had gotten drunk. A voodoo priest was incarcerated in the town jail for illegal religious practices. At night Brokaw and his companions took the priest and another prisoner to the outskirts of town, ordered them to dig graves, and shot them, as Wise noted, "just for excitement."[141]

This time, General Catlin did not hesitate to prosecute, and two general courts-martial were convened in Port-au-Prince. Only Johnson and McQuilkin went to trial. Brokaw, who showed signs of mental instability, was examined by a naval surgeon, pronounced "insane," and sent to St. Elizabeths Hospital in Washington, D.C.

At the trials another version of events emerged. According to the testimony, Brokaw had ordered the two privates, along with three *gendarmes,* to form a firing party and execute the two prisoners. Johnson and McQuilkin, doubting Brokaw's authority, shot "wide" so as not to kill, but managed to maim the prisoners. Brokaw, seeing that they were still alive, drew his pistol and performed the *coup de grace*.

Johnson and McQuilkin were convicted and given long sentences at hard labor.

But this was just the beginning of the affair. In his attempt to mitigate the private's guilt, Johnson's military defense counsel had offered that the unlawful killing of Haitians was a comparatively ordinary practice by the marines. The statement went into the record, and, Dopey Wise noted, "hell started popping."[142]

Up the chain of command the court-martial papers passed for their routine review. In late September they arrived on the desk of Commandant George Barnett. The statement regarding the random killing of Haitians leapt out at him. Barnett was incensed, and to the new brigade commander, John Russell, he sent a confidential letter: "It appears from the testimony in the general court-martial . . . that unlawful executions of Haitians have occurred. . . . You will issue immediate, necessary, and proper instructions regarding these unlawful actions." All very well and proper, but Barnett could not let the matter rest.[143]

Five days later, on October 2, he dictated a second letter for Russell, this time marked "Personal and confidential": "The court-martial of one private for the killing of a native prisoner brought out the statement by his counsel *which showed me that practically indiscriminate killing of natives* [italics added] has gone on for some time. I hope you will go into the matter personally . . . and not only to correct it, but absolutely correct it. I was shocked beyond expression to hear of such things and to know that it was at all possible that duty could be so badly performed by marines of any class. . . . I want every case sifted thoroughly and the guilty parties brought to justice. I think this is the most startling thing of its kind that has ever taken place in the Marine Corps, and I don't want anything of the kind to happen again." Barnett's conclusion's verily accused the Corps of practicing genocide.[144]

Further up the chain of command went the court-martial documents. On January 12, 1920, they arrived on the desk of Navy Secretary Josephus Daniels. The second letter to Russell, however, was not among them.

In Haiti, Colonel Russell closely investigated the allegations regarding Wells, Brokaw, Becker, and the "practically indiscriminate killings." He found they were isolated acts, divorced from the general standard of brigade and *gendarmerie* conduct, and that Wells seemed to be their main instigator. But Wells' court-martial was no longer possible. Haitian witnesses, even if they could be found, were considered to be notoriously unreliable. The enlisted marines to be summoned as interested parties or witnesses were no longer in the Corps and impossible to locate. Russell's report was duly sent to the commandant in mid-March; it never arrived.

In August Daniels' office made a query as to the disposition of the case. The Secretary requested the documentation from the commandant and Russell's report was nowhere to be found.

In the United States, the whole question of the occupation had been very much in the background until then, overshadowed by the aftereffects of the world war. But in the spring of 1920 it was slowly seeping into the newspapers. The *New York Evening Post*, consistently anti-interventionist, considered the occupation "more like bullying than helping." The influential liberal journal, the *Nation,* which seemed to serve as the propaganda organ of the disenfranchised Haitian *élite*, saw the intervention and occupation as unbridled imperialism. It noted that the only difference between the European, Japanese, and American variety was that the Americans "were Anglo-Saxon enough to mask . . . imperialism under high-sounding phrases." Infant civil rights organizations, led by the National Association for the Advancement of Colored People (NAACP), were bombarded by the Haitian *élite* with woeful tales of American perfidy and atrocity. Considering the *élite's* history, their new-found concern for Haiti's illiterate, malnourished masses was rather suspect. Daniels decided it was time for a high-level investigation.[145]

John A. Lejeune, the new and universally respected commandant of the Marine Corps, was ordered to Haiti. In July, 1920, Lejeune, accompanied by Brigadier General Smedley Butler, landed at Port-au-Prince. Following an inspection of the marines and *gendarmerie* in the capital, they traveled the length and breadth of the republic. "A state of peace and tranquility prevailing throughout Haiti," Lejeune noted. "We traveled through the country without a guard, and found no evidence of hostility on the part of the natives."[146]

He found the military situation, to be "in excellent condition." The marines and *gendarmerie* were actively patrolling the interior, and the generals found "the natives busily at work cultivating their farms and carrying their produce to market."[147]

Lejeune found Colonel Russell, the brigade commander, "an able, just, and humane officer, who issues the most comprehensive instructions requiring the kindly treatment of the inhabitants by our own men."[148]

Russell's missing report was unearthed in the brigade files, and Lejeune's synopsis entirely mirrored its findings. The abuses and atrocities were the isolated acts of ill-disciplined men, and on at least two occasions, of deranged men. In short, no matter what tales the Haitian *élite* were telling their American allies, the common Haitian peasant simply did not regard the marines as the sadistic oppressors they were now being portrayed. But before the Lejeune report arrived on Secretary Daniels' desk, the game of American presidential election politics had begun to play out. The occupation of Haiti as well as the entire question of Woodrow Wilson's aggressive foreign policy was a ready-made issue for the Republican outs. Their candidate, Warren G. Harding, told the crowds, "Thousands of native Haitians have been killed by American Marines."[149]

The Lejeune report to Secretary Daniels was made public on October 12, 1920. The Secretary and President Wilson were relieved, but their complacency was short-lived. George Barnett, no longer commandant but still on active duty, saw the very existence of the Lejeune-Butler mission as a sign of Daniels' distrust of his own investigations. He requested that Headquarters Marine Corps release his Haiti files.

Among the documents was Barnett's second letter to Russell, the one marked "Personal and confidential." Printed by the *New York Times* on October 14, Barnett's unfortunate use of the phrase "indiscriminate killing" received prominent space in a full-blown journalistic disaster. Vainly, the ex-commandant tried to exculpate himself. Although the words were his, *he* had not made the allegation; it had been made by the defense counsel of an indicted murderer. Barnett had really meant "unlawful," not "indiscriminate." "I am a soldier," he told the press, "and not an author. I feel certain that the brigade commander fully understood my meaning."[150]

But in the opinion of certain journals and the Republicans, the Marine Corps and the Navy Department stood fully condemned. The Democratic vice-presidential candidate was young Franklin Roosevelt, lately Assistant Secretary of the Navy, an architect of occupation policy, and one of the authors of the Haitian constitution. Republicans, Warren G. Harding trumpeted, would never impose democracy on the little West Indian republics at the point of a bayonet.

The charges fueled by the Barnett letter continued without abatement. The Marine Corps, so recently hailed for its heroic exploits on the battlefields of France, was now vilified as a bunch of baby killers. In an interview with the *New York Times,* travel writer Harry Franck distorted a few grains of truth in a huck-stering shill for his just published book, *Roaming Through the West Indies*. To a reporter, Franck told "how American Marines, largely made up of and officered by Southerners, opened fire with ma-chine-guns from airplanes upon defenseless Haitian villages, kill-ing men, women, and children in the open market place."[151]

The Lejeune report, which confirmed the findings of the here-tofore missing Russell investigation and cleared Barnett of any coverup, did little, if anything, to halt the clamor. Secretary Dan-iels ordered a full-dress court of inquiry. Headed by Rear Admiral Henry Mayo, lately commander in chief of the Atlantic Fleet, it was specifically charged with investigating whether (in Barnett's words) "practically indiscriminate killing of natives has been going on for some time." The court left for Haiti on November 3, 1920.[152]

The inquiry was even more exhaustive than the Lejeune-Butler mission had been, and arrived at similar conclusions. Two "unjustifiable homicides" had been committed and sixteen other "serious acts of violence have been perpetrated against citizens of Haiti." As in the previous reports, the Mayo court deemed them all isolated acts, "and in nearly all cases [the] responsible party [had been] brought before general court, convicted and sen-tenced." Regarding the "practically indiscriminate killing of na-tives," the members delivered an adamant rebuke to Barnett, finding "no proper grounds" for his statement.[153]

The court went further. The widespread charges of crimes and atrocities were "ill considered, regrettable and thoroughly unwarranted reflections on . . . the U.S. Marine Corps. . . . Now," the court concluded, "for the first time in more than a hundred years, tranquility and security of life and property may be said to prevail in Haiti."[154]

Like the Lejeune-Butler mission, the Mayo court of inquiry hardly dented the invective. Actually the clamor got worse. Through their political action committee called *Union Patriotique*, and the pages of the *Nation*, the Haitian *élite* contin-ued their campaign. Charlemagne Péralte, they asserted, had been crucified by the marines; and "outrages on pregnant women," "tortures of water and fire," and villagers "devoured by war dogs imported from the Philippines" were all common-place.[155]

In mid-1921 the United States Senate began its own exhaustive investigation into the occupations of Haiti and the Dominican Republic. Every person of stature with a role in the occupation —military and civilian, Haitian, Dominican, and American—was called upon to testify.

The Senate committee traveled to Haiti, and despite the constant bombardment of propaganda regarding "numberless abominable crimes," unearthed nothing to compromise the facts of the military reports.

The committee, far from condemning the original intervention of July 1915, considered it a wholly necessary operation for the protection of the Haitian people. The problem, as they saw it, was one of a singular lack of central policy and political direction.

Immediate evacuation was out of the question. Haiti, the committee felt, was hardly prepared to go it alone. "We are there," wrote committee chairman Senator Joseph Medill McCormick, "and in my judgment we ought to stay there for at least twenty years."[156]

The committee recommended a coordination of policy and the treaty services, including the marines and the *gendarmerie,* under a single high commissioner appointed by and directly responsible to the President of the United States. The post went to the judicious and capable ex–brigade commander John Russell.

With peace in Haiti, the role of the Marine Corps rapidly diminished, and the brigade, now reduced to the 2nd Marines, assumed the comfortable, if boring, existence of garrison troops at Port-au-Prince and Cap Haïtien. Most military functions were now the province of the *gendarmerie.* By 1922 its ranks included twenty-three Haitian officers, a number that slowly grew to 200 by the end of the occupation in 1934. The name *"gendarmerie"* is more suggestive of a police than a military capacity, so in 1928 the *gendarmerie* was accorded a new designation, worthy of the army it had become: the *Garde d'Haiti.* By the early 1930's its enlisted ranks mustered nearly 3,000 men, and mobile companies equipped with light armored cars were headquartered at the capital, the Cap, Gonaïves, and Hinche.

In 1929 the final disturbance of the occupation occurred, signaling the beginning of its end. In his attempt at revamping Haiti's educational system, Russell established the *Service Technique* to instruct the Haitian masses in the manual trades.

Its crown jewel was a teachers' college of agronomy, the Central School of Agriculture, in the Port-au-Prince suburb of Damien. As admission required literacy, there was hardly a peasant enrolled. The sons of the *élite*, having no sense of *noblesse oblige*, shunned the place. To induce the young *élite* into the school, a scholarship of twenty-five dollars per month was offered to each entering student. The not inconsiderable sum served its purpose. But once enrolled, the *élite* scions concentrated only on the academic curriculum; hired peasants slopped the hogs and shoveled the dung.

Seeking to right the imbalance, in the fall of 1929, the American head of the *Service Technique* reduced the scholarships for the *élite*, reserving the funds for the sons of backcountry peasants. This experiment greatly disturbed the student body. On October 31, accompanied by their Haitian instructors, they marched in a mass demonstration. Within a fortnight, students throughout Haiti, from kindergartens to the prestigious French *lycées*, were out on strike.

Simultaneously, President Louis Borno, nearing the last months of his eight-year term, decided his people were not yet ready for popular suffrage, and showed an increasing reluctance to step down. The opposition "parties," seeing in the student revolt a ready-made opportunity to jointly topple Borno and press for an end to the occupation, began fomenting a general strike. Throughout November, demonstrations, marches, and wildcat strikes hit the capital. Russell several times had to restrain Borno, who attempted to clap every opposition politician in jail. More importantly, through some judicious arm-twisting, he convinced the president to announce he would not seek office in the 1930 elections.

But the announcement had no effect, the unrest continued, and Russell became suitably alarmed at the military situation. Numbers of the marine brigade had been siphoned off to Nicaragua to deal with a nasty guerrilla war there, and its strength in Haiti was at an all-time low, less than 500 men. The *Garde d'Haiti* thus far had handled the situation alone, but Russell had grave doubts about it. On December 3 he cabled Secretary of State Henry Stimson, "Loyalty of the *Garde* now very questionable. . . . It is therefore requested that strength of the brigade be immediately increased by 500 until after inauguration of new president in 1930."[157]

The State Department considered Russell worried overmuch.

They were only half right. The *Garde* did remain loyal, but the next day workers at the Port-au-Prince customs house went on a rampage. The American collector and his deputy were badly beaten, and the files, equipment, and furniture were destroyed. Inevitably mobs gathered in the streets, and the customs house workers were joined in their strike by those in the office of the financial advisor. In mid-afternoon, Russell declared martial law, proclaimed a curfew, and ordered the marines to take charge of Port-au-Prince. From Hampton Roads the 1st Marine Provisional Battalion embarked and sailed for Haiti.

The punitive measures had their desired effect, and conditions in the capital quickly returned to normal. But in Les Cayes, along the southern crab claw of south Haiti, an ugly incident was taking form. The year's coffee harvest was a bad one, and that coupled with higher taxes on alcohol put the peasantry in a worse than usual state. Whipped up by anti-Borno and anti-occupation agitators, mobs overran several rural *Garde* stations and marched on the town. Early on December 7 the telephone lines were cut, but not before the local commander phoned brigade headquarters that the situation was "getting rapidly out of hand." American women and children took refuge in the *Garde* barracks.

At Port-au-Prince a marine platoon boarded their trucks for the ninety-mile trip over the good *corvée* road to Les Cayes. From the capital's Bowen Field, a flight of scout bombers roared off, climbed the *massif* and headed west. They flew over Les Cayes and commenced dummy runs over the town. For added effect their tiny, 25-pound bombs were dropped into the bay.

The truck-borne marines arrived in late afternoon. At the town's outskirts about twenty, with a pair of Browning automatic rifles, faced a surging mob of about 1,500 stone-throwing, machete-armed demonstrators. For half an hour the marines were pelted with stones. A spokesman for the mob came to the fore, demanded the release of the town's prisoners, and was refused. He thereupon bit a marine on the ear, was shoved off with a bayonet, and the mob charged.

The marines reacted by firing a volley over their heads. The mob halted, but just for a moment. Agitated by their leaders, they came again. This time the marines lowered their weapons and fired for effect. A dozen Haitians lay dead, and twenty-three were wounded. Instantly the rioters evaporated.

The *Nation* termed the incident the "Cayes Massacre," and

Under Secretary of State Joseph Cotton, ignoring the evidence, called the marines "a firing squad."[158]

In the meantime, Russell ordered *Garde* and marine reinforcements to all towns threatened by strikes and riots. But in the end the incident at Les Cayes proved the instant collapse of the movement. So quickly did calm descend upon Haiti that the 1st Provisional Battalion was turned back while still at sea.

In Washington, however, the uprising focused President Herbert Hoover's attention on the island. A Quaker humanitarian, he had inherited a distasteful occupation which stretched back through three administrations to Woodrow Wilson. The Haitian-American treaty still had six years to run; after 1936 the United States had absolutely no mandate to remain. For Hoover, Haiti, and the Marine Corps, that was too long to wait.

In February 1930 President Hoover appointed ex–governor-general of the Philippines W. Cameron Forbes to chair a commission with orders to end the occupation. The mission, Forbes wrote, "was laid out for me in no uncertain terms." The commission arrived at Port-au-Prince on the last day of the month and began an inspection and tour of the republic.[159]

Among their recommendations were the rapid Haitianization of the treaty services, and the turning of the *Garde d'Haiti* over to complete Haitian control by October 1, 1934. The marine brigade, which the commission carefully noted should not be reduced, would evacuate the republic thirty days thereafter, two years prior to the expiration of the treaty.

In accord with the commission's request for a civilianization of the occupation, in November 1930 Brigadier General Russell resigned his post, and was replaced as *ambassador* by Dr. Dana G. Munro, a career diplomat.

In early July 1934 the navy's transports and supply ships began the evacuation of the brigade's nonessential elements and civilian dependents. On August 1 on the Champ de Mars, where nineteen years before Captain van Orden had bivouacked the *Washington*'s landing force, a spruce and sparkling battalion of the *Garde d'Haiti* marched in review. With a flurry of salutes, drums, and bugles, the last American *Chef* turned over the command to his Haitian successor.

Two weeks later, on August 14, in front of brigade headquarters, a company of the 2nd Marines faced a company of the *Garde* across a flagpole. The band played the national anthems of both countries, and the guns of Fort Nationale boomed out a salute of forty-two guns. Slowly, down came the stars and stripes, and in its place rose the blue and red flag of the Republic of Haiti. The next morning, the marines formed up for the last time, and as they marched down to the wharf, into their transports, the *Garde* band played them out to "The Halls of Montezuma."

"Neither the Haitians, the American public, nor the marines themselves," noted the *Denver News*, "will feel very badly about it if they never go back."[160]

6:

DOMINICAN
REPUBLIC I
1916–1924

If the ox of a man of sound senses gored the ox of a
deaf-mute, an imbecile, or a minor, the owner is culpable; but if the ox of a deaf-mute, an imbecile, or a
minor gored the ox of a man of sound senses, the
owner is not culpable."

–The *Mishnah*

On April 30, 1916, Dopey Wise's 6th Company
and Eugene Fortson's 9th (artillery) Company marched down to
the waterfront at Port-au-Prince. At anchor lay the old transport
Prairie, her boats bobbing along the wharf ready to take the marines out to the ship. In a short briefing by Colonel Waller and
Admiral Caperton, the officers were introduced to the latest situation. "Wise," the colonel began, "there's a little trouble over in
San Domingo. It will probably be settled in a short time." There
weren't many details, but the admiral added some perspective.
"There's a revolution over there. You are to support the President
and have entire charge of the work ashore."[1]

The *Prairie* weighed anchor and three days later she steamed
into the open roadstead of Santo Domingo. Already in attendance
was the gunboat *Castine,* anchored in the mouth of the Ozama
River.

During the passage Wise had much to think about. "In the
back of my head . . . had been lurking the idea that some Marine
command might before long be due for annihilation on some
expedition like this," he later wrote. "We had been getting away
with murder. Little outfits of Marines, in the face of a hostile
population greatly outnumbering them, had been getting one foot
on the beach, and then, presently, getting the other foot planted
there. I didn't know how long we were going to be able to get

away with it. I made up my mind the annihilated outfit wasn't going to be mine."[2]

With the two warships' skippers, Wise landed at the customs house wharf, and the three men walked through the city to the American legation, where Ambassador William Russell "greeted us with considerable relief."[3]

Russell briefed the officers. The situation was delicate and confounding. The current president of the Dominican Republic was Juan Isidro Jiménez, whom an American observer described as "a man totally lacking in character or vision." A wealthy planter, he was a classic, faction-leading *caudillo*, the boss of the *Jimenistas*, a politico-military agglomeration which passed for a political party in the republic. In 1914 he took office as a result of freely held, American-supervised elections and thanks to the not so subtle presence of a regiment of marines lying off shore.[4]

As a *quid pro quo* to American support, President Woodrow Wilson demanded major internal reforms, especially in the Dominican Republic's corruption-ridden military and treasury. Jiménez agreed, but the Dominican Congress refused any cooperation and the capital was swept with constant threats of impeachment and rebellion.

Conditions rapidly deteriorated. In late 1915 Secretary Robert Lansing's State Department demanded the appointment of an American financial advisor to oversee the domestic purse. The department coupled this with a demand for the disbandment of the Dominican Republican Guard and its replacement by a nonpartisan, American-officered constabulary, the chief to be appointed by the President of the United States.

No Dominican politician could accept these conditions and survive. The demands were universally condemned and formally rejected as "an abdication of national sovereignty." Given the Dominican position, the State Department had but two choices: land the marines to carry out the reforms, or back down and lose face. The department opted for the temporary humiliation.[5]

By early 1916 the Jiménez government was in its death throes. Insurgency threatened in every province and armed rebels were in the field. In the Congress, each day brought threats of impeachment. Within the cabinet, War Minister General Desiderio Arias, a perpetual destabilizer and former *Jimenista,* grew increasingly insubordinate, constantly intriguing with the deputies to vote articles of impeachment.

On April 14, 1916, the long-awaited crisis broke. Jiménez, from his country home, moved to cut Arias' ever-increasing influence. On charges of disloyalty and venality in office, he ordered the arrest of two of the war minister's leading supporters, the chief of the Republican Guard and the commandant of the arsenal.

Arias reacted quickly. Forcing his way through the arsenal gates at pistol point, he took command of the facility and announced his refusal to obey the orders of the president. The bulk of the Republican Guard and the opposition factions followed suit. "Great excitement here yesterday," cabled Ambassador William Russell.[6]

For ten days nothing happened. President Jiménez, ill and discouraged, daily toyed with resignation and only strenuous arguments from Russell and loyal cabinet ministers prevented his doing so. The ambassador notified all factions that the United States government placed its support firmly with the president and that another revolution would not be tolerated.

On State Department orders, Russell insisted that Jiménez request American armed assistance; the Dominican president vacillated, asking only for a loan of arms and ammunition. Russell refused to consider this; the request must be confined to direct, armed intervention.

On May 1 Arias forced the decision. His troops surrounded the Chamber of Deputies and demanded a vote of impeachment. In a feeble, moot response Jiménez issued a proclamation charging Arias with treason and dismissed him from the cabinet. With his remaining soldiery, Jiménez abandoned his country house and advanced on the capital. Such was the situation and conditions when Dopey Wise arrived at the legation.

When Ambassador Russell finished his briefing, stressing that Jiménez must be restored to authority, Wise spoke up. " 'Does the State Department mean business this time? Or is this just another one of those bluffs?' I knew," he later wrote, "that for the last twelve years there had been just one revolution after another in San Domingo, and that time after time we had threatened to land Marines and take control. But we had never made good on the bluff. I didn't want to start in with something we weren't going to carry through."[7]

Assured that the State Department had no qualms this time,

the officers made their plans. Santo Domingo was not a sheltered harbor, but an open roadstead with crashing surf on its beaches. Commander Crosley of the *Prairie,* who was Wise's senior, suggested loading the men and the 9th Company's guns into the ship's boats, then heading upriver to land at the customs house wharf and assault the rebel position at Fort Ozama. Wise rejected the suggestion. Coming up the Ozama the boats would be naked to point-blank artillery and rifle fire. Also, the six-knot current would sweep away any damaged boat and likely drown all on board. Crosley was annoyed. "Hell," he exclaimed to Wise, "I'll go through that town alone and bring Arias out with me!" For the moment military courtesy was forgotten. "Nobody's stopping you," the captain of marines told his superior officer.[8]

Wise conducted a reconnaissance, and with Crosley's approval opted to land over open beaches at the foot of Fort San Gerónimo, about two miles below the city. "Three May, [nineteen] sixteen, ten p.m." noted Crosley's terse document, "Campaign Order No. 1. . . . A landing force from the *Prairie* will land in San Domingo City, D.R., to protect American interests and to support present constituted authority." Eight years of intervention, military government, occupation, and guerrilla war were about to begin.[9]

The Dominican Republic, wrote a thoughtful American observer, "is about the size of Ireland and has caused almost as much trouble."[10] The little nation had known virtually no internal peace. In the seven decades before Dopey Wise splashed ashore in 1916, she suffered through nineteen constitutions and forty-three presidents, only three of whom completed their terms in office. In her colonial period, dating from Columbus' discovery, she had been variously shunted through Spanish, French, and a beastly Haitian domination. After a brief spell of mid-nineteenth-century independence, she willingly placed herself back into the rotting Spanish colonial yoke.

Sovereign again in 1869, the republic slid into financial insolvency; American economic and military intervention followed, beginning with an infusion of foreign capital in the form of a loan from a consortium of British banks. The terms verged on extortion. The republic was fleeced, and the republic defaulted.

The customs house revenues, the country's only substantial income and the specie by which the debt was serviced, simply disappeared into the private accounts of whatever Dominican faction held office. New loans were floated to pay the old; and in what was becoming an internationally disturbing sequence, the Dominican Republic again defaulted.

In 1893 the United States became a player to prevent a Franco-German banking group from assuming the collection. To the State Department this seemed very much like the parable of the camel's nose under the tent flap: first the German banks, then a lease on a coaling station to defray the inevitable default, bringing the German Navy into a permanent Caribbean facility. This could not be permitted. The State Department suggested the republic's rail-road builder the New York–based San Domingo Improvement Company, take over the debt. Thus America pushed her nose under the tent flap.[11]

The company floated its own loan to pay the existing foreign debt, and to assure repayment took control of the customs houses. It was in vain. Company collectors skimmed the top for administrative fees, while local politicians and office-holders took their usual share. By 1900 the republic was again dead broke.

Desperately the Dominicans scrambled for solutions. The company collectors were sacked and the republic pledged the customs house revenues to repay the massive bailout loan to the San Domingo Improvement Company. Specific amounts were also pledged to the various European creditors. In all, nearly fifty percent of the revenue was slated for debt service. To no one's great surprise the republic defaulted. But in January 1903, after a "fierce and obstinate contest," a State Department proposal to establish a repayment arbitration commission was signed by the parties.[12]

In November 1903 insurrection brought an ex-priest, General Carlos Morales, to the presidency. Morales, a nominal *Jimenista,* had actually usurped the intended office from his insurgent *caudillo,* Juan Isidro Jiménez, whose forces were still in open revolt. The situation confounded and greatly annoyed both Theodore Roosevelt and the State Department. The current revolt and intervention in Panama required full attention, and the administration lacked the resources to deal with yet another temporary Dominican regime. No recognition was granted to either contender. "The so-called revolutions," noted Rear Admiral Charles Sperry, voicing the general service sentiment, "are nothing more nor less than struggles between different crews of bandits for the possession of the customs houses—and the loot."[13]

But American ambassador William Powell forced the issue.

He bluntly told Morales that unless all prior agreements, including the payment of the San Domingo Improvement Company claim, were "sacredly observed," the United States would not recognize his presidency. With this diplomatic club he bullied the president into forming a commission to negotiate a treaty, granting the United States rights to naval bases and for a measure of domestic financial control. When Morales agreed, Powell, to the great surprise and annoyance in the State Department, unilaterally recognized the new government in the name of the United States.[14]

The feeble republic presented the aspect of a state under siege. Weekly, United States warships landed their bluejackets and marines to protect American nationals and economic interests. The roadstead of Santo Domingo resembled nothing so much as an international naval review, with American, French, German, Dutch, and Italian men-of-war riding to their anchors, an ever-present threat and constant reminder of the nation's insurmountable and unpaid debts.

Rear Admiral Henry Clay Taylor, Chief of the Bureau of Navigation, was convinced that the Dominican Republic (and Haiti) were now "governments and nations only in name." Rear Admiral Charles Sigsbee, commanding the Caribbean Squadron, went further, suggesting that denial of Dominican sovereign rights was the only way for the United States to deal with the power vacuum. The Dominicans, he claimed to Secretary of State Hay, would never feel the need for effective self-government until a foreign power seized the customs houses and the republic experienced a taste of domination. "The Spaniard has intense and aggressive pride," he wrote. "The Negro is highly imitative and lacks a sense of proportion. Conjoin these qualifications and we have the Hispano-Negro, with his lofty declarations and his poor performance."[15]

But there was equal condemnation across the spectrum. Admiral Sperry curtly informed the State Department that the majority of American claims against the republic were the result of collusion between "foreign adventurers" and corrupt local officials. Neither the navy nor the American government, the admiral advised, should make any attempt at debt collection.[16]

Pressure on the republic was unrelenting. In January 1904 increasing European payment demands, coupled with the advance of Jiménez' rebels on the capital and key ports, brought a heightening of American activity. The Atlantic Training Squadron received orders "secret and confidential for the protection of American interests, especially in Haiti-Santo Domingo." In the War Department, the General Staff initiated a special study of the republic's roads and the condition of the railways.[17]

In the harbor of Santo Domingo, the gunboat *Newport* landed a force to protect the American legation. She was reinforced by the cruiser *Columbia*, whose armed boats escorted neutral commerce about the inland waters. The *Columbia*'s skipper and officers were granted a special privilege. "As a special mark of favor," penned Ambassador Powell, "the relics of Columbus will be opened to your view, a favor not generally accorded."[18]

The "neutral commerce" presented problems for the navy, which was charged with intercepting contraband of war. "It would seem from what I learn," Rear Admiral Barker wrote to the Secretary of the Navy, "that certain Americans are responsible in great measure for this unfortunate state of affairs in San Domingo, as they bring arms and ammunition to the different parties." Secretary Moody agreed. "Arms," he noted, "are concealed and entered as codfish, and distributed fairly to each faction, the government, *de facto,* paying all the bills."[19]

In the meantime, the Dominican treaty commissioners, appointed by Morales and the price for his recognition by the United States, arrived in Washington. There was no doubt that the republic was a hairsbreadth away from dissolution and political anarchy. But the Dominicans asked much and offered little. In return for American guarantees of Dominican independence plus direct payment by the United States of all the republic's debts, the commissioners promised Samaná and Manzanillo bays as naval coaling stations. The navy had long coveted Samaná to guard the Mona Passage, a strategic Atlantic gateway to Panama and the canal under construction. But with neighboring Puerto Rico now in American hands, Samaná had lost much of its allure. The navy didn't need new bases, and international events mooted the rest of the proposals. The treaty, as presented by the Dominican commissioners, was a dead issue.

President Roosevelt had no doubt that the onerous duty of wielding the big pencil of fiscal control, if not the big stick of empire police, would eventually fall to the United States. But he was reluctant to take the step, for 1904 was an election year, and especially so soon after the Panamanian intervention, he had no desire to provide his domestic opponents with a new chance to accuse him of expansionism. "Many honest people," he wrote in a letter to the president of Harvard College, would misunderstand his motives if he took "partial possession" of the Dominican Republic. For the moment, a direct United States role was out of the question.[20]

On February 22, 1904, the Permanent Court at The Hague submitted its findings in a seemingly unrelated matter: German, British, and Italian claims against Venezuela. Two years before, unable to collect their nations' debts, the European navies bombarded the Venezuelan coast, sank most of its minuscule fleet, and slapped a blockade over its ports. It was at President Roosevelt's behest that the parties, who detested one another, submitted the question for international arbitration.

The Hague court upheld the blockaders' claim to preferential treatment as regards payment of debts, and, by implication, condoned the use of armed force as a legitimate method of collecting money. For President Roosevelt and the United States, this decision presaged a major reassessment of hemispheric policy: the Roosevelt Corollary to the Monroe Doctrine. Its first application was to the unhappy Dominican Republic.

The Corollary formed the basic tenet that guided much of America's Caribbean policy for the next two decades. If the United States wished to prevent European intervention on the Venezuelan model, it must, Roosevelt argued, help the Caribbean republics sweep away their chronic disorder and fiscal mismanagement.

Since the rebirth of the United States Navy and the acquisition of large chunks of the late Spanish empire, the Monroe Doctrine was no longer an international joke, seen as all bluster and no guns; and in the face of The Hague decision, America had now to assume real responsibility for those states falling under its protective umbrella. Roosevelt first articulated the policy to Elihu Root. "If we are willing to let Germany or England act as the policeman of the Caribbean," he noted in a letter, "then we can afford not to interfere when gross wrongdoing occurs. But if we intend to say 'Hands off' to the powers of Europe, then sooner or later we must keep order ourselves."[21]

This was a preamble to the Corollary's public airing on May 20, 1904, at a New York dinner commemorating the second anniversary of Cuban independence. Root was the featured speaker, and his address a statement direct from the President: "All that we desire is to see all neighboring countries stable, orderly and prosperous . . . if [a nation] keeps order and pays its obligations, then it need fear no interference from the United States. Brutal wrongdoing, or an impotence which results in a general loosening of the ties of civilized society, may require intervention by some civilized nation, and in the Western Hemisphere, the United States cannot ignore this duty."[22]

I n the Dominican Republic, the continuing civil war lapsed into an uneasy peace. Certain northern ports, with their precious customs houses, remained under control of the *Jimenistas,* and no one expected the rickety peace to last. There was also no hope that the government could pay its debts without external aid.

In July came the hammer blow. The arbitration commission, in its decision on the San Domingo Improvement Company claim, announced in the company's favor: $4.5 million, to be paid by the republic in monthly installments. As a security bond, the commission pledged the revenues of the north coast customs houses.

In August the republic missed its first payment. Immediately came the company's demand for customs house revenues. The European creditors now clamored for their payment. In November the French and Belgians threatened to seize the customs house in the capital. In December Italy added her voice to the fray.

To Thomas Dawson, the new American ambassador, it was evident that the European nations would not idly watch the San Domingo Improvement Company receive its money while they got nothing. He was convinced the only road to Dominican solvency, and indeed eventual independence, lay with complete United States customs receivership. "Our only policy for the present," he noted to the State Department, "is to let the pressure of increasing financial difficulties bring about the inevitable result. Without our intervention they cannot pay, and unless they pay they cannot stay in power."[23]

Theodore Roosevelt agreed, but he felt that any further delay would only exacerbate an already dangerous situation. He took the European threats seriously; there must be no repeat of Venezuela. In late December he ordered that the question be put directly to Morales and the Dominican government, "discreetly but earnestly and in a perfectly friendly spirit." Were they "disposed to request" an American takeover of the customs and the distribution of funds to the various claimants?[24]

Without resorting to threats, Ambassador Dawson presented the proposal. Morales was a realist; he knew the European powers would accept no further promises, but would demand full and immediate payment, and he frankly admitted the necessity of handing over his country's receivership to the United States.

On January 21, 1905, a receivership agreement was signed by representatives of both governments. The United States undertook the collection of the Dominican customs revenues, disbursing forty-five percent to the republic for ongoing expenses. The remainder went toward adjusting the debt.

American popular opinion regarding the Monroe Doctrine as a vehicle for financial custodialship was singularly lacking. Then as now, there was general disregard and ignorance regarding the world outside the United States. The *Chicago Tribune* railed that Americans viewed the events in the Dominican Republic "with contemptuous indifference." The press, however, generally agreed with Roosevelt's policy. *Harper's Weekly* declared it "entirely unobjectionable." Some journals went further. The *New Orleans Picayune* noted, "It probably might save future trouble to annex the island outright and administer its affairs very much as Puerto Rico is governed." Others considered the Dominicans of no account whatever. The editor of one large New York daily referred to them as "a horde of naked niggers."[25]

The anti-expansionist press maintained its traditional view. The *Cleveland Plain Dealer* noted, "Uncle Sam is not yet to be made a sort of glorified bailiff for the western hemisphere." And in a direct attack on the Roosevelt Corollary itself, the *Indianapolis News* editorialized, "If this is not imperialism we do not know what to call it."[26]

On the morning of May 5, 1916, Dopey Wise's landing force prepared for the run ashore. There was a heavy surf, and a sailing launch, from which a line was tethered to a palm tree on the beach, was anchored beyond the breakers. In the method of a cable ferry, one of the *Prairie*'s whaleboats tied on to the line and trolleyed the men to the beach. "To say the least," Wise reported, "the boating was difficult."[27]

Wise established a base camp at the foot of Fort San Gerónimo, and leaving the bluejackets to hold it, marched with his two companies of marines to the American legation. Firing came from the north and west as Jiménez' remaining government troops vainly attempted to regain the city. Several shells and rifle bullets fell close to the legation grounds. Wise telephoned both factions and demanded they respect the American property. Firing ceased and the legation was declared a neutral zone.

Wise assessed the tactical situation. He had to take an ancient, walled city, held by Arias' 250 insurgents; further, "every male in town even boys were armed, easily making over a thousand rifles, with five gatlings, unlimited ammunition . . . plenty of [artillery] . . . and gunners who knew how to use it." His marines mustered barely 150 men. Government forces, led by General Pérez, counted about 800, but they were nearly out of cartridges, "and of course, our ammunition wouldn't fit their guns." At a council of war, Pérez asked the loan of 100 Springfields and 50,000 rounds of ammunition. Wise refused. "It didn't look so good," he later wrote, "particularly because I didn't know how far I could trust the President's men."[28]

At Fort San Gerónimo, Wise and Ambassador Russell conferred with Jiménez. Wise could see that Jiménez was in "a bad fix." He desperately wished to regain his capital, "but he didn't care much about getting it with the aid of Americans." Jiménez made his request to the captain of marines: confront General Arias and demand he surrender the city without bloodshed. "I told him Arias would laugh at me. He asked me if I'd try it anyhow." Wise agreed, provided that if Arias refused, the marines would attack in the morning and Jiménez must pledge his troops to fight alongside.[29]

With Ambassador Russell, Wise rode to Fort Ozama and was graciously received. According to Lieutenant Julian Smith, Wise "needed a shave, and Arias' barber was there, and he went and sat in the barber's chair and let Arias' barber shave him."[30]

Wise presented a bold front. He knew his meager resources stood little chance against the city's thick and well-defended walls. But he demanded the right to move his military supplies through rebel-held ground, and Arias agreed. Wise then lectured the general on the broader points of Wilsonian foreign policy. Revolutions in Santo Domingo must cease, the insurgents must evacuate the city, and Jiménez must be restored to office. This time, Wise observed to Arias, "the United States meant business and if he didn't do it we were going to put him out."[31]

"I do not intend to leave," Arias replied. "Oh, yes you will," shot back the captain of marines. Arias shrugged his shoulders and smiled politely at his guests. Ambassador Russell added the weight of the State Department: "These revolutions have got to cease and you Dominicans have got to run a good government." Arias continued smiling. "Has the United States sent people down here to teach us how to behave?" To this, Wise noted, "I didn't have any comeback."[32]

Wise returned to the beach and began his preparations for the morrow. General Pérez suggested the government forces renew their aborted attack, believing they required only artillery support for success. The 9th Company's 3-inch guns were brought ashore, and Captain Fortson established a fire direction center established atop the American legation, its status as a neutral zone conveniently ignored. Pérez would hold his position; with the dawn, Wise reported, "We were to use our field and machine guns against the city and when it was well shaken [the government troops] were to make their infantry attack." But again, Wise had his doubts, and he ordered up the 6th Company, part of the 9th, and sixty bluejackets as reinforcements.[33]

The peripatetic captain hiked back to Fort San Gerónimo and reported his preparations to President Jiménez. As Wise recalled, the president was in great anguish. "I cannot keep my word with you. I can never consent to attacking my own people!" Wise exploded, "You've put me in a jack pot. At your solicitation we have gone in and made another cheap bluff." According to Wise, he informed the president that if he did not want American help, his only course was to resign his office. Jiménez paced the room and agreed; he would sign the resignation document in the morning. Angrily Wise retorted, "You'll do no such damn thing. You'll sign it right now." A secretary was summoned, wrote the prepared phrases, and handed it to Jiménez for his signature. Within the hour the city was plastered with the declaration. The Dominican Republic was without a government.[34]

Russell cabled the news to the State Department. "The President, forced by family and Cabinet, resigned rather than face the responsibility for the loss of life . . . that would result from capture of the city by our forces. . . . This is not the end but the beginning of trouble."[35]

A second command confrontation now erupted between Wise and Commander Crosley of the *Prairie*. The senior officer was all for demanding the city's surrender and, if Arias refused, opening a naval bombardment. Wise considered this folly. Naval guns alone could hold no ground. His marines had that task and there were not enough. The bluejackets in the landing force were neutralized keeping watch over the ex-government soldiers "whose good will" Wise "doubted, in case of attack alone by us against their own people." And if Arias, by some chance, opted to surrender, the scanty landing force could hardly police a city of 30,000 people *and* keep the opposing factions at bay.[36]

Wise's arguments predominated and a temporary truce was arranged. The city was quiet, but Arias still controlled it from his bastion in Fort Ozama, and every day his political hold grew stronger. The ultimatum Wise rashly delivered at Jiménez' plea was proving hollow indeed. The prestige of the United States, Wise later wrote, "after those years of bluffs, would have been ruined in Santo Domingo. The whole republic would know that we had made one more bluff—and Arias had called it." There was only one solution and Ambassador Russell agreed. Minutes later the legation radio operator tapped a message to Admiral Caperton in Port-au-Prince, requesting the immediate dispatch of a battalion of marines.[37]

On May 12 the dispatch vessel *Dolphin* and the store ship *Culgoa* arrived, bringing with them Admiral Caperton, Major Newt H. Hall, and the 4th and 5th companies from Port-au-Prince. The next day came the collier *Hector* with the 24th Company from Guantánamo Bay.

In an atmosphere of cordial politeness Caperton and Russell met with General Arias, and the admiral tendered *his* ultimatum. "If the rebel forces now in the city . . . do not disarm . . . by 6 A.M. Monday, May 15, 1916, it is my intention to occupy the city and forcibly disarm the rebels therein." Arias gave no hint of compliance.[38]

The 400 marines plus the several ships' landing parties were formed into the 1st Provisional Regiment, with Newt Hall commanding, and Dopey Wise his executive officer. Together they drew their plan for a dawn, May 15, attack on the city. The troops would march inland from Fort San Gerónimo, skirting around to high ground. The old walls here were breached in several places, but to make easy egress certain, the *Prairie*'s bluejackets were outfitted as pioneers, with picks, shovels, and blasting gear. Once through the walls the marine companies would form a line of skirmishers and advance through the city, combing house by house and block by block down to the waterfront. Arias was informed that any resistance would be met by a naval bombardment.[39]

Arias was no fool, and did not wish to put the 300 year old walls of Fort Ozama to the test of modern naval ordnance. On the night of the fourteenth, with about 200 rebels, a number of convicts from the city jails, and "as much ammunition as they could carry," he slipped out of the city and headed north.[40]

At 6:00 A.M. the next morning Dopey Wise led the advance through the north wall breaches. All knew that Arias had gone, but some resistance and sniping was expected. Not a shot was fired. Lieutenant Smith remembered, "If Arias had fought hard, if it had been like it was in Vera Cruz [Mexico, 1914]—sniping from every house and everything, why we had a rough job ahead of us; and nobody was very happy over it."[41]

"Our troops have entered the city without opposition and are now in control," Ambassador Russell cabled the State Department. "Considerable anti-American sentiment." Official notice was given the people in a proclamation by Admiral Caperton. The citizens were requested to remain and cooperate in the preservation of life, property, and order. "The sale of all kinds of spirituous beverages to the American troops is strictly forbidden, and any infringement of this order shall be immediately punished."[42]

While Ambassador Russell conducted tedious, unsuccessful negotiations to establish a government acceptable to the United States, reinforcements continued to pour in. By the third week in May there arrived from Haiti the headquarters of the 2nd Marines, with five companies of infantry, and two of artillery. From the United States the marine detachments of the battleships *New Jersey, Rhode Island*, and *Louisiana* were transferred to other vessels and bound for the republic.*

The situation in Santo Domingo quieted down, but such was not the case throughout the country, especially in the north, where Arias received his main support. It was evident that a major United States military intervention was in the offing,

---

*On July 1, 1916, the 1st Marines in Haiti and the 2nd Marines in the Dominican Republic exchanged their regimental numbers. On December 1 Headquarters, 1st Marines, returned to the United States. Its companies in the republic were redesignated the 3rd Provisional Regiment.

and to prepare an entry into the almost entirely railroad-free hinterland, Admiral Caperton slapped a blockade on every Dominican port of consequence. Off Monte Cristi, Puerto Plata, and the towns ringing Samaná Bay, at least one man-of-war, crammed with a landing force, awaited orders.

On June 1 the orders came. Off Puerto Plata, where a ramshackle railroad ran south through the mountains to Arias' stronghold at Santiago, the gunboat *Sacramento* nosed her way through the blue-green swells. On board were 133 marines of the *New Jersey* and *Rhode Island* detachments.

The original plan called for a surprise dawn attack, and it was hoped this could be accomplished without loss of life to either side. But, reported Major Charles Hatch, the landing force commander, it was "considered necessary" to notify the rebels and take off American and foreign nationals.[43]

The rebels, 500 strong, "together with a number of irresponsible citizens" and released convicts, sheltered in Fort San Felipe and its outworks, supported by snipers in loopholed houses along the waterfront. General Rey, the rebel commander, publicly announced, Hatch recalled, "that he would resist our landing with every means within his power."[44]

At dawn the civilian refugees in the gunboat were ordered below hatches; "battle ports [were] secured, and the *Sacramento* cleared for action." On the main deck, the landing force mustered in light marching order: rifles, cartridge belts, canteens, and two Colt machine guns. At 6:15 A.M. they clambered into the boats and headed ashore. Neither Major Hatch nor Commander Roscoe Bulmer of the *Sacramento* were under any illusions as to their reception, and in an attempt to force a quick evacuation of the fort, the vessel opened fire with one of her popgun 3-pounders.[45]

A hail of rifle fire erupted from the beach. Heavy Winchester rounds peppered the boats. Much of the fire came from the waterfront houses and none of it was returned. As Bulmer reported, "to have done so, lives of non-combatants would have been in danger." But there were already several wounded in the boats, and Captain Hirshinger had taken a mortal slug in the head. The rebels now concentrated inside the fort. "To have exposed the landing force to their fire," Bulmer noted, "would have been suicidal, and would have resulted in an appalling number of casualties." He ordered his 4-inch guns to commence firing.[46]

As the high-explosive charges slapped into the masonry, the

enemy fire slackened. The frail boats continued toward the beach, and near disaster struck when the steam launch carrying the *New Jersey*'s marines grounded on a reef, a scant twenty yards from its objective. Hatch ordered everyone into the surf, "and each officer and good swimmer aided those who could not swim." Two men nearly drowned. In the muddle, the bluejackets landed first, formed skirmish line, and charged up the beach, with the marines right behind. Fort San Felipe was taken at bayonet point.[47]

In fairly good order, the rebels retreated south through the town, all the while keeping up an incessant harassing fire on the landing force. The two machine guns, under command of the *Sacramento*'s paymaster, were brought into stuttering action.

Hatch ordered the advance, and through continuous sniping the marines and bluejackets came uphill to the rebel position at the hospital. As reported, it was "always used as a fort." By semaphore, he signaled the gunboat for fire support. On board, the 4-inch guns banged away. Bulmer was careful to order excess elevation, and the shells passed high over the target, "as I did not wish to run the slightest chance of a shell going short and possibly hitting buildings or residences in the City." The rebels showed no signs of retreating further. Bulmer ordered a slight reduction in range. His gunners nudged their pointing wheels a fraction, "and several shots were then put through the hospital building, which produced the desired effect, and the Revolutionists evacuated this place."[48]

It was all over by 9:30. Hatch posted his sentries, "and we began making camp, sending to the ship for tentage and stores." On June 5, Captain Eugene Fortson arrived from Santo Domingo with the 4th and 9th companies. Preparations were quickly taken in hand for a reconnaissance down the line to Santiago.[49]

Compared to the fight for Puerto Plata, the landing at Monte Cristi, sixty-five miles west and near the Haitian border, was a relatively easy affair. On May 30 Dopey Wise took ship to assume temporary command of the *Louisiana* and *Memphis* (formerly the *Tennessee*) marine detachments, about 120 men. Off Monte Cristi he found them embarked in the ancient transport *Panther*, with two destroyers in company.

As was his custom, Wise went ashore to conduct a personal reconnaissance. The rebels, commanded by one Miguelito, controlled the town. The governor had been chased out, but there were no "outrages" and the place was "running along in a normal manner." Wise took himself to Miguelito's headquarters in the town hall. He found the rebel commander a well-dressed, heavily built man, with a pistol belted around his ample, civilian-clad girth.[50]

The captain of marines introduced himself. "We intend to run you out of town." Miguelito was unimpressed. "You won't have the easy time you had over in Haiti." Wise ended the conversation. "We won't have any trouble when we make up our minds."[51]

Dopey Wise returned to the *Panther,* and on June 1 landed without opposition. The landing force was quite small and only objectives north of the Yaque del Norte River were secured. The ferry and waterworks to the south were left in rebel hands. Wise's strength did not go unnoticed. "A few of the populace were still seen in the streets," noted the *Panther*'s skipper, Commander Harris Lanning. "They took careful notice and counted the force that we landed . . . they were very much surprised and became much emboldened."[52]

From the rebel camp came rumors of the rebels' intention to drive the marines out of town, burn the place out and kill anyone caught aiding the *norte americanos.* "The result of this propaganda," Lanning reported, "was remarkable. By nightfall, the town was reported as deserted. All houses were closed and no one was seen on the streets. People were seen moving along the beach with all their belongings."[53]

On the third, the rebels started burning property on the outskirts, set up a landward blockade, and prevented all food from coming in. "All peaceable citizens," Lanning continued, "were, as far as we could learn, completely terrorized." Every available man from the ships, 100 bluejackets, was ordered ashore.[54]

Citizens complained to Wise that there had been no trouble until the Americans came, that it was his fault, and his alone. Wise had no rejoinder. But it was folly and weakness to sit and wait for the rebels to make their threatened attack, and there was also the matter of getting food into the town. With a machine gun and the *Louisiana*'s marines, Wise reconnoitered south to the Yaque ferry; it was deserted. Leaving the main body to hold the position, he strapped the machine gun to a mule, and taking a squad probed further along the river. Presently they came upon one of Miguelito's pickets. "We were on a hillside," Wise wrote, "about three hundred yards away from them. I didn't want them to know I had a machine gun. We opened up on them with rifles. Several got away. I had an idea they would soon return with their friends."[55]

The machine gun was dismounted, set up in the waist-high scrub and sighted in. In less than half an hour about 200 rebels came over the ridge. "In the midst of them I recognized Miguelito, mounted on a big roan mule. I suppose eight or nine of us looked easy to them. Their front extended over a hundred yards." But the rebels, firing as they advanced, came on willy-nilly, in little bunches, with no order or discipline. "When they reached the road we opened up with the machine gun and sprayed it up and down their line. Evidently it was the first time they had ever encountered a machine gun. I could see the amazement on their faces. All up and down the line I could see them dropping." The rebels turned their backs and fled; the food blockade was lifted.[56]

Admiral Caperton now controlled the republic's ports. But from his and the State Department's perspective, that hardly meant stability or an end to American participation in Dominican affairs. Since the resignation of Jiménez, the presidency lay vacant as the factions of an incensed and hostile Dominican Congress vied for power. None of the proposed candidates, Arias among them, would have anything to do with the United States' demands for internal reforms. Seeing no hope for the elevation of a malleable candidate, Russell enacted one of the major demands by imperial fiat. All government internal revenues and disbursements were placed under the jurisdiction of the American customs receivership. In the capital there was political stalemate, to say nothing of an ill-disposed, unfriendly population.

In the military sphere, General Arias maintained firm control over substantial parts of the country, especially in the populous northern Cibao region, and was reported to be preparing his base, Santiago, the republic's second city, to withstand a siege. Admiral Caperton felt the need for substantial reinforcements. His subordinates felt the same. "I am absolutely certain that there will be no peace, quiet, or safety in this part of the Island until these revolutionists are put down," Lanning reported to his chief. "[It] will necessitate an advance on and seizure of Santiago and the extermination of the bands which infest the country around it."[57]

On June 4 orders arrived for Uncle Joe Pendleton, last seen blasting open the Nicaraguan railways, and now commanding the 4th Marines, to take his regiment south. At New Orleans they boarded the *Hancock,* and on the eighteenth, the anchor roared out hawsepipe off Santo Domingo. At a council of war, Caperton opted to hold the city with a skeleton force, and sent Pendleton north with every available man to clear the Cibao and take Santiago. The expedition was not a war against an enemy but a "police action" in support of the constitutional government. Rebel activities were to be put down without further alienating the people, and with a minimum of blood and property damage.[58]

In 1916 there were three routes into the Cibao. The first, the railroad west from Samaná Bay, was vulnerable to guerrilla attack, especially where it crossed ten miles of open swamp over a rickety causeway. The second and shortest route, south over the coastal mountain range from Puerto Plata, was rejected on account of the difficult terrain. Pendleton picked the third, an eastward march of seventy-five miles along the Monte Cristi–Santiago road. The terrain was level, albeit heavy with cactus and brush, and the road—packed earth, and barely capable of handling motor transport in the dry season—at least provided a wide track. Parallel to it flowed the shallow, twisting Yaque River and its meager flow of water. Finally, about twelve miles from Santiago, the railroad from Puerto Plata joined the road, continuing alongside it into the city.

On June 21 the *Hancock* arrived at Monte Cristi where Pendleton found logistic preparations for the march already well in hand. His chief of staff, Major Robert Dunlap, had come up from Santo Domingo with the 13th (artillery) Company and Dopey Wise's 6th Company, and together they organized the baggage train. In that era, a marine expeditionary force had no organic transport save for some two-wheeled hand carts; all contrivances had to be purchased on the spot. Motor transport was very much in its infancy. The 13th Company brought its pair of Jeffrey Quads to haul their 3-inch guns, and Pendleton's regiment arrived with a Holt tractor, on loan from the manufacturer. For a marching column that numbered over 800 men, this was hardly sufficient.

Dunlap and Wise bought or leased everything with wheels, four legs, or a motor. The local Ford agency, at a rather large profit, was stripped of its twelve Model T touring cars. To these invaluable vehicles, which for Pendleton performed the ubiquitous service akin to the World War II Jeep, the two officers added a pair of boxcar-like White trucks, five Studebaker wagon trailers, and twenty-four Dominican mule carts. Wise, remembering the water problems during his Boxer Rebellion service, confiscated the town's mule-drawn sprinkling cart. "It was," he noted, "the most important single item in the transport."[59]

Intelligence concerning the enemy was also singularly lacking. Reports coming from Admiral Caperton indicated Arias had with him 1,000 men in Santiago. From his own sources in Monte Cristi, Uncle Joe gleaned that only 100 rebels were entrenched ahead at kilometer post 27. Dopey Wise voiced the general concern: "the country was full of rumors that all the way up we would be opposed by anything from a dozen to thousands of armed Dominicans. We knew that the minute we marched out of Monte Cristi we would be cut off from our base and be absolutely on our own."[60]

On a blazing hot June 26 morning Uncle Joe ordered the column to march. A fifteen-man detachment, mounted on stringy local horses, as the rebels had already taken the best ones for themselves, clattered to the point. Behind them stepped the advance guard, the 2nd Battalion, 4th Marines. Then marched Uncle Joe with the main body, the 1st Battalion, plus the 13th (artillery), 28th (machine gun), and 29th (signal) companies. Bringing up the rear came the vehicle train guarded by Dopey Wise's 6th (provost) Company and a machine gun squad.

From the outset there were problems with the transport. The mules had no understanding of English and their marine drivers could not make them obey. Wise found the carts stalled and badly overloaded "with typewriters, field desks, personal trunks of officers who didn't know how much an animal could carry. We dumped them out." The trucks, because of their heavy loads and the awful road, traveled mostly in low gear and burned enormous amounts of gasoline—about a gallon per mile.[61]

At kilometer post 9 came the first sight of the rebels, small bands falling back in the face of the advance. At kilometer post 18 the 27th Company received some sniper fire. The marines brought a machine gun into action and the rebels scattered. Dopey Wise thought the best way to prevent sniping was to burn the houses along the line of march. In mid-afternoon the column halted. Up ahead about two miles along the road sat the twin hummocks of Las Trencheras. It was a strong, natural position, and through their field glasses, officers watched numbers of armed rebels milling about. Rather than attack with tired troops, Uncle Joe camped for the night.

At dawn the next morning, while patrols went forward to

reconnoiter the enemy positions, the 13th and 28th companies emplaced their artillery, machine guns, and observation post on a ridge overlooking the road. Pendleton planned for a frontal assault with two battalions abreast: Major Melville Shaw's 2nd Battalion on the left, north of the road, and Captain Arthur Marix' 1st Battalion, on the right, south of the road. He intended to attack shortly after first light. But the men had unwisely depleted their water during the night. Until the water cart returned from the muddy Yaque, the advance was stalled. As Pendleton reported, "it was inadvisable to start without it."[62]

The water party, however, came under heavy fire, and Pendleton could wait no longer. Just after 8:00 A.M., he ordered the battalions to advance to the line of departure. The ground was broken, much overgrown by cactus and heavy brush, and with visibility severely limited, the inward flanks soon lost touch. There were further obstacles. On the right, the 32nd Company came up against a hidden swamp, directly in its line of march. Meanwhile on the left, the 27th Company was slowed by grinding intestinal disorders, the result of an overindulgence in large quantities of liberated canned honey.

At 8:45 the artillery and machine gun companies opened long-range searching fire on the rebel lines. "All enemy," Pendleton noted, "immediately disappeared from the front of the trenches." Front to rear, left to right, the rebel field works were swept. The artillery, however, was equipped only with shrapnel charges, there were no high-explosive rounds in the caissons, and though it kept the enemy's heads down, they did little physical destruction.[63]

Major Shaw halted his 2nd Battalion to regain contact with Marix, and the Dominicans, seeing their opportunity, opened a heavy rifle fire at the stalled attack. "The rebels," First Sergeant Roswell Winans remembered, "kept up a fairly heavy fire but aimed too high. One of our men was burned on the back of the neck by a big lead slug."[64]

Uncle Joe, watching the action through his field glasses, ordered Major Dunlap to take command at the front. Grabbing a machine gun crew, Dunlap jumped into a Model T and sped down the road. Reaching the 2nd Battalion's position just as the inner flanks were again joined, Dunlap's machine gun opened a spray of drumfire on the trenches, and he ordered the advance to continue. The skirmish lines re-formed and the marines went forward.

The rebel fire faltered. Dunlap sounded a blast on his whistle, the marines halted, ceased fire, fixed bayonets, and with a cheer charged up the slopes into the trenches. The whole fight lasted about an hour. One marine was killed. Five dead rebels were later found in the woods. The Dominican casualties were probably much greater, but as First Sergeant Winans noted, "It seemed to be a religion with these people to carry off their dead and wounded."[65]

Dopey Wise brought up the vehicle train, Uncle Joe re-formed the column, and at 1:00 P.M. they pressed on to Santiago. Maddeningly, the enemy's mounted scouts reappeared, hovering on the flanks, just out of range. With their wretched animals, the fifteen horse marines could do little to drive the rebels off. One eager rebel did get in too close and was shot dead. At kilometer post 42 Pendleton called a halt, and the troops made camp in the order of march.

Shortly after 7:00 P.M. shooting erupted from all sides. Sergeant Winans remembered, "The night was terribly dark. I had just crawled under my mosquito net and gotten comfortably settled when the rebels commenced firing on our camp. Somebody ran right through my mosquito net stepping on my stomach en route." Some of the rebels were equally surprised. A large party blundered into a 13th Company machine gun post and faced annihilation. Just as the marines made ready to open fire, Jack, their barking mascot dog, gave them away. The rebels turned and fled into the night. "We could hear the enemy talking excitedly on a hill just to our front," Winans continued. "Sweeping fire was opened in that direction. Meanwhile a bunch of the enemy tried to rush Corporal Frazee at the outpost. But the gun pointer . . . simply made a sieve out of one and several more were hit, judging by their yells." In the inky gloom, the marines hardly had time to properly register their weapons. "One of our [machine] guns on the right flank did not have enough elevation. Lieutenant Randall . . . was taking a bath a few yards in front of it when the firing started. We went into action very quickly and a stream of steel jackets passed through the lieutenant's hat. . . . Mr. Randall said he dispensed with the rest of his toilet."[66]

The rebels, badly shaken by the automatic weapons, were driven off. Weeks later, General Arias told the marines his men had believed machine guns or *esperalvos*, "sprinklers" as they called them, could not be fired at night.

On the morning of the twenty-eighth, the march was delayed by the destruction of two bridges spanning a pair of trickling, forty-feet deep *arroyos*. Using materials from one bridge, the other was rebuilt. A driveway was cut into the ditch and corduroyed for vehicle transport. By mid-morning the next day, all work was completed. Leaving the 8th Company* to guard the bridges, Uncle Joe resumed the march.

At kilometer post 49 the column encamped for the night. "It was a rainy night," First Sergeant Winans recalled, "but I was fortunate enough to get ahold of an old door from a village nearby, which made the finest kind of dry bed." As for the troops, their kerosene lanterns went dry. But Uncle Joe, ever solicitous of their needs, replenished them from headquarters stores.[67]

On the morning of June 30 the column came under heavy fire from rebels hidden in the dense underbrush. The machine guns came into action and the rebels faded away. One marine was killed. A second fight erupted at noon, and again the "sprinklers" drove the enemy off. At dusk the marines trudged into the village of Jaibon.

Pendleton now made a critical decision. The column was nearing the halfway point to its objective, and his supply line to Monte Cristi stretched back over thirty miles, the absolute limit for the shuttling motor transport. The line of communications was also consuming a fair amount of troops for guard duty. Additionally, Pendleton had received a radio message that the marine force coming down the railroad from Puerto Plata was nearing the column rendezvous at Navarette. Pendleton opted to cut himself off from his base and form a "flying column." The guarding detachments were pulled in, and the Model Ts trundled back to Monte Cristi for a last supply run.

Uncle Joe rested his men and beasts for the coming trial. Animal fodder required constant attention. "Camp had to be made at times entirely with this consideration in view," he noted in his report. "With only grass as food, animals require a much longer time to feed and I fear much of the time [they] went hungry. Towards the end of the march all were busy gathering grass wherever it could be found, and the animals were given every opportunity to graze."[68]

---

*Its skipper was first Lieutenant Holland M. Smith, who commanded the III Amphibious Corps in World War II.

The machine gunners put the time to good use, though Sergeant Winans and his mates began by cursing the ammunition. Some of it dated back to 1907 and had been reloaded so many times that the cartridge cases expanded, jamming the guns. During the halt every gun was thoroughly broken down and cleaned; all rounds were removed from the belts, and contrary to regulations, polished and oiled.

Reconnaissance patrols pushed forward and drove back all rebel observation parties. In the process they captured several good horses which proved, as Uncle Joe noted, "invaluable to us." The patrols also captured a prisoner who gave exact information of a strong Dominican force dug in astride the road at the hamlet of Guayacanas.

On the morning of July 3 the flying column marched out. After about four miles, rebel pickets opened fire on the point. Reinforcements rushed up, the outposts were driven in, and the Dominicans broke contact. Ahead lay the lines of Guayacanas.

Pendleton halted the column and ordered Shaw's 2nd Battalion to deploy and attack. A reconnaissance of the enemy positions reported them, however, as far stronger than at Las Trencheras. Just beyond the village, the road cut through a low, straddling ridge, a fine natural position completely dominating the axis of advance. On and forward of the heights were the rebel trench lines, skillfully dug and camouflaged by the removal of excavated earth. The ground for 200 yards to its front was cleared of vegetation, giving an unobstructed field of fire. Astride the road, about 150 yards before the first trench, sat an undefended roadblock of felled trees.

At 9:00 A.M. the 2nd Battalion formed in companies abreast. A reinforcing platoon of the 28th Company's machine gunners, roughly in the center, moved forward to the roadblock. As with the fight at Las Trencheras there were problems. Before coming into the cleared ground, dense underbrush hampered the advance. It also confused the 13th Company's gunlayers. Shrapnel burst over the advancing marines' heads. Tree limbs were severed and fell amongst them, but fortunately there were no casualties.

The rebels commenced a hot and deadly fire. Again, as at Las Trencheras, Major Dunlap came forward with a machine gun crew. Outstripping the advancing companies they found themselves fully exposed on the open ground and took cover behind the fallen trunks. Corporal Joseph Glowin brought his machine gun into action and was almost immediately hit. He continued to fire, was hit again, and had to be forceably dragged off and taken to the rear. Dunlap took over and the gun jammed. A second crew rushed to the roadblock. As Pendleton noted, "this gun in turn jammed; the men exposed themselves to repair it but could do nothing."[69]

Roswell Winans' platoon came on at the run. "The enemy," he remembered, "were using mostly old-fashioned breech loaders, with big lead slugs, 'tin cans' we called them. . . . At our end of the log a Benet-Mercie [machine gun] had just commenced roaring. . . . It had no sooner opened up than all the bullets in the world seemed coming our way. The enemy was shooting mighty close too. . . . [They] had an immensely strong natural position and had they a few machine guns and some barbed wire they could not have been rooted out without great loss of life."

The first gun in Winans' platoon to open fire had its gun captain killed and the rest of the crew wounded. "A call went up for a hospital apprentice, as Corporal Frazee had been shot in the head. He had been working hard getting his gun pointer on the enemy and had just succeeded. 'You are right on them now, give them hell!' were the last words he said."[70]

Winans and his crew emplaced the heavy, spoke-wheeled Colt, and he mounted the seat and opened fire. "They seemed to be just missing me. I don't know how the other men felt, but I expected to be shot any minute and just wanted to do as much damage as possible to the enemy before cashing in." The last round in Winans' belt jammed the gun. In full view the sergeant stood up to clear the breech. "We faced the enemy as much as possible while repairing the guns, as we had a horror of being shot in the back." In a diameter of twenty feet another man was shot dead and seven more wounded. A third Colt was brought up, and with three machine guns pouring lead into the trenches, the marines finally achieved fire superiority.[71]

Under cover of the machine guns, the infantry companies advanced to within 150 yards of the trench line. On the marines' left, the 27th and 29th cut their way through dense cactus hedge and turned the enemy flank. With a loud cheer they burst through, charged the works, and carried the northern end of the line. "One of the sweetest sounds I have ever heard," Winans remembered, "was the cheering of the infantry battalion as it charged the right flank of the enemy." The rebel commander was killed in the charge and the Dominicans abandoned the entire position and fled east. For their heroism at the roadblock, Corporal Glowin and First Sergeant Winans were awarded the Congressional Medal of Honor.[72]

The flying column continued the march. The rebels had done an excellent job sabotaging the already dreadful road, and three man-and-truck-breaking hours were needed to travel something less than a mile. At dusk Uncle Joe ordered camp for the night. The next morning, July 4, the column moved out. Shortly before noon, a Model T bearing a Red Cross flag and four Dominican doctors approached the advance guard from the direction of Santiago. They had come to treat their wounded at Guayacanas. The physicians were blindfolded, and with a marine driver were passed through the lines.

In mid-afternoon the weary marines pulled into Navarette linking up with the Puerto Plata–Santiago railroad. After three days in the "air," the flying column reestablished its supply and communications with the coast. Pendleton's logistic problems were eased immeasurably. All his heavy equipment could now travel the final twelve miles by rail, relieving the strain on the animals and trucks.

At the station, Major "Hiking Hiram" Bearss made his report to Uncle Joe. Bearss had come down the line from Puerto Plata with a train of four boxcars, pulled by a locomotive, that to Dopey Wise, "seemed to be held together with hay wire." The adventures of the Puerto Plata "Railroad Battalion" almost rivaled those of the flying column.[73]

The original Puerto Plata landing force had been increased by Captain Eugene Fortson, a highly respected gunner, and the 4th and 9th (artillery) companies. On June 25 came Pendleton's orders to reconnoiter down the line, keep it in repair, and establish secure communications to Navarette. The next day Fortson mustered his command: five officers, 129 marines, a navy medical officer and his two hospital apprentices. Four Colts, a pair of Benet-Mercie machine guns, and a 3-inch artillery piece mounted on a flatcar formed the heavy ordnance. There was an immediate problem. The Dominican train crew had deserted their posts, and Fortson had to send to the *Sacramento* for a couple of men from her black gang (engine and boilermen) to man the engine. In mid-morning they clanged out of Puerto Plata.[74]

The track ran thirty miles up the coastal mountain range before plunging rustily down into the Cibao. There were two major bridges and a long tunnel; the destruction of any severed communications from the coast to the hinterland. The railroad was a Belgian cog model, built for the Congo. But the contract was never consummated, and the facility was sold to the San Domingo Improvement Company. The original cog rails were gone, ripped up during some past revolution and replaced with ordinary smooth rails. For the train, it meant the engine could pull only one car at a time up the steep grades to the mountain summit. Each round trip before the descent into the Cibao took at least an hour.

On the first day Fortson traveled ten miles meeting no resistance. The next morning, with foot patrols cautiously advancing along the tracks, the train inched its way up to the town of Llanos. While the engine headed back to haul up the second section, an enemy outpost opened fire on the stranded cars at extreme range. Fortson sent two squads forward to flush the snipers and opened fire with the 3-inch gun. Two hours later the engine returned and Fortson advanced. From three sides higher up the mountain, the Dominicans delivered a heavy rifle fire. Fortson brought his Colt machine guns into position, a squad of nine men pushed up the heights, and the rebels were driven out.[75]

The track ahead was torn up, the rails thrown down the embankment, and the ties burned. Fortson had the presence of mind to carry spares, and the marines set to making repairs. With a chuff of greasy smoke, the train continued down the line.

The next day, June 28, Hiking Hiram Bearss arrived with the *New Jersey*'s marine detachment and took command. Bearss determined to keep the enemy on the run giving them no time for further damage. But they were dug in, it seemed, on every crest. On the twenty-ninth, at Alta Mira, the 3-inch gun was again brought into play, shelling a rebel position for half an hour until the infantry were able to envelop the town. The train dragged itself up to La Cumbre, a critical position dominating the tunnel entrance.[76]

Scaling the peak, the 4th Company spotted about 200 rebels 3,000 yards away. They signaled the train, and Fortson unloaded his gun and brought it to bear on a shack overlooking the rebel lines. His third shot tore off a side, the fourth shot hit dead center. The rebels, with shrapnel charges exploding over their heads, quit the trenches and ran for the tunnel. Bearss gave them no time to regroup. While Fortson directed the fire, Bearss, furiously pumping a handcar, dashed forward at the head of his men into the tunnel mouth. It was 300 yards long, pitch-black, and as much a death trap as Butler's drainpipe at Fort Rivière. But without casualty or mishap they burst through, only to see the rebels in high flight down the tracks. As one marine noted, "It was the most fun Hiram had enjoyed in a long time."[77]

The action at La Cumbre ended rebel resistance on the railroad, and on July 3, one day before the flying column, the battalion chugged into Navarette.

At the rendezvous Pendleton quickly reformed and revictualed. The wounded were sent to Puerto Plata, and on the return journey the train brought the welcome reinforcements of the 24th Company. Preparations were made for the immediate march and battle for Santiago.

But on July 5 Dominican heralds arrived from Santo Domingo. General Arias had decided to accept defeat and Admiral Caperton's offer of amnesty and pardon. He would lay down his arms offering no further opposition. It was requested by all factions—rebel, "government," and Admiral Caperton—that the column not enter the city until the next day to permit Arias time to demobilize his forces.

To this, Uncle Joe only partially agreed. Santiago was fair belted with trench lines, old forts, and the Yaque and Quiningua rivers to its front. If Arias reneged, and held these defenses in any kind of strength, Pendleton would have to lay the city to a formal siege. And the defenses, Pendleton noted, "were excellent. . . . In the hands of well organized and brave troops they would have been hard to take." He had no reason to suppose the Dominicans would cut and run; they certainly hadn't done it yet. Uncle Joe ordered the column to saddle up and march for the outworks. "There the town lay ahead of us," Dopey Wise wrote, "right on the banks of the [Yaque]. Behind it rose a hill. On top of the hill was a big masonry fort dating back from the Spanish days. It looked like a fight ahead."[78]

But Arias made good his promise; the positions were empty. Signalers connected the command post with the city's telephone lines, and the heralds, accompanied by the new governor, arrived to arrange the entry. "At 2:40 p.m.," Pendleton noted in his report, "marched to the city, occupied the Castillo and Forteleza de San Luis. There was no opposition, and the attitude of the people was more friendly than otherwise."[79]

Dopey Wise was immensely relieved. "Those eleven days we had spent on the way had taken years off my life. If the Dominicans, with their knowledge of the country, had a couple of good leaders, they could have cut us to pieces anywhere along the route."[80]

Wise and Bearss were given charge of the railroad. Hiking Hiram reported it "in a deplorable condition; another two months under Dominican rule and the entire outfit would have been worthless and useless."[81] It also had no income. There was neither commercial traffic of Cibao goods, nor passengers to Puerto Plata. The only cargo was marine supplies, and that paid no fare. The two officers decided to make the railroad a going concern. The Cibao is a great tobacco area, and bales of the stuff sat idle in the city, waiting for export; and prices were high, the World War saw to that. With Wise supervising the loading at Santiago, and Bearss the unloading and export at Puerto Plata, there was no skimming of price or customs duty, and the profits rolled in. To the astonishment of the locals, the money was applied to improving the rail system and paying Dominican salaries, the first they had received in months. Passenger service was developed: first-class rode in the caboose, second in the boxcar, and third-class sat on the roofs.

The marines set about the mundane tasks of occupation. Sergeant Nichols of the 8th Company wrote from Puerto Plata, "Our duty here consists of unloading the monthly supply boats . . . and guarding the municipal prison. . . . [The] inmates are all kept in one big cell, and there is not a bed or a chair in it. . . . None of them have dishes, but many have cans which are used for everything from cups to finger bowls. . . . We hope to institute many reforms before we are here long, and show them the road to proper living."[82]

The occupation of Santiago ended the first military phase of the intervention. The northern ports and railroad towns in the Cibao each received their marine garrison. With the exception of San Francisco de Macorís, there was hardly a murmur of opposition; indeed many Dominicans welcomed the relative tranquility that for a time settled over the republic.

But Pendleton understood that ultimate success in the main-tainence of order depended on the people's attitude toward the occupation forces. He demanded that the marines conduct them-selves with the strictest probity in their intercourse with the pop-ulation. When a group of local merchants approached Captain Chandler Campbell with a stack of bar chits signed "George Wash-ington," "Abraham Lincoln," and "Woodrow Wilson," Campbell compared the handwriting to the signatures on the 13th Com-pany's payroll, and the gunners were compelled to honor their debts. Thereafter the merchants were directed to conduct business on a cash-only basis.[83]

In the capital, the political stalemate continued. The presi-dency was still vacant and Admiral Caperton publicly announced that the marines would remain until the financial and military reforms were adopted. The State Department hoped to attain these objectives by establishing a malleable client government that would bend to United States pressure in much the same manner as Haiti's. This, however, was proving impossible.

The Dominican Congress, overtly hostile, moved for an im-mediate election of an interim president, favoring Desiderio Arias or one of his principal supporters. Ambassador Russell cabled the State Department, "It would seem final elimination [of] Arias as a political or military factor must now be accomplished." Vainly he and Caperton requested the lawmakers delay their votes.[84]

On May 18 the Dominican Senate prepared to elect Dr. Fe-derico Henríquez y Carbajal, an avowed Arias partisan and chief justice of the Supreme Court. With Federico there would be no cooperation whatever in enacting the reforms. Also Federico was opposed by most of the provincial governors, who threatened revolt upon his election. Clearly, the United States could not per-mit it. Ambassador and admiral demanded the Senate postpone the election in a "demand . . . which will be enforced if ignored." The Dominicans relented, and Federico withdrew his candidacy.[85]

The scramble began anew for a suitable man. In late July, without consulting the Americans, the Senate elected Federico's brother, Dr. Francisco Henríquez y Carbajal, provisional presi-dent. For the United States the choice was not wholly unfavorable. A physician and sometime diplomat, Francisco had been living in Cuba and was relatively divorced from the recent revolutionary cycle. The new president, reported Caperton's relief, Rear Ad-miral Charles Pond, "poses as a scholar and writer but he is honest."[86]

Francisco generally agreed with the financial portion of the reforms, but he balked at placing the Republican Guard under command of American officers. Russell turned the screws. Without any attempt at compromise, he halted the disbursement of all customs receipts and internal revenue to the Dominican government. The results were disastrous. Government employees were stripped of their salaries, and bureaucratic functions, never a paragon of efficiency, stopped altogether. An overnight economic recession struck the merchants and people.

Desperately Francisco sought to reach an accommodation. He was willing to negotiate a full United States assumption of financial control, and even to employ American officers on a contractual basis to reform the Republican Guard. But he could not, on constitutional grounds, allow its chief to be appointed by the President of the United States. Admiral Pond was impressed by Francisco's sincerity and felt the future boded well. But the State Department found the compromise unsatisfactory. All controls, fiscal and military, must be "definitely assured and made binding." Ambassador Russell was of like mind. Only with an ultimatum could the United States accomplish its goals, and if the ultimatum were rejected, the marines would "take charge."[87]

August is the Caribbean hurricane season. On the twenty-ninth, in the harbor of Santo Domingo, the armored cruiser *Memphis* rode placidly to her anchor. Captain Ned Beach had taken the precaution of setting an emergency steaming watch and all boilers were primed. But no storm signs were observed and her liberty parties were ashore. The little *Castine* was moored to starboard and all seemed serene. Suddenly, at about 3:30 P.M., the sea rose and enormous swells began rolling in. "Good Lord, Yancey!" Ned Beach exclaimed to his executive officer. "Look at this!" A monstrous yellow wave of water and mud, perhaps seventy-five feet high, blotted the horizon and churned inexorably into the harbor. On the bridge, the ship's navigator, Lieutenant Commander Thomas Withers,* "noticed ahead, to the eastward, an immense wave or swell approaching. As this swell got close to the ship, its face became very steep, but the ship rode over it."[88]

The *Castine* immediately headed to sea, but the tremendous wave batted the craft like a paper boat. With her rudder jammed hard left, she was thrown bows-on toward the beach. Desperately

---

*Commander Submarines Pacific Fleet, 1940–1942.

her skipper backed down full emergency. Her screws bit the water, but out of control she drifted crazily backward onto the *Memphis,* seemingly doomed to smash herself against the cruiser's armored sides. "At no time," recalled Withers, "was the *Castine* more than 1000 yards from the *Memphis,* and yet from the bridge, 45 feet above the water, the *Castine* disappeared time and time again. Even her mastheads disappeared! To see the *Castine* fighting for her life was a terrifying sight."

The gunboat's skipper, Commander Kenneth Bennett, remembered, "In a few minutes we were struck by a number of the largest combing seas I have ever witnessed. . . . The well deck had water up to the engine-room hatches, which fortunately had been battened down, but . . . water got into the engine room and the engine crankpits were filled. The seas filled up the fireroom to the level of the lower furnace." Luckily the *Memphis'* 16,000 ton bulk provided a very temporary breakwater. The *Castine* regained control, slowly came around, turned under the cruiser's stern and clawed her way to sea. In the cruiser the men topside raised a cheer.

But on board the *Memphis,* the waves were crashing at half-minute intervals. They were so large and steep, Withers recalled, "They simply flowed over the ship. They flowed over our bridge many feet deep. They flowed over our stacks and flooded our fires." Mess tables were torn from their brackets. Men and ready ammunition were thrown to the deck. Fifteen minutes after the first wave hit, the *Memphis* touched ground. Several attempts to let go the port anchor were unsuccessful, and she began dragging her keel 200 feet with each succeeding wave.

With the boilers doused by seawater, all hope of saving the ship vanished. Although the machinery plant was flooded and useless, the black gang stayed at their posts until ordered up on deck. They paid dearly for their attention to duty. A coral pinnacle lanced through the double bottom, crushing a pair of boilers, and horribly scalded the fireroom watch standers. Ned Beach's sole thought now was to get his crew ashore. He ordered lifelines rigged, and the men huddled in the lee of the stacks and superstructure. There was no panic, and excellent order and discipline prevailed.

At 4:50 P.M., the *Memphis* washed ashore forty feet off the beach. From the port bridge wing, a quartermaster heaved a lead-line on which were bent heavy, hemp hawsers. On the landward end they could not be secured, as the violent motion of the ship would have snapped them like threads. Instead, they were man-handled by the ship's marines, who rushed from their temporary quarters at Fort Ozama, and by scores of Dominican civilians. It took nearly four hours to lift 750 men to safety. As the numbers on deck thinned, the lines were cast off until only one remained for the final party of twenty-two officers, two chiefs, and Ned Beach, who was the last man to leave the ship. "Three times during the wreck the crew cheered," Withers recalled, "once when the *Castine* got to sea; again when the first line reached the shore; and again, when Captain Beach landed safely." The dead numbered forty and the injured 204.*

In October 1916 the political situation in the republic, at least from the State Department's view, was far from satisfactory. Francisco's provisional presidency was due to expire at year's end, and it was evident that any new, "permanent" government would be dominated by the Arias faction. The general and his adherents were outspokenly pro-German, a fact that weighed heavily in the State Department. Additionally, the economic misery wrought by Ambassador Russell's disastrous stoppage of customs revenues signaled the distinct possibility of widespread disturbances; undoubtedly the marines would soon again be required for the odious task of suppression.

Although Admiral Pond was impressed by the "assurance of willing cooperation" among some government officials, the attitude was not universal. In Santo Domingo, a two-man marine patrol was fired upon by a number of locals spilling from a "gambling saloon." The marines returned the fire, killing three.[89]

Ambassador Russell's zeal in laying on the imperial rod compounded the troubles. On October 24, in an ill-advised effort to enforce a State Department threat holding Dominicans disturbing the peace "personally responsible," he ordered the arrest of some minor *caudillos*. Most were taken without incident. One, Ramón Batista, resisted. Armed townsmen came to his aid, opening fire on the small marine patrol. Batista and two marines were killed and several Dominicans wounded. "I understand that a woman was shot through the body," a marine officer testified, "when we

---

*The *Memphis* lay on her deathbed, a sad tourist attraction for over five years before being sold for scrap.

fired down a street after a man who was running with a pistol; some women threw themselves in front of him to protect him."[90]

These episodes inclined the State and Navy departments to place Santo Domingo, and perhaps the whole republic, under martial law. Admiral Pond, however, saw them as isolated events and advised against any extreme measures. Ambassador Russell traveled to Washington for a high-level, State-Navy conference.

The participants concluded that since Arias' rebels had been defeated and disarmed and a provisional government established, the continued presence of the marines in their current status was no longer justifiable. The United States must either conjure a reason for keeping the marines in place, one recognized under international law, or they must withdraw. With Francisco's temporary administration due to expire by year's end, and the threat of an Arias-dominated regime taking its place, Russell and the State Department's Latin American Division advocated unilaterally dismantling the republic's political infrastructure and establishing a formal United States military government. It was the best approach, they argued, for extracting the demands for reform and alleviating the economic distress. Without a doubt, the looming war with Germany and Arias' pro-German sympathies influenced the conferees. Yet the diplomats and naval officers realized the political difficulties of establishing a military government without justification, and the Dominicans had not really provided a reasonable excuse. The departments, with eager cynicism, awaited the disorders which would afford the necessity for military government.

In the republic, Provisional President Carbajal knew the *norteamericanos* were searching for any excuse to declare martial law. Congressional terms were about to expire, and he feared the absence of a legislature would furnish the provocation. He ordered new elections, and in the process the State Department found their excuse. The congressmen received their votes from electoral colleges, and most of these were controlled by Arias supporters.

Promptly Secretary Lansing placed the matter before Woodrow Wilson. "The situation in the Dominican Republic," he noted, "is approaching a crisis and we ought to determine immediately a course of action as otherwise revolution and economic disaster are imminent." He added the Department's recommendation to establish martial law "as the only solution of the difficulty."[91]

The President agreed "with the deepest reluctance." He replied to the Secretary, "I am convinced that it is the least of the evils in sight of this very perplexing situation." His was the patronizing bewilderment of an aggrieved schoolmaster about to apply a caning to a recalcitrant pupil. On November 27 secret instructions were given to the Navy Department to establish martial law in the republic.[92]

Two days later, Captain (later Rear Admiral) Harry Knapp, the new senior officer in Hispaniolan waters, issued the proclamation. His signature lay at the foot of the document, but the language and rationale came right from the halls of Washington's State, War, and Navy Building. "The United States Government," it solemnly noted, "with great forebearance and with a friendly desire to enable Santo Domingo to maintain domestic tranquility and observe the terms of the [customs receivership treaty of 1907] . . . is hereby placed in a state of military occupation . . . subject to military government." Dominican national sovereignty, de jure, was unchallenged. Her citizens were still subject to the local statutes, but they would now be administered by the Department of the Navy, with Knapp as military governor. It was all so much blather. The Dominican ambassador vehmently protested to Robert Lansing, calling it an "unexampled act in contempt of the sovereignty of the Dominican people."[93]

In one of his first orders Knapp strictly censored the press, telegraph, and mails, an edict considered necessary to prevent inciting public resistance. Personal possession of firearms and explosives was forbidden and revenue disbursements from the customs receivership were instantly resumed.

By radio, telegraph, and telephone, the proclamation went to every marine garrison in the republic. In Santiago, seat of American power in the north, marine provost patrols moved through the streets and bars, passing the word that liberty was canceled and that all hands were to return to barracks. Every company was put on alert. Municipal officials were summoned and informed that they were expected to carry on with their duties; if they refused, the marines would assume the offices.

In the towns there was hardly a protest, except for an incident at San Francisco de Macorís. Situated along the railroad some thirty miles southeast of Santiago, the town had a reputation for harboring opinions hostile to the American presence. The 31st Company was in garrison there since mid-summer. On its arrival, the local governor and *caudillo*, Juan Pérez, with several armed followers, had barricaded themselves in the local *fortaleza*.* Rather than taking quick action, the marine commander wavered. Occasional sniping pinged out from the walls, and still the lieutenant did nothing. Relations with the townsfolk, civil at first, deteriorated.[94]

By the time of the proclamation of martial law, the 31st was reinforced by elements of the 47th Company, and First Lieutenant Ernest Williams had taken command. His strength was three officers and 115 men. With his arrival, municipal order was restored. Pérez, however, continued obdurate in the *fortaleza*. Williams' fellow officers estimated that a full battalion of infantry with artillery support was necessary. Much like Smedley Butler at Fort Rivière, Williams damned the odds and planned a surprise attack.

He chose an assault group of twelve men, with orders to assemble that night at the command post. At the sounding of taps, they marched off as if on routine patrol. Around the *fortaleza* the main bodies took position. Williams and his dozen inched as close as was possible without creating suspicion. At the massive double doors of the ornate main gate, the Dominicans prepared to shut up for the night. Williams led his men forward at the rush and hurled his body at the closing timbers. The assault caught the defenders completely by surprise.

The Dominicans rallied quickly, and eight of Williams' men were hit by rifle fire. The main body of the companies charged into the courtyard, and a fierce, ten-minute fight ensued. Pérez and about 200 followers escaped over the walls, but another hundred threw themselves facedown and surrendered. Williams was later awarded the Congressional Medal of Honor for the attack.

With the *fortaleza* secure, Williams sent a patrol to guard the railroad station and telephone exchange. They arrived too late. The wires had already been cut, and Pérez, with most of his men, had escaped by train. Marines garrisoned the larger towns along the line and trapped Pérez. Caught between advancing companies converging toward the center, Pérez abandoned his train and scattered south.

As 1916 moved toward its close, the republic lapsed into an uneasy quiet. "Ninety-five percent of the people," Pendleton re-

---

*Every Dominican provincial capital had its *fortaleza*, or fortress. They were fairly large, quadrangular masonry structures, some dating from the Spanish period, and served as the military, police, and government center.

ported, "have wanted just what they are now getting but have been afraid to say so, fearing the small percentage of politicos and professional disturbers."[95]

O n the day of Admiral Knapp's proclamation establishing the military government, the Dominican Congress adjourned *sine die*. Its next session was scheduled for late February 1917, when a third of the senators and half of the deputies stood for reelection. But by executive order, Knapp, a judicially minded officer, and, in the Caperton mold hardly a tyrant, canceled the election and suspended the legislative body.

Acting naively for a man of his intelligence, Knapp waited for the senior government bureaucrats to come forward and cooperate in establishing the "Wilson plan" reforms. But to a one, they resigned their posts "with the distinct purpose," as a marine officer noted, "of embarrassing the military authorities." President Carbajal and his cabinet likewise literally cleaned out their desks and departed, never to return. As no Dominicans of "suitable character" were found as replacements, Knapp established the military government in the Presidential Palace and appointed marine and navy officers to the portfolios.[96]

Uncle Joe Pendleton assumed the combined Ministries of War and Navy, Interior and Police. Colonel Rufus Lane received Foreign Relations, Justice, and Public Instruction. Naval officers headed the Departments of Sanitation and Beneficence, Agriculture, and Immigration. Treasury and revenue functions passed to the American receiver-general of customs. The judiciary largely retained its independence. In all departments rank and file civil servants were encouraged to remain, and as Knapp ordered an immediate reinstatement of government salaries most did.

Like any intelligent colonial governor, Knapp kept the existing civil law and the provincial and local units of government retained a fair degree of responsibility. He was careful to prescribe that civil officials were not to be "disturbed in their offices" or have their authority lessened, save in cases of malfeasance.[97]

Knapp's first priority, and the first major occupational operation of the marine brigade, was to disarm the population. Every Dominican sixteen years and older, it seemed, went about with some sort of weapon. In a matter of weeks over 50,000 firearms were confiscated. After the deadline for their surrender, any local caught with a gun received a heavy twenty-five-dollar fine imposed by the military provost courts and a jail sentence of three to six months.

In much the same manner that Leonard Wood had implemented educational reforms in Cuba, Knapp attempted a total revamping of the Dominican Republic's educational system. Nationwide, only 18,000 children were enrolled, and most of these attended private, subsidized institutions in the cities. In the rural districts, total enrollment never exceeded 1,000 students. In a population of 750,000, ninety percent were illiterate and there was not a single public school worthy of the name.

Under Colonel Lane's direction and aided by a Dominican commission, all unworthy teachers were dismissed, salaries were improved, and government subsidies to favored institutions ceased. In a laudable attempt at reaching and educating the masses, Lane concentrated his efforts on primary and secondary education. Within a year he established nearly 500 rural schools and national enrollment increased to 100,000 students. Unlike the educational systems during the United States occupations of the Philippines, Puerto Rico, and to a degree, Cuba, all teaching was conducted in Spanish rather than English.[98]

One of the military government's more important successes, and one which removed a tremendous impediment to economic progress, was the adjudication of millions of dollars in outstanding claims against the republic. Knapp appointed a commission whose judgment could not be appealed. It could summon witnesses under oath, examine all public and private documents, impose fines or imprisonment for contempt, perjury, "or any other act tending to defeat its purpose." By 1920, when it completed its work, the commission had winnowed the myriad claims to a mere $6 million.[99]

And there were the usual public works projects and health programs attending an American occupation. Roads were built, port facilities improved, and public buildings given thorough cleaning and restoration. Of the existing jails, a naval officer noted, "The word inadequate is barely expressive of the condition"; a new penitentiary was opened in Santo Domingo. A national leper colony was also established. The republic had few lepers, but lacked facilities for those there were, and they had mingled in the streets, in daily contact with the population.[100]

Upon the establishment of the occupation, the republic was divided into northern and southern military districts, with the demarkation line generally along the crest of the Cordillera Central. The 4th Marines, headquartered in Santiago, garrisoned the north. The 3rd Marines, raised for the Vera Cruz occupation in 1914 and disbanded thereafter, was re-formed in Santo Domingo. Hiking Hiram Bearss assumed command and established his southern district headquarters in Fort Ozama. Together the two regiments formed the 2nd Provisional Brigade, commanded by Brigadier General Pendleton until his relief in late 1918.

The entire occupation had no unifying policy and the tasks of the brigade, beyond keeping order and training a constabulary, were ill defined. Frequent changes of command on all levels led to varying mission interpretations and there was little policy direction from the State and Navy departments.

According to Colonel George Thorpe, who later commanded the 3rd Marines, "It would [have been] a fine thing if troops in the Dominican Republic and Haiti, [had been] told exactly what their mission [was]. . . . Men can face a very black future if they but know what it is."[101]

Among the worst facets of the occupation were the operations of the provost courts within the military districts. In theory they were to adjudicate civil and criminal actions between the occupation forces and the population, as well as try those Dominicans accused of crimes against the military government. In practice they were notoriously capricious and were often presided over by marine officers with little or no knowledge of military or civil law. "The provost courts," noted an American civilian observer with much experience in Latin American affairs, "have gained the reputation of being unjust, oppressive and cruel, and seem to delight in excessive sentences." With their alien language, marine judges, and military procedure, the courts were regarded by the locals "with aversion and terror."[102]

While many officers attempted to judge and sentence fairly marine and indigenous defendants alike, this was not general practice. In more than a few cases Dominicans were denied counsel and investigating officers were unsympathetic to their complaints, accepting the testimony of marines, especially if they were fellow officers, at face value. One marine captain, accused of crushing a man's genitals with a stone and killing four prisoners in cold blood, was acquitted on a technicality. Admiral Knapp condemned this as a "shocking occurrence, utterly reprehensible."[103]

An essential task allotted to the brigade was the formation and training of a nonpartisan Dominican constabulary. The old Republican Guard had been a thoroughly corrupt institution; like the Haitian Army, its recruits were press-ganged into the ranks. At the time of the intervention, the army was budgeted for 900 infantry, cavalry, and mountain gunners, plus thirty-three musicians. A true muster roll, save for the band, would have given about half that number.

In April 1917 the United States military governor abolished the existing structure and appropriated half a million dollars for the organization of a Dominican Constabulary Guard. Former Republican Guardsmen were welcome, but until Dominicans of officer caliber were sufficiently trained, all command functions were assumed by the Marine Corps.[104]

Its name was soon changed to the *Guardia Nacional Dominicana*, and it began with an initial strength of something less than 1,000 men. Despised by the population as traitors and puppets and generally neglected by the brigade, the *guardia* never achieved the status or the ability of the Haitian *gendarmerie*. In large measure this was due to the shortness of the occupation (eight versus nineteen years) lack of funds, and the paucity of competent marine officers and sergeants, most of whom were soon shipped off to France and the World War.

"Our first enlisted men," a marine officer wrote, "were the most ignorant and crude specimens . . . the scum of the island. . . . As a general rule, the degree of intelligence increased with the decrease of the ebony tinge . . . all of our best non-commissioned officers were either of Porto Rican descent, or had a larger proportion of Spanish than of negro blood in their veins."[105]

Dominicans were permitted to apply for *guardia* commissions as second lieutenants, and one who did was a thief, forger, and pimp named Rafael Trujillo, who rose to become the corrupt, brutal dictator of the republic. Nearly sixty years later, Major General Omar Pfeiffer remembered, "My information which came from natives was that Trujillo was a crook, cheat, and so on, of the first water. . . . When he took men [of the *guardia*] out on patrol, he was given an allowance in cash to pay for [their] food. One of Trujillo's duties was to enforce sanitary regulations in isolated *bodegas*. . . . When Trujillo entered one of these places . . .

the first thing he did was to go to the shelves and look for specks of rust on tin cans and, finding it or not finding it, he appropriated enough . . . to feed his men and he kept the money in his own pocket. Other stories of the similiar nature were many."[106]

With no clear policy regarding the length and nature of the occupation, the effectiveness of the *guardia* was a key factor the United States government used to determine the time of the American withdrawal. In the summer of 1919 the *guardia,* according to the American ambassador, was "in no way fitted to insure law and order if our forces should retire." Rear Admiral Snowden, the new military governor, perhaps with an overwhelming urge to depart a thankless billet tending Naboth's vineyard, condemned the *guardia*'s critics as "visionaries or socialists."[107]

Organized resistance to the occupation had ended with Arias' surrender in July 1916, but this hardly meant an end to military operations. In the wild, eastern provinces of Seibo and Macorís, banditry was an age-old problem. Sparsely populated, and with the exception of the northern cultivated coast and the sugar plantations in the south, the region was dotted with isolated farms and scraggly hamlets. In an area larger than Puerto Rico, there were less than sixty miles of bad road. One marine officer described it as "almost in the same state of wilderness in which Columbus found it some years ago."[108]

Prior to the occupation, the Dominican Army and government had little effect on the bandits' predations. During periods of relative domestic peace, much like the Haitian *cacos,* they preyed upon convenient villages. In times of revolution, they aligned with whichever faction offered the most money. Indeed, according to Brigadier General Harry Lee, who later commanded the marine brigade and served as military governor, the various regimes had shown "a chronic attitude of passivity and tolerance towards them." Once a new government was installed it was customary to grant an amnesty to these "patriots," who immediately returned to brigandage.[109]

Locals followed an established custom of paying "protection," usually in kind. Peasants on tiny plots feared even to plant, for as soon as the crop matured, a marine officer observed, "some of the many roving 'generals' would appear with his following of vagabonds, and the crop would rapidly disappear into the insides of the 'outside' army. The farmer got it in the neck."[110]

A number of the bandits were displaced smallholders, thrown off their land in complicated deals by the foreign-owned sugar companies. The unemployed rural proletariat also swelled the rank; highway robbery at least provided some form of livelihood. The functioning of the sugar companies contributed to this vicious cycle. They were the region's largest employer, but work was restricted to the grinding season. Once a poor peasant became a wage-earner, he was reluctant to return to farming, especially as the roving bandits made that living unprofitable.

By no means were the bandits all economically disenfranchised peasants and workers. Most were outright professional criminals, full-time highwaymen called *gavilleros*; others were "peaceful" tillers who worked the soil by day and robbed and killed at night. The *gavilleros* and their cohorts coalesced around some dynamic personality or minor *caudillo* and operated in bands that generally numbered less than fifty men. Their arms varied from gang to gang. Some carried little more than machetes, others had pistols, the odd black-powder rifle, occasionally a Krag-Jorgensen, and even a modern Springfield or two.

The marines, even those who had seen Haitian service, were unprepared for what soon degenerated into a brutal and debilitating guerrilla war. Much of the onus for this can be placed on the American military's lack of a cohesive, centralized operational command.

Lieutenant General Edward Craig recalled his experiences commanding the 70th Company. "I could find nothing in the orders that defined the area I was supposed to patrol. I assumed that I could go anywhere in the district that I desired. I also found out that patrols were not coordinated. There might be a patrol operating in the same general area where I had a patrol, and I would know nothing about it. Consequently we had to exercise extreme caution in our patrols in this area."[111]

Initial marine tactics relied on small, scattered units, often mounted, and usually of less than thirty men. But locating the bandits, much less bringing them to battle in the wild, roadless country, proved almost impossible. Ambush was an ever-present danger, and though the vastly superior marksmanship of the marines invariably controlled the engagement, the foe remained elusive.

"Most of our contacts developed from the enemy's attacking," reported Colonel Thorpe. "It was looking for a needle in a haystack to expect to find the enemy in the dense brushwood or in the network of mountain trails."[112]

Lieutenant Pfeiffer observed the same problem, and described an aftermath that often turned grisly. "The bandits that we encountered were peaceable people by day, and bandits and thieves by night. When a group of four, six, or eight such people would come into a town or settlement, if there were inhabitants with sufficient courage, they would resist and kill [them]; those were the dead bandits that we would see the next day, sliced to pieces with machetes. But [the villagers] wouldn't inform, because they were afraid of retaliation."[113]

The smallness of the marine patrols emboldened the bandits and sometimes led to savage hand-to-hand fighting. At Dos Ríos a four-man detachment was surrounded and charged by "a large group." Marine fire and bayonets killed and wounded many, but three of the marines also died. The lone survivor, Private Rushford, wounded in the hip and both hands, managed to mount his horse and fought his way back to camp. Once safely at his base, according to Colonel Thorpe, "He wanted to return to the fight although both hands were useless and his horse, saddle and equipment literally varnished with blood."[114]

Intelligence regarding enemy movements was singularly lacking. The rural population, covertly hostile to the occupation at best and terrorized into silence by fear of bandit reprisals, refused to divulge any information. In their frustration the marines stoked the merely sullen attitudes of the locals into overt hatred. "The natives had no liking for the Marines," General Craig recalled. "We would find some that in order to obtain favors would be friendly, or if they were employed by the Marines—it meant their jobs. Others, of course, were between the Devil and the deep sea. If they gave information the bandits would kill them; and if they didn't give information the Marines would sometimes be hard on them."[115]

During an operation in January 1917 to capture the bandit chief Chacha, the skipper of the 1st Company, 3rd Marines, took three locals prisoner for concealing arms in the bush. He reported to Colonel Bearss, "Found natives . . . unfriendly and almost uncivilized and unwilling to give least information about anything. . . . By threats of force and by other threats made prisoners act as guides."[116]

But any cooperation with the marines brought atrocious retribution from the *gavilleros*. "This was because of the known fact," reported the southern district commander, "that a leading *gavillero*, Vicentino Evangelista, had stated he would kill any native making a report, and the confirming knowledge that he had on at least three occasions cut men to pieces who had made prompt reports."[117]

Captain Craig witnessed a particularly heinous episode. "My boy who took care of my meals, a native boy, came in one night with his ears cut off. He said they had cut his ears off across the street in the village because he worked for the marines. I grabbed my pistol and ran across the street to apprehend the man that did it. I found the man that did it still with the knife, and as I had my pistol in my hand, he grabbed it and started wrestling it away from me. [Sergeant] Hensley came up and shot him through the head just in time."[118]

In early 1917 Hiking Hiram Bearss led a large-scale sweep through the southern district attempting to bring Chacha and Vicentino to the ground. On January 10 he assembled his forces at San Pedro de Macorís, two companies of marines, half of them mounted on local horses, and headed inland. The locals, knowing the dire consequences of being caught with arms, immediately surrendered 400 rifles and pistols and even a small, ancient cannon. Bearss received information that Chacha was strongly entrenched at the Consuelo sugar plantation about twelve miles up the road. With mounted infantry in the van, he loaded his main body on board a train and advanced up the track. When they were a mile from Consuelo, a sniper fired from atop a nearby water tank. "Evidently," Bearss reported, [this was] "intended as a warning."[119]

Closer to the hamlet, bandits opened a heavy fire. Bearss detrained, formed a skirmish line astride the tracks and advanced. The bandits, however, disappeared into the bush, and Bearss, leaving the train and a small detachment, pressed on to Hato Mayor. Here he learned that Vicentino had passed through earlier in the day, heading northeast for the hills. At midnight on the twelfth, a deserter came into the lines and reported the location of Vicentino's band. Bearss immediately formed seventy men and marched north. In the predawn hours they came upon the empty camp. "I learned," he reported, "only after threatening the natives in the vicinity," that Vicentino had left the previous day. Bearss about-faced and returned to Hato Mayor, "having covered about 15 miles over extremely bad roads, through heavy rains."[120]

June 22, 1898: Aided by ships' boats of the naval covering force, a regiment of the II Corps' cavalry disembarks at Daiquiri, Cuba. (*National Archives*)

July, 1898: Officers of the Cavalry Division, II Army Corps, in Cuba. Left to right: Major General Joseph Wheeler, Colonel Leonard Wood, Lieutenant Colonel Theodore Roosevelt. (*Harper & Row*)

1898: A typical formation of the Cuban Liberation Army. Well-led but miserably equipped, its initial camaraderie with the United States Army soon collapsed amid culture clash and the *insurrectos'* constant pleading for the army's rapidly diminishing supplies. (*National Archives*)

Troopers of the 10th Cavalry, one of four black regiments in the United States Army. All distinguished themselves in the bloody battle for San Juan Hill. (*National Archives*)

Major General John R. Brooke, USA. The first American military governor of Cuba, the cautious Brooke directed the emergency food and sanitation programs that lifted the ravaged island out of the chaos of revolution. (*Author's collection*)

The intervention of 1906; the 28th Infantry at physical drill. (*U.S. Army Military History Institute*)

Bluejackets and marines along the line of transit during the Panama intervention of 1885. This expedition was the largest foreign operation undertaken by the United States in the period between the Mexican War of 1846–1847 and the Spanish-American War. (*Harper's Weekly*)

The gunboat *Nashville*. Her appearance at Colón, Panama, on November 3, 1903, guaranteed the success of the Panamanian revolt and Panama's immediate independence from Colombia. (*U.S. Navy*)

President-elect Taft greeted by Major Smedley Butler, USMC, (holding hat) and his officers in the Panama Canal Zone, 1909. At the time, Butler commanded the Marine Corps' "Panama battalion." (*National Archives*)

Circa 1920, Marines guard a wounded *caco*. (*National Archives*)

A Jeffery Quad (four-wheel drive) truck, one of two used to haul the guns of the 1st, 9th, and 13th marine artillery companies in Haiti and the Dominican Republic. The caisson and trail of a 3-inch field gun, hitched to the truck, are visible at left; all are mired in the mud of a Haitian road. (*National Archives*)

Brigadier General Joseph Pendleton, USMC. "Uncle Joe" commanded the American forces during the Nicaraguan intervention of 1912 and the marine brigade in the Dominican Republic from 1916 to 1918. A kindly warrior who continually looked to the welfare of his men, Pendleton was nonetheless a thoroughly hard campaigner. (*U.S. Marine Corps*)

Dominican guerillas, circa 1917. The guerilla bands who fought the marines were composed of traditional bandits, *gavilleros,* leavened with a portion of displaced farmers who were forced to eke out an existence by plunder. During the United States occupation, *gavillero* leaders adopted a patriotic mien, cloaking their depredations in national liberation rhetoric. (*National Archives*)

A typical rural scene, Dominican Republic, circa 1920. While a boy looks on, marines search a hamlet for ever-elusive guerillas.
(*U.S. Marine Corps*)

Captain Gilbert Hatfield, USMC, and members of the 16th Company following their heroic defense of Ocotal, Nicaragua, July, 1927. (*U.S. Marine Corps*)

Marines guard a ballot box, piled atop the jumble in the "bullcart," during
the Nicaraguan presidential elections of 1928. The election, supervised by
United States forces, remains the most honest election in Nicaragua's history.
(*U.S. Naval Institute*)

Troopers of the 82nd Airborne Division celebrate the capture of Grenada, October, 1983. (*U.S. Army Military History Institute*)

A Sheridan light tank moves through the impoverished El Chorillo section of Panama City; the *Commandancia* is nearby. (*Doug Pensinger, Army Times*)

On January 17 Bearss missed the *gavillero* by only an hour, but took several of the bandit's horses as well as a large quantity of ammunition. Some days later Bearss achieved a major success. At Consuelo, "Mrs. Chacha" came out of the bush and asked Bearss what guarantees he could offer should her husband submit. The colonel could guarantee his life, nothing more. Two days later Chacha surrendered.

Vicentino, however, remained in the field. In mid-March he attacked a marine patrol and was bloodily repulsed, losing eleven men. Publicly, he pledged to kill any *norteamericanos* that came his way, making good the threat when his band captured two civilian engineers and murdered both with machetes.

A major operation involving both the 3rd and 4th regiments, as well as a gang which was a rival of Vicentino and his supporters and was hired for the purpose, moved into the hills. One of the erstwhile *gavilleros*, Antonio Draiby, insinuated himself into Vicentino's band and arranged a parley. Accompanied only by Draiby, First Sergeant William West walked into the bandit camp and induced Vicentino to surrender. On July 5, Vicentino and nearly 200 bandits laid down their arms. All but forty-eight were released. Vicentino was held for trial on eleven counts of murder and numerous rapes. The *jefe* never had his day in court. Sent under guard to San Pedro de Macorís, he was shot while attempting to escape.

The operations against Chacha and Vicentino, successful in the capture of two prominent bandit chiefs, also netted over 1,500 rifles and pistols. "Whole province quiet," Bearss reported. "Natives well pleased and want troops to remain to prevent further uprisings." *Gavillero* activity essentially ceased, and except for the garrison at San Pedro de Macorís and a few scattered posts, the marines were withdrawn from the eastern provinces. An unwarranted optimism settled over the military government.[121]

In the spring of 1917 the United States went to war. As with the 1st Brigade in Haiti, most of the 2nd Brigade's best in the Dominican Republic were ordered home and shipped to France. Despondency settled on those who remained. "It is hard lines," wrote Uncle Joe to Commandant George Barnett, "to be in this service nearly thirty-nine years and then when the first real war of one's service comes, to be shelved down here."[122]

Quality and quantity declined. Junior officers were at a premium. In one instance, there were but two lieutenants for 150 men. And one of these had to be relieved for misconduct and his place temporarily filled by a navy medical officer. The new enlisted men, a goodly number of whom were draftees, were hardly the caliber of the old, long-service regulars. Many, General Pfeiffer recalled, "were disappointed and disgruntled because they had to serve in Santo Domingo instead of fighting in Germany." When Captain Craig arrived, he found them "very poorly trained. They were practically mutinous," and for a time, "I had to sleep with a BAR [Browning Automatic Rifle] by my bed."[123]

The deceptive calm that had settled over the republic was shattered in March 1918. A sergeant was ambushed and killed near Hato Mayor, and this began a renewed outburst of bandit activity. But now it was not mere predation. Political motives had taken root in some of the bands and their operations adopted overtones akin to a war of national liberation. The 3rd Marines' depleted garrisons took to the field. In numbers they were barely adequate as occupation troops, and reinforcements had to be ordered down from the 4th Marines in Santiago; 114 men, formerly a reinforced company, now made up a quarter of the regiment.

Hiram Bearss had gone off to France and Colonel Thorpe now commanded the 3rd Marines and southern district. As with a number of insurgent incidents in the Caribbean, Germany was seen as responsible for the local unrest. "Whoever is running this revolution is a wise man," Thorpe noted to General Pendleton. "He is certainly getting a lot out of the niggers. . . . It shows the handwork of the German."[124]

Regular methods of patrolling failed and Thorpe was forced to adopt drastic measures. In a decree reminiscent of Butcher Weyler's *reconcentrado* policy in Cuba and anticipating the free fire zone of the Vietnam War, Thorpe ordered all law-abiding locals in the southern district to gather their livestock and enough food for a month and to relocate in the garrison towns. After August 24 any armed Dominican found in the provinces of Seibo and Macorís would be deemed a bandit and arrested; those refusing to surrender would be shot.

With less than excellent troops and a severe paucity of junior officers, the order was ofttimes brutally carried out. In October 1918 a detachment of the 113th Company commanded by a sergeant approached a domicile north of Hato Mayor. "There were two bandit houses," the sergeant later reported, "and I would say, four men, four women and some children. . . . They did not have any property of importance." The peasants fled at the marines' approach. The patrol, continued the sergeant, "formed skirmish line and opened fire, but all got away except one woman and child and one horse and saddle." The incident brought forth an admonition from Ben Fuller (Commandant of the Marine Corps, 1930–1934), now commanding the brigade, to "exercise extreme caution in firing on fleeing parties which contain women and children."[125]

One of the most serious atrocities committed involved marine Captain Charles Merkel, the notorious "Tiger of Seibo." Merkel, who routinely tortured bandit suspects, was, according to Rear Admiral Snowden, "a German who used the well-known German methods on the native population." Finally arrested after the archbishop interceded with the military governor, Merkel was charged with four counts of murder and with beating and disfiguring a prisoner. Confined to quarters to await a general court martial, he committed suicide "with a small pistol concealed on his person." Unofficial accounts speak of two officers who visited the captain, leaving the pistol and one bullet on their departure.[126]

In early 1919 in order to better coordinate operations, the military government created the eastern district in Seibo and Macorís provinces. With the redrawn map came heavy reinforcements, the 15th Marines and the 1st (marine) Air Squadron with six Curtiss JN-6 Jennys. Their arrival in February brought the brigade to its peak occupational strength of 3,000 men.

The personnel and matériel rejuvenation of the brigade coincided with a general review of operational errors and the adoption of new tactics. The failure to suppress banditry was attributed to the constant difficulty of obtaining accurate intelligence of the enemy's movements, the impossibility of rapid communications between command posts and units in the field (until mid-1919, when the marines were equipped with field radios, and air detachments arrived, all communications were by mounted "runner") and the absence of effective regimental and brigade staff planning.

In the eastern district, the 15th Marines abandoned small, independent patrolling and adopted instead a system of large-scale sweeps, using all available forces. Superiority of numbers permitted fresh troops in constant field rotation and kept the bandits on the run. Each company carried at least one mule-mounted radio, enabling them to report exact positions down to squad level. The air detachment, with pilots sitting on iron stove lids as protection against sporadic ground fire, proved its worth in control and direction. "Aeroplane service," reported Colonel William Harllee, the district and regimental commander, "has enabled all companies . . . to move out promptly and simultaneously for concerted action with complete and definite instructions for operations."[127]

The new tactics were a qualified success. One three-month operation resulted in the collection, identification, and conviction of over 400 "habitual bandits." The process of "collection and identification," to use a phrase coined later, was hardly intended to "win the hearts and minds" of the people.

General Craig remembered, "Colonel Harllee put out operation orders which provided for patrols and companies to arrive in certain areas at specified times and to sweep these areas as a combined force. These patrols had orders to shoot any bandits seen, to bring in any prisoners that surrendered, and to gather in everybody between the ages of ten and seventy years of age for interrogation.

"The interrogation center was run by a Captain Louis Cukela, [who] spoke Spanish fluently. The prisoners were sent back to the center, where informers [many of whom were local prostitutes] were placed behind a canvas screen with a small hole they could look out of as each suspect was brought before him under a bright light, so the informers could not be identified. Whether these informers always correctly identified bandits or their own enemies, I never found out; but we did identify quite a number of bandits."[128]

Throughout the renewed campaign in the eastern district, the *gavilleros* continued their trade of preying upon the population. Caught between the marines and the bandits, locals moved to safer areas in the north and south. Colonel Harllee described the region as "a scene of desolation and long-abandoned homes, a sad and pitiful spectacle." The marines considered anyone on the run either a bandit or an accessory to banditry. When they discovered newly built shacks in the hills, these were often put to the torch. Locals fled at the sight of an approaching patrol, and whether armed or not, they drew fire. "People who are not bandits," Colonel Harllee erroneously claimed, "do not flee at the approach of Marines."[129]

New tactics or old, good troops or bad, the anti-bandit operations dragged on inexorably, taking a physical toll on the people and morally draining the marines. Over a thousand suspected bandits were killed or wounded, and hundreds more incarcerated. But like the later Viet Cong, many melted into the peasantry, "appearing" as Colonel Harllee noted "like any other citizen." Fatigued and frustrated, the marines began to regard all Dominicans as the enemy.

As national liberation ideology flourished in many of the bands, recruitment rose. But not all the recruits joined out of ideological fervor. One prominent civilian stated, "When someone . . . was killed, his brothers joined the *gavilleros* to get revenge on the Marines. . . . Some joined the ranks inspired by patriotism, but most of them joined the ranks inspired by hate, fear or revenge."[130]

In the spring of 1922 Brigadier General Harry Lee assumed command of the brigade. In one of his first orders, he abolished the system of hidden informers. Realizing that many in the bands had not enlisted for plunder, Lee offered pardons to all who surrendered their arms and returned to a peaceful life. Those charged with "criminal acts of a heinous nature" must take their chances before the provost courts. Lee also organized a special force of marine-officered Dominican civil guards, men who "have suffered some injury at the hands of the bandits and are eager to operate against them." The guards proved a reliable auxiliary, and in conjunction with regular marine units, they inflicted heavy casualties. Lee now granted an armistice, offering suspended sentences to all who remained on good behavior. Whole bands took advantage of the new leniency. By mid-year Lee's programs showed good result. There were still some professional *gavilleros* operating on the fringes of the sugar plantations, but by the summer of 1922 Lee could report the eastern district as finally "pacified."[131]

The occupation moved toward an unlamented end. On State Department orders the military government commissioned prominent Dominicans to draft the constitutional groundwork for new elections and the formation of a transitional government. The duties of the brigade were consequently reduced and the garrisons were pulled in and concentrated in the major cities. To fill the military vacuum, the *guardia*, since renamed the *Policía Nacional Dominicana*, finally received the full attention of the occupation authorities. A Dominican was appointed to its command, but training continued to be the responsibility of marine officers. A military academy of sorts was established at Haina. Results were mixed. There was difficulty in recruiting literate Dominican officer and noncommissioned officer candidates. The cadets shied away from any manual labor and were reluctant to participate in classroom studies. But in field subjects, musketry, small unit tactics, and drill, they became adept.

In August 1922 the 3rd and 15th regiments were disbanded, the former, in a much reduced capacity, readopted its original lineage of the 1st Marines. In July 1924, at the very close of the occupation, the regiment was redesignated 3rd Battalion, 6th Marines, just prior to its sailing for home. The same month saw the departure of the 1st Air Squadron. The bulk of the 4th Marines steamed for San Diego in August. On September 16, the last company of the regiment filed on board their transport at Santo Domingo, and the occupation of the Dominican Republic came to an end.

"There is no doubt as to what our mission is," First Lieutenant Robert Kilmartin, the brigade law officer, had lectured in 1922. "It is to help this Republic and its people." That indeed was the high-noted Wilsonian doctrine. But an accurate postmortem was delivered by the eminent academician, Dr. Carl Kelsey. "The Marine Corps is intended to be a fighting body and we should not ask it to assume all sorts of civil and political responsibilities unless we develop within it a group of especially trained men."[132]

7:

NICARAGUA II
1927–1934

There's no use sending a handful of our boys down
there to get butchered. If it's war let us call it that and
successfully conclude it.

–Father of a dead marine, *New York Times*
   January 5, 1928

In the years that followed Uncle Joe Pendleton's
victory at Coyotepe in 1912, Nicaragua enjoyed more than a
decade of peace and relative prosperity. Woodrow Wilson continued Taft's program of dollar diplomacy and the State Department
assisted the government in obtaining substantial loans from New
York banks. That the money was a principal prop to the continued
administration of Adolfo Díaz and the Conservatives only
strengthened America's commitment to ensure political stability
in the country. By the early 1920's the United States had seemingly
achieved its goal through her hold on the Nicaraguan economy.
Americans managed the customs service, the national bank, and
the railroad, as well as dominated the commission which parceled
Nicaragua's debts.

Political order was also maintained by the residence of a 100-
man marine legation guard in Managua. Though small, equal in
size to the landing force of a cruiser, its presence exerted a significant influence on internal politics and in effect guaranteed the
minority Conservative rule.

For much of their tenure, however, the legation-guarding marines were an ill-trained, ill-disciplined, and ill-officered aggregate
of recent recruits. Frequent street and bar fights with local ne'er-
do-wells and confrontations with the police stoked strong feelings
of resentment, especially among the Liberal outs. In the Managua

285

press, the marines were condemned as "barbarian oppressors" and were accused of bringing venereal disease to the capital. In February 1921, responding to the attacks, they sacked the offices and destroyed the press of *La Tribuna*. In December forty marines battled the municipal police, killing six. In both instances the perpetrators were arrested and convicted by courts-martial. But anti-Americanism, never far below the surface, swept the capital, and the United States ambassador was forced to request landing forces from the ships at Corinto. The entire legation guard was replaced and the State Department planned for its complete, permanent withdrawal.[1]

That, however, was contingent upon the Nicaraguan government's ability to maintain internal peace which was highly questionable. The presence of the legation guard had lulled the Conservative government into complacency. There was little interest in developing an efficient army; instead the muster declined in both numbers and fitness. By 1924 its strength had dwindled to less than 400 men. Recruitment was by the usual method of the region, the press-gang. "Occasionally," reported marine Captain Ross Rowell in 1916, "they round up the spectators at a fiesta or a baseball game or a band concert."* Twenty cents a day was deducted by the commanding officers from each soldier's pay for rations. When Rowell commented on this rather large (by Nicaraguan standards) allowance, the minister of war replied, "Oh yes; they live very well and the commanding officers are still able to make a very nice profit."[2]

In 1923, under United States auspices, the Central American states entered into a general treaty whereby the signatories agreed not to recognize any government which had come to power through revolution or coup. The treaty also spoke to the nations' responsibility for maintaining internal peace, which was the necessary condition for the State Department to initiate withdrawal of the Nicaraguan legation guard. "The first duty of the armed forces of the Central American Governments is to preserve order," noted the department's treaty text, and each of the signatories pledged to establish a nonpartisan national guard.[3]

In 1925 the State Department submitted to Nicaragua a detailed organizational plan for the establishment of a United

---

*This disproves the assertion of Lieutenant Colonel Oliver North, USMC, that the presence of baseball diamonds in Nicaragua in the 1980's corroborated the existence of Cuban military personnel because "Nicaraguans don't play baseball."

States–trained constabulary, the *Guardia Nacional*. American officers were not specifically mentioned, but "suitable instructors [hired on the State Department's recommendation] . . . with experience gained in other countries in organizing such corps" were. The plan specified a *Guardia Nacional* of twenty-three native officers and 393 men, a force which was to grow and eventually replace the entire "national police, navy and army of Nicaragua."[4]

This *guardia*, "a force to be trained free from political influence," was to be divided into a "Constabulary Proper" and a "Training Branch," with United States instructors supreme in the latter and holding absolute control over supplies, accounts, and enlistments. Violent opposition in the Nicaraguan Congress, however, wrought significant changes. The Nicaraguan army, partisan in the extreme, was retained, and the *guardia*'s American instructors were placed under command of the minister of war. The lucrative supply services were given to the minister of police. Not surprisingly, the State Department voiced opposition to what it rightly considered a prostitution of a noble goal. Yet as Nicaragua must eventually control its own forces and destiny, the State Department in the end agreed to cooperate on her terms.[5]

As the first *jefe* of the *guardia*, the State Department recruited Army Major Calvin Carter, lately of the Philippine Constabulary. In July 1925 Carter arrived in Managua to find 200 raw enlistees and nothing else. Ninety of the potential guardsmen failed their physical examination. For the remainder he could provide neither arms nor ammunition, and neither uniforms nor boots. The budget was totally inadequate and Carter was forced to exceed appropriations merely to obtain the basics, which included "mahogany boards for the men to sleep on."[6]

Despite hostility, suspicion, and the war ministry's attempted subversion of the new organization, Carter made good progress. He genuinely tried to recruit without regard to political affiliation. Within two months the infant *guardia* mustered eighteen officer cadets and 225 *rasos* (privates). Had the political situation remained calm, the *guardia* might well have fulfilled the State Department's hopes in insuring internal peace. But less than two months after Carter's arrival, to quote Smedley Butler, "revolution was on again."

In 1917 Adolfo Díaz had come to the end of his presidential term and was succeeded by his factional enemy, the popular Conservative general, Emiliano Chamorro. Formerly commander in chief of the army and Nicaragua's envoy to Washington, Chamorro had led or instigated more revolutions than anyone in Nicaraguan history. Constitutionally prohibited from succeeding himself in the 1920 elections, Chamorro engineered the election of his aged uncle, Diego. In 1923 Diego suddenly died and Vice President Bartolomé Martínez assumed the office.

Martínez, too, hoped to perpetuate himself in office, but was, of course, also prohibited by law from doing so. The State Department made it very plain that it would refuse recognition to anyone who assumed office in violation of the 1923 treaty. To prevent his arch-rival Chamorro, now a lawful candidate, from garnering the votes, Martínez formed a coalition party of relative moderates, the Conservative Republicans. For the offices of president and vice president, they nominated the Conservative Carlos Solórzano and the Liberal Dr. Juan Sacasa. Through force, intimidation, and wildly fraudulent ballot counting, the coalition ticket swept into office. Chamorro laid his plans for revolution.

In January 1925, in one of his first official acts, President Solórzano requested that the State Department not withdraw the legation guard. The plea was understandable. His government was a fragile, uneasy coalition, its army completely subordinate to factional interests, and the tiny, nonpartisan *guardia,* barely trained, provided no real buttress for domestic peace. In the towns there were rumors of *Chamorrista* revolt. If the marines left, noted the American ambassador, revolution would be "inevitable."

The State Department agreed. The marines would remain, but under the firm understanding that recruitment and training of the *guardia* be vigorously pressed. Six months was considered ample time for this, and whether or not the *guardia* proved capable, the marines would depart no later than September 1.

On August 4, 1925, the legation guard embarked at Corinto, and Nicaragua, it was hoped, was left finally to her own fates. "Peace," noted one meticulous historian, "reigned . . . for three weeks, four days and 13 hours."[7]

The night of August 28 witnessed a grand, champagne-flowing party at Managua's International Club. Everyone of note was there: Ambassador Charles Eberhardt of the United States, War Minister Moncada, and most of the cabinet; even President and Señora Solórzano made an appearance. As couples danced, there drunkenly swaggered and lurched into the ballroom "a threatening, coatless figure in boots, spurs, and military breeches, with a broad brimmed hat pulled well down over his face, flourishing a revolver in each hand." An armed rabble of men and boys shuffled in behind. Bellows of "Down with the Liberals!" were followed by shots into the ceiling; men leapt under the tables, women screamed and fainted.[8]

It was Gabry Rivas, brother and emissary of the commandant of La Loma fort, come to "liberate President Solórzano from the Liberal element in his government." War Minister Moncada and the senior government Liberals were placed under arrest.[9]

Major Carter turned out the *guardia* and urged President Solórzano to crush the revolt. Taking an escort of fifty men, he advised the shaken president to enter La Loma, parade General Rivas' troops and ask whether they would stand by their oath or turn traitor. When Carter offered to shoot the general "if he misbehaved," Solórzano declined. "Oh, but he is my brother-in-law."[10]

While the president waffled, Rivas sent an ultimatum: he would return to La Loma and release the prisoners once they were expunged from the coalition government. Vice President Sacasa had already fled into exile, and Solórzano bowed to the demands. Rivas kept his promise, and as a reward received $5,000 and a house in Managua.

Chamorro's role in the incident remains unclear. In any event, he was out of Managua and denied any complicity. But the situation had turned very much in his favor, and he returned to the capital to actively plot Solórzano's demise. On October 25 Chamorro personally led an armed force to the gates of La Loma, which were opened to receive him. By telephone he informed the president that any attempt at dislodgment would be answered by their opening fire on the presidential palace.

Major Carter again offered the *guardia* to evict the usurper and begged for enough ammunition to complete the task; again Solórzano demurred. For five days nothing much happened. Then, after breakfast on the sixth day, Carter's phone rang. It was Chamorro, inquiring whether the *guardia* would obey a presidential order to assault La Loma. "I shall take orders from the President," Carter replied. "Well," the general continued unfazed, "if he does order you to attack us will you please call me up and let me know?" Paralyzed with indecision, Solórzano still did nothing.[11]

Secure in La Loma fort, whose brooding hilltop walls dominated all Managua, Chamorro moved toward political consolidation. He informed the president that he might remain in office only if the coalition government were dissolved and the remaining Liberals ousted. Full amnesty must be given to all participants in the coup, and the government to tender Chamorro $10,000 for his out-of-pocket expenses. Once these matters were handled, the president must appoint Chamorro commanding general of the army. To all the demands, President Solórzano meekly acquiesced. At a total cost of twenty dead, and with a handsome profit for himself, Chamorro had become virtual dictator of Nicaragua.

Doubtless, Chamorro continued to have thoughts of outright seizing the presidency, but that might well result in United States intervention. He had already been told by Ambassador Eberhardt that no recognition would be tendered to anyone taking office in violation of the 1923 Washington treaty. Indeed, the ships of the Special Service Squadron, an aggregate of obsolescence from the heyday of the New Navy, were already beating about the coasts. But the general was a crafty fox, and skillfully wove his path around and through the intricacies of the treaty clauses.

First he had himself appointed minister of war, and when a Managua senator conveniently resigned, Chamorro was elected to fill the vacancy. Also, vacant, de facto, was the vice presidency. The Liberal Dr. Sacasa, though in exile, still held the office, and indeed, when he arrived in Washington to plead his case, was granted the proper honors. But the Nicaraguan Congress swiftly created a legal void by voting him a two-year banishment. It then declared Chamorro *primero designado*—first designate—the constitutional understudy filling the "absolute or temporary default" of the vice presidency. Solórzano was finished. Citing reasons of health, the Congress continued the charade and granted the president an indefinite leave. On January 16, 1926, Solórzano tendered his formal resignation and Emiliano Chamorro was proclaimed President of Nicaragua. Immediately he set about obtaining the vital recognition of the United States; the State Department refused.

Vociferous in their opposition to the American intervention in 1912, and to the presence of the marine legation guard, the Liberals now clamored for the marines' return, calling loudly for the United States to restore their political rights by force. In Washington, Dr. Sacasa established a government in exile, but the State Department refused recognition to him as well.

On May 2, 1926, the inevitable civil war burst forth. Supplied with Mexican arms, a force of Liberal exiles landed at Bluefields, captured the town and customs house after a bloody little battle, and rifled the vaults of the local branch of the National Bank. Within hours, the old peace cruiser *Cleveland* was wheezing north at fourteen knots from Panama. She arrived on the sixth, put ashore her landing force "to protect American lives and property," and proceeded to disarm the rebel troops within a declared "neutral zone," the first of several such entities established by American forces in Nicaragua. "Business resumed and feeling of confidence prevails," cabled the American consul.[12]

In Managua, Chamorro decreed a state of war, jailed his political opponents, and moved vigorously to crush the Liberal revolt. He expanded the army to over 5,000 men and marched east. On both sides, children and women were not exempt from recruitment. "Dear Colonel," wrote a junior officer in charge of a press-gang, "I am sending you herewith forty volunteers who will fight for the cause so dear to us. . . . It will greatly help me . . . to secure others if you will make sure to return the ropes."[13]

Uniforms, such as they were, consisted of red hatbands for the Liberals and blue for the Conservative government troops. Many kept the opposite hidden away, and if wounded or captured simply changed colors. "This," noted an observer, "was a form of insurance against an artistically inflicted death."[14]

As for the *Guardia Nacional,* they too were sent east. Chamorro had assiduously cultivated their loyalty, and as Ambassador Eberhardt reported, they were "fast disintegrating into a politically controlled machine of the present regime."[15]

But in the east the Liberals were gaining ground and the government was going broke. In late August the former war minister, José Moncada, captured the American company town of Puerto Cabezas, extended his political control down the coast, and drove the government forces inland. The action brought divisions within the Conservative ranks, with calls for Chamorro's resignation and some accommodation with the Liberal rebels.

In October, under the hounding sponsorship of the American legation, a fifteen-day truce was declared, and representatives of the government and rebels met in Corinto on board the venerable *Denver*. All sides agreed that Chamorro must go, but there was no agreement as to his replacement or what form a new government would take. Ex-President Adolfo Díaz, "our Nicaraguan," was unacceptable to the Liberals, and ex–Vice President Sacasa was equally repugnant to the Conservatives. In deadlock, the parley disintegrated, and the civil war continued.

The next month Chamorro surprised everyone and resigned in favor of Senator Uriza, the current *designado*. At the urging of the State Department, the expelled Liberals were officially reinstated in the government. But as most of these were either in exile or active revolt in the field, it was a hollow gesture. Within days, following strong recommendations from the legation and the State Department, the Nicaraguan Congress selected Adolfo Díaz *designado*, and Uriza promptly resigned in his favor. With "our Nicaraguan" in office, the United States immediately granted recognition to the new regime.

But the new coalition government failed utterly in ending the civil war. On December 1, bearing the Liberal standard, Dr. Sacasa returned from exile, landed at Puerto Cabezas with a small guard, and over the radio proclaimed himself Constitutional President of Nicaragua. From Mexico he received his only recognition, and a steady flow of munitions as well. The *Cleveland* and *Denver* were in port, and while Sacasa protested, their landing force surrounded his house "with bellicose display." The senior naval officer declared the town and the adjoining foreign concessions a neutral zone, "which comprised the district lying within rifle range of property of Americans and Foreigners"; he ordered Sacasa to disarm his guard or vacate the zone within twenty-four hours. "There will be no carrying of arms, ammunition, knives, etc." Faced with unpalatable choices, Sacasa chose to disarm and retain his capital. In a lengthy missive to the Secretary of State, his spokesman protested, "Would it not be more worthy of the greatness of your country to let the Nicaraguans determine their own affairs as they have a right to?"[16]

But this diplomatic defeat for the Liberals had little effect on the battlefield. In late December at Pearl Lagoon, midway between Puerto Cabezas and Bluefields, General Moncada subjected the government army to a stinging defeat. Hundreds were killed in four days of vicious fighting. Routed, the government forces fell back on Bluefields, where they found the neutral zone a welcome asylum. The wounded of both sides were collected by American naval personnel and taken on fruit barges to Bluefields for treatment.

Desperately Adolfo Díaz scrambled about for overt American assistance, but the State Department, having just slapped an arms embargo on Nicaragua and recently untangling itself from the Dominican Republic morass, shied away from any new, quicksand commitment.

Díaz then hit upon the one factor that was sure to get America's attention: the American fear of communist influence and its threat to the lives and property of American citizens. In 1926 that hemispheric bogeyman seemed to reside in Mexico. Alone, of all nations, it had recognized Sacasa and the Liberals as the legitimate government of Nicaragua, and a pipeline of munitions flowed steadily from Mexico to the rebel forces in the field. "This condition," Díaz stated, "places in imminent risk the sovereignty and independence of Nicaragua [and] places in peril the interests of North American citizens and other foreigners residing in our territory."[17]

The United States, lately in the grip of a domestic red scare, took the bait. The Associated Press saw in the Mexican interference "the spectre of a Mexican-fostered Bolshevistic hegemony intervening between the United States and the Panama Canal"; the State Department was "deeply concerned."[18]

For a time there actually seemed a prospect of war, and in Mexico one parliamentary leader said, "I do not believe there will be war between Mexico and the United States, but I should like to know what the United States is seeking—another [battleship] *Maine* [incident]?"[19]

The Mexican war situation was eventually defused, but the fear of Mexican meddling in Nicaragua still haunted the State Department. In early January 1927 it dismissed Díaz' suggestion that the presidency be given to a "third party," and insisted on his retention in office to prevent "a Mexican triumph."[20]

But in Nicaragua the civil war raged unabated, and while the United States sorted out its policy, hoping to avoid a major intervention, troop commitments nevertheless began. On January 6, in response to Díaz' plea, the peace cruiser *Galveston* landed her marines at Corinto and were welcomed by the Nicaraguan government as deliverers from the threat of a Liberal victory. Later that week, President Coolidge lifted the arms embargo, announced the sale of munitions to the Díaz government and the increase of American forces. On January 24 the first substantial units arrived; the 400 men of the 2nd Battalion, 5th Marines.

American neutrality was evaporating, and through shifting circumstances, United States forces were slowly being placed in a position of allies to Díaz, ready to take the field against the Liberal rebels. In mid-January Díaz proposed specific peace terms, including an agreement to hold free elections in 1928 under American supervision. American participation in the election, he said, "will spare Nicaragua the horrors of Bolshevism, lawlessness, religious persecution and general retrogression." He expressed his willingness to permit the Liberals to enter the government in the interim. From his neutral zone sanctuary at Puerto Cabezas, Dr. Sacasa agreed to cooperate, but first Díaz must resign and the office be filled by the ever phantom "third party." On this point there was deadlock, and the compromise died aborning.[21]

The Liberals, immobilized on the east coast because of the neutral zones, now moved westward. Across extremely difficult and unsustaining terrain, General Moncada, recruiting as he advanced (women and children among his levies) marched through central Nicaragua, and with 3,000 troops approached Matagalpa, a critical road junction leading to the capital. As his army drew near, joined "for the fun and the looting" by marauding bands, the substantial foreign colony scurried from their coffee plantations into the town. Battle with a nearby government force appeared likely, and to protect foreign lives and property, a reinforced company of marines rushed up from Managua in commandeered autos and trucks. Matagalpa was not yet a neutral zone, and the marine commander showed no inclination to prevent the fight, prompting one distraught American civilian to exclaim, "Hell, that's what you're here for!" News of the impending battle was telephoned to Managua and further marine reinforcements moved in and declared the town and its environs a neutral zone. The government and rebel forces maneuvered to avoid confrontation, but Moncada nonetheless advanced slowly on to the capital.[22]

In Managua the foreign minister proclaimed victory. "The military operations of the Government have been everywhere triumphant. . . . Now there is in arms only General Moncada. . . . As soon as he sallies forth into the open and inhabited country . . . his army will be destroyed." It was all so much bombast.[23]

On February 6 the Nicaraguan government suffered a crushing reversal at Chinandega, just north of Corinto, and a vital rail and telegraph link between Managua and the coast. About 500 government troops held the town, and were attacked by a rebel column variously estimated at between 600 and 2,000 troops. The street-to-street and house-to-house fighting was exceedingly brutal. The rebels blasted out the heart of the town, and hundreds were killed on each side. "[T]he right of way of the railroad," wrote an American observer, "was black with the flopping, squawking vultures which grow fat on Central American fields of honor."[24]

At the battle, two American freelance aviators flew in the service of the Nicaraguan government. The pilots were ex-barnstormers, whose aircraft, Rusty Rowell later noted, were "discards from the Checkered Cab Co., at San Francisco." One told the *New York Times*, "After I had figured out where the sharpshooters were hidden I heaved a bomb at them. The traffic jam that followed probably was the worst ever known in Chinandega. Men and women and children dashed up and down the streets, through the squares and back again. They seemed to be crazy, they ran so fast and aimlessly."[25]

American relief supplies were rushed to the town, and government forces arrived soon after. On February 19 a reinforced marine rifle company marched in. The next day, Rear Admiral Latimer, commanding the Special Service Squadron, put ashore his landing forces from the new light cruisers *Milwaukee*, *Raleigh*, and the veteran *Galveston*. Chinandega and León were declared neutral zones. The railroad, however, was not, being far too vital an artery for the movement of government troops. Latimer merely declared it "off limits," and prohibited fighting within 2,000 yards of the right-of-way. On the twenty-first, the Scouting Fleet's marine battalion, 204 officers and men, landed in Corinto from light cruiser *Trenton*. In Managua the marines occupied La Loma fort, "to afford better protection to foreign lives and property," according to Ambassador Eberhardt.[26]

The battle for Chinandega was followed by another government defeat, this time at the hands of Moncada at Muy Muy, midway between Matagalpa and the capital. Díaz' army faced dissolution, and his envoy in Washington formally requested United States intervention, at the very least to keep communications open between Managua and the sea. As more marines and bluejackets poured in, in effect doing exactly that, the State Department continued to withhold full military support for the Díaz government. The Nicaraguans, they instructed Admiral Latimer, were "exclusively responsible for maintaining order ... and the Díaz Government cannot expect the forces of the United States to participate in aggressive measures against the Nicaraguan revolutionists." Maintenance of order outside the neutral zones was to remain the "special and exclusive responsibility of the Government of Nicaragua"—for the moment anyway.[27]

But the United States' hand was being forced by the spectre of European intervention in Nicaragua. On February 22 the British chargé in Managua handed Eberhardt a note requesting concrete guarantees for the protection of the lives and property of British subjects. "[I]n the event of further street fighting, incendiarism, and pillage," he stated, "His Britannic Majesty's Government are reluctantly contemplating the despatch of a man-of-war to the western coast of Nicaragua."[28]

The note set off the alarm bells in the State Department. The commitment of American forces, though responsible for the establishment of neutral zones, was having little effect in keeping the peace. The Nicaraguan government had lost all control, groups of bandits and deserting soldiers pillaged the countryside, and the republic was collapsing into anarchy. When the British announced that the cruiser HMS *Colombo* would shortly arrive at Corinto, Secretary Kellogg sought to calm British fears. The United States, he informed His Majesty's minister in Washington, was perfectly capable of handling the situation, and its forces "will be pleased to extend to British subjects such protection as may be possible and proper under the circumstances."[29]

More reinforcements were ordered. On February 26 the destroyer tender *Melville* anchored at Corinto and disembarked Major Ross "Rusty" Rowell's Observation Squadron 1 (VO-1M): eight officers, eighty-one enlisted men, and six deHavilland 4B reconnaissance bombers. With wings removed, the planes were loaded on flatcars for the trip to Managua. There was no proper airdrome and the squadron temporarily established itself at the capital's baseball park.

As Rowell noted, "Everything was under canvas. We had no shelter whatever for the airplanes. ... Yet we were able to operate and to keep the ships flying practically every day. ... We were sent daily over the front to observe the hostilities. That was a fine opportunity, and we thought we had secured excellent reserved seats for the show. We enjoyed it until we found that we were as much under fire as were the Nicaraguan aviators." In late May,

VO-1M was augmented by the six machines of Observation Squadron 4 (VO-4M), and the units, under Rowell's command, were designated Aircraft Squadrons, 2nd Brigade.[30]

The 2nd Marine Brigade had been forming since March. In the first week the transport *Henderson* landed the brigade staff plus the 1st and 3rd battalions, 5th Marines, at Corinto. Brigadier General Logan Feland, veteran of the Great War and the pacification of the Dominican Republic, took command of all American forces ashore in western Nicaragua. By mid-month, the Navy Department announced that there were over 2,000 troops in the country, established in every section to keep the peace.

But there was no peace, only bloody deadlock. Moncada advanced slowly on the capital, and Díaz, whose army was now equipped with 3,000 Krags and three million rounds of ammunition, bought on credit at fire sale prices, could not match the Liberals in the field. Rusty Rowell noticed "The Federals were constantly reporting victories, but after every victory we would learn that the war zone had gotten several miles closer. Things got to the point where you could almost hear the firing from the capital." And one bluejacket observed, "It was obvious that had we not arrived to declare the various towns neutral, the Liberals would have swept the Conservatives out of control in short order."[31]

But the marines and the cruisers of the Special Service Squadron and Scouting Fleet could not remain in Nicaraguan limbo forever. In late March President Coolidge took a personal hand to negotiate an end to the strife and sent former Secretary of War Henry Stimson to Nicaragua. Stimson was an excellent choice, having recently settled a nasty border dispute between Chile and Peru, and closely observed conditions in the Philippines in the company of its governor-general, Leonard Wood.

In April Stimson met with Coolidge and Secretary Kellogg to outline the mission. The President very much wanted to retain Díaz in office, but was willing to risk a Liberal victory at the polls if the Americans supervised the 1928 elections. Stimson was given extremely wide latitude in negotiating a settlement. "The president's only instructions [to Stimson] other than to investigate and report were that if I should find a chance to straighten the matter out he wished I would try to do so."[32]

He arrived in Nicaragua on the *Trenton* on April 15 and was met at quayside by Admiral Latimer and Ambassador Eberhardt.

On the train to Managua the envoy noted, "A large portion of ... Chinandega was in ashes. Almost every man or boy whom one met ... was armed. It was a common sight to see a farmer driving his cattle ... with a military rifle strapped across his back, while the butt ends of revolvers and automatics produced telltale creases in the garments of such male Nicaraguans as one met or did business with in town."[33]

Stimson immersed himself in conversations with everyone—Conservatives, Liberals, American military personnel, and civilians—and thoroughly investigated the situation. By April 21 he arrived at what he considered acceptable terms of peace. These included: an immediate ceasefire and general amnesty for the Liberal rebels; inclusion of Liberals in Díaz' cabinet; disarmament of both sides; retention of the marines until a new *guardia*, under the command of U.S. Marine officers, was formed to replace them; and finally, American-supervised elections in 1928. The following day, President Díaz agreed to all points.

It now remained to convince the Liberals to sign the document. Stimson concentrated his efforts, not on Sacasa's shadow government, though Sacasa expressed his willingness to negotiate, but on General Moncada, the Liberals' field commander. The peace conference was held at Tipitapa, on the southeast shore of Lake Managua. Along the Tipitapa River, the marines manned a line preventing the Liberal troops from advancing further, serving notice that the United States was determined to keep Díaz in office, and that they had no choice but to accept Stimson's terms.

Publicly Moncada balked, but in private conversations with Stimson he admitted "that neither he nor the Government could pacify the country without help of the United States." The fact that Moncada had his eye on the presidency in the 1928 elections added no small measure to his cooperation.[34]

On May 4 Stimson and Moncada met under the branches of a large blackthorn tree. To Stimson's points the Liberal general now added a requirement of his own: Díaz must appoint Liberal *jefes políticos*, civil governors, in the country's six Liberal-dominated provinces; Stimson agreed. But Moncada, fearful of appearing to capitulate to the Americans too easily, requested that Stimson publicly enumerate his terms in the form of a threatening note which would stress the point regarding the disarming of Liberal armies in the field. Again Stimson complied. "The forces of the United States," he penned to the general, "will be authorized to accept the custody of the arms of those willing to lay them down, including the Government, and to disarm forcibly those who will not do so." The next day Moncada announced to his army acceptance of the American terms, and Díaz proclaimed a general amnesty.[35]

The government forces retired southward, and Moncada's army, with the exception of one "general" and his troops, began turning in their arms to the marines. "It is expected," reported General Feland, "that approximately 80% of the revolutionists will give up their arms, the other 20% will take to the hills as followers of individual leaders."[36]

Ten dollars was promised every soldier who surrendered his rifle, and within two weeks nearly 12,000 rifles and 303 machine guns had been deposited by both sides. For many there was an easy profit in the sale and resale of weapons. One marine officer remembered, "We would put [the rifles] in the government warehouse and [then would find] that they were being issued out the back . . . as fast as we were storing them in the front." Still, the operation was successful beyond all expectations. According to Ambassador Eberhardt, the marines "effected a wonderful disarmament with a minimum of bloodshed or friction."[37]

Not everyone was pleased though. In the United States, the National Citizens' Committee on Relations with Latin America lambasted Coolidge and the State Department claiming that "stripped of diplomatic disguises this policy comes easily within the definition of imperialism as every normal American understands the term." Of the Stimson mission, the committee was equally harsh, calling it "little more than a beautiful funeral for Nicaraguan sovereignty." The liberal Republican Senator George Norris found the whole intervention, "shocking to every peace-loving citizen in civilization."[38]

Meanwhile, the obdurate Liberal commander who refused to obey Moncada's order headed north to the Honduran frontier with 200 followers. "Moncada," he had recently written to a friend, "will at the very first opportunity sell out to the Americans. We must . . . save [the revolution]." His name was Augusto César Sandino, and his men called themselves *Sandinistas*.[39]

This rebel, a complex man and the bane of Nicaraguan governments both Conservative and Liberal, a man the marines and *guardia* would chase through the northern wilds for six frustrating years, had grown to maturity during the Zelaya era. The illegitimate son of a southwestern landowner and a peasant girl, Sandino had dreams of grandeur and eventually dropped his matronymic Calderón for the more regal César. A description circulated among the marines in 1928 of a "well built slight wiry type" man with "exceptionally small" feet, "two or more front [teeth] showing gold work," and "right thumb crippled so that it lies flat against the index finger." According to "five different persons, all of whom have seen him within the past year," Sandino was bound up with nervous energy and "pace[d] the floor most of the time . . . boasting of past achievements, and what he will eventually do to the Yankees."[40]

In 1920 the as yet apolitical Sandino shot a man in the leg, settling a personal score, and fled to Honduras. Then, as later, he worked for American companies, usually as a mechanic. He was considered by his employers a good worker of solid, sober habits. Three years later Sandino was in Mexico. At the Tampico oilfields he acquired an education in the lack of social and economic justice for the victims of American capitalism. He also evidenced a complex messianic personality and regarded himself as a savior of the Indo-Latin peoples.

In 1926 the Liberal revolt against Chamorro brought Sandino, with $500 and a Smith & Wesson revolver, home to Nicaragua. He did not immediately turn to revolutionary activities, but instead found work as paymaster's assistant at the American-owned San Albino gold mine in the northern department of Nueva Segovia. "Not that he appeared to be especially qualified to fill such a position," his employer later said, "but . . . he appeared too well educated to work as a peon."[41]

Sandino soon began to appeal to the political consciousness of the miners, encouraging them to demand cash wages instead of the customary company-store scrip. They found the new man very sympathetic to their plight and his support among the disaffected workers grew.

Sandino decided that the time for a fuller commitment had come. The Sacasa-Moncada rebellion was in full swing. Though hardly an establishment Liberal, Sandino bought enough arms from Honduran gunrunners to outfit twenty-nine men and took to the field. His first foray met with abject failure. Sandino and his men attacked the nearby government garrison at Jícaro and were thrown back; most of the band deserted their charismatic leader. This incident convinced Sandino that he could not accomplish his goals independently, so he journeyed east with his remaining men to Puerto Cabezas and offered his services to Dr. Sacasa.

The doctor and his field commander General Moncada were not particularly receptive. Sandino demanded much in the way of arms, and brought little to the cause of *Liberalismo*. Moncada treated the new recruit disdainfully, and later, after hearing Sandino speak of "the necessity for the workers to struggle against the rich and other things that are principles of Communism," with outright distrust.[42]

When the Liberals advanced out of the Puerto Cabezas neutral zone, Sandino had but six men in his command. With the aid of the town prostitutes, they salvaged some rifles from the harbor bottom and followed in the tail of Moncada's army. While the general planned his westward march to Managua, certain Liberal leaders began to press for Sandino's promotion. He had proven himself resourceful and was clearly committed to the overthrow of the Conservative Díaz government. Unimpressed, Moncada nevertheless agreed to Sandino's elevation. During the advance on Managua, Sandino, recruiting as he marched, covered the army's right flank. Instead of the traditional red hatband of *Liberalismo*, Sandino's men wore the syndicalist black and red. Twice in hard battle he met superior machine gun–equipped government forces and still emerged the victor.

Moncada, perhaps fearing the ascension of a potential rival or perhaps merely annoyed with his egocentric personality, ordered Sandino to occupy Boaco, the next town on the road to Managua. But he kept to himself the information that it was strongly entrenched with government troops. Sandino suspected the setup and wisely skirted the place.

By then Henry Stimson had arrived in Nicaragua and the negotiations for the Peace of Tipitapa were well along. General Moncada saw that it would be difficult to induce Sandino to surrender his arms and disband his forces in compliance with American demands. He summoned Sandino to his headquarters and offered him the governorship of Jinotega Department as well as ten dollars a day for each day he had served in the Liberal army and the mules he had requisitioned during the civil war. Sandino refused the gifts, but agreed to comply with Moncada's decision to disarm and disband.

But on May 12, when Moncada and his generals presented their signed agreement to Stimson, Sandino's signature was not among them. "I decided to fight," he wrote, "understanding that I was the one called to protest the betrayal of the Fatherland."[43]

United States government officials and military commanders in Nicaragua only vaguely grasped the obstacles they would face in their efforts to restore peace, maintain law and order, and train a new *guardia*. The government and rebel armies had voluntarily disbanded, and it seemed that at most the marines could expect scattered outbreaks of endemic banditry. "From a military standpoint," noted Secretary of the Navy Curtis Wilbur, "the disarmament was almost complete." What guns remained, "were held illegally by the ignorant, irresponsible, and criminal." As for Sandino, this was not the first time was he consigned to ignominy. "A fugitive from justice," Wilbur stated, holed up with "not more than 200 of the worst element in the revolutionary army."[44]

The first clash, though not with Sandino, occurred almost immediately. In the early, dark hours of May 16, 1927, a couple of hundred marauding bandits and demobilized Liberal soldiers swept into La Paz Centro, a railroad town midway between Corinto and Managua. The marine detachments from the Scouting Fleet's battleships *Florida* and *Arkansas* were camped outside, and the townspeople came to them for help. Captain Richard Buchanan, the marines' skipper, ordered his bugler to sound the call to arms, and with forty men he advanced into the town. "Buchanan did a very gallant thing," said the commandant of the Marine Corps, Major General Lejeune. "He went right into that town in the dead of night, and the town was full of these [bandits]. They were looting the stores and houses." The fight lasted two hours, Buchanan and a private were killed. Fourteen dead bandits lay strewn in the mud streets. But the actual number of bandits was not known, according to Lejeune. "They do not like to leave their dead around. They have a superstition about the vultures which are everywhere in that country eating dead men, and they always carry their dead off if they can possibly do it; take them away and bury them at the first opportunity."[45]

Police action against endemic banditry or not, heavy reinforcements for the brigade were already at sea. The newly raised 11th Marines, half of which formed in Haiti, landed at Corinto on the nineteenth and quickly deployed along the railroad. In a matter of weeks forty-three towns in western Nicaragua had marine garrisons.

By late May, Sandino's cause, even to himself, appeared hopeless. Most of his remaining band surrendered their rifles for the ten-dollar bounty, and he was down to thirty men. To throw the marines into the sea was a ludicrous impossibility, but perhaps with the Yankees' help, he thought, he might be able to rid the government of the equally despised Adolfo Díaz. From his northern fastness, he wired General Feland. "For peace to be durable we propose that the two parties leave the affairs of the Republic in the hands of [an] American governor until absolutely free elections have been [held]."[46]

Feland responded by sending elements of the 5th Marines north from Matagalpa with orders to disarm what remained of Sandino's band, or failing that to force him over the border into Honduras. On May 23 they occupied Jinotega, capital of Jinotega department, without opposition. The day the marines marched in, General Moncada arrived to offer peace. Sandino was nearby at Yali, and the general cabled a request that he enter the marines' lines and confer. Sandino dismissed the offer. He did agree, however, to disarm, "provid[ed] the United States takes over the government of Nicaragua, appoints a military Governor," and "discharges" the Conservatives and Liberals currently holding office. It was not the last time he was to demand an American military government as preferable to those whom he considered home-grown traitors. This, of course, the United States refused to consider under any circumstances. The recently ended fiasco in the Dominican Republic precluded any of that.[47]

Moncada made a last attempt and persuaded Sandino's father, Gregorio, to journey to Yali and convince his son to give up the fight. It came to nothing. "[H]is troops applauded him and cheered him," Don Gregorio remembered. Feeling his honor impugned by the American rebuffs, Sandino pledged his life to the liberation of Nicaragua and declared he had no option other than resistance. He withdrew northward into the mountain jungles of Nueva Segovia department and prepared for protracted guerrilla war.[48]

Under the terms of the Stimson-Moncada Agreement, six Liberal *jefes politicos* were assigned to the provinces as civil governors. The *jefe* for Nueva Segovia, Arnoldo Ramírez, refused to enter his provincial capital, Ocotal, without a marine escort. This northern department, even without Sandino, had collapsed into anarchy. Bands of demobilized soldiers, joined by the usual highway robbers that infested the border region, roamed and pillaged. Feland, in what Marine Corps historian Robert Heinl termed a "non-campaign," already had plans to send Major Harold "Biff" Pierce with a fifty-man patrol to pacify the region; they served as escort for Ramírez as well.

Feland directed Pierce to disarm everyone in accordance with the Stimson-Moncada agreement. "But," he cautioned, "do not fire a shot unless imperatively necessary; and conciliate with firmness, tranquilize without force of arms, avoid combat if possible."[49]

The first leg of the operation was by truck from Managua to Matagalpa, the rest of the way was on mule back. At Matagalpa, Pierce spent four days organizing his transport and baggage train, made up of fifty riding mules, fifty-six pack mules, eleven local *muleros*, mule skinners, and a pair of guides, whom the marines nicknamed "Matamoras" and "The Turk."

On June 5 the patrol entered San Rafael del Norte, near the border separating Jinotega and Nueva Segovia. The telegrapher here was none other than Sandino's wife Blanca. There is an unconfirmed account that in conversation she told Ramírez her husband would not open fire on the marines, "but that some of his people whom he might not be able to control might do so."[50]

As Pierce continued north, shadowers hovered out of sight on his flanks and rear, and evidence accumulated of Sandino's close presence. But there was no engagement. Small groups of disbanded Liberals were found "plundering cattle." After confiscating and burning their weapons, the patrol picked its way through the mountains and arrived at Ocotal on June 9.

The town was under some sort of siege. A Liberal garrison held the place, but a Conservative force was in the vicinity, and occasionally fired a shot in its direction. Neither side seemed eager to disturb the status quo. Pierce relieved the garrison of their firearms, and reported to the brigade, "I find no police here, no system of civil law whatsoever in effect. The Government Office is in a state of disorder, and I believe no attention has been paid to the rights of the people. The soldiers have subsisted simply by taking any property desired."[51]

With no landing strip as yet at Ocotal, no telegraph cable to the south, and field radios only short-range primitives, a plane from Aircraft Squadrons, 2nd Brigade, flew over for the message pickup, the first of unnumbered hundreds of such ground-to-air communications. A slack string was looped about a headless nail, one each, parallel to the ground, atop a pair of white-flagged poles, held vertical, about sixty feet apart. In the center of the string hung a message pouch. The aircraft came in low and slow, trailing a weight which tangled itself into the slackline, plucking all off the nails. It was then reeled in.* Along with his recommendation that a full rifle company be sent up as a garrison, Pierce ended his message with a "Request plane be directed to drop a United States Flag as soon as possible, together with a set of halyards, for our use."[52]

After disarming the town soldiery, Pierce invited the Conservative commander to come in and surrender. The next day, 168 ex-government soldiers, led by a small troop of cavalry, marched into Ocotal with trumpets bleating and flags unfurled. "Pretty good-looking little army for Nicaragua," Pierce noted.[53]

On June 13, in response to a report of a Sandino kidnapping at Telpaneca, about twenty miles southeast, Pierce made ready to move. But Ramírez, the *jefe político*, refused to remain without a marine guard; if Pierce provided none, he would return to Matagalpa. Pierce detached Captain Gilbert Hatfield and eight marines and pushed on to Telpaneca.

The twenty map miles stretched to near thirty. Two grueling days were spent following mountain-jungle trails that were little better than hog tracks; in the rainy season even the mules found the path treacherous. The kidnapping proved to be a false report, but Sandino had been in Telpaneca, leaving with $720 in cash and the looted goods from the local *bodega*. From the locals, Pierce and the marines first learned of Sandino's command post; they called it El Chipote, and it was, well, somewhere.

Pierce, considering his mission accomplished, returned to Matagalpa and made his report. Sandino's forces, he rightly noted, were small but well armed with "plenty of ammunition and explosives." But Biff Pierce made an error many of his superiors

---

*The author, in 1962, while serving in the 1st Battalion, 6th Marines, held one of the poles in exactly the same manner and process during numerous Caribbean training exercises. The aircraft, L-4 Piper Grasshoppers, flew in at about fifty feet, or less if the pilot was particularly skillful. It is a somewhat scary situation; the holders face away from the aircraft to avoid flinching and dropping the pole.

were wont to make. Sandino, he continued, "is not a strong leader and his band is probably composed of foreigners and fugitives from justice." He concluded that the rebel would find it extremely difficult to hold them together during the rainy season. "All places of importance are denied to him by the Marines . . . he will not be able to cause any serious trouble."[54]

The same complacency existed in the south. "Fresh fruits and meats in abundance in the markets," noted an 11th Marines intelligence report from León. "Friction between troops and civil population, none . . . the new *Jefe Politico*, Anastacio Somoza, was installed in office today."*[55]

With peace seemingly at hand, the chain of command, Feland, Lejeune, and the Navy Department, considered the forces in Nicaragua excessive. The strength of the total marine corps was less than 18,000 men and the civil war in China necessitated shipment of another brigade (commanded by Brigadier General Smedley Butler) overseas to protect American citizens and interests. The Corps was stretched very thin. While orders at Managua were still calling for Sandino to be "disarmed forcibly," others emanated from Washington disbanding the 2nd Battalion, 5th Marines, and the entire 11th Marines. In all, over a thousand troops were withdrawn, leaving Feland's 2nd Brigade with only 1,800 men, including the air squadrons. Further reductions, Feland warned Lejeune, must not take place until after the elections, "The rebellious chief is still carrying on," he concluded.[56]

The first of Stimson's three specific goals (which, indeed, were the specific purposes of the intervention), ending the civil war, had been basically accomplished. There now remained two objectives: the re-formation of a nonpartisan *guardia*, and the supervision of free elections. When all were fulfilled, the marines were expected to go home.

After a somewhat promising start, Major Carter's original *guardia* was politically co-opted during the Chamorro presidency. When Díaz assumed office in late 1926, he dismissed the *jefe* and his American assistants, in effect disbanding the organization. By emergency decree Díaz created a new *guardia* in late July 1927,

---

*This was Somoza senior, founder of the brutal dynasty. An ingratiating, bilingual Liberal, a former baseball umpire and lavatory inspector, he had much impressed Stimson with his energy and resourcefulness.

and Lieutenant Colonel Elias Beadle, USMC, was promoted to brigadier general in the Nicaraguan service with the title *jefe director*. During its tenure under Beadle and his immediate successors, the *guardia* evolved into a fairly decent military organization: Its corruption by the *Somocistas* lay several years in the future.

As the sole force agency of the republic, ninety-three officers and 1,136 enlisted men were considered a minimum requirement. Supreme "command" was vested in the president of Nicaragua, but recruiting, training, promotion, discipline, operations, quartermaster, and administration functions all came under the purview of the *jefe director*. As was the case in the Haitian *gendarmerie*, with the lure of additional pay and increased (Nicaraguan) rank, volunteer officers and enlisted men of the Marine Corps and Navy Medical Department were detached from brigade and fleet duties for service with the new *guardia*. The enlisted marines were given initial appointments as cadets, and if qualified, commissioned as second lieutenants in the Nicaraguan service.

Beadle made a priority of inculcating the American military norms of political neutrality and national patriotism into the minds of the Nicaraguan recruits, and before each new man took his oath, he received a lecture on these qualities. All were constantly subjected to Beadle's maxim, "Friendliness and justice promote security; friendship and favoritism promote insecurity." When one guardsman was found shouting political *vivas* outside a Managua café, Beadle ordered his summary dismissal and the unfortunate *raso* was made an object lesson for the entire *guardia*.[57]

Between the Nicaraguan guardsmen and their marine officers there developed a reasonably close rapport. So long as the *gringo* proved himself brave in combat, he could well count upon the loyalty and steadfastness of his *guardia* troops. Obedience to non-commissioned and company-grade officers was an early problem. One marine historian noted, "The Nicaraguan soldier of the past had been used to receiving orders from nothing less than a colonel. Majors, captains, and lieutenants were as scarce as hen's teeth in the old Nicaraguan armies, and sergeants and corporals were simply words under the old system." The Americans found, however, that confidence led to obedience. The Nicaraguan guardsman could be led, if led well, and by and large he was. By late June, after a few days' training, the 1st Company, made up of three marine officers, and fifty enlisted *guardia*, were sent north to Ocotal.[58]

But any leisurely plans Beadle and the brigade had for complete training of the *guardia,* or for settling down to await the election results, were thrown into turmoil.

On June 30 word came to Managua that Sandino, with fifty men, had seized his old workplace, the American-owned San Albino gold mine. According to the reports, he relieved the management of 500 pounds of dynamite, with fuses and caps, to "kill Yankees." From the mine, Sandino issued his first proclamation to the people of Nicaragua and all Latin America. The "bonds of nationality," he claimed, gave him the right to rectify the republic's myriad problems, which were also those of "Central America and all the continent that speaks our language." He vehemently denounced the Conservative government of Adolfo Díaz and hailed those "people who have not committed treason, who did not falter or sell their rifles to satisfy the ambition of Moncada." As for the marines, they were "a bunch of dope fiends . . . come to murder us in our own land." If they wished a fight, he accepted the invitation to combat; "I, myself, am provoking it."[59]

Sandino's defiance attracted scores of local and regional Central American recruits, and with the loot obtained from the mine and the recent foray into the *bodega* at Telpaneca he was well equipped for offensive operations. The mine owners appealed to the marine brigade for protection.

Prior to the seizure, General Feland had continued with his "non-campaign" and planned to order up another large patrol of seventy-five marines and 150 *guardia* into Nueva Segovia department. "I am not planning a campaign, in the usual sense of the word," he wrote Lejeune on June 30, "but I am trying to force [Sandino] out of the country by successively occupying the towns which he claims." Major Oliver Floyd was in command, and Feland originally intended the expedition to be primarily a *guardia* operation, with the marines present "principally to look after him and the Marine officers with him, and to give a little backbone to the outfit." The next day came the news of Sandino's incursion at San Albino.[60]

Feland immediately ordered out the patrol. Orders are one thing, reality another, and for eleven days Floyd and Major Victor Bleasdale (captain, USMC), commanding the *guardia* contingent, mucked about in Matagalpa, gathering pack animals and recruits.

The *guardia* enlistments were handled by the local *jefe politico* and were mostly local Indians, and supposed volunteers. Floyd suspected that most of the 150 formed on parade had been "drafted."

"The ignorant Indians from the interior," wrote a Marine Corps historian, "were stoic-looking people because their faces were so blank and expressionless; but continued observation . . . forced the conclusion that they had much more common sense and natural cunningness than the Anglo-Saxon credit them with." Bleasdale picked fifty men, among them an aged, former Conservative general as mess officer.[61]

On July 11 the Nueva Segovia expedition consisting of eighty marines, seventy-four *guardia,* nineteen horses, 172 mules, and twenty-four oxen pulling four bull carts, headed northwest for Estelí and Telpaneca. Sandino's jungle intelligence service passed the word. "Just received a warning from San Rafael from my own wife," he notified one of his "generals," "that one hundred Constabularies are coming by that way."[62]

O cotal, capital of Nueva Segovia, the northernmost marine and *guardia* garrison, sits 2,000 feet up a broad valley, less than twenty miles from the Honduran border. In good times 1,400 people inhabited the town, but in 1927 only a few families remained. On June 27 Captain Hatfield's original eight men were reinforced by a detachment of the 16th Company, bringing his marine strength to forty-one men. On July 11, the day the Nueva Segovia expedition began its march, the command was further augmented by the *Guardia Nacional*'s 1st Company. The marine billets were in the town hall, a two-story adobe building facing the little earthen plaza. The *guardia* were quartered in a "barracks," across the mud, down a side street. A fine brick and adobe Romanesque church, built with a three-story belfry and fronted by a waist-high wall, faced the plaza's east side.

Hatfield did not remain idle. His men constructed an airstrip near the town's western edge, a regular air liaison service was established with Managua, and the telegraph put into operation with the surrounding towns. About twelve miles northeast, right up on the Honduran border, lay San Fernando and Sandino. On June 25 Sandino opened communications with Ocotal, writing, as Ambassador Eberhardt put it, "insultingly," to Hatfield.

Addressing the reports (which proved false) that Hatfield was arming local *Conservativos,* Sandino wired, "Shall I wait here for you or shall I go to you?" Unimpressed, the captain of marines replied, "It is not true that I am arming Conservatives to attack you . . . as I need no other help than that of the Marines. . . . What I do need are quick running horses to be able to take you in your mountains . . . assuring you that we shall not run away. . . . I thank you for your letter, and trusting that you will soon come and salute me personally, I am yours respectfully, G.D. Hatfield, Capt., USMC."[63]

Hatfield's response triggered the more unsavory aspects of Sandino's personality. In reply, Hatfield received a letter with a crudely drawn cartoon, which Sandino adopted as his official seal, of a guerrilla brandishing a machete over the neck of a prostrate marine. It was signed, "Your obedient servant, who wishes to put you in a handsome tomb with flowers." To his new adherents, Sandino offered the prize of Ocotal and the chance to drink "Yankee blood."[64]

The mutual baiting continued. On June 27 Hatfield wrote, "It has occurred to me that if you are honest in your desire to defend the rights and insure the happiness of your people, you might be willing to come in and talk with me." Hatfield guaranteed Sandino's safety, allowing the rebel to bring "a reasonable number of men" as bodyguards. "Hoping that you are a patriot and not a robber," Hatfield sent it off. From "El Chipote via San Fernando," Sandino wired back. He would not come for a meeting like "a dove deceived by a few grains of rice at the door of a trap." He prodded Hatfield in turn. If Hatfield wished a conference, then Hatfield could come into the mountains with 500 marines, but "make your wills beforehand."[65]

"Bravo! General," the captain of marines rejoined. "If words were bullets and phrases were soldiers, you would be a field marshal instead of a mule thief." He invited Sandino to wire him again "when you have something more than the ravings of a conceited maniac." On July 11 Hatfield offered Sandino another opportunity: To surrender "with honor in spite of your insolent replies." He warned Sandino that the marines were prepared to hunt him down and to have no illusions in the matter. The rebel answered in kind. "Your threats seem very pale to me. . . . I shall have the honor of sprinkling the soil of my native country with the blood of traitors and invaders." Sandino, however, left himself a convenient exit. If the United States turned the government over to a "true Liberal," he promised to "put down my arms peacefully."[66]

On the fifteenth, Sandino issued his operation orders for the capture of Ocotal. It was a well-conceived plan involving nearly his entire force, which was estimated at something over 300 men, with 120 rifles and at least two machine guns. Thoroughly modern in his tactical outlook, he assigned one detachment to destroy the airstrip. These men, he wrote, "shall put five pounds of dynamite in the machine of each one of the airplanes, shall also dig five holes in the camp, and shall put five pounds of dynamite in each one . . . and then everything will be thrown far up into the air."[67]

For the main attack on the town Sandino chose his inner cadre, about sixty veterans of the late civil war. Each soldier carried two rifles, one for himself, the other to arm any supporters within. As for *Conservativos* found within, "General Salgado shall be in charge of driving out of the houses all of [those] people who may be hidden." Traditional Central American battles involved a high degree of drunkenness among the troops. The abstemious Sandino would have none of it. He warned, "It is prohibited to drink liquor and the one who does so I shall receive it as if it were an outrage to our country."[68]

Late on July 16 Sandino moved with his troops down from San Fernando to positions around Ocotal, establishing his command post on a small hill on the outskirts, just east of the church.

Hatfield knew the attack was coming and made his defensive preparations. The marines and *guardia* were put through hours of drill, and, as he reported, "always slept with arms and ammunition at hand." Officers stood watch-and-watch (four hours on, four hours off) instead of the usual officer-of-the-day duty, and also slept fully clothed.[69]

At 1:15, in the black, first hours of July 16, the marine sentry on post in front of the city hall noticed a "suspicious movement." He investigated, and a shattering fusillade rent the night. Within three minutes of the opening shot, the marines and *guardia*, Hatfield noted with grim satisfaction, were at their "battle stations . . . receiving fire from all directions, and from well located snipers in addition."[70]

"The outlaws," joined by some 100 residents, "had evidently infiltrated the town during the early part of the night and expected to effect a complete surprise." Two, or possibly three, machine guns, sited on the flanking hills and in the office of the *jefe politico*, swept the plaza and streets fronting the marine and *guardia* barracks, effectively isolating the positions. With shouts of "Death to the Yankees!" and "Viva Sandino!" individual *Sandinistas* ran forward to hurl dynamite bombs through the barrack windows. From the *guardia* quarters, First Lieutenant Bruce (first sergeant, USMC) emplaced a Lewis light machine gun in the street and, completely unprotected, engaged the rebels in the *jefe*'s office. The entire area was swept by a murderous crossfire. "The officers," Hatfield wrote, "had to pass through this barrage to join their units."[71]

After the initial wild melee, both sides settled into their positions while the *Sandinistas* began looting the houses. At about 3:00 A.M. the rebel bugles sounded the assembly, bringing a relative lull which was punctuated by desultory sniper fire. In Hatfield's opinion, Sandino was altering his plan of attack.

In about an hour, with the gray streaks of the false dawn, "General" Rufo Marín led the renewed assault. Advancing from the church into the plaza under a heavy covering fire, the rebels reached the buildings and walls adjoining the marine position at the city hall and the *guardia* barracks. But the marine and *guardia* fire took an extremely heavy toll, and dozens of *Sandinista* bodies littered the earthen plaza. In three insane, frontal rushes, Marín led the city hall charge and was shot dead. Confusion swept the rebel ranks, the attack fizzled, and the *Sandinistas*, some turning to loot, withdrew back across the plaza. This second attack lasted over four hours. One marine was killed by a sniper, who in turn, Hatfield reported, "was killed by Sergeant Blackburn with fire from his pistol and was found with four .45-calibre bullet wounds in his head and neck."[72]

A few minutes after 8:00 A.M., a rebel carrying a flag of truce approached with a message from Sandino. Firing ceased, but the marines and *guardia* remained at the ready, with orders to allow no shifting of enemy positions during the parley. With supreme arrogance, Sandino complimented Hatfield's "brave fight." The marines and *guardia,* he stated incorrectly, were short of water and he offered a guarantee of immunity if they threw their weapons into the street and surrendered. "But," Hatfield said, "if we did not surrender in sixty minutes, he would fire the town and show us an amount of rifle fire that we had never dreamed of." Hatfield told him to "Go to hell." Marines, he said, "did not know how to surrender and that water or no water we would stick it out until killed or captured, and that firing would be resumed as soon as the flag bearer had turned the nearest corner."[73]

Under a tropical downpour the battle resumed. There were no further rushes on the marine and *guardia* positions, but a machine gun from the church belfry raked the city hall and snipers worked their way ever closer. At about 10:00 A.M. the skies cleared, and in place of the clouds flew Lieutenant Hayne "Cuckoo" Boyden and his wingman, Marine Gunner (warrant officer) Mike "the Polish Warhorse" Wodarczyk, up from Managua on a regular reconnaissance flight. They found the Ocotal airstrip strangely deserted; there should have been marines down there laying panels giving wind direction and other landing instructions. The pilots continued east for a few seconds and saw, below, the town under siege. As soon as Hatfield heard the engines, he ordered coded panels laid on the ground inside the city hall compound, their message, "Being attacked by Sandino."[74]

While Wodarczyk covered him from the air, Boyden, in an act of marked courage, landed at the airstrip where he received a situation report from a group of excited locals. Amidst scattered rifle fire, Boyden took off. The two planes commenced a strafing run on the *Sandinista* positions; then, low on fuel but at full throttle—125 mph—roared off for Managua.

They landed at the baseball diamond airfield at about noon and made their reports to Rusty Rowell. For Ocotal, there were no reinforcements in reach. Floyd's column was at least fifty miles away near Estelí, so it was the planes or nothing. "At that time," Rowell remembered, "we had only five airplanes, of the D.H. type, capable of fighting. The distance was 110 miles and the weather was bad, but there was nothing to do but to go."[75]

Rowell led his planes north. In addition to full machine gun magazines, each plane carried four 25-pound bombs beneath their wings. "We took off for Ocotal," he wrote, "with all we could carry in the way of bombs and machine guns. It was a bad day. Storms abounded us on all sides. We could not stay on course and were obliged to wend our way through the mountains." The flight arrived over Ocotal at 2:00 P.M. The marines and *guardia* had been fighting for sixteen straight hours, with neither food nor sleep. Rowell continued, "As we came in, I closed the column up into a tight 'Vee' formation. We thought we would at least make *them* think that our morale was high."[76]

Rowell had no real idea of Hatfield's position; his only information was that the garrison was under siege. "It was vital to learn quickly where the enemy's lines ended, and where ours were too, as we had only gas enough to stay there about 45 minutes." Rowell circled the town and spotted Sandino's command post above and behind the church. "I went in first, leading the attack, and as I went down I could see the enemy troops firing in groups. They were absolutely unconcerned. Just before I dropped the first bomb, I actually saw a puff of smoke come from a man sitting on a horse and smoking a cigar. After the first bomb dropped, things changed."[77]

The five fabric-covered biplanes dropped as low as 300 feet, bombing and strafing as they zoomed in. By the second pass, the *Sandinistas* were consumed by utter panic. "I never saw such a wild rout, and probably never will again. . . . As soon as they broke, we closed in and worked at close range to make every bomb count. After we finished with the bombing my crowd got so interested chasing the groups out of town and down the road, that I could hardly get them gathered together to go home. It was a complete rout for Sandino." Many threw away their rifles scrambling to safety, but certainly not all. The planes were hit repeatedly by small arms fire, and Rowell counted forty-four bullet holes in his wings and fuselage.[78]

Sandinista casualties were estimated at up to eighty killed, and perhaps twice that number wounded. It was history's first dive-bombing attack in tactical support of ground troops.

In Ocotal, rebels on the hills kept up an annoying fire until the early evening. Then, with the exception of seven snipers crouching behind the church wall, all withdrew. Lieutenant Bruce persuaded these to surrender; all but one complied, and he was killed running away by the last shot of the battle. Hatfield counted his losses: one dead (Private Obleski, who was buried with military honors behind the city hall barracks and "a cross and fence erected over his grave"), one marine and four *guardia* wounded, and four *guardia* captured, their fates unknown. Patrols fanned the area and counted enemy dead. More than fifty corpses lay in the streets and plaza. From the number of funerals and the increased size of the cemetery, Hatfield estimated the *Sandinistas* had suffered about 300 dead in total, "a fact evidenced by practically every Liberal family in town being in mourning."[79]

By any reckoning, Ocotal was a stunning little victory. Sandino, in his first significant offensive, had been bloodied well beyond expectations. Unfortunately, this only confirmed the incorrect American assessment. "It is not supposed that Sandino will offer much further serious resistance," Eberhardt cabled to the State Department, "quite possible that in his fanaticism he will continue his outlawry though quite unlikely on any large scale any time soon." At home, the press also misread the man and his cause. National liberation movements were little understood at the time. Sandino's support was concentrated in sparsely populated northern and eastern Nicaragua, a traditionally anti-government region; he never gained the widespread support of the Nicaraguan peasantry, who wished only to be left alone by everyone. Sandino's movement was principally anti-capitalist and anti-government, be it Conservative or Liberal. His fight against the American intervention, the prop of the Nicaraguan government, was only incidental to his basic revolutionary aim to topple whatever elitist establishmentarian regime happened to be in place in Managua. But this was completely misread. Sandino activities, the *New York Times* noted, "cannot be considered to have any political significance whatsoever." The *Sandinistas* were "in effect nothing more than common outlaws."[80]

The battle intensified the operations of Major Floyd's Nueva Segovia expedition. Still camped around Estelí, he received word of the Ocotal fight and sent forward a mounted relief detachment of fifty marines; the rest of the column and baggage train followed on. From Ocotal, where he rested and watered his men and animals, Floyd continued east for the San Albino mine, hoping to catch Sandino and finally put an end to the rebellion. He very nearly succeeded.

On July 25 the column marched for San Fernando. Aware of the advance, Sandino planned an ambush. He placed forty rebels in the town, posted a sentry on an outlying knoll, and sat back to await developments. Floyd, too, had received intelligence data and knew a substantial rebel force occupied the town. By mid-afternoon the point had come up to the knoll in a cautious and well-spread-out advance. The *Sandinista* sentry, however, had left his post to dally with a young Indian woman in a nearby shack. Within San Fernando the rebels sought relief from the beating sun and lounged in the comparative cool of the mostly deserted houses. Unnoticed, the marine advance guard continued into the town.

Victor Bleasdale and his orderly, marine Private Rafael Toro, rode point and were the first to enter. The place seemed entirely empty save for an elderly couple "who showed no indication of fear of an impending battle." When the old man headed for a nearby house, it aroused Bleasdale's suspicions and he galloped forward to question him. Alerted by the hoofbeats the loafing rebels poured into the plaza and opened fire. Bleasdale (described by a pro-*Sandinista* American journalist as a man who "literally ate cold steel and fire, and enjoyed it") and Toro were completely exposed. There was nothing to do but charge into the rebel midst. Toro received a mortal wound. But the advance guard came at a run and eleven *Sandinistas* were killed. It was another rout and Sandino considered himself lucky to escape with his life.[81]

Following the engagement, Floyd noted his observations to brigade command. If the Nueva Segovia expedition were to continue, he penned, "I will have to wage a real blood and thunder campaign and I will have casualties every day. . . . I will be involved in a small real war. . . . All people encountered are unquestionably strong for Sandino." Again, in a complete intelligence botch, no one listened.[82]

Due to the difficulty in evacuating Private Toro to Managua, the column halted its advance for two days. On July 27, aircraft message drops reported machine gun–equipped rebel concentrations some miles to the northeast, right along the line of march. One group opened automatic fire on the planes; they countered with a dive-bombing and strafing attack which left "six dead or seriously wounded" on the jungle trail. The column entered the area in early afternoon and was ambushed with machine gun fire by perhaps 150 *Sandinistas*; this was, after Ocotal, the largest guerrilla force yet encountered. The fight lasted ninety minutes; most of the time with the entire column, including the baggage train, standing in the direct line of automatic fire. Once more the rebels took flight, leaving five dead, twenty horses and mules killed or captured, and large quantities of ammunition. There was also a prisoner, "an ignorant youth . . . captured while pretending to be dead." The only armed *Sandinista* captured by the expedition, he was later permitted to return to his home.[83]

After further brushes with small outposts, the column, with aircraft cover, trekked into Jícaro, Sandino's provisional capital. The rebel renamed the town Ciudad Sandino and completely looted it before his departure. There was no opposition, save for some dozen rebels in the surrounding hills who had been left to detonate dynamite mines in the town; they were soon scattered by aerial bombing. Sandino responded to the virtually uncontested occupation of his capital with braggadocio. "In respect to the bombs you heard, it is nothing," he wrote to a subordinate, "because I have 120 men surrounding Ciudad Sandino to see if we can take some of the cargoes that the Machos* bring from Ocotal. . . . I have everything mined and I am only waiting for the Machos so that after the mines explode, we can attack them from the flanks and take the town anew. . . . Try to hide some of the [looted] merchandise of Messrs. Garcia."[84]

Without a shot fired, the marines occupied the San Albino mine on August 1; what few rebels remained took to the bush. Sandino's morale touched bottom, and after his string of defeats he seriously contemplated surrender and exile in Mexico.

While at San Albino, Floyd received orders to locate and attack Sandino's El Chipote mountain redoubt. Air reconnaissance located an area that seemed a probable site of the much talked about fortress, and Floyd received a full report. For three days, over difficult terrain and heavy rains, the column traversed a forty-five-mile clockwise circuit. At one point they actually passed fairly close to the fortress, and a local guide indicated its position. Bleasdale volunteered to take part of the column and investigate. But Major Floyd, according to marine historian Robert Heinl, was "an officer who was somewhat of a student of classic war." His answer to Bleasdale was no. "I will never divide my force in the presence of the enemy." Notwithstanding that dictum, Floyd had reasons for doubt. El Chipote was not on any map, as he reported to brigade. "Everyone talks about El Chipote. No one who talks has ever been there; ask any man where El Chipote is and he will give you answer, then upon further questioning it will develop that he has not been there and that even his informant never was there. Sandino is a notorious prevaricator . . . there was never in this country a place known as El Chipote until Sandino's recent regime."[85]

The Nueva Segovia expedition had pacified much of the department, though this proved temporary. Following Ocotal and its aftermath, many of Sandino's men gave up the fight and returned to their villages. Only scattered banditry remained, and General Feland viewed the situation as an opportunity for the

---

*Nicaraguan slang for male mules, strong but impotent animals, and Sandino's epithet for the marines.

guardia to begin exercising its constabulary functions "with slight assistance from the Fifth Regiment of Marines, to police the entire department."[86]

On August 9 he published an offer of general amnesty: "to those who were deluded by Sandino into the belief that his revolt was in the interest of your country and those of you who supported him." Feland guaranteed immunity from punishment from any acts committed while under Sandino's orders to all his followers who gave up their weapons. "Let all good people," he concluded, "with a single mind think of and work for the good of Nicaragua." Once again each rebel who turned in a weapon would receive ten dollars. Thousands of copies of the statement were printed and dropped by aircraft throughout the Nueva Segovia department. It bore results; many rebels accepted the offer. Two weeks later, Feland turned command of the depleted brigade over to Colonel Louis Gulick and departed for the United States.[87]

Yet there were some who remained suspicious of the peace. In early September, Lieutenant George O'Shea led a small patrol south from Jícaro into the mountainous region around Quílali to investigate. O'Shea's instinct as well as captured *Sandinista* documents told him that Sandino was gathering his forces for further operations. O'Shea had come within an eyelash of discovering El Chipote.

But for a month it seemed the prognosticators were right. "Sandino's power is broken," noted a brigade intelligence report. "There should be no further trouble of any nature in the entire republic." The steady attrition of the brigade continued apace, the last of the 11th Marines leaving on September 6.[88]

The village of Telpaneca sits within the mountains, on a bend of the Coco River, about ten miles southeast of Ocotal. In September its little garrison counted twenty-one marines and twenty-five *guardia,* the whole commanded by Captain Herbert Keimling (first lieutenant, USMC); here Sandino renewed his offensive.

Midnight passed and in the first hour of September 19, as Private Handzlik remembered, "the town was blanketed by a heavy fog which permeated the buildings." The gloom shrouded 200 guerrillas who infiltrated past the sentries, right up to the doors and windows of the marine and *guardia* barracks fronting the plaza. At 1:00 A.M., preceded by an intense burst of automatic fire, grenades, and homemade dynamite bombs, the *Sandinistas*, screaming *"Muera los Estados Unidos . . . Este por Marinos,"* charged the front doors. "The first [rifle] shot," Handzlik continued, "hit Private Russell who was sleeping near the front door. . . . Russell after he was wounded jumped up and grabbed his rifle and fired three shots and was shot again right near the heart. He laid down his rifle and went to his bed to lay down and die, which he done about three or four minutes after the fight started."[89]

Behind the rebel riflemen came a second line with machetes. Captain Keimling was in his adjoining office. "As I reached the doorway, Sergeant Eadens shoved me back saying, 'Here they come,' and shot a bandit whose rifle was pointed at me. As the bandit staggered back, he shot Private Glasser. . . . [We] grabbed him and dragged him into the office. . . . Eadens and I worked in reliefs guarding the door and bandaging the wounded man."[90]

Leaving Eadens in charge, Keimling stepped into the fire-swept plaza to coordinate the defense. "Found everybody at their posts and in the best of spirits, passing jokes." A brave Lewis gunner, completely exposed, was already mowing the enshadowed attackers as they crisscrossed the bare expanse. "Look at the bozo coming down the hill, skipper," said the gunner. The rebel lobbed a twenty-five stick dynamite bomb through a window and, with its fuse still burning, a *guardia raso* heaved it back, sighted his rifle and shot the late grenadier. Between rushes on the *guardia* barracks, the cook, Private Romero, took time to brew coffee for the embattled defenders.[91]

Above the blasting din, Keimling bellowed orders for his men to "fire as fast as possible for ten minutes and then to fire at flashes caused by the enemy rifle fire. . . . After the first fifteen minutes everybody settled down and shot like veterans."[92]

Keimling returned to his command post just in time to throw some grenades at a group rushing the rear of the building. These he said were not an undisciplined horde. "Several bandit groups fired by command and did some pretty good shooting." Word was passed that the Lewis gun was jammed. Keimling continued, "Sergeant Eadens gave me his rifle and said, 'Captain, guard the door, I'll fix it,' and did so in the open, under fire, without any shelter."[93]

The fog lifted at 2:30 A.M. and within half an hour the rebels began taking their dead in retreat. Keimling estimated the enemy had suffered fifty dead and wounded, including "General" Salgado, one of Sandino's leading subordinates. His own losses were two marines killed, one *guardia* seriously wounded.

Taken together, the battles of Ocotal and Telpaneca should have alerted brigade command to the fact that Sandino, far from being whipped or deserted by the bulk of his troops, had the capacity to mount full-scale attacks with automatic weapons and was, indeed, an extremely dangerous foe. But brigade command felt otherwise and did little other than to increase patrolling in Nueva Segovia. General Beadle of the *guardia* also misread the portents. With support from President Díaz, he withheld the bulk of the *guardia* for duty as rural police in the more peaceful southern and eastern provinces. It was left to the undermanned 5th Marines and Rowell's planes to deal with Sandino.

As for the rebel *jefe*, he had learned some bloody lessons and resolved never again to "stand his ground" and fight on the enemy's terms. It would now be guerrilla war, hit and run. And if he were cornered in the mountains, there was the convenient Honduran border to slip across until he was ready to strike again. At El Chipote he regrouped and gathered recruits. The strategic turning point for both sides had arrived.

In mid-morning, October 8, Second Lieutenant Earl Thomas and his observer-gunner, Sergeant Frank Dowdell, passed north of Quílali on routine patrol. Nearby flew their wingman, Mike Wodarczyk. Both aircraft were the improved 02U Vought Corsair, the metal fuselage model of the old fabric-covered DH. For reasons unknown, Thomas and Dowdell's plane suddenly lost altitude and glide-crashed into the jungle sides of Zapotillo ridge. Wodarczyk circled about, marked the position with an X on a map, and dropped it to his waving comrades. The downed airmen destroyed the plane's two machine guns, as they were far too heavy to hump through the jungle, torched the craft, and headed for Quílali; no American ever saw them alive again.

Sandinista defectors later revealed that the two marines were shadowed along the difficult trails. Thomas and Dowdell fought off fifteen of them with their pistols, killing five. They conscripted a pair of locals to act as guides. On the trail, one swung his machete and badly cut Thomas, and was instantly shot by Dowdell. But the other managed an escape, and more guerrillas gathered. In the end, the two marines were surrounded by forty rebels and shot it out until their ammunition was exhausted. Captured,

Thomas and Dowdell were tried before a *Sandinista* court martial, probably tortured, and then shot. Thomas' body they hanged from a tree and photographed. Sandino then set an ambush for the inevitable rescue patrol.[94]

Twelve miles north at Jícaro, Lieutenant O'Shea mustered eight marines, ten *guardia,* and Dr. John O'Neill, USN; "all the available men able to stand the trip." The best saddle animals were already out with regular patrols, so O'Shea made do with four borrowed horses and a mule. Packing three days' rations, they set out by forced march for Quílali. He expected a fight, but hoped to arrive at the crash site before great numbers of the enemy could assemble. But after less than twenty miles, they halted for the night. "The men," O'Shea said, "were . . . in an exhausted condition, six of the marines and several of the *guardia* weakened by a recent attack of malaria."[95]

Up with the dawn, the patrol marched to the foot of the Zapotillo ridge, just three map miles north of Quílali, but at least double that over the "ridge of difficult mountains." Aircraft indicated the general crash site, but were forced to break off for lack of gas. A passing woman and boy also pointed to the general area atop the ridge. O'Shea gave it some close scrutiny and found "no movement or anything suspicious." The patrol moved up the trail. After about 100 yards, heavy firing erupted from their right and rear. This was Sandino's ambush, "about 200 bandits who seemed to be well armed and had plenty of ammunition. It was my intention," O'Shea reported, "to go forward and take the hill."

He soon thought better of it and reversing direction turned back. But there were at least 100 rebels occupying the hill and the road he had just traversed, "and we could hear more coming in the distance, yelling as they came." O'Shea launched an attack on the band blocking his retreat and drove them off. "Rifle [grenades] and hand grenades," he said, "were of great assistance." During this assault to the rear, the little force came under heavy, continuous fire. The *guardia* sergeant received a bullet in the head and died instantly. A dynamite bomb exploded ten feet between O'Shea and a private, but neither were injured. In the melee, Dr. O'Neill and a Thompson submachine gun—wielding marine dropped back to await the rush from the main guerrilla force. It came, and the doctor hurled it back with a volley of well-placed grenades. O'Shea had the patrol nearly through, back to the trail from whence they came. "I was leading with hand grenades, and since the brush along the road seemed to be full of the enemy it was necessary to throw them only a short distance." The *guardia*, O'Shea reported, behaved "splendidly. . . . One of them continued to fire his rifle after half of the barrel had been blown off."

Back on the trail the firing died away. All but one of the pack animals had been killed, and O'Shea took the path north for San Albino. They marched straight into seventy-five rebels who immediately attacked. The trail was very narrow, not much more than a goat track, and it was impossible for the patrol to deploy. At the point, O'Shea, with Dr. O'Neill and Private Golak, met the attack head-on, broke it with automatic fire, and drove the *Sandinistas* to the next hill.

But behind the patrol, the enemy on the Zapotillo ridge had reorganized and closed in. O'Shea was trapped. "Believing that our only way out lay ahead [toward San Albino] I decided to push forward. Dr. O'Neill, at his own request, led this attack." A machine gun stuttered up, pinning the patrol, until a rifle grenade, fired with great accuracy, killed the enemy gunner. Taking fire at very close range, they pushed ahead another 200 yards; two more guardsmen fell dead. From all sides in the dense jungle distance they heard the sounds of *Sandinista* reinforcements closing in.

To remain in position was to die, but there was no room to maneuver, and as a last resort, O'Shea decided to take to the jungle. "I had hesitated to do this because of the thick brush, the danger of becoming split up and lost, and our unfamiliarity with the country. Our guides had left during the fight and I had lost my compass."

By early evening, having fought continuously for two and a half hours, against overwhelming odds, O'Shea turned left, led his men down a very steep ravine, and slipped between the enemy bands. They took a prisoner who was fully armed and equipped. "[We] were afraid to shoot him for fear of giving away our position." The patrol marched and stumbled until midnight when it was finally safe to rest. At 6:00 A.M. they resumed. In midafternoon, having been without food for over a day, very welcome aircraft flew over and dropped rations. Just before midnight on October 10 the patrol trod wearily into Jícaro. "We arrived . . . suffering from exposure and complete exhaustion, bruised, cut up by thorns and bitten by insects." Cautious estimates put the number of *Sandinistas* engaged at 400, with the patrol killing at least forty, and possibly up to sixty.

On O'Shea's return steps were immediately taken for additional patrols to discover the whereabouts of El Chipote and bring Sandino to bay, and if possible to investigate the crash site on Zapotillo ridge. On October 18 Lieutenant Moses Gould led a sixty-eight-man marine and *guardia* force north from Matagalpa to Quílali; five days later, hoping to catch the rebels in a pincer, Lieutenant C.J. Chappelle, following O'Shea's route, brought a similar column south from Jícaro for a rendezvous.

At the deadly Zapotillo ridge, he was hit and surrounded by about 150 *Sandinistas*. Forced into a defensive laager, Chapelle fought it out for two days. The hardship was not without some comic relief. In the midst of the battle, a Corsair air-dropped his orders to flight training: report immediately, any delay to count against accumulated leave.

The heavy growth made it virtually impossible for the planes to spot the besiegers, and a message was dropped to Chappelle: "Where is the enemy?" In what passed for a clearing, Chappelle ordered the panels laid. "He is north, south, east, and west. Request you bomb." Then, with adroit cooperation from Rusty Rowell's planes which swept the way ahead, scattering the rebels and forcing them to take to the bush, Gould's column broke the siege.[96]

On October 24 the combined patrols reached the crash site. Other than the plane's motor and metal parts, they found nothing but torched remains. Reversing march back to Jícaro, they were met by an enemy force estimated at 250, which they severely mauled and routed with perhaps sixty dead and wounded.

Although none of the patrols had found the elusive El Chipote, O'Shea, Gould, and Chappelle gave a fair approximation of its position. On November 23, using a map drawn by O'Shea, Rusty Rowell reconnoitered the area with two aircraft and found it about five miles northeast of Zapotillo ridge. "Chipote," he reported, "is a hill wooded at the top with several long thatched houses. . . . A large amount of washing . . . immediately attracted attention, due to the size of the wash in relation to the number of houses in the vicinity."[97]

Also clearly out of proportion were the large number of men, about 200, he saw running for cover. All around the houses were piles of freshly turned earth, "evidently machine gun nests" and rifle pits. Rowell led the attack, while puffs of rifle smoke marked the rudimentary anti-aircraft fire. "One [bomb] hit was made close to one machine gun nest and four men were seen to fall." The planes circled to the east side of the hill and received additional ground fire. "The fire was returned by the rear guns and all [enemy] action in the vicinity promptly ceased." There were probably numerous civilian casualties among the guerrillas' camp followers, one of whom was Sandino's Salvadoran mistress. Slightly injured in the head, a small piece of her skull was removed by the doctor, which Sandino then had embedded in a finger ring of San Albino gold. War in its pre-automotive age was as cruel to animals as to humans. Rowell spotted the rebel horse corral, which he "strafed with good results." Indeed, Sandino later claimed it was not the air attack *per se,* but the stench of the rotting carcasses that forced him to evacuate the position.[98]

Having located El Chipote, Colonel Gulick felt the campaign was nearing its end and he launched a two-pronged assault to finally bring Sandino to heel. The columns, marching from the south and west, would converge on Quílali, an overgrown and abandoned hamlet. There they would establish a base of operations and, with air support, storm the fortress. This plan led to disaster.

At mid-morning on December 30 Captain Richard Livingston's southern column, made up of 114 marines, an unknown number of *guardia,* and a pack train of about 200 mules, reached to within a scant mile of the Quílali rendezvous. It was the dry season but that fact seemed to have little relevance along the trail, the grandly named Camino Real. The mules, General Lejeune said, "always put their feet in the same holes, and those holes get full of water and each hole becomes a quagmire . . . and they had trouble . . . getting bogged; [the men's] minds were more on the mules, I think, than anything else."[99]

Down and to their left flowed the 200 foot wide Jícaro River. A steep ridge rose immediately to the right. In front, as the point approached the tumbledown shacks, a scraggly banana grove straddled the way.

When nearly up to the grove, the leading private in the point spotted "suspicious movements" in the brush. The point dropped to the ground, and, Lieutenant Gould reported, "a perfect storm of fire" erupted from enemy positions to the front and from the left across the river. Captain Livingston fell wounded and Gould assumed command. Forward in the banana grove a machine gun opened to enfilade the entire column. But the weapon had been improperly sited and most of its rounds spewed harmlessly into the river. Actually, the enemy had at least two machine guns, and as Gould uncomfortably discerned, there were "unidentified weapons, sounding similar to our trench mortars and mountain battery guns."[100]

The rebels, estimated at 400, were well concealed; each man lay behind an individual parapet of rocks piled around closely spaced tree stumps. But they had opened fire too early. Intending to ambush the entire column, they instead engaged only the point and the advance guard. The marines reacted quickly. Machine guns were dismounted from the pack mules, while a right-flanking detachment of riflemen worked around the rebel foxhole line, rolling it up into the banana grove. In the face of this determined counterattack, the enemy broke in retreat. Five marines and two *guardia* were killed, and twenty-three marines and two guardsmen wounded. The pack train had been heavily shot up. Enemy losses were "unknown, but believed to be heavy." Under Gould's command, the column collected its dead and injured and continued into Quílali.

Although the *Sandinista* attack had been imperfectly executed, the marines were nonetheless conscious of their foe's newly found battle prowess. "The discipline maintained, the morale, and the accuracy of the fire of the bandits," Gould reported, "as well as the tactical dispositions of their troops were far above anything displayed by them in any of their actions heretofore." Worse was to come.[101]

The western column from Telpaneca, First Lieutenant Merton Richal with forty-two marines, twenty *guardia* led by Lieutenant Thomas Bruce of Ocotal fame, and a 100-mule pack train had their first encounter with the enemy at midday, December 30. As the point of the single-file column reached a hill crest somewhere north of the Zapotillo ridge, about fifty well-hidden rebels opened fire on the left flank. At no time were more than three of the enemy visible and this at ranges that never exceeded fifty feet. The action lasted half an hour before the enemy withdrew in the face of superior fire.

On New Year's day 1928, Richal's column continued the last six miles south to Quílali, marching roughly between the ridge on its right and the Jícaro River to the left. Lieutenant Bruce commanded the point, which rounded a curve in the trail just after noon, and he spotted movement ahead. Bruce drew his pistols and was immediately killed by an overwhelming avalanche of machine gun fire, rifle fire, and dynamite bombs. About 400 guerrillas had completely surrounded the column. "The bandit forces were well disciplined," reported Gunnery Sergeant Brown, "and when Lieutenant Bruce was killed they were able to rush our point and advance guard at the command of their leader." The head of the column fell back on the main body. One guardsman tried to remain with the dead lieutenant but was overwhelmed by machete-wielding bandits and so badly slashed that he required the amputation of his left arm.[102]

Richal ordered his heavy weapons dismounted. Along with the machine guns, a Stokes trench mortar and a 37-mm mountain gun kept the charging enemy from following their temporary advantage. Amid the carnage, the column re-formed into a skirmish line and slowly regained fire superiority.

Richal ordered the advance and launched a counterattack on an enemy-occupied hummock directly to his front. Leading the assault, he was shot in the left eye, the bullet exiting through his nose. With Bruce dead and Richal badly wounded, Gunnery Sergeant Brown took command. The marines and *guardia* gained the heights, then dug in to defend against a completely encircling foe. They recovered Bruce's body, mutilated with machetes and looted of its pistols, field glasses, and compass. "Buried on the spot," Brown later reported, "field burial regulations complied with."[103]

By field radio "Gunny" Brown raised Quílali, and a relieving force immediately marched to their aid. But they would not arrive until late the next day. In the offing, Rusty Rowell's planes flew constant air cover over the battered and surrounded patrol, bombing and strafing the enemy until the relief column fought its way through. After spending the night on the hill, the combined columns, covered all the way by the protective umbrella of patrolling aircraft, limped into Quílali.

Of 174 officers and men, eight were dead, and thirty-one—including every surviving officer—wounded, eighteen seriously. The stampeded pack trains had taken a good portion of the reserve ammunition and medical supplies. If the badly wounded men were not evacuated, most would surely die. Worse, the rebels had crept in on the heels of the withdrawal and had taken the hamlet under direct small arms fire. In another first in the history of warfare, it was decided to evacuate the wounded by air.

Rowell personally reconnoitered the area and concluded that an aircraft might, *just* might, land on the scraggly mountain trail that passed for the main street. Tools were air-dropped, and after a feverish day's work, the troops demolished the abandoned shacks and managed, "in spite of the almost impossible conditions obtaining," to hack a strip 200 feet long and 100 feet wide. It was potted with holes, and the takeoff end plummeted into a deep ravine.[104]

At Managua, Lieutenant Christian Schilt volunteered for the mission. To save weight, the machine guns on his Corsair were removed, as was all extraneous equipment (which wasn't much in those days). To facilitate landing on the pitted strip, the landing gear was replaced by the larger wheels of the older DH.

On January 6 Schilt, covered by an ever-present wingman, flew in. He attempted a standard landing, but found it impossible; there were just too many holes. He circled the town, brought the plane in at ten feet, stalled the engine, and dropped like a stone. The Corsair had no brakes so Schilt relied on the marines rushing onto the strip to keep the plane from nosing into the ravine. Takeoffs were the same. The marines held the wing tips while Schilt revved the engine and "catapulted" the plane into the air. On the eighth landing the tail skid assembly collapsed; the ninth badly damaged the center landing struts. For three days, under constant rifle fire, Schilt completed ten missions. He carried out the badly wounded, brought in first a relief commander and then 1,400 pounds of provisions and medical supplies. For his "almost superhuman skill" and heroism, Schilt received the Congressional Medal of Honor.

Reprovisioned, the mauled columns evacuated Quílali and, under continuous air cover, trudged north to San Albino to regroup and rethink coming operations.

The extrication of the columns and Schilt's exploits could not hide the fact that Sandino had inflicted a severe blooding on the marines and *guardia*. "Undoubtedly," noted the report of the Marine Corps' Division of Operations and Training, "we had made an error in under-estimating the bandit combat strength." Rear Admiral David Sellers, commanding the Special Service Squadron, felt the Quílali battles "established the fact that Sandino's forces are even better equipped and organized than there has been reason to think."[105]

In the United States, and indeed throughout the world, Sandino's stock rose. Like Ho Chi Minh after him, Sandino was idolized in the United States by a vocal left, while isolationists severely chastised America's interventionist policy. Senator Burton K. Wheeler of Montana considered the Coolidge administration guilty of "a dishonorable program of brutal bluff and bully. What right," he continued, "have we to send our boys into a foreign country to stamp out banditry? If we are to use them to stamp out banditry, let's send them to Chicago to stamp it out there. As far as I'm concerned, I wouldn't sacrifice the lifeblood of one American boy for all the damn Nicaraguans."* Looking at the broader issues, Representative Huddleston of Alabama asked members of the House, "What are we doing in Nicaragua anyway? The people do not know and unfortunately Congress doesn't know. The people would have us away from there and leave Nicaragua to a settlement of her own disturbances."[106]

Latin American sympathies came down solidly with the *Sandinistas*. The Buenos Aires *La Critica* castigated the "Colossus of the North. . . . Argentina must express its solidarity with the victims of Yankee imperialism." And in civil-war ravaged China, one of Chiang Kai-shek's Russian-trained formations bore the name "Sandino Division."[107]

Among those in favor of United States action in Nicaragua was the ranking Republican of the House Committee on Naval Affairs, who saw it as necessary for the legacy of public esteem. The amount of men and money to "clean up" the rebels was unimportant compared "with the maintenance of American world prestige."

Public demonstrations abounded. Picketers massed in front of the White House carrying signs reading, "Wall Street and not Sandino is the Real Bandit." Letters were mailed to marine units embarking for Nicaragua, pleading with them not to fight, but to join Sandino in his "war for freedom."[108]

Soap boxes and posturing aside, it was clear that if the marines were not going to withdraw immediately, they could not very well remain and conduct an active campaign without substantial reinforcements. The first arrived in early January, 176 marines stripped from the vessels of the Special Service Squadron. But that was hardly enough. On orders from the Secretary of the Navy, the 11th Marines, recently disbanded, re-formed on the Atlantic

---

*Wheeler's isolationism knew no bounds, and in a later decade he led the losing and short-sighted fight to prevent Lend-Lease aid to an embattled Britain.

and Pacific coasts, and by cruisers and transports were rushed to Corinto. Ailing General Feland, now commanding at Parris Island, was again picked to command the brigade. Air reinforcements were also on the move. In mid-February the brand-new aircraft carrier *Saratoga* interrupted her shakedown cruise to bring Marine Observation Squadron 6 through the Panama Canal to Corinto. Nothing was neglected. The dearth of pack animals in Nicaragua was so acute that the U.S. Army was persuaded to loan sixty of its big, tough mules, with full equippage. These, however, proved very much a mixed blessing. Unlike the scrawny Nicaraguan beasts, who subsisted on any sort of forage, these army mules ate only oats and hay. A six-month supply shipped to Corinto required a convoy of 225 bullcarts to transport the fodder inland.

Pending Feland's arrival, Colonel Gulick changed tactics. He laid aside the original plan to assault El Chipote with a combined infantry-air attack, and the primary mission assigned to Rusty Rowell's planes was to destroy the fortress from the air; the riflemen would then mop up. An air reconnaissance reported more than 1,000 "armed bandits" dug in with machine guns and cleared fields of fire. The mountain itself rose 3,000 feet and had "approaches through the worst kind of ravines." Rowell considered his numbers somewhat thin, as he had only four of the new Corsairs, and didn't want to use the old, fabric-covered DHs. "I didn't think much of going up against a hill of that size with those four planes. It looked to me as if we didn't have enough firepower to cover the situation." Gulick rightly thought otherwise. "You go ahead and put on the show," he said.[109]

On January 14 the airmen loaded up with 50-pound demolition and 17-pound fragmentation bombs, and flew northeast from Managua through heavy cumulus clouds. Luckily "there was a nice hole in the clouds right over the bandit mountain." Rowell gave the signal, and in almost vertical dives, the planes went in. "They saw us coming. . . . The first thing I saw was a barrage of sky rockets. Eight or ten of them rose in the sector that I was after." Each rocket was attached to a stick of dynamite, and though very "annoying," none exploded.[110]

Atop the summit Rowell noticed numerous perfectly round, barrel-sized holes, without any parapets—individual bomb shelters which were fairly impervious to attack. But the guerrillas were bunched in several large wooden shacks, easy targets. "We went down through the clouds and caught them beautifully. We sprayed the mountain top with machine gun fire and after the first 50-pounder hit, things started to move." After one shack collapsed under the impact of a 50-pound bomb, "the bandits came out in droves from the others. We kept after them until they had gotten over in the ravines and we had no more ammunition."[111]

At a critical point, Rowell's engine coughed and stalled. He managed to get it going again and flew to Ocotal for temporary repairs. All seemed in order, but on the flight back to Managua it happened again. Landing safely, Rowell and his mechanics disassembled the engine and found a house fly stuck in the carburetor.

Following the air assault, rumors of Sandino's death received wide circulation and credence. On the nineteenth, Rowell flew over the mountain and saw nothing but "squadrons of vultures."[112]

That day a battalion-sized column moved methodically south from San Albino to El Chipote. First Lieutenant Kenyon led the advance guard 20th Company, occupying successive positions in the direct line of approach. Kenyon made good progress, all the while firing rifle grenades ahead at possible points of ambush. At noon they reached the Murra River valley leading up to the heights. "I was walking with Gunnery Sergeant Brooks ahead of the point," he reported, "when fire broke out from concealed places on the crest from what sounded like one machine gun and a section of rifles." The marines hit the deck and deployed. "All rifle fire was held up by my orders until the enemy could be seen." Rifle grenadiers adjusted the special bubble sights* and let fly their missiles "where smoke was spitting." The guerrillas maintained fire for twenty minutes, and the grenadier at Kenyon's side was shot through "the fleshy part of both buttocks." Swept by automatic rifles, rebel fire slackened and Kenyon ordered the advance. Of the enemy, only a few were seen "jumping into the brush as they fled from their position." No dead or wounded guerrillas were found. But two days later air reconnaissance reported "vultures eating four bodies near the location of the contact."[113]

The rumors concerning Sandino's death were scotched at Santa Rosa, just west of the mountain. Captured documents in-

---

*Very much like a small carpenter's level attached to the rifle stock.

cluded a recent letter in Sandino's handwriting. This, General Lejeune said (echoing Mark Twain's quip to the Associated Press when Twain got word of his own reported demise), "caused us to feel that the reports of his death had been 'greatly exaggerated.' "[114]

On January 23 Kenyon extended his outpost line over the Murra and onto the trails leading to the summit. The mule-packed rations had run out, and the marines subsisted on "forage," captured enemy stocks of coffee, beans, and fruit. A section of the 8th (machine gun) Company arrived the following morning, and the marines spent the day preparing "to move toward the position known as the main fort." In early evening a reconnaissance patrol advanced up the slopes and destroyed an enemy observation post with Stokes mortar fire. At nightfall the remainder of the battalion closed upon Kenyon's advance line.

At dawn they continued up the slopes. In one abandoned outpost Kenyon found a goodly amount of saddles and other equipment taken from Livingston's and Richal's stampeded pack trains, as well as "a considerable amount of 1927 issue expended 30-30 ammunition and pieces of flying machine parts." The methodical advance continued, and the following day Kenyon led a patrol to the summit. They had finally reached the mythical El Chipote, and missed the enemy garrison by what seemed only minutes. Kenyon reported "A freshly butchered beef was found hanging near the house said [by a prisoner] to have been the headquarters of General Salgado and a chicken still limp and undressed was on the floor of the quarters near the fireplace."[115]

On January 28 the battalion came down from the mountain and marched the eight miles to Quílali. It was evident that the rebels had recently been here as well. The temporary airstrip, so laboriously constructed, was holed, ditched, and pitted along its entire length. "The pits were filled," the column about-faced and trudged back north to San Albino. The campaign to capture El Chipote had reached its anticlimactic end.

With the arrival of the 11th Marines, as well as five all-metal Fokker trimotor aircraft, the first transports allotted to the Marine Corps, aggressive patrolling began throughout Nueva Segovia. Marines garrisoned practically every town, including, for a time, San Rafael, where Blanca Sandino continued her job as telegraph operator. She was considered no great security risk, as all military traffic was encoded.

Air activity was stepped up. "We constantly had patrols after them," Rusty Rowell said, "but an Indian in the jungle is a hard fellow to capture." Yet "the planes were able to keep them off the roads in the daytime, out of villages, and out of organized positions." After the capture of El Chipote, the *Sandinistas* adopted some novel tactics to avoid attack from the air. "One trick was to have a woman with two babies in her arms stand in front of the combatant group. . . . Some stunts worked and some did not. We had orders not to bomb them in towns. . . . When the bandits found that out, they would ambush our troops and then run into a town. We finally had to bomb a group in a town. After we bombed that outfit the game was spoiled." Notwithstanding that policy, there were continuous canards in the press regarding the marines' bombing defenseless villages, and even to using poison gas.[116]

When Feland arrived in mid-January 1928, he divided Nicaragua into three military districts. The northern area, scene of most active operations, comprised as well all of western Nicaragua, north of the line Estelí-Jinotega. It was allotted to the 11th Marines; Colonel Robert Dunlap, last seen in 1916 with Uncle Joe's flying column on the road to Santiago in the Dominican Republic, established his regimental headquarters at Ocotal. The 5th Marines garrisoned and patrolled the southern area, generally south of the Estelí-Jinotega line, with headquarters in Managua. The relatively quiescent eastern area, headquarters, Puerto Cabezas, formed a vast, sparsely settled region. It stretched far inland from the Atlantic coast, shifting nebulously westward to any point where troops could be supplied from its ports. It was assigned to Major Harold Utley and the marines of the Special Service Squadron, reinforced by the 5th Regiment's 51st Company.

On January 20, with the reinforcements still shaking down, Admiral Sellers made a final appeal for Sandino's surrender. After informing the guerrilla *jefe* of the United States' "solemn obligation to preserve order," he mentioned the state of the American forces, which "have recently been very largely augmented with men and munitions" and the United States' "intention to utilize fully all of the vast resources that our government has placed at our disposal." Referring to Sandino's loss of El Chipote and his refusal in the past to disarm and disband, the admiral continued, "The unnecessary sacrifice of human lives is a very serious matter . . . while heretofore you have refused, in the light of subsequent events you might now be willing to consider the advisability of discontinuing the present armed resistance . . . and . . . follow the example of your countrymen of both political parties who . . . agreed to settle their differences in a high-minded and patriotic manner without further bloodshed."[117]

Sellers entrusted a rebel prisoner called Lobo with the letter, first freeing him on his promise to deliver. Sandino received the missive at San Rafael where he was visiting his wife in the marines' temporary absence. He composed his reply to "Mr. D.F. Sellers, Representative of Imperialism in Nicaragua." Because "special circumstances" prevented his delivering it personally, Sandino enlisted Carleton Beals, a visiting American reporter from the liberal, pro-*Sandinista* journal *The Nation*.

This was no mere civil war, Sandino lectured the admiral. "Don't believe that the present struggle has for an origin . . . the revolution just passed. Today this is a struggle of the Nicaraguan people in general, to expel the foreign invasion of my country." As for the terms of the Stimson-Moncada treaty, "We have reiterated a thousand times our ignorance of them. The only way to put an end to this struggle is the immediate withdrawal of the invading forces from our territory . . . and supervis[ed] elections by representatives of Latin America instead of by American Marines."[118]

Between receipt and response, Sandino, chased from the north, moved south into the more settled agricultural region around Jinotega and Matagalpa. Echelons of the 5th Marines at Managua rushed up by forced march and motor transport to the threatened area. Mounted units of the 11th Marines scoured the territory in the Coco River valley to cut off any retreat.

Captain Maurice Holmes' 52nd Company trotted north out of Estelí bound for the Coco towns. "Our point had cleared the [Estelí] river . . . the main body was in place, and a squad and a half of Marines were spread where we intended the pack train to go. The rear point went into action at once trying to herd mules back where mules didn't want to be. Lots of men believe . . . that soon we would have straightened out fine except for the air service. Two of those planes zoomed just over our heads as the pack train was approaching the river; by the time we had recovered enough mules to supply a good share of the ten days' rations . . . it was almost 4:00 p.m."[119]

By nightfall the company had covered all of five miles. Riding and pack animals were unsaddled, evening chow served up, and the marines prepared their beds. "And from sleeping in the grass in Nicaragua," Holmes mused, "may the good Lord deliver us. When morning came, I pulled 36 ticks of various sizes from their burrows which ran from my eyelids to my toes."

The pack train of scrawny local mules proved a constant drag on their progress. "The end of our second day found us about 18 miles to the north and I wonder how we got that far." Nicaraguan *muleros* accompanied nearly every patrol and column, and to Holmes it seemed their cry " *'Alto! Alto! Una carga discompuesta,'* came up from the rear every 200 yards. I would have enjoyed detailing an escort to that pack train and letting it catch up at the bivouac if I could have squared it with my conscience. But with the exception of a few noncoms, all [marines] were recruits who had to be trained as we went."

It was a monotonous trek. "About the only contacts to break the otherwise complete isolation from the world were the patrols of two planes . . . which came over us almost daily." At Yalaguina, just before the Coco, with rations nearly gone, Holmes sent part of the company with the train to Ocotal for replenishment. Over the hamlet, the ubiquitous Corsairs dropped a message. "I was to take all of the 52nd Company I could immediately lay hands upon, beat it to Yali, and there check Sandino's retreat to the north. . . . Other companies were to converge on the boy if possible and tag him before he could run back to his base."

Unencumbered, Holmes marched the twenty-five miles southeast to Yali in less than two days. "I learned that friend Sandino had departed . . . the preceding Thursday night, taking with him all the loot he could pack including all the whiskey and beer stocks. We could tell by this that we had to deal with a very selfish man."

At Yali, Holmes received a report of an impending night attack and he deployed accordingly. He sent half a dozen *muleros* down the trail to man a listening post, then stationed four squads of marines in ambush positions enfilading the main approaches. Holmes held the remainder in reserve, behind a thick-walled adobe house. The night passed quietly.

The next day a message drop ordered the company to Jinotega, twenty miles further southeast. "Sandino had moved ahead of our information pausing only to snatch morsels of loot and pass out his catchy bits of propaganda. Well the patriots reckoned he really had triumphed since he was right there telling them so and multitudes decided they would get on his bandwagon. It looked better yet when he began commandeering . . . supplies from some of the foreign-owned coffee plantations near Matagalpa, so they marched in the ranks of the army with stalwart devotion and delirious morale. When [his] column swung north, however, and whispers . . . indicated a return to the fastness of . . . El Chipote, the increment of patriots decided they could serve their country better at home."

From Jinotega, Holmes, reinforced with a half company, headed south on the bullcart trail to Matagalpa. "Between 5:00 A.M. and 10:30 A.M. . . . we got the mounts bridled, saddled, and held in columns of twos. . . . Flushed with this success, I proudly gave the order for mounting in unison—and spent an hour and a half . . . thereafter attempting to mount at will."

Holmes completed the eighteen-mile march in just over nine hours. "I attribute our speed to the lucky find of 80 sets of rowel spurs . . . the regulation spur never bluffed those little mules beyond the first hour on the trail; as a matter of fact, the rowelled spur meant nothing to any one of them after he decided he had marched enough that day."

From Matagalpa it was again north, this time in company with the whole of the regiment's 1st battalion. They established temporary bases along the line of march, and patrols pushed out ten and twenty miles in all directions. In Holmes' entire mission, he "had not heard one shot fired in anger."

As the marines drove north, Sandino withdrew with his main body. But a detached column, mainly recently recruited locals, pivoted northwest to strike in the area south of the Coco, below and roughly between Ocotal and Quílali. These "part-time bandits," the future Major General Julian Smith wrote, "were always ready to furnish food and information or to join the regulars for an opportunity to loot, or for an especially important raid."[120]

On February 28 1st Lieutenant Edward O'Day, 2nd Battalion, 11th Marines, left Estelí in command of what, for Sandino, was an inviting target: thirty-six marines, a navy pharmacist's mate, twenty-two *muleros* with ninety-five mules—the provision train for the garrisons at San Rafael and Yali.

Completing the resupply mission, the empty pack train plodded its slow path westward. Near the hamlet of Bromaderos, the column entered a flat, open space, hugged on either side by ranges of low hills. It was an ideal spot for an ambush and O'Day ordered the column to close up. When the entire train, front to back, lay exposed in the clearing, the guerrillas opened fire from three sides. O'Day recalled, "The first shot of the skirmish was directed at the undersigned." The mules immediately stampeded, and the marines bolted for a low ridge to their left and returned fire.[121]

They were vastly outnumbered. O'Day estimated that he faced "beyond doubt" at least four machine guns, 600 rifles, and a "large quantity of dynamite bombs, of which at least 200 were thrown." For an hour the rebels kept up an incessant fire. Then using staff college tactics the enemy machine guns laid down a base of fire; the bandits formed a skirmish line, and charged. They reached no further than the base of the ridge before being hurled back, "leaving several groups [of dead] in vicinity." Before rejoining their lines, the surviving *Sandinistas* dallied to loot the wandering mules. In the early evening they charged again. As the Duke of Wellington said of the French, "They came on in the same old way, and we beat them in the same old way."

With the night, O'Day continued to hold his position. Five marines were dead and eight wounded. "The Marine dead," he reported, "were whacked over the head with bolos by the bandit skirmishers, splitting their skulls wide open. . . . Existing instructions pertaining to deceased marines were complied with to the best extent practicable."

During a lull the guerrillas engaged in a bit of psychological warfare. Speaking an "irregular English . . . [they] made a specialty of harassing the Marines with slurs and insults." There were other sounds from the enemy lines. "Someone with a tenor voice complimented the bandits for their work. This was repeated in loud tones all along the line."

When it was full and truly dark, O'Day sent a runner to summon help. At a hamlet about seven miles away, the runner encountered Captain William MacNulty's patrolling 57th Company. Leaving his pack train and all extra equipment under guard, MacNulty marched to the relief. It took an hour and a half to reach the edge of the ambush site. MacNulty heard no firing, "only a few native yells." With the dawn he conducted a reconnaissance and moved forward. In the field were a pair of O'Day's mules, one still carrying a load of ammunition. "I called to Marine Gunner Allen to shoot it," MacNulty said, "which he did." The rifle shot brought forth a call, "Who is there?" MacNulty halted his company and got the point under cover. "Captain MacNulty with the 57th Company," he yelled back. Out of the bushes stepped an exhausted Lieutenant O'Day.

MacNulty aimed his machine gun to sweep the crest of the enemy's hill line, then formed his troops and counterattacked. Covered by the machine gun, the marines advanced by short rushes, slamming straight into the guerrillas' right flank. Many had departed during the night and he estimated the enemy's current strength at 200 rifles. The dead he counted at ten, the wounded, at least thirty. "The entire command," he noted, "conducted themselves in the most soldierly manner. . . . Most . . . were recruits with less than four months' training, yet they responded instantly to orders and the line never faltered in its advance."

On May 18 a two-plane patrol located the main *Sandinista* force at Murra, about twenty miles north of Quílali and hard by the Honduran frontier. The next day, shuttling back and forth from the forward airfield at Ocotal, the planes subjected the guerrilla concentrations to continuous bombing and strafing attacks. The airmen reported heavy casualties inflicted, but one of the two-seaters' observers was shot in the foot, and thereafter a sheet of plate armor was fitted under the seats of the brigade's attack aircraft.

The air assault at Murra forced Sandino further east and he marched his bands into the undefended gold-mining districts in north-central Nicaragua. En route, he penned a strange note to the marine commanders in the Jinotega-Matagalpa area. He offered them $2 million if they would "protest to your government about the occupation of our territory, and then evacuate the towns occupied by you and concentrate in Managua." The letter and gift were ignored.[122]

On April 12 a rebel column occupied the American-owned La Luz and Los Angeles gold mines, looting a number of Chinese stores in the process. Troops and aircraft from the northern and eastern areas rushed to the scene. But Sandino slipped away, this time back to the west, in the region of the middle Coco River and the Honduran frontier. It is the most difficult terrain in Nicaragua, a region where daytime visibility in the jungles is a bare twenty feet. Here he would rest his forces, refit from Honduras, and establish supply dumps in the nearly inaccessible river towns.

Hoping to discover Sandino's exact whereabouts, patrols from the northern area probed eastward. On May 9 Captain Robert

Hunter led mule-mounted elements of his 47th Company: twenty-seven marines, plus a navy hospital corpsman, a marine *guardia* officer, and nine guardsmen out of Quílali. The *guardia* were questionable. Cadet Ollie Blackburn (gunnery sergeant, USMC), a veteran of the Battle of Ocotal, spoke no Spanish, and was an unknown quantity to his men. The guardsmen themselves were the worst of the Quílali garrison, as their betters were exhausted after constant patrolling. The train comprised eleven pack mules, loaded with ten days' rations and ammunition.

Sandino had received advance intelligence of the patrol, and fearful of its penetrating into the Coco "rest area," he ordered Manuel Girón to intercept. A professional Guatemalan soldier-of-fortune, Girón, according to Captain Victor Bleasdale, was "a high type guerrilla officer [and] probably the most able that ever served under Sandino."[123]

The patrol advanced in the normal order of march for jungle trails. A submachine gun–toting corporal and four privates, spaced twenty yards between each man, formed the point. Twenty yards back came the main body, bunched much closer together, with only a mule's length between. Next plodded the pack mules, and finally the rear guard of a sergeant and four privates.

At least three times, individual guerillas or small groups were spotted; each time either *guardia* or marines fired too soon. The guerrillas made their escapes and doubtless provided Girón with information of the patrol's approach. On the morning of May 13 the patrol cleared camp. In his report, Second Lieutenant Earl Piper wrote, "Passed several houses, some of which were occupied by apparently friendly natives. Others had evidently been deserted in a hurry." By late afternoon, "after traveling through heavy timber and underbrush . . . reached scene of combat."

The patrol marched north on the Bocaycito trail, cresting a hill which was well wooded save for a house and a small clearing around it. The point, with Hunter in company, descended the far side leading to a ravine. When about halfway down the slope, they began receiving random fire from the dense jungle to their right and from hidden guerrillas in the ravine to their front.

The point immediately dismounted, and, leaving their mules, returned fire while falling back to establish a firing line on the crest. Behind them the main body dismounted and formed line to defend itself on the trail. For ten minutes the firefight continued, the guerrillas all the while remaining invisible in the dense growth. When hostile fire ceased, Hunter, who was a veteran of both the World War and the Dominican pacification, assumed the enemy had gone, yet he ordered no confirming reconnaissance.

Within minutes a heavy volume of rifle and automatic fire from at least 100 guerrillas in the ravine and atop a hill to the left front opened on the point. Hunter, Piper, and four marines bounded forward to reinforce the position. The guerrillas had come up to the point's abandoned mules, and to prevent their capture, the marines stood up and fired, exposing themselves in turn to heavy, well-directed shooting from the ravine. A corporal fell dead.

The navy hospital corpsman picked up the dead man's Thompson submachine gun, but being unfamiliar with the piece, could not fire. Hunter grabbed the weapon. As Lieutenant Piper reported, "On his way back to the . . . crest [Hunter] stopped and in a standing position, fired into the bandits and felled two of them but in turn was shot in the chest by a bandit Thompson at a range of 50 yards," Slammed to the ground by a 45-caliber slug, Hunter regained his feet, continued toward the firing line on the crest and was hit again. The hospital corpsman dragged him to cover and dressed his wounds.

While the marines engaged the enemy to their front, flanking guerrilla parties lobbed dynamite bombs from the jungle. The marines replied with hand grenades. At 4:30 P.M., hostile fire died away. They buried the corporal. Aside from Captain Hunter, only one other marine was slightly wounded.

Lieutenant Piper took command and prepared to spend the night on the hill. "The night was a trying one." Within a seventy-five-yard perimeter, the men were paired in foxholes, one man awake while the other slept. The patrol was very short on water, as they had only what remained in their canteens, and most of that was needed for the badly wounded captain. There was a nearby stream to their rear, but Piper considered it too dangerous to send a party.

At daybreak Piper reconnoitered the position and found it empty of the enemy. But he got no solace from this, and rightly assumed the guerrillas lay in ambush along the trail to his front and rear. Yet there was nothing to do but about-face and retrace their steps back to Quílali. Air support would have been a godsend, but none had been assigned to follow the patrol. Improvising a stretcher for Hunter from a navy hammock and two poles, the patrol started back.

To the point Piper assigned a Thompson gunner and a rifle

grenadier. All marched on foot, leading their mules. Fifteen minutes after they set out, the guerrillas opened fire from the rear and both flanks. The patrol dashed for cover in a streambed, and at last they refilled their canteens. Captain Hunter was placed in a well-defiladed position, but, Piper reported, "though fatally wounded, [he] leaped from his stretcher and insisted in participating in the fire fight and had to be overpowered and returned to his stretcher." For forty-five desperate minutes, the outnumbered patrol fought back. In front, things went well: "Sergeant Brown made some grenade throws that made his comrades inquire if he was the world's champion discus thrower." But the rear guard nearly collapsed. The marines and *guardia* were pinned down by automatic fire and the guerrillas slowly closed in; some actually coming at the rush. The *guardia* could not face it, and though Cadet Blackburn tried to hold them in position, they scattered into the jungle. The last guardsman to bolt took an enemy dumdum round in his head. Deserted by his men, Blackburn stood up and engaged the enemy with his pistol until reinforcements from the main body came up, and with rifle grenades reduced the threat to the rear.

Hostile fire ceased at 9:00 A.M. and the patrol continued its retreat. They had marched less than 100 yards when the rear was again taken under fire. The enemy were determined to isolate the pack train, but rifle grenade fire held them off. During this phase, Piper said, the guerrillas began yelling in Spanish, calling the marines " '*muleros*' and many other unkind names and told them that they were going to cut all their throats before they got out of Nicaragua."

At mid-morning the *Sandinistas* withdrew northward. Just then an aircraft flew overhead at 500 feet. Some of the marines frantically waved their arms but there was no time to lay the panels and the plane flew off. The march resumed and six of the deserting *guardia* returned. The patrol halted for the night. Captain Hunter's wounds were draining his life away and he hovered near death. On May 15 the patrol reached the hamlet of La Flor, and Piper concluded they could go no further without killing the captain. Again planes appeared, and this time they spotted the patrol. Terrain made it impossible for a message pickup so panels "Help" were laid out. Camp was made behind a log barricade and the patrol settled in to await relief. "Gave men all rest possible," Piper noted in his report. Even Captain Hunter seemed to be recovering.

On the seventeenth, the planes dropped very welcome rations and medical supplies and preparations were made to carry the captain out in a Loening OL-8 amphibian which would land in the Coco. But the next day Captain Hunter died. The relief column finally arrived on May 22, seven days after the plane spotted the "Help" panels. For his conduct during the engagements, Captain Hunter received a posthumous Navy Cross.

Sandino's main force foray into the mining district moved operations eastward. To deny Sandino free rein in the jungle fastness of the Coco River valley and simultaneously seal the Honduran border, Captain Merritt "Red Mike" Edson, the ice-eyed skipper of the *Denver*'s marines, proposed a daring mission. "We had no information about the Coco River or the country through which it flowed," he told the eastern area's Major Utley. "Why not send a reconnaissance patrol upstream from Cape Gracias, using the ship's boats if necessary."[124]

The Coco, rising in western Honduras and flowing down to the Atlantic, is the longest river in Central America. As it nears the ocean it is wide and sluggish in the dry season, with an average depth of fifteen feet. In the rainy months it climbs three-fold, overflowing its banks and flooding the countryside. Year-round the river is navigable by shallow-draft motor craft as far up as Huaspuc, a distance of eighty-five miles on the map, but more than double that in tortuous, twisting miles on the water. The upper river, beyond Awasbila to Poteca at the very tip edge of the northern area, is strewn with deadly rapids and even the local Indians fear to travel there.

From start to finish, Edson's Coco adventure employed nearly every conceivable form of transport: coastal schooner, gas motorboat, native dugout canoes, poling boats which were "sometimes right side up and almost as often bottom side up; old shank's mare with our food and clothing, if we had any," mules, and aircraft. He never used an automobile or the local bull cart, "because such things as bull cart trails did not exist in the area . . . and automobiles were to northeastern Nicaragua what rocket ships are to us—dreams of the future."

Edson began the patrol on March 7 with a small reconnaissance force, five marines from the *Denver* in a flat-bottomed boat powered by an engine salvaged from a Model T Ford; supplies were carried in a native dugout canoe, lashed alongside the boat. Orders were to travel as far as Huaspuc, and further if Edson deemed it necessary. The journey up the lower river was uneventful. All the Miskito Indian villages were abandoned save for a few women, the men having taken to the bush.

Once at Huaspuc Edson intended to press on, but on learning that Sandino was actively recruiting along the upper river he opted to return to Cape Gracias. Coming down water, he noticed the Indian men had returned, "having learned that the Marines intended them no harm in any way, and they quite willingly helped [us]."

Edson had little time before the next mission. Reports arrived of guerrilla bands raiding the lumber camps west of Huaspuc, and along the Huaspuc River, a tributary flowing into the Coco from the mining region to the south. Edson was ordered up the river to close the Huaspuc and Coco rivers' junction.

On August 7 he loaded 38 marines into a pair of motor craft and, chugging westward, he reached Huaspuc in six days. On learning that 200 *Sandinistas* were coming downriver to ambush him, Edson established an outpost and pushed on with seven men for Awasbila. The river began taking its toll. "Personnel O.K.," he radioed. "Lost one BAR, two rifles, 200 rations . . . four packs complete and all clothing of men in patrol."

About the last day of April Edson established air contact. Responding to rumors that the patrol had been annihilated, Christian Schilt landed on a sandbar about fifty miles above Huaspuc and found all well. On May 2 orders came to ascend the Huaspuc tributary toward the mining region and intercept any guerrilla bands retreating northward. The patrol traveled in large native dugouts, which proved unwieldy in the stream. There were a few minor skirmishes with small bands of guerrillas, but the main enemy forces had gone.

The patrol spent the next ten days in an Indian village. They were entirely without their usual rations: "For ten days we subsisted on the three B's: bananas for fruit, beans for cereal and beef as the pièce de résistance for breakfast; bean soup, broiled beef and bananas for dinner; and a slum made of all three for supper. A little real monkey meat . . . was added occasionally for variety."

To pursue the guerrillas required mules. Edson sent a foot patrol to find some, and they came back empty. But on May 19 an overland column arrived from Puerto Cabezas with thirty extra beasts in their pack train. Edson mounted most of his men and moved southwest into the heart of the mining region. There was no trail connecting the villages so the marines had to cut their own. At Casa Vieja they were joined by another overland column and together trekked through trackless jungle scrub northwest to Bocay on the Coco, about fifty miles beyond Awasbila.

Here reinforcements arrived on June 4, the 59th Company and the *Galveston*'s marines. While at Bocay Edson received orders to return to Puerto Cabezas and take command of the *Rochester*'s* marine detachment and he returned to the coast by plane. On June 28 the ancient, coal-eating flagship arrived bearing General Feland.

Feland told his officers that air reconnaissance had definitely located the *Sandinista* concentrations around Poteca. "Major Utley tells me that you would like to go to Poteca. Can you get there from this coast?"

"Yes, sir," Edson replied. "It can be done."

"Well, I am going to give you the chance to do it."

Poteca, far up the Coco, was the very edge of the northern area, beyond which lay Honduras. Though only sixty miles from the 11th Marines' Jícaro River line, there were no overland trails and the Coco was the only means of approach. Brigade intelligence estimated 400 guerrillas in the vicinity.

At the height of the rainy season, the Coco presented a veritable spate. "The Río Coco," Edson said, "was higher than it has been for several years; its numerous rapids presented the most difficult task that has yet been encountered by our advancing troops; the supply situation introduced an almost impossible problem."

On July 23 Edson, with the *Denver* detachment of forty-six marines and a navy hospital corpsman, pushed upriver from Bocay in large native dugouts fitted with outboard motors. At times the river rose thirty feet in twelve hours, and for days they were forced to huddle on the soaking banks. On August 1 the ration boat swamped while shooting the Callejon rapids. For six days, until an airdrop, the men ate little but coffee and flour. It rained every day and night. But August 5 "was welcomed joyously." It dawned sunny bright, and Edson gave his men a thorough rest and time to wash and dry their clothes.

In early afternoon, August 7,** the patrol cleared Lliliquas, an Indian hamlet nearly at the end of their journey. As on overland

*The old armored cruiser *New York*, commissioned in 1893.
**Fourteen years to the day when Edson would lead his 1st Marine Raider Battalion ashore at Tulagi, just across Ironbottom Sound from Guadalcanal.

formations, the boats proceeded in an order of march fifty yards apart. A four-man point rode the first; Edson, his first sergeant, and two runners came second; the third and fourth boats contained the advance guard and main body; the fifth carried the hospital corpsman and sick; bringing up the rear in the sixth boat were the cooks, messmen, and rations. On the flanking banks, foot patrols regulated the speed of the advance. "It is absolutely necessary . . . to put out flank patrols," Lieutenant Jesse Cook said. "The men, while still in the boats, are at the mercy of anyone on shore—the boats are hard to manage, easily capsized and the danger of travel in them is sufficient without adding that of machine gun fire from an ambush." Indeed, the enemy waited.

Sandino gave the mission to Manuel Girón, who had proved his worth in the May ambush of Hunter's patrol. Girón, with thirty men and a machine gun, entrenched himself on the northern bank; another thirty took position on his left, though too far away for effective support. Sandino and a reserve force of another thirty men with three automatic weapons stood on the south bank.

As Edson's boats and flankers hacked and breasted their way upriver, a pair of OL-8 amphibians spotted the rebel concentrations and dove in bombing. Girón's north bank units held their positions, but not Sandino. He retired with his men upriver to Wamblam, where his mistress waited.

Edson's men distinctly heard the bombing and return gunfire and cautiously poled ahead. At 1:00 P.M. his north bank flankers nearly fell into the enemy foxholes. One of Girón's lieutenants rashly exposed himself, firing too soon, and the battle was on. Edson beached his boats and the marines advanced up the riverbank. The rebels fought doggedly and well. Lieutenant Cook noticed many wore regular uniforms and "were evidently well trained for they held the positions assigned them until almost stepped on by the Marines."

The fight lasted nearly three hours, until each guerrilla was personally winkled out of his hole. "Individuals," Cook said, "had to do some fast thinking and faster firing." Girón retreated westward, leaving fifty-four rifles, fourteen dead, four wounded, and five prisoners. "One *hombre* when found, said in very good English, 'I'm just a hard working man, Sandino makes me fight.'"

Marine losses were one killed and three wounded; the wounded were evacuated to Puerto Cabezas in the Loening amphibians. Ten days later the patrol arrived at Poteca. Here Edson seized a large cache of Sandino's quartermaster stocks and then pushed on to Santa Cruz, only fifteen miles from Quílali. Edson considered the battle of August 7 a watershed in the campaign. "This decisive defeat," he said, "marks the end of organized outlaw resistance in Nicaragua."

The expedition *down* the Coco to rendezvous with Edson was a far more difficult endeavor. The Indians considered the stretch of river east of Ocotal unnavigable. In fact it was considered so dangerous that volunteers were called for. On September 4 Captain Peter Geyer led forty-five marines and navy surgeon O'Neill out of Ocotal in four homemade boats, fitted with outboard motors. All ammunition and supplies were equally divided, each boat being a self-contained unit.

From the very beginning, disaster loomed. Rapids were near continuous and boat No. 2 jammed between the rocks. A stream anchor thrown to steady the craft only served to pull it under. Everything went overside, and the men leapt in to salvage what they could. "In order to do so," Geyer said, "they had to swim the rapids, about 150 yards of white water containing many sunken rocks barely below the surface. The entire outfit worked late during the night, diving, salvaging and bringing ashore all stores and equipment. It was pitch dark, raining and bitterly cold. The work was extremely dangerous." Everyone suffered cuts but there were no serious injuries, a fact Geyer attributed to the new kapok life jackets.

The next day they floated the boat and to patrolling aircraft signaled "All well." It took two fatiguing days to reach Telpaneca. "The mere carrying of a line from a boat to the shore was heartbreaking toil," Geyer remembered. "Every man who went into the water was cut and lacerated. . . . Rocking, tugging, pushing and hauling at the boats from dawn till sundown very nearly had the unit exhausted by nightfall." For three days the men rested and repaired the boats, and extra anchors and tackle were delivered by air.

On the eleventh, they were back in the river and on the fourteenth, there was another airdrop of shoes, nails, oakum, pitch, and line. The next day the marines portaged over a 600 yard rapid. The sixteenth was spent entirely in rapids. Boat No. 1 swamped and block and tackle were needed to raise it; twice the lines snapped. The seventeenth saw the worst rapids to date, "like a staircase," Geyer noted, "with water cascading over it. River bottom drops nine feet in 50 yards." Boat No. 2 went under. "Nearly lost Private Davis when sucked under boat by current. Infections. Some fever, diarrhea. Continued water exposure infects wounds."

A plane came over in mid-morning on the eighteenth. Panels were laid calling for a message pickup, and two privates held the poles. The pilot, however, began dropping rations. Geyer yelled a warning to his men, but they either did not hear, or could not get out of the way fast enough. A thirty-five-pound sack of rice fell square on Private First Class DeHart. "Hit in head and shoulder," noted Geyer's report, "face cut against pick up pole. Wounds multiple and cerebral concussion. Dr. O'Neill immediately attended."

The next day No. 2 boat again caught on the rocks and it was impossible for swimmers to reach it. The river rose three feet, the boat cast loose and drifted downstream. Four marines jumped into the river "across current which was vicious, twelve miles per hour." They fastened a line to No. 4 boat and worked it into the current. In minutes the river rose another foot. A heaving line was thrown and tangled. Private Moore jumped in to free it, going hand over hand down the stopline to a point twenty feet from the bank. He could go no further and called for help. A life jacket was lowered, but he was unable to grab it. Private Guthrie jumped in from the opposite bank, but was swept downstream. Moore slipped his grip on the stopline and tried to swim to the far bank. Guthrie, again on shore, jumped in to assist, and grabbed an arm. But the current was too strong. The two men were swept away and apart. Guthrie came to land about 100 yards downriver. Moore disappeared. A foot patrol going three miles down found nothing. "They further reported," Geyer said, "that three-fourths miles downstream was an exceedingly bad rapid, through which it was practically impossible for a man to pass alive."

On September 20 the message pickup station was underwater, and a hilltop position had to be cleared. "River still rising," Geyer reported, "part of camp flooded. . . . Will have to wait to get last boat down rapid. DeHart no change [he was delirious and running a 104 degree fever]. No bandits." Despite the adversity, the marines' spirits remained high. Geyer ended his message, "Morale Excellent."

Day followed day, boats swamped, the river at one point rose five feet in two hours. "Sores and cuts refuse to heal," read Geyer's next message pickup, "Lieutenant Roberts suffering with bad case of dermatitis venenata." The captain and half the command were pocked with skin ulcers. On September 25 rapids and a forty-foot jutting rock made it impossible to portage along the flooded banks, and the patrol dragged their burdens through four miles of trackless jungle.

On the twenty-seventh, they received a mail and ration drop, and with them information that Moore's body had washed up at Huaspuc with "three bullet holes in head." The next day an overland patrol with a full pack train arrived to evacuate the sick, more than half the men, and to inform Geyer that regiment had canceled the expedition; "abandoned [it]," Colonel Dunlap explained to the men, "not because you have wanted to turn back, but because the perils and dangers yet to be encountered . . . appear to be too great to warrant higher command authorizing any further advance."

Geyer loaded everyone and everything onto the mules and burned his boats. On October 9 they were finally back at Ocotal. "Entire unit played out," he wrote. "Men who are still left in terrible physical condition. Shoes entirely worn out. Men need rest and lots of it. Morale is still excellent. The spirit is and has been unbelievable."

The time for the 1928 elections drew near and the brigade braced for its expected disruption by the *Sandinistas*; it never happened. As with the American-supervised balloting in Cuba and Haiti, the election was a model of democratic efficiency. Early in the year Calvin Coolidge dispatched his special emissary, Brigadier General Frank McCoy, United States Army, to take charge of the operation. McCoy was described by Carleton Beals as "one of these iron-willed, super logical, single-track types whose stern jaw carried not an ounce of compromise."[125]

McCoy, whom the navy and Marine Corps much resented for impinging on what they considered their turf, assembled a Spanish-speaking staff of junior officers: twenty-five army, twenty-nine navy, four Marine Corps, and ten civilians, and set about assembling the election machinery.

Dr. Harold Dodds of Princeton University crafted the election law and Conservative President Adolfo Díaz proclaimed it by executive decree. But his Conservative compatriots resented it. A minority party, they knew well that a fair election would mean a Liberal government. The close supervision the American authorities maintained precluded the methods traditionally employed by the party in power in order to win the election. Further, Conservative prestige had plummeted among the populace. "To an ignorant voter," Dr. Dodds said giving his explanation for the decline in popularity, "a government which could not favor its workers was not entitled to respect." In fact, McCoy so stretched traditional methods that he permitted the Liberal outs free use of the national telegraph and telephone system; these had always been the exclusive tools of the governing party.[126]

Internal squabbles within the Conservative ranks brought forth a compromise candidate, a wealthy planter named Adolfo Bernard who was known as the "Sugar King of Nicaragua." He had no real chance. The clear choice for the Liberals was General José María Moncada.

To assure a peaceful process, additional reinforcements were culled from every available command. From the Battle Fleet came 950 marines. For special duty in electoral supervision, 270 bluejackets received several months' intensive training in Spanish.

McCoy scheduled voter registration for the two weeks beginning September 23. Seventy percent of the franchise was illiterate so the ballots were designed, Dodds noted, "to enable a man to mark the party of his choice even if he was not able to read and write." To prevent repeaters, each voter, upon registration, had to dip a finger into a pot of yellow dye. President-elect Hoover, touring Latin America, happened to be in Corinto during the period and said to the marine officer who devised the dye scheme, "I lived once in New York and proposed it as a cure for one of Tammany's bad habits, but everybody said it would be insulting."[127]

During the registration, there occurred one incident of disruption by the *Sandinistas*. At San Marcos, near Jinotega, a small guerrilla band killed four Liberal campaign workers and then moved about the region killing indiscriminately. The 45th Company threw out patrols, and by effectively screening the polling places forced the band back into the bush.

McCoy assigned two Spanish-speaking ensigns to each departmental electoral board. The electoral boards were subdivided into 432 precinct boards. Within each precinct was the *mesa*, the voting table. At each *mesa*, an enlisted marine or bluejacket served as *presidente de la mesa*.[128]

On November 3 McCoy prohibited the sale of liquor and all depositories were placed under *guardia* control. The next day Nicaragua voted. This time, instead of the yellow dye, voters dipped their fingers into a pot of red ink and Mercurochrome. *Sandinistas* passed the canard that the stuff was poisoned. But as a Marine Corps historian noted, "only a few superstitious Indians believed them."[129]

Throughout the day, the planes of Aircraft Squadrons, 2nd Brigade, maintained constant contact between the precincts and McCoy's Managua election headquarters. There was a near total absence of the customary intimidation, bribery, and fraud. At day's end the ballots were collected, and under marine escort taken to Managua by plane, lake steamer, trucks, bullcart, and mule.

Fully ninety percent of the franchise voted, the greatest number in Nicaragua's history. Moncada received 76,696 votes, 20,000 more than his Conservative rival. The peace of Tipitapa had come full circle.

The new year, 1929, ushered in ever-increasing difficulties. Lieutenant Colonel Clyde Metcalf, commanding the eastern area, wrote, "it was becoming more and more evident that the marines in Nicaragua had been called upon to perform an almost impossible task. . . . They were expected to maintain order—taken to mean the eradication of banditry—without any control over the civilian population . . . officers conducting the campaign were practically unanimous in their opinion that the military situation had reached a stalemate."[130]

In Washington, President-elect Hoover made prompt withdrawal a priority, and in Congress the pressure for it mounted by the day. But in Managua, American authorities feared chaos if the marines were pulled out too soon; the *guardia* must be brought to a higher level of strength and competence before any major reductions in the brigade could be contemplated.

Sandino's bands, chased hither and yon, were compressed, for the time being, into the regions along the Honduran border. On January 1 Moncada, with the full approval of brigade command, shifted the deployment policy of the *guardia*. It would now assume full duties in the field and leave the marines essentially to police and support duties. Immediately the various ships' detachments were withdrawn, and the 2nd Battalion, 5th Marines, temporarily disbanded.

Moncada, however, distrusted the *guardia*; they were, after all, "nonpartisan," and thus had no innate loyalty to *Liberalismo*. With General Feland's concurrence, he began recruiting a corps of *voluntarios*. Their chief virtue, Moncada claimed, was their ability to distinguish "bandits" from "law-abiding inhabitants." Not surprisingly, the new formation met with the strenuous objections of Ambassador Eberhardt, and the *guardia jefe*, Elias Beadle. This private army of Moncada's directly contravened the Tipitapa agreements, and it took no genius to predict that if given free rein it would eventually supersede the *guardia*. Faced with the American legation's political opposition, Moncada trimmed back. The *voluntarios*, he told Eberhardt, would only number "a few hundred," and would not operate independently, but as brigade saw fit.[131]

Feland's acquiescence to the *voluntarios* made public the already deep fissures within the American politico-military establishment in Managua. Eberhardt saw the brigade commander as greatly overstepping his responsibilities, and called him Moncada's "virtual Minister of War and advisor on military and other matters." And Feland's support of the *voluntarios* constituted "a campaign of interference which has seriously damaged the prestige of the Legation, the Guardia, and the Marine Corps itself and which threatens to jeopardize our whole Nicaraguan program." Acting with Eberhardt's advice, the State and Navy departments ordered Feland's and Beadle's relief. Brigadier General Dion Williams, a veteran tropical soldier whose career stretched back to the Battle of Manila Bay, and Colonel Douglas McDougal, lately *chef* of the *Garde d'Haiti*, assumed the brigade and *guardia* commands.[132]

On February 3 the marines achieved a major coup by capturing Manuel Girón. Oddly enough, it was accomplished by another veteran of the Haitian occupation, Lieutenant Herman Hanneken, killer of Charlemagne Péralte. Hanneken, with a small patrol of eight men, had camped by a stream not far from San Albino. While half of them bathed, the others stood guard against the ever possible guerrilla ambush. In mid-morning they spotted a mounted man, head down, asleep in the saddle, ambling down the bank. The swimmers bolted from the water, grabbed their rifles and slipped into the bush. The dozing Girón was pounced and taken prisoner.

A month later he was tried by a Nicaraguan court martial composed of *voluntario* officers, and sentenced to be shot. "I still have my doubts as to the legality of this trial," Hanneken said many years later. Girón died bravely; when asked if he had any last words, he replied to the Nicaraguan officer, "No, you son-of-a-bitch!"[133]

The *voluntarios* were a short-lived organization. Prone to execute "bandit collaborators," they were denounced by the Conservative press as cutthroats and "more bloody" than Sandino's most sanguinary subordinates. By summer, Moncada was forced to disband the corps, and most of the men went to work on road-building projects.

In late May Sandino surprised everyone, *Sandinista*, American, and Nicaraguan government alike, by taking a year's leave in Mexico. Hoping to receive massive military support, he was offered instead political asylum, a house in Yucatán, and little else.

To keep up *Sandinista* morale during his absence, pamphlets were periodically distributed throughout Nicaragua announcing his imminent return. He would lead the uprising against "foreign intervention and the exploitation of the country by the money powers of Nicaragua and Wall Street."[134]

"These pamphlets," said Brigadier Williams, "have all the hackneyed phrases of the communism [sic] and advocate division of property, downfall of government and the soviet rule . . . [they are] doubtless inspired . . . by documents issued by the radical groups of Europe and America."[135]

But there was no doubt that the *Sandinistas* had nevertheless become confused and demoralized through the absence of their leader. Most of the leading *jefes* disbanded and crossed the border for temporary internment in Honduras. Only one band was left to carry on, taking the best rifles and automatic weapons. The rest they stored in the mountains.

With the onset of the spring and the six-month rainy season, guerrilla activity diminished to the extent that only what Williams considered "standard" banditry remained. Increasingly, the *guardia* replaced the marine garrisons in the northern area and newly created central area. The advanced posts in northern Nueva Segovia were also withdrawn. The eastern area pulled in, eliminating the detachments along the Coco and holding west only so far as the mining district.

Major force reductions continued through the summer. The 3rd Battalion, 11th Marines, which were spread from Managua to Ocotal and beyond, disbanded in June; regimental headquarters and the remaining two battalions sailed from Corinto in August. By September 1929 United States military forces had been reduced from nearly 6,000 on the previous election day to 2,215.

Bandit and guerrilla activity, the two at times indistinguishable, traditionally increased with the dry season and its coffee harvest. But active patrolling kept depredations very much to a minimum. General Williams was pleased that "not one single successful raid was accomplished by any of the four bandit groups still known to exist."[136]

But in Nueva Segovia banditry was an age-old occupation; the *Sandinista* rebellion merely served to provide it with a patina of legitimacy. "The new Guardia Nacional," General Williams said, "left these bandits but little time to carry on their depredations or to gain needed rest and the profits were taken out of their trade . . . but it was very difficult to make any close estimate as in many cases a native was a bandit one day and a worker on some coffee *finca* the next day."[137]

In guerrilla war it is virtually impossible to bring the main body of the enemy to battle unless the enemy wishes it. *Guardia* and marine patrols swept back and forth through Nueva Segovia with but minor brushes against small numbers. In an attempt to deny the bandit-guerrillas of sustenance and rural support, President Moncada decided to experiment with a *reconcentrado*, always a hated policy and always doomed to fail. In May 1930 orders went out to the Ocotal area; all locals were to leave their farms and bring their cattle and property into the garrison towns. Anyone found roaming about after June 1 would be considered a bandit.

In Managua, Matthew Hanna, the new American ambassador, an ex–West Pointer as well as education director under Leonard Wood during the Cuban occupation, vehemently protested the measure. It didn't work for Butcher Weyler during the 1895 Cuban revolution; it didn't work for the military government in the Dominican Republic; and it wouldn't work for Moncada in Nicaragua. (It wouldn't work for the Americans in Vietnam, either.) From Matagalpa, the American consul watched the refugees stream out of the restricted areas in a "distressful stampede." But Hanna continued the pressure, and on June 5 the *reconcentrado* orders were quietly withdrawn.

In late May Sandino returned to Nicaragua and the war burst forth anew. On June 18 he led 400 men to a mountaintop just north of Jinotega. A pair of patrolling marine aircraft spotted the concentration and dove to the attack. After expending their ammunition the aircraft dropped a warning message to the town garrison and flew to Managua to raise the alarm. Six planes flew to the mountain and attempted to keep the rebels pinned until the Jinotega column arrived. But the column came too late. Darkness settled in and contact was broken. One guerrilla later taken prisoner said, "We would have captured Jinotega were it not for the airplanes." Sandino, however, was wounded in the leg by a bomb fragment and required the attention of a doctor brought across the border from Honduras.

A general *guardia* offensive produced mixed results. As always some guerrilla bands were scattered, but operations had to be curtailed to provide enough troops for congressional election duty in the fall. The voting turnout, though somewhat less than in 1928, was still quite substantial, and the Liberals gained seats in both houses.

On the last day of 1930 the guerrillas struck a blow that brought far-reaching consequences. A heavily armed marine patrol of ten men started from Ocotal to repair the telephone lines connecting the town with San Fernando. They were ambushed by a *Sandinista* band and eight of the marines were killed; two were wounded and managed to escape. The enemy collected enormous booty: two BARs, a Thompson submachine gun, three Springfield rifles, and eight fully laden mules.

The incident spurred an immediate policy assessment in Washington. Henry Stimson, now Secretary of State, summoned Hanna, Williams, and McDougal home for a conference. Understanding that a military victory over Sandino was impossible without a vast commitment of troops, the Hoover administration was determined to get the marines out of Nicaragua as soon as was practicable. Opposition to the Nicaraguan campaign in the Depression-wracked United States was no longer confined to the editorial pages and halls of government. Large *Sandinista* fund-raising rallies, coordinated by the leftist All-American Anti-Imperialist League, thronged public squares in New York and Washington; hundreds were arrested by the police.

But an immediate evacuation of Nicaragua might well cause a collapse of the Moncada government which the United States had done so much to install, thus Stimson devised a plan for a *phased* pullout. By June 1, 1931, he would withdraw all marines except "an instruction battalion in the city of Managua and the aviation force"; the remainder would depart following the 1932 Nicaraguan presidential elections. In mid-February Stimson slashed the brigade by 1,000 men, and its only ground unit, the 5th Marines, was reduced to its headquarters and an oversized 1st Battalion, with a total of 745 men in five companies.[138]

Not surprisingly, Moncada opposed the reductions and plan for withdrawal. Sandino remained in the field, unbeaten, and without the marines an expanded *guardia* would require enormous resources; in a time of worldwide Depression, little Nicaragua hardly had the money for that.

In the midst of it all, nature struck. At 10:19 A.M. on March 31 the earth opened beneath Managua. For two and a half minutes, a dozen quaking shocks rent the city asunder; its heart, a three-by-five-mile area, was reduced to stones and ashes. The American legation crumbled to its foundation. The scene, described by the chargé, was one of "desolation and terror. People in the street were screaming or appeared to be numbed by shock."[139]

Because the people of Managua are used to earthquakes, many, not realizing the intensity, neglected to seek shelter; nearly 2,000 died and 3,500 were injured. The city maintained no fire department and damage to the pumping system made any fire-fighting endeavor nearly impossible. Marines and *guardia* in the city turned out to rescue trapped citizens and fight what fires they could. The municipal hospital collapsed and the injured were taken to the marine field hospital on the Campo de Marte. Here the marine field kitchens fed the city until United States and Central American Red Cross personnel relieved them of the duty. American medical assistance flew up from the Canal Zone and the carrier *Lexington* launched her planes off the east coast with relief supplies for the city.

From Jinotega, *guardia* Captain Lewis "Chesty" Puller (first lieutenant, USMC) drove down through crowds of fleeing refugees. "These people went away from their city as far as they could," he said, "to the oceans, and Honduras and Costa Rica." At Managua, he was assigned to collect and burn the dead with fuel oil.

Sandino felt no compassion for his dead countrymen. The earthquake, he announced to his followers, "clearly demonstrates to the doubters that divine gestures are guiding our actions in Nicaragua."[140]

While the world's attention was focused on Managua, Sandino launched an offensive to the east with the object of seizing Cape Gracias at the mouth of the Coco. From bases near Bocay, 150 guerrillas pushed downstream toward the coast. From the mining district a second band, looting and pillaging as they went, advanced into the Wawa River country just upstream from Puerto Cabezas. Here a marine and *guardia* patrol was ambushed near Logtown. Aircraft located the enemy and killed seven, but did not stop them. A *guardia* detachment rushed up from Bluefields, and to protect the town in their absence, the *Sacramento* put ashore her landing force. There were several major clashes along the logging railroad between the *guardia* and guerrillas, and air support proved decisive. But for a time it seemed that Puerto Cabezas itself was in imminent danger of capture. Civilians took to the craft in the harbor, and their fear was only alleviated when the gunboat *Asheville* landed her bluejackets.

To the north, the Coco River band of forty men with ten rifles overran the small *guardia* post fronting Cape Gracias and took the town without firing a shot. Marine aircraft disturbed their looting but did little damage to the rebels. The brunt of the guerrilla operations at the cape fell upon the Standard Fruit Company. A dozen employees were killed, including eight Americans. Most of the *guardia* were fighting south around Logtown and Puerto Cabezas, and the company begged for United States protection. Henry Stimson said no. Though a Republican to his fingertips, he considered the American entrepreneurs on the Mosquito Coast "a pampered lot of people who think they have a right to call for troops whenever any danger apprehends." Still, he agreed to send the *Asheville* north, but the rebels had already gone.[141]

Stimson's refusal to recommit substantial American forces inaugurated a radical departure from a policy stretching back to the nineteenth century isthmian treaties with Colombia. The United States government, he cabled the legation, "cannot undertake general protection of Americans throughout [Nicaragua] with American forces. To do so would lead to difficulties and commitments which this Government does not propose to undertake." There would be no more marines for Nicaragua.[142]

Emboldened by the lack of American response, the *Sandinistas* raided every department north of Managua, hitting and plundering a series of undermanned *guardia* posts. *Guardia* and civilian prisoners received summary Sandino machete justice, usually dismemberment, decapitation, or disembowelment. "Liberty," said the messianic *jefe*, "is not conquered with flowers." The "bandit situation," cabled the American chargé, "appears as grave, or graver than at any time I have been in Nicaragua."[143]

In August guerrilla bands moved to within striking distance of the Managua–Corinto railroad. Three months later they crossed it and Managua panicked. Moncada called for volunteers, who were incorporated as *guardia* auxiliaries. Stimson authorized the marines to serve as train guards; it seemed the old intervention cycle was being renewed, but the Secretary held fast in his refusal to commit more troops. The *guardia* marched north from León and, following several inconclusive skirmishes, the guerrillas melted away.

Election day drew near. President Moncada, constitutionally prohibited from succeeding himself, proposed a convention to modify the inconvenient law. The Nicaraguan Congress, packed by the Liberals, would doubtless have promulgated the president's wishes. This infuriated the Conservatives and they threatened an election boycott. Ambassador Hanna averted the crisis by bringing members of both factions to dinner at the legation. "All the loss of American lives and treasure," the chargé ruminated, "would avail nothing in bringing peace to Nicaragua so long as this senseless enmity between the two parties continued."[144]

President Moncada arrived accompanied, the chargé noted, by "aides and by a squad of guards armed with rifles and submachine guns. The guards proceeded to station themselves at strategic locations inside and outside the Legation."[145]

The Conservatives' guest list included Adolfo Díaz and Emiliano Chamorro. What began at the soup course as a three-way mutual detestation ended amicably by dessert, and Moncada dropped his idea for a constitutional convention. In Washington the Hoover administration went ahead with plans to supervise the election. But Congress refused to allocate funds for 500 additional troops and the burden again fell upon the *guardia* to provide election security.

The spring and summer of 1932 witnessed almost continuous fighting in nearly every Nicaraguan department; there were over 100 clashes between April and September. Nicaraguan politicians, perhaps in part because they put aside their hereditary fractiousness, knew that whoever won the election still had to deal with Sandino. They hammered together an arrangement whereby the victor would share the spoils and responsibility of government with the minority party, and they called for a united front against *Sandinismo*. The temporary coalition also knew there was no chance of a *guardia* military victory in the field and attempted another course. They made an offer to the rebels to participate in the elections and subsequent government. "Peaceful and conciliatory methods are to be preferred," noted the political leadership, "and an effort will be made to treat with Sandino along these lines immediately."[146]

Sandino agreed to the gist of their overtures, but he communicated counteroffers that ended all hope of cooperation. He insisted that *all* marines be withdrawn prior to the election; and, if not satisfied with the voting, he vowed to forcibly install his own presidential choice, an elderly exile long removed from the political fray, to head a government of "national unity." The coalition rejected the counteroffer and the parties nominated their standard war horses, Adolfo Díaz for the Conservatives and Dr. Juan Sacasa for the Liberals.

In the weeks prior to the election, guerrilla raids increased to alarming proportions. In September they hit a railroad construction camp northeast of León and struck about the banks of Lake Managua.

At Jinotega, Chesty Puller's *guardia* Company M (Mobile) embarked on what would be called a "search and destroy" mission during the Vietnam War. Company M was the most successful of all the *guardia* formations, taking the war directly to the enemy in a series of constant, aggressive patrols. Puller, to guardsman and *Sandinista* alike, went by the nickname "El Tigre," and Sandino laid a price of 5,000 pesos on his head. Of El Tigre and Company M the wildest atrocity stories abounded. Puller was accused of offering a bounty to his troops for *Sandinista* ears, which the *guardia* allegedly wore as trophies on their belts.

In late September an aged local pointed out to Puller what purported to be an old Indian trail. Puller investigated and found sections newly hacked, unconnected, and seemingly headed nowhere; he knew it was a main guerrilla supply route. Puller fitted the company for an extended march, and with forty men and eighteen pack mules headed out of Jinotega.

Along the trail they found well-prepared but abandoned guerrilla camps and pushed on. "We were picked up by two bandit scouts," Puller said, "who kept ahead of us for a day and a half. . . .

From the time we were picked up, I knew that we would be ambushed at any moment."[147]

The first clash came at mid-morning on September 26. At Río Ayubal a guerrilla band estimated at eighty men fired one rifle volley and bolted. Puller believed "this was an effort to get the officers of the company."[148]

An hour later, as Puller and his men crossed another stream, the major contact began. Puller was the second man in the point. The guardsman in front shouted the alarm and the two men dropped to the ground. Directly ahead, Puller saw an enemy machine gunner take aim and fire. "I wasn't as good a man as that Indian [guardsman] ahead of me," he remembered. "He saved my life by yelling, and I could have saved Rodriquez, but I just dropped. When I looked behind me I saw a sheet of blood; those machine gun bullets had stitched the bugler's body, every two inches, running from the groin up to the head. They literally cut him to pieces."[149]

By the volume of their fire, Puller estimated the patrol faced at least 150 guerrillas with at least seven automatic weapons, numerous rifle and hand grenades, a couple of hundred dynamite bombs, "and a great quantity of rifle ammunition." Aside from the dead bugler, three guardsmen, including his second in command, Bill Lee, who was shot in the head and arm, fell wounded. Fire from the front was matched by a storm of grenades and bombs the guerrillas hurled down a steep ridge to the right.[150]

For about fifteen minutes the company lay in its exposed position and returned fire. "During the fight," Puller recalled, "when a bandit was hit, you could hear the machete men being called to drag them off. The machete platoons were also being urged to charge the company." Bill Lee, thought to be dead, regained consciousness and managed to slash a Lewis gun off a pack mule. He used it, as Puller said, "with telling effect." Under Lee's base of fire, Puller ordered his men to charge the ridge, and they advanced up the slope against a withering hail. Gaining the heights, more guerrillas opened fire on their rear. The guardsmen faced about and raked the opposite ridge with their rifles and grenades. Enemy fire slackened and then ceased. Puller counted sixteen enemy dead and traces of many more wounded. "The company cleared the bandits from their position, went forward to a ridge that crossed the road, established outposts, took care of the wounded, and buried [in a concealed grave] *Raso* Rodriquez."[151]

If not for the wounded, Puller would have continued the pursuit. The men fashioned litters from clothing, blankets, and poles and prepared to march back to Jinotega. "We will take these men back," he said, "eight men to a stretcher, so that no one will be worn out. No stretcher is to be put on the ground without orders from me. Any man who drops a stretcher will be shot." Some years later Puller expounded on this before a class of new Marine Corps officers, "You can never stop, you've got to keep going, when you're carrying wounded on the trail."[152]

On the back march to Jinotega, the company was ambushed again by at least eighty guerrillas. "The [enemy] Indians," Puller noted, "were brave and intelligent, and laid perfect traps, but they were excitable, and not accustomed to [their] weapons. They usually fired high. If we'd been in their shoes, we'd have wiped out any passing patrol." Bill Lee, momentarily recovered from his wounds but lacking the use of an arm, brought the Lewis gun into action. The fight took ten minutes and the enemy broke contact, leaving one dead and eight wounded. On October 1, after marching 120 miles, Company M returned to Jinotega. So far had evacuation procedures progressed in the war against Sandino that the wounded were loaded into a trimotor Ford "Tin Goose" for a quick flight to the field hospital at Managua.[153]

On November 6, 1932, the voters elected the Liberal Dr. Juan Sacasa President of the Republic of Nicaragua. Nine days later Sacasa announced the first Nicaraguan *jefe* of the National Guard, Anastasio Somoza.

One of President Moncada's last official acts was the dedication of a new railroad line from León northeast to El Sauce, and rumors circulated of a Sandino plan to disrupt the ceremony and tear up the line. A day after Christmas, Puller, with seven marine officers and sixty-four picked guardsmen, entrained for El Sauce to secure the area. Not all the spikes were driven into the track, and when the engineer hesitated to cross a bridge, Puller held a pistol to the man's head.

In late afternoon as the train pulled up the last grade, 100 guerrillas were already in the town ransacking the shops. Their *jefe*, hearing the approach of the train and thinking it lightly guarded, sent half his men to effect a capture. When the engine passed some ruins, the rebel machine guns opened fire from both sides of the track. Bill Lee, atop the boxcar, called for a BAR; it jammed after one round. Lee jumped down, hit the receiver with a rock, and commenced firing.

Mounted rebels circled the train, firing "Indian fashion" from under the necks of their horses. "I'll bet this is the first Indian attack on a train in fifty years," Puller said amidst the racket. The guardsmen piled out of the coach and deployed left and right into an advancing skirmish line. After an hour they threw the enemy back, leaving thirty-one dead *Sandinistas* and capturing sixty-three horses. It was the last fight of the intervention.[154]

President Moncada and party arrived three days later and insisted Puller conduct him on a tour of the battlefield. "I [had] spent the better part of two days cleaning up," Puller said. "I dragged the animal carcasses down the hill for burial, and even had them level up the torn earth." But the president seemed disappointed. A marine officer came up to Puller, "Where are all the bodies—and the dead animals? It doesn't look like much of a battlefield. He wants to see some gore."[155]

On January 1, 1933, the inauguration of Dr. Sacasa took place on the field fronting La Loma fort. Hours before, at dawn, Cuckoo Boyden led out Flight C—five Corsairs, one Boeing FB-5 fighter, and a Tin Goose loaded with mechanics—for the hopping flight to Quantico, Virginia. In all, three flights took off that day, a total of twenty-two aircraft. The next morning, the 1st Battalion, 5th Marines, boarded their transports at Corinto, and the Nicaraguan intervention came to an end. In six years, United States forces had engaged in 150 combats and suffered 136 dead from all causes.

The lessons of Nicaragua remained with the Marine Corps for decades. The campaign underscored the necessity for tactics utilizing small units with limited means and this theory of fighting marked the technique of the Corps through the 1930's, serving them well in the jungles of Guadalcanal. And for years afterward every new officer was required to learn Spanish or at least "bullcart Spanish" as the old salts called it.

The marines also made giant strides in aviation in Nicaragua. Many of the aerial tactics and techniques they employed had been used before, but never to the same degree of coordination and frequency as the Aircraft Squadrons, 2nd Brigade.

Most important were the strong political motives of the Nicaraguan foe. For the first time, the United States and its force agency, the Marine Corps, encountered a modern, charismatic guerrilla leader with an international reputation. Ruthless, self-serving, and mentally unbalanced, Sandino nevertheless embodied a nationalistic ideal that could not be defeated on the battlefield. It was a lesson learned by Henry Stimson in 1932 and forgotten by Lyndon Johnson in 1965.

Immediately after the marines had gone, the Sacasa government opened negotiations with Sandino. The president was pessimistic but sincere; General Somoza and the *guardia* were openly hostile toward Sandino. On February 2 Sandino flew to the capital and, amidst the rejoicing of the citizens, signed a truce. He agreed to surrender a portion of his weapons, and save for a personal guard of 100 men, to disband his soldiery, which now numbered 1,800 followers.

On February 21, 1934, following a dinner with President Sacasa, Sandino, his brother Sócrates, and two former *Sandinista* generals were kidnapped on Somoza's orders. They were taken to the airfield and killed by a *guardia* machine gun firing squad.

8:

DOMINICAN REPUBLIC II
1965

It's bad enough we can't tell a good guy from a bad guy, but on top of that they're all over the place!

—U.S. marine

Between 1933 and 1965, United States forces played no role in active combat or pacification in Central America or the Caribbean basin. Indeed, the second Nicaragua campaign ends the classic period of the Banana Wars, and what follows are but epilogues. Yet the success of Fidel Castro's Cuban Revolution in 1959 inevitably brought rising tensions to the area, as well as to the White House and State Department.

In 1961 the brutal Dominican dictator and former National Guardsman, Rafael Trujillo, was assassinated by disgruntled subordinates. Only two out of twenty conspirators survived the subsequent manhunt, initiated and directed by the dictator's son. For a time the Trujillo family attempted to retain their hold, but their grip weakened and a provisional government took the reins. When a coup by the Trujillo family attempted its ouster, President Kennedy, with the tacit consent of most hemispheric governments, ordered naval and Marine Corps units to the Dominican coast.

In December 1962 the intellectual and ardently nationalist leftist reformer Juan Bosch was elected president. Within seven months he was ousted by a rightist military coup, which heralded several short-lived juntas. The failed juntas, in turn, elevated a civilian businessman, Donald Reid Cabral, who, with military support, assumed the presidency.

But the Dominican people, having had, with Bosch's brief term, their first taste of democracy in three decades, were restive

362

and unhappy with Reid Cabral. Plot and counterplot against him formed, flared, and died with dizzying rapidity. A United States Army intelligence report concluded, "It is extremely doubtful that the Dominican Republic, still in a state of political immaturity, will achieve any semblance of political stability in the foreseeable future."[1]

In April 1965 a small group of officers and enlisted men loyal to Juan Bosch arrested the army chief of staff, seized the radio station, and proclaimed a revolution. Although Reid Cabral had taken office with the army's support, the army did nothing to maintain his power. After desperately requesting American military intervention, Cabral resigned and went into hiding. The army then moved to crush the rebels, and large-scale street fighting ensued in the capital.

The United States' response to events reflected Lyndon Johnson's obsessive fear of the spread of Castro-style communism; it was incorrectly assumed, mainly through highly inaccurate embassy reports, that Bosch was a Castro-supporting communist. But for the Johnson administration, the prospect of dealing with corrupt, reactionary military juntas was even more odious.

On April 27 Dominican army units, including tanks, converged on the rebel centers and rumors of Bosch's return brought out the Dominican Air Force in a strafing attack on the Presidential Palace. For a time the American embassy came under fire. That noon, the rebel leadership entered the American embassy and requested that Ambassador William Tapley Bennett use his good offices in ending the conflict. The rebels had been willing to agree to a cease-fire, but quickly changed their minds when subjected to the ambassador's insulting remarks regarding their "irresponsibility"; they then resolved to continue the fight.

The situation rapidly deteriorated. Armed mobs of every faction roamed the streets of Santo Domingo, sniping at each other from the rooftops. A military junta organized at San Isidro airport made vain attempts at putting the rebellion down. At the Duarte Bridge, just upstream from old Fort Ozama, the rebels stopped the army's advance. There came another appeal for American intervention, this time by the anti-Bosch, San Isidro officers. The communists, they claimed, had taken over the revolt. While there were certainly communists in the rebel ranks, their numbers and influence were greatly exaggerated.

With the army and police temporarily neutralized, Santo Domingo was left without any semblance of order. Diplomats from the embassies of Mexico, Peru, Guatemala, and Ecuador feared for the security of their nationals. Ambassador Bennett offered the service of an American evacuation, and they gladly accepted.

The embassy reports, coupled with the San Isidro plea, convinced Lyndon Johnson that not only were American lives in jeopardy, but the prestige and security of the United States were on the line. He invoked his ill-formed Johnson Doctrine, which permitted unilateral intervention in any Latin American country menaced by an internal communist threat. "The American nations," he said in a television address, "cannot, must not, and will not permit the establishment of another communist government in the Western Hemisphere." It was nothing but a reconfigured, dusted off version of the old Roosevelt Corollary.[2]

Off the east coast of Puerto Rico, in the lee of Vieques Island, lay the Caribbean Ready Group: the ships and embarked units of Amphibious Squadron 10. The broad pennant of Captain James Dare, PhibRon 10's commodore, flew from the old *Essex* class carrier *Boxer*,* her configuration hardly changed from the last years of World War II. But now, instead of fighters and torpedo bombers, she carried the twenty-one helicopters of a marine medium helicopter squadron, HMM-264, the Black Knights. Around the carrier lay the rest of the squadron, an odd-looking lot of old and new. Most striking were the asymmetrical dock landing ships *Raleigh* and *Fort Snelling*, each capable of flooding their well decks and disgorging landing craft heavily laden with tanks, artillery, and heavy equipment. More familiar in appearance was the LST *Wood County*, her sides girthed with portable mooring piers. Two World War II veterans completed the squadron: the high-speed transport *Ruchamkin*, originally a destroyer escort, and the freighter-like attack cargo ship *Rankin*. All were in the final stages of backloading the troops, the reinforced battalion landing team formed around the 3rd Battalion, 6th Marines, BLT 3/6, less Company M at Guantánamo Bay.

Around midnight on April 24 Captain Dare received a message alerting the squadron to the potentially dangerous situation in Santo Domingo. In the morning there came orders to steam with the *Boxer* and "appropriate ships" for the evacuation of approximately 1,200 American civilians.[3]

In conference with BLT commander Lieutenant Colonel Poul Pedersen, Captain Dare recalled, "The big question became: What

---

*The author served on board with BLT 1/6 in 1962.

should [we] land in order to assure an orderly, safe evacuation? [We] did not know what the opposition looked like, nor even how many there were. Indications were that the dissident Dominicans were rather grouchy with each other and not with Americans. If [we] were to land an armed contingent, [we] might really start something." To meet all possible contingencies, Dare sent the *Rankin* and *Fort Snelling* to cover the north and east coast ports. But as it happened, all the action occurred at Santo Domingo.[4]

While the ships steamed, the Joint Chiefs of Staff increased the readiness condition of the army's 82nd Airborne Division's 3rd Brigade at Fort Bragg, North Carolina.

In the early hours of the twenty-sixth, PhibRon 10 arrived on station, ten miles to sea and out of sight. Not knowing what reception they might receive from government or rebel forces, the ships assumed a threat readiness, with partial air and surface batteries manned and ready; they were repeatedly snooped by the Dominican Air Force. "At least some of the local force knew who was there," Dare said.[5]

Ashore, the embassy alerted all American citizens to prepare for evacuation at the Hotel El Embajador, which was at the extreme western end of the city. Fronting a golf course and polo field, it made an excellent site for a helicopter landing zone. But at sunrise Dare received welcome permission from the Dominican Navy giving free access to the port of Haina, about six miles down the coast. He adjusted his evacuation plans and gave the job to the *Ruchamkin* and *Wood County*.

At Santo Domingo, the other ships moved closer in, five miles offshore, and watched government planes bomb and strafe the rebel positions around the Presidential Palace. At the El Embajador, armed rebels entered the hotel, where Americans were already gathered, searching for an "anti-Communist" editor who was reported hiding amongst the evacuees. They terrorized civilians, fired some shots into the ceiling and threatened to shoot the men. Just before noon, Admiral Thomas Moorer, Commander in Chief, Atlantic (CINCLANT), ordered Dare to begin the evacuation.

To assure an orderly process, and at the same time to prevent any escalation of violence, Dare and Pedersen decided to land a "control element" with the ships at Haina, unarmed squads from Company K "in fatigue dress." Orders were, "No helmets, no pistol belts."[6]

In early afternoon the evacuation commenced. Bus, truck, and auto convoys brought the civilians to Haina, and by 6:30 P.M. nearly 600 American nationals were taken on board the *Ruchamkin* and *Wood County*. During the operation Ambassador Bennett requested that the *Boxer* and *Raleigh* move within easy visual distance of downtown Santo Domingo. "This show of force," said Dare, "was conducted under circumstances which would turn any skipper's hair grey. As the . . . ships approached, it seemed as though the ambassador had the con. He repeatedly called for a closer view of the U.S. ships."[7]

The next day, in late afternoon, sniper fire erupted around the embassy. Worse, the National Police informed Ambassador Bennett that they could no longer give protection along the evacuation route from the hotel to Haina. The ambassador requested that operations be switched to the polo field and requested 300 marines to bolster embassy security. "From that minute on," said the skipper of HMM-264, Lieutenant Colonel Fred Kleppsattel, "we were really in business."[8]

Within minutes a pathfinder element and another of Company K's unarmed squads were in the air. For Kleppsattel, this was cutting it a bit thin, and he received permission to carry the marines' automatic weapons in stowed boxes on board his helicopters. After bringing in the first evacuees from the polo field, the Black Knights loaded up with two of L Company's platoons, fully armed and reinforced with two squads of Company K, and headed back. All day the shuttling continued, women and children flown out, and the remainder of K and L companys plus the battalion headquarters and two sections of 81mm mortars flown in. They secured the hotel area without incident. For the first time in history, armed marines had landed by "vertical envelopment" in combat conditions into an unsecured perimeter. Just after midnight, Colonel Pedersen sent a "clutch" platoon from Headquarters and Service Company to reinforce the embassy guard.

The Haina evacuees had been shifted to the *Raleigh* for a "safe haven" at San Juan, Puerto Rico, but the *Boxer* was jammed with the polo field people, 684 of them. It had been a long day for the Black Knights. "Following debriefing," Kleppsattel said, "the pilots hit the pad wherever they could find a soft spot. The ship had given all available cabin spaces to the women evacuees. Many of the weary pilots slept in the ready room chairs or in their aircraft on the hangar deck."[9]

Late that night, at Camp Lejeune, North Carolina, orders came to activate the headquarters of the 4th Marine Expeditionary Brigade. BLTs 1/6 and 1/8 would go by air, BLT 1/2 by sea. PhibRons 8 and 12 loaded up 1/2 and the brigade's heavy equipment and headed south. Provisional Marine Air Group-60—one attack, one fighter, and two helicopter squadrons—would provide additional support.

In early afternoon on the twenty-ninth, the embassy came under heavy rebel small-arms fire, which was returned by the marines. Ambassador Bennett called for more forces and the 3rd Airborne Brigade boarded their big C-130 Hercules transports and prepared to drop at San Isidro airfield, the junta headquarters, northeast of the city.

The *Raleigh*, with I Company on board, returned from San Juan; the *Rankin* and *Fort Snelling* came in from the quiet points about the coasts. With all forces concentrated, Dare and Pedersen commenced Operation BARREL BOTTOM, the expansion of the landing zone perimeter at the polo field. At high speed, the ships moved to their assault positions off the mouth of the Haina River and began offloading I Company and the BLT's tanks, trucks, artillery, and Ontos* antitank vehicles into landing craft. Once on the beach, the units formed an armored column and headed northeast for the polo field.

Shortly after midnight on April 30 the 3rd Airborne Brigade began its landing at San Isidro. Plans had originally called for a parachute drop, but with the field in "friendly" hands, this was altered to an air landing en route. Major General Robert York, commanding the 82nd, was designated commander of all United States ground forces.

Once in, the airborne brigade secured the airfield and then advanced west to the Duarte Bridge, which crossed the Ozama River, establishing cordons and roadblocks to deny the rebels access to the bridge. With the airborne troops in the east and the marines in the west, the city center remained essentially a no-man's-land.

Vice Admiral Kleber Masterson, commanding the Second Fleet, broke his flag in the *Boxer,* took overall command of the operation, and ordered a linkup of the forces; nothing larger than

---

*Ontos, the Greek word for "thing," was a small, extremely potent tracked vehicle mounting six 106mm recoilless rifles.

small-caliber arms were to be fired unless higher authority gave permission.

In three prongs and preceded by tanks, Ontoses and armored landing vehicles (LVT), BLT 3/6 advanced from the polo field to positions beyond the embassy. Near the old city airport, I Company took some rebel fire and requested permission to use heavy-caliber weapons. Hours later permission came, though for 3.5-inch rocket launchers only. Under heavy rebel fire, 3/6 moved forward, hugging garden walls and moving from tree to tree.

The linkup was established between the embassy and the Duarte Bridge, and the whole area from the polo field to the embassy was declared an international safety zone. Immediately north of the zone, a thin, two-mile strip connected the marine and airborne units. The marines called it the Corridor; the airborne troopers named it after their divisional nickname, the All American Express. Holding the strip and moving through it occupied the troops for the rest of the mission.

The marines and soldiers sealed off the Corridor's side streets by building roadblocks of anything they could find: overturned cars, some ancient Dominican field guns, furniture, logs, cement blocks, coils of barbed wire. Key intersections were covered by machine guns and 106mm recoilless rifles. Along the way the locals painted every wall with political slogans. There were several that read YANKEES, GO FIGHT IN VIETNAM, as well as the more common YANKEE GO HOME. When asked to comment on the sentiments expressed by the Dominican graffiti, one 82nd trooper said, "I think it's a good idea. I'm ready to go home any time. But I guess we're going to be around awhile yet, so I just ignore it."[10]

Snipers became extremely bothersome. A sergeant from A Company, BLT 1/8, told a reporter, "Bedcheck Charlie didn't hold taps last night. Usually he pops out of somewhere right about dusk and fires a few rounds into the street and our area. But last night he took a break. The people were pretty happy, and didn't drag all the kids in. They sat on the steps and sang, played guitars, and just generally lived it up. I thought they'd finally get around to roping off the Corridor and having a street dance."[11]

But when the snipers reappeared, the business became deadly serious. "Turn those glasses on the door and keep them there," yelled a marine on the street to another on a rooftop.

"It's opening! Sight in on him," yelled back the roof observer.

But the marines didn't shoot; orders said the rebels must fire first. A round whizzed by, the door shut, and the sniper disappeared. "Lost him," said the marine on the street. "Have to wait until his next shot."

From the roof came another hail. "The door's opening again. Stand by." Another shot, but the door didn't close fast enough. From atop a tank turret came the dull bop, bop, bop of a .50 caliber machine gun.

"You're too low, come up—come up! Good! You're on!" The door was torn from its hinges.

"That should take care of him," said the marine on the street. "I don't think he got out of there. He's either stupid, brave or dead, but if you want to bet, I'd say he's dead."[12]

From the onset of hostilities the United States worked to arrange a cease-fire but this was always frustrated by the rebels. Ambassador Bennett's relations with them were of the worst kind, prompting Lyndon Johnson to send ex-Ambassador John Martin, a political liberal with close ties to the anti-Trujillo factions, to open negotiations with them. With Martin came an Organization of American States (OAS) Peace Committee, with representatives from Argentina, Colombia, Guatemala, and Panama. On May 5 they brought the rebels and junta together to sign a formal truce, the Act of Santo Domingo. A provisional government was established under the aegis of the junta. But within a fortnight the junta broke the peace and drove the main rebel body from the capital. The United States forces holding the zone were accused, depending on who hurled the charges, of aiding both sides in the action.

In mid-month a majority of the OAS voted for Operation PUSH AHEAD, the reduction of United States forces and their replacement by an Inter-American Peace Force (IAPF). On May 14 the first contingent, a Honduran rifle company, arrived. By the end of May they were bolstered by detachments from Costa Rica, El Salvador, and Nicaragua. Brazil provided the largest unit, a full reinforced infantry battalion. Its commander, Brigadier General Hugo Alvim, assumed command of all OAS ground forces, which now included nearly 15,000 American airborne troops, and 8,000 marines.

On May 26 United States forces began their withdrawal. First to go were the first to come, BLT 3/6. By June 9 the last had returned to their bases. "BLT 1/6 arrived at Morehead City," [North Carolina], reported its skipper, "and offloaded for Camp Lejeune."[13]

9:

GRENADA
1983

We are a zero-defect military and we simply cannot
accept that any mistakes could have been made.

–Anonymous American officer

Tiny Grenada sits at the bottom of the Windward
Islands, at the southeastern extremity of the Caribbean. Note-
worthy as the supplier of one-third of the world's nutmeg, Grenada had never, before 1983, played a role in the hemispheric
politics of the United States, and until granted dominion status
in 1974, remained an obscure backwater of the British Empire.

Since decolonization, its government, headed by Prime Minister Sir Eric Gairy (an eccentric man who believed in UFOs)
dominated the island's politics and remained firmly pro-West. Yet
within five years, Gairy's penchant for self-aggrandizement, and
his free use of gangs to intimidate the citizenry, cost him virtually
all popular support.

In March of 1979, Maurice Bishop, leader of the leftist opposition New JEWEL (Joint Endeavor for Welfare, Education
and Liberation) movement, took advantage of Gairy's temporary
absence from the island and staged a bloodless coup. He assured
the Grenadans economic and political reforms, promising to turn
the island into a socialist democracy. With its new government,
the nation lurched sharply leftward. Both Bishop and Deputy
Prime Minister Bernard Coard were protégés of Fidel Castro,
and Cuba quickly offered diplomatic, military, and economic assistance.

A month after the coup, the first Cuban military shipments

arrived: 3,400 AK-47 rifles, 200 machine guns, 100 assorted heavy weapons, including anti-aircraft and antitank guns, half a dozen Russian BTR-60 armored cars, and a mountain of ammunition. More important and troublesome to the United States was Cuba's promise to construct a major airfield at Point Salines, on the island's southwest tip. When completed it would be capable of handling the biggest of jumbo jets. According to Bishop, it was intended to encourage a fledgling tourist industry. The United States was not convinced. The field clearly had military potential, and indeed Cuba planned to use it as a refueling and logistic depot for its troop lifts to Africa.

By year's end, Bishop had officially sanctioned Grenada's political realignment by declaring a new revolutionary course, based on the Cuban model. He concentrated all power in the New JEWEL, stifled the opposition, and reneged on his promise to hold free elections. East Bloc and "nonaligned" advisors poured in: Cubans, Russians, North Koreans, East Germans, Bulgarians, and Libyans. Cuba provided the largest contingent, nearly 800, most of whom were a paramilitary construction battalion for work on the airfield.

In May 1980 Coard traveled to Moscow and signed a treaty permitting the Russians to land and service long-range reconnaissance aircraft when the Point Salines airfield was finished. In the United States, the agreement stoked some fears of a Caribbean "Red Triangle," with Cuba, Nicaragua, and now Grenada holding the points. The State Department considered the situation irritating, but hardly of crisis proportions. Aside from providing additional economic and security assistance to Grenada's tiny neighboring democracies who were concerned over the course of events, they turned their attention elsewhere.

But in Ronald Reagan's White House, the anticommunist crusaders, notably Assistant Secretary of State Elliott Abrams, and CIA director William Casey, became obsessed. The CIA initiated a propaganda and economic plan to destabilize Bishop's government. It was very similar to the one used against Fidel Castro when he first came to power, and had the Grenadan plan been put into effect would have had the same result: none, save for pushing it further, if that were possible, into the red camp. The Senate Intelligence Committee refused to give the CIA authority to implement the plan; Grenada was just not that important. Ronald Reagan disagreed. "It isn't nutmeg that's at stake in the Caribbean and Central America," he said in the spring of 1983, "it's U.S. national security."[1]

By that time, Prime Minister Bishop had grown disillusioned with the increasingly Marxist tone of his government and sought closer ties to the West. In June, to defuse the ever-increasing bellicosity coming from the Reagan White House, he journeyed, without invitation, to Washington and met with several high-ranking members of the National Security Council (NSC).

The visit widened an already divisive split within the New JEWEL movement over the communist connection. On October 13 Bernard Coard, who led the East Bloc faction, ordered Bishop to resign, charging the prime minister with failing to carry out the directives of the Grenadan Central Committee. Bishop refused, and on Caord's orders he was placed under house arrest. Several cabinet ministers resigned in protest and were in turn arrested. The next several days saw large-scale, pro-Bishop demonstrations. It has been suggested that Fidel Castro initiated the anti-Bishop coup but there is no evidence to support this. The Russians, however, might have had some advance knowledge.

On the day of the coup the State Department convened an interagency conference to discuss the status of the nearly 1,000 Americans in Grenada, of whom about 600 were students at the St. George University School of Medicine. There was no indication that they were in any danger, but it was thought best to prepare contingencies for evacuation.

The following morning Rear Admiral John Poindexter, the NSC's deputy chief, chaired a Crisis Preplanning Group of mid-level staffers from both the NSC and the Joint Chiefs of Staff (JCS). The participants included an obscure NSC Marine Corps officer, Major Oliver North, and his partner, Constantine Menges, a right-wing ideologue, transferred from the CIA where he had been known as "Constant Menace." Using the pretext of rescuing the students, Menges, it seems, put forward the idea of a military operation to topple Grenada's Marxist government. The U.S. military's adoption of this confused, dual mission would result in a bungled, uncontrolled operation, employing massive resources that far exceeded the importance of the tiny island nation to the United States.

That evening, Vice President Bush convened the Special Situations Group, the executive branch's highest crisis management unit made up of senior White House staff, cabinet members, NSC,

CIA, and representatives of the Joint Chiefs of Staff. Uppermost on the agenda was a worst-case scenario whereby the students would be taken hostage in a mirror image of the Teheran embassy debacle. The main military options discussed were a "surgical strike"—a "permissive" or "nonpermissive" evacuation of the students—or, barring that, a full-scale, single, or dual-purpose, invasion.*

General John Vessey, the old World War II soldier and Chairman of the Joint Chiefs of Staff, warned that a surgical strike would be impossible; the whole island would have to be taken, and the Grenadan military, such as it was, would hardly sit placidly by. Defense Secretary Caspar Weinberger was opposed to any military operation. There was no legal justification, he maintained, for an invasion. Fear of the students' safety and the obvious military nature of the Point Salines airfield were not enough.

Still, JCS began to shift forces. The carrier *Independence* battle group and PhibRon 4, carrying the 22nd Marine Amphibious Unit (MAU),** which was built around the 2nd Battalion, 8th Marines (BLT 2/8), were diverted from their voyage to the Middle East and ordered south. Then, if only for political reasons, an informal consensus within the Special Situations Group began shifting to Vessey's purely military view. The CIA's William Casey was very enthusiastic. "Hey, fuck it," he allegedly said, referring to Coard and the New JEWEL. "Let's dump these bastards."† The JCS were ordered to plan a nonpermissive evacuation, and operational control was vested in Commander in Chief, Atlantic (CINCLANT), Admiral Wesley McDonald.[2]

If the medical students were to be the official reason for military action, in whatever form, it behooved the planners to get a complete roster and as much background information on them as possible; that job was given to Menges and North of the NSC.

To obtain this information, Menges and North plugged into the right-wing, anticommunist crusader network. They enlisted a

---

*A surgical strike has a precise, narrowly defined target. A permissive evacuation is undertaken with the tacit acceptance of the local government, while a nonpermissive evacuation is opposed by defending forces. "Single" and "dual-purpose" refer to the nature of the mission, specifically whether to evacuate the students only, or to invade and topple the Grenadan government as well.

**A MAU is a marine battalion landing team, BLT, with a larger headquarters and air-support component.

†Ben Bradlee Jr., the author of *Guts and Glory: The Rise and Fall of Oliver North*, gives no citation for the Casey quote.

New York janitor who happened to live near the Long Island administrative offices of the St. George University School of Medicine but had no connection to the school. Thrilled beyond measure with his assignment, the janitor and a colleague obtained an appointment with the school's chancellor. The freelance NSC "agents" were skeptically received and quickly shown the door.

But on the eighteenth, with no diplomatic intelligence from the island indicating any threat to the students, the State Department sent a formal note to Grenada requesting assurances for the safety of American citizens. The minister of external affairs replied the next day. "The interests of United States citizens . . . are in no way threatened by the present situation . . . which the Ministry hastens to point out is a purely internal matter." The State Department found little comfort in the cable, but there remained no hard evidence to show that Americans were endangered in any way.[3]

Bishop and his supporters were not so fortunate. That day, crowds numbering in the thousands converged on Bishop's residence to free him from house arrest. Guards first fired over the marchers' heads, then permitted Bishop to leave. The crowd, with Bishop and former members of his cabinet, flowed out of town to Fort Rupert, where other supporters were reportedly detained.

The place was garrisoned by a small body of regular Grenadan soldiery, the Peoples' Revolutionary Army (PRA), who obligingly gave up their weapons and permitted Bishop to enter and liberate his colleagues. But then PRA reinforcements rolled up: three armored cars and a truck full of troops. They deployed before the fort and the cadet commanding officer gave the order to open fire. "Oh God," Bishop said in his last recorded words, "they have turned their guns on the masses." Over 100 Grenadans fell, with at least fifty dead (including the cadet and two other PRA soldiers, shot by their own men, probably by accident). Taken inside the fort, Bishop and three prominent supporters were forced to kneel on a basketball court and shot. His ex–minister of education, Jacqueline Creft, was beaten to death. The PRA removed the bodies and, with great secrecy, buried them in a garbage pit.[4]

Over Radio Free Grenada, the PRA commander, General Hudson Austin, with advice from Coard, announced a twenty-four-hour shoot-on-sight curfew and the formation of a new government, the Revolutionary Military Council, of which he was chairman. From Bridgetown, Barbados, the closest American diplomatic post, Ambassador Milan Bish notified the State Department, "There appears to be imminent danger to U.S. citizens . . . due to the current deteriorating situation . . . reports of rioting . . . (possibly deaths), automatic weapons discharged, Soviet-built armored personnel carriers in the . . . streets. . . . Embassy Bridgetown recommends that the United States should now be prepared to conduct an emergency evacuation of U.S. citizens."[5]

The situation was indeed grave and an evacuation seemed prudent, yet there were no hard reports that the students or other Americans and western nationals had received any threats or were the objects of any violence.

On October 20 the Joint Chiefs of Staff met to discuss contingencies. Their estimates of potentially hostile forces on the island were extremely vague, ranging from 250 armed Cuban construction workers and perhaps 300 Grenadan troops to one ludicrously inflated estimate of 11,200 well-equipped Cuban and indigenous personnel. In actuality, the Cubans numbered less than 800 and the PRA 600, with about 2,500 paramilitary Grenadan militia.[6]

At first, using the lower end of the estimates, the JCS considered two plans for evacuation of the students. The first, advanced by the Joint Special Operations Command (JSOC), involved elite Special Forces only. It was heatedly opposed, and correctly so, by CINCLANT, who advocated instead a navy and Marine Corps mission as the most logical and economic means for carrying out the evacuation. The second option would employ the *Independence* task force and BLT 2/8 embarked in PhibRon 4, which were already at sea. If additional forces proved necessary, a second battalion landing team and its amphibious squadron were close at hand on regularly scheduled deployment at Vieques Island, Puerto Rico.

The operationally sound CINCLANT plan was unfortunately shelved. The army and air force also wanted a piece of the action, and with no dominant leadership, the JCS opted for an unsatisfactory compromise. They divided Grenada operationally in half. Army Special Forces, followed by the 1st and 2nd Ranger battalions, were assigned the southern half. Their principal objectives were the Point Salines airfield and the rescue of the students, all of whom were thought to be at the True Blue Campus, near the field's eastern end. The marines were given the upper half of the island, whose major facilities included the small Pearls Airport and the town of Grenville on the northeast coast. Total ground, air, and support forces (excluding ships' crews) numbered 6,500, and overall tactical command remained with CINCLANT.

The JCS imposed total operational security (OPSEC) on what was now histrionically called "Operation URGENT FURY." The chiefs met for the next five days, and, fearing leaks, they so closely held to OPSEC that notes were never removed from their Pentagon meeting room. The JCS thus convened in a virtual vacuum, providing information to the White House and State Department, but *incomplete* data to CINCLANT staff, JSOC, and the specific naval and marine commanders at sea. Army logistic commands were kept completely out of the informational loop, and the selective intelligence given to the operational forces precluded adequate, interservice planning. It all had the unfortunate result of leading to confusion for all involved in the mission.

At 3:00 A.M. on October 21 CINCLANT ordered the *Independence* battle group and PhibRon 4 to deploy in Grenadan waters. If they did not receive further instructions by midnight on the twenty-fourth, they were to reverse course and resume the voyage to the Middle East. To electronically hide the task forces, CINCLANT further ordered the vessels to initiate immediate complete emissions control (EMCON). This involved a shutdown of all transmitting devices including active radar. From that moment the forces afloat could do nothing to question any CINCLANT decision. Worse, besides the order to steam for a specific grid reference, the task force and MAU commanders had no idea of their mission: was it evacuation of the students only; or did the JCS have additional political and military aims? There were no operational orders of any kind. Passive electronics were not effected by EMCON, so the officers tuned in the BBC's World Service from which they learned of Bishop's murder and the chaotic situation on the island. In the absence of any information from CINCLANT, the BBC proved of inestimable value. As one marine officer said, "Ninety percent of the intelligence I had before we went ashore came from the BBC." Forced to draw their own conclusion about the nature of the mission, the commanders assumed it would be an evacuation operation involving navy and marines only.[7]

In Washington, Defense Secretary Weinberger vainly searched for a justification for military intervention to evacuate the students; after all, it had been eight days since Bishop's death, and not a single threat had been aimed at any American on the island. It is alleged that Major Oliver North provided the solution. Six members of the Organization of Eastern Caribbean States (OECS) were then meeting in Barbados to discuss the Grenadan situation.* These tiny island nations—Antigua, Dominica, St. Vincent and the Grenadines, St. Lucia, St. Kitts-Nevis, and Monserrat—rightly considered themselves vulnerable to Grenada's revolutionary activities. Reportedly it was North who suggested that the OECS be pursuaded to request a United States intervention not merely to rescue the students but to topple the Coard government as well. The United States would then be less susceptible to charges of unilateral hemispheric interference.

On October 22, the commanders afloat met on board PhibRon 4's flagship, the amphibious assault carrier (LPH) *Guam.* There was a significant problem: no one had any maps of Grenada. A frantic search through the ships' libraries produced a five-by-eight-inch map, updated to 1895, in a recent tourist brochure. Unable to communicate with CINCLANT and with incomplete information from the JCS, the navy and marine officers were completely ignorant of the army and air force's participation. They devised their own operation for a simultaneous helicopter assault on Point Salines airfield with a surface landing on Grand Anse beach, between the airfield and St. George's. This would effectively isolate the True Blue Campus, their ostensible goal, from the capital and all points north.

Sunday, October 23, was a busy day. The OECS conferees received a State Department note concerning American assistance and voted unanimously to request its intervention. Jamaica and Barbados, though not member states, offered 300 troops and constabulary to join the invading forces.

In Washington, Frank McNeil, ambassador to Costa Rica, was summoned to the State Department. The OECS appeal had just arrived, and, to gauge the mood of OECS leaders, McNeil, as presidential emissary, was ordered to Barbados. He was to make it clear to them that President Reagan had as yet made no decision regarding their request for assistance. The JCS was still reluctant to commit forces immediately and this would give them more time to prepare.[8]

---

*Grenada was a member of OECS, but was not invited to the conference. Barbados, though *not* a member, is nevertheless the strongest of the tiny eastern Caribbean states, and for that reason was chosen as the meeting place.

As McNeil made ready to leave for Barbados news came of the marine catastrophe in Beirut: 241 men of BLT 1/8 dead. McNeil opined that the political consequences of the disaster precluded any Grenadan intervention. While it has been suggested that the decision to invade Grenada was made specifically to counter the disaster at Beirut with a success, it was actually the opposite. Had there been significant political fallout from the deaths in Beirut, a Grenadan invasion would have been extremely unlikely; the administration would not have been able to take such a risk vis-à-vis public opinion. But with President Reagan's glib assumption of "responsibility" for the slaughter of BLT 1/8, there followed little effective political or military opprobrium, and the planning for Grenada continued unabated.

At Barbados, McNeil conferred with the Caribbean envoys, "particularly with respect to the students [and then] recommended [to the State Department the] sending in [of] the troops, so long as it was done quickly before surprise was lost." There was finally a political justification for the incursion beyond the safety of the students. McNeil "found the reasoning of the OECS leaders entirely persuasive as to the dangers to the neighboring small islands if the thugs who massacred Bishop and his followers kept power. But . . . the make-or-break factor for me was the students."[9]

For the mission CINCLANT activated Joint Task Force (JTF) 120, with Vice Admiral Joseph Metcalf III, Commander of the Second Fleet, in tactical charge. Additional command levels invariably result in confusion, and professional opinion is mixed regarding the necessity of Metcalf's presence on site, especially since the *Independence* group already had a rear admiral in command. But this was to be, with the exception of marine command, a top-heavy operation.

In the afternoon a CINCLANT/JSOC team flew to the *Guam* to conduct a briefing. Here the skippers afloat learned of the operation's expansion to include the army, air force, and every sort of exotic special troops. The team brought with them one current map of the island. But the photocopier in the *Guam* could only reduce the image, making the map too small to be read. More were promised, but none arrived until after the marines were ashore.

The intelligence summary was a joke. Neither the rear admiral commanding the *Independence* battle group, nor the PhibRon 4 commodore, nor the marine officers had the vaguest idea of hostile numbers, arms, or deployment. When they requested permission to land their own embarked navy SEAL (sea, air, land) team for an on-site reconnaissance, CINCLANT refused. All pre-invasion work would be conducted by JTF-120 command-level SEAL teams and the army's Task Force 160, a super-sophisticated, high-tech helicopter unit known as the Night Stalkers.

Concurrent with the *Guam* conference, the Joint Chiefs of Staff received further "intelligence" suggesting larger Cuban and Grenadan forces than previously reckoned. No photo reconnaissance had produced this latest estimate, and there were no covert American agents on the island. The source remains unknown, and in any event, was completely incorrect. Possibly the hostile numbers were intentionally inflated to justify sending additional troops. But in a stroke, the JCS nearly doubled the size of the invasion force, adding the 1st and 2nd battalions, 325th Airborne Infantry, 82nd Airborne Division; they would follow in the Rangers at Point Salines.

On the twenty-fourth, a very curious communication arrived in Washington from Sir Paul Scoon, the figurehead governor-general of the Dominion of Grenada, and as such the personal representative of Great Britain's Queen Elizabeth, who was still the island's nominal chief of state. It had come on a roundabout route, confidentially via Barbados, to whose prime minister it had originally been addressed. "I am requesting your help," Scoon penned, "to assist me in stabilizing this grave and dangerous situation. It is my desire that a peace-keeping force should be established in Grenada. . . . In this connection, I am also seeking assistance from the United States, from Jamaica and from the OECS." It was extraordinary that Scoon sought aid from the United States rather than from Great Britain, to whom he owed his allegiance, especially as he had no reason to suppose the British would refuse. The letter was not made public by the State Department until October 27, two days after the invasion, with Scoon safely in American hands. Many in the British government viewed the communication, and its release date, with suspicion; might it have been drafted at the United States' behest? Probably not, but the letter did serve the Reagan administration as an additional prop to justify the intervention.[10]

That evening, from Washington, Vice President Bush's Special Situations Group initiated a conference call to Augusta, Georgia, where President Reagan, Secretary of State Shultz, and NSC chief

Robert McFarlane were spending a golfing weekend. The decision was made for full-scale intervention, not only to evacuate the students, but to overthrow the Coard-Austin clique and re-establish a democratic regime. To avoid the personal onus for any possible failure and the situation President Carter found himself in after the Iran hostage rescue fiasco, the President vested full responsibility for the operation with the Joint Chiefs of Staff. The President, however, saw fit to personally notify Britain's Prime Minister Margaret Thatcher of what was to come. Her response bordered on the apoplectic and she charged the United States with contravention of international law and gross meddling in the internal affairs of an independent state.

Late that day, Admiral Metcalf hoisted his flag on the *Guam*. In a final briefing to the forces afloat, photo reconnaissance revealed that the marines' initial objective, Pearls Airport, was defended by a number of ZSU-23 antiaircraft guns. Lieutenant Colonel Ray Smith, the marine skipper, consulted the tourist brochure and switched landing zones to a nearby racetrack. One marine officer recalled, "We had no intelligence on that and had no idea whether it was defended or not."[11]

The marines, no longer merely rescuers, but the agents of political and military change, were instructed to tell the Grenadans on landing, "We are here to neutralize the People's Revolutionary Army, to evacuate Americans, and to restore peace to Grenada. We do not want to have to hurt anyone but we will certainly kill anyone who resists us. Remain in your homes, do not gather in large groups, and do not take any hostile action towards us."[12]

On the *Guam*, the regular evening movie was preempted and replaced with *Sands of Iwo Jima*, starring John Wayne.*

In the first hours of October 25 Operation URGENT FURY commenced. The Night Stalkers, prepositioned at Barbados, flew thirty-five men of the army's Delta Force (Special Forces Operations Detachment) onto the airfield at Point Salines. They were quickly spotted and the alarm was raised throughout the island. The Cuban labor troops and PRA brought heavy rifle and machine gun fire to bear, pinning and surrounding the Deltas in a small ravine. In four hours, six Deltas were dead and sixteen

---

*These films are often shown in the Marine Corps. During the author's time in the Corps in the early 1960's, they were treated with hooting derision, and the term "John Wayne" connoted an exhibition of false heroics.

wounded. With the dawn, an Air Force AC-130 Spectre gunship*
responded to appeals and laid a devastating covering fire.

Simultaneous with the Delta landing, the command-level navy
SEAL teams met their own failures. The eight men slated to assault
the Radio Free Grenada transmitter on Grand Anse beach was
ambushed; two were killed and two wounded. The remaining six
aborted the mission and the radio continued to broadcast the
alarm.

Off Grenville in the marine zone, the SEALs attempted a
dangerous low-altitude water drop (LAPESing: low altitude parachute extraction system). The first four men were knocked un-
conscious and drowned. The second element landed safely,
climbed into their outboard-engined rubber dinghy, and headed
for the beach. But a fishing boat happened by, and the SEALs
cut the dinghy engine, which later refused to start. They floated
out to sea and were picked up by helicopter eleven hours later,
the entire mission proving a complete failure. On learning the
details, Colonel Smith, on board the *Guam,* reverted to the original
plan and ordered his own embarked SEALs ashore.

At Point Salines, the Rangers came on in the wake of the Delta
Force. Presupposing a secured air field, the dark, H-hour air
landing was slated for 4:30 A.M. During the planning phase, this
assault was scheduled in two waves, the 1st Battalion leading, the
2nd Battalion following. But in the elbowing for bigger pieces of
the pie, it was agreed that elements of both units would land
simultaneously in the first wave. This unfortunately broke apart
skilled tactical teams and unit cohesiveness, and resulted in tre-
mendously confused command and control.

Informed of the Delta plight while still en route, and aware
that the field was not yet secure, the Rangers opted to parachute.
Everyone and everything in the big C-130's had to be hastily and
excruciatingly rerigged. With the inevitable delay, the sun dawned
over the island, rerigging still incomplete.

On approaching Point Salines, the two leading aircraft were
met by small arms fire and turned away after releasing only a
dozen men. The third plane, with the command and support
elements, continued over the zone, completing its drop at the
western end of the runway. The Rangers immediately came under

---

*A variant of the C-130 transport, fitted with a stunning variety of ground-support weap-
onry.

heavy fire and were unable to relieve the Deltas, still pinned down in the ravine. The first wave, which at most should have taken thirty minutes, took a full two hours. Further, instead of advancing to clear out the resistance pocket at the runway's eastern end and *then* moving to the nearby True Blue Campus, they dug in to await reinforcements.

Worse yet, the Rangers carried none of their organic mortars, an inconceivable yet calculated omission. They would rely instead on naval gunfire and close air support from the *Independence* group. But no naval liaison teams were alerted until forty-eight hours before the drop, and they did not arrive in time to initially deploy with the Ranger battalions. When they finally landed, it was without the proper codes, radio frequencies, or call signs to communicate with the supporting ships. Eventually the Rangers were forced to resort to verbal orders via helicopter, civilian ham radio links, and in one extreme case, a round-robin telephone credit card call to Fort Bragg, routed through Washington to the *Guam*. On the ground the Rangers' disorganization turned to bewilderment, and one military historian likened their condition to "something close to panic." On board the *Guam*, Admiral Metcalf, apprised of the debacle at Point Salines, diverted the Air Force transports to fly in the 325th Airborne Infantry.[13]

Another catastrophe loomed. At 6:30 A.M., well after first light, the Night Stalkers, in nine UH-60 Black Hawks, carrying Delta forces, passed over the island to capture Richmond Hill Prison, just east of St. George's and physically dominated by the main PRA depot, Fort Frederick. The Black Hawks were to hover just over the yard and the troops then to drop on ropes and liberate the Grenadan political prisoners reportedly held within. It was yet another example of the hazy duality of mission, and it went terribly wrong.

The liberation of the prisoners was planned as a night operation. It has been suggested, however, that the orders for the operation were written using confusing local time zones rather than Greenwich Mean Time (in military parlance, ZULU Time). The sun provided perfect targets for the PRA anti-aircraft gunners in Fort Frederick. One Black Hawk was shot down crossing the coast, and at least one more was shot down during the attack. The drop was aborted, but later in the day an *Independence* air strike on Fort Frederick mistook and leveled old Fort Matthew. The building had been converted to a mental hospital but was then flying a PRA flag; twenty-one patients were killed.

But in the north, in contrast, the marines carried out a near flawless operation. The plan was for the helicopters of HMM-261 to ferry E and F companies of BLT 2/8 to the Pearls racetrack, while Company G, in the LST *Manitowoc,* assaulted Grenville from the sea. In the *Guam,* the pilots and crews readied their machines. Fortunately most of the squadron's senior sergeants had seen combat in Vietnam, and these veterans were distributed among the crews. One officer recalled, "In case there were any early jitters, which you'd obviously have on the first combat experience for any of these young guys, they would have that old hand right there to steady them or if they looked to him, they'd know exactly what to do."[14]

At 2:00 A.M., the embarked SEALs went ashore to reconnoiter and sent back the message: "Walk Track Shoes." Decoded, it meant the heavy surf and swampy beaches were barely suited to landing craft, and the plan was altered for a helicopter assault only; G Company would remain at sea in reserve.

At 5:20 A.M., the marines went in. The first UH-46 Sea Knight helicopter sank into the spongy ground, a jeep-mounted TOW antitank weapon tipped over, and that was all for mishaps. The marines came under some scattered fire from Pearls Airport, but their Sea Cobra attack helicopters from the *Guam* quickly silenced these positions. In half an hour the airport was secured, along with a Cuban transport plane and its twelve-man crew.

At Pearls and Grenville the locals welcomed the marines as liberators from a regime they considered nothing less than thugs and gangsters. They led the troops to hidden stores of weapons and identified members of the PRA, many of whom had changed into civilian clothing.

In mid-morning, to ascertain truly the capability of the beach, a single LVT armored amphibian rumbled down the *Manitowoc*'s bow ramp. The amphibian made it across the beach, but not without a mighty endeavor. Fortuitously G Company and the remaining thirteen LVTs stayed on board.

From the other side of the island came more bad news. The commander of the SEAL team which was ordered to rescue Governor-General Scoon from his supposed confinement radioed alarming news to the *Guam.* The team, he informed Metcalf, had reached Scoon at his residence outside St. George's. But they were now surrounded, taking heavy fire from armored vehicles, and eight of his thirteen men were wounded. Two Sea Cobras immediately set off from Pearls to raise the siege and were shot down; three marines were killed, the only marine fatalities in the whole operation.

To Admiral Metcalf it seemed that every operation, save for the marine landing, had gone seriously awry, in good part because the strictly military nature of the evacuation had been mottled over with political goals. The SEAL/Special Forces operations were a disaster and the Rangers were still sorting themselves out on the Point Salines runway. When Metcalf dispatched four Sea Cobras to break up resistance, the marines found it extremely difficult to communicate with the army due to different radio frequencies and map variations. Finally, the report of the SEALs at the governor-general's residence indicated that they were a step away from surrender or annihilation.

Leaving E Company to mop up the area around Pearls and Grenville, Metcalf ordered a dual strike to the southwest at Grand Mal Bay, just north of the capital. Helicopters from Pearls would bring in F Company, while G Company (reinforced) would storm the beaches from the *Fort Snelling* and *Manitowoc*. If successful, it would not only relieve the siege of the SEALs but would place the island's government, population, and military concentrations between the eventually converging forces at Point Salines and the marines at Grand Mal.

Leaving the dock landing ship *Trenton* to support E Company in the north, Metcalf took the rest of PhibRon 4 around the island. H-hour for the Grand Mal operation was scheduled for 4:00 P.M. But a bare half hour before that someone realized the marines had not yet been briefed for their new mission so the time was pushed back to 6:30, then again to nearly midnight.

Once the ships got under way, communications between Metcalf and the marines at Pearls and Grenville unraveled. Ashore, Ray Smith, skipper of BLT 2/8, received no details of the impending attack. He intended to go in with G Company and desperately looked for a helicopter to take him out to the now departed ships. When he finally found a chopper, its navigation and communications gear failed, and it took four hours to locate the *Guam*, by which time Smith was "so frustrated [he] could barely see."[15]

In the meantime, just after 2:00 P.M., the leading elements of the 325th Airborne Infantry began flying into Point Salines. They, too, expected a secured airfield and were very surprised at their reception. The runway was full of construction debris which the

Rangers were supposed to have removed. Instead, the Rangers were still dug in at the runway's west end, while the Cuban and PRA defenders on the east end raked each incoming plane with their ZSU-23's and automatic small arms.

Because the rubble-strewn runway could handle only one plane, which took half an hour to unload, at a time, the follow-on aircraft spent precious minutes and fuel circling the island. Continuing the ill-advised practice of top-heavy control, Major General Edward Trobaugh, commander of the 82nd Airborne Division, arrived in one of the first planes. Trobaugh was amazed at the situation; the Rangers had done little, if anything, to secure the airfield. According to CINCLANT, "Securing, in Ranger terms, was a little less than he would have liked . . . because when he landed . . . the battalion commander for the Rangers was only about 50 meters down the road from where he got off the airplane."[16]

It took a full hour for Trobaugh's paratroopers to link up with the Rangers. The Cubans counterattacked with a pair of BTR-60's, both of which were destroyed. Dislodged from position after position and suffering heavily, the Cubans radioed Havana for permission to surrender. "For the glory of the revolution," came the reply, "no!"[17]

At an inching crawl, with heavy air support, the troops moved eastward, down the runway toward the True Blue Campus. By day's end, having advanced one mile since the dawn, the Rangers and airborne troops reached the student quarters and established a perimeter for the night. Questioning some of the 130 students, they learned that True Blue was not the only school facility. About 500 more were living at the Grand Anse Campus about four miles northeast of the airfield and at Lance-aux-Epines in the St. George's area. This came as a big surprise to everyone.

In the midst of the battle for Point Salines, the Night Stalkers, running low on fuel, landed on the *Guam*. Attempting to grasp defeat from what was hardly yet the jaws of victory, the *Guam* refused them fuel, supposedly on CINCLANT orders, because the interservice bureaucracy had not yet transferred the required funds. Fortunately the *Guam*'s air officer disregarded the farce and on his own initiative ordered up the avgas.

At 11:20 P.M., G Company made ready to go ashore at Grand Mal. The embarked SEALs reported the beach suitable for landing craft, and, indeed, there were no problems. But once established on the beachhead, Special Forces intelligence reported two phantom battalions of hostiles facing the marines north and south. Company F was still en route in their helicopters; Company G, loath to sit it out and wait, dug in a platoon at the landing zone, while the bulk of the company, mounted in LVTs, advanced with five tanks down the road to St. George's and points south.

They reached the governor-general's residence at 3:00 A.M. the following morning. Contrary to the report, there was no siege; neither were there any wounded SEALs. "In fact, they had not been surrounded but had simply panicked and lied to get help," charged a marine officer.[18]

In mid-morning the students at True Blue were evacuated and the Rangers moved east, about two miles, to Frequente. Here they found a complex of warehouses stacked to the ceilings with Cuban and Soviet weaponry: rifles, mortars, machine guns, anti-aircraft guns, rocket launchers. Many of the crates had been disguised as ordinary imports; CUBAN ECONOMIC OFFICE, read the labels.

Along the coast the marines continued their advance on St. George's, skirting the town from the landward side. Approaching Fort Frederick, they watched groups of men climbing down the far walls. The marines entered unopposed, and like the Rangers, unearthed large quantities of East Bloc weapons and ammunition. They also found a cache of documents, including an arms agreement signed by Nicaragua, Cuba, Grenada, and the Soviet Union.

While BLT 2/8 cleaned up the area around St. George's, the crews of HMM-261 prepared to carry the Rangers on to the Grand Anse Campus. "The Iranian hostage rescue attempt was on everyone's mind," said one of the marine officers. "We were coming out with something, or there was not going to be [a helicopter] left." The squadron's skipper expressed the same determination. "Regardless of what happens to any of our aircraft or any of the Rangers on that beach, it's going to go down."[19]

Intelligence reported hostiles of unknown strength in defensive positions between the campus and its very narrow fronting beach. To crush it quickly the commanders planned an overwhelming attack by all forces, with the exception of the ground elements of BLT 2/8. Following an artillery and air bombardment, the Rangers and Airborne would assault the campus from the landward side, while nine of HMM-261's Sea Knights flung more Rangers at the beach.

At 4:00 P.M. the Sea Knights lifted off from Point Salines for the short flight to Grand Anse beach. Five minutes later the artillery barrage and air strikes from the *Independence* leveled the area, which included two tourist hotels occupied by PRA forces. Friendly fire ceased, at least officially, twenty seconds before the choppers touched down. But as the choppers maneuvered onto the crowded growth that came right up to the water's edge, heavy small arms and anti-aircraft fire opened up, shooting down one and badly damaging another. "I am absolutely convinced," said a senior marine officer, "the only people firing at us were our forces and that is what shot us down."[20]

As each big Sea Knight landed, the Rangers poured down the rear ramp and rushed the campus buildings. The students, nearly 200 of them, were evacuated without casualty.

The following morning, D+2, BLT 2/8 completed its operations in the strongpoints ringing St. George's. G Company entered unoccupied Richmond Hill Prison, then moved several hundred yards south to attack Fort Adolphus. This place *was* occupied; the marines could see a strange flag on the walls. Colonel Smith considered using TOW antitank missiles and 50 caliber machine guns to prep it before the assault. Admiral Metcalf suggested naval gunfire and air strikes; Smith said no. "I'm not sure what stopped us from doing it," he said. "The only thing that stopped us from going in and prepping it, is that we had been so successful without shooting that I recall consciously making a decision: 'It's working, let's just keep doing it the way we're doing it.' " G Company advanced cautiously until a single man walked out of the fort: the Venezuelan ambassador. The flag on the walls was the flag of Venezuela, and the fort their temporary embassy.[21]

In the afternoon, in order to permit BLT 2/8 to continue the advance southward, Admiral Metcalf moved the boundary line to accommodate operations. Thus the marines, with only twenty percent of the invasion forces, would occupy eighty percent of the island. Their tactical area was now so great it forced Ray Smith to land part of his support force, Battery H, 10th Marines,* as a provisional rifle company to garrison St. George's. The marines entered the capital without opposition. With help from the locals, they took into custody Bernard Coard and several high-ranking

---

*The reader will recall the genesis of the 10th Marines, the 1st, 9th, and 13th artillery companies in Haiti and the Dominican Republic.

Central Committee and New JEWEL members, as well as a number of PRA soldiers who had changed into civilian clothes.

The boundary change dictated the marines' next mission, the Ross Point Hotel, on the coast between the capital and Grand Anse beach. Reports indicated approximately 400 American, British, and Canadian civilians desiring evacuation. The movement would also enable BLT 2/8 to link up with forward elements of the 82nd Airborne.

Company F moved out and by evening secured the resort without resistance. But instead of 400 mixed civilians, they found twenty-four Canadians, few of whom had any wish to leave. Seeing no signs of the 82nd, the marines formed a defensive perimeter and bedded down for the night.

Leading elements of the 2nd Battalion, 325th Airborne Infantry, arrived in the morning. Their officers had not been told of the boundary change, but had instead been briefed that the hotel area was to be considered a free-fire zone—shoot anything that moved—and until they met F Company, they were prepared for a reconnaissance in force. "After all," said the airborne battalion commander, "what you kill you don't have to carry." Indeed, many locals had left their homes when they heard that the 325th planned to "blow the town away." "Yes," recalled an airborne artillery officer. "The worst of the Vietnam excesses came back to haunt us." The marines were appalled and bitterly complained to Admiral Metcalf to exercise some control over the airborne units.[22]

The last significant action on Grenada occurred later in the day, the Ranger assault on Calvigny Barracks, on the southeast coast. Thought to be a hostile bastion holding as many as 600 Cuban and PRA troops, the attack began with damaging *Independence* air strikes, naval gunfire, and the airborne's 105mm artillery. Eight army Black Hawk helicopters brought in the troops. The first landed safely. The second and third crashed into each other and fell amidst the Rangers on the ground, killing four, while the whirring blades lopped arms and legs off several others. The barracks, as it happened, were empty.

By nightfall of the twenty-eighth, resistance ceased and Grenada passed to the control of the United States and OECS peacekeeping forces. For BLT 2/8 there was a final mission. Unconfirmed intelligence reported PRA troops, and perhaps some North Koreans, on Carriacou, an island just off Grenada's northern tip. Metcalf ordered the marines to conduct a full-scale air and surface assault before daylight, November 1. There was no opposition, let alone North Koreans. The people, many of whom had worked in the United States or had relatives there, welcomed the marines warmly. Some even suggested to Colonel Smith that he run up the American flag and annex the place. Smith paroled the local PRA garrison, nineteen men already in civilian clothes who readily gave themselves up, and ordered them to return to their homes.

On November 2, BLT 2/8, its supporting units, PhibRon 4, and the *Independence* task group resumed their voyage to the Middle East.

Total casualties in Operation URGENT FURY are difficult to calculate, especially as much of the operation is still classified. A low estimate counts eighteen Americans killed and 116 wounded. Grenadan dead are estimated at 110, of whom twenty-four were civilians. The Cuban labor battalion suffered twenty-five killed and fifty-nine wounded; the remainder were repatriated.[23]

In the following months the United States Army awarded 8,612 various medals to its participants, although not more than 7,000 had ever set foot ashore.

"I can't say enough in praise of our military," said President Reagan, forever basking in the glow of heroes real and imagined, in a speech at the Cherry Point Marine Air Station. "Army Rangers and paratroops, Navy, Marine and Air Force personnel, those who planned a brilliant campaign and those who carried it out." A senior intelligence officer put it somewhat differently. "It was Ollie North's charade. Whatever was screwed up was the fault of North, the Navy and the gutless JCS. [Special Forces] should not have been used and their performance was absolutely horrible."[24]

AFTERWORD: THE PANAMA INVASION 1989

"Do you want to spend the rest of your life having nuns wash your underwear?"

–Msgr. José Sebastián Laboa

The Panama Canal is no longer the linchpin of America's hemispheric defense. Strategic geography, however, remains fairly constant, and the transcontinental waterway will, in all likelihood, forever remain under the defensive umbrella of the United States.

Inevitably and immediately following the signing of the 1903 Hay–Bunau-Varilla Treaty, the Panamanians sought modifications, especially in the clauses that gave the United States perpetual control of the Canal Zone. Significant amendments in 1936 and 1955 provided Panama a measure of authority over canal operations. But in 1964 an insult to the Panamanian flag at an American high school in the Zone led to alarming riots and brought into clear focus the unequal partnership between the two countries.

Beginning with Lyndon Johnson, four successive Presidents attempted major renegotiations of the treaty with various Panamanian governments. In the late 1970's, President Jimmy Carter, in a marked demonstration of political courage, negotiated full transfer of the Canal and Canal Zone to Panama in the year 2000.

Of enormous help in convincing the Panamanians to accept the terms of the treaty, in particular the extended time of transfer, was the strong, popular chief of their defense forces and de facto national leader, General Omar Torrijos. Like Carter, Torrijos had

390

put *his* prestige, if not his life, on the line for the treaty; without him, it would likely not have been signed.

Torrijos, however, was a chronic alcoholic who seemed to place little value on his life. At the time of the negotiatons, he was constantly attended by the chief of Panama's military intelligence bureau, Manuel Antonio Noriega, who was described by a United States Army officer on the scene as "the hood ornament on Torrijos' jeep." When the negotiations had reached a critical point, Torrijos' alcoholism, coupled with his penchant for high-risk flying, became disturbing to the Americans. "My God," said one diplomat to the United States officer, "what do we do if Torrijos dies?" "You shoot Noriega," replied the officer.[1]

In July of 1981 the American diplomat's fear came to pass when General Torrijos died in a plane crash whose causes remain a mystery. By the fall of 1989, corruption-soaked narcotics trafficker Manuel Noriega had risen from chief of Panamanian military intelligence to commander of the Panama Defense Forces (PDF) and to the legislatively rubber-stamped "Maximum Leader" of Panama.

Since his cadet days at a Peruvian military academy in 1960, Noriega had graced the payrolls of American intelligence agencies; by the mid-1970's he was known as "rent-a-colonel." Although he was identified as a double agent who passed classified information to Cuba, Libya, Warsaw Pact states, and later to the *Sandinistas*, the CIA considered Noriega's worth to exceed any information he might divulge. Against suggestions that Noriega be "terminated permanently," i.e., killed, were arguments for his retention. During the Carter administration, however, CIA chief Stansfield Turner dropped Noriega from the payroll; he was reinstated upon Ronald Reagan's assumption of the presidency.

By this time Noriega was known to be deeply involved in international narcotics trafficking, but in the Reagan administration that privately counted for little, particularly because Noriega formed a vital link in the succor of the anti-*Sandinista*, *contra* rebels in Nicaragua. Indeed, according to an American military contractor, the United States purchased large amounts of Warsaw Pact weaponry, mostly small arms, on the open market in Poland for shipment via Panama to the *contra* rebels.[2]

But Manuel Noriega was not, as some commentators have implied, a creation of the American intelligence community. "The American military intelligence groups," stated a former United

States Army officer with wide experience in Latin American affairs, "were using a lot of Panamanian sources, keeping their eyes on a lot of people, and so there was a lot of 'incest,' everybody gathering information on everybody. It wasn't like we created Noriega, he was going to be the G-2 [chief of Panamanian military intelligence] whether we liked it or not, and as the G-2, he had a valid excuse for dealing with American intelligence. You hear these newsmen pompously say that Noriega was our creation, they're full of shit. Dealing with someone like him comes with the intelligence territory. Anyone who knows these 'Arabs' with Spanish names knows what they're dealing with." But as of this writing, in January 1990, with Manuel Noriega in American custody, "there will be a lot of embarrassed Congressmen around, and they'll be in a low hover. Though I don't think [Noriega] can touch [President George] Bush. Instincts tell me [Bush] is too well insulated."[3]

By 1987 Noriega's virtually public corruption and private double-dealing with outright terrorist organizations, such as the more radical factions of the Palestine Liberation Organization and the Colombian M-19 group, a strange amalgam of Marxist-Leninists and drug cartel enforcers, had become acutely discomfiting to American policy-makers, and his services to American intelligence agencies were abruptly concluded. Noriega was further estranged from American officials when, on February 15, 1988, federal grand juries in Florida handed down indictments charging the general with thirteen counts of narcotics trafficking and associated racketeering.

One month later, in an attempt to topple Noriega by indirect methods, Ronald Reagan imposed severe economic sanctions on Panama. These, however, inflicted far more harm upon Panama's poor, working, middle, and peasant classes; Noriega and his ruling coterie were left relatively unscathed. According to retired General Frederick Woerner, then commanding the United States Southern Command (SOUTHCOM), headquartered in Panama City, "We enforced [the sanctions] quite ineffectively because we didn't want to hurt U.S. business."[4]

In Panama a largely democratic and increasingly vocal civilian opposition with public and covert support by the United States seemed likely to defeat the dictator's political machine in the May 7, 1989, presidential elections. As the ballots were counted, it was clear that Noriega's hand-picked presidential candidate was being trounced three to one at the polls. Fearful of defeat, Noriega ordered the PDF and his personal, thuggish paramilitary organization, the so-called Dignity Battalions, to seize the ballot boxes, close the polls, and brutally intimidate the opposition and its supporters. The election, he declared, was null and void due to "foreign interference." Presidential candidate Guillermo Endara and his running mates sought refuge in the embassy of the Papal Nuncio in Panama City.

Following the election, American military personnel and their dependents, whenever caught off their bases in the Canal Zone, were subjected to harassment and in some cases detention and beatings by the PDF. In one incident, the PDF attempted to tow and detain a Zone schoolbus filled with American children and were only prevented by the timely arrival of American military police.

In Washington, amid brave words, hollow threats, and the dispatch of a mixed brigade from the army's 7th Infantry Division (Light), 5th Infantry Division (Mechanized), and a 2nd Marine Division light armored infantry company to reinforce the Canal Zone garrison, the administration of President George Bush looked on helplessly, apparently powerless to influence events and subject to Noriega's constant, infuriating taunting. Yet these reinforcements brought an immediate and significant drop in the harassment of American citizens, from fifty-five incidents in May to twelve in June.

On July 20 the Pentagon announced that General Frederick Woerner, increasingly critical of both the Reagan and Bush administrations for what he considered a "policy vacuum" in regard to Panama, would shortly be replaced in SOUTHCOM by General Maxwell Thurman. "The military option [to overthrow Noriega] was always an option, nobody denied that," said the retired general. "[But] I felt that there was a full range of options that could be applied that might have made the military option unnecessary." Yet, according to Woerner, President Bush's senior policy formulators "buried the damn things. . . . Breaking diplomatic relations is a pretty logical step," but at the time the administration considered even that "overly bold."[5]

Within the Panama Defense Forces, cells of opposition to Noriega brewed among a number of middle-level officers. To be sure, this was not a democratic political opposition. The corrupted PDF had supped well at the public trough, and was reportedly linked at most levels to narcotics trafficking; its officers were more concerned about their personal promotions than with the creation of a fundamental opposition to the dictator's regime. The apparent leader of the cabal was the commander of the Urraca Battalion, Major Moisés Giroldi Vega, who ironically had played a pivotal role in crushing an anti-Noriega revolt in March of 1988.

Since the nullified election, President Bush had been urging the PDF to "do everything they can to get Mr. Noriega out of there." But he offered no concrete assistance. According to published reports, United States intelligence agencies maintained no conduits to the military malcontents.

On October 3, 1989, Giroldi Vega staged *his* abortive coup. Politically, and perhaps militarily, the United States was caught flat-footed, unprepared, and one reason was the state of SOUTHCOM upon General Thurman's arrival. A Pentagon source has said that under Woerner and his predecessors, SOUTHCOM resembled "a sleepy hollow of a headquarters, full of people who could speak Spanish but could not tie their shoes"; a billet for officers, passed over for promotion, in their final tour of duty.[6]

When the shooting began, General Thurman placed United States troops in the Canal Zone on their highest state of alert. He ordered attack helicopters to fly over Panama City and heavily armed formations to block key access routes to the north and west, isolating PDF bases from Noriega's headquarters at the *Comandancia* in the city's southern slum district of El Chorillo. Because Noriega was thought to be somewhere else, probably in the combined American-Panamanian facility at Fort Amador, the eastern corridor to Torrijos-Tocumen International Airport and the PDF's Albrook air base was left unguarded. Coming from the east, the PDF's 7th Company and Battalion 2000,* unblocked and unmolested, enveloped the rebels from the rear and utterly crushed the coup.

While Noriega continued to strut about, heightening his barrage of taunts at the United States and brandishing a machete before crowds of cheering supporters, President Bush received severe, bipartisan castigation for his lack of will in seizing the strategic moment and militarily supporting the coup. Bush told the nation that to "unleash" America's armed forces was "not

---

*So called for the year the Panama Canal and Canal Zone are to pass into complete Panamanian control.

prudent, and that's not the way I plan to conduct the military or foreign affairs of this country." So it seemed.[7]

Immediately after the failed coup, incidents of PDF harassment against the United States military personnel, dependents, and residents increased. Perhaps Noriega felt he could now act with impunity toward an apparently gun-shy Bush administration, perhaps he felt compelled to display his macho qualities in front of his supporters, or perhaps he was goaded into escalating the tension by *agents provocateurs*. Noriega's reported use of greater and greater amounts of cocaine might also explain much of his posturing and belligerent, eventually self-defeating behavior. "I don't think he was bolted down tight," said an experienced American officer, "but he was very crafty and street-smart."[8]

Spurred by the escalation in attacks against United States citizens, General Thurman made the first of several trips to Washington to persuade the Chairman of the Joint Chiefs of Staff, General Colin Powell, of the need for a major military operation to overthrow Manuel Noriega. Previously, the chief had been opposed to a unilateral American invasion, but Thurman turned him around. A military operation, Thurman argued, need not depend on an indigenous revolt or civil uprising. According to a JCS officer, "Thurman convinced everybody that we did not need to be in that condition. If we decided to go, we'd go for our own reasons, on our own timetable, not because some guy stood up and said, "I'm running the country now.""[9]

Unlike the patchwork, extemporaneous Grenada intervention, a contingency plan for an invasion of Panama for the specific purpose of defending the canal has existed in some form for decades. The most recent plan, Operation BLUE SPOON, had been drawn during the Reagan administration, reportedly for a full-scale military intervention and occupation of the Canal Zone. General Thurman lobbied hard for dusting off BLUE SPOON. He convinced Powell that if intervention came, it was imperative to launch a full-scale operation and not to opt for a highly risky surgical strike merely to remove Noriega while still leaving in place the disreputable PDF and Noriega's fraudulently installed government.

Notwithstanding glib commentators who ignorantly bemoan an army's incapacity for subtlety, precisely targeted surgical strikes are best performed by those military forces, unlike the United States', whose very existence is predicated upon them, such as the

Israeli army. Since Ulysses Grant's Civil War Wilderness Campaign in 1864, the doctrine of the United States Army has invariably eschewed the scalpel for the meat axe. "Thurman felt quite rightly," an administration source stated, "that if you're going to go in, the safest way both to end the violence quickly and to protect the Americans down there would be to do it with massive force. Do it suddenly and quickly . . . to disable the PDF."[10]

With Powell and the JCS convinced of the military correctness of BLUE SPOON, specific invasion planning commenced at least two months prior to the December 20, 1989, D-day. Noriega's movements were continually tracked by Delta Force and SEALS, and indeed he must have felt like a hunted animal, sleeping fitfully by day, and moving to three or four different locations each night. An American human rights worker met with Noriega some weeks prior to the invasion and described the general as either, "someone who hasn't slept for twenty days or who has become a consumer of his own product [cocaine]. . . .He had that look of Joan of Arc as they lit the kindling."[11]

On December 15 the immediate events that triggered the invasion began when Panama's hand-picked National Assembly declared Manuel Noriega the *de jure* head of state, draping him with the title of Maximum Leader. Then in an act of collective political insanity if not suicide, the assembly, citing "aggression against the [Panamanian] people," declared the republic "in a state of war" with the United States. "We the Panamanian people," Noriega exhorted, "will sit along the banks of the canal to watch the dead bodies of our enemies pass by."[12]

In its initial reaction, the Bush administration, at least in public, derisively dismissed the Panamanian pronunciamento as akin to the mouse that roared. The administration would cite the declaration of war as one of its legal justifications for the intervention.

The following day, Saturday, December 16, witnessed a pair of savage incidents involving the PDF and American servicemen and dependents. Four unarmed, off-duty American officers lost their way while driving to a restaurant in Panama City. Stopped at a PDF checkpoint near the *Comandancia*, a hostile crowd gathered while a Panamanian soldier attempted to pull one of the officers from the car. The driver put the gas pedal to the floor, and as the vehicle sped forward the PDF opened fire, mortally wounding marine Lieutenant Robert Paz.

The confrontation was witnessed by an American naval officer and his wife, who were taken into custody by the PDF, blindfolded, and brought to the *Comandancia*. Both were brutalized. "A senior member of the PDF," stated a White House official, "came in without a word, hit [the officer] in the mouth and kicked him in the groin, sort of as a 'Hello.' " As his shrieking wife watched, the naval officer was beaten. "They brutalized his wife," continued the White House source. "They said they were going to rape her. Then they made her stand up against the wall [with her arms over her head] for thirty minutes until she collapsed; then [they] slammed her head against the wall."[13]

The death of Lieutenant Paz and the torture of the navy couple erased any doubts the Joints Chiefs might have had regarding overt military action against Manuel Noriega. They had previously considered the dictator not worth expending American lives in battle. "But once [the PDF] murdered that serviceman and brutalized the others," said a senior administration source, "there was a real shift in the Pentagon's thinking."[14]

President Bush was horrified by the reports and, according to reliable accounts, they were the final straws that led him to order the invasion. "Enough is enough," the President said. "I can't just sit back and wait until this thing deteriorates further." On December 17 he reviewed several options, including a covert strike to kidnap Noriega. This the President rejected because of the difficulty in claiming the operation had been launched to protect American lives. Worse, if the covert strike failed, and there was no reason to suppose that it wouldn't, the lives of American citizens in the Canal Zone would be in a far worse predicament. Finally, failure would bring total embarrassment to the administration, which, considering the lack of decisive action manifested during the October coup attempt, it could ill afford. That day, at lunch with the Vice President and Defense Secretary Richard Cheney, President Bush reported, "the die was pretty much cast" for BLUE SPOON (renamed JUST CAUSE by Cheney) and for full-scale intervention.[15]

President Bush convened at the White House with his military and civilian advisors on Sunday, December 17, disguising the meeting as a discussion regarding an expanded role for the military in the escalating drug war. The legal justifications for the intervention were considered, and there were two essential props: first, the right generally recognized under international law for a nation state to protect the lives of its citizens abroad; and second, the rights conferred by the 1979 Panama Canal treaties (indeed, rights and duties stretching all the way back to the Bidlack-Mallarino and Hay–Bunau-Varilla treaties) for the defense of the line of transit.

Noriega's and the PDF's increasingly obnoxious conduct, combined with the declaration of the state of war, provided a reasonably justifiable threat to American citizens throughout Panama. There was also a recent, though unconfirmed, report from a reliable intelligence mole inside the PDF that Noriega, aided by Cuban military advisors, had organized a 250-man urban commando unit specifically trained to assault American neighborhoods within the Zone.

As for danger to the Canal, Pentagon sources admitted there was no real threat to the waterway, and the intervention was neither designed nor executed toward that end. Had it been so, American invasion forces would have numbered upward of 100,000 troops, five divisions, about five times the number actually committed, which would have necessitated a near-total air force–navy mobilization of transport capability; it probably could not have been done.

The real threat in Panama, much ignored in the press, and seemingly not considered by the Bush administration, was the continued integrity of the 1979 Carter-Torrijos Canal treaties. The author has no doubt that had conditions in Panama continued to deteriorate, with Noriega and the PDF maintained in their kleptocracy—a government of thieves—and with hardly any possibility of the establishment of a democratic government, the United States Congress would have abrogated the treaty and refused sovereign transfer of the Canal and Zone to Panama in 2000.

Operation JUST CAUSE was far better conceived, organized, and executed than Operation URGENT FURY in Grenada, not least because there was no unnecessary ideological baggage. The clear, immediate purpose of the mission, the military removal of Manuel Noriega from office and power, had only the most peripheral, if any, connection to the containment of the Cuban and Nicaraguan revolutions. As such, operational success was directly contingent upon the engagement of United States forces with Noriega's power prop, the PDF, in regular battle.

Ideally, these symbiotic targets, Noriega and the PDF, would be attacked simultaneously, physically isolating them from each otehr, and leaving each relatively impotent at their supreme moment of crisis.

Unlike the muddled leadership of the Grenada incursion, the senior American command echelons for JUST CAUSE were kept strictly within definite spheres of responsibililty, and there was no interservice bickering or elbowing for pieces of the operational pie. "It is my understanding this situation was brought about by the Chairman of the Joint Chiefs of Staff, General Colin Powell," said a highly decorated airborne officer, now on duty at the Pentagon. "I'm very pleased to see a guy like him who grasps both the political and military sides of a problem. He's also a decision-maker, and it's about time we got a guy like that in there."[16]

Of the approximately 24,000 United States military personnel allocated for JUST CAUSE (the equivalent of a heavily reinforced infantry division), 13,000 from all services were already stationed or training in the Canal Zone. The Zone's in-place, primary combat components comprised the army's 193rd Infantry Brigade, and a battalion each of the 82nd Airborne Division's 1st Brigade and the 7th Special Forces Group. Marine units counted D Company, 2nd Light Armored Infantry Battalion, and K Company, 3rd Battalion, 6th Marine Regiment.

The invading units from the United States, 11,000 troops, came under the command of the XVIII Airborne Corps, a highly mobile, quick response JCS "contingency" formation having no specific geographic region of responsibility. For the initial assault in Operation JUST CAUSE, General Powell and his planners cobbled together from the east, west, and gulf coasts: two battalions of the 75th Ranger Regiment; the remainder of 82nd Airborne Division's 1st Brigade; four battalions of specially trained urban warfare specialists from the 7th Infantry Division (Light): and one battalion from the 6th Infantry Regiment, 5th Infantry Division (Mechanized). Added to these were sundry special operations and logistic units: army Delta Force; navy SEALS; the 16th Military Police Brigade; components from twenty-one wings of the Air Force's Military Airlift Command; twenty-six Strategic Air Command air refueling squadrons; and lethal AC-130 Specter gunships from the 919th Special Operations Group, Air Force Reserve.

The particular capabilities of each unit had been carefully

considered and meticulously pieced into an intricate jigsaw puzzle whose completion spelled at least military success for the operation. "Airborne, Rangers, light infantry, Marine and in-place units," said the respected defense analyst Edward Luttwak, "could all be exploited without paying the usual price of diversity because of different mindsets (if not different radio sets). We could have had the full JCS salad—indeed we could have had a Belgian fire brigade too—but without any harm done this time."[17]

Against this crushing meat axe, the PDF, though hardly a defenseless scallop of veal, especially if the operation degenerated into protracted guerrilla warfare, could in no way match forces in the open field of regular battle. The full PDF mustered between 12,000 to 15,000 men, but only a quarter counted as combat troops. These, generally well trained, with modern, light weaponry including twenty-eight Cadillac-Gage armored cars, were organized into an airborne group and eight light infantry companies. Less than a thousand men combined to form the PDF's air force and two-ocean navy, for the most part equipped with a few reconnaissance aircraft, unarmed helicopters, and small miscellaneous patrol craft.

The remainder of the PDF formed the paramilitary police and eighteen of Noriega's personal Dignity Battalions (or as they were soon called by the American troops, Dingbats). Little better than armed street gangs, the Dignity Battalions were organized in units numbering anywhere from a dozen to 150 people. In Panama City, they were concentrated in the poorer sections.

At the time of this writing, it is extraordinarily difficult for the historian to sift and evaluate information, the overwhelming amount of which remains classified. Indeed, it took twelve years before the Marine Corps declassified its synopsis of the 1965 Dominican Republic intervention. But from the data available, the first American troop deployments probably began on December 18, when a navy SEAL team was reportedly infiltrated into Panama City to ferret out Noriega's whereabouts. Quietly, but hardly secretly, over the next forty-eight hours, the bulk of the CONUS-based* Rangers and units of the 5th, 7th, and 82nd divisions began landing at American bases in the Canal Zone.

Without much doubt, the heightened activity alerted Noriega to the distinct probability of an invasion. According to a U.S. government official in the Zone, "The word was all over Pan-

---

*CONUS, the military abbreviation for Continental United States.

ama. . . . Some knew about it earlier, but it was public knowledge before dark." Indeed, by 6:00 P.M., December 19, congressional offices in Washington were receiving calls from the isthmus asking what time the Americans would begin the attack.[18]

According to some sources Guillermo Endara, the apparent winner of the nullified presidential elections of the previous May, was notified of the invasion at 10:00 P.M., three hours prior to H-hour. The news came, said Endara, "like a kick in the head. It was not the best thing I would have thought. . . . We were not really consulted." Reportedly, Endara and his two vice-presidential running mates were then sworn into office by a Panamanian judge at an undisclosed American base. It is not known under what conditions, but at 12:15 A.M., December 20, forty-five minutes to H-hour, Endara requested United States military intervention in Panama.[19]

The American formations divided into four task forces: Bayonet, Red (with a subgroup, Task Force Pacific), Semper Fidelis, and Atlantic. H-hour was slated for 1:00 A.M., and all PDF targets were to be attacked with simultaneous, overwhelming, crushing assaults.

Because the initial penetration operations were theoretically carried out in unison, it is difficult to construct a chronology. It seems, however, that General Thurman, concerned over losing the element of surprise, ordered Task Force Bayonet—two infantry battalions, four Sheridan light tanks, and a SEAL team—to begin their advance on the PDF's Panama City complexes at Fort Amador and its downtown *Comandancia* a few minutes early.

The SEALs, who had rehearsed the operation some weeks before at the same location, dropped with their motor craft into the dark Pacific and headed for Panama City's downtown Paitilla Airport, used mainly for private, executive aircraft, and the place where Noriega based his personal LearJet. It was a key avenue of potential escape, and it was the SEALs' mission to cork it.

The airfield was stubbornly defended by the PDF, against whom the lightly armed SEALs could not long fight without reinforcement. Engaged in close, fierce combat, the SEALs managed to put a round from their new, shoulder-fired Lightweight Multipurpose Weapon (AT-4) into the cockpit of the LearJet, searing the interior and melting the windows from within. Suffering four dead and eleven reported wounded, the SEALs desperately clung to one end of the field and awaited relief.

Their succor, when it eventually arrived, came from sub–Task

Force Pacific: a battalion of the 75th Rangers, and two battalions of the 82nd's 1st Airborne Brigade. At H-hour, covered by the ferocious fire of AC-130 gunships, the Rangers dropped onto the runways of Panama City's Torrijos-Tocumen International Airport, a complex that included the PDF's Albrook airfield—another Noriega escape hatch—and considered an *entrepôt* for possible Nicaraguan or Cuban reinforcements. Nearby, at Fort Cimarron, across the Pacora River bridge, sat the barracks of Battalion 2000, the unit instrumental in smashing the abortive October revolt, and one of Noriega's most loyal formations.

The Rangers secured large parts of the air facility, but without reinforcements they too could not hold out against any sustained counterattack, nor could they gain control of the Pacora River bridge to isolate Battalion 2000 from the main theater of operations in and around Panama City. Fighting continued, and command of the airport, bridge, and the eastern corridor to the SEALs in Panama City now depended on who arrived first—the two in-flight battalions of the airborne brigade, or the PDF's Battalion 2000.

With timely accuracy, the lead airborne battalion dropped into the firefight, and one nineteen-year-old soldier had a difficult time coming to grips with reality. "It just didn't dawn on me," he plaintively explained to a hometown reporter. "Most of this was to get college money. I didn't really plan to go to war. I'm shocked."[20]

While fighting for the air complex continued, Battalion 2000 began moving west out of Fort Cimarron, toward the Pacora River bridge and the thin cordon of Rangers and paratroopers. The airborne's follow-on battalion was still in-flight, three hours off, making up time on account of North Carolina ice.

Almost two centuries ago, Napoleon considered luck a tangible military asset; in Operation JUST CAUSE, the unforeseen operational glitches that had dogged America's armed expeditions over the past decade, Grenada being a prime example, were expertly and professionally, and probably with some luck as well, overcome. While loading the troops at North Carolina's Pope Air Force Base, the four C-141 jet StarLifters and three C-130 Hercules transports were subjected to a potentially mission-killing, wing-icing freezing rain. Constant spraying by special deicer trucks limited the delay to three hours. Then once aloft, the lead StarLifter suffered a malfunction of its navigational equipment, and pathfinding was switched in flight. According to Lieutenant

Tracy Mead, whose plane took over the duty, "It went more smoothly than day-to-day training."[21]

In the offing, the battling Rangers and paratroopers on the ground had called in the AC-130 Specter gunships for direct fire support against Battalion 2000. The aircraft's awesome weaponry, which includes a 105mm gun, obliterated the van of the Panamanian column. What remained of Battalion 2000 about-faced and rushed headlong back to Fort Cimarron.

At 5:00 A.M., nearly four hours late, the seven transports flew into the still-disputed drop zone. The planes headed into their approach and prepared to loose the paratroopers 500 feet over the runways when PDF anti-aircraft fire rose to meet them. Ordered in preflight assignments to make one pass only, the transports were radioed by the ground control team to cease the drop and were directed onto a second approach, out of the line of fire.

The second pass brought further problems to the lead and another aircraft. In the leading plane, with only a few paratroopers away, a trooper fell in the exit hatch, and the man behind him caught his gear in the plane's internal jump rigging; the thirty-five remaining paratroopers were blocked. Having already made one more pass than originally ordered, all assumed the mission was aborted. What occurred in the second plane is not known to the author, but both veered away and commenced mid-air refueling from Strategic Air Command Stratotankers.

While the two aircrews prepared their return to Pope, new orders arrived for yet a third pass over the field, this time in a direction that served to confuse the PDF's anti-aircraft gunners. The remaining paratroopers jumped without mishap.

With the big airfield complex secured and Battalion 2000 routed, the airborne troops were finally able to go to the relief of the SEALs at Paitilla. According to reports in the *Army Times*, this did not happen until late December 22. A high-speed convoy with Company D, 4th Battalion, 325th Airborne Infantry mounted in the army's new High Mobility Multipurpose Wheeled Vehicles (HMMWV), or "Hummer," rushed through the streets of Panama City, often coming under fire, and broke through to Paitilla.

There came immediate controversy, especially from civilian proponents of special operations units, regarding the heavy casualities among the SEALs and the agonizing delay of their relief. Elite units such as Delta Force, SEALs, and Rangers, when used as assault troops must either be withdrawn or relieved very quickly, because they do not have the capability to hold against a sustained counterattack. As explained by Dr. Harry Summers, formerly of the Army War College: "We can't have it both ways. The emphasis of surprise, stealth, and the use of elite units is undercut by a major Cecil B. de Mille operation. 'Mission Impossible' is a TV show, it is not reality."[22]

Simultaneous with the actions at the airfields, the landward prong of Task Force Bayonet, spearheaded by Sheridan tanks and infantry in armored personnel carriers (APC), roared out of the American bases toward the El Chorillo slums and the *Comandancia*. "The [assault] time," said Lieutenant Colonel Jim Reed of the 4th Battalion, 6th Infantry, "was one o'clock in the morning. We had to move it up because it appeared something was up. We caught [the PDF] still pulling weapons out of trunks of cars and whatnot. We had a company of tanks—Sheridans—back on the high ground [overlooking the *Comandancia*]. There was a Marine platoon attached to me. Later that day, we had a reinforced Ranger Company that . . . cleared [the *Comandancia*] room by room . . . by the time we got in, there were only four dead bodies there."[23]

Army psychological warfare units (PsyOps) broadcast appeals for the PDF within the *Comandancia* to surrender, which they largely ignored. Instead, according to Lieutenant Colonel Reed, "they fired a few [buildings] up. I got a Marine LAV [Light Armored Vehicle] attached to me and I used it to break down a wall. . . .We received very heavy fire." During the fight for the *Comandancia*, its buildings were subjected to pulverizing fire by artillery and infantry heavy weapons, until the night sky over the twisting, ancient streets of El Chorillo was ablaze with a cauldron of fiery light. Whole blocks were obliterated in the flames. Much of this "collateral damage" was blamed, probably correctly, on retreating units of the PDF who lit backfires to cover their withdrawal, and marauding bands of the Dignity Battalions, who simply torched the neighborhood during a frenzy of looting.

Resistance at the *Comandancia* collapsed on the morning of Thursday, December 21. Inside Noriega's office, the troops unearthed, according to General Thurman, "a ready supply of pornography in his desk," a photo of Adolf Hitler, a bucket of blood and other voodoo paraphernalia of which Noriega was an alleged practitioner, and what was purported to be fifty kilos of cocaine. This later turned out to be nothing but tortilla flour.[24]

Sporadic fighting continued throughout the neighborhood. It was too early to tell, General Powell said, whether the residual shooting came from "an armed resistance force or . . . individuals who now are just criminals and thugs running around the countryside."[25]

Hundreds of urban refugees, soon to number in the thousands, began their wandering to schools, churches, and hospitals seeking safety from the carnage.

Streaking through the night skies, unseen and with the most lethal precision—indeed the surgical accuracy so hungered after by civilian commentators—a flight (real numbers are unknown, probably from two to eight) of Air Force F-117A Stealth fighter-bombers, "Wobbly Goblins," knifed into their attack over Río Hato. The jungle-edged Pacific-coastal town about sixty miles southwest of Panama City housed a major concentration of the PDF, the heavily armed 6th and 7th companies. These units had been reinforced to about 600 men, and were extensively equipped with sixteen Cadillac-Gage armored cars, eleven Warsaw Pact ZPU-4, quad-barreled, anti-aircraft machine guns, sundry mortars, infantry machine guns, East Bloc rocket-propelled grenades, and what one American officer later described as "tons of ammo." The base also contained the PDF's basic training facility.

Río Hato was a prime military target whose neutralization and isolation from the political locus of the fighting, Panama City, was vital to the success of the intervention. Because the PDF maintained neither military ground-to-air radar, nor fighter interceptors, the Pentagon planners also considered it a perfect, virtually no-risk combat test for the Stealth fighter.

Critics have maintained that the $50 million apiece Stealth fighters were hardly a cost-effective weapon for the Río Hato assault, especially since the PDF had no counter systems capable of defeating American *conventional* attack aircraft. The Stealth raid, said an unnamed congressional defense authority, was "pure pap—a gimmick."[26] A senior, highly decorated air force fighter pilot, when asked if Stealth was militarily justified in the Río Hato attack, claimed, "There are other things we could have used. I won't say it's a flip of a coin to use Stealth or conventional jet attack aircraft, because there are a lot of operational factors you have to consider when using any system. Can it do the job, and do the job effectively? Can it do it at minimal or no loss; can it do it in a timely manner? You must consider all these questions in a military situation."[27]

There is also the inescapable matter of a new weapon that has yet to be combat-tested, and cost-effectiveness or tactical necessity aside, the opportunity had suddenly arisen. "Yes," continued the officer, "especially something like that, like Stealth, that has received the press and interest it has, and the amount of money put into it. You always want to use it for something, and anytime you use technology like that, you want to try it out at an easy level. I won't say a 'milk run' level, but you want to try it where you are not going to take losses the first time out. You want to try to walk before you run. So I think from a lot of aspects, Stealth was probably justified. True, we could have used a lot of other things instead, but well, why not try it? And we apparently did."[28]

Sometime between midnight and 1:00 A.M., the Stealths, which had begun their flight at Tonopah, Nevada, dropped a ton of ordnance around the PDF facilities at Río Hato and disappeared into the night. Behind them lumbered fifteen C-130 transports of the 317th Tactical Air Wing, carrying a battalion of the 75th Rangers.* The 317th had been chosen for the mission because it was one of only two wings equipped with the Adverse Weather Aerial Delivery System (AWADS), allowing near pinpoint accuracy of troop and gear drops in zero-visibility weather or total darkness.

They had been flying south for seven hours in total radio-emission silence. Yet during the repeated, passive electronic frequency changes, several air crews were cut out of communications entirely. These crews, according to the flight's lead navigator, "just hung in there. The discipline was incredible." When asked to compare the mission to Grenada, the air tactics officer of the 317th stated, "We did a lot better [here]."[29]

Wheeling into their approach, the thirteen troop-carrying aircraft lined up about 200 yards to the right of Río Hato's runway, thereby permitting the easterly wind to drop the Rangers square on the tarmac. The two equipment-laden planes flew a few hundred yards to the right, furthest away from the PDF barracks,

---

*Some accounts indicate only two companies of Rangers engaged at Río Hato. The author has chosen, for the sake of military logic, and the ninety-two-man capacity of the C-130, to accept the larger figure of a battalion. At Río Hato, thirteen aircraft carried troops, two carried equipment.

and directly over the battery of ZPU-4 anti-aircraft guns, which lacked the capability of firing straight up.

The PDF gunners, however, threw up a heavy barrage at the troop carriers, and within the planes, crews and Rangers heard and felt the ominous "chink, chink" vibrations as small arms rounds struck the fuselages. Seven planes were hit, none seriously, though a Ranger in the lead aircraft received a bullet in the leg. Because aircraft on a drop approach cannot dodge fire, but as an Air Force officer said, must "bear down and be gritty," the planes never veered an inch while their navigators guided them in by radar in complete darkness.[30]

The Rangers dropped from about 500 feet and encountered a determined defense. With no initial thought of surrender, the PDF staged an orderly fighting retreat. The Rangers blew open barracks doors with a new, Swedish, shoulder-fired rocket. The primary PDF tactic was to withdraw through the rear of the building and take up a new position in nearby trenches or gullies. When the Rangers worked through and exited, the PDF opened fire, then retreated to the next barracks to repeat the procedure. According to the Rangers' commanding officer, Colonel Buck Kernan, the fighting was "savage." The PDF, he continued, "were gutsy. They hid in a bunch of draws behind the buildings and fired when we came out. . . . These guys were jungle fighters, highly trained and disciplined."[31]

In one barracks the Rangers found 180 unarmed recruits cowering in the corners, and they were taken prisoner without casualty. With the dawn, AC-130 gunships roared over the jungle canopy. This so intimidated the escaping members of the PDF that large groups came out of hiding to surrender. By day's end, the Rangers were relieved by the 7th Infantry Division's 2nd Brigade, and with it concluded the army and air force's little victory at Río Hato, a Banana Wars' battle as hard fought as any in the ninety-one years since Fighting Joe Wheeler's dismounted cavalry had charged up Kettle Hill.

It was only a few minutes flying time to a landing at Howard Air Force Base, near the coast, just west of the Canal's Pacific entry. Ground fire had put holes in several wing tanks, and the planes, said an observer, were "losing fuel as if faucets had been turned on." An experienced air force sergeant, who specialized in battle repair, climbed a ladder and under a constant shower of high octane avgas, moved from hole to hole plugging the leaks with special putty. He was at it for three hours, and every fifteen minutes he was hosed down by a fire truck.[32]

Still by night, midway along the Canal, in what seems the only objective in the intervention directly contingent upon the security of the waterway, a battalion of the 82nd Airborne division, half of Task Force Atlantic, seized the critical Madden Dam and hydroelectric station near the east bank at Sierra Tigre. These paratroopers were already in Panama for jungle training at the time of the invasion, and probably boarded their aircraft at the Jungle Operations Training Center not far from Colón.

On the Canal's west bank, the second element of Task Force Atlantic, a battalion of the 7th Infantry Division, moved up from the Howard–Fort Clayton complex and captured Gamboa Prison, near old Matachin, and liberated some fifty political prisoners.

This battalion (the author believes) also had the mission of seizing the government radio station, Radio Nacional, which continued until its capture, in late afternoon, to broadcast fighting appeals to the PDF from Noriega and his government. "We're in trench warfare now," Noriega declared in his last speech, "and we will maintain the resistance. We must resist and advance. . . . Our slogan is to win or die, not one step back."[33]

Most of the 600 marines in Panama were organized into Task Force Semper Fidelis, and encountered what one marine called, "a mix of fire fights and friendliness."[34]

The task force was assigned a multiplicity of missions within a six-square-mile area on the west bank of the Canal. "We have to ensure we use the minimum force the situation demands," said Colonel Charles Richardson to his officers, "and that our men conduct themselves as professionals. . . . The Panamanian people are not our enemies. They are good people. We will treat them that way."[35]

The marines quickly secured their primary target, the access highway and Bridge of the Americas, the sole avenue of approach into Panama City from the west. The marines' secondary objectives were PDF bases near the Arrajian Tank Farm, a large fuel depot just west of Howard and a major supplier to American installations. Mounted in LAVs, each fitted with a 25mm, rapid-firing gun, the marines assaulted the fuel compound, and according to an officer, "moved room to room to rout the Panamanians." Reforming the LAV column, the marines moved three miles to the PDF barracks at the town of Arrajian. Their way was blocked by a fuel tanker truck, athwart the highway, behind which about thirty PDF troops had taken up a defensive position. The marines opened fire, assaulted the road block, and completed their tasks by 4:30 A.M.[36]

While U.S. forces successfully isolated and neutralized the bulk of the PDF, downtown Panama City degenerated into chaos. Dignity Battalions twice raided the Marriott Caesar Park Hotel, and about a dozen Americans, mostly journalists, were taken hostage and held for some hours. But it was not for another eighteen hours that units of the 82nd Airborne arrived at the Marriott. In the confused fight for the hotel, a Spanish news photographer was killed, and another badly injured. Some sources indicate the paratroopers were shooting at one another; army press reports speak of heavy sniper activity.

The American high command has been faulted, perhaps rightly, for failing to provide immediate security to the civilians at the Marriott. Generals Powell and Thurman responded that their first priority was to smash the PDF. A Pentagon spokesman explained it somewhat differently, "There are 23,000 [civilian] Americans down there. There are a lot of other places there too."[37]

Jets and attack helicopters obliterated whole blocks of Panama City's northeastern San Miguelito neighborhood, site of a PDF barracks, and a stronghold of the Dignity Battalions; thousands of refugees roamed and ran aimlessly about. Widespread arson and looting erupted, much of it reportedly perpetrated by the Dingbats. Americans on the spot as well as those watching the scenes on television in the United States were both amused and shocked by the spectacle. "It was an amazing sight," said an American soldier, "amazing and comical. Those people were out there looting their asses off. They had armfuls of televisions, pillows, anything they could get. When they saw us, they shouted, 'Viva Bush! Viva the United States!' "[38]

While the American forces in the city were contained battling snipers and roaming, vandalizing bands of Dignity Battalions, the looting continued for perhaps two days, during which time whole neighborhoods were taken over by the paramilitary gangs. The municipal police, as part of the PDF, had disappeared from their posts, presumably to take up arms against the invasion, and there was no one to keep order. Mobs of civilians, from children to the elderly, stripped stores clean. "Somebody's going to take it anyway," one looter told a reporter. Even in a relatively prosperous Third World country such as Panama, there is a great deal of severe poverty, and those who have nothing will enrich themselves when the opportunity presents.[39]

For this lapse, too, opprobrium has been leveled at the high command. The author asked Lieutenant Colonel Fitzsimmons why the urban depredations were not immediately confronted. "I've wondered about that myself," the bullet-headed paratrooper at the Pentagon responded, "I think it's intolerable. There had to be some military reason why we could not respond, but I don't know what that reason is. My guess is that General Thurman either didn't think about it, or somebody on his staff didn't think about it, or the plan that we had to deal with it, if we did think about it, fell through for some reason."[40]

"This city has been raped," said a local citizen, "both by the U.S. Army and by looters."[41]

A phenomenon of Operation JUST CAUSE that received the overwhelming attention of the American press was the role of women in direct combat support. The thirty-nine participating female soldiers were assigned to the military police (MP) companies and moved in right behind the assault troops. There was nothing unusual about their state of mind, which mirrored that of every American soldier since the band of half-trained Massachusetts minute companies took their stand on Lexington Common in April 1775. "Will I ever see my kid and husband again," mused a member of the 988th MP Company as she boarded her transport at Fort Bragg. "I was never so scared in all my life."[42]

During the consolidation phase of the intervention, the first forty-eight hours, the MPs were subjected to sporadic, harassing sniper fire from isolated pockets of the PDF and drive-by shootings by the always dangerous Dignity Battalions. "It used to scare me really, really bad the first two days or so," said a female member of the 988th MP Company. "You jumped at anything. You'd just continuously be jumping. Now you hear a shot, it's like, 'Oh well, it ain't at us so we don't have to worry about it.' "[43]

The incident that received the most attention concerned Cap-

tain Linda Bray, commanding officer of the 988th. The company
was ordered to capture a PDF guard dog kennel in the area of
Fort Amador, a major PDF facility on the east bank of the Canal's
Pacific entry. According to initial press accounts, Bray, with one
platoon, gave the PDF defenders thirty seconds to surrender.
When after two minutes they continued their sniping, Bray ordered her troops to open fire. After the MPs' heavy automatic
weapons had fairly riddled the structure, Bray reportedly manned
a Hummer-mounted machine gun and crashed through the gate.
Some accounts indicated three Panamanian soldiers were killed
within.

The little action stirred a wide controversy, not merely because
a woman commanded in combat, though that was certainly significant in itself, but also because there was some question of
whether it had really occurred as reported. As of this writing, the
author does not know. "It didn't happen anything like it's been
reported in the news media, and this is from an MP source,"
Lieutenant Colonel Fitzsimmons said. "If I understand correctly,
Bray, the young female captain, was away from the platoon at the
time of the incident. A military police platoon is equipped with
more machine guns than a [standard] infantry platoon, so when
they returned fire, they basically took the building apart. The big
joke is that all they did was wound a schnauzer. It's my understanding she was ten minutes away when it started, and arrived
sometime later, during the time of shooting. That she crashed
down the gate with a jeep while she manned the M60 machine
gun, we also believe that not to be true. You know that sometimes
in the heat of battle, young captains are going to tell you that they
were heroes, thinking they are telling only you, and not thinking
they are telling the whole world and that it's going to be on the
front page of the *New York Times* the next day."[44]

By the close of the first day, December 20, a
fresh brigade of the 7th Infantry Division flew in to relieve the
assault troops. Though widespread looting and urban chaos
still reigned in Panama City, most of the military objectives of
Operation JUST CAUSE had been accomplished, and the principal concentrations of the PDF had been neutralized or destroyed. Hundreds of Panamanian soldiers had surrendered, and
hundreds more had changed into civilian clothes to melt into the
population. The amount of firearms confiscated, both from the

PDF and the general citizenry, General Thurman described as "astonishing." As has occurred throughout the history of the Banana Wars, a reward was offered for guns, and uncounted thousands were surrendered. In the western districts of Panama City, Colonel Linwood Burney, commanding the 7th Infantry Division's 2nd Brigade, told a correspondent, "There are about 1,200 Dignity Battalion and PDF members [in our area of operations]. We've picked up 33,875 weapons. . . . It's an impossible amount." As another officer said, "We're seeing everything from muzzle-loaders to new Uzis." The troops found not only firearms, but homemade mortars and alarm clocks and devices for the manufacture of time and letter bombs.[45]

The plight of the staggering number of urban refugees became an immediate and overwhelming problem and seems not to have been adequately prepared for. This lapse proved a major operational glitch, draining support forces from the combat arms. Extended fighting within Panama City, coupled with the Dignity Battalions' depredations, caused severe food and medicine shortages. In a matter of days, 12,000 destitute, bombed-out Panama City civilians crowded the stadium and grounds of the Zone's Balboa High School. Sanitary facilities were woefully inadequate, and the stench of rotting garbage permeated the area. United States forces were able to provide only the most basic food and water requirements. The situation was only alleviated when the refugees were moved to larger facilities and makeshift shelters at the former PDF facility at Albrook field.

The Dignity Battalions continued to pose considerable problems. General Thurman considered their predations "centrally controlled," an allusion to the still at large Manuel Noriega. On December 23, 2,000 additional 7th Infantry Division troops were flown into the Zone to counter the protracted resistance. But it was not just because of their looting and arsonist activities that the United States determined to smash the Dingbats in Panama City.

"Bandits," such as the *gavilleros* encountered during the Dominican Republic intervention of 1916–1924, can quite easily don the mask of national liberators, and it would be folly to assume the Dignity Battalions would not do the same. The Dingbats, personally loyal to Manuel Noriega, not yet run to ground, posed a real threat of imposing a debilitating guerrilla war which could entail a United States combat presence in Panama the American public and its armed forces could neither countenance nor sustain. "The limit of [American] force is very real," said the army's chief planner, Lieutenant General Thomas Kelly. The Dignity Battalions, General Thurman seconded, "would have given the U.S. a significant challenge."[46]

The key to the neutralization of the Dignity Battalions along with isolated pockets of the regular PDF, indeed the key to the major immediate political goals of the intervention, remained the capture or death of Manuel Noriega—and he was nowhere to be found.

For months prior to the invasion, Noriega had been constantly tracked by members of Delta Force and SEAL Team 6. Operation JUST CAUSE proved an open secret in Panama (a downside to having bases on site), but Noriega, though aware of the buildup, seemed to dismiss the probability of an imminent attack. He likely considered the heavy reinforcements landing at Howard Air Force Base as a logical, if posturing, United States reaction to the increasingly violent incidents between the PDF and zonal Americans.

At 1:00 A.M., H-hour, December 20, according to very sketchy accounts, Noriega was first reported to be in Colón inspecting PDF installations. The story then quickly changed, and he was reported to be with a prostitute at a PDF officers' club in the northern reaches of Panama City, in or near the international airport–Albrook airfield complexes. When, as the British say, the balloon went up, Noriega left the club with an unknown number of bodyguards and proceeded to drive around the city.

For those columnists who bemoaned the absence of the "cool coup," some sources do indicate that the initial plan was for Delta Force to kidnap Noriega immediately prior to H-hour, and that the massive military invasion to neutralize the PDF was merely a follow-on backup to the kidnapping. But military operations seldom unfold as predicted, and when the scalpel of the hoped-for surgical strike by the Delta Force failed, it was left to the traditional meat axe to complete the job. "A plan exists only up to the time of execution," commented General Powell, "then you're into [football line of scrimmage] audibles." Regarding the initial escape of the dictator, General Kelly said, "He's a crafty devil. . . . We had a pretty good idea where he was last night. We went there, and he wasn't there." The Bush administration attempted what is called spin control and lamely claimed the immediate capture of Noriega was not a paramount objective, which is of course arrant nonsense. Still, the President of the United States put a bounty of $1 million on the elusive Maximum Leader's head.[47]

Noriega's escape might have been very finely timed. In the first minutes of the invasion, U.S. troops burst into one of his hideouts. "There was still a candle burning," said an American officer. Noriega, it was reported, had escaped in the company of four Brazilian female voodoo practitioners.[48]

Throughout the isthmus, the avenues of escape were slammed shut. SEALs were stationed at key ports, air force special units stood ready to intercept any escape attempt by air, and Green Beret Special Forces combed the alleys of Panama City.

For the wider political ramifications, the hunt for Manuel Noriega was cast as a criminal justice dragnet rather than a military operation. "If we hunt him down as a criminal by people who professionally hunt down criminals, then it looks better," said a senior soldier in Washington. "We don't want to make him a fugitive bandit being hunted by marines. He's not Pancho Villa [or César Sandino, he might have added], he's John Dillinger."[49]

The Bush administration's legitimate fears of Noriega igniting a guerrilla war in Panama collapsed on Christmas Eve. "So exhausted from the chase, he could barely speak," according to a bodyguard, Noriega telephoned the Papal Nuncio from a nearby Dairy Queen restaurant, and with "ten associate thugs," as a Justice Department spokesman put it, he requested political asylum. Noriega's wife and about sixty-five of the dictator's entourage sought and were granted the safety of the Cuban embassy.[50]

Immediately, United States troops descended upon Panama City's Paitilla district and cordoned the area surrounding the Papal Nunciature with armored vehicles and flesh-tearing hoops of concertina razor wire. The American soldiers were joined by hundreds of anti-Noriega Panamanians, banging pots, cheering, jeering, and honking car horns. "Mission accomplished; that coward," exclaimed a cab driver. It was not that simple. True, the Maximum Leader had been run to ground, but he still had to be winkled out of his hole.

The Vatican was no great supporter of Manuel Noriega, whom it considered an arch violator of human rights; indeed the Panama City Nunciature had provided refuge to Noriega's political opponents following the voided May 1989 elections. But the Vatican nunciatures around the world traditionally provided a temporary refuge to anyone claiming religious or political persecution. "It's a very complex problem," stated a Vatican diplomat. "I don't think [the Nuncio] could directly hand Noriega over to the Americans, who are an invading army."[51]

The key individual who emerged in the delicate negotiations over what would become of Manuel Noriega was the Papal Nuncio, Monsignor José Sebastián Laboa. A Basque Spaniard, seasoned Church diplomat, and former *advocatus diaboli*, or "devil's advocate," in the verification of miracles, Laboa applied both subtle and direct pressure on the dictator, what Americans call the good cop–bad cop routine.

Inside the Nunciature, Noriega was immediately disarmed and permitted neither alcohol, save for a single glass of beer, nor narcotics, to which he is allegedly addicted. He was allowed neither to receive nor to make any telephone calls, and in the stifling heat and humidity of Panama City, he was confined to a bare bedroom with no air-conditioning and a broken television.

Outside the Nunciature, United States troops initially employed crude PsyOps. To deprive Noriega, a reported opera aficionado, of sleep, and generally keep him in a high state of agitation and enraged impotence, loudspeakers blasted rock and roll and country and western music around-the-clock. The song "You're No Good" seemed a particular favorite. The noise drove the Nunciature staff crazy as well; "a very serious matter," they protested, and it was turned off after about three days.

Negotiations between the United States and the Vatican proceeded with some acrimony. Vatican officials blamed the Bush administration for the impasse, terming its forces "an occupying power," without lawful rights to demand the surrender of the fugitive. A Church spokesman, however, explained that Noriega, who now claimed the status of an ousted head of state, was being urged to leave of his own free will. "At the same time," he continued, "we cannot force Noriega to leave nor . . . can we consign him to U.S. forces, which would be a decision against the principles of international law." If the demand for Noriega were based on criminal indictments, the diplomat said, it was up to the new Panamanian government to seek custody, but no request was forthcoming. Indeed, it was contrary to Panamanian law to surrender one of its citizens to a foreign power.[52]

There would never be a request from the government of Guillermo Endara for the ousted Maximum Leader; politically they could not afford it. For as long as Noriega remained in Panama, be he an internal refugee in the Nunciature under indictment, at trial, or in jail, he would continue to exert an extremely destabilizing influence on a country whose new political infrastructure, with its shaky popular mandate, had, after all, been established by the gringos.

On December 29, in the midst of the negotiations and for no apparent reason, American troops smashed into the Nicaraguan embassy in Panama City. An embarrassed but still bellicose George Bush called it "a screwup" that should not have occurred, but in light of the assault he disingenuously wondered why the Nicaraguan ambassador was "up to his eyeballs" in weaponry. Found on the premises were shoulder-fired antitank rocket launchers, grenade launchers, about a dozen each of AK-47 and Belgian FN assault rifles, some Uzi submachine guns, and a large variety of ammunition. The State Department, apparently unsure of the motive behind the break-in, claimed the weapons were "in excess of normal requirements for defending the [embassy]." But their spokesman declined to enumerate what constituted "normal requirements." In Managua, the Nicaraguans retaliated for the outrage by expelling twenty American diplomats.[53]

But day by day Monsignor Laboa turned the screws. First he told Noriega that he had given the Americans permission to storm the Nunciature should Noriega attempt to hold its personnel as hostages. When the dictator's associates within began surrendering of their own accord, the priest floated the suggestion that the entire Nunciature staff might just walk away, leaving Noriega alone in the deserted compound. Finally he asked the former Maximum Leader, "Do you want to spend the rest of your life having nuns wash your underwear?"

Whatever it was, Noriega had had enough. At 8:50 P.M., January 3, 1990, Manuel Noriega, in a wrinkled uniform and holding a Bible and toothbrush, walked out of the Nunciature and placed himself in American custody. "He really looked like a whipped and beaten little man," said a diplomat on the scene. The ex-dictator was hustled aboard a Blackhawk helicopter for the few minutes flight to Howard Air Force Base, where he was formally placed under arrest by agents of the United States Drug Enforcement Administration, and was read his constitutional "Miranda" rights in Spanish.

Via Air Force C-130 transport, Noriega was flown to Miami and arraigned before a Federal magistrate as prisoner 41586.

According to conflicting reports, the casualties of Operation JUST CAUSE were: twenty-three American military dead and 323 wounded; 297 "enemy forces" killed and 123 wounded; and an estimated 300 Panamanian civilians killed.

For the United States and for Panama, were these casualties worth the intervention? That question might well be asked of every intervention discussed in this book. An uncertain future follows the short-term military success of JUST CAUSE. This future must include an understanding of what exactly America's long-term interest in Latin America is to be. Since 1903 the United States has maintained what amounts to a colonial presence in Panama. Because of this presence, and the Canal revenues, many Panamanians live better than citizens of most Third World countries. Yet Panama lacks bedrock democratic traditions. The government of Guillermo Endara will survive only so long as the United States continues its political and economic support.

For the very short term, the cycle is familiar. "I have got to start putting the same effort into bringing these towns along," commented Colonel Burney, surveying his new fief around Río Hato, "making sure there is a mayor, making certain there is a security force, making certain they have all the public services, a fire department . . . electricity, those kinds of things. Once we've done that, then we'll be able to put in a [U.S. Army] civil affairs team [to organize the local government infrastructure]. We'll have to make certain the mayor is supported, the political appointees are comfortable with the [new Panamanian] security forces, etc." How little things have changed since that day in July of 1898 when Leonard Wood rode into Santiago de Cuba.[54]

NOTES

1. EMPIRE BY DEFAULT 1898

1. 55th Congress, 2nd Session, *Consular Correspondence Respecting the Condition of the Reconcentrados in Cuba, the State of the War in That Island, and the Prospects of the Projected Autonomy* [hereinafter cited as *Consular Correspondence*], p. 87; Walter Millis, *The Martial Spirit*, p. 102; Lawrence Shaw Mayo, *America of Yesterday: The Diary of John D. Long*, p. 162.
2. John K. Winkler, *W.R. Hearst*, p. 144.
3. Millis, *Martial Spirit*, pp. 31–32.
4. Frederick Funston, *Memories of Two Wars*, p. 100.
5. French Ensor Chadwick, *The Relations of the United States and Spain: Diplomacy* [hereinafter cited as *Diplomacy*], pp. 474–75; Charles E. Chapman, *A History of the Cuban Republic*, p. 81.
6. Millis, *Martial Spirit*, p. 41.
7. Roger Butterfield, *The American Past*, p. 276.
8. Samuel Eliot Morison, *The Oxford History of the American People*, p. 799.
9. *Consular Correspondence*, p. 30.
10. Department of State, *State Papers Relating to the Foreign Relations of the United States*, [hereinafter cited as *Foreign Relations*] 1897, pp. XI–XXII, *passim*.
11. Henry F. Pringle, *Theodore Roosevelt*, p. 176.
12. *Consular Correspondence*, p. 19.
13. Chadwick, *Diplomacy*, p. 533.
14. *Ibid.*, p. 534; Millis, *Martial Spirit*, p. 95.
15. *Consular Correspondence*, p. 85.
16. Chadwick, *Diplomacy*, p. 538.

17. Elbert J. Benton, *International Law and Diplomacy of the Spanish-American War*, p. 74.
18. *Foreign Relations*, 1898, p. 1011.
19. Winkler, *W.R. Hearst*, pp. 152–53.
20. Hyman G. Rickover, *How the Battleship Maine Was Destroyed*, p. 45; Mayo, *America of Yesterday*, pp. 163–64.
21. 55th Congress, 2nd Session, *The Report of Naval Court of Inquiry Upon the Destruction of the United States Battle Ship* Maine [hereinafter cited as *Report of the Court of Inquiry*], p. 281; Rickover, *How the Battleship* Maine *Was Destroyed*, pp. 94–95.
22. Millis, *Martial Spirit*, pp. 108, 110.
23. Mayo, *America of Yesterday*, p. 169.
24. Pringle, *Theodore Roosevelt*, p. 178.
25. L. White Busbey, *Uncle Joe Cannon*, p. 186.
26. *Ibid.*
27. *Foreign Relations*, 1898, p. 684.
28. *Report of the Court of Inquiry*, p. 281.
29. Chadwick, *Diplomacy*, pp. 576–77.
30. *Ibid.*, pp. 579–81.
31. *Ibid.*, p. 581.
32. *Ibid.*, p. 582.
33. *Ibid.*, p. 583.
34. *Ibid.*, p. 585.
35. *Foreign Relations*, 1898, p. 762.
36. Herbert H. Sargent, *The Campaign of Santiago de Cuba*, Vol. III, p. 158; Russell F. Weigley, *History of the United States Army*, p. 568.
37. French E. Chadwick, *The Relations of the United States and Spain: The Spanish-American War* [hereinafter cited as *Spanish-American War*], Vol. 1, p. 10.
38. *Ibid.*, pp. 39–40.
39. Frank Freidel, *The Splendid Little War*, p. 43.
40. Nathan Sargent, ed., *Admiral Dewey and the Manila Campaign*, p. 19.
41. H.W. Wilson, *The Downfall of Spain*, p. 62.
42. E.B. Potter, *Sea Power: A Naval History*, p. 177; Richard S. West Jr., *Admirals of American Empire*, p. 224.
43. Chadwick, *Spanish-American War*, Vol. 1, p. 173.
44. Carlos G. Calkins, "Historical and Professional Notes on the Naval Campaign of Manila Bay in 1898," United States Naval Institute *Proceedings* [hereinafter cited as *USNIP*], June 1899, *passim*.
45. *Ibid.*
46. *Ibid.*
47. Chadwick, *Spanish-American War*, Vol. 1, pp. 305–307.
48. Freidel, *Splendid Little War*, p. 61.
49. *Ibid.*, p. 64.
50. *Ibid.*, p. 68.
51. *Ibid.*, p. 89.
52. *Ibid.*, p. 93.
53. Richard Harding Davis, *The Cuban and Porto Rican Campaigns*, pp. 193–94.
54. Freidel, *Splendid Little War*, p. 135.

55. Frederick Remington, "With the Fifth Corps," *Harper's*, November 1898.
56. Theodore Roosevelt, *The Rough Riders*, p. 130.
57. *Ibid.*, p. 131.
58. Freidel, *Splendid Little War*, pp. 162–63.
59. Roosevelt, *Rough Riders*, p. 136.
60. *Ibid.*, p. 138.
61. Chadwick, *Spanish-American War*, Vol. 2, p. 106.
62. Francis A. Cook, "The *Brooklyn* at Santiago," *The Century Magazine*, May 1899, p. 96.
63. Robley D. Evans, "The *Iowa* at Santiago," *The Century Magazine*, May 1899, p. 50.
64. Chadwick, *Spanish-American War*, Vol. 2, p. 128.
65. John W. Philip, "The *Texas* at Santiago," *The Century Magazine*, May 1899, p. 90.
66. Chadwick, *Spanish-American War*, Vol. 2, p. 145.
67. *Ibid.*, p. 153.
68. West, *Admirals of American Empire*, p. 7.
69. Freidel, *Splendid Little War*, p. 234.
70. *Ibid.*, p. 255.
71. Benton, *International Law*, pp. 222–23, 232; Charles E. Hill, *Leading American Treaties*, pp. 331, 335–36.

2. CUBA 1899–1917

1. Hermann Hagedorn, *Leonard Wood*, Vol. I, p. 184.
2. *Ibid.*, pp. 184–85.
3. *Ibid.*, pp. 187, 190.
4. *Ibid.*, p. 187.
5. *Ibid.*, pp. 187–88.
6. *Ibid.*, pp. 188–89.
7. *Ibid.*, p. 189.
8. *Ibid.*, pp. 192, 198.
9. Department of War, *Report of Major General J.R. Brooke on Civil Affairs in Cuba: 1899* [hereinafter cited as Brooke Report], Part I, pp. 3–4; *New York Tribune*, December 30, 1898.
10. Brooke Report, Part I, p. 5; David F. Healy, *The United States in Cuba, 1898–1902*, p. 55.
11. Hugh L. Scott, *Some Memories of A Soldier*, pp. 233–34.
12. Healy, *United States in Cuba*, p. 58.
13. Department of War, *Annual Reports of the Secretary of War, 1899–1903*, p. 113.
14. Brooke Report, Part III, pp. 372–73; Frederick Palmer, *Bliss, Peacemaker. The Life and Letters of General Tasker Howard Bliss*, p. 62.
15. Louis A. Pérez Jr., "Supervision of a Protectorate: The United States and the Cuban Army, 1898–1903," *Hispanic American Historical Review* [hereinafter cited as *HAHR*], May 1972, p. 254; *New York Tribune*, May 28–29, 1899.

16. Healy, *United States in Cuba*, p. 88.

17. *Ibid.*, pp. 90, 102.

18. James Harrison Wilson, *Under the Old Flag*, p. 468.

19. *Ibid.*, pp. 490–91.

20. *Ibid.*

21. *Ibid.*; Brooke Report, Part I, p. 12.

22. Hagedorn, *Leonard Wood*, p. 214; Pérez, "Supervision of a Protectorate," p. 256.

23. Pérez, "Supervision of a Protectorate," p. 256.

24. Healy, *United States in Cuba*, p. 105.

25. Phillip C. Jessup, *Elihu Root*, pp. 286–87.

26. *Annual Reports of the Secretary of War, 1899–1903*, p. 110; Brooke Report, Part III, p. 363.

27. Department of War, *Civil Report of Brigadier General Leonard Wood, Military Governor of Cuba, for the Period from December 20, 1899, to December 31, 1900*, Vol. I, pp. 66–74, *passim.*

28. Healy, *United States in Cuba*, pp. 185–86.

29. *Annual Reports of the Secretary of War, 1899–1903*, p. 225.

30. Jessup, *Elihu Root*, p. 306.

31. Healy, *United States in Cuba*, p. 148; Allan R. Millet, *The Politics of Intervention: The Military Occupation of Cuba, 1906–1909*, p. 45.

32. Chapman, *History of the Cuban Republic*, pp. 136–37; Richard D. Challener, *Admirals, Generals, and American Foreign Policy, 1898–1914*, pp. 94–95.

33. Pérez, "Supervision of a Protectorate," p. 263.

34. Healy, *United States in Cuba*, p. 178.

35. *Annual Reports of the Secretary of War, 1899–1903*, pp. 256, 454.

36. Chapman, *History of the Cuban Republic*, p. 190.

37. *Ibid.*, pp. 191–92.

38. Millett, *Politics of Intervention*, p. 60.

39. *Ibid.*, p. 68.

40. *Foreign Relations*, 1906, p. 471.

41. Jessup, *Elihu Root*, p. 481.

42. Ralph E. Minger, "William Howard Taft and the United States Intervention in Cuba in 1906," *HAHR*, February, 1961, pp. 76–77; Millett, *Politics of Intervention*, pp. 66–71.

43. William Inglis, "With the Rebel Leader in the Cuban Hills," *Harper's Weekly*, September 29, 1906.

44. Department of War, "Report of William H. Taft, Secretary of War, and Robert Bacon, Assistant Secretary of State, of What Was Done Under the Instructions of the President in Restoring Peace in Cuba," in *Annual Reports of the War Department*, Vol. I, 1906 [hereinafter cited as Taft-Bacon Report], pp. 444–45.

45. Allan Nevins, *Henry White: Thirty Years of American Diplomacy*, p. 255.

46. Taft-Bacon Report, pp. 444–45.

47. *Foreign Relations*, 1906, p. 476.

48. Roosevelt to Secretary of the Navy. September 12, 1906, National Archives and Records Service, Record Group 45, Area File 8, Caribbean [hereinafter cited as NARS, RG 45, AF 8].

49. Commander John C. Colwell to SecNav, October 6, 1906, NARS, RG 45, AF 8, [hereinafter cited as Colwell Report].

50. *Ibid.*

51. *Ibid.*

52. *Ibid.*

53. *Ibid.*

54. Jessup, *Elihu Root,* p. 533; Colwell Report.

55. *Foreign Relations,* 1906, p. 479; Taft-Bacon Report, pp. 446–47.

56. *Foreign Relations,* 1906, pp. 480–81; Taft-Bacon Report, pp. 491–92.

57. Taft-Bacon Report, pp. 491–92.

58. *La Correspondia,* Cienfuegos, Cuba, September 6, 1906, NARS, RG 45, AF 8; Eduardo Guzmán to George R. Fowler, September 10, 1906, NARS, RG 45, AF 8.

59. W.R. Fullam to Secretary of the Navy, September 14, 1906, NARS, RG 45, AF 8; Fullam, September 20, 1906, NARS, RG 45, AF 8.

60. Fullam to Secretary of the Navy, September 15, 1906, NARS, RG 45, AF 8; Fullam to Lieutenant J. V. Klemann, USN, September 16, 1906, NARS, RG 45, AF 8.

61. Secretary of the Navy, *Annual Report* [hereinafter cited as SecNav, *Annual Report*], 1906, pp. 1097–1098; *Army and Navy Register,* October 13, 1906.

62. Roosevelt to SecNav, September 14, 1906, NARS, RG 45, AF 8.

63. Jessup, *Elihu Root,* p. 534.

64. Minger, "William Howard Taft," pp. 80–81.

65. *Army and Navy Register,* September 22, 1906.

66. *New York Times,* September 22, 1906.

67. Taft-Bacon Report, pp. 473–75.

68. *Ibid.,* pp. 474–76.

69. William Inglis, "The Collapse of the Cuban House of Cards," *Harper's Weekly,* October 20, 1906.

70. Taft-Bacon Report, p. 486; Joel Thacker, *Interventions in Cuba Under the Platt Amendment,* unpublished manuscript, History and Museums Division, United States Marine Corps [hereinafter cited as H&MD], p. 4; Clyde Metcalf, *History of the United States Marine Corps,* p. 318.

71. *Army and Navy Register,* October 8, 1906.

72. Lt. Wm. P. Upshur, USMC, October 5, 1906, Southern Historical Collection, University of North Carolina.

73. Albertus A. Catlin, *With the Help of God and a Few Marines,* p. 249.

74. Taft-Bacon Report, p. 531.

75. *Army and Navy Register,* October 13, 1906.

76. Taft-Bacon Report, p. 488.

77. *Ibid.,* p. 533.

78. Millett, *Politics of Intervention,* p. 129; Department of War, *Annual Report,* 1908–1909, Vol. III, pp. 242–43.

79. *New York Times,* November 14, 1906.

80. *Army and Navy Journal,* May 4, 1907.

81. National Archives and Records Service, *The Bureau of Insular Affairs and Its Functions With Respect to Cuba,* p. vii.

82. *Army and Navy Journal,* November 24, 1906; Millett, *Politics of Intervention,* p. 136.
83. Department of War, *Annual Report,* 1907, Vol. III, pp. 321, 323, 333.
84. Chapman, *History of the Cuban Republic,* p. 272–73.
85. Louis A. Pérez Jr. "Politics, Peasants, and People of Color: The 1912 'Race War' in Cuba Reconsidered," *HAHR,* August 1966, p. 531.
86. *Foreign Relations,* 1912, p. 244.
87. *Ibid.,* p. 245.
88. Pérez, "Politics, Peasants, and People of Color," p. 532.
89. Robert D. Heinl, *Soldiers of the Sea,* p. 153.
90. *Foreign Relations,* 1912, p. 248.
91. *Ibid.,* pp. 250–51.
92. Alexander A. Vandegrift, *Once a Marine,* pp. 35–36.
93. Pérez, "Politics, Peasants, and People of Color," p. 537.
94. Metcalf, *History of the United States Marine Corps,* p. 331.
95. *Foreign Relations,* 1917, pp. 350–51.
96. *Ibid.,* p. 356.
97. *Ibid.,* p. 364.
98. Dudley W. Knox, "An Adventure in Diplomacy," *USNIP,* February 1926, pp. 273–79, *passim.*
99. *Ibid.,* pp. 281–83.
100. *Ibid.,* p. 283.
101. *Ibid.,* pp. 282–83.
102. *Foreign Relations,* 1917, p. 363.
103. Chapman, *History of the Cuban Republic,* pp. 378–79; Thacker, *Interventions in Cuba,* p. 18; Metcalf, *History of the United States Marine Corps,* p. 334; *Foreign Relations,* 1917, p. 382.
104. *Foreign Relations,* 1917, p. 407.

3. PANAMA 1885–1904

1. SecNav, *Annual Report,* 1898, Vol. II, p. 47.
2. *Ibid.*
3. C.N. Offley, "The Work of the *Oregon* During the Spanish-American War," *Journal of the American Society of Naval Engineers,* 1903, p. 1154.
4. Charles E. Clark, *My Fifty Years in the Navy,* p. 264.
5. *Saint Paul Pioneer Press,* April 24, 1898.
6. SecNav, *Annual Report,* 1898, Vol. II, p. 50.
7. *Ibid.,* p. 51.
8. *Ibid.*
9. Freidel, *Splendid Little War,* p. 44.
10. Clark, *My Fifty Years in the Navy,* pp. 274–75.
11. *Ibid.,* p. 277.
12. Miles P. DuVal Jr., *Cadiz to Cathay,* pp. 451–52.
13. Daniel Ammen, *The Old Navy and the New,* pp. 229–30.
14. 58th Congress, 2nd Session, Senate Document 143, *Use by the United States of a Military Force in the Internal Affairs of Colombia* [Note to reader: This is

a comprehensive collection of State and Navy department orders, reports, and letters covering the period from the earliest interventions until the end of 1902, hereinafter cited as *Military Force*], pp. 83–86.

15. *Ibid.*, p. 52.
16. Metcalf, *History of the United States Marine Corps*, p. 49.
17. Frank E. Evans, "The First Expedition to Panama," *Marine Corps Gazette* [hereinafter cited as *MCG*], June 1916, pp. 125, 128.
18. Kenneth J. Hagan, *American Gunboat Diplomacy and the Old Navy: 1877–1889*, p. 173.
19. *Ibid.*
20. *Military Force*, p. 113; Paolo Coletta, *Bowman Hendry McCalla: Fighting Sailor*, pp. 43–44.
21. *Military Force*, pp. 112–13.
22. Hagan, *American Gunboat Diplomacy*, p. 176.
23. *Military Force*, p. 67.
24. Hagan, *American Gunboat Diplomacy*, p. 179.
25. SecNav, *Annual Report*, 1885, Vol. II, pp. 24–25.
26. *Military Force*, pp. 144–45.
27. H.C. Reisinger, "On the Isthmus: 1885," *MCG*, December 1928, p. 234; *Military Force*, p. 107.
28. *Military Force*, pp. 105, 142.
29. *Ibid.*, p. 117.
30. *Ibid.*, p. 118; SecNav, *Annual Report*, 1885, Vol. I, p. XVI.
31. *Military Force*, p. 121.
32. *Ibid.*, pp. 119–21, 140.
33. *Ibid.*, p. 120.
34. *Ibid.*, p. 121.
35. *Ibid.*, p. 120.
36. *Ibid.*
37. Reisinger, "On the Isthmus," p. 232.
38. *Military Force*, p. 123.
39. *Ibid.*, p. 141.
40. *Ibid.*, p. 124.
41. *Foreign Relations*, 1885, p. 280; Robert Coontz, *From Mississippi to the Sea*, p. 92.
42. *Military Force*, p. 126.
43. *Ibid.*
44. *Ibid.*, p. 131.
45. 63rd Congress, 2nd Session, Senate Document 474, *Diplomatic History of the Panama Canal*, pp. 272–76 [hereinafter cited as *Diplomatic History*].
46. Lawrence O. Ealy, *Yanqui Politics and the Isthmian Canal*, p. 43.
47. Alfred Thayer Mahan, *The Influence of Sea Power Upon History: 1660–1783*, p. 30.
48. Ealy, *Yanqui Politics*, p. 44.
49. *Ibid.*, pp. 44–45.
50. *Diplomatic History*, pp. 289–91.
51. Ealy, pp. 44–45; Dana G. Munro, *Intervention and Dollar Diplomacy in the Caribbean; 1900–1921*, p. 38.

52. *Diplomatic History,* pp. 292–94.
53. Challener, *Admirals, Generals, and American Foreign Policy,* p. 151; SecNav, *Annual Report,* 1902, p. 466.
54. Challener, *Admirals, Generals, and American Foreign Policy,* p. 151.
55. *Military Force,* p. 186.
56. *Ibid.,* p. 70.
57. *Ibid.,* p. 201.
58. Challener, *Admirals, Generals, and American Foreign Policy,* p. 150; *Military Force,* p. 202.
59. *Military Force,* p. 203.
60. *Army and Navy Register,* December 14, 1901.
61. *Military Force,* p. 206.
62. *Ibid.,* pp. 203–206.
63. *Ibid.,* pp. 202–203
64. *Ibid.,* p. 203.
65. *Ibid.,* p. 270; Department of War, *Notes on Panama,* pp. 193–94.
66. *Military Force,* p. 270.
67. *Ibid.,* p. 211.
68. *Ibid.*
69. *Ibid.*
70. *Ibid.,* pp. 213–18.
71. *Ibid.,* p. 218.
72. *Ibid.,* p. 222.
73. Munro, *Intervention and Dollar Diplomacy,* pp. 38–44.
74. Philippe Bunau-Varilla, *Panama: The Creation, Destruction, and Resurrection,* pp. 189–91.
75. *Military Force,* p. 282.
76. Challener, *Admirals, Generals, and American Foreign Policy,* p. 153.
77. SecNav, *Annual Report,* 1902, pp. 992–93.
78. *Military Force,* p. 284.
79. *Ibid.,* pp. 286–87.
80. *Ibid.,* pp. 287, 295–96; *Army and Navy Register,* September 27, 1902.
81. *Military Force,* p. 295.
82. SecNav *Annual Report,* 1903, p. 1231; *Army and Navy Register,* October 11, 1902.
83. *Military Force,* p. 288.
84. *Ibid.,* p. 290.
85. *Ibid.,* p. 300.
86. *Ibid.,* pp. 304–305.
87. *Ibid.,* pp. 299, 305; SecNav, *Annual Report,* 1903, p. 1230.
88. *Military Force,* p. 305.
89. *Ibid.,* pp. 310–12.
90. *Ibid.,* pp. 311, 313, 317.
91. *Ibid.,* pp. 319–21.
92. *Ibid.,* p. 321.
93. William R. Thayer, *The Life and Letters of John Hay,* Vol. 2, pp. 327–28.
94. *New York Times,* November 15, 1902.
95. DuVal, *Cadiz to Cathay,* p. 188.

96. *Ibid.*, p. 196.
97. 62nd Congress, H.R. No. 32, *Story of Panama*, "Hearings on the Rainey Resolution, Before the Committee on Foreign Affairs of the House of Representatives, 1913," p. 322 [hereinafter cited as *Story of Panama*].
98. DuVal, *Cadiz to Cathay*, p. 215.
99. *Ibid.*, p. 218.
100. *Foreign Relations,* 1903, pp. 133–34.
101. *Ibid.*, 1903, pp. 137–41.
102. Pringle, *Theodore Roosevelt*, p. 311.
103. *New York World,* June 14, 1903.
104. *Story of Panama,* p. 349.
105. *Foreign Relations,* 1903, p. 120; David McCullough, *The Path Between the Seas,* p. 342.
106. DuVal, *Cadiz to Cathay*, pp. 261–62.
107. *Washington Post,* September 2, 1903.
108. DuVal, *Cadiz to Cathay*, p. 286; Thayer, *Life of John Hay,* Vol. 2, p. 322.
109. Dwight C. Miner, *The Fight for the Panama Canal Route: The Story of the Spooner Act and the Hay-Herran Treaty,* p. 348.
110. *Ibid.*, pp. 348–50.
111. *Ibid.*, p. 351.
112. *Ibid.*
113. *Ibid.*, p. 357.
114. Bunau-Varilla, *Panama*, pp. 310–11.
115. DuVal, *Cadiz to Cathay*, p. 299.
116. Bunau-Varilla, *Panama*, pp. 312, 320.
117. *Ibid.*
118. Secretary William Moody to Rear Admiral Henry Glass, October 15, 1903, Record Group 45, Area File 8, Caribbean, National Archives and Records Service [hereinafter cited as NARS, RG 45, AF 8].
119. Miner, *Fight for the Panama Canal Route,* pp. 354–59; Pringle, *Theodore Roosevelt,* p. 321.
120. Pringle, *Theodore Roosevelt*, p. 321.
121. Moody to Glass, October 19, 1903, NARS, RG 45, AF 8.
122. John A. Lejeune, *The Reminiscences of a Marine,* p. 152.
123. *Story of Panama,* p. 380.
124. Bunau-Varilla, *Panama*, p. 329.
125. *Ibid.*, p. 330.
126. *Ibid.*, p. 331.
127. *Ibid.*
128. Asst. Secretary Charles Darling to Commander John Hubbard, October 30, 1903, NARS, RG 45, AF 8; *Story of Panama,* p 381.
129. DuVal, *Cadiz to Cathay*, p. 321.
130. *Diplomatic History,* pp. 362–63; *Story of Panama,* p. 382.
131. *Story of Panama,* p. 386.
132. *Ibid.*, p. 388.
133. *Ibid.*
134. *Ibid.*, p. 390
135. Miner, *Fight for the Panama Canal Route,* p. 365.

136. *Story of Panama*, p. 390.
137. *Ibid*, pp. 392–93.
138. *Ibid.*, p. 394.
139. *Ibid.*
140. *Diplomatic History*, p. 346.
141. *Story of Panama*, p. 440.
142. *Ibid.*, p. 397.
143. *Ibid.*, pp. 441–42.
144. *Ibid.*, pp. 442–43.
145. *Ibid.*, pp. 435, 442–43.
146. *Ibid.*, pp. 442–43.
147. *Ibid.*
148. *Ibid.*, p. 444.
149. *Ibid.*, pp. 453–54.
150. *Ibid.*, p. 435.
151. Lejeune, *Reminiscences of a Marine*, pp. 154–55.
152. *Ibid.*, p. 157.
153. *Ibid.*; DuVal, *Cadiz to Cathay*, p. 337.
154. *Foreign Relations*, 1903, pp. 225–26.
155. *Diplomatic History*, p. 296.

4. NICARAGUA I 1912

1. Challener, *Admirals, Generals, and American Foreign Policy*, p. 293.
2. Frederick Palmer, *Central America and Its Problems*, p. 178.
3. Challener, *Admirals, Generals, and American Foreign Policy*, p. 293.
4. Munro, *Intervention and Dollar Diplomacy*, pp. 175–77.
5. Challener, *Admirals, Generals, and American Foreign Policy*, pp. 288–89.
6. Lowell Thomas, *Old Gimlet Eye: The Adventures of Smedley D. Butler*, p. 126.
7. Challener, *Admirals, Generals, and American Foreign Policy*, p. 299.
8. Thomas, *Old Gimlet Eye*, pp. 127–28.
9. *Ibid.*
10. *Ibid.*, pp. 130–31.
11. *Ibid.*
12. *Ibid.*, p. 130.
13. Munro, *Intervention and Dollar Diplomacy*, pp. 188–89.
14. *Foreign Relations*, 1911, p. 661; Thomas, *Old Gimlet Eye*, p. 138.
15. *Foreign Relations*, 1912, p. 1013.
16. *Ibid.*, pp. 1028–1031.
17. *Ibid.*, pp. 1032–1033.
18. *Ibid.*, p. 1038.
19. *Ibid.*, pp. 1039–1040.
20. Thomas, *Old Gimlet Eye*, p. 139.
21. Butler's account of the incident is taken from Thomas, *Old Gimlet Eye*, pp. 140–50, *passim*.
22. Vandegrift, *Once a Marine*, p. 40.
23. Thomas, *Old Gimlet Eye*, p. 150.
24. *Ibid.*, p. 140.

25. R. Adm. W.H.H. Southerland to Col. Joseph H. Pendleton, "Campaign Order No. 4," September 4, 1912, Pendleton papers, H&MD.
26. Southerland, "Memorandum for Commanders of Expeditionary Forces Operating in Nicaragua," September 4, 1912, Pendleton papers, H&MD.
27. Thomas, *Old Gimlet Eye*, pp. 147–48.
28. Southerland to Pendleton, September 11, 1912, Pendleton papers, H&MD; *Foreign Relations*, 1912, p. 1045.
29. *Foreign Relations*, 1912, pp. 1028–1029, 1059–1060.
30. *Ibid.*, pp. 1059–1060.
31. Vandegrift, *Once a Marine*, p. 41.
32. Thomas, *Old Gimlet Eye*, p. 154.
33. Pendleton to B.F. Zeledón, September 18, 1912, Pendleton papers, H&MD.
34. B.F. Zeledón to "Admiral Commanding American Forces in Nicaraguan Waters," September 18, 1912, Pendleton papers, H&MD.
35. Thomas, *Old Gimlet Eye*, p. 154.
36. Maj. Smedley D. Butler to Pendleton, "Beyond Masaya," September 19, 1912, Pendleton papers, H&MD.
37. *Ibid.*
38. *Ibid.*; Butler to Pendleton, "Report of duties performed," November 15, 1912, Pendleton papers, H&MD; *Foreign Relations*, 1912, p. 1062.
39. Thomas, *Old Gimlet Eye*, p. 160.
40. *Foreign Relations*, 1912, pp. 1059–1060.
41. Zeledón to Pendleton, October 3, 1912, Pendleton papers, H&MD.
42. Pendleton to Butler, October 3, 1912, Pendleton papers, H&MD.
43. Thomas, *Old Gimlet Eye*, pp. 166–67.
44. Joseph H. Pendleton, "The Battle of Coyotepe," *Army and Navy Register*, May 16, 1914.
45. *Ibid.*
46. *Ibid.*
47. Butler to Southerland, October 4, 1912, Pendleton papers, H&MD.
48. Thomas, *Old Gimlet Eye*, p. 166–67.
49. Pendleton to Lt. Col. Charles G. Long, "Orders," October 5, 1912, Pendleton papers, H&MD.
50. Long to Southerland, "Occupation of León," October 6, 1912, Pendleton papers, H&MD.
51. Lt. Cmdr. H.G.S. Wallace to Long, October 10, 1912, Pendleton papers, H&MD.
52. *Ibid.*
53. Long to Southerland, "Occupation of León"; Long to Pendleton, October 7, 1912, Pendleton papers, H&MD.
54. Pendleton to Southerland, "Report on Matagalpa Expedition," November 3, 1912, Pendleton papers, H&MD.
55. Challener, *Admirals, Generals, and American Foreign Policy*, p. 309.

5. HAITI 1915–1934

1. Edward L. Beach, *Admiral Caperton in Haiti*, p. 5.
2. *Ibid.*, pp. 1–2.

3. Robert D. Heinl and Nancy Heinl, *Written in Blood* [hereinafter cited as Heinl and Heinl], p. 388.
4. *Foreign Relations*, 1915, pp. 499–500.
5. SecNav, *Annual Report*, 1920, p. 224.
6. Lowell Thomas, *Old Gimlet Eye*, p. 181.
7. *Foreign Relations*, 1915, pp. 462–63.
8. *Ibid.*
9. Beach, *Admiral Caperton in Haiti*, p. 5.
10. Heinl and Heinl, *Written in Blood*, p. 386.
11. 67th Congress, 1st and 2nd sessions, Senate. *Inquiry Into the Occupation and Administration of Haiti and Santo Domingo* [hereinafter cited as Senate *Inquiry*], Vol. I, p. 290.
12. *Ibid.*
13. Beach, *Admiral Caperton in Haiti*, p. 6.
14. Heinl and Heinl, *Written in Blood*, p. 390.
15. *Ibid*, p. 392.
16. Beach, *Admiral Caperton in Haiti*, pp. 10–11.
17. *Ibid.*, pp. 12–14.
18. Maj. Gen. Walter Greatsinger Farrell, USMC (Ret.), interview with the author, September 1987 [hereinafter cited as Farrell interview].
19. Heinl and Heinl, *Written in Blood*, p. 397.
20. *Foreign Relations*, 1916, p. 315; Beach, *Admiral Caperton in Haiti*, p. 18.
21. *Foreign Relations*, 1916, p. 315; Heinl and Heinl, *Written in Blood*, p. 397.
22. Farrell interview.
23. Senate *Inquiry*, Vol. I, pp. 306–307; *Foreign Relations*, 1916, p. 314.
24. *Foreign Relations*, 1916, pp. 315–18.
25. Rear Adm. William B. Caperton, *History of U.S. Naval Operations Under Command of Rear Admiral W.B. Caperton, USN, Commencing June 5, 1915, Ending April 30, 1919*, p. 44 [hereinafter cited as Caperton, *Operations*]; SecNav, *Annual Report*, 1920, p. 246; USS *Washington*, deck log, July 27, 1915.
26. Coffey, R.B., "A Brief History of the Intervention in Haiti," *USNIP*, August 1922, pp. 1326–1327; Senate *Inquiry*, Vol. I, pp. 307–309.
27. *Foreign Relations*, 1915, pp. 475–76.
28. SecNav, *Annual Report*, 1920, p. 246.
29. Heinl and Heinl, *Written in Blood*, p. 403.
30. Beach, *Admiral Caperton in Haiti*, pp. 24–25; Coffey, "A Brief History of the Intervention in Haiti," p. 1334.
31. *Foreign Relations*, 1915, pp. 477–78.
32. Heinl and Heinl, *Written in Blood*, p. 406.
33. SecNav, *Annual Report*, 1915, p. 763; *Annual Report*, 1920, pp. 249–50.
34. Caperton, *Operations*, p. 53.
35. Beach, *Admiral Caperton in Haiti*, pp. 27–28.
36. *Ibid.*, pp. 32–34; Heinl and Heinl, *Written in Blood*, pp. 408–409.
37. SecNav, *Annual Report*, 1920, p. 251.
38. *Foreign Relations*, 1915, pp. 477–78.
39. SecNav, *Annual Report*, 1920, p. 252.
40. Beach, *Admiral Caperton in Haiti*, p. 36.

41. *Ibid.*
42. SecNav, *Annual Report,* 1920, p. 253.
43. *Ibid.,* pp. 253–54.
44. Beach, *Admiral Caperton in Haiti,* p. 44; Caperton, *Operations,* pp. 64–65.
45. Beach, *Admiral Caperton in Haiti,* pp. 56–58; Caperton, *Operations,* pp. 64–65.
46. Beach, *Admiral Caperton in Haiti,* p. 57.
47. *Ibid.,* pp. 61–63.
48. *Ibid.*
49. SecNav, *Annual Report,* 1920, p. 255.
50. Frederic Wise, *A Marine Tells It to You,* p. 129.
51. Beach, *Admiral Caperton in Haiti,* p. 68.
52. *Ibid.,* p. 72; Caperton, *Operations,* p. 87.
53. Caperton, *Operations,* p. 88; SecNav, *Annual Report,* 1920, p. 256.
54. David F. Healy, *Gunboat Diplomacy,* p. 115.
55. Wise, *A Marine Tells It to You,* p. 130.
56. Faustin Wirkus, *The White King of La Gonave,* p. 17.
57. *Foreign Relations,* 1915, pp. 449–51; SecNav, *Annual Report,* 1920, p. 255.
58. Caperton, *Operations,* p. 89, 114; SecNav, *Annual Report,* 1920, p. 257.
59. The account is taken from Fred E. McMillen, "Some Haitian Recollections," *USNIP,* April 1936, pp. 522–23.
60. The account is taken from Frederic Wise, "The Occupation of a Haitian Town," *USNIP,* December 1931, pp. 1629–31; Wise, *A Marine Tells It to You,* p. 134; SecNav, *Annual Report,* 1920, p. 264.
61. Caperton, *Operations,* p. 68.
62. SecNav, *Annual Report,* 1920, p. 259; David N. Buckner, *A Brief History of the 10th Marines,* pp. 5–6.
63. SecNav, *Annual Report,* 1920, p. 260.
64. Lowell Thomas, *Old Gimlet Eye,* p. 183.
65. *Ibid.,* pp. 183–84.
66. *Ibid.,* pp. 185–86.
67. SecNav, *Annual Report,* 1920, p. 262.
68. *Ibid.,* pp. 262–63.
69. *Ibid.,* p. 263.
70. Col. L.W.T. Waller to L.W.T. Waller Jr., October 17, 1915, Waller papers.
71. *Ibid.*
72. Senate *Inquiry,* Vol. I, p. 613.
73. The account of Butler's reconnaissance is taken from Butler to Commanding Officer, 1st Marines, December 7, 1915, "Report of Operations, October 9th, 1915, to November 27th, 1915, inclusive," Waller papers; SecNav, *Annual Report,* 1920, pp. 265–66; Thomas, *Old Gimlet Eye,* pp. 194–98.
74. SecNav, *Annual Report,* 1920, p. 266.
75. Lt. S.D. McCaughey, USN, "Haitian Blacks, No. 1," November 2, 1915, Waller papers.
76. *Ibid.*
77. Waller to Waller Jr., November 2, 1915, Waller papers.
78. SecNav, *Annual Report,* 1920, p. 267.

79. *Ibid.*
80. *Ibid.,* p. 268.
81. Thomas, *Old Gimlet Eye,* p. 200.
82. *Ibid.,* p. 202.
83. The account of the storming of Fort Rivière is taken from Butler to Commanding Officer, 1st Marines, "Report of Operations, October 9th, 1915, to November 27th, 1915, inclusive," Waller papers; SecNav, *Annual Report,* 1920, p. 269; Thomas, *Old Gimlet Eye,* pp. 200–208.
84. *Foreign Relations,* 1915, p. 494.
85. *Ibid.,* p. 450.
86. Burke Davis, *Marine! The Life of Chesty Puller,* p. 21.
87. Vandegrift, *Once a Marine,* pp. 49–50.
88. Waller to SecNav, "Treatment of Haitians by Marines," September 18, 1920, Waller papers.
89. Wirkus, *White King of La Gonave,* pp. 23–24.
90. SecNav, *Annual Report,* 1920, p. 272.
91. Waller to SecNav, "Treatment of Haitians by Marines."
92. SecNav, *Annual Report,* 1920, p. 274; Waller to SecNav, "Treatment of Haitians by Marines."
93. SecNav, *Annual Report,* 1920, p. 272; Waller to SecNav, "Treatment of Haitians by Marines;" Wirkus, *White King of La Gonave,* p. 27.
94. Beach, *Admiral Caperton in Haiti,* p. 15; Lester D. Langley, *The Banana Wars: An Inner History of American Empire, 1900–1934,* p. 156.
95. Brig. Gen. Eli Cole to R. Adm. Harry Knapp, April 8, 1917, Waller papers.
96. SecNav, *Annual Report,* 1917, p. 770.
97. *Ibid.,* p. 771.
98. *Ibid.*
99. Heinl and Heinl, *Written in Blood,* p. 449; SecNav, *Annual Report,* 1920, p. 237.
100. Senate *Inquiry,* Vol. I, pp. 530–31.
101. James H. McCrocklin, *Garde d'Haiti: Twenty Years of Organization and Training by the United States Marine Corps,* p. 95; Thomas, *Old Gimlet Eye,* p. 238.
102. Vandegrift, *Once a Marine,* pp. 52–53.
103. Farrell interview.
104. SecNav, *Annual Report,* 1920, p. 278.
105. Wise, *A Marine Tells It to You,* p. 311.
106. Heinl and Heinl, *Written in Blood,* p. 451.
107. Wise, *A Marine Tells It to You,* p. 310.
108. SecNav, *Annual Report,* 1920, p. 287.
109. Wise, *A Marine Tells It to You,* p. 301.
110. *Ibid.,* p. 309.
111. *Ibid.*
112. *Ibid.,* pp. 309–310.
113. *Ibid.,* p. 310.
114. Farrell interview.
115. Heinl and Heinl, *Written in Blood,* p. 455.
116. Wise, *A Marine Tells It to You,* pp. 311–12.
117. *Ibid.,* pp. 318–19.

118. *Ibid.*, p. 320.
119. Metcalf, *History of the United States Marine Corps*, p. 397; Wise, *A Marine Tells It to You*, pp. 321–23; Heinl and Heinl, *Written in Blood*, p. 458.
120. SecNav, *Annual Report*, 1920, pp. 290–91; Wise, *A Marine Tells It to You*, pp. 321–23; Farrell interview.
121. Farrell interview.
122. *Ibid.*
123. SecNav, *Annual Report*, 1920, p. 304.
124. *Ibid.*, p. 287; Heinl and Heinl, *Written in Blood*, p. 459.
125. Farrell interview.
126. *Ibid.*
127. SecNav, *Annual Report*, 1920, p. 298; Heinl and Heinl, *Written in Blood*, p. 460.
128. Heinl and Heinl, *Written in Blood*, p. 460.
129. SecNav, *Annual Report*, 1920, p. 297.
130. *Ibid.*, pp. 298–99.
131. *Ibid.*, p. 300.
132. Senate *Inquiry*, Vol. I, pp. 654–55.
133. SecNav, *Annual Report*, 1920, pp. 303–304.
134. *Ibid.*
135. Senate *Inquiry*, Vol. II, pp. 1808–1809.
136. SecNav, *Annual Report*, 1920, p. 313.
137. Carl Kelsey, "The American Intervention in Haiti and the Dominican Republic," *Annals of the American Academy of Political and Social Science*, 1921, p. 138.
138. Farrell interview.
139. Wise, *A Marine Tells It to You*, pp. 303–304.
140. *Ibid.*
141. *Ibid.*, p. 304.
142. *Ibid.*, pp. 304–305
143. SecNav, *Annual Report*, 1920, p. 306.
144. *Ibid.*, p. 179.
145. John W. Blassingame, "The Press and American Intervention in Haiti and the Dominican Republic, 1904–1920," *Caribbean Studies*, July 1969, p. 39.
146. SecNav, *Annual Report*, 1920, p. 242.
147. *Ibid.*
148. *Ibid.*, pp. 244–45.
149. *New York Times*, Sept. 21, 1920.
150. SecNav, *Annual Report*, 1920, pp. 180, 182.
151. *New York Times*, Oct. 15, 1920.
152. Record of Proceedings of a Court of Inquiry . . . Into the Conduct of the Personnel of the Naval Service That Has Served in Haiti, in Senate *Inquiry*, Vol. II, p. 1587.
153. *Ibid.*, pp. 1667–68
154. *Ibid.*
155. Heinl and Heinl, *Written in Blood*, p. 471.
156. *Ibid.*, p. 472.
157. *Ibid.*, p. 495.

158. *Ibid.*, p. 496.
159. *Ibid.*, p. 497.
160. *Army and Navy Journal*, August 18, 1934.

6. DOMINICAN REPUBLIC I 1916–1924

1. Wise, *A Marine Tells It to You*, pp. 138–39.
2. *Ibid.*
3. *Ibid.*, p. 139.
4. Selden Rodman, *Quisqueya: A History of the Dominican Republic*, p. 103.
5. Bruce J. Calder, *The Impact of Intervention: The Dominican Republic During the U.S. Occupation of 1916–1924*, pp. 6–7; Sumner Welles, *Naboth's Vineyard*, Vol. II, pp. 760–763.
6. Welles, *Naboth's Vineyard: The Dominican Republic 1844–1924*, Vol. 2, pp. 766–67; *Foreign Relations*, 1916, p. 221.
7. Wise, *A Marine Tells It to You*, pp. 139–40.
8. *Ibid.*, p. 140.
9. W.S. Crosley to distribution list, May 3, 1916, History and Museums Division, Headquarters, USMC, Dominican Republic Geographic File [hereinafter cited as H&MD DomRep File].
10. Samuel Guy Inman, *Through Santo Domingo and Haiti: A Cruise with the Marines*, p. 18.
11. Munro, *Intervention and Dollar Diplomacy*, pp. 78, 81–82.
12. *Ibid.*, pp. 84–86.
13. Challener, *Admirals, Generals, and American Foreign Policy*, p. 20.
14. Munro, *Intervention and Dollar Diplomacy*, pp. 88–89; *Foreign Relations*, 1904, p. 268.
15. Challener, *Admirals, Generals, and American Foreign Policy*, pp. 124–25.
16. *Ibid.*, p. 127.
17. *Ibid.*, pp. 126–27.
18. William Powell to Cmdr. James Miller, Jan. 20, 1904, NARS, RG 45, AF 8.
19. R. Adm. Albert W. Barker to Moody, Feb. 15, 1904, *ibid.*
20. Munro, *Intervention and Dollar Diplomacy*, p. 92.
21. *Ibid.*, p. 77.
22. Philip C. Jessup, *Elihu Root*, Vol. I, p. 469.
23. Munro, *Intervention and Dollar Diplomacy*, pp. 98–99.
24. *Foreign Relations*, 1905, pp. 311–12.
25. Blassingame, "The Press and American Intervention," pp. 28–37, *passim*.
26. *Ibid.*, p. 38.
27. Wise to the Major General Commandant, "Report of Operations of a Provisional Battalion . . . Ashore at the American Legation, Santo Domingo City, D.R., May 5th to May 11th, 1916 [hereinafter cited as Wise, "Operations Ashore"], H&MD DomRep File.
28. *Ibid.*; Wise, *A Marine Tells It to You*, pp. 141–42.
29. Wise, "Operations Ashore"; Wise, *A Marine Tells It to You*, p. 142.
30. Julian Smith, Oral History Collection, History and Museums Division, Headquarters, Marine Corps [hereinafter cited as Smith Oral History].

31. Stephen M. Fuller and Graham A. Cosmas, *Marines in the Dominican Republic 1916–1924*, pp. 7, 9; Wise, *A Marine Tells It to You*, p. 142.
32. Wise, *A Marine Tells It to You*, pp. 142–44.
33. Wise, "Operations Ashore"; Fuller and Cosmas, *Marines in the Dominican Republic*, p. 9.
34. Wise, *A Marine Tells It to You*, pp. 142–44.
35. *Foreign Relations*, 1916, p. 225.
36. Wise, "Operations Ashore."
37. *Ibid.*; Wise, *A Marine Tells It to You*, p. 144.
38. *Foreign Relations*, 1916, p. 226.
39. Headquarters First Provisional Regiment, Santo Domingo, D.R, May 14, 1916, "Field Order #1," H&MD DomRep File.
40. *Foreign Relations*, 1916, p. 226.
41. Smith Oral History.
42. *Foreign Relations*, 1916, p. 227–28
43. Major Charles B. Hatch to Commander, Cruiser Squadron, June 4, 1916, "Report of Landing at Puerta Plata, D.R., June 1, 1916," H&MD DomRep File [hereinafter cited as Hatch Report].
44. *Ibid.*
45. Commander Roscoe C. Bulmer to Commander, Cruiser Squadron, June 4, 1916, "Report of Landing at Puerto Plata, D.R., June 1, 1916," H&MD DomRep File [hereinafter cited as Bulmer Report].
46. *Ibid.*
47. Hatch Report.
48. Bulmer Report.
49. Hatch Report.
50. Wise, *A Marine Tells It to You*, pp. 146–47.
51. *Ibid.*
52. Commander Harris Lanning to Commander, Cruiser Squadron, June 6, 1916, "Report of Operations and Conditions, Monte Cristi, D.R.," H&MD DomRep File [hereinafter cited as Lanning Report].
53. *Ibid.*
54. *Ibid.*
55. Wise, *A Marine Tells It to You*, pp. 148–49.
56. *Ibid.*
57. Lanning Report.
58. Kenneth W. Condit and Edwin T. Turnbladh, *Hold High the Torch: A History of the 4th Marines*, pp. 2, 39–41.
59. Colonel Joseph H. Pendleton to Commander, Cruiser Squadron, July 20, 1916, "Report of Provisional Detachment, U.S. Expeditionary Forces . . . Operating Ashore in Santo Domingo, June 26th to July 6th, 1916," H&MD DomRep File [hereinafter cited as Pendleton Report]; Condit and Turnbladh, *Hold High the Torch*, pp. 44–45; Wise, *A Marine Tells It to You*, pp. 149–150.
60. Condit and Turnbladh, *Hold High the Torch*, p. 43; Wise, *A Marine Tells It to You*, p. 150.
61. Condit and Turnbladh, *Hold High the Torch*, pp. 45–46; Wise, *A Marine Tells It to You*, p. 151; Pendleton Report.
62. Pendleton Report.

63. Condit and Turnbladh, *Hold High the Torch*, pp. 49–50; Pendleton Report.
64. Roswell Winans, "Campaigning in Santo Domingo," *Recruiters' Bulletin*, March 1917.
65. Pendleton Report; "March From Monte Cristi to Santiago," H&MD DomRep File; Winans, "Campaigning in Santo Domingo."
66. Pendleton Report; Winans, "Campaigning in Santo Domingo."
67. Winans, "Campaigning in Santo Domingo."
68. Pendleton Report.
69. *Ibid.*; Condit and Turnbladh, *Hold High the Torch*, pp. 54–57.
70. Winans, "Campaigning in Santo Domingo."
71. *Ibid.*
72. *Ibid.*; Condit and Turnbladh, *Hold High the Torch*, pp. 57–58.
73. Wise, *A Marine Tells It to You*, p. 153.
74. Eugene Fortson, "Report of Operations of Fourth and Ninth Companies from June 21, 1916 to . . . July 9, 1916," H&MD DomRep File [hereinafter cited as Fortson Report].
75. *Ibid.*; "Engagements at Llanos, Periz, and Quebreda Honda," H&MD DomRep File.
76. "Engagement at Alta Mira," H&MD DomRep File.
77. Condit and Turnbladh, *Hold High the Torch*, p. 62; Fortson Report; Heinl, *Soldiers of the Sea*, p. 184.
78. Pendleton Report; Wise, *A Marine Tells It to You*, p. 153.
79. Pendleton Report.
80. Wise, *A Marine Tells It to You*, p. 153.
81. Condit and Turnbladh, *Hold High the Torch*, p. 59.
82. John H. Nichols, "Hiking and Fighting," *Recruiters' Bulletin*, November 1916.
83. Condit and Turnbladh, *Hold High the Torch*, p. 64.
84. *Foreign Relations*, 1916, pp. 227–28.
85. *Ibid.*, pp. 222–30.
86. Munro, *Intervention and Dollar Diplomacy*, p. 309.
87. *Ibid.*, p. 310.
88. The account of the *Memphis* disaster is taken from Edward L. Beach, *The Wreck of the Memphis, passim*; Thomas Withers, "The Wreck of the USS Memphis," *USNIP*, July 1918, *passim*; Ivan Musicant, *U.S. Armored Cruisers: A Design and Operational History*, pp. 186–88.
89. Condit and Turnbladh, *Hold High the Torch*, p. 65; *Foreign Relations*, 1916, p. 239.
90. Munro, *Intervention and Dollar Diplomacy*, p. 312; "Board of Inquiry into the Deaths of Captain William K. Low and First Sergeant Frank L. Atwood," H&MD DomRep File.
91. *Foreign Relations*, 1916, pp. 240–42.
92. *Ibid.*, pp. 242–43.
93. *Ibid.*, pp. 246–47.
94. The incident at San Francisco de Macorís is taken from Condit and Turnbladh, *Hold High the Torch*, pp. 70–75; Clyde Metcalf, *History of the United States Marines*, pp. 353–54; Fuller and Cosmas, *Marines in the Dominican Republic*, p. 26.

95. Pendleton to Commandant of the Marine Corps, December 18, 1916, H&MD, Pendleton papers.
96. Charles J. Miller, "Diplomatic Spurs: Our Experiences in Santo Domingo," *Marine Corps Gazette* [hereinafter cited as *MCG*], February 1935, p. 45; C.C. Baughman, "United States Occupation of the Dominican Republic," *USNIP*, December 1925, p. 2309.
97. Miller, "Diplomatic Spurs," February 1935, pp. 45–46.
98. Baughman, "United States Occupation," p. 2314; Carl Kelsey, "The American Intervention," p. 173.
99. Baughman, "United States Occupation," pp. 2311–12.
100. *Ibid.*, p. 2316.
101. George C. Thorpe, "Dominican Service," *MCG*, December 1919, p. 325.
102. Bruce J. Calder, "Caudillos and *Gavilleros* versus the United States Marines: Guerrilla Insurgency during the Dominican Intervention, 1916–1924," *HAHR*, November 1978, pp. 670–72.
103. *Ibid.*
104. Marvin Goldwert, "The Constabulary in the Dominican Republic and Nicaragua," *Latin American Monographs*, September 1961, pp. 2–4, 8–9.
105. Edward A. Fellowes, "Training Native Troops in Santo Domingo," *MCG*, December 1923, pp. 230–31.
106. Maj. Gen. Omar T. Pfeiffer, USMC, Oral History Transcript, 1974, Marine Corps H&MD, Oral History Collection [hereinafter cited as Pfeiffer Oral History].
107. *Foreign Relations,* 1919, Vol. II, pp. 100, 120.
108. Henry C. Davis, "Indoctrination of Latin-American Service," *MCG*, June 1920, p. 154.
109. Calder, "Caudillos and *Gavilleros*," p. 653
110. Davis, "Indoctrination of Latin-American Service," p. 155.
111. Lt. Gen. Edward A. Craig, USMC, Oral History Transcript, H&MD Oral History Collection [hereinafter cited as Craig Oral History].
112. Lt. Col. George C. Thorpe to Commandant of the Marine Corps, "Certain Gallant Services in Santo Domingo," May 14, 1919, H&MD DomRep File.
113. Pfeiffer Oral History.
114. Fuller and Cosmas, *Marines in the Dominican Republic,* p. 38.
115. Craig Oral History.
116. "Report of operations of detachment of 1st Company Under Command of First Lieutenant Roben, in Province of Seibo, Santo Domingo, January 14–February 1, 1917," H&MD DomRep File.
117. District Commander, Southern District, to Commanding General 2nd Marine Brigade, December 30, 1921, "Reports requested by Senate Committee re-Santo Domingo," H&MD DomRep File.
118. Craig Oral History.
119. Commander U.S. forces Operating in Province of Macorís. Consuelo, D.R., to Brigade Commander, Second Provisional Brigade, USMC, February 2, 1917, "Report of Operations in the Province of Macorís, D.R." H&MD DomRep File [hereinafter cited as Bearss, Macorís Report].
120. *Ibid.*
121. Bearss Macorís Report.

122. Pendleton to Barnett, April 9, 1917, H&MD, Pendleton Papers.
123. Pfeiffer Oral History; Craig Oral History.
124. Thorpe to Pendleton, August 18, 1918, H&MD, Pendleton Papers.
125. Calder, "Caudillos and *Gavilleros*," p. 667.
126. Fuller and Cosmas, *Marines in the Dominican Republic*, p. 33.
127. District Commander, Eastern District, to Commanding General, Second Brigade, U.S. Marines, Santo Domingo City, D.R., January 2, 1922, "Control of Field Forces by Regimental Headquarters, 15th Regiment," H&MD DomRep File.
128. Craig Oral History.
129. Calder, "Caudillos and *Gavilleros*," pp. 666–67.
130. *Ibid.*, p. 669.
131. Condit and Turnbladh, *Hold High the Torch*, p. 93; Fuller and Cosmas, *Marines in the Dominican Republic*, p. 45.
132. Robert C. Kilmartin, "Indoctrination in Santo Domingo," *MCG*, December 1922, p. 377; Kelsey, "The American Intervention," p. 198.

7. NICARAGUA II 1927–1934

1. Allan R. Millett, *Semper Fidelis: The History of the United States Marine Corps*, pp. 239–40.
2. Richard Millett, *Guardians of the Dynasty: A History of the U.S. Created* Guardia Nacional de Nicaragua *and the Somoza Family*, pp. 33–34.
3. *Foreign Relations*, 1927, Vol. III, pp. 288–89.
4. Goldwert, "The Constabulary in the Dominican Republic and Nicaragua," p. 24.
5. *Ibid.*, p. 26.
6. R. Millett, *Guardians of the Dynasty*, p. 44.
7. Harold N. Denny, *Dollars for Bullets: The Story of American Rule in Nicaragua*, p. 203.
8. *Ibid.*, pp. 206–207.
9. *Ibid.*
10. *Ibid.*; R. Millett, *Guardians of the Dynasty*, p. 45.
11. Denny, *Dollars for Bullets*, p. 210.
12. *Foreign Relations*, 1926, Vol. II, p. 786.
13. Goldwert, "The Constabulary in the Dominican Republic and Nicaragua," p. 23.
14. Denny, *Dollars for Bullets*, p. 225.
15. R. Millett, *Guardians of the Dynasty*, p. 47.
16. Situation reports, untitled, December 23, 1926, History and Museums Division, Headquarters, Marine Corps, Nicaragua Geographic File [hereinafter cited as H&MD Nicaragua File]; *Foreign Relations*, 1926, Vol. II, pp. 815, 817.
17. *Foreign Relations*, 1926, Vol. II, pp. 809–810.
18. Denny, *Dollars for Bullets*, pp. 243–44.
19. *Ibid.*, p. 246.
20. R. Millett, *Guardians of the Dynasty*, p. 53.

21. Denny, *Dollars for Bullets,* pp. 267–68.
22. *Ibid.,* p. 278.
23. *Ibid.,* p. 275.
24. *Ibid.,* p. 270.
25. *Ibid.*
26. *Foreign Relations,* 1927, Vol. III, pp. 312–13.
27. *Ibid.,* p. 309.
28. *Ibid.,* p. 314.
29. *Ibid.,* p. 313.
30. Ross E. Rowell, "Marine Air in Nicaragua," *MCG,* May 1985, pp 82, 84.
31. *Ibid.,* p. 85; R. Millett, *Guardians of the Dynasty,* p. 53.
32. Henry L. Stimson, *American Policy in Nicaragua,* p. 42.
33. *Ibid.,* p. 46.
34. *Foreign Relations,* 1927, Vol. III, p. 337.
35. *Ibid.,* p. 338.
36. Situation Reports, untitled, May 1, 1927, H&MD Nicaragua File.
37. *Foreign Relations,* 1927, Vol. III, pp. 349–50.
38. *New York Herald Tribune,* May 14, 1927; Lejeune Cummins, *Quijote on a Burro: Sandino and the Marines, a Study in the Formulation of Foreign Policy,* p. 114.
39. Joseph O. Baylen, "Sandino: Patriot or Bandit?" *HAHR,* August 1951, p. 399.
40. Headquarters, Eastern Area, Nicaragua, June 9, 1928, "Description of Sandino," H&MD Nicaragua File.
41. Neill Macaulay, *The Sandino Affair,* pp. 54–55.
42. *Ibid.*
43. *Ibid.,* p. 61.
44. SecNav, *Annual Report,* 1928, p. 65.
45. "Testimony of the Major General Commandant Before the Senate Committee on Foreign Relations," *MCG,* March 1928, pp. 49–50 [hereinafter cited as Lejeune Testimony]; Robert Heinl, *Soldiers of the Sea,* p. 266.
46. Macaulay, *The Sandino Affair,* p. 65.
47. *Ibid.*
48. *Ibid.,* p. 66.
49. Edwin North McClellan, "He Remembered His Mission," *MCG,* November 1930, pp. 30–32.
50. *Ibid.*
51. *Ibid.*
52. *Ibid.*
53. *Ibid.*
54. Macaulay, *The Sandino Affair,* pp. 69–70.
55. 11th Marines Intelligence Report, León, Nicaragua, June 10, 1927, H&MD Nicaragua File.
56. Edwin North McClellan, "The Nueva Segovia Expedition," part I, *MCG,* May, 1931, p. 22; Macaulay, *The Sandino Affair,* p. 70; Situation reports, June 21, 1927, H&MD Nicaragua File; Robert Emmet, *A Brief History of the 11th Marines,* pp. 3–4; James M. Yingling, *A Brief History of the 5th Marines,* p. 15.

57. Goldwert, "The Constabulary in the Dominican Republic and Nicaragua," p. 39.
58. H.C. Reisinger, *"La Palabra Del Gringo!: Leadership of the Nicaraguan National Guard,"* USNIP, February 1935, p. 216.
59. *Foreign Relations,* 1927, Vol. III, p. 440; Macaulay, *The Sandino Affair,* pp. 74–75.
60. Macaulay, *The Sandino Affair,* pp. 73–74.
61. Edwin McClellan, "The Nueva Segovia Expedition," I, p. 23.
62. *Ibid.,* p. 24.
63. *Foreign Relations,* 1927, Vol. III, p. 441; Macaulay, *The Sandino Affair,* p. 71.
64. Denny, *Dollars for Bullets,* p. 313; *Foreign Relations,* 1927, Vol. III, p. 441.
65. Macaulay, *The Sandino Affair,* pp. 71–72.
66. *Ibid.,* pp. 72, 75–76.
67. U.S. Marine Corps, Division of Operations and Training, "Combat Operations in Nicaragua," I, *MCG,* March 1929, pp. 21–22.
68. *Ibid.*
69. *Ibid.,* p. 18.
70. *Ibid.*
71. *Ibid.,* pp. 18–19.
72. *Ibid.,* pp. 19–21.
73. *Ibid.,* p. 20; Captain Gilbert D. Hatfield at Ocotal, December 22, 1960, H&MD.
74. Heinl, *Soldiers of the Sea,* p. 269; Vernon E. Megee, "The Genesis of Air Support in Guerrilla Operations," *USNIP,* June 1965, p. 54.
75. Rowell, "Marine Air in Nicaragua," p. 87.
76. *Ibid.*
77. *Ibid.*
78. *Ibid.*; Megee, "The Genesis of Air Support in Guerrilla Operations," p. 54.
79. "Combat Operations in Nicaragua," I, p. 21.
80. *Foreign Relations,* 1927, Vol. III, p. 440–42; *New York Times,* July 19, 1927.
81. McClellan, "The Nueva Segovia Expedition," II, *MCG,* August 1931, p. 8; Macaulay, *The Sandino Affair,* pp. 74, 85.
82. Macaulay, *The Sandino Affair,* pp. 85–86.
83. *Ibid.,* p. 86; McClellan, "The Nueva Segovia Expedition," II, p. 8–9.
84. McClellan, "The Nueva Segovia Expedition," II, p. 9.
85. Heinl, *Soldiers of the Sea,* p. 273; McClellan, "The Nueva Segovia Expedition," II, p. 11.
86. McClellan, "The Nueva Segovia Expedition," II, p. 11.
87. Brig. Gen. Logan Feland, "To the People of the Setentrion," August 9, 1927, H&MD Nicaragua File.
88. Macaulay, *The Sandino Affair,* p. 89.
89. Statement of Pvt. L.C. Handzlik, nd, H&MD, Nicaragua File.
90. Capt. H.S. Keimling, (GNN), "Statement of the Battle of Telpaneca," nd, H&MD Nicaragua File.
91. *Ibid.*
92. *Ibid.*

93. *Ibid.*
94. Heinl, *Soldiers of the Sea*, p. 271; Macaulay, *The Sandino Affair*, p. 93; for a poignantly excellent fictional account, see John Thomason, "Air Patrol," in his compendium *Fix Bayonets!*
95. The account of O'Shea's patrol is taken from First Lt. George J. O'Shea, "Attack on O'Shea's Patrol," nd, H&MD Nicaragua File.
96. Rowell, "Marine Air in Nicaragua," p. 89.
97. U.S. Marine Corps, Division of Operations and Training, "Combat Operations in Nicaragua," II, *MCG*, June 1929, p. 83.
98. *Ibid.*
99. Lejeune Testimony, p. 53.
100. "Combat Operations in Nicaragua," II, pp. 85–86.
101. *Ibid.*
102. *Ibid.*, pp. 87–88.
103. *Ibid.*, pp. 88–89.
104. *Ibid.*, p. 90; Edwin H. Brainard, "Marine Corps Aviation," *MCG*, March 1928, p. 33.
105. "Combat Operations in Nicaragua," II, p. 90; *New York Times*, January 4, 1928.
106. *New York Times*, January 18, 1928; January 10, 1928.
107. *Ibid.*, January 4, 1928.
108. *Ibid.*, January 4, 1928; Denny, *Dollars for Bullets*, pp. 326–27.
109. Rowell, "Marine Air in Nicaragua," p. 91.
110. *Ibid.*
111. *Ibid.*
112. *New York Times*, January 20, 1928.
113. "Combat Operations in Nicaragua," II, p. 92.
114. Lejeune Testimony, p. 58.
115. "Combat Operations in Nicaragua," II, pp. 93–94.
116. Rowell, "Marine Air in Nicaragua," p. 91.
117. *Foreign Relations*, 1928, Vol. III, p. 563.
118. *Ibid.*, p. 569.
119. Maurice Holmes, "With the Horse Marines in Nicaragua," *MCG*, February 1984, pp. 36–42, *passim*.
120. Macaulay, *The Sandino Affair*, p. 111.
121. The account of O'Day's patrol is taken from U.S. Marine Corps, Division of Operations and Training, "Combat Operations in Nicaragua," III, *MCG*, September 1929, pp. 173–77, *passim*.
122. Macaulay, *The Sandino Affair*, p. 115.
123. The account of Hunter's patrol is taken from Victor F. Bleasdale, "La Flor Engagement," *MCG*, February 1932, pp. 30–37, *passim*.
124. The account of the Coco patrol is taken from Merritt A. Edson, "The Coco Patrol," *MCG*, August 1936, pp. 18–40, *passim*, *MCG*, February 1937, pp. 35–58, *passim*; Edwin N. McClellan, "The Saga of the Coco," *MCG*, November 1930, pp. 71–79, *passim*.
125. Carleton Beals, *Banana Gold*, p. 293.
126. Harold W. Dodds, "American Supervision of the Nicaraguan Election," *MCG*, June 1929, pp. 120–22.

127. *Ibid.*; Goldwert, "The Constabulary in the Dominican Republic and Nicaragua," p. 32.
128. Edwin N. McClellan, "Supervising Nicaraguan Elections, 1928," *USNIP,* January 1933, pp. 37–38.
129. Bernard C. Nalty, *The United States Marines in Nicaragua,* p. 27.
130. Metcalf, *History of the United States Marine Corps,* p. 439.
131. Macaulay, *The Sandino Affair,* p. 139.
132. *Ibid.,* pp. 136–37.
133. *Ibid.,* pp. 138, 141; Nalty, *The United States Marines in Nicaragua,* p. 28.
134. Dion Williams, "The Nicaraguan Situation," *MCG,* November 1930, p. 21.
135. *Ibid.*
136. *Ibid.*
137. *Ibid.*
138. Yingling, *A Brief History of the 5th Marines,* p. 19; Macaulay, *The Sandino Affair,* pp. 183–184.
139. Willard Beaulac, *Career Diplomat,* pp. 128–130.
140. Macaulay, *The Sandino Affair,* p. 191.
141. Henry Stimson and McGeorge Bundy, *On Active Service in Peace and War,* p. 182.
142. *Foreign Relations,* 1931, Vol. II, p. 808.
143. Macaulay, *The Sandino Affair,* p. 212; *Foreign Relations,* 1931, Vol. II, p. 828.
144. Beaulac, *Career Diplomat,* p. 126.
145. *Ibid.,* pp. 126–27.
146. Macaulay, *The Sandino Affair,* p. 231.
147. Jim Boyce, "Combat Patrol: Nicaragua," *Leatherneck,* October 1982, p. 42.
148. *Ibid.*
149. Davis, *Marine!,* p. 68.
150. Boyce, "Combat Patrol: Nicaragua," pp. 42–43.
151. *Ibid.*; Heinl, *Soldiers of the Sea,* p. 286.
152. Davis, *Marine!,* p. 69; Heinl, *Soldiers of the Sea,* p. 286.
153. Davis, *Marine!,* p. 53.
154. *Ibid.,* p. 74.
155. *Ibid.,* p. 75.

8. DOMINICAN REPUBLIC II 1965

1. Jack K. Ringler and Henry I. Shaw Jr., *U.S. Marine Corps Operations in the Dominican Republic: April–June, 1965,* p. 7.
2. *Ibid.,* p. 50.
3. James A. Dare, "Dominican Diary," *USNIP,* December 1965, pp. 37–38.
4. *Ibid.,* p. 39.
5. *Ibid.*
6. *Ibid.*
7. *Ibid.,* p. 41.
8. Gene Young, "*Boxer*'s First Round," *Leatherneck,* July 1965, p. 29.
9. *Ibid.*

10. Paul Berger, "The Corridor," *Leatherneck*, August 1965, p. 24.
11. *Ibid.*
12. *Ibid.*, pp. 28–29.
13. Ringler and Shaw, *U.S. Marine Corps Operations in the Dominican Republic*, p. 130.

9. GRENADA 1983

1. Ben Bradlee Jr., *Guts and Glory: The Rise and Fall of Oliver North*, p. 173.
2. *Ibid.*, p. 174.
3. Committee on Armed Services, House of Representatives, *Lessons Learned as a Result of the U.S. Military Operations in Grenada* [hereinafter cited as *Lessons Learned*], p. 11.
4. Lee E. Russell and M. Albert Mendez, *Grenada 1983*, p. 5.
5. *Lessons Learned*, p. 11.
6. Michael J. Bryon, "Fury from the Sea: Marines in Grenada," *USNIP*, May 1984, p. 123.
7. James Adams, *Secret Armies*, p. 226.
8. Frank McNeil, *War and Peace in Central America*, p. 173.
9. *Ibid.*, p. 174.
10. *Lessons Learned*, p. 12.
11. Adams, *Secret Armies*, p. 230.
12. *Ibid.*
13. *Ibid.*, p. 233.
14. Ronald Spector, *U.S. Marines in Grenada 1983*, p. 7.
15. *Ibid.*, p. 14.
16. *Lessons Learned*, p. 36.
17. "The Battle of Grenada," *Newsweek*, November 7, 1983, p. 72.
18. Adams, *Secret Armies*, p. 236.
19. Spector, *U.S. Marines in Grenada*, p. 18.
20. Adams, *Secret Armies*, p. 242.
21. Spector, *U.S. Marines in Grenada*, p. 21.
22. Adams, *Secret Armies*, p. 241; anonymous interview with the author.
23. Bryon, "Fury from the Sea," p. 119.
24. Russell and Mendez, *Grenada 1983*, p. 37; Adams, *Secret Armies*, p. 245.

AFTERWORD. THE PANAMA INVASION 1989

1. Statements of Colonel John D. Waghelstein, U.S.A., June 6, 1989.
2. Anonymous interview, January 16, 1990.
3. Interview with Colonel John D. Waghelstein, U.S.A., Ret., January 10, 1990 [hereinafter cited as Waghelstein interview].
4. *Army Times*, January 1, 1990.
5. *Ibid.*
6. *Newsweek*, October 16, 1989; *Army Times*, January 1, 1990.
7. *Newsweek*, January 1, 1990.

8. Waghelstein interview.
9. *Army Times*, January 1, 1990.
10. *Newsweek*, January 1, 1990.
11. *Ibid.*
12. *Ibid.*; *New York Times*, December 21, 1989.
13. *Newsweek*, January 1, 1990; *New York Times*, December 18, 1989.
14. *Newsweek*, January 1, 1990.
15. *Newsweek*, January 1, 1990; *New York Times*, December 21, 1989.
16. Interview with Lieutenant Colonel Ed Fitzsimmons, U.S.A., January 9, 1990 [hereinafter cited as Fitzsimmons interview].
17. *Army Times*, January 1, 1990.
18. *Minneapolis Star Tribune*, December 21, 1989.
19. *Ibid.*, December 24, 1989; *New York Times*, December 21, 1989.
20. *Minneapolis Star Tribune*, December 23, 1990.
21. *Air Force Times*, January 8, 1990.
22. Dr. Harry Summers, National Public Radio, January 11, 1990.
23. *Army Times*, January 15, 1990.
24. *Ibid.*, January 1, 1990.
25. *Ibid.*
26. *Newsweek*, January 8, 1990.
27. Anonymous interview.
28. *Ibid.*
29. *Air Force Times*, January 8, 1990.
30. *Ibid.*
31. *Ibid.*, January 15, 1990.
32. *Air Force Times*, January 8, 1990.
33. *Minneapolis Star Tribune*, December 21, 1989.
34. *Newsweek*, January 1, 1990.
35. *Navy Times*, January 1, 1990.
36. *Ibid.*
37. *Minneapolis Star Tribune*, December 21, 1989; *Army Times*, January 8, 1990.
38. *Newsweek*, January 1, 1990.
39. *Minneapolis Star Tribune*, December 22, 1989.
40. Fitzsimmons interview.
41. *Minneapolis Star Tribune*, December 22, 1989.
42. *Newsday* (Long Island, New York), December 28, 1989.
43. *Army Times*, January 8, 1990.
44. Fitzsimmons interview.
45. *Army Times*, January 1, 1990.
46. *Ibid.*
47. *Minneapolis Star Tribune*, December 22, 1989; *Newsweek*, January 1, 1990.
48. *Newsweek*, January 1, 1990.
49. *Minneapolis Star Tribune*, December 22, 1990.
50. *Ibid.*, December 27, 1989.
51. *Ibid.*, December 25, 1989.
52. *Ibid.*, December 30, 1989.
53. *Ibid.*, December 31, 1989.
54. *Army Times*, January 15, 1990.

BIBLIOGRAPHY

UNPUBLISHED GOVERNMENT DOCUMENTS

Department of the Navy, Area File of the Naval Records Collection, 1775–1910: Record Group 45, Area 8, Caribbean. National Archives and Records Service, Washington, DC.

Ringler, Jack K. and Henry I. Shaw, Jr. *U.S. Marine Corps Operations in the Dominican Republic—April–June 1965.* History and Museums Division, U.S. Marine Corps, Washington, DC.

United States Marine Corps. Geographic Area Files: Dominican Republic, Haiti, Nicaragua. History and Museums Division, Headquarters, U.S. Marine Corps, Washington, DC.

PUBLISHED GOVERNMENT DOCUMENTS

55th Congress, 2nd Session, Senate Document 207 (serial 3610). *The Report of the Naval Court of Inquiry Upon the Destruction of the United States Battle Ship Maine.* Washington, DC, 1898.

55th Congress, 2nd Session, Senate Document 230 (serial 3610). *Consular Correspondence Respecting the Condition of the Reconcentrados in Cuba, the State of War in that Island, and the Prospects of the Projected Autonomy.* Washington, DC, 1898.

58th Congress, 2nd Session, Senate Document 143 (serial 4589). *Use by the United States of a Military Force in the Internal Affairs of Colombia.* Washington, DC, 1904.

63rd Congress, 2nd Session, Senate Document 474 (serial 6582). *Diplomatic History of the Panama Canal.* Washington, DC, 1914.

67th Congress, 1st and 2nd sessions, *Inquiry Into Occupation and Administration of Haiti and Santo Domingo* [Hearing]. Washington, DC, 1922.

445

67th Congress, 2nd Session, Senate Report 794, (serial 7954). *Inquiry Into Occupation and Administration of Haiti and Santo Domingo* [Report]. Washington, DC, 1922.

71st Congress, 3rd Session, Senate Document 288 (serial 9347). *United States Marines in Nicaragua.* Washington, DC, 1931.

98th Congress, 2nd Session (HASC No. 98–43), *Full Committee Hearing on the Lessons Learned as a Result of the U.S. Military Operations in Grenada.* Washington, DC, 1984.

Buckner, David, N. *A Brief History of the 10th Marines,* History and Museums Division, U.S. Marine Corps, 1981.

Condit, Kenneth W. and Edwin T. Turnbladh, *Hold High the Torch: A History of the 4th Marines.* Historical Branch, G-3 Division, Headquarters, USMC. Washington, DC, 1960.

Department of State. *State Papers Relating to the Foreign Relations of the United States.* Washington, DC, various years.

Department of the Navy. *Annual Report of the Department of the Navy.* Washington, DC, various years.

———. *Dictionary of American Naval Fighting Ships,* eight vols. Washington, DC, 1970–1981.

Department of War. *Annual Report of the Department of War.* Washington, DC, various years.

———. *Annual Report of Charles E. Magoon—Provisional Governor of Cuba.* Washington, DC, 1907.

———. *Five Years of the War Department Following the War with Spain, 1899–1903: As Shown in the Annual Reports of the Secretary of War.* Washington, DC, 1904.

———. *Notes on Panama.* Washington, DC, 1903.

———. *Records of the Bureau of Insular Affairs Relating to the United States Military Government of Cuba 1898–1902 and the United States Provisional Government of Cuba 1906–1909.* Washington, DC, 1943.

———. *Report of Maj. Gen. J.R. Brooke on Civil Affairs in Cuba: 1899.* Washington, DC, 1900.

———. *Report of Brig. Gen. Leonard Wood on Civil Affairs in Santiago and Puerto Principe, Cuba.* Washington, DC, 1900.

Emmet, Robert, *A Brief History of the 11th Marines.* Historical Branch, G-3 Division, Headquarters, USMC. Washington, DC, 1968.

Frank, Benis M. *A Brief History of the 3rd Marines.* Historical Branch, G-3 Division, Headquarters, USMC. Washington, DC, 1961.

Fuller, Stephen M. and Graham A. Cosmas. *Marines in the Dominican Republic 1916–1924.* History and Museums Division, U.S. Marine Corps, 1974.

Hewes, James E. Jr. *From Root to McNamara: Army Organization and Administration, 1900–1963.* United States Army Center of Military History. Washington, DC, 1975.

Johnson, Edward C. *Marine Corps Aviation: The Early Years 1912–1940.* History and Museums Division, U.S. Marine Corps, 1977.

Jones, William K. *A Brief History of the 6th Marines.* History and Museums Division, U.S. Marine Corps, 1987.

Kane, Robert, J. *A Brief History of the 2nd Marines.* History and Museums Division, U.S. Marine Corps, 1970.

Nalty, Bernard C. *The United States Marines in Nicaragua.* Historical Branch, G-3 Division, Headquarters, USMC, Washington, DC, 1968.

Rickover, Hyman G. *How the Battleship* Maine *Was Destroyed.* Naval History Division, Dept. of the Navy, Washington, DC, 1976.

Spector, Ronald H. *U.S. Marines in Grenada 1983.* History and Museums Division, U.S. Marine Corps, 1987.

The Story of Panama: Hearings on the Rainey Resolution before the Committee on Foreign Affairs of the House of Representatives. Washington, DC, 1913.

Yingling, James M. *A Brief History of the 5th Marines.* Historical Branch, G-3 Division, Headquarters, USMC, Washington, DC, 1968.

PRIVATE PAPERS, MANUSCRIPTS, INTERVIEWS, AND ORAL HISTORIES

Barnett, George. *Soldier and Sailor Too.* Unpublished manuscript. History and Museums Division, U.S. Marine Corps.

Beach, Captain Edward L., USN. *Admiral Caperton in Haiti.* Unpublished manuscript, 1919. Captain Edward L. Beach, Jr., USN (Ret.), Washington, DC.

Caperton, Rear Adm. William B. *History of U.S. Naval Operations Under Command of Rear Admiral William B. Caperton, USN, Commencing June 5, 1915, Ending April 30, 1919.* Subject File ZN, National Archives, Washington, DC.

Craig, Lt. Gen. Edward A., USMC. Oral History Collection, History and Museums Division, U.S. Marine Corps.

Ellsworth, Harry. *One Hundred Eighty Landings of United States Marines: 1800–1934.* History and Museums Division, U.S. Marine Corps.

Farrell, Maj. Gen. Walter Greatsinger, USMC (Ret.). Interview with the author, October 1987, San Diego, CA.

Fitzsimmons, Lt. Col. Ed, USA. Interview with the author, January 1990.

Metcalf, Clyde. *American Naval Interventions on the Isthmus of Panama.* Unpublished manuscript. History and Museums Division, U.S. Marine Corps.

Pendleton, Maj. Gen. Joseph H., USMC, miscellaneous papers. History and Museums Division, U.S. Marine Corps.

Pfeiffer, Maj. Gen. Omar T., USMC, Oral History Collection. History and Museums Division, U.S. Marine Corps.

Qualy, Lt. Col. Thomas, USA (Ret.). Interview with the author, January 1990.

Smith, Lt. Gen. Julian C., USMC, Oral History Collection. History and Museums Division, U.S. Marine Corps.

Thacker, Joel. *Interventions in Cuba Under the Platt Amendment.* Unpublished manuscript. History and Museums Division, U.S. Marine Corps.

Upshur, Maj. Gen. William P., USMC, miscellaneous papers. Southern Historical Collection, University of North Carolina, Chapel Hill, NC.

Utley, Maj. Gen. Harold H., USMC, miscellaneous papers. History and Museums Division, U.S. Marine Corps.

Waghelstein, Col. John, USA (Ret.). Interview with the author.

Waller, Maj. Gen. Littleton W.T., USMC, miscellaneous papers. Col. L.W.T. Waller II, USMC (Ret.), La Jolla, CA.

SECONDARY SOURCES: BOOKS

Adams, James. *Secret Armies.* New York: Atlantic Monthly Press, 1988.

Ammen, Daniel. *The Old Navy and the New.* Philadelphia. J.B. Lippincott, 1891.

Beach, Edward, L. *The Wreck of the* Memphis. London: Jarrolds, 1967.

Beals, Carleton. *Banana Gold.* Philadelphia: Lippincott, 1932.

Beaulac, Willard. *Career Diplomat.* New York: Macmillan, 1951.

Benton, Elbert J. *International Law and Diplomacy of the Spanish-American War.* Baltimore: Johns Hopkins Press, 1908.

Bradlee, Ben Jr. *Guts and Glory: The Rise and Fall of Oliver North.* New York: Donald I. Fine, 1988.

Bunau-Varilla, Philippe. *Nicaragua or Panama.* New York: Knickerbocker Press, 1901.

———. *Panama: The Creation, Destruction, and Resurrection.* New York: McBride, Nast, 1914.

Busbey, L. White. *Uncle Joe Cannon.* New York: Henry Holt, 1927.

Butterfield, Roger. *The American Past.* New York: Simon and Shuster, 1957.

Calder, Bruce J. *The Impact of Intervention*: The Dominican Republic During the U.S. Occupation of 1916–1924. Austin: University of Texas Press, 1984.

Callcott, Wilfred H. *The Carribean Policy of the United States: 1890–1920.* Baltimore: Johns Hopkins Press, 1942.

Carter, William H. *The Life of Lieutenant General Chaffee.* Chicago: University of Chicago Press, 1917.

Catlin, Albertus A. *With the Help of God and a Few Marines.* New York: Doubleday, 1919.

Chadwick, French Ensor. *The Relations of the United States and Spain: Diplomacy.* New York: Scribner's, 1909.

———. *The Relations of the United States and Spain: The Spanish-American War.* New York: Scribners, 1911.

Challener, Richard, D. *Admirals, Generals, and American Foreign Policy, 1898–1914.* Princeton: Princeton University Press, 1973.

Chapman, Charles E. *A History of the Cuban Republic.* New York: Macmillan, 1927.

Clark, Charles E. *My Fifty Years in the Navy.* Boston: Little Brown, 1917.

Coletta, Paolo. *Bowman Hendry McCalla: A Fighting Sailor.* Washington, DC: University Press of America, 1979.

Collum, Richard. *History of the United States Marine Corps.* New York: L.R. Hamersly, 1903.

Coontz, Robert. *From Mississippi to the Sea.* Philadelphia: Dorrance, 1930.

Cosmas, Graham A. *An Army for Empire: The United States Army in the Spanish-American War.* Columbia: University of Missouri Press, 1971.

Craige, John Houston, *Cannibal Cousins.* New York: Minton, Balch, 1934.

Cummins, Lejeune. *Quijote on a Burro: Sandino and the Marines, a Study in the Formulation of Foreign Policy.* Mexico City: privately published, 1958.

Davis, Burke. *Marine! The Life of Chesty Puller.* Boston: Little, Brown, 1962.

Davis, Richard Harding. *The Cuban and Porto Rican Campaigns.* New York: Scribners, 1898.

Denny, Harold N. *Dollars for Bullets: The Story of American Rule in Nicaragua.* New York: Dial Press, 1929.

Draper, Theodore. *The Dominican Revolt: A Case Study in American Policy.* New York: Commentary Report, 1968.

DuVal, Miles P. Jr. *Cadiz to Cathay: The Story of the Diplomatic Struggle for the Panama Canal.* Palo Alto, CA: Stanford University Press, 1940.

Ealy, Lawrence O. *Yanqui Politics and the Isthmian Canal.* University Park: Pennsylvania State University Press, 1971.

English, Adrian J. *Armed Forces of Latin America.* London: Jane's Publishing, 1984.

Evans, Robley D. *Sailor's Log.* New York: Appleton, 1901.

Foraker, Joseph B. *Notes of a Busy Life.* Cincinnati, OH: Stewart & Kidd, 1916.

Freehoff, Joseph C. *America and the Canal Title.* New York: Privately published, 1916.

Freidel, Frank. *The Splendid Little War.* Boston: Little, Brown, 1958.

Funston, Frederick. *Memories of Two Wars.* New York: Scribners, 1911.

Graber, D.A. *Crisis Diplomacy.* Washington, DC: Public Affairs Press, 1959.

Hagan, Kenneth J. *American Gunboat Diplomacy and the Old Navy: 1877–1889.* Westport, CT: Greenwood Press, 1973.

Hagedorn, Hermann. *Leonard Wood.* New York: Harper & Bros., 1931.

Hart, Albert Bushnell and Herbert Ronald Ferleger, eds. *Theodore Roosevelt Cyclopedia.* New York: Roosevelt Memorial Association, 1941.

Healy, David F. *Gunboat Diplomacy in the Wilson Era: The U.S. Navy in Haiti, 1915–1916.* Madison: University of Wisconsin Press, 1976.

———. *The United States in Cuba, 1898–1902: Generals, Politicians, and the Search for Policy.* Madison: University of Wisconsin Press, 1963.

Heinl, Robert D. *Soldiers of the Sea.* Annapolis, MD: United States Naval Institute, 1962.

Heinl, Robert D. and Nancy G. Heinl. *Written in Blood: The Story of the Haitian People 1492–1971.* Boston: Houghton Mifflin, 1978.

Hill, Charles E. *Leading American Treaties.* New York: Macmillan, 1922.

Inman, Samuel Guy. *Through Santo Domingo and Haiti: A Cruise with the Marines.* New York: Committee on Co-operation in Latin America, 1919.

"I Took The Isthmus," Ex-President Roosevelt's Confession, Colombia's Protest and Editorial Comment by American Newspapers on "How the United States Acquired the Right to Build the Panama Canal." New York, 1911.

Jenks, Leland Hamilton. *Our Cuban Colony: A Study in Sugar.* New York: Vanguard Press, 1928.

Jessup, Philip C. *Elihu Root.* New York: Dodd, Mead, 1938.

Johnson, Willis F. *Four Centuries of the Panama Canal.* New York: Henry Holt, 1906.

Karsten, Peter. *The Naval Aristocracy.* New York: The Free Press, 1972.

Knox, Dudley W. *A History of the United States Navy.* New York: G.P. Putnam's Sons, 1936.

Langley, Lester D. *The Banana Wars: An Inner History of American Empire, 1900–1934.* Lexington: University Press of Kentucky, 1983.

———. *The United States and the Caribbean 1900–1970.* Athens: University of Georgia Press, 1980.

Lejeune, John A. *The Reminiscences of a Marine.* Philadelphia: Dorrance, 1930.

Lieuwen, Edwin. *Arms and Politics in Latin America.* New York: Council on Foreign Relations [Praeger], 1961.

Lockmiller, David. *Magoon in Cuba: A History of the Second Intervention, 1906–1909*. Chapel Hill: University of North Carolina Press, 1938.

Macaulay, Neill. *The Sandino Affair*. Durham, NC: Duke University Press, 1985.

Mahan, Alfred Thayer. *From Sail to Steam: Recollections of a Naval Life*. New York: Harper and Bros., 1907.

———. *The Influence of Sea Power Upon History: 1660–1783*. Boston: Little, Brown, 1898.

Mayo, Lawrence Shaw. *America of Yesterday: The Diary of John D. Long*. Boston: Atlantic Monthly Press, 1923.

McCrocklin, James H. *Garde d'Haiti: Twenty Years of Organization and Training by the United States Marine Corps*. Annapolis, MD: Naval Institute Press, 1956.

McCullough, David. *The Path Between the Seas*. New York: Simon and Schuster, 1977.

McNeil, Frank. *War and Peace in Central America*. New York: Scribners, 1988.

Mersky, Peter B. *U.S. Marine Corps Aviation*. Baltimore: Nautical & Aviation Publishing Co., 1983.

Metcalf, Clyde H. *A History of the United States Marine Corps*. New York: G.P. Putnam's Sons, 1939.

———, ed. *The Marine Corps Reader*. New York: G.P. Putnam's Sons, 1944.

Millett, Allan R. *Semper Fidelis: The History of the United States Marine Corps*. New York: Macmillan, 1980.

———. *The Politics of Intervention: The Military Occupation of Cuba, 1906–1909*. Columbus: Ohio State University Press, 1968.

———. "The United States and Cuba: The Uncomfortable 'Abrazo,' 1898–1968," in Braeman, John, *et al.*, eds., *Twentieth-Century American Foreign Policy*. Columbus: Ohio State University Press, 1971.

Millett, Richard. *Guardians of the Dynasty: A History of the U.S. Created Guardia Nacional de Nicaragua and the Somoza Family*. Maryknoll, NY: Orbis Books, 1977.

Millis, Walter. *The Martial Spirit: A Study of Our War with Spain*. Boston: Houghton Mifflin, 1931.

Miner, Dwight C. *The Fight for the Panama Canal Route: The Story of the Spooner Act and the Hay-Herran Treaty*. New York: Octagon Books, 1966.

Munro, Dana G. *Intervention and Dollar Diplomacy in the Caribbean: 1900–1921*. Princeton: Princeton University Press, 1964.

Musicant, Ivan. *United States Armored Cruisers: A Design and Operational History*. Annapolis, MD: Naval Institute Press, 1985.

Morison, Samuel Eliot. *The Oxford History of the American People*. New York: Oxford University Press, 1965.

Naval Actions and History: 1799–1898. Boston: Military History Society of Massachusetts, 1902.

Nevins, Allan. *Henry White: Thirty Years of American Diplomacy*. New York: Harper & Bros., 1930.

Palmer, Frederick. *Bliss, Peacemaker: The Life and Letters of General Tasker Howard Bliss*. New York: Dodd, Mead, 1934.

———. *Central America and Its Problems*. New York: Moffat, Yard, 1913.

Perkins, Dexter. *The Monroe Doctrine*. Johns Hopkins Press, Baltimore, MD, 1937.

Potter, E.B. *Sea Power: A Naval History*. Annapolis, MD: Naval Institute Press, 1981.

Pringle, Henry F. *Theodore Roosevelt*. New York: Harcourt, Brace, 1931.

Puleston, W.D. *Mahan: The Life and Work of Captain Alfred Thayer Mahan, U.S.N.* New Haven, CT: Yale University Press, 1939.

Rodman, Selden. *Quisqueya: A History of the Dominican Republic*. Seattle: University of Washington Press, 1964.

Roosevelt, Theodore. *The Rough Riders*. New York: Scribners, 1925.

Russell, Lee E., and M. Albert Mendez. *Grenada 1983*. London: Osprey Publishing, 1985.

Sargent, Herbert H. *The Campaign of Santiago de Cuba*. Freeport, NY: Books for Libraries Press, reprinted 1970.

Sargent, Nathan, ed. *Admiral Dewey and the Manila Campaign*. Washington, DC: Naval Historical Foundation, 1947.

Scheina, Robert L. *Latin America; A Naval History, 1810–1987*. Annapolis, MD: Naval Institute Press, 1987.

Scott, Hugh L. *Some Memories of a Soldier*. New York: Century, 1928.

Sherrod, Robert. *History of Marine Corps Aviation in World War II*. Washington, DC: Combat Forces Press, 1952.

Stimson, Henry L. *American Policy in Nicaragua*. New York: Scribners, 1927.

Stimson, Henry L. and McGeorge Bundy. *On Active Service in Peace and War*. New York: Harper & Brothers, 1947.

Thayer, William R. *The Life and Letters of John Hay*. Boston: Houghton Mifflin, 1915.

Thomas, A.J. Jr., and Ann Van Wynen Thomas. *The Dominican Republic Crisis 1965*. Dobbs Ferry, NY: Oceana Publications, 1967.

Thomas, Lowell. *Old Gimlet Eye: The Adventures of Smedley D. Butler*. New York: Farrar & Rinehart, 1933.

Thomason, John W. *Fix Bayonets!* New York: Scribners, 1970.

Vandegrift, Alexander A. *Once a Marine*. New York: Ballantine Books, 1964.

Weigley, Russell F. *History of the United States Army*. Bloomington: Indiana University Press, 1984.

Welles, Sumner. *Naboth's Vineyard: The Dominican Republic 1844–1924*. New York: Payson & Clarke, 1928.

West, Richard S. Jr. *Admirals of American Empire*. Indianapolis, IN.: Bobbs-Merrill, 1948.

Wilson, Herbert W. *The Downfall of Spain: Naval History of the Spanish-American War*. Boston: Little, Brown, 1900.

Wilson, James Harrison. *Under the Old Flag*. New York: Appleton, 1912.

Winkler, John K. *W.R. Hearst: An American Phenomenon*. New York: Simon and Schuster, 1928.

Wirkus, Faustin. *The White King of La Gonave*. New York: Doubleday, Doran, 1931.

Wise, Frederick, *A Marine Tells It to You*. New York: J.H. Sears, 1929.

SECONDARY SOURCES: PERIODICALS

Air Force Times, various editions.

Army and Navy Journal, various editions, 1906–1907.

Army and Navy Register, various editions, 1900–1915.

Army Times, various editions.

Ashby, Timothy. "Grenada: Soviet Stepping Stone." *Proceedings* of the United States Naval Institute, December 1983.

"The Battle for Grenada." *Newsweek,* November 7, 1983.

Baughman, C.C. "United States Occupation of the Dominican Republic." *Proceedings* of the United States Naval Institute, December 1925.

Baylen, Joseph, O. "Sandino: Patriot or Bandit?" *Hispanic American Historical Review,* August 1951.

Berger, Paul. "The Corridor." *Leatherneck,* August 1965.

———. "Peace Force On Line." *Leatherneck,* August 1965.

———. "Rebels Fire First." *Leatherneck,* July 1965.

Blassingame, John W. "The Press and American Intervention in Haiti and the Dominican Republic, 1904–1920." *Caribbean Studies,* July 1969.

Bleasdale, Victor F. "La Flor Engagement." *Marine Corps Gazette,* February 1932.

Boyce, Jim. "Combat Patrol: Nicaragua." *Leatherneck,* October 1982.

Boyden, Hayne, D. "Some Forced Plane Landings in Santo Domingo." *Marine Corps Gazette,* June 1922.

Brainard, Edwin H. "Marine Corps Aviation." *Marine Corps Gazette,* March 1928.

Brooks, Charles T. "War in Nicaragua." *Marine Corps Gazette,* February 1933.

Bryon, Michael J. "Fury from the Sea: Marines in Grenada." *Proceedings* of the United States Naval Institute, May 1984.

Buell, Raymond L. "Reconstruction in Nicaragua." *Information Service,* Foreign Policy Associaton, November 12, 1930.

Bullard, Robert. "The Army in Cuba." *Journal of the Military Service Institution of the United States,* September 1907.

Calder, Bruce J. "Caudillos and *Gavilleros* versus the United States Marines: Guerrilla Insurgency during the Dominican Intervention, 1916–1924. *Hispanic American Historical Review,* November 1978.

Calkins, C.G. "Historical and Professional Notes on the Naval Campaign of Manila Bay in 1898." *Proceedings* of the United States Naval Institute, June 1899.

Conard, Charles. "A Year in Haiti's Customs and Fiscal Service." *Proceedings* of the United States Naval Institute, April 1923.

Cook, Francis A. "The *Brooklyn* at Santiago." *The Century Magazine,* May 1899.

Dare, James A. "Dominican Diary." *Proceedings* of the United States Naval Institute, December 1965.

Davis, Henry. C. "Indoctrination of Latin-American Service." *Marine Corps Gazette,* June 1920.

Division of Operations and Training, HQMC. "Combat Operations in Nicaragua." *Marine Corps Gazette,* March, June, September 1929.

Dodds, Harold W. "American Supervision of the Nicaraguan Election." *Marine Corps Gazette,* June 1929.

Duncan, G.A. "The Corps of Civil Engineers, U.S. Navy, in Haiti." *Proceedings* of the United States Naval Institute, March 1930.

Edson, Merritt A. "The Coco Patrol," *Marine Corps Gazette,* August and November 1936, February 1937.

Evans, Frank E. "The First Expedition to Panama." *Marine Corps Gazette,* June 1916.

Evans, Robley, D. "The *Iowa* at Santiago." *The Century Magazine,* May 1899.

Fellowes, Edward A. "Training Native Troops in Santo Domingo." *Marine Corps Gazette*, December 1923.

Goldwert, Marvin. "The Constabulary in the Dominican Republic and Nicaragua." *Latin American Monographs*, September 1961.

Gray, John, A. "The Second Nicaraguan Campaign." *Marine Corps Gazette*, February 1933.

Harrington, Samuel M. "The Strategy and Tactics of Small Wars." *Marine Corps Gazette*, December 1921.

Holmes, Maurice. "With the Horse Marines in Nicaragua." *Marine Corps Gazette*, February 1984.

Inglis, William. "The Armed Struggle for Control in Cuba." *Harper's Weekly*, September 22, 1906.

———. "The Collapse of the Cuban House of Cards." *Harper's Weekly*, October 20, 1906.

———. "With the Rebel Leader in the Cuban Hills." *Harper's Weekly*, September 29, 1906.

Jennings, Kenneth A. "Sandino Against the Marines: the Development of Air Power for Conducting Counterinsurgency Operations in Central America." *Air University Review*, July–August, 1986.

Kaltenbeck, R.W. "The Little Airlift." *Marine Corps Gazette*, August 1949.

Kelsey, Carl. "The American Intervention in Haiti and the Dominican Republic." *Annals of the American Academy of Political and Social Science*, 1922.

Kilmartin, Robert C. "Indoctrination in Santo Domingo." *Marine Corps Gazette*, December 1922.

Knox, Dudley W. "An Adventure in Diplomacy." *Proceedings* of the United States Naval Institute, February 1926.

Lane, Rufus H. "Civil Government in Santo Domingo in the Early Days of the Military Occupation." *Marine Corps Gazette*, June 1922.

"Marine Corps Aviation, a Record of Achievement." *Marine Corps Gazette*, November 1930.

"The Marines Return from Nicaragua," *Marine Corps Gazette*, February 1933.

McClellan, Edwin, North. "He Remembered His Mission." *Marine Corps Gazette*, November 1930.

———. "The Neuva Segovia Expedition," parts I and II. *Marine Corps Gazette*, May, August 1931.

———. "Operations Ashore in the Dominican Republic." *Proceedings* of the United States Naval Institute, February 1921.

———. "The Saga of the Coco." *Marine Corps Gazette*, November 1930.

———. "Supervising Nicaraguan Elections, 1928." *Proceedings* of the United States Naval Institute, January 1933.

McMillen, Fred E. "Some Haitian Recollections." *Proceedings* of the United States Naval Institute, April 1936.

Megee, Vernon E. "The Genesis of Air Support in Guerrilla Operations." *Proceedings* of the United States Naval Institute, June 1965.

Meyer, Leo J. "The United States and the Cuban Revolution of 1917." *Hispanic American Historical Review*, May 1930.

Miller, Charles J. "Diplomatic Spurs: Our Experiences in Santo Domingo." *Marine Corps Gazette*, February, May and August 1935.

Minger, Ralph Eldin. "William Howard Taft and the United States Intervention in Cuba in 1906." *Hispanic American Historical Review,* February 1961.

Minneapolis Star Tribune, various editions.

Mulcahy, Francis P. "Marine Corps Aviation in the Second Nicaraguan Campaign." *Proceedings* of the United States Naval Institute, August, 1933.

Navy Times, various editions.

Newsweek, various editions.

New York Herald-Tribune, various editions.

New York Times, various editions.

Nichols, John H. "Hiking and Fighting." *Recruiters' Bulletin,* November 1916.

Offley, C.N. "The Work of the *Oregon* During the Spanish-American War." *Journal of the American Society of Naval Engineers,* 1903.

Pendleton, Joseph H. "The Battle of Coyotepe." *Army and Navy Register,* May 16, 1914.

Pérez, Louis A. Jr. "Politics, Peasants, and People of Color: The 1912 'Race War' in Cuba Reconsidered." *Hispanic American Historical Review,* August 1986.

———. "Supervision of a Protectorate: The United States and the Cuban Army, 1898–1903." *Hispanic American Historical Review,* May 1972.

Philip, John W. "The *Texas* at Santiago." *The Century Magazine,* May 1899.

Reisinger, H.C. "*La Palabra Del Gringo!* Leadership of the Nicaraguan National Guard." *Proceedings* of the United States Naval Institute, February 1935.

———. "On the Isthmus: 1885." *Marine Corps Gazette,* December 1928.

Remington, Frederick. "With the Fifth Corps." *Harper's,* November 1898.

Rowell, Ross E. "Marine Air in Nicaragua." *Marine Corps Gazette,* May 1985.

St. Paul Pioneer Press, various editions.

Schoenrich, Otto. "The Present Intervention in Santo Domingo and Haiti," in Blakeslee, George H., ed., *Mexico and the Caribbean,* New York: Clark University Addresses, 1920.

"Testimony of the Major General Commandant Before the Senate Committee on Foreign Relations." *Marine Corps Gazette,* March 1928.

Thorpe, G.C. "American Achievements in Santo Domingo, Haiti, and Virgin Islands," in Blakeslee, *op cit.*

———. "Dominican Service." *Marine Corps Gazette,* December 1919.

Walraven, J.C. "Typical Combat Patrols in Nicaragua." *Marine Corps Gazette,* December 1929.

Webb, Percey [sic]. "When The Marines Did Duty at Panama." *The Marines Magazine and Indian,* October 1921.

Williams, Dion. "The Managua Disaster." *Marine Corps Gazette,* August 1931.

———. "The Nicaraguan Situation." *Marine Corps Gazette,* November 1930.

Winans, Roswell. "Campaigning in Santo Domingo." *Recruiters' Bulletin,* March 1917.

Wise, Frederick. "The Occupation of a Haitian Town." *Proceedings* of the United States Naval Institute, December 1931.

Withers, Thomas. "The Wreck of the U.S.S. *Memphis.*" *Proceedings* of the United States Naval Institute, July 1918.

Young, Gene. "*Boxer's* First Round." *Leatherneck,* July 1965.

INDEX